Soviet Strategies in Southeast Asia

SOVIET
STRATEGIES
IN SOUTHEAST ASIA

*An Exploration of Eastern Policy
under Lenin and Stalin*

BY CHARLES B. McLANE

PRINCETON UNIVERSITY PRESS
PRINCETON, NEW JERSEY
1966

Printed in the United States of America
by Princeton University Press, Princeton, New Jersey

To Carol

Preface

A DISTINCTIVE feature of Khrushchev's foreign policy was the fresh attention his regime directed to the emerging nations of Asia and Africa. This interest is usually dated from 1955, soon after Khrushchev gained the Soviet leadership. In that year the Russians acclaimed the first Afro-Asian conference at Bandung, reversing their earlier stand on neutralism and acknowledging the validity of non-alignment; they welcomed in Moscow former "running dogs" of American and British imperialism such as Nehru and U Nu; Khrushchev and Bulganin made what was described in the Russian press as a "triumphal tour" of the Asian sub-continent; more ominously, Moscow's determination to play a more vigorous role in the Near East and North Africa was revealed in a critical arms agreement between Czechoslovakia and Egypt. Since 1955 the Kremlin has made it clear that no part of the colonial, former colonial, or semi-colonial world lies outside the scope of its interest. This interest has been manifested in greatly expanded trade with Asia, Africa, and South America, in widening diplomatic contacts with the new nations, in an elaborate system of cultural and aid programs, not excluding military assistance to selected countries, and in many other ways.

No one need doubt that Khrushchev's attention to the developing nations affected world affairs. It promoted the identity of these nations and gave new stature to their spokesmen. It quickened the desire of subject peoples for independence and in some cases hastened the process of independence. It caused affluent Western powers, the United States in particular, to devote more energy and funds than they might otherwise have allocated to the modernization of the once underdeveloped world. A new spotlight was cast on the emerging nations. Vast competition among the Great Powers was launched for their allegiance, or at least for their good will. The bipolar world of the post-war era was replaced by a world of infinitely varied and complex relationships between states. A shift in Soviet foreign policy once again influenced the course of international relations, much as

Preface

Andrei Zhdanov's articulation of the "two camp" thesis in 1947 fixed the character of international relations during the Cold War. It is important to understand the origins of the Russian shift. Some Western observers, struck by the speed with which Moscow in the mid-1950's abandoned its hostility toward unaligned nations such as India, Egypt, and Indonesia, have tended to think of Russian interest in the developing nations as of comparatively recent origin, dating from Khrushchev's ascendancy. Others, consumed by resentment of what they felt to be Russia's presumptuous and meddlesome intervention in an already troubled arena of international politics, have viewed Soviet motives as designed principally to embarrass the Western Powers and have discounted any genuine interest Moscow might have in Asia and Africa. In point of fact, concern with the colonial—or, as it was called, the Eastern—question can be traced back to the first years after the Russian Revolution. The East, it is true, did not engage Moscow's attentions as persistently as the West, either in a revolutionary sense or in the Russians' periodic search for normal diplomatic intercourse (which was in any case out of the question where the nations concerned were dependent). Nor were Soviet policies in the East normally based on as much detailed knowledge of local conditions as were policies with respect to more developed countries; the social and political systems of Burma and Indochina, for instance, were never as familiar to Russians as those of England and France—even with the distortions often arising from their Marxist-Leninist outlook. The Russians did, however, devise theories of social and political development in the colonial and semi-colonial East which they fitted into their general philosophy of world affairs and which they sought to apply as opportunities arose. Indeed, in the sense of suggesting to the subject peoples of the East an alternative to a dependency they increasingly wished to rid themselves of, the Soviet Union may be said to have taken a *constructive* interest in the colonial world some years before a similar concern developed in the West. The present study, then, is a search for origins. What was the nature of Moscow's interest in the East under Lenin and Stalin, before Khrushchev's more decisive concern with Eastern affairs in the mid-1950's? How did Soviet colonial policies—that is, policies toward colonial and semi-colonial countries—unfold in one sector of the Eastern world? Do these policies suggest a pattern of Soviet behavior in the East at large?

The selection of Southeast Asia as a proving-ground of Soviet strategies in the East has not been made at random. It followed, in the first instance, from the author's having had some prior acquaintance with the area—an acquaintance that grew during the years while research was in progress and, in particular, during two extended visits in 1961 and 1962 that took the author to each of the countries treated in this study, in several cases more than once. The selection of Southeast Asia in any case needs no apology. Many considerations make this area well suited to the purposes of the present study. Its proximity, for instance, to China and India, two persistent targets of Moscow's strategies in the East, give special pertinence to parallel strategies in Southeast Asia; the Chinese revolution in particular, vividly mirrored in the course of events in Southeast Asia, at times stimulated and at times frustrated Soviet policies. It was in Southeast Asia that the first Communist thrust in the East after World War II, an outgrowth of Zhdanovism, took place. The startling contrasts in Southeast Asia, meanwhile, posed a demanding test of Russian ingenuity. The widely divergent conditions which influenced the development of local nationalist and Communist movements made it impossible for the Russians to rely on fixed formulas and so bring to light different facets of their colonial strategies. The fact too that the Russians competed in Southeast Asia with several varieties of foreign imperialism meant that their policies reflected the complex interplay of Stalin's dual concern with revolution abroad and normal relations with the Great Powers. These circumstances, among others, make Southeast Asia an excellent prism through which to study Soviet policies in the East.

It is easier by far to indicate what the present study sets out to accomplish than to foretell with confidence how it is to be done. The search for materials that might shed light on Soviet strategies has been extensive and for certain periods, if it does not sound immodest to say so, exhaustive. Yet the evidence is uneven and sometimes fragmentary. It is useful to review briefly at this juncture the types of sources that have been consulted. Most relate, of course, to Southeast Asia, but Soviet activity elsewhere in the colonial and semi-colonial world (notably in China and India) has not been overlooked. Chapter One, for instance, is given over entirely to the evolution of Moscow's Eastern policies during the decade following the Russian Revolution, with little specific reference to Southeast Asia; succeeding chapters open with a discussion of Moscow's general objectives in the East at a given stage, seen in the context of Stalin's world-wide strategies.

The principal evidence on which this study relies is extracted from Russian publications, especially contemporaneous Soviet and Comintern (later Cominform) periodicals, which are unencumbered by afterthought and hindsight. To the uninitiated the Russian press is often incomprehensible, a mixture of half-truths and what appear to be willful self-deceptions. It is, however, the permanent record of Soviet strategies and accordingly the constant companion of any student of Russian affairs. Even with the yawning gaps where Southeast Asia is concerned, Russian periodicals provide the fullest testimony of Moscow's policies there.

Evidence of Moscow's strategies in the East is not, of course, confined to what is recorded in Soviet and Soviet-controlled publications. Since Russian policy may reasonably be said to embrace any activity that Moscow approves (or in some cases merely refrains from disapproving), however initiated, efforts to discover it in Southeast Asia inevitably lead to consideration of the course of local nationalist as well as Communist movements and the encouragement given these movements by metropolitan and other Asian parties. A few primary records of local Communist movements in Southeast Asia shed light on these matters, although the authenticity of such records is often difficult to establish. The files of former colonial administrations, where they are open to scholars, are also of value despite their tendency to exaggerate both the extent of local Communist activity and Soviet responsibility for it. Materials relating to metropolitan Communist parties such as the French and British, and to Asian parties such as the Chinese and Indian, further illuminate Communist strategies in Southeast Asia. The author has made what use he could of this scattered documentation but is much indebted to students of Southeast Asian affairs who have already sifted through it and published their findings. It would have been impossible for this writer, working alone, to trace Russian policies in Southeast Asia without ready access to the work, for instance, of George M. Kahin and Ruth T. McVey on Indonesia; of Renze L. Hoeksema on the Philippines; of I. Milton Sacks on Indochina; and of Gene Z. Hanrahan and Lucien Pye on Malaya. (These studies and others are listed in the Bibliography.) The gaps that remained have been filled as well as possible by evidence the author himself was able to gather in interviews during 1961 and 1962 with several dozen Southeast Asians, ranging from prominent opponents of Communism (such as Phoumi Nosavan of Laos and the late Ngo Diem Nhu of South Vietnam) to former Communist leaders serving jail sentences for insurrection (such as Luis Taruc and José Lava of the Philippines); their testimony, of course, supplements data based on documentary sources yet it has often provided insights into Southeast Asian affairs not otherwise available. (A list of these informants as well as a brief itemization of the topics that the author discussed with them is also included in the Bibliography.)

Raw data relating to Russian policies in Southeast Asia, thus, are not lacking. Great care, however, must be exercised in the use of these data. No service is done future students of Southeast Asian affairs by a painstaking reconstruction of Soviet strategies based on data that cannot be verified. The trick, in short, lies not in discovering new "evidence," engaging as this enterprise may be, but in making the evidence sustain a plausible argument. To this end the author has sought to underplay the evidence at hand and to avoid the temptation of rendering a fuller account of Russian policy in Southeast Asia than the facts will support. Whether or not he has succeeded the reader must judge for himself.

The list of individuals to whom the author owes a debt of gratitude in connection with the present study is both long and impossible to give here in full. Some informants are listed in the

Bibliography as interviewees, and the author's gratitude to them, to the humble as well as to the illustrious, is very real. Others, however, often the most helpful and the most generous with their time and expertise, are government officials in Southeast Asia and should not be named. It must suffice to acknowledge the latter *incognito* but no less warmly. Acknowledgment is made of the permission given the writer by the Ministry of External Affairs of the Government of Malaya to inspect certain early records of Malayan Communism, records which greatly enriched his understanding of the evolution of this movement; this permission was arranged through the good offices of Professor Anthony Short of the University of Malaya, who is currently engaged in research on the Malayan Emergency. The assistance of a former student, John B. Starr, who as a Senior Fellow of Dartmouth College accompanied the author on his 1961 visit to Southeast Asia, should also be acknowledged here. Travel grants for the 1961 and 1962 visits were awarded, respectively, by the Russian Research Center of Harvard University and by the Cultural Affairs Program of the Southeast Asia Treaty Organization. Grants from Dartmouth College covered the costs of a brief trip to Leningrad in 1961 in search of materials and, subsequently, of preparing the manuscript. Mrs. Joan Erdman was indispensable in organizing the Index. None of these individuals or institutions, of course, bear responsibility for any shortcomings of the present study.

The author's very lively sense of gratitude, finally, should be expressed to his wife, Carol Evarts McLane, who has read the manuscript from beginning to end for style and coherence, suffered with forbearance the domestic inconvenience of authorship, and offered solace beyond any call of duty. On plea of modesty she avoided the intended dedication to her of an earlier volume which she helped to shape no less than this; the writer and husband has determined that her modesty should not prevail a second time.

Contents

Contents

Contents

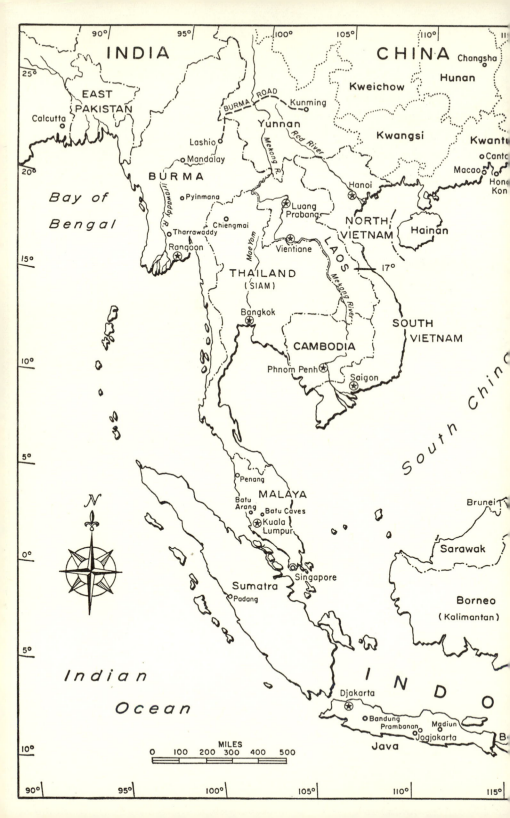

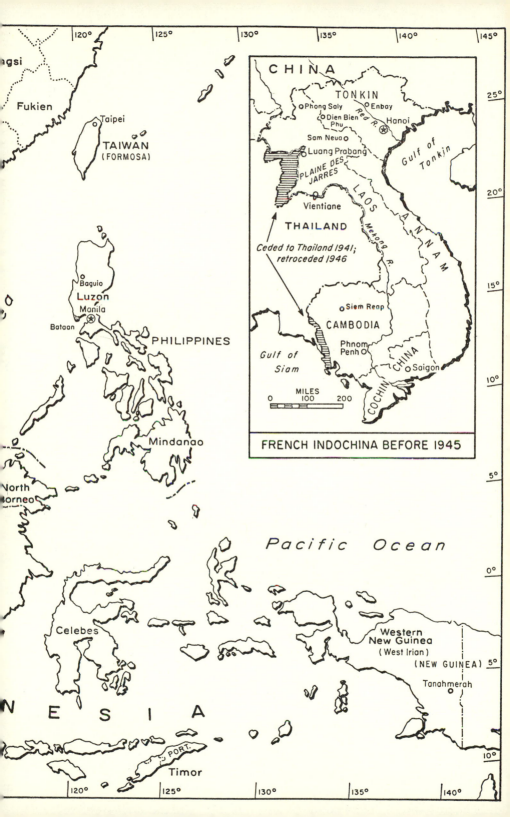

CHINA

TONKIN

Phong Saly   Enbay

Dien Bien
Phu   Red R.   Hanoi

Sam Neua   Gulf of
Tonkin

Luang Prabang

PLAINE DES
JARRES   L A O S   A N N A M

Vientiane   Mekong R.

THAILAND

*Ceded to Thailand 1941;
retroceded 1946*

Siem Reap

CAMBODIA

Phnom
Penh   CHINA

Gulf of
Siam   Saigon

MILES
0   100   200   COCHIN

FRENCH INDOCHINA BEFORE 1945

Fukien

Taipei

TAIWAN
(FORMOSA)

Baguio

Luzon

Manila

Bataan

PHILIPPINES

Mindanao

North
Borneo

Pacific   Ocean

Celebes

Western
New Guinea
(West Irian)

(NEW GUINEA)

Tanahmerah

N   E   S   I   A

PORT.

Timor

Soviet Strategies in Southeast Asia

CHAPTER ONE

The Evolution of Soviet Eastern Policy: 1917-1928

W HATEVER one may think of the relationship between theory and practice in Soviet foreign policy, the deference Moscow pays to theory compels us to know what it is, or what it is said to be. It is possible to discover this without succumbing to the Marxian notion that theory, or ideology, is derived from certain immutable laws. In reality, as the following discussion will show, much of Soviet theory, and indeed much of Soviet practice itself, is contrived, answerable to no fixed logic and as fluid as theory and practice are in less pretentious systems.

In particular, we need to understand something of early Soviet theories regarding the "East," which embraces the area of our focus. Moscow did not initially devote much attention to Southeast Asia, but when it did the strategies devised were in the context of a set of theories already formulated for the "East" in general. The theories were not without contradictions, but they were nonetheless consulted more or less systematically. They are, in consequence, relevant to our study, and it is the purpose of the present chapter to review them, together with some of the general strategies founded on them.

The word "East" did not always have an exact meaning for Moscow. In the months immediately after the Bolshevik Revolution, for instance, the East (*Vostok*) appears to have signified no more than the Asian parts of the former Russian Empire, especially Tataria and Turkestan. By mid-1918 the term was being used to describe the Muslim world both inside and outside the Soviet Union. By the end of 1918 the word was freely used, as in Stalin's much-quoted article "Don't Forget the East,"[1] to describe all of Asia, including China. Thereafter the concept grew gradually to embrace, as a leading Soviet Orientalist wrote in 1921, "the entire colonial world, the world of the oppressed peo-

---

[1] The article first appeared in *Zhizn' natsional'nostei*, No. 3, November 24, 1918; a partial English translation is in Eudin and North, *Soviet Russia and the East*, pp. 156-7.

ples not only of Asia but of Africa and South America—in a word, that entire world the exploitation of which nourished the might of capitalist society in Europe and the United States."[2] On occasion it was even suggested that countries such as Germany, Austria, and Hungary, by virtue of their defeat in World War I and their subsequent "exploitation" by the victorious capitalist powers, qualified as Eastern countries.[3] Normal usage, however, limited the East to colonies and semi-colonies (principally in Asia, since that was the focus of Soviet Eastern policy in the 1920's) and we will follow that usage in the present chapter.

PRE-REVOLUTIONARY MARXIAN VIEWS OF THE EAST

Marx had nothing to say on the focal area of this study, and in all likelihood could not have distinguished one Southeast Asian country from another. He did, however, comment—at wide intervals—on China and on Ireland, and from these comments it is possible to gain an idea of how the colonial (or national) question fitted into his scheme of world revolution.

As early as 1853 Marx saw in the Taiping rebellion in China the possibility of a sufficient contraction of British trade to trigger revolution in England and eventually throughout Europe. The Taiping rebellion, he wrote, "will throw the spark into the overloaded mine of the present industrial system and cause the explosion of the long-prepared general crisis [in England], which, spreading abroad, will be closely followed by political revolution on the Continent." He continued: "It would be a curious spectacle, that of China sending disorder into the Western World while the Western Powers, by English, French and American warsteamers, are conveying 'order' to Shanghai, Nanking and the mouths of the Grand Canal."[4]

Doubtless Marx was more intrigued by the hypothetical "spectacle" than seriously persuaded his prediction would come true, but there is here the genesis of an idea that was to re-emerge in

[2] M. N. Veltman (Pavlovich) in *Novyi Vostok*, No. 1, 1922, p. i.
[3] See the article by M. Rafail in *Lenin i Vostok*, p. 13.
[4] Karl Marx, "Revolution in China and in Europe," *New York Daily Tribune*, June 14, 1853; cited in *Marx on China: 1853-1860* (London, 1951), p. 7.

4

Soviet thinking after 1917: the idea that revolutions in colonial and semi-colonial countries, by denying markets and resources to imperialist powers, could cause revolutions in Europe. Marx from time to time returned to the thesis, especially in his comments on Ireland. Summarizing his views on Ireland in 1870, he wrote: "After occupying myself with the Irish question for many years, I have come to the conclusion that the decisive blow against the English ruling classes (and it will be decisive for the workers' movement all over the world) *cannot* be delivered *in England* but *only in Ireland*. . . . Ireland is the bulwark of the *English landed aristocracy*. The exploitation of that country is not only one of the main sources of this aristocracy's material wealth; it is their greatest *moral* strength. It, in fact, represents the *domination of England over Ireland*. Ireland is therefore the great means by which the English aristocracy maintains *its domination in England itself*. . . . The overthrow of the English aristocracy in Ireland involves as a necessary consequence its overthrow in England. And this would fulfil the preliminary condition for the proletarian revolution in England."[5]

Lenin was attentive to certain of Marx's views on Ireland (notably that Ireland must first secede from England before a free alliance between the two nations could be brought about),[6] but he gave little attention to Marx's argument concerning colonial revolution as the means of revolution in the metropolitan. His *Imperialism, the Highest Stage of Capitalism* (written in 1916), where one would surely expect to find discussion of such a thesis, contains none. The implication there is that revolution would occur first in Europe and only subsequently in the colonies. The East in fact drew little attention from Lenin prior to

[5] *Karl Marx and Frederick Engels: Selected Correspondence* (Moscow, 1956), p. 285; letter to S. Meyer and A. Vogt, April 9, 1870 (emphasis in original).

[6] Lenin used this argument to show that his support of secession within the Czarist Empire, prior to the Russian Revolution, was not in pursuit of any idea of small states but, on the contrary, to prepare the conditions for large states united "on a truly democratic, truly international basis"; see, for instance, his article in November 1915, entitled "The Revolutionary Proletariat and the Right of Nations to Self-Determination," in *Sochineniia*, XXI, p. 377 (unless otherwise indicated, all references to Lenin's *Sochineniia* are to the Fourth Edition, 1947-50).

5

1917. An article in 1913 entitled "Backward Europe and Advanced Asia," in which Lenin claims the existence of a "mighty democratic movement" everywhere in Asia, should not mislead us; it seems clearly to have been written in hostility toward the projected Great Power loan to Yuan Shih-kai, at the expense of the new Chinese Republic, and his claim is not repeated in other writings of this period.[7] In 1916 Lenin included colonies and semi-colonies in his general formula on the right of self-determination, arguing that their struggle for liberation "in its political expression signifies nothing more nor less than the recognition of this right"; but he did not suggest that national liberation in the East was as vital in the revolutionary process as self-determination in the subject countries of Europe, such as Poland and Ireland.[8] The most that Lenin ever argued before the Russian Revolution, concerning the relationship between revolutions in the colonies and in Europe, was that the social revolution could occur only in "an epoch of civil war against the bourgeoisie in the advanced countries *combined with* a whole series of democratic and revolutionary movements . . . in the underdeveloped, backward and oppressed nations."[9] And even assertions such as this occur too rarely in Lenin's pre-revolutionary writings to warrant the assumption that he placed much reliance on colonial upheavals.

The discussion of the national question before 1917, which is of course the only clue to any Bolshevik "colonial policy," involved mainly the legalistic question of a "right" to independence. The question had two parts, as Lenin stated it in 1913: "the right of nations to self-determination and the attitude the socialist proletariat should adopt towards this right."[10] The voluminous writ-

[7] The article was first published in *Pravda*, May 18, 1913; see *Sochineniia*, xix, pp. 77-8. Lenin also wrote several articles on the Chinese revolution itself, generally critical of Sun Yat-sen and seeing no great future in his leadership; *e.g.*, "Democracy and Narodism in China" (July 1912) and "Regenerated China" (November 1912), *ibid.*, xviii, pp. 143-9, 371-2.

[8] Lenin, "The Socialist Revolution and the Right of Nations to Self-Determination" (March 1916), *ibid.*, xxii, pp. 139-40.

[9] Lenin, "Concerning a Caricature of Marxian and 'Imperialist Economics' " (October 1916), *ibid.*, xxiii, p. 48 (emphasis added).

[10] Lenin, "The Right of Nations to Self-Determination," *ibid.*, xx, p. 396.

ing on the national question among Marxists, which is heavier in polemics than in consistency, underscores at least one important consideration—the need to distinguish between the right itself and the political advisability of exercising it. On the latter point Lenin acknowledged that there might be different attitudes by Marxists in different countries. "The right to unite," he wrote in April 1917, applying the prevailing Bolshevik formula on self-determination to Poland, "implies the right to secede. We Russians must emphasize the right [of Poland] to secede, while the Poles must emphasize the right to unite."[11] This was probably as succinct a statement as could be made, and it remained, in theory at least, the Bolshevik formulation on self-determination as long as the national question was in the forefront. The only significant modification of the formula after the Bolshevik Revolution was the not surprising stipulation that, at least in the portions of the former Czarist Empire to which the Bolsheviks laid claim, the right of self-determination was properly exercised only by elements sympathetic to the revolution—which meant, of course, that it was not to be exercised at all.

If a Bolshevik "Eastern policy" may be inferred from these pre-revolutionary writings, it amounted simply to an alleged "right" of colonies and semi-colonies to seek independence from their oppressors. The Bolsheviks were committed to support this effort (except perhaps in the "Eastern" portions of Russia itself), and they trusted that the colonial risings would occur close enough to risings in Europe so that the world-wide social revolution could unfold simultaneously. The question of whether to support bourgeois democratic or proletarian elements in the colonies had not yet arisen in Bolshevik calculations, inasmuch as colonial proletariats did not exist and even bourgeois democratic movements, according to Lenin in 1916, "have either hardly begun, or are far from being completed."[12] The "policy" had the virtue of simplicity and showed none of the deviousness of paral-

[11] Lenin, *ibid.*, xxiv, p. 265; from Lenin's speech on the national question at the All-Russian Conference of the RSDLP, May 12, 1917.

[12] Lenin, "The Socialist Revolution and the Right of Nations to Self-Determination," *ibid.*, xxii, p. 140.

lel policies for revolution in Europe; it proved, however, either too virtuous or too naïve for political realities in the East.

BOLSHEVIK BEACONS IN THE EAST

After coming to power, the Bolsheviks inevitably directed a portion of their attention eastward, first to the Asiatic peoples of Russia itself, later to all the peoples of Asia and the Near East. As early as May 1918, Stalin, People's Commissar for the Nationalities, spoke of the new Tatar-Bashkir Soviet Republic as "a living beacon to the Muslim peoples of the East, lighting the path to their emancipation from oppression."[13] In November 1918, addressing the First Congress of Muslim Communists in Moscow, Stalin was more explicit about the role Russia's Islamic peoples could play beyond the borders of the Soviet republics. "No one," he said, "can erect a bridge between the West and the East as easily and quickly as you can. This is because a door is opened for you to Persia, India, Afghanistan and China. The liberation of the peoples of these countries from the yoke of the imperialists would . . . undermine imperialism at its very foundation."[14]

Stalin returns here—and he appears to have been the first Bolshevik to do so—to Marx's long-neglected thesis that colonial revolution, especially in Asia, could hasten revolution in Europe. There was no agreement among Soviet leaders, however, that revolution in the East was *essential* to revolution in the West or would necessarily precede it. This, indeed, remained a question on which there would be differences of opinion for many years. Trotsky, for instance, speaking at the founding congress of the Communist International in March 1919, stated: "The workers and peasants not only of Annam, Algeria, Bengal but also of Persia and Armenia will obtain the possibility of independent existence only on the day when the workers of England and France will have overthrown Lloyd George and Clemenceau and

[13] Stalin, *Sochineniia*, IV, p. 92.
[14] *Zhizn' natsional'nostei*, November 24, 1918, p. 2, cited in Eudin and North, *Soviet Russia and the East*, p. 77; for reasons not clear, the text of the address is not included in Stalin's *Sochineniia*.

8

taken the state power into their hands."[15] A few weeks later Zinoviev, in a mood of extreme optimism generated by recent events in Hungary and Bavaria, wrote that within a year Europe would be Communist "and the struggle will have spread to America, perhaps to Asia too."[16] Clearly Trotsky and Zinoviev believed national liberation in the East was contingent on Communist successes in Europe.

Other Bolshevik spokesmen argued in an opposite sense. In 1918 an early Soviet volume on revolution in the East considered that "the Persian revolt can become the key to a general revolution."[17] In May 1919 an article appearing in *Zhizn' natsional'-nostei* (organ of Stalin's Commissariat for the Nationalities) described Marx as having foreseen that "the Communist revolution must be preceded by a number of national revolutions of the oppressed peoples, and first of all India and the peoples of the East."[18] It is unlikely that Marx ever made so firm a prediction, but it is instructive that an authoritative Soviet writer makes the claim. After Russian Turkestan (Central Asia) had been recovered by the Bolsheviks in September 1919, an editorial in *Zhizn' natsional'nostei* observed that this success offset the recent loss of the Ukraine because the Soviet Union now bordered on Afghanistan and "from Afghanistan the road leads to Hindustan [India], the possible key to world revolution."[19] Another writer in *Zhizn' natsional'nostei*, an Asian protégé of Stalin, charged that it was a strategic blunder to give priority to the revolution in the West when the weakest link in the capitalist chain was the East.[20]

[15] *Der I Kongress der Kommunistischen Internationale: Protokoll* (Hamburg, 1921), p. 5; cited in Boersner, *The Bolsheviks and the National and Colonial Question*, p. 66.

[16] *Kommunisticheskii internatsional*, May 1, 1919; cited in Degras, *Communist International*, I, p. 51.

[17] Troianovsky, *Vostok i revoliutsiia*, p. 47, cited in Eudin and North, *op. cit.*, p. 92.

[18] Palinkaitis, "Turkestan i revoliutsii Vostoka," *Zhizn' natsional'nostei*, May 26, 1919, p. 2, and in Eudin and North, *op. cit.*, p. 161.

[19] *Zhizn' natsional'nostei*, September 21, 1919, p. 1, cited in *ibid.*, p. 161.

[20] *Zhizn' natsional'nostei*, October 5 and 12, November 2, 1919; cited in Richard Pipes, *The Formation of the Soviet Union: Communism and Nationalism, 1917-1923* (Harvard, 1954), p. 169. The writer was Mirza Sultan-Galiev, a Tatar.

Lenin and Stalin themselves, addressing the Second Congress of Muslim Communists in November 1919, spoke with only slightly less enthusiasm of the revolutionary role of the Eastern colonies. Lenin, for instance, stated that "without the help of the toiling masses of all suppressed colonial peoples, especially the peoples of the East, the English, French, and German workers will not succeed."[21]

It is not easy then to fix a consistent Bolshevik attitude toward the East during the first years after the Revolution. This should surprise no one. There was still relatively wide freedom of expression at this time, within certain limits established by the Revolution, and honest differences of opinion among Bolshevik leaders were not unusual. Moreover, as the fortunes of the Civil War shifted back and forth on the Eastern and the Western fronts, it was natural for Soviet spokesmen to respond by shifting their emphasis between East and West. It was equally natural when Russians addressed assemblies of Asians, such as the two congresses of Muslim Communists, for them to accent the role of the Muslims in establishing "beacons" and "bridges" to the rest of Asia. Muslims themselves, such as Mirza Sultan-Galiev, emphasized the revolutionary potential of the East as a matter of course. The focus of the Bolsheviks, however, measured by any reasonable analysis of their propaganda and of the energy they expended during these years, remained in Europe. It was there that the first concrete steps were taken to extend the revolution; it was from Europe, not Asia, that delegates came in 1919 to found the Third International. As Bukharin stated the argument for an Eastern orientation shortly after the founding of the International: "If we propound the solution of the right of self-determination for the colonies . . . we lose nothing by it. On the contrary, we gain. The most outright nationalist movement . . . is only water for our mill, since it contributes to the destruction of English imperialism."[22] Whatever, at any event,

[21] Lenin, *Sochineniia*, xxx, p. 140; Stalin's address is in his *Sochineniia*, iv, pp. 279-80.
[22] Cited in Degras, *The Communist International*, i, p. 138; from Bukharin's speech before the Eighth Congress of the Russian Communist Party.

10

was *said* of revolution in the East—as support, prerequisite, or consequence of revolution in the West—little was accomplished there beyond the perimeter of Bolshevik control.

In the last analysis, the attitudes expressed by Lenin and Stalin must be taken as the most authoritative—Stalin's, because of his closeness to the Eastern question in his role as Commissar for the Nationalities; Lenin's, because he was Lenin. Stalin, the first Bolshevik to draw attention to the East after the Revolution and to reintroduce Marx's thesis of a link between revolutions in Asia and Europe, leaves no question as to the ultimately greater importance of Europe. Note, for instance, his formulation of the problem in his article "Don't forget the East," referred to above: "At a time when the revolutionary movement is rising in Europe, when old thrones and crowns are tumbling and giving way to revolutionary Soviets of workers and soldiers . . . , the eyes of all are naturally turned to the West. It is there, in the West, that the chains of imperialism, which were forged in Europe and which are strangling the whole world, must first of all be smashed. It is there, in the West, that the new socialist life must first of all be forged."[23] Only after this reminder does Stalin come to the point of his article: "Yet the East should not be forgotten for a single moment, if only because it represents the 'inexhaustible' reserve and 'most reliable' rear of world imperialism." Stalin added very little to this formulation in subsequent years.

Lenin, in the meantime, although perhaps less consistent than Stalin on the Eastern question in the years before the Second Comintern Congress in 1920, appears to have given a similar priority to Europe. On the eve of the Second Congress he gave this answer to a direct question by a Japanese correspondent concerning the best chances of Communist success, in the East or the West: "True Communism can succeed only in the West at the present time. However, the West lives at the expense of the East; the European imperialist powers prosper chiefly as a result of their Eastern colonies. At the same time they are arming their

[23] Stalin, *Sochineniia*, IV, p. 171.

11

colonies and teaching them how to fight, and in doing so they are digging their own graves in the East."[24]

THE EASTERN QUESTION AT THE SECOND COMINTERN CONGRESS: 1920

The increasing attention given the Eastern question by Soviet spokesmen ensured its being included conspicuously on the agenda of the Second Comintern Congress in July and August 1920. Lenin himself, early in June, drafted theses on the national and colonial question, which were published prior to the congress. Following a discussion of the theses in the Commission on the National and Colonial Question, Lenin personally introduced them to the full congress on July 26. Adopted with minor changes, Lenin's theses became the major statement of Comintern policy in the East for many years.[25]

The discussion of the colonial question during the Second Congress reveals many differing viewpoints which Lenin's theses could not wholly resolve. Had the question put to the congress been simply "Shall there be greater attention to the East?" there would have been negligible disagreement. Subsidiary questions, however, inevitably injected themselves into the debate and in the end all but submerged the basic query: How *much* attention to the East? Was the East to be considered more important than the West? Was revolution in Asia to precede revolution in Europe, or vice versa? These were issues which, as we have seen, had already been debated to some extent by Bolshevik spokesmen and which were now for the first time being discussed in an international Communist forum. The widened forum raised new questions: What responsibility for nurturing revolutionary movements in the colonies fell on the metropolitan parties? What allies in the East were Communists to seek?

Lenin's draft touched, though often vaguely, on most of these questions. Developments since the end of the war, he argued, showed that promises by capitalist states to honor the principles

[24] *Lenin i Vostok*, p. 63; the interview, with Katsuchi Fuse, took place on June 4, 1920.

[25] The text of the draft is in Lenin, *Sochineniia*, xxxi, pp. 122-9; the theses as adopted are in *Vtoroi Kongress Kommunisticheskogo Internatsionala*, pp. 491-5, and are widely reprinted and translated in other sources.

12

of equality and self-determination were fraudulent, that national boundaries would continue to be altered—or not altered—in accordance with the economic interests of the imperialist powers, and that the "so-called League of Nations is nothing but the insurance contract by which the victors in the war mutually guarantee each other's spoils." Accordingly Comintern policy on the national and colonial question must seek "the closest alliance of all national and colonial movements of liberation with Soviet Russia, the precise form of this alliance to correspond to the stage of development of the Communist movement among the proletariat of each country or of the bourgeois democratic liberation movement of workers and peasants in the backward countries or among backward nationalities." In the case of countries able to create soviet regimes, Lenin proposed a temporary form of federation with the Soviet Union, such as the RSFSR, and argued that without such a federation "it will be impossible for the Soviet Republics to survive, surrounded as they are by the imperialist powers of the world which from a military viewpoint are incomparably stronger."

Lenin does not appear to have had the colonies of the East specifically in mind in this proposed federation for he returns to the special problem of the "more backward feudal or patriarchal or patriarchal-peasant nations" later in the theses.[26] In paragraph 11 he advances six policies for these areas:

a. "All Communist Parties must support the bourgeois democratic movement of liberation in these countries," primary responsibility to fall on the workers of the country on which the backward nation is dependent.
b. The influence of the priesthood and of similar reactionary and medieval elements must be resisted.

[26] The extent to which the "national" or "Eastern" question still referred to Europe, rather than Asia, is also suggested by Stalin's response to Lenin's draft, which was sent to him for comment prior to publication: in a short letter to Lenin (Stalin was in South Russia at the time) he virtually ignores the Asian colonies and confines himself to the argument that confederation, not federation, will better ensure the union of future soviet republics in Europe to the USSR and thus make the theses "more elastic." The text of Stalin's letter is in Lenin, *Sochineniia*, 2nd ed., xxv, p. 624, translated in Eudin and North, *op. cit.*, pp. 67-8.

13

c. Pan-Islamic and like tendencies must also be resisted.
d. The peasantry must be supported and peasant movements given a more revolutionary character through the formation of soviets.
e. Any tendency to paint bourgeois democratic movements in Communist colors must be avoided. "The Communist International must support bourgeois democratic national movements in the colonies and backward nations only on condition that elements of future proletarian parties in these countries . . . be grouped together and educated to appreciate their special tasks: to struggle against the bourgeois democratic movements in their countries. The Communist International must enter into temporary alliance with bourgeois democracy in the colonies and backward countries, but must not merge with it and must above all preserve the independence of the proletarian movement even if it exists only in the most rudimentary form."
f. The deception of the imperialist powers in creating ostensibly independent states which are in fact wholly dependent must be systematically exposed.[27]

At Lenin's request, supplementary theses were prepared by the Indian delegate M. N. Roy[28] and discussed by the commission prior to presentation to the congress. Roy's theses were not fundamentally in conflict with Lenin's, but they treated two aspects of the problem differently. First, Roy placed more emphasis than Lenin had on the dependence of European revolutions on Asian. "Super-profit obtained from the colonies," he asserted, "is the mainstay of modern capitalism. It will not be easy for the European working class to overthrow the capitalist order until the latter is deprived of this source of super-profit. . . . Consequently, the Communist International must widen the sphere of its activity."[29] This idea was reiterated throughout the supplementary

---

[27] Lenin, *Sochineniia*, xxxi, pp. 122-9; the portions quoted are translated from the text, the remainder paraphrased. It should be noted that these are the original theses, before revision.

[28] Roy, who was to become one of the most active, and controversial, Asians in the world Communist movement during the 1920's, was 22 at this juncture; he had recently arrived in Moscow from the United States and Mexico, where he had already engaged in revolutionary activities. Lenin, who was attracted to Roy as an authentic Asian revolutionary, evidently felt that Roy's views would support and amplify his own.

[29] *Vtoroi Kongress Kommunisticheskogo internatsionala*, p. 497; an English

14

theses. Secondly, Roy's theses noted, as Lenin's did not, that peasant-proletarian movements were already growing in the colonies parallel to bourgeois democratic movements. He was accordingly more insistent than Lenin that the Comintern's efforts be directed primarily to the former. "The foremost and immediate task," he stated, "is to form Communist parties which will organize the peasants and workers and lead them to the revolution and to the establishment of soviet republics."

These were the two sets of theses which were presented first to the Commission on the National and Colonial Question and later to the full congress.

Although the time of the commission was largely taken up with lengthy reports of revolutionary developments in the colonies,[30] the delegates did from time to time discuss the two sets of theses. Attention was drawn especially to Roy's argument—which he stated with particular force in introducing his theses—concerning the dependence of European revolutions on Asian. His argument was repudiated by most speakers, including Lenin. Although Lenin himself had made the same argument on previous occasions (for instance, in his remarks to the Second Muslim Congress in 1919), he now felt that Roy went "too far in declaring that the destiny of the West will depend exclusively upon the degree of development and the strength of the revolutionary movement in the Eastern countries."[31]

Lenin and Roy also disagreed on the substance of paragraph

---

translation is in Eudin and North, *op. cit.*, pp. 65-7. This is the final version of Roy's theses, after revisions made in the commission; the original is not extant so far as is known.

[30] A report on Indonesia, for instance, was delivered by Maring, on Persia by Sultan-Zade, on China by Lan, on Korea by Pak, etc. Summaries of these reports may be found in *The Second Congress of the Communist International, as Reported and Interpreted by the Official Newspapers of Soviet Russia*, pp. 40-6. Approximately a dozen Eastern delegates (excluding those from within the Soviet Union) attended the Second Congress, of a total of 217 (voting and non-voting); two, Pak and Sultan-Zade, were elected to the 26-man Executive Committee, and Maring was elected to represent Java.

[31] *Ibid.*, p. 44, citing *Petrogradskaia Pravda*, July 29, 1920; it is not clear whether the passage quoted represents Lenin's exact words (in translation) or a paraphrase of them.

15

11-a of Lenin's theses: the obligation to support alliances with all liberation movements in the colonies. Roy's analysis of the mass revolutionary movements emerging in Asia, especially in India, led him to propose the elimination of this recommendation in its entirety. The course of the debate on Roy's proposal is not clear, but a compromise appears to have been worked out. This was to substitute for "bourgeois democratic" the term "national revolutionary," not only in the paragraph under discussion but throughout Lenin's theses. In explaining the change to the full congress, Lenin appeared wholly satisfied with the substitution, arguing that it now permitted the necessary distinction to be made between revolutionary and merely "reformist" movements.[32]

The Commission on the National and Colonial Question also discussed the problem of soviets in backward countries. In his opening address to the congress Lenin referred to "the beginning of a soviet movement throughout the entire East, in the whole of Asia, among all colonial peoples."[33] Since no soviets outside the Soviet Republic had been formed at this juncture, apart from the abortive efforts in 1919 in Bavaria and Hungary, Lenin was doubtless using the term freely to describe revolutionary movements in general. Yet he continued to insist, later in the congress, that "the idea of soviet organization is a simple one." The discussion in the commission, Lenin reported, had demonstrated that "we must base the theses of the Communist International on the assumption that peasant soviets, the soviets of the exploited, are applicable not only in capitalist countries but also in countries with pre-capitalist conditions and that it is the absolute duty of Communist parties, and of elements preparing to form Communist parties, to propagate the idea of peasant soviets and soviets of toilers everywhere, including the backward and colonial countries."[34] Concerning the related question of whether colonies must pass through a capitalist stage before reaching socialism, Lenin said that the commission had decided after "lively debates" that, "if the victorious revolutionary proletariat conducts

[32] Lenin, *Sochineniia*, xxxi, pp. 216-7.
[33] *Ibid.*, p. 209.
[34] *Ibid.*, p. 218.

16

systematic propaganda among the backward peoples and if the Soviet [i.e., Russian] government comes to their help with all means at its disposal, then it is incorrect to assert that a capitalist stage of development is unavoidable for backward nationalities."[35] To these propositions, it may be imagined, there would have been no objections from M. N. Roy.

The discussion of the national and colonial question during the fifth and sixth plenary sessions of the full congress, following the deliberations of the commission, should have been more or less routine. It was not. Unexpected opposition arose to portions of the theses, and each of the two sessions ended more acrimoniously than any others during the entire congress. A brief review of the discussion, from the stenographic record of the congress, is instructive.[36]

Lenin reported for the commission, expanding somewhat on his theses, the text of which had already been given to the delegates. Maring, the secretary of the commission, read the few changes in wording agreed upon by the commission. Roy then read his supplementary theses, which had not been previously circulated, and commented briefly on them. His approach was more moderate than it had been during the debate within the commission. He no longer argued, for instance, that Asian revolutions must precede European but asserted merely that the colonial question was urgent because its resolution would hasten Communism in Europe. Whether the coming revolution in India, for instance, would be Communist or not was less important than the impetus it would give to the collapse of British imperialism, "which would be of enormous significance to the European proletariat." In short, Roy had abandoned his earlier position, which gave the appearance—rightly or wrongly—of pitting East against West, and now argued that the East was important because it could *help* the West.

[35] *Ibid.*, p. 219.
[36] The full official record is *Vtoroi Kongress Kommunisticheskogo internatsionala; stenograficheskii otchet (1921)*, reprinted in 1934 as *Vtoroi Kongress Kominterna*. An abbreviated English record of the congress is *Second Congress of the Communist International: Proceedings* (1921).

Following Roy, John Reed spoke about the American Negro, and Fraina about Latin America. Radek then took the floor. Two of his remarks deserve notice. The first concerned an assertion made before the commission by a British delegate, Quelch, that British labor would not support any uprising in India. If the assertion was meant to reveal the cowardly position of British labor, Radek pointed out, it was acceptable, but did not "exonerate the British comrades for being passive." He then made a remark often quoted in later years: "The International will judge the English comrades not by the articles they write in *Call* and *Workers' Dreadnought* [two British Communist publications] but by the number of comrades who are thrown into prison for agitation of the colonial question." Radek also sought to reassure the colonial delegates present that Comintern tactics in the East were not, as Roy and others implied, "an auxiliary device in our struggle against European capitalism," but a distinctive and separate feature of the world struggle. He went on to support Lenin's notion that capitalism could be bypassed in the East, opening the way for a direct transition to socialism.

At this juncture the Italian delegate Serrati, charging that most of the speeches thus far had been irrelevant (he singled out John Reed's speech in particular), moved that the list of speakers on the colonial question be closed. The motion raised a storm of protest led by the Dutch representative Wynkop, the most outraged of the delegates, and supported by Maring, Radek, and others. Maring called attention to the irony of Serrati's seeking to silence the delegates from the East when he had not taken the trouble to attend sessions of the commission. Sensing the certain defeat of his motion, Serrati withdrew it and the meeting adjourned at 2:30 a.m.—an hour which perhaps explains the frayed tempers during the final minutes of the session.

The sixth session opened peaceably enough with a new round of reports by delegates from Eastern countries, most of whom had already been heard in the commission. Early in the session an Italian delegate, Graziadei, proposed an amendment to paragraph 11-a of Lenin's theses, the same previously challenged by Roy in the commission: instead of requiring that Communist

18

parties "support" national revolutionary movements, Graziadei argued, they should be required merely to "show active interest" in them. The purpose of the amendment was not made clear, but, to judge from subsequent reference to it by an Irish delegate, Graziadei was motivated by the same considerations that would later prompt Serrati to deny any responsibility of the European parties for colonial movements. The proposal in any case attracted little attention and was never brought to a vote.

Following a second unsuccessful attempt by Serrati to close debate, Maring, drawing on his long experience in Indonesia, delivered one of the major—and surely one of the most pertinent—speeches during the debate on the Eastern question. "There is no question in all the proceedings of the congress," he began, "of greater importance for the development of the world revolution than the colonial and national question." He then discussed the revolutionary movement in Indonesia in some detail before turning to the two sets of theses before the congress: "I find no distinction between the theses of Comrade Roy and those of Comrade Lenin. They are alike in essence. The difficulty lies only in finding the precise formula for the relationship between the revolutionary national and the socialist movements in the backward countries. The difficulty does not exist in reality. In actual practice we find it necessary to work together with the revolutionary nationalist elements and our work would be half done if we should deny the nationalist revolutionary movement and play the dogmatic Marxists."

Maring closed with the first concrete proposals for an Eastern policy: publication of the theses in various Oriental languages, especially Chinese and Hindi; the establishment of a Bureau of Propaganda for the Far East and Near East; and the summoning of Eastern leaders to the Soviet Union for periods of half a year to study Marxism. "Moscow and Petrograd," he concluded, "have become a new Mecca for the East."

Serrati in the meantime had not said his final word. Following a series of interventions which had little to do with the theses under discussion (including a sharp exchange between several Jewish delegates on the integrity of the Jewish Socialist Bund),

19

the controversial Italian volunteered an explanation of his objection both to the unnecessarily prolonged debate on the Eastern question and to the theses themselves. The theses, he said, were vague; the very expression "backward countries," used throughout the theses, was ambiguous as well as chauvinistic. His main objection, however, was that the proposed alliance with bourgeois democracy in the colonies was a dangerous policy for proletarians. "A struggle for national liberation carried on by the democratic bourgeoisie, even when insurrectionary methods are used, is not a revolutionary movement. . . . The movement for national liberation can be revolutionary only when the working class maintains its own class lines. . . . Only by means of a proletarian revolution and through a soviet regime can the subject nations obtain their freedom. This cannot be done by temporary alliances of Communists with bourgeois parties called nationalist revolutionaries." Serrati announced that because of lack of clarity in the theses he would abstain from voting.

The congress was not prepared to let the matter rest there. Attacks on Serrati's position now multiplied in intensity. Zinoviev denied "that the theses, which are nothing but a summary of propositions of Marx and Engels, can furnish any ground for misinterpretation" and went on to impugn Serrati's standing with Italian workers. Wynkop accused Serrati of calling Lenin's theses "counter-revolutionary" and "compromising." Roy, identifying himself wholly with Lenin in the crisis, made the same charge. At length, obviously stung by the abuse directed against him, Serrati again took the floor. Wynkop and Roy, he said, had misunderstood him: if he felt the theses were "counter-revolutionary," he would surely vote against them. As it was, he merely felt that they "could serve as a source of misinterpretation by chauvinists and nationalists" and therefore he proposed to abstain from voting. Serrati pointed out that he had long opposed such formulations as those in the theses because he found them in contradiction with the principles of "revolutionary socialism"; he was resigned, he said, to the fact that the congress must vote on—and pass—the theses, but his conscience did not permit him to join the majority. The question, Serrati continued, could not be objectively discussed under the circumstances. Nonetheless he had been on the point of offering the following substitute resolution: "The congress sends its fraternal greetings to all the peoples suffering under the oppression of the imperialist powers. It stands ready actively to support every movement directed against all exploiters and it declares that in this struggle against capitalist oppression the proletariat may take advantage of every national insurrection in order to turn it into a social revolution." Such a resolution, he said—he did not make it clear whether he intended it as a substitute for the theses altogether, or for paragraph 11-a of Lenin's theses—would obviate the need for any firm policy of alliance with the bourgeoisie while giving some freedom of action to the colonial proletariat to "take advantage" of favorable local situations. He closed with a rebuke to Zinoviev for questioning the responsibility of delegates at the congress to workers at home.

Zinoviev, chairing the session, allowed time for a few final insults to be leveled at the Italian—before calling for a vote on the theses as recommended to the congress by the Commission on the National and Colonial Question. They were passed unanimously, with three abstentions, and the Second Congress passed on to other business.

The foregoing must destroy any notion that Lenin's famous theses were final or definitive. They were adopted as he presented them to the congress largely, it may be imagined, because of his great prestige. But the debate on them, as well as on Roy's supplementary theses, revealed a variety of viewpoints on the colonial question which must have confounded any observer attempting to form a concrete idea of Moscow's Eastern policy. Lenin, who evidently left the meetings after presenting his theses, was not present to give direction to the deliberations and in consequence they meandered aimlessly. From an ideological standpoint, Serrati, in insisting on traditional class differentiations, exhibited the purest orthodoxy and greatest consistency. But his view was unacceptable to a congress bent on exploring and glorifying the "mysterious East." As Radek said, in protesting one of

Serrati's efforts to close debate: "We are concerned with the *political* significance of the colonial question"—by which he meant that what was decided at the congress was less important politically than the fact that Eastern delegates were heard and that the Third International, unlike its predecessors and its contemporary rivals, was considering the colonial question at all. Serrati's influence, moreover, was undermined by his evidently arrogant manner and by his direct assault on Lenin's theses.[37]

It is useful, given the importance of the deliberations in 1920 on the future course of Soviet policies in the East, to attempt a recapitulation of the divergent views expressed during the Second Congress:

On the question of *how* important the East was, at one extreme would be Roy, Maring, Wynkop, Pak, and perhaps other Asian delegates, arguing that the Comintern should devote its major efforts to the East. Serrati would be at the opposite extreme, along with a handful of Europeans, arguing that revolution in the East was impossible—and therefore irrelevant to Marxists—until completed in Europe. Lenin's position was intermediate, reflecting his obvious bewitchment with the East, especially its size,[38] and his feeling that it had been neglected, but with no conviction that activity in the West should be curtailed to allow more attention to the East. Zinoviev, Radek, Bukharin, and most of the European delegates associated themselves with Lenin.

On the question of *why* the East was important, the alignment defies easy classification. Roy again stands at one extreme, with his argument that European revolutions are contingent on Asian. However, the shift in his position during the discussion in the Colonial Commission and in the congress suggests that he stressed the contingency in order to persuade reluctant Europeans that an investment in colonial movements would in the end

---

[37] Serrati, known as a "maximalist" in Italian socialist circles, quarreled incessantly with both socialists and Communists until his final break with the Comintern in 1923.

[38] Lenin, it should be noted, referred several times during the Second Congress, as on other occasions, to the 70% of the world's population living under colonial rule; e.g., *Sochineniia*, xxxi, pp. 202, 216.

22

benefit them. By the same token, it is possible that Lenin, together with Radek and others, *minimized* the connection between Asian and European revolutions in order to avoid giving the idea to Asians that their efforts were merely "auxiliary." Radek, Maring, Sultan-Zade, and others reflected an emotional commitment to the East, evidently generated by the congress itself, and indicated that there was something noble and uplifting in the West helping the East. Lenin and Zinoviev, on the other hand, were more pragmatic and indicated merely that timely uprisings in Asia might facilitate revolution in Europe and prove the best way of saving the Soviet Republic.

On the question of *alliance with the bourgeoisie*, an issue which was to remain in the forefront of Soviet Eastern policy for the next three decades, the felicitous rephrasing in Lenin's theses—substituting "national revolutionary" for "bourgeois democratic"—allowed the differences to be somewhat obscured. The differences nonetheless existed. Lenin here would appear at one extreme (though, to be sure, with the majority) in encouraging alliance with "national revolutionary" movements in the East.[39] Roy, along with Sultan-Zade, would permit such alliances only under very restrictive conditions, emphasizing instead more vigorous support of bona fide peasant-proletarian movements. Serrati, with whom it may be noted Roy was in closer accord on this point than with Lenin, would reject the alliances altogether. Indeed it was precisely his suspicion of such alliances that led him to deprecate any serious effort at all in the East: unless there was a proletariat strong enough to stand alone, there could be no Marxist revolution. The most realistic comment on the matter was doubtless Maring's reminder that in actual practice it was not too difficult to decide whether to ally with bourgeois nationalists or not.

On one issue all but Serrati and his handful of supporters appeared to agree: the European parties must devote more attention

---

[39] Although the Second Congress left no doubt about the intent henceforth to substitute "national revolutionary" for "bourgeois democratic" in all Comintern pronouncements, in actual practice both terms continued to be used interchangeably.

23

to the colonial question, especially those parties in countries with colonies. And yet the accomplishments in this area in the years following the Second Congress were negligible.

FROM THE SECOND COMINTERN CONGRESS TO THE FOURTH: 1920-1922

Despite the rejection by the Second Congress of Roy's thesis concerning the dependence of European revolutions on Asian, the idea continued to appear in Soviet commentaries on the East. An authoritative article in *Zhizn' natsional'nostei*, for instance, appearing less than a month after the close of the congress, re-iterated Roy's argument as though it had never been disputed. "It is necessary," the article stated, "to break and destroy the capitalist front by means of organizing the revolution and the revolutionary fighting forces behind the capitalist lines. . . . This new field of revolutionary work will mean striking a blow in the rear of the rapacious Entente and this *in turn* will clear the way for the triumphant march of the proletariat of the West."[40] In October, two months after the Second Congress, Stalin himself asserted that "the more developed proletarian West cannot finish off the world bourgeoisie without the support of the peasant East."[41] Several years later, in a retrospective glance at the era following the Civil War and Intervention, Stalin acknowledged that the forward momentum of revolution had been stopped when Red Army troops failed at Warsaw in 1920 and that it had been neces-sary to reestablish contact with the base, especially "the heavy reserves in the East which are the main rear of world capital-ism. . . . One of two things: either we succeed in stirring up, in revolutionizing the remote rear of imperialism—the colonial and semi-colonial countries of the East—and thereby hasten the fall of imperialism; or we fail, and thereby strengthen imperialism and weaken the strength of our movement. That is how the question stands."[42] Statements such as these show that whatever formulation the Second Comintern Congress attempted to give to

[40] *Zhizn' natsional'nostei*, September 2, 1920, p. 2; cited in Eudin and North, *op. cit.*, p. 17 (emphasis added).
[41] Stalin, *Sochineniia*, IV, p. 351; from an article in *Pravda* on the government's policy on the national question in Russia.
[42] Stalin, *Sochineniia*, V, p. 237; from an address to the Twelfth Congress of the CPSU in April 1923.

the matter, a sense of urgency concerning revolution in the East as a means of hastening revolution in Europe persisted in certain quarters. In Stalin's case, indeed, the conviction appears to have grown stronger as time passed.

In the years following the Second Congress, special efforts were made to encourage revolutionary movements in the East. In September 1920, for instance, a Congress of Toilers of the East, attended by nearly 2,000 Muslims from the Near East and Central Asia, convened in Baku; the congress was addressed by Zinoviev, Radek, and other Comintern spokesmen who pressed the delegates to declare a "holy war" against imperialism.[43] The Baku congress established a Council for Propaganda and Action to coordinate Comintern activities in the East and to publish a journal, *Narody Vostoka*. The council was soon subdivided into three sections, located in Baku, Tashkent, and Irkutsk, with responsibilities, respectively, for the Near East, Central and South Asia, and the Far East; Southeast Asia was not included in this early effort to make concrete contacts with revolutionary movements in the East. In January 1922 a Congress of Toilers of the Far East, attended by representatives from Korea, China, Japan, Mongolia, and Java, met for a week in Moscow and Leningrad; this congress too, like the Baku congress, was dominated by Comintern spokesmen who stressed the themes of the Second Congress.[44] Similar conferences of Asian youth and of Asian women were held in Moscow at about this time.[45] Meanwhile, the Red International of Labor Unions (RILU, or Profintern) was established in 1921 and the Peasant International (Krestintern) in 1923, both of which in due course were to play an important role in carrying out Soviet policies in Asia.[46]

[43] For the proceedings see *Pervyi s"ezd narodov Vostoka: stenograficheskii otchet*; although called the "First Congress," it was not followed by others.

[44] The official record of the congress is *Pervyi s"ezd revoliutsionnykh organizatsii Dal'nego Vostoka* (1922). Like its predecessor at Baku, this congress was the first and last; it was prompted by the Washington Naval Conference, which convened in November 1921, and no machinery was set up for the implementation of Comintern policies in the Far East.

[45] *Ibid.*, pp. 293-314, 333-42; for a fuller discussion of these early Soviet efforts to organize Asian revolutionaries, see Eudin and North, *op. cit.*, pp. 79-81, 145-7.

[46] At least three Asians attended the founding congress of the *Krestintern*, and one of them, Nguyen Ai Quoc (Ho Chi Minh), was elected to the presidium; *ibid.*, p. 267.

During this period the Soviet government also established schools and training centers for Asian revolutionaries, an effort that perhaps stemmed from Maring's recommendation at the Second Congress. During the winter of 1920-1921, for instance, a training school for Indian revolutionaries was organized in Tashkent by Roy, a member of the Comintern's three-man Turkestan Commission; thirty-six Indians are reported to have attended the school. In 1921 the Communist University of Toilers of the East (*KUTV*) was formally launched and by January 1923 was reported to have had 800 students, mainly from Asia. There were also a number of institutes for Russians training in Oriental studies, both for future revolutionary work and for research. Among these were: the Narimanov Institute of Oriental Studies in Moscow (formerly the Armenian Institute), dating from 1919; the Oriental Institute of Leningrad; the Scientific Association of Oriental Studies, founded in 1921 under M. P. Veltman (M. Pavlovich); and various military schools and faculties devoted to Eastern affairs.[47]

In addition to these institutional facilities in the Soviet Union, both for Asians seeking more knowledge of Communism and for Russians seeking more knowledge of Asia, Comintern agents made a number of direct contacts with Asian revolutionary movements. Gregory Voitinsky, for instance, was sent to China in the spring of 1920 to contact Chinese Marxists with a view to organizing a Communist party. In 1921 Maring arrived in Shanghai as the Comintern's representative in the Far East; he attended the founding congress of the Chinese Communist Party in July 1921 and remained in China for several years before being replaced by Voitinsky. Another Soviet agent named Dalin conferred with Sun Yat-sen in Shanghai in mid-1922.[48] These early contacts with Chinese Communists and Nationalists, it should be noted, occurred before Adolf Joffe's fateful negotiations with Sun Yat-sen in January 1923, which opened the door to a flood of Soviet ad-

[47] The work of these institutions is described in *ibid.*, p. 86-8.

[48] For an account of the activities of these early Soviet agents in China based on Chinese Communist materials, see Wilbur and How, *Documents on Communism, Nationalism and Soviet Advisers in China*, pp. 79-90 *passim*.

visers and Comintern agents in China during the remainder of the decade. Roy in the meantime maintained contact with Indian revolutionaries he met in Tashkent during 1920 and 1921, after their return to India. He also arranged for a British Communist, Charles Ashleigh, to visit India in September 1922, but Ashleigh's mission was frustrated by his arrest and deportation.[49] Similar contacts were made in Persia, Turkey, Afghanistan, and other Eastern countries.[50]

These widely varied activities of the Soviet government during the years immediately following the Second Congress testify to a growing interest in the East which can doubtless be traced to the decisions of the congress and to Lenin's theses. The impact of Soviet activity, however, should not be exaggerated. Very little was changed in the course of events in Asia until 1925 or 1926, and the total number of Asians directly exposed to Soviet influence remained negligible. These years, in retrospect, must be looked upon as years of preparation, when the ground-work was being laid for a future assault on the East; no one, after all, should have imagined that decisions reached by a conclave in Moscow, made up largely of Europeans, would immediately affect social processes in Asia involving hundreds of millions. A question of greater consequence, in attempting to comprehend Soviet Eastern policy during these years, is whether Moscow was demonstrating an interest proportionate to the importance attached to the East in official pronouncements or merely responding, in a perfunctory way, to warnings that the colonial world must not be overlooked.

As the Third Congress approached, the Comintern's Executive Committee (ECCI) issued a circular on the agenda which attached continuing importance to the Eastern question. "The Third Congress will have to deal with the Eastern question not only theoretically, as the Second Congress, but as a practical matter," the circular declared. "Without a revolution in Asia there

[49] See Overstreet and Windmiller, *Communism in India*, pp. 39, 42.
[50] An account of early Soviet efforts in the Near East may be found in Eudin and North, *op. cit.*, pp. 91-120.

27

will be no victory for the world proletarian revolution. This must be firmly grasped by every proletarian Communist."[51]

But these proved to be words, no more. The Third Congress, meeting in June and July 1921, gave slight attention to the colonial question. Lenin touched on the matter only casually in two of his four speeches during the congress.[52] Trotsky, who drafted the principal theses on the world situation adopted by the congress, also gave the Eastern question cursory treatment.[53] The resolutions and manifestos adopted at the close of the congress ignored the East altogether and the new Executive Committee included no representative from the East. The colonial question reached the agenda only during the next to last session, and the discussion appears to have given little satisfaction to anyone. Roy, one of the three Eastern delegates who spoke, used the five minutes allotted to him to protest the "opportunist way" in which the colonial question was being treated; a Bulgarian delegate dismissed his protest, reminding him that the Eastern question had after all been thoroughly discussed at the Second Congress and at Baku.[54] Roy also complained that no American or European delegates had attended the single meeting of the Commission on the National and Colonial Question held the preceding day. This meeting, given over largely to developments in the Near East, evidently reaffirmed over Roy's objections the policy of close—but temporary—alliance with the colonial bourgeoisie, the tactic approved by the Second Congress; the meeting does not appear to have taken concrete steps to implement the 1920 theses.[55]

[51] *Kommunisticheskii Internatsional*, June 1921; translated in Degras, *Communist International*, I, p. 223.

[52] Lenin, *Sochineniia*, xxxii, pp. 430, 457-8.

[53] See Section 26 of "Theses on the World Situation and Tasks of the Comintern" adopted by the Third Congress; translated in Degras, *Communist International*, I, p. 234.

[54] *Protokoll Des III Kongress Der Kommunistischen Internationale*, pp. 1018, 1035; cited in Page, *Lenin and World Revolution*, p. 198.

[55] The only account of the meeting known to the writer is taken from the memoirs of the Chinese delegate at the Third Congress, Chang T'ai-lei; see Boris Shumiatskii, "Iz istorii Komsomola i Kompartii Kitaia," *Revoliutsionnyi Vostok*, No. 4-5, 1928, pp. 218-22. A summary of the portion of the article dealing with the meeting of the commission may be found in Eudin and North, *op. cit.*, p. 144.

28

The Second Comintern Congress to the Fourth

During the sixteen-month interval between the Third and Fourth Comintern Congresses, from July 1921 to November 1922, the Eastern question came before the ECCI only half a dozen times, as compared to the more than sixty occasions when European problems were discussed.[56] The Comintern's only directive regarding the East during this period was an ECCI resolution dated March 4, 1922, urging all parties in countries with overseas colonies, especially the British Communist Party, to establish colonial commissions "for the purpose of supplying regular information about colonial affairs, of establishing regular contact with the revolutionary organizations of the colonial countries, and of making this contact practically operative."[57] This was evidently the first specific Comintern instruction on Eastern policy since the Second Congress, two years earlier.

The colonial question received considerably more attention during the Fourth Comintern Congress, in November and December 1922. The Fourth Congress could record a certain progress in the East. A pro-Soviet regime had been established in Mongolia. Strike movements had gained headway in China and India. The Near East was in ferment as a result of the Turkish revolution of Kemal Pasha. Communist parties now existed in eight or ten Eastern countries. The number of Eastern representatives at the congress was larger than heretofore and included delegates from countries not previously represented.[58]

Zinoviev, who delivered the keynote address during Lenin's illness, touched briefly on the colonial question, but the principal discussion of the issue occurred at two sessions midway through the congress. Ravensteyn of Holland introduced the theses on the Eastern question which had been previously drawn up by

[56] See *Fourth Congress of the Communist International*, pp. 9-10; the Eastern areas discussed were: Near and Far East (three times), China, Japan, and South America (once each).

[57] *Inprekorr*, April 1, 1922, p. 9; translated in Degras, *Communist International*, I, pp. 326-7.

[58] The Eastern nations represented at the congress included China, Japan, India, Java, Turkey, Egypt, Tunisia, and Persia; Katayama and Safarov were elected to represent the Orient on the ECCI, with Roy as alternate. See *Fourth Congress of the Communist International*, p. 296.

delegations from the colonial countries in collaboration with the Eastern section of the ECCI. The theses attempted no conscious departure from Lenin's theses at the Second Congress, but they analyzed developments in the East in far greater detail and in effect altered several of Lenin's formulations. The Fourth Congress theses, for instance, took cognizance of greater variety in national revolutionary movements that had been acknowledged two and a half years earlier. The Comintern still undertook to support "every national revolutionary movement against imperialism," but the danger of confusing these movements with "feudal-bureaucratic," "feudal-agrarian," and "feudal-patriarchal" elements was underscored. Pan-Islamic movements, which Lenin had singled out for attack in 1920, were now largely exonerated. "In Muslim countries," the theses declared, "the national movement at first finds its ideology in the religio-political watchwords of pan-Islam . . . but to the extent that the national liberation movements grow and expand, the religio-political watchwords of pan-Islam are increasingly replaced by concrete political demands." Ravensteyn stressed this new positive approach to pan-Islamic movements and stated that "the international proletariat therefore acclaims the political aspirations of the Mohammedan nations." The change in Comintern policy on this issue was to have significant consequences in Indonesia.[59]

The theses went on to enumerate the tasks of colonial Communist parties with regard to the agrarian question, the labor movement, and, in particular, the united front—the general strategy adopted by the Fourth Congress for all sections. In the East, because of the prospect of a protracted struggle with imperialism, the form of the united front was to differ from that in the West by being anti-imperialist rather than proletarian (that is, "from above" rather than "from below"). This, of course, was the justification for the recommended alliance with national revolutionary movements. Refusal to enter into such alliances, "on the ground

[59] Impetus for the change may have come from the Indonesian delegate Tan Malaka, who requested clarification of the Comintern's view on the Islamic question in the light of recent developments in the Muslim world; see below, p. 84. He was supported by another Muslim delegate, a Tunisian; see *Fourth Congress of the Communist International*, p. 214.

30

of the ostensible 'defense' of independent class interests," was labeled "opportunism of the worst kind"; remaining aloof from the class struggle "in the name of 'national unity' or of 'civil peace' with bourgeois democrats" was equally reprehensible. The colonial parties, the theses proclaimed, have a dual task: "they fight for the most radical possible solution of the tasks of a bourgeois democratic revolution, which aims at the conquest of political independence; and they organize the working and peasant masses for the struggle for their special class interests, and in doing so exploit all the contradictions in the nationalist, bourgeois democratic camp." The Fourth Congress, then, came no closer than its predecessors to formulating a clear directive to Asian revolutionary leaders on the conditions necessary to justify an alliance with nationalist movements; the pitfalls on each side of Moscow's razor-thin line were equally hazardous. The theses closed with a fresh reminder to the metropolitan parties that they must assist the colonial movements, but not by forming overseas European Communist organizations, which were considered "a concealed form of colonialism."[60]

Discussion of the theses was far milder than during the stormy sessions of the Second Congress, perhaps because Serrati, though present, took no part in the debate; perhaps because Moscow's hold over the Comintern was surer than it had been in 1920. Ravensteyn's attention was directed mainly to the Near East, which continued to be the major focus of the Comintern's Eastern policy. Roy, delivering the principal supporting speech, appeared more subdued than on previous occasions. He no longer argued, for instance, that revolution in the East must precede revolution in the West, but merely that any efforts the European parties made in the East "would not be gratuitous . . . because capitalism is today very closely linked with the situation in the colonial countries."[61] Nearly all speakers, Eastern and Western alike, underscored the urgency of more attention to the East by the Euro-

---

[60] An English text of the "Theses on the Eastern Question" adopted by the Fourth Congress may be found in *Inprecor*, December 22, 1922, pp. 979-90; also in Eudin and North, *op. cit.*, pp. 231-7, and Degras, *Communist International*, 1, 383-93.

[61] *Inprecor*, December 22, 1922, p. 990.

pean sections. At the close of the discussion the theses were passed unanimously and without amendments.[62]

The more extended treatment of the Eastern question during the Fourth Congress, as compared to the Third, should not be interpreted as the signal for any significant turn in Comintern policy. The Comintern's principal focus remained, as before, in Europe. The officials of the organization were predominantly European, its strength lay in the European parties, and the current crises were European—for instance, the Ruhr and German reparations. Both before and after the Fourth Congress the Comintern, to judge from its published records, devoted incomparably more attention to these problems than to developments in the East.[63] The Fourth Congress, moreover, exhibited no great confidence, as earlier congresses had, in the prospects of revolution either in the West or the East. Lenin, in his only appearance before the congress, urged moderation and caution: "I submit that after five years of the Russian revolution the most important thing for all of us to do is to study, Russians and foreign comrades alike. We have only now gained the opportunity of studying. I do not know how long this opportunity will last; I do not know how long the capitalist powers will allow us to study in peace. But we must use every moment of respite from fighting and war to start learning from the beginning."[64] Radek echoed Lenin's sentiment. In his remarks on the colonial question he cautioned the Chinese comrades "not to indulge in too rosy expectations or to overestimate your strength. . . . Neither the question of socialism, nor of a soviet republic, are now the order of the day." The current task facing the Chinese was the more prosaic one of organizing the worker's movement and regulating

[62] Ravensteyn's and Roy's speeches are given in full in *ibid.*, December 22, 1922, pp. 979-90; a summary of the debate on the colonial question is in *ibid.*, December 7, 1922, pp. 894-5. See also *IV Vsemirnyi Kongress Kommunisticheskogo Internatsionala*, pp. 250 ff., and *Fourth Congress of the Communist International*, pp. 204-24.

[63] In 1922 *Inprecor*, for instance, carried fewer than fifteen articles on Eastern problems, as against hundreds on European affairs; in 1923 the increase in Eastern coverage was negligible.

[64] Lenin, *Sochineniia*, XXXIII, p. 393.

the party's relations with the revolutionary bourgeoisie preparatory to a prolonged struggle against imperialism.[65] The actions of the Comintern, in retrospect, appear to be a surer measure of Moscow's commitment to the East than the existence in Russia of various Oriental institutes and universities for Asians, and the presence in Asia of half a dozen Soviet agents. Through the Fourth Congress at least, to judge from all evidence, Soviet attention continued to be focused on Europe, despite the waning prospects of revolution there. It is a caution against too great a reliance on theory as an indicator of Soviet policy, for the theory throughout this period—at least as it was articulated by such spokesmen as Stalin, Radek, Roy, and others—continued to emphasize the critical importance of the East.[66]

A TARGET IN THE EAST AND THE COMINTERN'S RESPONSE: 1923-1924

During the interval between the Fourth and Fifth Comintern Congresses, Moscow acquired an objective in the East which was materially to affect the course of Soviet policy. The objective was China. For several years after the Russian Revolution, Soviet interest had centered first on the Muslim world and later in India. Roy, the principal spokesman for the East in Moscow, helped to sustain interest in India through the Fourth Comintern Congress.[67] Following this congress, however, a series of reverses in India, including the arrest of most of the Communist leaders in the so-called Cawnpore Conspiracy, all but eliminated any chances of success there.[68] It was during this period of acute frustration in India that Moscow's attention was drawn to China. Soviet policy in China in the 1920's has been extensively dealt

[65] *Fourth Congress of the Communist International*, pp. 223-4.

[66] For a contrary view on the shift of Soviet attention to the East during the Fourth Congress, see Whiting, *Soviet Policies in China, 1917-1924*, p. 97.

[67] It should be noted that, despite his occasional differences with the official Comintern line, Roy continued to be held in high esteem by Comintern spokesmen, at least through the Fourth Congress; see, for instance, the favorable remarks on Roy at that congress by Zinoviev and Radek in *Fourth Congress of the Communist International*, pp. 26 and 224.

[68] For a detailed account of Soviet efforts in India during this period, see Overstreet and Windmiller, *Communism in India*, pp. 53-69.

with elsewhere[69] and needs no detailed treatment here. Moreover, Moscow's actions in China—despite the fact that the Chinese revolution was for some years the major focus of Soviet interest in the East—are not necessarily representative of Soviet Eastern policy in general for reasons we will explore. It will therefore satisfy our purposes to note from time to time certain crucial landmarks in the Sino-Soviet relationship without attempting to retell the long and extremely complex story.

Diplomatic exchanges between Sun Yat-sen's revolutionary government in Canton and the Soviet government date from the formation of the two regimes within two months of each other in late 1917 and early 1918. In the early 1920's these links were strengthened by interviews between Sun Yat-sen and Soviet agents such as Voitinsky and Maring, although the primary mission of these agents was to hasten the development of Chinese Communism. Sun was also in correspondence with Chicherin, the Soviet Foreign Minister, despite the fact that Soviet policy during the early 1920's was moving toward normalization of relations with Peking, the seat of the internationally recognized government of the Chinese Republic; in September 1923 the arrival of Leo Karakhan in Peking marked the resumption of formal diplomatic relations between Russia and China. Sun Yat-sen in the meantime, having abandoned hope of assistance from the Western powers in his struggle against Peking, had met another Soviet emissary, Adolf Joffe, in January 1923 and concluded with him the Sun-Joffe agreement which became the basis of Soviet-Kuomintang collaboration. This agreement assured Moscow's aid to the revolutionary regime in Canton, and the latter's acceptance of it, on condition that Moscow not consider China suitable terrain for "the Communistic order or even the soviet system." In the autumn of 1923 Mikhail Borodin, Moscow's representative to the Kuomintang, arrived in Canton and became almost immedi-

---

[69] E.g., Whiting, *Soviet Policies in China, 1917-1924*; Brandt, *Stalin's Failure in China, 1924-1927*; Schwartz, *Chinese Communism and the Rise of Mao*; North, *Moscow and Chinese Communists*; Wilbur and How, *Documents on Communism, Nationalism and Soviet Advisers in China, 1918-1927*; Eudin and North, *op. cit.*

ately the dominant figure, after Sun himself, in the revolutionary regime.

In China, then, there was established by 1924, without benefit of mass organizational efforts and without too much reliance on theory, a working alliance between Moscow and a major revolutionary movement in the East. One might imagine that this first significant breakthrough in the East would be accompanied by a prompt reorientation of the Comintern's interests and energies. This was not the case. The Comintern as such appears not to have been directly involved in the Sun-Joffe negotiations. Joffe, a Soviet diplomat dispatched initially to Peking where he opened the negotiations subsequently concluded by Karakhan, evidently used diplomatic rather than Comintern channels in reporting his progress and received instructions in the same manner. Indeed it is likely that the terms of the agreement with Sun Yat-sen were worked out largely on his own initiative.[70] The Comintern, at any event, indicated no foreknowledge of the agreement and even after its announcement showed little interest. On January 12, 1923, an ECCI directive to the Chinese Communists—the first explicit instruction to the Chinese comrades, incidentally, and dated a fortnight before the Sun-Joffe agreement—gave no hint of the approaching alliance between Moscow and Sun's organization.[71] Another directive to the Chinese Communists in May, on the eve of their Third Congress, was phrased in a manner that suggests as much suspicion of Moscow's new Chinese allies as confidence in them; the directive, for instance, explicitly warns the Communists against Sun's possible accommodation with the

[70] For an account of Joffe's mission in China, see Whiting, *op. cit.*, pp. 181-207.

[71] The text of the resolution is in *Strategiia i taktika Kominterna v natsional'no-kolonial'noi revoliutsii*, p. 112, translated in Degras, *Communist International*, II, pp. 5-6. The resolution attempted to settle a tactical dispute which had divided the Chinese leadership for some months—the question of Communists' holding dual membership in the CCP and the Kuomintang. This proposal appears to have originated with Maring a year earlier, probably in response to a suggestion by Sun Yat-sen himself that while a formal alliance between the two parties was at that time inappropriate, Communists would be welcomed in the Kuomintang as individuals; see Wilbur and How, *Documents on Communism, Nationalism, and Soviet Advisers in China*, p. 83.

militarists.[72] The Comintern press, in the meantime, made no mention of the Sun-Joffe agreement and, as observed above, gave limited coverage of Chinese affairs during 1923; in 1924 there were fewer than half a dozen items on China in *Inprecor* until the introduction of a special section in October entitled "Hands off China!"

Above all, for our purposes, there was no evident impact of the Sun-Joffe formula on the Comintern's general approach to colonial policy. To judge from the Comintern's few pronouncements on the Eastern question between the Fourth and Fifth Congresses, the 1920 theses remained in force, muddied somewhat by the theses adopted by the Fourth Congress. Alliance with national revolutionary movements was still desirable and, in some countries, such as China, might go as far as dual membership in Communist and bourgeois parties; but the risks of such collaboration were sounded as frequently as the virtues. The Comintern, as an organization, appeared to take the position that what Soviet diplomats did in Peking, Shanghai, or elsewhere was their own affair; it should not, however, be confused with the business of waging revolution.

The Fifth Comintern Congress, the first without Lenin and the last in which honest differences of opinion were freely aired, did little to clarify an Eastern policy. Like its predecessors, the congress was concerned mainly with European problems, especially the German question in the wake of the abortive rising in the Ruhr in October 1923. The composition of the congress was also predominantly European, even more so than at earlier congresses since representation was now weighted to reflect actual party strength.[73] The "Russian question"—that is, the attitude to

[72] *Strategiia i taktika Kominterna* . . . , p. 114 and Degras, *Communist International*, II, pp. 25-6; the instruction is concerned mainly with the need to give more attention to the Chinese peasantry in view of the agrarian nature of the Chinese revolution.

[73] According to the report of the Mandates Commission, 5 of the 41 countries represented (Germany, France, Italy, Czechoslovakia, and Russia) accounted for nearly two-thirds of the 336 voting delegates, and Russia alone accounted for approximately one-third; delegates from the East numbered fewer than ten. See *Inprecor*, August 12, 1924, p. 608.

be taken toward the opposition within the Russian Party centering around Trotsky—overshadowed the congress. The issue,
which had been thoroughly debated during the Thirteenth Congress of the Russian Communist Party just prior to the Comintern Congress, was not debated in any open sessions of the congress but was the subject of a resolution which passed unanimously; the resolution endorsed the action of the Thirteenth Congress condemning "the platform of the opposition as petty-bourgeois and its conduct as a threat to the unity of the party and
consequently to the proletarian dictatorship in the Soviet Union."[74]
Only a naïve foreign delegate would not have appreciated the
consequences to his career of failing to acknowledge the ascendency of the new Soviet triumvirate—Stalin, Zinoviev, and Kamenev.

These circumstances provided a poor atmosphere for a fruitful
discussion of colonial problems. Zinoviev, reporting for the ECCI,
barely touched on the Eastern question, an oversight that caused
two Eastern delegates, Nguyen Ai Quoc (Ho Chi Minh) of Indochina and Sen Katayama of Japan, to utter muted protests.[75]
Manuilsky, who delivered the report on the national and colonial questions, conceived the central problem in terms of the
right of self-determination and related notions; he accordingly
drew his illustrations mainly from the Balkans and Central Europe and touched only casually on the problem of colonies overseas. Two full sessions of the congress were set aside for a discussion of the report, but they failed to place Eastern policy in
a clearer perspective. Of the two dozen interventions during the
day-long debate, all but five were by Europeans and the principal focus of their interest continued to be the Balkans and

[74] Excerpts translated in Degras, *Communist International*, II, p. 140. This
volume, pp. 96-161, includes full or partial translations of the principal resolutions passed by the congress, with helpful commentaries by the author. An abridged
account of the proceedings, without resolutions, is *Fifth Congress of the Communist International* (London, 1924). *Inprecor*, Nos. 41-64 (July 16-September
5), 1924, gives an abridged account of all discussion in plenary sessions as well
as the final English text of the resolutions. The fullest and most authoritative
record of the Fifth Congress is *Piatyi vsemirnyi kongress Kommunisticheskogo
Internatsionala; stenograficheskii otchet* (2 vols).

[75] See *Inprecor*, July 17, 1924, p. 424, and July 24, 1924, p. 500.

Central Europe. The discussion ended in a personal feud, wholly irrelevant to national or colonial questions, between the German delegate Sommer and Karl Radek, the principal scapegoat of the congress.[76] An Irish delegate, urged by Zinoviev to take the floor because of the congress' interest in Ireland, said bluntly: "I have failed to notice it. The congress seems interested only in those parties which have the largest membership."[77] The delegates from the East, it may be imagined, identified themselves with this view.

Roy, again the chief spokesman for the East, was troubled in particular by the formulation given in the draft resolution on Zinoviev's report. He quoted the resolution as stating that "in order to attract the peoples of colonial and semi-colonial countries to the struggle of the proletariat, the Executive Committee must maintain direct contact with the national liberation movement." This, Roy argued, violated the sense of Lenin's 1920 theses, which stated that "the nature of the support must be determined by existing conditions." Conditions have in fact changed, Roy continued. In India, for instance, nationalist elements which in 1920 had been sufficiently revolutionary to be suitable allies of the Communists (Roy had denied this at the time, it should be recalled) had now deserted the liberation movement. He flatly contradicted Manuilsky's appraisal of a nationalist revival in India; on the contrary, Roy said, the past year had seen the "worst depression" in the national movement. It was the workers and especially the peasants who had become revolutionary, and it was with them that the Comintern should establish "direct contacts."[78] Roy indicated that Manuilsky was equally in error in his analysis of the situation in other colonies.[79]

[76] Radek, a sympathizer with Trotsky, had been sharply attacked earlier in the congress by Zinoviev and others for his part in the Ruhr uprising; he had responded with a vigorous counterattack on Zinoviev's report. The exchange between Sommer and Radek during the debate on the national question was a continuation of the same quarrel.

[77] *Inprecor*, July 26, 1924, p. 524.

[78] Roy had altered his view during the preceding year or two on the role of workers in the East and said, according to one version of his speech, that "it is mere romanticism to speak of a revolutionary proletariat" in the colonies (*Fifth Congress of the Communist International*, p. 196); his emphasis had now shifted to the revolutionary potentialities of the peasantry. His new estimate, however,

Roy's concern was, of course, not new. He had from the outset opposed too rigid a commitment by the Comintern to national movements in the colonies; he had given ground at the Second Congress, at Lenin's insistence; now, standing virtually alone at the Fifth Congress, he was making a desperate attempt to check a policy that appeared to him to go even further than the 1920 formula. The tide, however, was running against Roy. Moreover, his tactless attack on Manuilsky, and implicitly on Zinoviev, made it comparatively easy for Manuilsky, who was riding the tide, to dismiss Roy's objections in the closing session of the congress.[80] Roy, Manuilsky said, exaggerated the importance of social movements in the colonies at the expense of national movements. Even if his allegation were true that a sharpening of the class struggle could be demonstrated in India, it was not true that the national movement in the colonies had everywhere run its course and lost its usefulness. "In regard to the colonial question," Manuilsky continued, "Roy reflects the nihilism of Rosa Luxemburg. The truth is that a just proportion should be looked for between the social movement and the national movement. Can the right of self-determination become a contradiction to the interests of the revolution?"[81]

---

in no way altered his negative view of the national movement, in India and elsewhere.

[79] The full text of Roy's speech is in *Piatyi vsemirnyi kongress Kommunisticheskogo Internatsionala*, I, pp. 604-18; abbreviated versions may be found in *Inprecor*, July 25, 1924, pp. 518-9, and in *Fifth Congress of the Communist International*, pp. 196-8. The speech, it should be noted, was unusually long and was interrupted at one juncture by an Indonesian delegate who proposed a limitation of Roy's time.

[80] Roy, as the principal speaker on the national and colonial question after Manuilsky, was offered an opportunity to speak before Manuilsky in the summing up of the debate, but refused; his position was that he should follow, not precede, Manuilsky inasmuch as the latter was planning to refute his argument. "If an opportunity is denied me to reply to Comrade Manuilsky's remarks against me," he announced, in obvious ill humor, "then I have absolutely nothing further to say here on this question." *Piatyi vsemirnyi kongress Kommunisticheskogo Internatsionala*, II, p. 963; the incident is passed over in the accounts in *Inprecor*, August 12, 1924, p. 608, and *Fifth Congress of the Communist International*, p. 271.

[81] The phrasing here is from the abbreviated report; the full text makes the same point more circuitously.

What Manuilsky appeared to be saying, whether intentionally or not, was that nationalism in Asia, no matter what forces were behind it, provided a surer source of harassment to Russia's enemies in Europe than any colonial proletarian or peasant movements yet in sight. Asian Communists accordingly should not obstruct the development of Asian nationalism in the pursuit of their social goals. At one juncture Manuilsky argued that Communists in Asia should be prepared "not only to collaborate with petty-bourgeois parties but to *take the initiative in organizing them* in backward countries."[82] Such views, needless to say, were more narrowly European and more contemptuous of the revolutionary aspirations of Asians than any previously accepted by the Comintern. They passed unchallenged, however, except by Roy. The great majority of the delegates, we must assume, were too preoccupied with other problems to become involved in what appeared to be a private feud between Manuilsky and Roy over an obscure detail of Eastern policy.

On one point regarding colonial policy there was general agreement at the Fifth Congress—the need to give more attention to the East. In paying lip-service to this recurrent thesis, the European delegates doubtless felt they were discharging their obligation to the East. Manuilsky, for instance, was caustic in his attack on the French Communists for their failure to implement the Comintern's colonial policies and only a shade less severe on the British. "The Russian comrades," he said, "are grateful to you for launching the slogan 'Hands off Soviet Russia' at the time of the armed intervention [1918]. But the entire International would rejoice even more if you were now to launch another no less courageous call: 'Hands off the colonies.' "[83] He closed his report with a reminder that "the time for declarations of a general character have passed; we have now a period of creative, revolutionary work in the colonies and among national minorities."[84] Both Eastern and European delegates underscored and expanded his

82 *Piatyi vsemirnyi kongress Kommunisticheskogo Internatsionala*, I, p. 590 (emphasis in original).

83 *Fifth Congress of the Communist International*, p. 193.

84 *Ibid.*, p. 195.

remarks during the discussion of the national question. Meanwhile, the congress formalized the sentiment by acknowledging, in the resolution on the ECCI report, the inadequacy of work in the colonies thus far and demanding "not only the further development of direct links between the Executive and the national liberation movements of the East, but also closer contacts between the sections in the imperialist countries and the colonies of those countries."[85] The words, of course, have a hollow ring measured against the meager attention given to the East by the Fifth Congress, which failed even to propose a separate resolution on the colonial question.[86]

The inattention to the East at the Fifth Congress deserves comment, especially since the time spent on both the *national* and colonial questions has led some students of Soviet policy to emphasize the growing Comintern commitment to the East revealed at this congress.[87] It is entirely understandable, of course, that the congress should show concern with the national question in the Balkans and Central Europe. This was an important problem facing the Comintern and one of particular interest to the large number of delegates from these areas, many of whom were attending a Comintern congress for the first time. The issue, moreover, seemed particularly relevant in light of the recent formation of the Union of Soviet Socialist Republics, which Manuilsky called "a great experiment in solving the national question under the proletarian dictatorship."[88] It was also appro-

---

[85] Degras, *Communist International*, II, p. 106.

[86] Manuilsky, in his concluding remarks on the national and colonial question, proposed that a commission including himself, Bukharin, Stalin, Roy, Katayama, and others be appointed to prepare definite theses. It is doubtful, however, that the commission met. Reporting at the ECCI plenum following the congress, where residual business was dealt with, Manuilsky recommended that the final resolution on the national and colonial question be referred to the Presidium; that was the last heard of the matter. The only resolution to emerge from the discussion of Manuilsky's report in the congress was one on the national question in Central Europe and the Balkans, which reaffirmed "the right of every nation to self-determination, even to the extent of separation"; text in *Inprecor*, September 5, 1924, pp. 682-5.

[87] See, for instance, Eudin and North, *op. cit.*, p. 271.

[88] The last portion of Manuilsky's report on the national question was given over to this theme; see *Fifth Congress of the Communist International*, pp. 194-5.

priate for the national question to be linked to the colonial question, as it had been at previous congresses. The colonial question, we have seen, was an outgrowth of the national question, as this question had been formulated before 1917, and was an extension of it in the context of overseas empires in Asia and Africa. The Comintern had not troubled to make rigid distinctions between the two, or between either and the Eastern question.

What is more difficult to understand is why the national question in Europe should have virtually submerged the colonial question in Asia. This had not occurred at previous congresses. While discussion of the East, to be sure, had never matched the attention given to the West, when there had been discussion of the Eastern (or national, or colonial) question, it had concerned Asia, not Europe. The argument had been that revolution in Asia was, if not a prerequisite for revolution in Europe, at least a vital accompaniment to it. This idea is conspicuously absent in most of the discussion of the colonial question during the Fifth Congress. Moreover, the Fifth Congress took place at a time when revolutionary prospects in Europe were at their lowest point since the war and when a more serious look at prospects in the East might have been anticipated.

This was also a time when the tempo of events in China was accelerating daily. Yet the congress' treatment of developments in China was casual: a recent strike of railway workers in Hankow, leading to several executions, was made the occasion for a hastily drafted "Manifesto Against the Oppression of the Peoples of the Orient," which was introduced midway through the congress and adopted unanimously, without discussion;[89] Manuilsky noted that the Comintern had authorized Chinese Communists to join the Kuomintang, and he chided the Chinese comrades for their continuing opposition to this policy on the grounds that it led to "class collaboration";[90] one of the two Chinese delegates at the congress—both minor figures in the CCP—described recent developments in China during the debate on Manuilsky's report, emphasizing the gains resulting from Communist-Kuo-

[89] *Inprecor*, July 17, 1924, p. 416.
[90] *Ibid.*, August 4, 1924, p. 570.

mintang collaboration but making no reference to the Soviet-Kuomintang alliance.[91] It is not a little extraordinary that the records of the Fifth Congress show no other significant discussion of the country where Moscow was on the threshold of enjoying its greatest success to date.

In speculating on the reasons for the Comintern's neglect of the East during the Fifth Congress, one must bear in mind not only the attitudes of those to whom the Eastern question was entrusted but also attitudes which had been heard previously and now for one reason or another were not. Zinoviev, for instance, had never shown himself a student of the East; accordingly his making little of the colonial question in reporting for the ECCI was to be expected. Manuilsky, a Ukrainian speaking soon after the unification of the Ukraine with the RSFSR, was presumably more drawn to the national question in neighboring Balkan and Central European states than to related questions in distant colonies of which he evidently had little knowledge at the time. Maring, a staunch spokesman for the Eastern orientation of the Comintern in earlier years, was absent.[92] Radek, another champion of the East, was in disgrace. Trotsky, whose discouragement over the course of events in Europe was bringing him to a reappraisal of revolutionary possibilities in Asia, was inactive.[93] Roy had stood too persistently in opposition to the Comintern's formula for alliance with "revolutionary nationalists" to carry significant

[91] *Ibid.*, July 26, 1924, p. 526.

[92] Maring had left China in 1923 to return to Holland, where he continued for a time to serve as Comintern representative; subsequently he broke with Moscow.

[93] During a speech in May, marking the third anniversary of the Communist University of Toilers of the East, Trotsky said: "If Europe is going to be kept in the present state of decomposition by this narrow-minded, aristocratic Mac-Donaldism of the upper strata of the working class, the center of gravity of the revolutionary movement will be transferred to the East. And then it will become evident that . . . it will require a revolution in the East . . . to give an impetus to the revolution of the European proletariat"; L. Trotsky, "Prospects and Tasks in the East," *Inprecor*, May 29, 1924, p. 307. Trotsky appeared briefly at the opening session of the Fifth Comintern Congress and drafted one of the manifestos passed by the congress, but declined to take part in the proceedings as long as the "Russian question" remained unresolved; see Degras, *Communist International*, ii, p. 141.

43

weight at the Fifth Congress. The remaining Eastern delegates were sycophants, such as Katayama, or too newly arrived on the scene, such as Nguyen Ai Quoc and the Javan Semaoen, to speak with authority. Lenin, who perhaps would have insisted on a clearer formulation on the East, was dead.[94] Stalin, whose occasional observations on the East revealed a commitment in that direction unmatched by any major Soviet spokesman, was presumably too preoccupied with succession politics to speak forth.[95]

There was thus no authoritative voice at the Fifth Congress to drive home to the delegates the arguments in behalf of the East which had been advanced in the past and which should have been even more compelling in 1924. Without this stimulation, the delegates followed their normal habit of concentrating their attention on European affairs; they were in any case still predominantly European and believed themselves faced with problems of the utmost urgency in the West. Discussion of the East, including China, was accordingly reduced to little more than a ritual.

Two further considerations are important in interpreting the lack of attention to China during the Fifth Congress. First, if it is true that the channels for handling the delicate maneuvers in China were outside the Comintern, it may have been a matter of policy for open forums of the International not to discuss China in too great detail. The multi-level policy in China was

[94] In his last published article, in March 1923, Lenin once again spoke of the vast population of the "revolutionary and nationalist East" and the need to "civilize" (that is, "indoctrinate") the East through Marxism before the next overt clash between Russia and the West; *Sochineniia*, xxxiii, p. 458. Lenin died on January 21, 1924, five months before the Fifth Comintern Congress.

[95] Stalin for the first time took part in the work of a Comintern congress but confined his activities to the work of the Polish Commission, of which he was chairman; he did not address any plenary meetings of the congress. His influence was nonetheless felt, and he was mentioned by several speakers as an authority on the Eastern question. Manuilsky, for instance, coupled his name with Lenin's as co-architect of the Second Congress theses in 1920; Nguyen Ai Quoc referred to Stalin's having labeled as "counter-revolutionary" the argument that "the victory of the proletariat in Europe is possible without a direct tie with the liberation movements in the East"—one of the few references made during the congress to this thesis. See *Piatyi vsemirnyi kongress Kommunisticheskogo Internatsionala*, i, pp. 589 and 654.

necessarily a Soviet responsibility and no purpose was served in having this policy openly debated by foreign delegates not fully conversant with all the subtleties of Moscow's strategy. Secondly, the development of Soviet policy in China spanned the period when power in Russia was passing from Lenin first to the triumvirate and thence to Stalin, and must therefore be associated with Stalin; it is not certain at what juncture Stalin became personally involved in the China policy, but it is reasonable to assume that this had occurred as early as the Fifth Congress. Stalin had never been active in the Comintern; several of his major rivals, notably Zinoviev and Trotsky, had been. Moreover, both Trotsky (despite his remarks on the eve of the Fifth Congress) and Zinoviev, like the rest of the Comintern, had been traditionally oriented to Europe; Stalin, we know, had on numerous occasions spoken in favor of greater attention to the East. It was therefore natural for Stalin, especially in working out a policy in China that might encounter some resistance in the Comintern, to rely on agencies where his control was more secure—for instance, the Commissariat of Foreign Affairs. In short, if Stalin was not the direct architect of Soviet policy in China in 1923 and 1924, there are reasons to imagine that he was closer to it than any high officials in the Comintern; for the time being he wished to keep matters this way.

Whatever the reasons for the Comintern's apparent exclusion from the China policy, the policy itself represented an unmistakable shift in Soviet strategies in the East. It greatly enlarged perspectives for revolution in Asia. In due course it transformed Soviet Eastern policy from a purely abstract formulation of interest into a concrete program in which not only the Russian government but the Comintern, the *Profintern*, and other Soviet-oriented organizations would participate.

STALIN'S ADVENTURE IN CHINA AND THE TURN TO THE EAST: 1925-1927

Events in China during 1925 and 1926 continued to favor Soviet policies there. The May 30th incident, for instance, quickened the revolutionary mood in all segments of the population.[96] Strikes

[96] On May 30, 1925 a dozen Chinese demonstrators were shot down in

45

in Canton and Hong Kong during the latter part of 1925 and most of 1926 disrupted the Chinese economy. Sun Yat-sen's death in March 1925 led to prolonged struggle for control of the Kuomintang but did not prevent the launching of the long-awaited Northern Expedition in mid-1926, the effort of all elements associated with the revolutionary regime in Canton to overthrow the government in Peking. Soviet political and military advisers under Borodin, despite Chiang Kai-shek's effort in March 1926 to curb their power, played an important role in the preparation of the expedition.[97]

These dramatic events had the effect of distracting the Comintern's attention increasingly from European problems and focusing it in Asia. Stalin's part in shifting the focus of revolutionary strategy to the East must not be overlooked; were it not for his growing identification with the China policy, at a time when he was becoming master of the Soviet establishment (including its outlying institutions such as the Comintern), even the stirring developments in Canton, Shanghai, and elsewhere might not have been enough to redirect the Comintern's attention.

Stalin's general view of the East during these years was singularly uncomplicated. In an article in *Pravda* in March 1925, one of Stalin's earliest comprehensive statements on international affairs since Lenin's death, he concluded that because of temporary stabilization in the West, revolutionary prospects were greatest in the East. A major task of all Communist parties accordingly was "to devise concrete forms and methods of drawing the working class in the advanced countries closer to the national

---

Shanghai while protesting the killing of textile workers during a recent strike against a Japanese-owned mill; the incident led to a wave of anti-foreign and anti-government sentiment throughout China, which in turn brought on new reprisals.

[97] During Borodin's brief absence from Canton in March, Chiang Kai-shek, evidently goaded by Rightist advisers, summarily arrested dozens of Chinese Communists and placed the Soviet advisers under house arrest. On Borodin's return the crisis was resolved and explained away as a "misunderstanding"; Chiang reaffirmed his loyalty to the Soviet-Kuomintang alliance. For an account of the episode and a judgment of Chiang's role in it by one of the Soviet advisers, see Wilbur and How, *Documents on Nationalism, Communism, and Soviet Advisers in China*, pp. 248-53.

revolutionary movement in the colonies and dependent countries."[98] There was, of course, nothing new in this recommendation, which had been repeated at regular intervals since 1920 by the Comintern and by most Soviet spokesmen. If anything had changed, it was that because of the "respite" gained by the West revolutionary activity in the East need no longer be considered prerequisite to, or supplementary to, parallel activity in the West. The niceties of the question which had diverted the Second Congress—where will revolution first occur: in Europe or Asia?—could be ignored. Revolution in Asia was now valid in its own right, because the most favorable terrain for revolution had shifted, at least for the time being, from the advanced industrialized nations to the underdeveloped world.

From 1925 to the end of 1927 Stalin returned again and again to this thesis.[99] The thesis, to be sure, became increasingly overburdened with tactical considerations, especially as the revolution in China grew more complex; these considerations were important, as we shall see, but they did not alter the focus of Moscow's attention. It is this Eastward focus, not the tactical maneuvering in China, which constitutes the principal shift in Soviet revolutionary strategy during the period we are reviewing.

Favorable prospects for revolution in China, then, and the emergence of a Soviet leader already inclined to look Eastward

[98] Stalin, *Sochineniia*, VII, p. 57.

[99] The greater part of Stalin's published pronouncements on the East occur from 1925 to 1927. While most of them relate to China, they also are expressive of Stalin's general view of the growing importance of the Eastern question, especially in Asia. The more important of these statements, contained in volumes VII-X of Stalin's *Sochineniia* are: a report to a Party meeting in Moscow (May 9, 1925); a speech at the Communist University of the Toilers of the East on the political tasks of the university (May 18, 1925); an interview with a Japanese correspondent on the revolutionary movements in the East (July 4, 1925); report to the Fourteenth Congress of the CPSU (December 18, 1925); a speech before the Chinese Commission of the ECCI during the Seventh Plenum on the prospects of the Chinese revolution (November 30, 1926); propaganda theses on the Chinese revolution (April 21, 1927); a speech at the Sun Yat-sen University (May 13, 1927); an address before the Eighth ECCI Plenum on the Comintern's tasks in China (May 24, 1927); an article in *Pravda* reviewing recent policies in China (July 28, 1927); a speech delivered before a joint meeting of the Central

combined to give a new focus to Moscow's revolutionary policies following the Fifth Comintern Congress. Moscow was also gaining new instruments with which to implement these policies. The development of Oriental studies, for instance, greatly improved the quality of political and economic analyses of Eastern countries, which had previously been treated in largely abstract terms. In 1926 Mikhail Veltman (Pavlovich), the acknowledged dean of Soviet Orientalists, noted that the Oriental Institutes in Moscow and Leningrad already possessed facilities for the study of the Near East (Turkey, Persia, and Arabia), the Middle East (Afghanistan and India, with plans soon to cover Tibet and Sinkiang), and the Far East (China and Japan); he added that "the time is not far off when we will begin a more searching study of Siam, Indochina, and the Dutch Indies."[100] The work of students trained at these and other Oriental institutes began to appear with growing frequency not only in the principal Orientalist journal, *Novyi Vostok* (founded in 1922), but also in regular Soviet periodicals; a growing number of pamphlets and monographs on Eastern countries also began to appear in Russia from 1925 on. China, understandably, was the country most extensively dealt with in these studies, but there was a generous spilling over of scholarly interest in other parts of the East.[101] The prevailing attitude of the Orientalists was one of unmitigated exuberance over the revolutionary potentialities of the East; reading their commentaries, one might well wonder whether Moscow had wholly abdicated its traditional interest in Europe. The lead-

---

Committee and Central Control Commission of the CPSU (August 1, 1927); and the political report to the Fifteenth Party Congress (December 3, 1927).

[100] *Novyi Vostok*, No. 10-11, 1926, p. ix; Pavlovich's article marked the fifth anniversary of the Moscow and Leningrad institutes.

[101] From 1917 to 1924 not more than a half dozen books and pamphlets on China had been published in the Soviet Union; in 1925-1927 more than 40 appeared. Articles on China appearing in Soviet periodicals numbered approximately 60 through 1924 and more than tripled during the following three years; see Skatchkov, *Bibliografiia Kitaia*, pp. 97-109. Increase in coverage of other Asian countries roughly parallels that for China. In the 29 issues of *Novyi Vostok* published between 1922 and 1930 (all but six published after 1924), coverage was as follows: Near East, 105 articles; China, 90; India, 30; Japan, 27; Africa, 27; and Southeast Asia, 4.

ing article in a volume of articles by Soviet Orientalists commemorating the first anniversary of Lenin's death proclaimed that "Lenin taught us to stand facing the East"—an interpretation of Lenin's teaching that might be difficult to support but which nonetheless characterizes the official view in 1925.[102] Pavlovich, in a contribution to the same volume, turns into an epigram the ancient charge that Mensheviks are European Communists and Bolsheviks Asiatic Communists. "*All* Communists," he writes, "are now becoming Asiatic."[103]

The Comintern was also better equipped than previously to follow current developments in the East. Growing numbers of Asians, for instance, took part in the work of the Comintern apparatus between the Fifth and Sixth Comintern Congresses (1924-1928). During these years there were normally a half-dozen Asians on the ECCI and often two or three on the Presidium.[104] In 1925 the Eastern Department was said to have had on its staff twenty-four Asians representing eight countries.[105] This greater capacity to interpret events in the East was reflected in *Inprecor*, which, like the rest of the Soviet press, more than tripled its coverage of Eastern affairs between 1924 and 1927. In the meantime the universities for training Asians in revolutionary strategy continued to attract students from the East, many of whom took part in the congresses and plenary meetings of the International and often worked in the Comintern apparatus before returning to their countries.[106] The Comintern's apparatus outside Russia,

[102] *Lenin i Vostok*, p. 14.

[103] *Ibid.*, p. 16.

[104] For the composition of the principal Comintern organs during this period, see Degras, *Communist International*, II, pp. 572-4.

[105] See *ibid.*, p. 247.

[106] The Communist University of the Toilers of the East, founded in 1921, remained in operation throughout the 1920's and drew students especially from Japan, India, and Korea, and to a lesser degree from Indonesia. Chinese students were normally enrolled in the Sun Yat-sen University (later called the Communist University for the Toilers of China), founded in 1925 and claiming a student body of 800 by 1928; see Eudin and North, *op. cit.*, pp. 86-7. How important these universities were in Moscow's calculations from 1925 to 1927 is suggested by the fact that Stalin during these years addressed the Communist University of Toilers of the East twice (May 1925 and May 1927) and Sun Yat-sen University once (May 1927).

it may be imagined, was also strengthened during the latter half of the 1920's, although authoritative evidence of its activities is extremely meager. The Far Eastern Bureau (*Dalburo*) in Shanghai continued in existence, to judge from infrequent references to it, and is reported to have been active in Singapore as well as in China.[107] Apart from the Soviet agents in China assisting Borodin, a number of British agents were sent to India in 1925 and 1926 in the Comintern's behalf,[108] and Comintern representatives are reported also to have been present in Southeast Asia.[109]

Despite these improved facilities for treating the colonial question, the Comintern was slower in bringing the question into the open than Soviet Orientalists. Lip service, to be sure, was paid to the growing importance of the East; during the Fifth ECCI Plenum in March 1925, Zinoviev, who had ignored the colonial question at the Fifth Congress eight months earlier, singled out the revolutionary upsurge in the Orient as the second most important factor—after the Russian Revolution itself—determining the current international situation. "The awakening of the East," he said, "will put an end to the isolation of the [European] working class."[110] Lenin, he declared, in his last years "clearly saw that from the East a great reserve army of the revolution was marching and that perhaps the revolution would change its route and enter by other gates."[111] However, neither at the Fifth Plenum nor at the Sixth, in February and March 1926, was there

---

[107] Reported Comintern activities in Singapore are discussed in the next chapter.

[108] For a discussion of Comintern activity in India via the Colonial Committee of the CPGB, which frequently clashed with Roy's *émigré* Indian organization in Berlin, see Overstreet and Windmiller, *Communism in India*, pp. 74-90 *passim*.

[109] The Indonesian Tan Malaka claims to have been appointed Comintern representative in Southeast Asia as early as 1923 and to have spent several years in the area on this assignment; see Willard A. Hanna, American Universities Field Staff Report WAH-1-'59 (April 6, 1959). Nguyen Ai Quoc is reported to have had this assignment at the end of the 1920's; "Basic Paper on the Malayan Communist Party," Vol. 1, Part 2, p. 6. The activities of both Tan Malaka and Nguyen Ai Quoc are discussed in the next chapter.

[110] *Inprecor*, April 24, 1925, p. 501.

[111] *Ibid.*, April 17, 1925, p. 446.

open discussion of tactics to be applied in the Orient. On both occasions discussion of the colonial question, as during plenary meetings of the ECCI in the past, was conducted in closed sessions of the Colonial Commission, whose minutes were not published; the delegates attending the Fifth and Sixth Plenums heard only brief reports of these deliberations. The only substantive resolution on an Eastern problem adopted during the two years following the Fifth Congress, although the Colonial Commission was said to have recommended half a dozen or more, was the Sixth Plenum's resolution on China. This resolution reaffirmed the official Soviet policy of Communist-Kuomintang collaboration, over certain lingering objections to the policy within the CCP, and called the Kuomintang "a revolutionary bloc of workers, peasants, intellectuals and the urban democracy" and the Canton government "a model for the future revolutionary democratic structure of the country." The resolution was adopted unanimously and without discussion.[112]

The Comintern's attention to the East, then, during the two years following the Fifth Congress, can be considered no more than a pale reflection of activity going on there; in no sense is there evidence of a vigorous effort to guide the activity. Stalin evidently continued to be reluctant to designate the International as the instrument of his policies in the East, especially in China. The Comintern was useful to Stalin in organizing general propaganda campaigns, such as the "Hands off China" effort launched in the summer of 1924, and in issuing occasional protest mani-

---

[112] An English text of the resolution is in Degras, *Communist International*, II, pp. 277-9. Dorsey, an American, reported for the Colonial Commission at the Fifth Plenum, noting that reports had been heard on a number of colonies and resolutions drafted on four—India, Java, Egypt, and the American colonies; none was published. Roy was *rapporteur* for the Eastern Commission at the Sixth Plenum and noted that five sub-commissions had unanimously approved several resolutions to submit to the plenum; only the one on China was published. The official records of the Fifth and Sixth Plenums, which do not include the minutes of the Colonial and Eastern Commissions, were published, respectively, in *Rasshirennyi plenum Ispolkoma Kommunisticheskogo Internatsionala* (1925) and *Shestoi rasshirennyi plenum Ispolkoma Kominterna* (1927); Dorsey's and Roy's reports may be found, respectively, on p. 472 and pp. 508-9. English transcripts of the two plenums were carried at the time in *Inprecor*.

festoes,[113] but so long as it remained under Zinoviev's domination it could not be entrusted with critical policy decisions. Stalin's tactics in China, moreover, encountered opposition in the Comintern not only from the Chinese Communists (as noted above) but from such spokesmen on Eastern affairs as Roy, and of course from Trotsky. An open discussion of China within the ECCI, where free speech was still more respected than in the CPSU, could only provide Trotsky and his followers a gratuitous forum from which to assail Stalin's leadership.[114] Doubtless such a consideration led Stalin to refrain from taking up the Eastern question at the Fifth and Sixth Plenums, and perhaps to use his influence to keep it off the agenda, although he was willing to take part in less controversial aspects of the ECCI's work.[115] The same consideration perhaps also explains why Borodin and the other Soviet agents in China, to judge from the evidence available, continued to maintain contact with Moscow not through Comintern channels but through Soviet government agencies directly responsible to Stalin.[116]

[113] The only statements on the East released by the Comintern during the 21 months between the Fifth Congress and the Sixth Plenum were of this type: a protest, directed to British workers, against the Labor Government's efforts to throttle the revolutionary regime in Canton (September 4, 1924); a manifesto, issued jointly with the *Profintern* and Young Communist International, against atrocities by foreign imperialists in China (June 8, 1925); and a protest against the British blockade of Canton, adopted at the beginning of the Sixth Plenum. English texts of these statements may be found in Degras, *Communist International*, II, pp. 169-70, 218-20, 248-9.

[114] Trotsky, it should be noted, although removed as Commissar of War in January 1925, still had opportunities of making himself heard as a Politburo member as well as a candidate member of the ECCI—positions he held until the end of 1926; Zinoviev and Kamenev, who joined Trotsky in the Left Opposition early in 1926, also retained membership in the Soviet Politburo— Zinoviev until July and Kamenev until October 1926. Zinoviev was not discharged as President of the Comintern until October; see the brief resolution on his dismissal in *ibid.*, pp. 308-10.

[115] Stalin participated in the work of the Czech and Yugoslav Commissions of the Fifth Plenum and the French and German Commissions of the Sixth Plenum; he was also a member of the Eastern Commission but there is no record of his having taken part in its deliberations. He did not speak at any of the open sessions of either plenum, and only his speech before the German Commission, in March 1926, was published at the time (*Kommunisticheskii internatsional*, No. 3, 1926). See Stalin, *Sochineniia*, VII, pp. 410-2, and VIII, pp. 391-2.

[116] A letter dated May 22, 1925, from one of the Soviet advisers in Canton

Stalin's Adventure in China

By the end of 1926 the struggle within the CPSU was sufficiently resolved, with the removal of the Left Opposition from all important posts, for Stalin to make free use of the Comintern to implement his strategies in China. China, accordingly, was a principal topic at the next ECCI plenum, the Seventh, meeting in November and December 1926. Bukharin, replacing Zinoviev as the principal Russian spokesman in the Comintern, devoted a large portion of his keynote report on the international situation to the Chinese revolution; he saw the world revolution, despite capitalist stabilization, moving forward in three parallel columns —in Russia, in England (where the restlessness of British miners was giving Moscow cause for hope), and in China. Three sessions of the full plenum were set aside for debate on the Chinese question, in addition to the deliberations of the Chinese Commission. Roy called the Chinese issue "certainly the most important question before this plenum."[117]

Stalin, for the first time, played a conspicuous role in the Seventh Plenum. He not only gave the report on the Russian Question, a three-hour denunciation of the Left Opposition followed by a three-and-a-half-hour reply to the discussion but took part in the work of several commissions, including the Chinese Commission. Stalin's speech before this commission, midway through the plenum, was his first attempt in a major public statement—

to Mikhail Frunze, Commissar of War, complains of the too rigid control over the Soviet advisory group exercised by Karakhan, the Russian ambassador in Peking; see Wilbur and How, *Documents on Communism, Nationalism, and Soviet Advisers in China*, pp. 339-40. A telegram from the Soviet Commissariat of Foreign Affairs to the Soviet representative in Peking, dated November 12, 1926, informed the latter that Borodin was to take his orders directly from Moscow and that any separate activities by the Comintern's Far Eastern Bureau should be cleared with him; see *Documents Illustrating the Hostile Activities of the Soviet Government and Third International against Great Britain* (Cmd. 2874), pp. 29-30, cited in Eudin and North, *op. cit.*, p. 368. If the authenticity of these two captured documents may be accepted, as leading scholars argue they should be, they clearly show that communication between Moscow and the Soviet advisers with the Kuomintang was not through Comintern channels.

[117] *Inprecor*, December 30, 1926, p. 1603. An English transcript of the Seventh Plenum was carried in special issues of *Inprecor*, running from December 3, 1926 to February 3, 1927; the official Russian stenograph is *Puti mirovoi revoliutsii: Sedmoi rasshirennyi plenum Ispolnitel'nogo Komiteta Kommunisticheskogo Internatsionala*, 2 vols. (1927).

the speech was soon published in the Comintern journals[118]—
to attach a specific theory to the tactics being applied in China.
The Chinese revolution, Stalin argued, fell somewhere between
the 1905 Revolution in Russia and the Bolshevik Revolution of
1917. It was fundamentally still a bourgeois democratic revolution, despite certain advantages it had over the 1905 Revolution,
and it was this circumstance which justified the continued alliance between the Chinese Communists and the Kuomintang. It
would be a "profound mistake," Stalin said, for Communists to
withdraw at the present juncture from the Kuomintang, a policy
strenuously urged by Trotsky and his supporters. By the same
argument Stalin also ruled out peasant soviets in China, a policy
urged by Pavel Mif. On the other hand, reversing a policy in
force until the eve of the Seventh Plenum, Stalin urged a far
more vigorous effort "to unleash revolution in the countryside,"
on the grounds that "the more quickly and thoroughly the
Chinese peasantry is drawn into the revolution, the stronger and
more powerful the anti-imperialist front in China will be."[119]

Stalin did not speak during the discussion of the Chinese question at the regular sessions of the plenum. His views, however,
were reflected in the course of the debate. The principal report
on China, delivered by T'an P'ing-shan, revealed, to be sure,
striking differences with Stalin's interpretation of the Canton
regime, but this did not prevent T'an from accepting Stalin's
dictum on continued alliance with the Kuomintang.[120] At no

[118] *Kommunisticheskii internatsional*, December 10, 1926, and *Inprecor*, December 23, 1926.

[119] In October Stalin had sent a telegram to the Chinese Communists directing them to restrain the peasants and not to harass the Kuomintang generals
during the Northern Expedition. Subsequently Stalin acknowledged that the telegram was a mistake and claimed that the order had in any case been canceled
soon after the telegram was sent. As Professor North puts it, "this 'cancellation'
was the line laid down by the Seventh Plenum"; North, *Moscow and Chinese
Communists*, p. 90.

[120] For a comparison of Stalin's and T'an P'ing-shan's views, see Brandt,
Stalin's Failure in China, pp. 99-100. Earlier in the year T'an had clashed with
Borodin over the restraint imposed on the Chinese peasantry by Soviet policies,
but in Moscow he appears to have been won over to Stalin's more cautious
view; subsequently he was made one of the principal scapegoats, along with Ch'en
Tu-hsiu, for the collapse of the Wuhan government in mid-1927.

time during the plenum was this policy seriously challenged, by either Asian or European delegates. Even Roy, who normally could be counted upon to question the wisdom of alliances with bourgeois parties, fell into line.[121] No reference was made to the episode when the alliance had been gravely imperiled by Chiang Kai-shek's action in Canton the preceding March. Nor was attention called to the contradictory policy of urging alliance with the Kuomintang at the same time the rebellious peasantry was to be "unleashed"—a contradiction which has been singled out by students of the Chinese revolution as the major cause of Stalin's failure there.

Several possible reasons for the Seventh Plenum's failure to articulate even a perfunctory challenge to Stalin's policies may be noted. In the first place, very limited information on developments in China during this period appears to have been made available to Comintern delegates by Soviet officials; if it is true that Soviet rather than Comintern channels were used for instructions and reports to and from China, it was inevitable that what little Comintern delegates learned would be heavily slanted to support Stalin's policies.[122] Secondly, the presence at the plenum of a representative of the Kuomintang, now affiliated with the Comintern as a sympathizing party, may well have inhibited the delegates; until they had adequate grounds, they would not have wished to jeopardize the alliance with the Kuomintang by debating it before someone whose subsequent reports to Chiang

[121] Roy, who had come from Berlin to attend the plenum, was sent to China early in 1927 to explain the decisions of the Seventh Plenum to the Chinese Communists; for a short period, then, he abandoned his traditionally independent role in the Comintern to serve as one of Stalin's agents.

[122] The Comintern evidently had only two major representatives in China during 1926, as contrasted with dozens representing the Soviet government. These were Pavel Mif, who spent most of the year organizing party schools throughout the country, and Gregory Voitinsky, head of the ECCI's Eastern Department, who was sent to China following the Sixth Plenum to combat anti-Kuomintang sentiment within the CCP; see Degras, *Communist International*, II, pp. 276, 337. Mif, as we have seen, was taken to task by Stalin during the Seventh Plenum for his views on peasant soviets in China. Voitinsky appears to have been more closely identified with the Soviet government than the Comintern and showed himself willing to sublimate any independent views he had to do Stalin's bidding; see Brandt, *Stalin's Failure in China*, p. 91.

could easily destroy it without further ado.[123] Finally—and this alone would have been enough—the influence of Stalin, working in the background of the plenum, was enough to curb open debate on the merits of his China policy. By the end of 1926 diversity of opinion could not continue where his authority made itself felt. The Seventh Plenum debate on China, accordingly, gave the appearance of a rather elaborate dumb show, organized to give an official stamp of approval to a policy previously decided upon—indeed, already in force—though not widely approved. The theses on the Chinese question, needless to say, also reflected Stalin's views.[124]

The broader aspects of the Eastern question received little attention during the Seventh Plenum. Only Manuilsky attempted to apply the lessons of the Chinese revolution to the rest of Asia, regretting the lack of attention the Comintern had given to the East in the past. "We were too much of a European International," he said, "inclined to see all the problems of world politics and of international workers' movements through the prism of European relations."[125] Manuilsky's change of attitude on this matter was perhaps symptomatic of a general reorientation of the International; but for the time being, to judge from the record of the Seventh Plenum, the reorientation was confined to China. India, for instance, was almost totally ignored. Even the insurrection in Java, in progress while the Seventh Plenum was in ses-

---

[123] Shao Li Tse was the Kuomintang representative; in his speech during the discussion of the Chinese question he reaffirmed, from the Kuomintang viewpoint, the alliance with the Communists. See *Inprecor*, December 30, 1926, p. 1604.

[124] Roy claims authorship of the theses, together with Bukharin and Andrei Bubnov, a member of Stalin's Politburo recently returned from China; another source credits the theses to Bukharin and Stalin. See North, *Moscow and Chinese Communists*, p. 90. T'an P'ing-shan, reporting for the Chinese Commission, stated that the theses were drawn up from six reports and drafts submitted to the commission; during the discussion, he said, opposition had appeared from both Right and Left on the peasant question—the Right fearing the alliance with the Kuomintang would be endangered by an active peasant policy, the Left insisting on a call for peasant soviets. Both views were rejected, as was the demand of the Trotskyists that the Chinese Communists leave the Kuomintang; *Inprecor*, January 27, 1927, p. 174.

[125] *Ibid.*, December 30, 1926, p. 1593.

sion, attracted minimum attention, apart from Semaoen's brief report on it at the opening session.[126]

Having elected, at the Seventh Plenum, to make the International the instrument of his policies in China, Stalin went to some trouble to identify his policies as the Comintern's and to give the appearance of working through the Comintern. Major policy pronouncements were issued by the ECCI—for instance, the resolutions on Chiang Kai-shek's coup in Shanghai in April and on the defection of the Wuhan government in July.[127] In May, at the height of the crisis in China, the Eighth ECCI Plenum provided the principal forum for a review of Soviet strategies. It was not Stalin's intention, however, that the International should take independent action in China, and, so far as is known, it did not. Stalin's instructions, worked out with his closest colleagues within the Soviet Politburo, were evidently transmitted in coded telegrams directly to Borodin in Wuhan; the Comintern, whose liaison with Soviet party leaders is reported to have been erratic during this period,[128] was brought onto the scene as the occasion required to give a formal stamp of approval to Stalin's schemes.

The reasons for Stalin's behavior in 1927 have been extensively analyzed by students of the Chinese revolution. No consensus exists, but most explanations rely on one of two opposing arguments. The first is that at a critical juncture in the Chinese revolution Stalin's choice of alternative policies was limited by the fact that the course which had the most to recommend it, the Leftist course, had been appropriated by the Opposition, and was therefore politically unacceptable. As the rivalry between Stalin and Trotsky grew more intense, it became increasingly difficult for even the most trusted of Stalin's supporters to urge this

[126] *Ibid.*, December 1, 1926, pp. 1430-1. The ECCI passed a resolution on the Javan uprising on the eve of the Seventh Plenum but took no further action until after the insurrection had failed; the episode is discussed in the next chapter.

[127] *Ibid.*, April 16, 1927, p. 859, and July 28, 1927, pp. 983-5.

[128] See Degras, *Communist International*, II, p. 367, citing the memoirs of a Swiss Communist, Humbert-Droz, who worked on the ECCI at the time.

policy on him for fear of being labeled Trotskyite.[129] There is little reason to doubt, in retrospect, that Stalin's position within the Soviet Union was secure against any pressure Trotsky could bring to bear on him as late as the spring of 1927; at the time, however, it should be recalled, the struggle still appeared to many to be fought out on issues. This was particularly so within the International, where the tradition of free speech had not yet been wholly extinguished. Trotsky's arguments on China were compelling, especially after Chiang's coup in mid-April. It was the force of his arguments at the Eighth ECCI Plenum, we may imagine, which led to the decision (presumably Stalin's) to suppress publication of the proceedings—the first time this had happened since the founding of the International in 1919.[130] The same considerations held Stalin fixedly to his course through June and into July, despite the fact that the collaboration he insisted on between the Chinese Communists and the Wuhan government was by that time no more than a fiction. Indeed, in the context of this interpretation, by July Stalin was even more circumscribed than previously because of the Opposition's greatly stepped up assault on his policies at a time when their bankruptcy was becoming more and more evident. When even the fiction of the Wuhan alliance was destroyed, Stalin still avoided for as long as he could the course Trotsky had urged. Instead, with extraordinary disdain for the record, he asserted the absolute correctness of the Comintern's (that is, his) policies in China and laid the failure there at the feet of the Chinese Communists, who had incorrectly applied them. By this reading of events, Stalin showed himself willing to sacrifice the entire revolution in China rather than risk the possible consequences of allowing Trotsky's policies to prevail.

[129] The failure of a Comintern delegation visiting China early in 1927 to report its suspicions of Chiang Kai-shek, for instance, is attributed to such a fear; see Brandt, *Stalin's Failure in China*, p. 112.

[130] Stalin's address was carried in *Bol'shevik*, No. 10 (May 31), 1927, and the principal resolutions were published in *Inprecor*, June 9 and June 12, 1927, and in *Vosmoi plenum Ispolnitel'nogo komiteta Kommunisticheskogo Internatsionala* (1927). No other record of the Eighth Plenum was published in Russia so far as is known; Trotsky's speeches and Zinoviev's theses on China were later released abroad.

Would Stalin have taken a more aggressive line in China had there been no Trotsky? The second argument raises doubt that he would have. Stalin, it has been noted, introduced theory (or ideology) into the Chinese question relatively late in the episode, only at the Seventh Plenum at the end of 1926; the presumption is that he did so to fortify policies already in existence, notably support of Chiang Kai-shek and alliance with the Kuomintang. It may, however, be argued that Stalin, who throughout his life was deferential to theory, was in some degree a captive of the theoretical formulations on China which he advanced. So long as the revolution in China remained bourgeois democratic—and even Trotsky raised no strong objection to this interpretation—it followed, from the ideological argument, that only the tactics appropriate to such a revolution could succeed. There is no reason to imagine that Stalin was uninfluenced by this consideration. One could, indeed, enquire how it came about that the policies of collaboration with the Chinese bourgeoisie were adopted in the first place, long before the Seventh Plenum, as long ago as the Sun-Joffe agreement in 1923; surely Trotskyism had not always compelled Stalin to pursue the policies he followed in 1927.

Whatever the origins of Stalin's strategy in China, during the climax of the revolution in 1927 he continued to apply, or to adjust, the formula he had enunciated at the Seventh Plenum. In April, for instance, he argued that Chiang's coup in Shanghai signified merely "that the revolution had entered the second stage of its development . . . away from the revolution of an *all-national* united front." It was still, however, bourgeois democratic, not socialist; accordingly, the line was changed only to exclude the Right (Chiang Kai-shek and his supporters) and "to concentrate all power in the hands of a *revolutionary* Kuomintang . . . [that is,] a bloc between the Left Kuomintang and the Communists."[131] At the Eighth Plenum in May, in a speech redolent with personal invective against Trotsky, Stalin described the bourgeois demo-

[131] Stalin, *Sochineniia*, IX, pp. 225-7; from "Questions of the Chinese Revolution" (April 21, 1927). The Wuhan coalition, which was such a bloc, was finally formed in May 1927, after much pressure on the Chinese Communists from Moscow.

cratic revolution in China as "a combination of two streams of the revolutionary movement: the struggle against feudal survivals and the struggle against imperialism." Since the Left Kuomintang identified itself with this dual struggle, alliance with it was mandatory.[132] As late as early July, when the Wuhan coalition existed in name only, Bukharin (whose views at this juncture were identical with Stalin's) still supported this regime and praised Communist participation in it.[133] Allowing for a certain amount of subterfuge in these public pronouncements, which did not always tally with secret instructions to Borodin,[134] they may still be read as an expression of Stalin's view that the Wuhan government, at least until mid-July, represented the proper vehicle for the Chinese revolution. Even when the alliance ended, it led to no agonizing reappraisal in Moscow. The revolution in China, Moscow reasoned, was still bourgeois democratic. All that had changed was that the national bourgeoisie had now defected in its entirety to the imperialist camp—a possibility Stalin claimed he had foreseen. This meant, as Stalin stated on August 1, that where the first stage of the revolution had been anti-imperialist, and the second anti-imperialist and anti-feudal, now "the spearhead of the revolution is turned mainly against internal enemies, primarily against the feudal landlords." But it was the *same* revolution, Stalin asserted—that is, still bourgeois democratic—and the prospects for its ultimate success were undiminished.[135]

Was it stubbornness, in the face of Trotsky's relentless opposition, that caused Stalin to cling to a strategy that seems, in retrospect, to have been long foredoomed? Or was it commitment to

[132] *Ibid.*, pp. 285-6.

[133] *Inprecor*, July 7, 1927, p. 873.

[134] On June 1, 1927, for instance, five and a half weeks before Bukharin's article, an instruction had been cabled to Borodin to press more actively Communist infiltration of the Wuhan Army, preparatory to seizing control of the Wuhan government itself. Stalin subsequently released a text of the telegram (see *Sochineniia*, x, pp. 32-3) and it is mentioned also in other sources; see Brandt, *Stalin's Failure in China*, p. 133. Roy's showing this telegram to Wang Ching-wei, the Left Kuomintang leader who headed the Wuhan government, is generally believed to have precipitated the final break with the Communists in mid-July.

[135] Stalin, *Sochineniia*, x, pp. 25-6; speech before a joint plenum of the Soviet party's Central Committee and Central Control Commission.

theory—call it principle? Despite a prevailing view that it was the former, it is manifestly impossible to say with certainty; nor is it likely that Stalin knew himself. The importance, in any case, which Stalin may have attached to his theories need not rest on any objective judgment of their insight or of their relevance to China—nor, of course, on Stalin's tedious justification of them in later years. Had Stalin's strategies, by some miracle, succeeded, this would have been vindication enough, and all objections would have vanished, much as objections to Lenin's strategies in the spring of 1917 dissolved in the autumn; in the meantime, the hypothesis that Trotsky's formula in China would have succeeded is quite unproven. In this connection, it is worth remarking that Stalin and Trotsky were perhaps not so far apart in their judgment of China as has been argued. Their differences were magnified at the time by the bitter rivalry between them; in later years the differences were magnified to an even greater degree by appreciation of Stalin's failure. Yet in March 1927, at the moment when he was launching his most bitter attacks on the Kuomintang alliance, Trotsky wrote: "The Communists cannot, of course, relinquish their support of the National [i.e., Wuhan] government and of the National Army. Nor does it seem that they can give up their participation in the National Government."[136] Later in the year, after the Wuhan government had been dissolved, Trotsky revealed himself no less optimistic than Stalin that ultimate victory in China would be achieved, despite past failures.[137] The two were, after all, trained in the same school.

The Chinese revolution of 1925-1927 had a great impact throughout Asia. It gave impetus to revolutionary movements in Southeast Asia which, except in Indonesia, had attracted little attention earlier in the decade. Moreover, since the energies of the Chinese Communists were not wholly exhausted in the Kuomintang and Wuhan episodes—as evidenced, for instance, in the Canton uprising late in 1927 and the soviets of Mao Tse-tung and his fol-

[136] From a document dated March 22, 1927, cited in Brandt, *op. cit.*, pp. 160-1.
[137] See for instance a manuscript dated September 1927, cited in *ibid.*, p. 161.

lowers in south China[138]—developments in China continued for some years to stimulate other Asians. The course of the revolution also demonstrated the energy that Moscow was capable of bringing to bear in the East, given favorable opportunities; Soviet Eastern policy was not, after all, mere talk. But when all this is duly acknowledged, the immediate relevance of Stalin's strategies in China to Soviet policies in the East generally should not be exaggerated. In the first place, they were conditioned not only by a bitter political struggle in Moscow but by special circumstances in China which had no exact parallel elsewhere in Asia; this meant that the China strategies were not readily transferable. Moreover, the personal attention Stalin devoted to China in 1926 and 1927 was unique. Stalin never again engaged himself so totally in an Eastern revolution. Eastern revolutionaries, it may be argued, were the beneficiaries of his neglect—that is another question—but his unwillingness again to involve himself to such a degree in the East had several consequences: it meant, for instance, that directives to the colonies in later years often lacked the authority of those issued to the Chinese Communists in 1925-1927; it meant, too, that, lacking this authority, the directives tended to be more equivocal; and, for Asian revolutionaries, it meant that the support Moscow had given the Chinese revolution (though it proved, in the end, to be a mixed blessing) could no longer be counted upon. For these reasons, although the impact of the Chinese revolution per se was formidable, the Russian experience in China provided fewer guides to strategies in other Asian countries than might be imagined.

Moscow's persistent preoccupation with China inevitably diverted attention for a time from other trouble spots in the East. The Comintern issued only two directives during 1927 relating to Asian movements other than in China: a resolution in July seeking to resolve a doctrinal dispute within the Japanese Communist Party on its size and character (a dispute very similar to that which divided the Russian Social Democrats in 1903);[139]

---

[138] The soviet slogan in China had been authorized by Moscow in August 1927 (although Mao, on his own initiative, had called for soviets before he knew of Moscow's decision) and continued in use for the next decade.

[139] The text of the resolution was given in *Inprecor*, January 12, 1928, pp.

and a belated comment in November on the Indonesian uprising a year earlier.[140] India continued to attract negligible attention in Moscow. Only after the Chinese revolution had quite obviously failed, though before the failure was widely acknowledged, did Soviet spokesmen attempt to draw some lessons from the Chinese experience which might be useful elsewhere. The lessons were mainly negative. Bukharin, addressing the Fifteenth Congress of the CPSU in December 1927, noted that while "the experience of the Chinese revolution has brought us into actual touch with a diversity of problems of colonial revolutions in general, . . . [it] shows very clearly how cautious one must be in deciding on concrete political tactics, how necessary it is to take into careful consideration the peculiarities of development in this or that country." In India, for instance, where the correlation of class forces was seen as wholly different from China's, it would be "unpardonable folly if we tried to mechanically transfer the experience of our Chinese tactics."[141] This was not, however, an admission of error in China. On the contrary, the China policy was once again vindicated by the Fifteenth Congress, and the cause of the "temporary" set-back in China laid to the improper execution of Moscow's directives. Stalin, at the same congress, enunciated his doctrine of the "ebb and flow" of revolutions, a doctrine that was to prevail in Soviet analyses of the East for the next half-dozen years: "Clearly the revolutionary awakening of the colonial and dependent countries presages the end of world imperialism. The fact that the Chinese revolution has not yet led to direct victory over imperialism cannot be of decisive significance for the prospects of the revolution. Great popular revolutions never achieve final victory in the first round of their battles. They grow and gain strength in the course of flows and ebbs. That has been so everywhere, including Russia.

50-54; it was drafted by a special ECCI commission attended by Japanese Communists and presided over by Bukharin.

[140] *Ibid.*, December 8, 1927, pp. 1562-3. In January 1927 the uprising on Java extended to Sumatra, where it lasted several weeks; the lack of Soviet response to the Indonesian revolution of 1926-27 is discussed in the next chapter.

[141] *XV S"ezd VKP(B)*, p. 606, cited in Eudin and North, *op. cit.*, p. 391.

So it will be in China."[142] Stalin went on to note that the most important consequence of the Chinese revolution was that it "has awakened from age-long slumber and set in motion hundreds of millions of exploited and oppressed peoples" in India, Indonesia, and elsewhere in the East.

Stalin might have added that the Chinese revolution also aroused from long "slumber" a Comintern which in the past had persisted in searching for revolution in the West rather than in the East. This, indeed, emerges as one of the principal residual consequences of the Soviet experience in China. Preoccupation with China, it is true, distracted Moscow for several years from any serious consideration of the wider dimensions of Asian revolution; but it also had the effect of directing a larger share of the Comintern's attention to Asia. It would take more than the failure of a single revolution to dislodge this interest. Bukharin, it turned out, was quite correct in predicting, at the Fifteenth Party Congress, that the colonial question would appear "in all its magnitude" on the agenda of the forthcoming Comintern congress.[143]

HARDENING OF SOVIET POLICY IN THE EAST: SIXTH COMINTERN CONGRESS: 1928

A number of circumstances combined to make the year 1928 a watershed in the evolution of Soviet Eastern policies. In the first place, Moscow's failures in China (which were compounded by the abortive Canton uprising in December 1927)[144] led inevitably to a reappraisal of certain traditional concepts of Soviet Eastern policy, notably the validity of alliances with bourgeois parties like the Kuomintang. This policy, in effect since 1920 with some variation in application depending on local conditions, had

[142] Stalin, *Sochineniia*, x, p. 283.

[143] *XV S"ezd VKP(B)*, p. 609.

[144] The Canton insurrection was launched by the Chinese Communists on December 11 and led to their control of the city for two days, under a hastily organized "soviet of workers', soldiers', and peasants' deputies," before the arrival of Kuomintang forces; Soviet advisers, notably Heinz Neumann, played an important role in the planning and carrying out of the uprising, the suppression of which led to exceptionally high Communist casualties.

yielded too meager success to go unchallenged. At the same time, the corresponding policy in the West, the united front from below, had run into difficulties in England, the Comintern's principal focus in Europe since the Fifth Congress, and this gave further impetus to change.[145] Within Russia, the final dispersal of the Trotskyist opposition at the end of 1927 (seventy-five Trotskyites were expelled from the party at the Fifteenth Congress, and Trotsky began his exile in Central Asia soon thereafter) left the way open for a turn to the Left which had been politically impracticable earlier. The decision to liquidate the New Economic Policy (NEP) in favor of planning also facilitated more radical approaches in foreign policy. Meanwhile the war danger which Moscow increasingly asserted during 1928, and perhaps even believed, tended to produce sharper distinctions between class allies and class enemies than had been articulated in recent years. All of these considerations led to a marked shift to the Left during the year.

The Ninth ECCI Plenum in February 1928 gave an early indication of the new course. A resolution on the Chinese question, for instance, which Stalin and Bukharin had a hand in drafting, proclaimed that despite setbacks the CCP "must prepare itself for a violent surge forward"; the party's immediate task was "to organize and carry through armed mass risings, for the tasks of the revolution can only be solved by rebellion." The resolution cautioned against premature insurrections, noting that "to play with revolts . . . is the surest way to bring disaster to the revolution," but the tone of the document remained militant. Even the uprising in Canton, whose failure was laid to a multitude of blunders committed by Comintern agents and Chinese Communist leaders alike, was considered "an heroic attempt of the proletariat to organize a soviet government in China."[146]

---

[145] The united front in Great Britain was expressed in the Anglo-Russian Trade Union Council, formed in 1925; after some early successes, notably during the General Strike of 1926, the alliance was dissolved by English labor leaders in October 1927.

[146] *Inprecor*, March 15, 1928, pp. 321-2; the resolution on China was offered by Stalin and Bukharin, representing the CPSU, and Li (Li Li-san?) and Sian

During the spring there was additional evidence of a shift in Soviet policies. In March, for instance, the Fourth Profintern Congress in Moscow adopted a militant line on trade union activities and gave special attention to labor movements in the East. In May the ECCI instructed the Japanese Communists, in the face of bitter persecution by the government, to strengthen their illegal apparatus and step up the tempo of their struggle with the social democrats.[147] A Comintern document released in July, on the eve of the Sixth Congress, reported a surge of revolutionary activity throughout the East, especially in India.[148]

The Sixth Comintern Congress, meeting in Moscow from mid-July to the beginning of September 1928, was the climax of this gradual process of radicalization in the Comintern's Eastern policy. The colonial question, as Bukharin had predicted, occupied a prominent place on the agenda of the congress. More than a quarter of the sessions were devoted to a discussion of the revolutionary movements in the colonies—no less, for instance, than were given to Bukharin's keynote address on the international situation, which also gave much attention to the East. More Asian delegates than ever before attended the congress (including four Indonesians and one Vietnamese), and many more than previously were elected to the Comintern's leading organs.[149]

The most important of the scores of theses, resolutions, and manifestoes adopted by the Sixth Congress was doubtless the

---

(Hsiang Chung-fa?), representing the CCP. The abbreviated record of the Ninth Plenum in *Inprecor* (February 25, 1928) and *Pravda* (February 28, 1928) omits the debate on the Chinese question, both in the Chinese Commission and during the plenum proper; no stenograph of the Ninth Plenum, which like the Eighth was attended by fewer than 100 delegates, was published.

[147] *Inprecor*, June 14, 1928, pp. 617-8.

[148] *The Communist International Between the Fifth and Sixth World Congresses*, p. 477.

[149] The new ECCI, for instance, included 13 Eastern delegates as full members and 9 candidates, of a total, respectively, of 59 and 43; the ECCI elected at the Fifth Congress in 1924, made up of 44 full members and 26 candidates, included only 5 members from the East and no candidates. The 27-man Presidium included 5 representatives from the East, as contrasted with a single member elected in 1924. See Degras, *Communist International*, II, pp. 572-5.

long program drafted by Bukharin. It represented the first attempt to articulate with some precision the trend of the world revolution in the present era and to formulate the grand strategy of the future. It attempted to be no less than a new *Communist Manifesto* geared to the Twentieth Century. The document included a classic Marxian analysis of the inevitable collapse of capitalism, despite evidence of momentary stabilization, and fitted the colonial question into the general scheme of world revolution without attempting to determine whether revolution in the East preceded or followed revolution in Europe. Rebellions in China, Indonesia, and India, the program stated, "are links in the chain of international revolution, constituent parts of the profound general crisis of capitalism." The tasks in the East—which were to appear again and again in the programs of the parties in Southeast Asia during succeeding years—were listed as:

1. The overthrow of foreign imperialism, of feudalism, and of the landlord bureaucracy.
2. Establishment of the democratic dictatorship of the proletariat and peasantry on the basis of soviets.
3. Complete national independence and political unification.
4. Cancellation of state debts.
5. Nationalization of large undertakings belonging to the imperialists.
6. Expropriation of large landowners, of church and monastery estates, nationalization of all land.
7. Introduction of the eight-hour day.
8. Establishment of a revolutionary workers' and peasants' army.[150]

Bukharin's program had too grandiose a design to provide practical guidance to colonial movements in their day-to-day activities; this, indeed, was one of the complaints most frequently raised against it throughout the congress. The document, however, represents a landmark in the history of the Comintern.

[150] Cited from the translation in *ibid.*, p. 507. The official stenographic record of the Sixth Congress is *Shestoi kongress Kominterna*, 6 vols. (1929); an English transcript of the 46 plenary sessions of the Congress, plus the resolutions, theses, etc., was carried in *Inprecor* during the fall of 1928.

If it accomplished little else, it demonstrated that reverses in China and England, and indeed in virtually all areas where the Comintern had been active during the decade, had not changed Moscow's commitment to the world revolution—at least in words.

More earthly advice on tactics was left to the theses on the revolutionary movement in the colonies, drafted by Otto Kuusinen. For the first time in several years China was not the principal focus of discussion, although, as previously, the Comintern's policy there was stoutly defended. Kuusinen, in introducing the theses, singled out India to illustrate his arguments because, as he said, it was a "classical colonial country" and because revolution there was imminent.[151] As finally adopted the theses were many times longer than any comparable theses adopted at earlier congresses and plenums. They discussed, in considerable detail, not only the general theories of colonial development but also the specific tasks in many individual countries. The colonial world, the theses stated, had become "an unquenchable blazing furnace of the revolutionary mass movement." Colonial movements were now indissolubly linked with the proletarian movements of the advanced countries, which opened to the colonial peoples the possibility of avoiding the capitalist stage of development. But only "through struggle and struggle alone" could the possibility become a reality. During the present stage of revolution—which was bourgeois democratic, not socialist—the "basic strategic aim was the hegemony of the proletariat." This required Communist parties, and the formation of such parties where none existed was accordingly a major task for all sections. The Comintern itself undertook to "give an absolutely special attention" to this problem. Trade union organization ranked second in importance, among the immediate tactical objectives in the East, and the colonies were referred to the Profintern for advice in this matter. The peasantry, called "a driving force of the revolution," was to be an ally of the worker; revolutionary peasant organizations were to be developed, but joint workers' and peasants' parties were discour-

[151] *Inprecor*, October 4, 1928, pp. 1225-34.

aged. "The Communist Party can never build its organization on the basis of a fusion of two classes," the theses stated. When appropriate, the solidarity of workers and peasants should be given expression in "carefully prepared and periodically convened joint conferences of representatives of revolutionary peasant unions and of trade unions." At the moment of revolution, however, alliance with the peasantry was mandatory; the formation of soviets of workers' and peasants' deputies was then "a fundamental task" of the colonial parties. On the matter of alliance with the "petty-bourgeois intelligentsia" the theses were extremely wary. Despite the historic role of these elements in the struggle against imperialism, which was seen as continuing even to the present day in a few countries such as India and Egypt, "only a few in the course of the struggle are able to break with their own class and rise to an understanding of the tasks of the class struggle of the proletariat."[152] The theses ended with a discussion of the tasks in individual countries—notably China, India, Indonesia, and Egypt—and with a fresh reminder to the parties in imperialist countries to take up the cause of the colonies and combat the inroads into colonial movements made by social democrats.[153]

Taken as a whole, Bukharin's program and Kuusinen's theses, together with the other resolutions adopted by the Sixth Congress, offer no startling, new formulations insofar as analysis of the world situation is concerned. Nor should it be imagined that they would. The same sort of delegate—if not the same delegates —attended this meeting who had attended previous meetings of the International. Meanwhile, the world situation had altered gradually enough so that many of the concepts advanced in mid-1928 were implicit, and very often spelled out, in earlier Comin-

---

[152] Bukharin's program, interestingly, took a more eclectic stand on this point. "Temporary compromises with the national bourgeoisie are permissible," the program stated, "if they do not hamper the revolutionary organization of the workers and peasants and if they serve the struggle against imperialism"; cited from English text in Degras, *Communist International*, II, p. 522.

[153] The quoted portions of the theses are taken from the American Communist translation, *The Revolutionary Movement in the Colonies* (New York, 1929).

tern pronouncements. What is chiefly significant about the Sixth Congress is that it affirmed the *tactical* drift to the Left evident since the latter part of 1927 and directed all sections to follow this course. The fact that Stalin took no visible part in the congress (though elected to the principal Comintern organs) and that Bukharin, who dominated the proceedings from beginning to end, was already at odds with Stalin did not lessen the significance of these decisions. During the greater part of the seven-year interval between this congress and the Seventh (and last) the Comintern's analysis of the world situation remained largely unchanged and the tactical line remained militant. Succeeding plenums reaffirmed this line. Soviet revolutionary policy, in the East as elsewhere, assumed a character of more or less chronic belligerency.

Moscow's Eastern strategies during the 1920's, it should be noted, were not the exclusive responsibility of the Comintern or of networks of operatives working directly under Stalin. Other Moscow-oriented agencies, whose activities were less publicized than the Comintern's, were also active in the East. One of these was the Profintern. From its founding in 1921 a major objective of the Profintern had been to gain the affiliation of labor movements in colonial and semi-colonial countries. In 1922, during the Second Profintern Congress (running concurrently with the Fourth Comintern Congress), it was first proposed that a conference of Pacific workers be convened in the Far East.[154] A year and a half later, in June 1924, such a conference was held in Canton under Profintern auspices—the Conference of Transport Workers of the Pacific; it was the first international gathering in Asia of Asian revolutionaries. Only three countries were represented—China, Java, and the Philippines—and no permanent machinery was set up to ensure that the ties established at the conference would continue.[155] However, it was

[154] *Inprecor*, December 7, 1922, p. 892.

[155] Reference was made, during the Third Profintern Congress in July 1924, to a "bureau" recently established in Canton, but there is no evidence that it ever functioned; see *Third World Congress of the Red International of Trade Unions: Resolutions and Decisions*, p. 22.

a beginning. A manifesto was adopted by the conference calling on the toiling masses of the East to form unions and affiliate with "the revolutionary workers of the world."[156] The following May, in the midst of the disorders in Shanghai, a group of Chinese unions, numbering approximately a million workers, became the first Asian organization to affiliate with the Profintern.

A more ambitious effort to organize colonial workers in East Asia was made in May 1927, when after a number of delays labor representatives from China, Japan, and Indonesia, as well as from Russia, the United States, England, and France, assembled in Hankow at the first Pan Pacific Trade Union Conference.[157] Lozovsky (S. A. Dridzo), head of the Profintern, delivered the keynote address, stressing the importance of the Chinese revolution to the international labor movement; the Asian delegates reported on the labor movements in their respective countries. At the close of the conference a permanent secretariat was established, the Pan Pacific Trade Union Secretariat (PPTUS), whose tasks were to establish a "lasting and militant alliance" between the workers of the East and West, to defend the USSR against imperialism, to struggle against the war danger in the Pacific, and to publish a trade union journal, the *Pan Pacific Worker*.[158] Between the Hankow and Vladivostok conferences, the latter held in August 1929, the PPTUS conducted a variety of activities in the Far East under the supervision of its secretary, Earl Browder. It was this organization rather than the Comintern which provided the first significant links between Moscow and several of the countries in Southeast Asia, notably the Philippines.

[156] G. Voitinsky, "First Conference of Transport Workers of the Pacific," *Inprecor*, September 11, 1924, pp. 704-5.

[157] An organization meeting called the previous October in Sydney had accomplished very little because so few delegates had been able to attend; the conference was then set for Canton early in May, but was later shifted to Hankow, where it conducted seven sessions between May 20-26.

[158] *Pan Pacific Worker*, July 1, 1927, p. 1-10 (the title of this journal changed several times during the five years of its publication); see also *Resolutions and Decisions of the Pan Pacific Trade Union Conference* (Hankow, 1927).

71

In Moscow, in the meantime, the Profintern gave regular coverage of activities in the East through its principal journals, *Krasnyi internatsional profsoiuzov* and *Mezhdunarodnoe rabochee dvizhenie*; in 1927 it began publication of an English-language journal, *Eastern and Colonial Bulletin*, which reached a wider audience in the colonies. Delegates from the East attended the Third and Fourth Profintern Congresses, held in Moscow, respectively, in July 1924 and March 1928. At the latter congress approximately fifty of the 421 delegates represented colonial or semi-colonial countries, thirty of them from Asia; the congress devoted three of its twenty-two sessions to a discussion of labor movements in the East, passed special resolutions on trade union problems in China and India, and elected Eastern delegates to a quarter of the seats on the Profintern's Central Committee and Politburo.[159]

A somewhat different activity in the East was undertaken by the League against Imperialism and for National Independence, an organization appealing to nationalists and intellectuals from the colonial countries. The League (which was variously called the Anti-Imperialist League or the League to Struggle Against Imperialism and Colonial Oppression) was organized at a congress which convened in Brussels, under Comintern auspices, in February 1927. One hundred and seventy-four delegates representing 134 organizations attended the congress, including several who were to play major roles in the nationalist movements of their respective countries in later years: for instance, Jawaharlal Nehru of India and Mohammed Hatta of Indonesia, both of whom were named to the first Executive Committee. Communists, it was said, constituted only 10 percent of the delegates at the Brussels congress. A unanimous resolution revealed the militant mood of the congress. "The collapse of imperialism," it stated, "has set in. The working class and the masses of the oppressed peoples are its gravedigger. . . . The representatives of the colonial and dependent peoples declare that they will develop the fight against imperialism into mass actions of the

[159] *IV Kongress Profinterna*, pp. 538, 588, 592.

workers of their countries."[160] Following the congress a head-quarters was established in Berlin, headed by a German Communist, Willi Münzenberg, and plenary meetings of the Executive Committee were held at intervals during the next two years. In the meantime national sections of the Anti-Imperialist League were established in many colonies, as well as in several European countries. Following the Second Congress, which met in Frankfurt in July 1929 and adopted a more militant strategy of reliance on revolutionary trade union movements in the colonies, the League lost the support of many moderate nationalists and ceased to serve as a device to link Communists and non-Communists in a broad anti-imperialist front in the East.[161]

In addition to the Profintern (and its affiliates) and the Anti-Imperialist League, a number of other Moscow-oriented organizations conducted parallel activities in the East: the Peasant International (Krestintern), the Communist Youth International, the International of Women, and others. The records of these lesser agencies are too meager to give a clear idea of how effective they were, but it is likely that each enlarged somewhat the range of Moscow's influence. Coordination of these scattered activities was presumably left to the Communist International.[162]

CONCLUSIONS

Before we turn from the general to the particular, it is appropriate to make a few observations on the foregoing account of

[160] *Inprecor*, February 25, 1927, p. 324; other materials relating to the Brussels congress may be found in *ibid.*, February 4, 1927, and February 17, 1927. See also G. Gautherot, *Le Bolchévisme aux colonies et l'impérialisme rouge*, p. 209.

[161] For accounts of the Frankfurt congress, see *Eastern and Colonial Bulletin*, No. 8-9, August-September, 1929 and *Pan Pacific Monthly*, No. 30-31, September-October, 1929, pp. 22-4.

[162] According to an anti-Comintern source, which cites an official Soviet year-book for 1927, the Oriental sections of the Profintern, Krestintern, Communist Youth International, International of Women, and VOKS, as well as the Association of "Hands off China," the Anti-Imperialist League and the colonial committees of major European parties, were all directly responsible to the Eastern Department of the ECCI; Permanent Bureau of the International Entente Against the Third International, "Charts Representing the Soviet Organizations Working for Revolution in All Countries" (Geneva, October 1928), p. 45.

Evolution of Soviet Eastern Policy: 1917-1928

Soviet policy in the East, especially on aspects of this policy which may shed light on strategies in Southeast Asia. This was the purpose of our review. Moscow's activities in Southeast Asia, we knew in advance, would prove too haphazard, and the record of them too fragmentary, to enable us to piece together a significant account without some framework of larger Soviet objectives. Such a framework has now been provided, but it needs interpretation.

1. Russia's turn to the East was very gradual. It cannot be dated with precision. It was not primarily the consequence of the Comintern's frustration in Europe, although this is sometimes argued by students of Soviet foreign policy. Nor was it necessarily in response to theories—which abounded in the years following the Russian Revolution—concerning the dependence, in one degree or another, of European revolution on revolution in the East. (We shall, however, return to this thesis.) These circumstances doubtless helped to create attitudes congenial to greater activity in the East, but they do not explain why in the last analysis the activity was undertaken. The passage of time assisted Moscow's Eastern orientation. By the middle of the 1920's the impact of the Russian Revolution was greater throughout the colonial world than it had been immediately after 1917; national movements in the East, many of them launched only during or after World War I, had had a chance to mature; time was necessary for the colonies to grow responsive to so novel an approach to international affairs as the Comintern's. Meanwhile, in Russia, time led to a clearer understanding of the East and a greater competence to analyze Eastern political and social movements; Soviet formulations on the East, for all their artifice, were more sophisticated in 1925 than in 1920. The most decisive circumstance, however, in Moscow's turn to the East was the coincidence of favorable opportunities for revolution in a single country, China, occurring at a time when Stalin, who was already disposed to look to the East, was coming to power in Russia. But for this coincidence, it is by no means certain that the International, oriented as it was to Europe, would have come

to give the East so much consideration. Once engaged, the Comintern's attention to the East remained relatively constant—at least so long as revolution abroad continued to be a serious preoccupation in Moscow, which spans the period covered in the present chapter.

In Southeast Asia, then, we should not expect to discover much Soviet concern before the middle of the 1920's. Whatever interest was then shown would be over-shadowed during 1926 and 1927 by Moscow's preoccupation with China. Only from 1928 on would it be reasonable to expect Soviet activity of any consequence.

2. Lenin's part in shaping Soviet Eastern policy should not be exaggerated. His 1920 theses on the Eastern question have been intensively studied—by both Communist and non-Communist Orientalists—as an authoritative early statement of Soviet policy in the East. On inspection, however, the theses show many formulations on the Eastern question and many specific policy recommendations which had little bearing on the problems actually encountered in the East in subsequent years. The importance which Lenin attached to the question of a federation of soviet republics proved quite irrelevant; his treatment of the relationship of Communists to "national revolutionary" movements was too ambiguous to enlighten anyone and made this issue a source of misunderstanding and confusion for many years; his injunction against certain movements such as Pan-Islam had presently to be set aside; and his rather premature call for soviets was simply ignored, until Stalin chose to launch the slogan in China in 1927 and, some years later, elsewhere in Asia. After the 1920 statement, Lenin gave no further systematic consideration to the Eastern question; when he discussed the East at all, it was normally to call attention to the enormous potential for revolution represented by its suppressed millions. Effective tactical guidance by Lenin must therefore be judged minimal. His contribution lay rather in directing the Comintern's attention for the first time to the vast world beyond Europe. The fact that Lenin had taken up the Eastern question,

no matter how clumsily, was enough to give it a certain vogue; all Communists, as Pavlovich put it, became in one degree or another "Asiatic."

3. The spirited controversy in the first years of the Soviet regime concerning the relationship of revolutions in Europe and Asia was left unresolved. During the Second Congress, in 1920, the question had seemed clear enough—were Asian revolutions a prerequisite for the more important risings anticipated in Europe, or merely the inevitable accompaniment?—and the various positions taken on the question were also unambiguous. The issue, however, was never debated outside the realm of pure theory; it was never brought down to the context of revolutionary realities in Asia proper. The loudest supporters of the Asia-first thesis, such as Roy, appear to have felt that only by arguing the vital importance of Asia to Europe could Europeans, preoccupied with their own affairs, be persuaded to assist movements in the colonies. When the East acquired significance in its own right, especially through China, the argument was no longer heard; the most that was ever seriously claimed of the Chinese revolution of 1925-1927, for instance, was that it would stimulate revolutionary activity elsewhere in Asia, which it in fact did. Yet there is some irony in the fact that, had the revolution in China succeeded, the impetus to world-wide revolution would have been greatly magnified, especially in the weakened condition of the capitalist states during the years of the depression. This possibility Moscow did not actively consider. The East *versus* West issue, far from being resolved on either the theoretical or practical level, had simply ceased to exist as such.

4. The Comintern's part in the formulation and execution of Soviet Eastern policy in the 1920's deserves comment. The usual presumption of students of the USSR is that Soviet and Comintern policies are synonymous, despite Moscow's disclaimers; as a rule, this is so. In the mid-1920's, however, Stalin's limited experience with the Comintern and the fact that two of his principal rivals, Trotsky and Zinoviev, were at home there meant

that the International was inevitably bypassed during Stalin's climb to power. From 1922, when Lenin's illness forced him from active participation in public affairs, until late 1926, when Stalin's ascendency was assured, the Comintern played a relatively minor role in the determination of Soviet foreign policy. This did not mean, of course, that it languished entirely. The prestige enjoyed by the Comintern from Lenin's patronage during the first few congresses was more than sufficient to protect it during any brief eclipse; moreover, the years of its "eclipse" were filled with plenary meetings of the ECCI and substantial expansion of staff so that any lessening of its importance would hardly have been noticeable to the casual observer. By the end of 1926, with the Left Opposition impotent (if not yet silenced), Stalin felt secure enough to adopt the Comintern as the principal instrument of his revolutionary policies, which were taking on special significance at that time because of events in China.

If there was a moment of truth in Stalin's relationship to the Communist International, it was during the Eighth ECCI Plenum of May 1927. The plenum was evidently necessary because of the deteriorating situation in China, because there was growing uneasiness over Moscow's policies, and because many of the sections felt (quite correctly) that they were ill-informed about events in China. For Stalin to have ignored the Comintern at this critical juncture would have been to risk the demoralization of an edifice which had been laboriously constructed during the past eight years to guide the world revolution when the time came. Stalin accordingly allowed his China policies to go on review, persuaded, we may presume, that if he did not accept the challenge of defending them before the ECCI the Comintern might pass into oblivion by default. How formidable was the challenge is not clear since the Eighth Plenum left no detailed record. Nor is it clear why Stalin's opponents were given the floor at this plenum when they had been denied it six months earlier during the Seventh Plenum. Perhaps, again, it was part of Stalin's decision to bring both foreign and domestic issues to the ultimate test: Trotsky's leadership or his. Trotsky lost—not, we may be sure, on the merits of his argument alone—

77

and the Comintern was preserved as Stalin's agency for revolution. Had Stalin, for reasons not easily imaginable, lost in the encounter, it goes without saying that the International would have ceased to play a significant part in Soviet strategies abroad, if, indeed, it could have survived at all.

Political institutions in dictatorships have, of course, no authority other than that invested in them by the dictator. The Comintern was no exception. Its survival at the end of the 1920's as the principal vehicle for Stalin's revolutionary strategies merely reflects his decision to adapt the organization to his purposes, much as Lenin adapted the soviets to his in 1917. The fact that after the Ninth ECCI Plenum early in 1928 Stalin played no visible part in Comintern affairs means simply that, secure in his own power, he had no further doubts that the International could be counted upon to serve him faithfully as the occasion arose. The Comintern grew increasingly sterile in the process of its adjustment to its new role; but in this its fate was no different from that of all other institutions which Stalin embraced.

For our purposes, then, in contemplating Soviet strategies in Southeast Asia, we may treat with some diffidence Comintern pronouncements in the mid-1920's which give the impression of being supported by an undisputed authority; this should apply to analyses of the political situation throughout Southeast Asia no less than to the policies recommended to local revolutionary movements. We should respect, instead, Stalin's observations on Southeast Asia—but unfortunately these will be few indeed. From 1927 on we can be confident that the formulations given by the Comintern (or its affiliates), while they are subject as always to subsequent revision, represent an authentic Soviet attitude at the time.

5. Finally, with regard to the importance of theory—the question with which this chapter began—it is not sufficient to argue either that theory *determined* Soviet policies in the East or that it merely *graced* them. There is evidence to support both arguments. No formula has ever been devised to explain when a

given Soviet action relies on doctrine and when doctrine is appealed to subsequently to rationalize the action. The versatility of theory in Soviet behavior, or perhaps the versatility of its practitioners, is such that few have satisfactorily explained its function. When one considers, for instance, that the action which had possibly the most far-reaching consequences in Soviet Eastern policy during the 1920's—Joffe's agreement with Sun Yat-sen in 1923—was accomplished without reference to theory and was even in violation of certain current doctrines (concerning too firm alliances with bourgeois parties), it is not easy to sustain an argument that theory is all-important. On the other hand, what if ideology had not initially directed the attention of Russians to the East, for which they have never shown a convincing sympathy? To overlook evidence capable of supporting either argument is to court gross oversimplification of Soviet behavior and to risk misunderstanding Moscow's motives. It is the misfortune of students of Russian revolutionary policy that they must continue to be attentive to theory, for the clues it sometimes provides, with little hope of being able to work out a formula that will be helpful at all times. The problem, needless to say, is as irksome in studying Soviet strategies in Southeast Asia as elsewhere.

CHAPTER TWO

Early Soviet Policies in Practice: Southeast Asia in the 1920's

THE question now to be considered is whether Soviet efforts in Southeast Asia in any sense corresponded to the promises made in Lenin's theses of 1920 and in periodic statements issuing from Moscow during the following decade. Moscow's revolutionary interests, we know, were global; its capacity, however, actively to promote revolution throughout the world was limited, even if active revolution was judged to serve best the Kremlin's purposes. Assistance to workers in Germany and France meant assistance withheld from revolutionary movements in Java and Indochina. A meager flow of aid to Southeast Asia might, then, reflect no more than a system of priorities in Moscow; it need not imply Soviet indifference. The purpose of the present chapter in any event is to discover what specific policies, if any, were devised for Southeast Asia and how, if at all, they were implemented.

Our study will begin with Indonesia, the second largest colonial possession in the world (after India) and one in which by 1917 there already existed a lively nationalist movement.

A REVOLUTION FAILS IN INDONESIA

Indonesian Communism developed initially under the wing of *Sarekat Islam*, a nationalist-religious organization formed in Java as early as 1912. By 1920 *Sarekat Islam*, numbering two and a half million members, had become a significant force in the colony's political life. It played havoc, for instance, with the Dutch government's "ethical policy," a program devised early in the century to liberalize the colonial administration in the Indies by introducing economic, social, and political reforms: faced with the alleged excesses of *Sarekat Islam*, Dutch officials felt constrained to reimpose restrictions on political activity, which led in turn to new disorders and more controls. From 1920 on an upward spiral of mistrust and hostility marked

80

Dutch-Indonesian relations. These circumstances favored aggressive Soviet strategies in Indonesia based on Lenin's theses of 1920 and other Comintern formulations of this era.

On the eve of World War I the Dutchman Hendrik Sneevliet, later known as Maring, had organized in Java the Indies Social Democratic Association, the first Marxist organization in Asia. Sneevliet's group, composed at first only of Dutch settlers, shared with *Sarekat Islam* the central objective of Indonesian independence. The two accordingly were able to remain allied for a number of years, and dual membership was not uncommon; it was in all likelihood Sneevliet's success with this tactic in Java that led him, as the Comintern representative in China some years later, to urge it there. By 1919, at the Fourth Congress of *Sarekat Islam*, rivalry between the Marxist and nationalist leaderships had become increasingly evident. The Marxists, influenced by the Russian Revolution, sought a more radical program than the moderate leaders of *Sarekat Islam* could accept, and on this issue the alliance was dissolved. In May 1920, on the eve of the Comintern's Second Congress, the social democrats reorganized themselves as the Communist Party of the Indies (*Perserikaten Kommunist di India*, or PKI). Two native Javanese were elected President and Vice-President, Semaoen (or Semaun) and Darsono, and two Dutchmen, Bergsma and H. V. Dekker, Secretary and Treasurer; Maring had by this time been deported for having written articles in praise of the Bolshevik Revolution.[1]

The PKI was thus the first national Communist party in Asia (formed more than a year before the Chinese Communist Party), and it remained for some years the largest.[2] At the end of 1920 the PKI formally affiliated with the International. The

[1] Authoritative accounts of the origins of the Communist movement are in substantial agreement on details. See Kahin, *Nationalism and Revolution in Indonesia*, pp. 71-4; McVey, *Development of the Indonesian Communist Party and its Relations with the Soviet Union and the Chinese People's Republic*, pp. 5-7; and Blumberger, *Le Communisme aux Indes Néerlandaises*, pp. 10-22.

[2] In 1924, at the Fifth Comintern Congress, the membership of the PKI was given as 2,000, as contrasted with 800 in the Chinese Communist Party; *Fifth Congress of the Communist International*, pp. 268-9.

great distance between Moscow and Java, however, the watchfulness of the Dutch, and the shortage of Comintern operatives combined to make direct contacts exceedingly difficult. No Comintern agents, insofar as is known, reached Indonesia during the 1920's. A procession of Indonesian Communists, on the other hand, represented the PKI at international meetings throughout the 1920's and so secured some liaison with Moscow from the outset.[3] Although most of these Indonesians were in exile at the time of their contact with international Communist organizations, it is reasonable to imagine that collectively they provided enough information about developments in Indonesia to enable the Comintern to formulate specific policies for the PKI—had it been the Comintern's wish to do so.

During the early years of its existence the PKI faced three specific problems on which it would have welcomed Moscow's guidance: its relationship to the Islamic, or Pan-Islamic, movements; the relative emphasis to be attached to proletarian and peasant formations in the revolutionary movement; and the timing of any uprising it might venture to lead. Moscow offered advice on each of these problems, but rarely in time to be of help to the PKI.

The question of relations with the Islamic movement in Indonesia was greatly complicated after 1920 by the sharply increased rivalry between the Islamic and Communist leaderships for control of local branches of *Sarekat Islam*. Since the division between the parties in 1920 had been, as two students of Indo-

---

[3] Indonesia was represented at the Second Comintern Congress (unofficially) by Maring and an unnamed delegate; at the Third by Darsono; at the Fourth by Tan Malaka; and at the Fifth by Semaoen and an alternate named Josef. Semaoen had previously represented Indonesia at the Congress of Toilers of the Far East in Petrograd in 1922; following his exile from Indonesia in 1923 he lived in Moscow and attended all Comintern congresses and most plenums of the ECCI from that time on, as did Musso following his exile in 1925. Tan Malaka and Alimin, meanwhile, attended the Canton Conference of the Transport Workers of the Pacific in 1924; Alimin was also present at the Pan Pacific Trade Union Conference in Hankow in 1927 and was elected to the Secretariat. Further possibilities of liaison between Moscow and the PKI existed through Maring, the Comintern's representative in Shanghai from 1921 to 1923, and later through Tan Malaka, who claims to have been the Comintern's representative in Southeast Asia from 1925 to 1927.

nesian Communism suggest, "at the summit,"[4] the local organizations continued to be fair game for each. The competition for control was so bitter that by the end of 1922 it was no longer possible even to contemplate an alliance between the PKI and *Sarekat Islam* as such. Lenin's advice to Asian Communists to ally under appropriate circumstances with "national revolutionary" movements accordingly had little relevance in Indonesia.

The problem was further compounded for the PKI by Lenin's sharp attack on Islam in his theses at the Second Comintern Congress. Lenin's position in effect discouraged the PKI from seeking support in the most promising quarter available to it— the local branches of the nationalist movement where inevitably Islam was strongest. Had the Indonesians heeded Lenin's warning, they would have damaged their prospects for a mass following, perhaps irrevocably. They did not, however, take the advice too literally and continued to work as before within the Islamic community. This was, of course, in the spirit of Maring's judgment at the Second Comintern Congress that the problem of working out a relationship with local national revolutionary elements (such as *Sarekat Islam*) was greatly simpler "in actual practice" than in theory. "Our work," Maring told the congress, referring to the situation in Indonesia before the split between *Sarekat Islam* and the social democrats had become final, "would be half done if we should deny the nationalist revolutionary movement and play the dogmatic Marxists."[5]

Moscow's position on Islam nonetheless remained a source of embarrassment to Indonesian Communists, and they sought first to explain it away, then to reverse it. Following the 1920 Congress of Toilers of the East at Baku, where Soviet spokesmen appealed to Muslims in the Near East to ally with Bolsheviks in a "holy war" against British imperialism, PKI cadres in Java pointed to the congress as evidence that Moscow was not hostile to Islam as such, but only to bourgeois movements in

[4] Benda and McVey, *The Communist Uprising of 1926-1927 in Indonesia*, p. xvi.
[5] See above, p. 19.

the colonies riding behind the banner of pan-Islam.[6] In 1922, Tan Malaka, attending his first Comintern congress, sought clarification of Moscow's view of pan-Islam and left no doubt that in his view the 1920 formulation needed revision: "Pan-Islamism now means the fraternity of all Muslim nations and the liberation struggle not only of the Arabic, but also the Indian, Javanese, and all other oppressed Muslim nations. This fraternity is called the liberation struggle against the British, French, and Italian capitalists, consequently against world imperialism. Such is the meaning of pan-Islamism. . . . Just as we are willing to support a national war, we also want to support the liberation struggle of the aggressive, very active 250 million Mohammedans who are subject to the imperialist powers. Therefore I ask once more if we should support pan-Islamism in this sense and in how far we are to support it."[7]

Although there was no official reply to Tan Malaka, the Fourth Congress' theses on the Eastern question included a restatement of the issue: in due course, the theses stated, the "religio-political watchwords" of pan-Islam are replaced by "concrete political demands"; this, it was implied, made possible an alliance between Islamic and Communist movements.[8] There is some evidence that the Comintern actively encouraged such an alliance in Indonesia. At the Fifth Comintern Congress in 1924 Manuilsky remarked that the Comintern had "allowed the Communists in Java to take an active part in the work of the local workers' peasants' party there."[9] This party is not identified by name, but it seems clear in the context of Manuilsky's remarks, which link this activity in Java with Communist-Kuomintang collaboration in China, that he had *Sarekat Islam* in mind. His exact meaning, however, is obscure, and even if such a directive were given the PKI in 1922 or 1923 it came too late to reverse the widening rupture between the nationalist and Communist

[6] Blumberger, *Le Communisme aux Indes Neérlandaises*, p. 18.

[7] *Inprecor*, December 5, 1922, p. 876.

[8] The text of the theses may be found in Degras, *Communist International*, I, p. 385; see also above, p. 30.

[9] *Fifth Congress of the Communist International*, p. 188.

A Revolution Fails in Indonesia

leaderships "at the summit." The most that can be claimed of Moscow's shift on the Islamic question, at least insofar as Indonesia is concerned, is that by lifting the stigma on Islam the Comintern removed a handicap under which the PKI had been operating and allowed the Communists to register significant gains at the local level during 1922 and 1923. To argue, however, that the Comintern's restatement on Islam was inspired by Tan Malaka's protests, or was designed primarily to achieve the effect it did in fact achieve in Java, would be to exaggerate Indonesia's significance to Moscow at this juncture. It is more appropriate to consider the Indonesians the beneficiaries, and only incidentally the architects, of a policy change that was overdue.

With regard to the other problems confronting the PKI, the apportioning of energy between the peasant and labor movements and the timing of an uprising, Moscow's guidance appears to have been non-existent until the spring of 1925. On the former issue there were, of course, standing instructions in force for Communists everywhere: "first, the winning over of the workers; then of the peasants and artisans."[10] But no Comintern directive, as far as is known, took account of special circumstances in Indonesia. Such circumstances existed. In its struggle with *Sarekat Islam* for control of the national movement early in the 1920's, the PKI inevitably established extensive contacts with the peasantry, which constituted the mass base of the movement. When the struggle reached a climax in 1923, the Communists created a rival organization, *Sarekat Rakjat* (People's Association), composed of Communist-led peasant formations which had broken away from *Sarekat Islam*.[11] This organization, which two students of Indonesian Communism describe as the outer, and incomparably larger, of two "concentric circles" constituting the party's support,[12] engaged most of the PKI's at-

[10] See, for instance, Radek's address at the Fourth Comintern Congress in 1922; *Inprecor*, December 7, 1922, p. 895.

[11] For a discussion of these developments in the Comintern press, see the articles by Bergsma in *ibid.*, August 16, 1923, p. 607, and September 27, p. 699.

[12] See Benda and McVey, *op. cit.*, pp. xxiii-xxiv.

tention during 1923 and 1924. By the end of the latter year its strength greatly exceeded that of the trade unions (the inner circle) and peasant influence accordingly surpassed proletarian in party councils.

This situation, hardly unknown in Communist movements in the colonial world, evidently troubled the orthodox Indonesian leaders enough to cause a general review of party policies at a conference held in Jogjakarta in December 1924. According to a subsequent Dutch account of the conference, the party leadership (which was then dominated by Alimin and Musso) pressed for the immediate dissolution of *Sarekat Rakjat* and urged that the party redirect its energies to the neglected trade unions. Rank and file cadres at the conference, understandably enthusiastic about the flourishing peasant organization they had created, rejected the proposal and rebelled against their leaders. In the end a compromise was worked out which satisfied both sides: *Sarekat Rakjat* was to be dissolved less ostentatiously, its most reliable members to be absorbed gradually into the PKI; the party in the meantime was to turn its energies to the labor movement.[13]

Apart from the doctrinal considerations that quite obviously motivated the party leaders at Jogjakarta, there were also certain tactical considerations arising from the government's current campaign against the Communists, especially against the party leaders. Semaoen and Tan Malaka had by this juncture already been exiled; other leaders were under surveillance. The PKI, in short, was gradually being forced into a clandestine existence, despite its legal status under laws still surviving from the "Ethical" era. Should the party be compelled to go underground entirely, it would have to fall back on its "inner circle" of support, as Lenin had in 1903; the PKI would have to forego the luxury of a mass organization like *Sarekat Rakjat* which it could not effectively control. The proposed dissolution of this organization, then, may be seen as an essential step in preparations for the rigorous discipline of an illegal existence. Certainly the revolt of

---

[13] See the Dutch government report entitled (in English translation) "The Course of the Communist Movement on the West Coast of Sumatra" (1928); cited in Benda and McVey, *op. cit.*, pp. 124-5.

rank and file cadres at Jogjakarta demonstrated only too plainly the need of a stricter sense of party discipline.

There is irony in the fact, if accounts of the Jogjakarta conference are accurate, that a meeting which brought to the surface the sharpest intraparty rivalries yet revealed in the short history of Indonesian Communism and which decreed the liquidation of the party's most promising organized support should also move toward insurrection—a venture which needless to say required maximum unity within the PKI and support far outside party circles. In advancing the slogan for a soviet republic in Indonesia, party leaders set in motion processes which would reach their melancholy climax two years later. No Soviet instruction, we should remind ourselves, inspired the Jogjakarta decisions, at least insofar as is known. Had there been guidance from Moscow—on the peasant question, on insurrection, or on both—the subsequent course of Indonesian Communism might have been very different; there seems little doubt, at any event, that the PKI was following a course which would not have found approval in Moscow.[14]

The decisions taken at Jogjakarta at last moved Moscow to formulate a more specific policy for the PKI. When and how the decisions were made known to Moscow is not clear (Soviet sources made no mention of the Jogjakarta conference either at the time or subsequently), but the Comintern appears to have been fully informed of them by the time of the Fifth Enlarged Plenum of the ECCI, which convened in Moscow in March and April 1925. The Indonesian situation was discussed within the

[14] Students of Indonesian Communism are not in agreement on the possible influence on the PKI of Comintern strategy during 1924. Kahin, *op. cit.*, p. 77, for instance, argues that the resolutions of the Fifth Comintern Congress and of the Pan Pacific Transport Workers' Conference (Canton) held earlier in the year inspired the PKI to adopt a more militant strategy; see also Siswadji, *The Impact of Comintern Policy on the Indonesian Communist Movement*, p. 29. Benda and McVey, *op. cit.*, p. xxix, on the other hand, conclude that the PKI leadership, already inclined toward a militant program, distorted these resolutions to justify its action; in this connection they call attention to the observation by Voitinsky, the Russian observer at Canton, that the Indonesian delegation there (which included Alimin) was "Leftist"—that is, imprudent. The author identifies himself in this instance with the argument of Benda and McVey.

87

Colonial Commission and a resolution on Indonesia was prepared for the Fifth Plenum and adopted unanimously. The text of the resolution was not published, perhaps to avoid embarrassment to the PKI, but its contents were described as follows by a spokesman for the Colonial Commission (the American Dorsey): "In Java . . . the principal task confronting the Communist Party is the strengthening of its proletarian basis by the introduction of industrial workers and revolutionary intellectuals; secondly, to define its attitude toward the revolutionary national movement, particularly the *Swaraj Islam* [*sic*]; thirdly, to work out a practical platform of main demands: independence, withdrawal of foreign troops, the establishment of the People's Assembly, universal suffrage, and the eight-hour day. The party is to work for the formation of a revolutionary national bloc and gradually to separate itself organizationally from the Swarajites [*sic*] in Java."[15]

An unpublished letter from the Comintern to the PKI dated May 4 amplifies this brief description of the ECCI resolution. The letter makes it clear, for instance, that *"Swaraj Islam"* refers not to *Sarekat Islam*, as might at first be expected, but to *Sarekat Rakjat*. This is evident in the similar phrasing used in Dorsey's summary and in the May 4 letter to describe the PKI's relationship to the organization in question. The latter reads: *"Sarekat Rakjat* must be *gradually separated* from the Communist Party of Indonesia and be converted into a genuine national, revolutionary organization working in conjunction with and under the intellectual leadership of the Communists."[16]

The May 4 letter also reveals more clearly than the official summary of the ECCI resolution that Moscow was not satisfied with the way the PKI leadership was handling the peasant question in Indonesia. It stated: "The experience of the international Communist movement has shown that there is not a single country in the world where the proletariat can count on success

---

[15] *Inprecor*, April 28, 1925, p. 513.

[16] The letter is quoted in part in the West Sumatran report of 1928, referred to above, and appears to be authentic; see Benda and McVey, *op. cit.*, p. 139 (emphasis added).

88

in the struggle unless it obtains the active support of the majority of the peasantry. The peasantry has its own interests; consequently the whole of the peasantry can be drawn into the antiimperialist struggle only if this fight is conducted in defence of its interests. In general these interests coincide with the interests of the whole of the Indonesian people, and do not contradict the interests of the proletariat. A platform must be drawn up for the general national struggle which must give first consideration to the interests of the peasantry."[17] Similar instructions, it is reported, were sent at this time by the Krestintern, urging the PKI to devote greater attention to the peasant question.

The Fifth Plenum, to judge from these accounts of its resolution on Indonesia, appears clearly to have repudiated any strategy in Indonesia—such as the decision at Jogjakarta looking to the liquidation of *Sarekat Rakjat*—that would have isolated the party from its main base; a separation of peasant and proletarian organizations was permissible, even desirable, but not the elimination of the peasant organs. The question of an early uprising in Java, meanwhile, was not mentioned in the resolution, as reported, and perhaps would not have been even if discussed within the Colonial Commission. Moscow's negative view of such a venture, however, is suggested in Stalin's remarks at the Communist University of the Toilers of the East on May 18. Speaking of the dangers of Left deviation, which he described in this context as "overrating the revolutionary potentialities of the liberation movement and underrating the importance of an alliance between the working class and the revolutionary bourgeoisie against imperialism," Stalin said: "The Communists in Java, who not long ago erroneously put forward the slogan of a soviet government for their country, suffer, it seems, from this deviation. This is a deviation to the Left, pregnant with the risk of isolating the Communist Party from the masses and of transforming it into a sect. A determined struggle against this deviation is a necessary condition for the education of truly revolutionary cadres for the colonies and dependent countries of the East."[18]

[17] *Ibid.*, p. 138.
[18] Stalin, *Sochineniia*, VII, p. 151.

If there was any doubt that the Fifth Plenum's resolution on Indonesia constituted a rebuke to the PKI leadership for its decision at the Jogjakarta conference, Stalin's remarks must clearly have removed it. The fact that this was the only published comment he was ever to make on the Indonesian Communists adds force to the point.

Comments in Moscow on Indonesian developments following the Fifth Plenum of the ECCI continued to indicate dissatisfaction with the performance of the PKI. Bergsma wrote in *Inprecor* in October 1925 that, although the PKI had "altered its tactics . . . in accordance with the latest resolution of the enlarged executive [i.e., the Fifth Plenum], . . . success has not yet been reached in welding the national and revolutionary movement into a united anti-imperialist bloc."[19] A Comintern report published early in 1926 again raised the charge of "Left deviation," recalling that "until very recently" the PKI had insisted on the establishment of soviets as the "immediate task."[20] "Our Java comrades devote too little attention to the notion of a united front. . . . The PKI despite all its activity has not yet begun to work effectively with the peasants, drawing them into the nationalist movement. The errors committed by the PKI with regard to nationalist organizations are repeated with regard to the peasantry. . . . If the party does not adopt a correct policy *vis-à-vis* the peasantry in time, the latter will pass the party by, as has already happened to some extent among the more radical nationalist elements. Only the full and unconditional carrying out of the resolution of the March Plenum of the ECCI can change the isolated position of the party and gather around it all the active anti-imperialist forces of the Indonesian people."[21]

These counsels of moderation were overlooked by the PKI. Possibly they were misunderstood in Indonesia. It is more likely, however, that conditions in the colony—which Moscow, in turn, seems to have misunderstood—frustrated a policy of moderation

---

[19] P. Bergsma, "The Revolutionary Movement in Java," *Inprecor*, October 8, 1925. Bergsma had been exiled from Java in 1923 and was living in Holland.
[20] *Otchet Ispolkoma Kominterna* (1926), p. 357.
[21] *Ibid.*, p. 390.

at this time. During 1925 the Dutch government intensified its repression of the Communists, which culminated in a ban in November on all meetings of Communist and Communist-led organizations; Comintern spokesmen periodically, and of course ineffectually, protested these measures.[22] Under the circumstances the PKI leaders still in Indonesia could follow Soviet advice only at their peril. It is not the time to speak of united fronts and alliances with the bourgeoisie when one's very existence is being threatened. Semaoen, speaking at the Sixth Enlarged Plenum of the ECCI in February 1926, attempted to explain the PKI's troubles to his largely European listeners. He denied that charges of Right or Left deviation were justified in the case of the PKI; the party's difficulties, he said, arose from the fact that government terror in the preceding year alone had led to 3,000 arrests, including 500 Communists, plus 50 killed and 150 wounded. Any revolutionary movement faced with such setbacks would suffer from inertia.[23]

Plans for the rebellion meanwhile moved inexorably forward. In October 1925 a meeting of the Central Committee at Prambanan reaffirmed the decision taken at Jogjakarta ten months earlier and set June 18, 1926, for a general uprising.[24] Local units, where they could be contacted, were alerted, but for the most part Communist liaison was in disarray. A series of premature strikes in December 1925 forced Alimin and Musso, the last of the major PKI leaders remaining in Java, to flee from the colony. Singapore, where most of the party leaders assembled, now became the directing center for the revolt, despite total lapses of information at times on critical developments in Indonesia. As

[22] E.g., Bergsma, "Sharpening of the Class War in Indonesia," *Inprecor*, March 5, 1925, p. 260; "Down with the White Terror in Indonesia" (a statement by the Eastern Bureau of the Comintern), *ibid.*, March 19, 1925; "The Struggle of the Indonesian Proletariat" (a statement by the Profintern), *ibid.*, November 12, 1925.

[23] *Shestoi rasshirennyi plenum Ispolkoma Kominterna*, p. 70.

[24] Some sources, both Communist and non-Communist, trace the origins of the uprising to the Prambanan meeting rather than to the conference at Jogjakarta in December 1924; e.g., G. J. van Munster, "The Background and History of the Insurrection in Java," *Inprecor*, December 16, 1926; and Kahin, *op. cit.*, p. 80.

91

two students of the 1926-1927 uprising have expressed it, the PKI had been "a movement which, having gained momentum towards a goal, has become possessed by that momentum and finds that it cannot alter or slow down its course."[25]

The events leading to the 1926-1927 risings on Java and Sumatra, which are exceedingly complex, need concern us only as they relate to Moscow's role in the episode. The PKI leaders, already divided over the question of insurrection as early as the Jogjakarta conference, became even more so during 1925 and 1926. Alimin and Musso appear to have been determined to go forward at all costs with the rebellion. Tan Malaka, on the other hand, who claimed to have been the Comintern's representative in Southeast Asia, opposed the plan, and Alimin's secret visit to him in Manila in February 1926 failed to move him. Tan Malaka prepared a document, which he entrusted to Alimin, outlining his objections to the Prambanan plan and urging a more moderate course in keeping with the Comintern's instructions to date.[26] Alimin, on his return to Singapore, failed to show this statement to his colleagues, it is asserted, and even represented Tan Malaka as having approved the plan. At a meeting in April, accordingly, the plan for a rebellion was once again affirmed by the exiled leaders in Singapore, the date for the rising now set ahead to the end of the year, and Alimin and Musso departed for Moscow to seek the Comintern's approval and, hopefully, financial support.

Tan Malaka, in the meantime, came himself to Singapore in June (evidently after the departure of Alimin and Musso) and, learning of the advanced stage of preparations for the uprising, began immediately to undermine them. He succeeded in persuading several exiled leaders to dissociate themselves from the

[25] Benda and McVey, *op. cit.*, p. xxvii.

[26] As set forth in a pamphlet published about this time, Tan Malaka's argument was that the PKI had neither the mass support nor sufficient Marxist indoctrination to carry off an insurrection; the venture would "lead the party to a *Putsch* or to anarchism, and ultimately it will be completely destroyed." The pamphlet, entitled *Massa Actie* (Singapore, 1926), is quoted in Kahin, *op. cit.*, pp. 82-3.

project and through them also deterred a portion of the leadership in Indonesia, including several members of the Central Committee which was then located in Bandung. Other local leaders, to complicate matters still further, determined to go forward with the insurrection regardless of decisions in Singapore or even of Moscow's approval.[27]

What transpired during the Alimin-Musso visit to Moscow in 1926 remains obscure.[28] If they were given an opportunity to present their case for a rebellion, it is doubtful that the Russians responded sympathetically. At this juncture, united front tactics were being applied in China with notable success, or so Stalin believed; it seems quite unlikely that Moscow would have jeopardized gains in China, where much was at stake, by authorizing an opposing strategy in Java—a strategy, that is, that could only have alienated the national bourgeoisie throughout East Asia. Why, indeed, should Moscow have done so? Its reading of the situation in Indonesia prior to 1926 had not indicated a need for violence; it is difficult to imagine what Alimin and Musso could have revealed of developments in Java to cause Soviet officials to alter their views. Moreover, the fact that neither Alimin nor Musso subsequently made reference to Moscow's views, after so long a journey explicitly to learn them, does not suggest an affirmative response. Their silence, however, need not be construed as implying beyond doubt a negative reply. A very real possibility, in the confused circumstances surrounding the succession crisis in Moscow, is that the Comintern simply procrastinated and sent the two Indonesians back to Singapore with a few conundrums and a recommendation that they work out what they could. A complaint of Comintern inaction made by

[27] The foregoing account is drawn chiefly from Blumberger, *Le Communisme aux Indes Neérlandaises*, pp. 66ff., which is drawn in turn chiefly from Dutch sources; see also Kahin, *op. cit.*, pp. 79ff., and Benda and McVey, *op. cit.*, "Introduction."

[28] Mention of the trip is made by an Indonesian delegate, Manawar (presumably Musso), at the Sixth Comintern Congress; see *Inprecor*, October 17, 1928, p. 1325. The principal source of information on the visits, however, is Alimin's testimony published in 1947; see Kahin, *op. cit.*, p. 83.

an Indonesian delegate at the Sixth Comintern Congress lends support to this last hypothesis.[29]

Moscow's decision, if there was one, probably would not have greatly affected the course of events in Indonesia. A number of local leaders, we have seen, were prepared to go forward with the scheduled uprising come what may.[30] It accordingly broke out in Java, following a loosely prepared time-table, on November 12 and in Sumatra, after some delays, early in 1927. Alimin and Musso, in the meantime, arrived back in Malaya only in mid-December (more than a month after the insurrection in Java had broken out) and were arrested by British authorities before they could reach Singapore to report on their findings in Moscow. It is evident, then, that a nearly total breakdown of communications between the scattered and divided PKI forces in Southeast Asia crippled the rebellion before it properly began.

Despite its earlier caution, the Comintern responded promptly and sympathetically to the Javan uprising once it had begun. Within ten days the ECCI (during its Seventh Plenum, then in session) issued a manifesto on the revolt linking it to the revolution in China and claiming Communist leadership of a united front including "the overwhelming majority of the population, proletariat, peasantry, intellectuals, and petty bourgeoisie." Despite Dutch repression, the manifesto continued, "the Indonesian people are rising against inhuman and intolerable conditions. . . . The Communist International greets the Indonesian revolutionary struggle and will support it to the utmost." The manifesto closed with an appeal to workers in all countries to support the revolt with mass demonstrations. "The Indonesian rebels are your vanguard. . . . Do everything you can to support them in their fight."[31] In its resolution on the Dutch question, also dis-

[29] The complaint, made by a delegate known as Padi (probably Alimin), is discussed below.

[30] This appears to have been the case on Sumatra, for instance, where, according to the official Dutch report of 1928, local leaders during the months before the uprising were only irregularly in contact with the party's central organs in Java and never with the PKI organization in Singapore; see Benda and McVey, *op. cit.*, pp. 145ff.

[31] Degras, *Communist International*, II, pp. 311-12; translated from *Inprekorr*, November 23, 1926, p. 2506.

Lenin and Zinoviev (on second step) with delegates to Second Comintern Congress 1920; M. N. Roy is in center (Courtesy of Hoover Library)

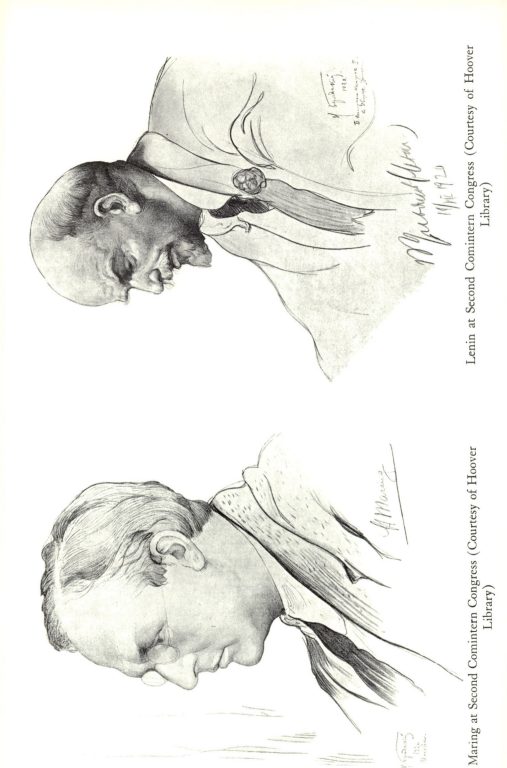

Maring at Second Comintern Congress (Courtesy of Hoover Library)

Lenin at Second Comintern Congress (Courtesy of Hoover Library)

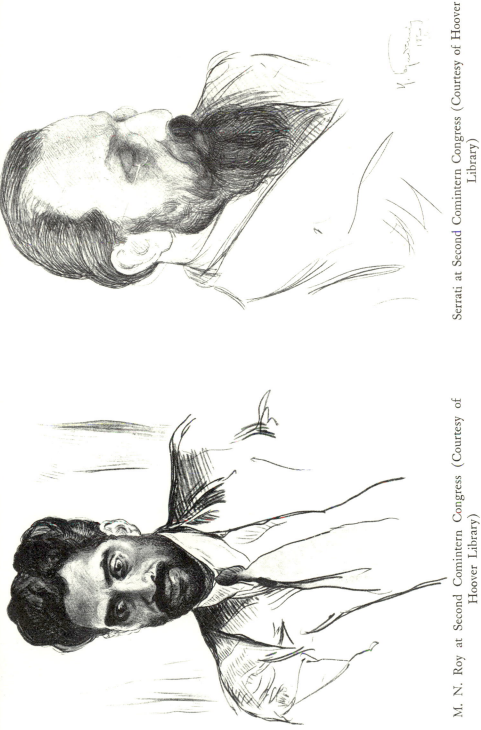

M. N. Roy at Second Comintern Congress (Courtesy of Hoover Library)

Serrati at Second Comintern Congress (Courtesy of Hoover Library)

Tan Malaka, 1947 or 1948 (Courtesy of Professor George M. Kahin)

Musso, after being shot during Madiun rising, October 1948 (Courtesy of Professor George M. Kahin)

Chen Peng, during Baling talks, 1955 (Courtesy of Professor Anthony Short)

Luis Taruc, following surrender in 1954 (Courtesy of Professor Alvin Scaff)

cussed at the Seventh Plenum, the ECCI admonished "every honorable Dutch worker to support the Communist Party in its struggle for the freedom and independence of the suppressed Indonesians, especially during their present heroic and blood-letting insurrection."[32]

Soviet and Comintern journals also gave the uprising immediate and sympathetic coverage. A Dutch Communist, writing in the November 25 issue of *Inprecor*, gave a few preliminary details of the insurrection and complained that the Dutch party was rendering "ineffective assistance" to the Indonesians in their hour of crisis; Indonesia, he wrote, is the "Achilles' heel" of Holland.[33] A week later Semaoen, writing of the events from Moscow, where he was attending the Seventh Plenum, blandly noted that the uprising "came as a surprise" and traced it to Dutch suppression of the Indonesians' celebration of the anniversary of the Bolshevik Revolution on November 7.[34]

The Comintern's effort, to judge from these early accounts, was to make the rebellion appear spontaneous and, above all, based on a broad united front of all elements of the population. In fact, the base of the rising seems to have been exceedingly narrow. Dutch sources estimate that no more than 5,000 were actively involved in the disorders.[35] Whether or not this figure is a low estimate—Semaoen later claimed a party membership of 9,000 at the time of the insurrection with an additional 100,000 in *Sarekat Rakjat*[36]—the uprising on Java was suppressed within three weeks and on Sumatra in about four.

For some months after the Indonesian rebellion, accounts published in Moscow continued to treat it enthusiastically. Semaoen, for instance, wrote in a Profintern journal in January 1927 that despite the defeat of the rising in Java it signaled the approaching bankruptcy of Holland's "moral authority" in the colony.

[32] *Puti mirovoi revoliutsii*, II, p. 460.

[33] Gerald Vartez, "The Insurrection in Java," *Inprecor*, November 25, 1926.

[34] Semaun, "The Rebellion in the Dutch East Indies," *ibid.*, December 2, 1926, pp. 1437-8.

[35] See Kahin, *op. cit.*, p. 84.

[36] *Inprecor*, October 4, 1928, p. 1246 (Semaoen's report to the Sixth Comintern Congress).

"The next revolutionary outbreak," he concluded, "will put an end to Dutch imperialism in Indonesia."[37] A pamphlet released by the Profintern in mid-1927, also written by Semaoen, still considered the Javan and Sumatran risings as the critical "turning-point in Indonesia's revolutionary-liberation movement" and the beginning of a new "stage of open rebellions" against Dutch rule.[38]

By the end of 1927, however, the magnitude of the debacle had become too obvious to ignore, and greatly sobered estimates of the 1926-1927 uprisings began to appear. In November, on the first anniversary of the rebellion, the ECCI issued a post-mortem on it after "an extremely careful investigation" of its lessons. The rebellion was undoubtedly of "enormous significance," the ECCI statement reads, as the first "conscious and organized attempt to overthrow the rule of the Dutch occupation by armed force." But the PKI had made many errors. "The whole course of the revolt betrayed the lack of an earnest political and organizational preparation of this movement as a whole. It is highly characteristic that the revolt was conducted under the general slogan of the fight against Dutch imperialism, and without a concrete political and economic slogan which would have mobilized broad masses and would have made the revolt the last and deciding point of a *general strike* and a peasant insurrectionary movement."[39] Moscow, it is apparent from this statement, had reverted to its 1925 estimate of the Indonesian situation: what had been required was a broad united front and the mobilization of the peasants, as the ECCI had pointed out in the resolution passed by the Fifth Enlarged Plenum; the PKI's failure to carry out this instruction was the cause of the Javan and Sumatran disasters. The new tasks, now that the PKI was illegalized and its members dispersed, was to rebuild from the bottom a new party organization, "even at the cost of the greatest sacrifices."

[37] Semaun, "Vokrug vosstanie na Iave," *Krasnyi internatsional profsoiuzov,* January 1927, p. 76.

[38] Semaoen, *Indoneziia v tsepiakh imperialisma,* p. 40.

[39] "The ECCI on the Tasks of the Communists in Indonesia," *Inprecor,* December 8, 1927, p. 1562.

Subsequent appraisals of the 1926-1927 uprisings followed this analysis with few variations.[40]

On whom was Moscow to pin responsibility for the failure in Indonesia? There was no dearth of candidates: Alimin and Musso, for having urged so ill-considered a revolt in the first place; Tan Malaka, for having systematically thwarted the uprising once the decision had been made to prepare for it; local leaders in Indonesia, for having moved ahead without adequate instructions; Dutch Communists, for having failed to guide and restrain the Indonesian comrades. Meanwhile, if Moscow could find no convenient scapegoat at hand, the many rival factions within the PKI were only too willing to suggest names. Tan Malaka, for instance, is known to have felt a lingering resentment against Alimin for having failed to report his opposition to the uprising to PKI leaders in Singapore in the spring of 1926; Alimin and Musso were no less resentful of Tan Malaka's betrayal of the uprising in the last half of 1926 when they were in Moscow.[41] All, it may be imagined, were jealous of Semaoen's easy access to the Comintern leadership in Moscow during the years preceding the rebellion.[42] Semaoen in turn had showed himself in earlier meetings of the ECCI bitterly resentful of the patronizing attitude of Dutch Communists toward the PKI leadership.[43] The Comintern did not, however, prior to the

[40] See, for instance, Galperin, "Gollandskaia Indiia," *Novyi Vostok*, No. 20-21, 1928, pp. 55-85, and *The Communist International Between the Fifth and Sixth World Congresses* (July 1928), pp. 478-83. The same points also occur in recent critiques of the 1926-27 insurrection by the present leadership of the PKI; e.g., Aidit, *The Birth and Growth of the Communist Party of Indonesia*, pp. 9-11.

[41] See Kahin, *op. cit.*, pp. 82ff., citing subsequent statements by Tan Malaka and Alimin as well as miscellaneous Dutch government sources.

[42] Semaoen was first elected to the ECCI at the Fifth Comintern Congress in 1924. He evidently fell briefly from favor in 1927, following his negotiation of an agreement with Mohammed Hatta in December 1926 (during the Javan uprising) which would have submerged the PKI within Hatta's émigré student organization in Holland, *Perhimpoenan Indonesia* (PI). According to Hatta, Semaoen was "exiled" for a time to the Crimea for having made this agreement without authorization, but soon regained his position in the Comintern as the principal spokesman on Indonesia; interview with Hatta, March 27, 1961.

[43] "Don't meddle in our affairs!" Semaoen warned the Dutch comrades at the

Sixth Congress, select a scapegoat from the list of eligible candidates—perhaps because it was too preoccupied with failures in China. The PKI leaders, accordingly, including most of the principals in the 1926-1927 rebellion, were able to gather unscathed in Moscow in July 1928 to attend the Sixth Comintern Congress.

Indonesia did not figure conspicuously in the deliberations of the Sixth Congress, concerned as the latter was with Bukharin's program and other more urgent matters. Semaoen delivered the main report on Indonesia. He revealed little that was not already familiar to the delegates concerning the course of the PKI since 1920 and the causes of failure in the 1926-1927 risings. He now acknowledged (as he had not a year and a half earlier) the "extreme ultra-Left tendencies" of the PKI at the time of the Jogjakarta conference, when the call for soviets was first put forth. These tendencies had now been corrected and the outlook for Indonesian Communism, Semaoen asserted, was greatly improved. Mistakes in the past had been inevitable, he pointed out, because "there have been only very loose contacts with the Comintern."[44] Another Indonesian delegate, using the pseudonym Padi and believed to be Alimin, carried the latter point a step further: Moscow, he argued, should assume responsibility for failures in Indonesia since the PKI had been obliged from the outset to devise its strategies "without any guidance from the Comintern." He continued: "We consider it to be a serious mistake that during the uprising [of 1926-1927] . . . the Comintern remained inactive. The blame cannot be put on our Dutch party because our comrades did what they could to support the rebellion. The Comintern ought to have instructed all its sections . . . to support the uprising and to make a campaign with demonstrations, through the press, etc., in favor of it. But this has not

---

Sixth ECCI Plenum, for instance; "Study the colonial policy of brotherly parties like those in the Soviet Union, France and the United States." *Shestoi rasshirennyi plenum Ispolkoma Kominterna*, p. 71.

[44] *Stenograficheskii otchet VI Kongressa Kominterna*, vyp. 4, pp. 54-74; also *Inprecor*, October 4, 1928, pp. 1243-7.

been done. It is a sad experience of the Comintern and we hope that such a mistake will not occur again."[45]

If this blunt criticism of the Comintern bordered on indiscretion, the remarks by another Indonesian delegate, using the pseudonym Alphonso, were outspokenly provocative. Alphonso, who beyond much doubt was Tan Malaka,[46] took sharp issue with a number of points in Bukharin's "genuinely opportunist program." He challenged, for instance, the recommendation (in his words) "to repeat what has been done in China; that is, an alliance with the bourgeoisie until our party is destroyed." He opposed the "temporary agreements" with the bourgeoisie which the program authorized under certain conditions. He insisted that "we must form soviets in any struggle of the working class *versus* the capitalist class," not merely when conditions were favorable, as Bukharin (and Stalin) had argued. "As far as I can judge," Alphonso concluded, "this draft program is not a Communist program . . . it is a plan to weaken the proletarian movement, which is the latest plan of the *Mensheviki* of 1928."[47] Bukharin responded by charging Alphonso with making "secret propaganda for Trotskyism," a charge which the Indonesian hotly denied, though he did acknowledge belonging to the "Left wing."[48]

The exchange, which was the sharpest during the entire Sixth Congress, is puzzling. Assuming "Alphonso" to have been Tan Malaka, it is curious that he should have adopted so vigorously

[45] *Stenograficheskii otchet VI Kongressa, vyp.* 1, pp. 276-8; also *Inprecor,* August 11, 1928, p. 849.

[46] Most students of Indonesian Communism so assume: e.g., Kahin, *op. cit.,* p. 85, and McVey, *Development of the Indonesian Communist Party and Its Relations with the Soviet Union and the Chinese People's Republic,* p. 12. The only reason for questioning this judgment is Tan Malaka's own testimony, in an autobiography written in the 1940's, that he did not return to Russia after his departure in 1923; see Willard A. Hanna's summary of the autobiography in American Universities Field Staff, WAH-1-'59, p. 7. The autobiography, however, is not noted for its accuracy.

[47] *Stenograficheskii otchet VI Kongressa, vyp.* 3, pp. 57-8; also *Inprecor,* September 28, 1928, p. 1186.

[48] *Ibid.,* October 4, 1928, p. 1254.

Leftist a position when a year and a half earlier he had worked with equal vigor to discourage the Indonesian insurrection as a "Left deviation." Doubtless there was some obscure personal antagonism between the two disputants, and doubtless, too, there were overtones of the Stalin-Trotsky rivalry, which was still very much in evidence during the Sixth Congress. Had Alphonso sought to challenge Bukharin alone, his attack would perhaps not have been inappropriate, inasmuch as Bukharin himself was soon to fall; but an attack aimed equally at Stalin's policies in China and his 1925 dictum on soviets in Indonesia (which had not yet been altered) was an act of political suicide. The Sixth Congress, at any event, marked the turning point in Tan Malaka's career. The other Indonesian delegates at the congress formally dissociated themselves from his attack on Bukharin.[49] Tan Malaka himself, though elected as alternate to the ECCI at the end of the Sixth Congress,[50] soon left the ranks of the PKI and increasingly became identified as the evil genius of the 1926-1927 debacle. In Tan Malaka Moscow had at last found its scapegoat.

The tasks for the PKI, as set forth in the Sixth Congress' "Theses on the Revolutionary Movement in Colonial and Semi-Colonial Countries," deserve to be quoted in full since they represent Moscow's last known instruction to the PKI:

> In Indonesia the suppression of the rising of 1926, the arrest and exile of thousands of members of the Communist Party, greatly disorganized its ranks. The need for rebuilding the destroyed party organization demands from the party new methods of work, corresponding to the illegal conditions created by the police regime of Dutch imperialism. The transference of the center of gravity of all activity of the party to the places where the town and village proletariat is aggregated—to the factories and plantations; the restoration of the dissolved trade unions and the struggle for their legalization; special attention to the partial *practical* demands of the peas-

[49] *Stenograficheskii otchet VI Kongressa, vyp.* 3, p. 121.

[50] *Inprecor*, December 12, 1928, p. 1676; the other Indonesians elected to the ECCI—all were given their usual names—were Musso, a regular member as well as a member of the Presidium, and Darsono, an alternate.

antry; the development and strengthening of the peasant organizations; work within all the mass nationalist organizations, in which the Communist Party must establish factions and rally round it national-revolutionary elements; decisive struggle against the Dutch social democrats who, utilizing the support of the government, are attempting to secure a base for themselves in the native proletariat; winning over the numerous Chinese workers for the class struggle and national-revolutionary struggle and the establishment of connections with the Communist movements in China and India—these are some of the most important tasks of the Indonesian Communist Party.[51]

These tasks were not fulfilled. The 1926-1927 insurrections had in effect broken the back of the Communist movement in Indonesia, although the Comintern and the handful of Indonesian leaders abroad were slow to acknowledge it. The arrests, internments, and imprisonments following the insurrection had taken a heavy toll of Communist cadres throughout the colony.[52] The mobility even of Indonesian Communists abroad became sharply restricted after 1927, as collaboration between foreign police organizations in the Far East improved. By the end of the 1920's the PKI had become so demoralized that primary responsibility for such activity as it was able to keep up was assigned, in the absence of a visible leadership within Indonesia, to the Comintern's outpost in Singapore—itself a shadowy organization. Of the four PKI leaders in exile, Darsono, as well as Tan Malaka, was soon to break with Moscow.[53] Semaoen, Ali-

---

[51] *The Revolutionary Movement in the Colonies*, pp. 53-4.

[52] According to Dutch sources, of the 13,000 arrested after the insurrections (including both Communists and non-Communists as well as many who had no part in the disturbances) 4,500 were sentenced to prison and an additional 1,308 interned, the majority of the latter at the famous colony at Tanah Merah; see Kahin, *op. cit.*, p. 86.

[53] Darsono remained in Europe until 1950 when he returned to Indonesia, after independence, to take a part in the new republic's Foreign Office, where (at the time of writing) he still works. Tan Malaka, according to Professor Kahin, had organized an independent Communist organization in Bangkok even before the Sixth Congress; this organization, known as *Pari* (*Partai Repoeblik Indonesia*), served as his base of operations for a few years but had no striking success in Indonesia. *Ibid.*, pp. 85-6.

min, and Musso remained in Russia attached to the International. Musso replaced Semaoen after the Sixth Congress as the chief spokesman for the PKI. His articles appeared periodically in Comintern and Profintern publications and are a measure of the frustrations of Indonesian Communism. He complained bitterly of Dutch terrorism in Java, which he said had virtually forced "the dissolution of the Communist Party and the revolutionary trade unions."[54] He excoriated *Sarekat Islam* for condoning the government's terror and considered all Muslim leaders the "deadly enemy of Communism"; only the newly formed Indonesian Nationalist Party (PNI) was spared his criticism.[55] Musso also pleaded, as other Indonesians had during the Sixth Comintern Congress, for "concrete steps at last" by Moscow to relieve the intolerable plight of the Communists in Indonesia.[56] The plea, needless to say, was of no avail. By 1930 Moscow's attention was elsewhere. Moreover the fortunes of the PKI had fallen too low to be susceptible of immediate improvement by any assistance within the power of the Comintern or of the dispersed Indonesian leadership abroad to offer. Except for a brief effort to revive the PKI in the mid-1930's, Indonesian Communism was to remain largely inert until after World War II.

DEFAULT IN INDOCHINA

Indochina, asserted an Annamese delegate named An at the Sixth Comintern Congress in 1928, "is a country which seems to

[54] Musso, "The White Terror in Indonesia," *Eastern and Colonial Bulletin*, February-March, 1929, p. 13 (also *Inprecor*, March 8, 1929). According to Musso, 5,000 workers and Communists had been jailed on terms ranging from six to twenty years, 3,000 were exiled to New Guinea, and numerous executions of Communists had taken place.

[55] The PNI, formed by Sukarno and others in 1927 in the wake of the Communist rebellion, had grown to 10,000 by 1929 and was the most militant of the Indonesian parties. In an article early in 1928 (that is, before the Sixth Comintern Congress), Musso had spoken of it as representing the "true nationalism of Indonesia"; see Musso, "The Consolidation of the National Organization in Indonesia," *Eastern and Colonial Bulletin*, March 15, 1928, pp. 8-9. His 1929 comment was more restrained, but still tacitly acknowledged the leading role of the PNI.

[56] *X plenum Ispolkoma Kominterna*, vyp. 3, p. 169. Other articles and statements by Musso during this period are listed in *Bibliografiia Iugo-vostochnoi Azii*, pp. 150-1.

be forgotten by the whole world."[57] He could be pardoned for thinking so, judging as he did from the meager attention given to Indochina in foreign Communist circles.

Initial responsibility for guiding the Annamese lay with the French Communists, in accordance with directives laid down by the Second Comintern Congress in 1920. Opportunities for contact between French Communists and Annamese revolutionaries were good. During World War I the French government had brought to the metropolitan in various capacities some 100,000 Vietnamese, many of whom inevitably came into contact with French Socialists and future Communist leaders.[58] Nguyen Ai Quoc, who as Ho Chi Minh was subsequently to lead the Vietnamese Communists, was present at the French Socialist congress in 1920 at Tours and was a member of the majority which broke away to form the French Communist Party. At the latter's First Congress in December 1921 Nguyen is reported to have urged the formulation of a specific policy for the French colonies, evidently to no avail.[59] At the Fifth Comintern Congress in 1924, it will be recalled, Manuilsky criticized the French for their inaction on the colonial question. A French delegate acknowledged the shortcoming but was unmistakably irritated at the manner in which the attack was delivered. The guidance of colonial movements, he pointed out, was "a complicated organizational question which cannot be solved by a congress speech"—such as, he implied, Manuilsky's.[60] Nguyen, who was also present at the congress, pressed again for a French policy on the colonial question and proposed five steps the FCP might take to initiate one:

1. To have a section for colonial discussion in *L'Humanité*.
2. To intensify propaganda and recruiting among natives.
3. To send natives to the Communist University at Moscow.
4. To organize the natives working in France.
5. To oblige party members to take an interest in colonial questions.[61]

[57] *Inprecor*, October 25, 1928, p. 1357.
[58] See Thompson, *French Indochina*, p. 480.
[59] Walter, *Histoire du parti communiste français*, p. 73.
[60] *Fifth Congress of the Communist International*, p. 202.
[61] As reported in *ibid.*, p. 205.

The measures, though presumably unobjectionable, were not acted on; nor were they specifically referred to by other speakers. The Indochinese question continued to lie dormant insofar as French Communists were concerned during the years between the Fifth and Sixth Comintern Congresses. Their preoccupation with domestic affairs and intraparty crises evidently diverted attention from France's principal colony in Asia, although interest was shown in the neighboring Chinese revolutionary movement as well as in developments in French colonies in North Africa. Kuusinen, for instance, gave qualified approval at the Sixth Comintern Congress to French Communist activity in North Africa, calling it "the best work in the colonial sphere."[62] He made no reference, however, to Indochina; nor did the French delegates who attended the congress—presumably because they had nothing to report. The only delegate at the Sixth Congress to support the Annamese complaint of neglect was a Chinese Communist who spoke of the "unfortunately inadequate work of the FCP in Annam";[63] the remark passed unnoticed according to the records of the congress.

Whether the French were goaded by complaints of their neglect of Indochina or on their own initiative recognized a more urgent need to offer guidance to the fledgling Vietnamese Communists, the FCP did at last begin to take interest in the Indochinese movement after the Sixth Congress. During 1929, for instance, a series of articles written by Jacques Doriot for *L'Humanité* analyzed recent developments in Indochina and spelled out the immediate tasks facing Vietnamese revolutionaries. The tasks were geared, Doriot pointed out, to an agrarian revolution, as in China, but were addressed primarily to workers. "Indochinese Communists," he wrote, "must sharpen the economic and political struggle of the working class, bring the peasantry into this struggle, and place before both the objectives of the agrarian revolution: confiscation of land belonging to wealthy landowners, native and French alike; achievement of an eight-hour day; and termination of the barbaric methods of exploiting

[62] *Inprecor*, November 21, 1928, p. 1542.
[63] *Ibid.*, August 25, 1928, p. 967.

104

the workers."[64] If the advice was doctrinaire and hardly relevant to the problems facing Vietnamese Communist leaders at this juncture (during their efforts to unify the scattered forces of Indochinese Communism), it did at least indicate the beginning of a sustained French interest in the Indochinese question; this interest was to have significant consequences in the next decade.

Moscow, in the meantime, was no more attentive to the Vietnamese movement during the 1920's than were the French Communists. The records of Comintern congresses and plenary sessions of the ECCI reveal no specific discussion of Indochina, other than An's report at the Sixth Congress. At the preceding congress, in 1924, Indochina was evidently so far from the Comintern's consideration that even Nguyen Ai Quoc made no reference to his homeland in his remarks on French colonial policy.[65] Soviet and Comintern publications, insofar as this writer has been able to discover, included no coverage of Indochina before 1925; thereafter coverage was irregular and of little consequence until the early 1930's.[66] The article on Annam in the 1926 volume of *Bol'shaia sovetskaia entsiklopediia* called the nationalist uprisings to that date "disorganized and unplanned . . . only in rare circumstances acquiring a class character"; the toiling masses of Annam, the entry concluded, are "politically inert."[67] Some attention was given to Indochina in the organs of the Pan

[64] Cited in Dantsig, *Indokitai*, p. 104; Dantsig's 1931 study—the earliest monograph on Indochina published in the USSR—relies heavily on the Doriot articles for coverage of developments in the colony. Doriot, who had been present at the First Pan Pacific Trade Union Conference in Hankow in 1927, was considered within French Communist circles as an authority on Far Eastern questions.

[65] Nguyen did, however, report on Indochina at the Third Profintern Congress, immediately following the Comintern meeting; *III Kongress Krasnogo Internatsionala profsoiuzov*, pp. 297-9.

[66] The earliest articles on Indochina in the Soviet press appeared in mid-1925, one, for instance, on mining in *Novyi Vostok*, No. 28, 1925, another on the labor movement in *Mezhdunarodnoe rabochee dvizhenie*, No. 22, 1925. The official *Bibliografiia Iugo-vostochnoi Azii* lists fewer than half a dozen articles on Indochina in all Russian language publications during the 1920's, most of them concerned with French imperialist policies in the colony. *Inprecor* includes occasional items on Vietnam from 1926 on, but few of these touch on revolutionary activity or programs.

[67] *Bol'shaia sovetskaia entsiklopediia*, II (1926), pp. 773-6.

Pacific Trade Union Secretariat, but again with little insight into the real problems confronting Vietnamese Communism. Stalin, whose attentiveness to developments abroad is a sure indicator of Soviet interest, made a single reference to Indochina in his published speeches and articles during the 1920's—a passing remark in a speech in 1925.[68]

Moscow's inattention to Indochina cannot be attributed to lack of opportunities to learn about developments there. Nguyen Ai Quoc, following his arrival in Moscow in 1923, presumably served as spokesman for the Vietnamese revolutionary movement no less than Tan Malaka and Semaoen served in that capacity for the Javan. He remained two years in the Soviet capital, as an official of the Krestintern, before being sent to Canton as an aide to Borodin; in 1927 he is reported to have returned briefly to Moscow, presumably to discuss Vietnamese affairs with Comintern officials.[69] In addition to Nguyen there were an undetermined number of Vietnamese who attended one or another of the universities for Asians in Russia during the mid-1920's.[70] There were also Vietnamese students in France through whom Moscow, via the French Communists, could have learned of developments in Indochina.[71] Meanwhile periodic reports on the colony pre-

[68] Stalin, *Sochineniia*, VII, p. 100.

[69] Nguyen's travels in the 1920's are obscure and accounts vary. Certain of his activities in Moscow—such as his attendance at various international congresses—are proven by published records. His role in Canton, however (to which we will return), is meagerly documented. The fullest and probably most authentic biography seen by this writer is entitled (in English translation) "President Ho Chi Minh," published in Vietnamese in Hanoi in 1960; portions of it were translated for the writer in Saigon in February 1962. See also S. R. Mohan Das, *Ho Chi Minh: Nationalist or Soviet Agent* (Bombay 1950), cited in Trager, *Marxism in Southeast Asia*, p. 109.

[70] Vietnamese informants interviewed by the author in Saigon in 1962 mentioned by name a number of Indochinese known to have attended schools in Moscow in the 1920's—among them, for instance, a Professor Nguyen Khanh Toan, who subsequently was a member of the Central Committee of the French Communist Party.

[71] Three Vietnamese, for instance, are reported to have attended the Sixth Comintern Congress in 1928 as members of the French delegation; *Inprecor*, November 21, 1928, p. 1532. The Vietnamese were also represented from time to time at meetings of the Anti-Imperialist League in Europe; see *ibid.*, February 25, 1927, p. 328.

sumably reached Moscow after the mid-1920's from such Soviet-controlled organizations in the Far East as the Dalburo, the Pan Pacific Secretariat, and the South Seas Communist Party (discussed below). The fact that these opportunities to keep abreast of events in Indochina led to no sustained Russian interest in the colony suggests an obvious conclusion: in the scheme of Soviet strategies in East Asia, Vietnam was not critical—or less critical than other areas. Moscow's capacity to cultivate Asian revolutionary movements, it has been observed, was not unlimited; Indochina's was for the present expendable.

The Chinese Communists, finally, were as inattentive to their neighbors as were the French and Russians. The Chinese revolution, needless to say, served as a powerful stimulant to revolutionary, and especially Marxist, activity in Vietnam. The Annamese delegate who spoke at the Sixth Comintern Congress made a special point of acknowledging it: "China," he said, applying an ancient proverb, "is the dawn of Indochina."[72] But specific guidance from China during these years is no easier to discover than from Paris or Moscow. Subsequent Soviet claims of "constant ties" during the 1920's between Vietnamese and Chinese Communists,[73] it must be assumed, were made either gratuitously or in ignorance. The Chinese themselves throw doubt on such claims: a Chinese delegate at the Sixth Comintern Congress (the same who criticized the French for their inattention to Vietnam) acknowledged, with regrets, that "there is either very weak connection or none at all" between his party and other Communist, or proto-Communist, movements in Asia, including Indochina.[74]

There was some irony in the fact that Indochina received so little attention from the three "fraternal" parties who might have assumed responsibility for the incipient Communist movement there. Revolutionary prospects during the 1920's, seen from the Marxian viewpoint, were not inferior to those in colonies and semi-colonies which received some help from international Com-

[72] *Ibid.*, October 25, 1928, p. 1358.
[73] E.g., *Programmnye dokumenty Kommunisticheskikh partii Vostoka* (1934), p. 113; the claim is made in the Soviet editor's note introducing a Vietnamese Communist document.
[74] *Inprecor*, August 25, 1928, p. 967.

munism. As in Indonesia, for instance, a nationalist movement had been growing since the war. It consisted of three more or less distinct groups: a moderate reformist element centered on the Constitutional Party of Cochin China, which was made up largely of well-to-do landowners and native officials and believed in a measure of collaboration with the French; a more radical element which followed the leadership of the veteran nationalist Phan Boi Chau and repudiated cooperation with the French; and the overseas Indochinese in France who were under the influence of French Socialist, and to a lesser degree French Communist, circles.[75] The lines between these groups were never precisely fixed and there was a certain migration from one to another. The attitudes and policies of these nationalist forces also tended to shift with changing political conditions in Indochina. During the administration of the French Socialist Alexander Varenne in 1925-1927, for instance, the proposals put forth by the nationalists were moderate; on his recall, the tendency was to seek more radical solutions, a circumstance favoring the new Marxist organizations which sprang up in the country in the latter half of the 1920's. Moscow was consistent in repudiating Varenne's regime, which one writer called a mixture of "gingerbread and the whip,"[76] but offered no advice on the course Vietnamese Marxists might take in opposing it—especially with regard to alliance with other nationalist groups. Lacking such guidance, the Marxists made little effort either to ally with other nationalist elements or to unite their own scattered forces. Until the end of the 1920's the independence movement in Indochina was accordingly characterized by a state of chronic drift, by a proliferation of revolutionary organizations all vying with one another (a heritage, perhaps, of French political experience), and by the inevitable dissipation of whatever opportunities presented themselves.

[75] The early Vietnamese organizations are discussed in detail in Professor Sacks' chapter in Trager, *Marxism in Southeast Asia*, pp. 115-24.

[76] Dantsig, *Indokitai*, p. 100; for Soviet criticism of Varenne during his administration, see *Inprecor*, September 2, 1926, p. 1029; February 4, 1927, p. 253; and November 24, 1927, p. 1248.

The part played by Nguyen Ai Quoc in uniting the Vietnamese Marxists takes on special significance because of his known association with the Comintern and the presumption that he was serving in the Far East as Moscow's agent. When he arrived in Canton in 1925, officially as an interpreter on Borodin's staff but presumably with additional responsibilities vis-à-vis the Vietnamese nationalist movement, he was not unknown in Indochina. His name, meaning "Nguyen the Patriot," had been used early in the 1920's as the collective pseudonym for a series of articles written by Vietnamese nationalists for *L'Humanité*, copies of which, it is reasonable to imagine, found their way to Indochina via returning students.[77] His brochure *Le procès de la colonisation française*, one of the first Marxist analyses of European colonialism in the Far East written by an Asian, was published in Paris early in 1925 and copies of it may have reached Vietnam before Nguyen's arrival in Canton; it soon became, in any case, an authoritative document among Vietnamese nationalists and stimulated interest in Marxism.

In June 1925 Nguyen Ai Quoc conferred in Canton with Phan Boi Chau on recent developments in Indochina and reviewed with him the program of the recently created Vietnam Nationalist Party.[78] About the same time he founded, also in Canton, the Vietnam Revolutionary Youth League. This organization, designed to attract the more radical faction within the nationalist movement, was to play a key role in revolutionary developments in Indochina for the next three or four years; it was the immediate precursor of the Communist Party of Indochina. Its initial manifesto stated, in part: "The Vietnam Revolutionary Youth League is the vanguard of the people's revolution and will organize the proletariat of the country into a powerful army and lead it in the struggle against exploitation and oppression, in the struggle for its rights and for power. We aim to transfer fac-

[77] According to Vietnamese sources, Ho Chi Minh's real name was Nguyen Tan Thanh, and besides Nguyen Ai Quoc he also used at different times the pseudonyms Ly Thuy and Song Man Cho; see Trager, *op. cit.*, p. 316, n. 17.

[78] Min' Shan', "Oktiabr'skaia revoliutsiia i natsional'no-osvoboditel'naia bor'ba narodov Indo-Kitaia," *Sovetskoe vostokovedenie*, No. 5, 1957, p. 51, citing Phan Boi Chau's memoirs.

tories to the workers, land to the peasants, the sources of all wealth to the people, and power to the mass organizations—soviets of representatives of all toiling classes in the country." The ultimate objective, the manifesto concluded, was the "creation of a dictatorship of the proletariat."[79]

The Youth League's manifesto was more militant, it appears, than the policies Nguyen actually set for the organization during the first two years of its existence. According to one student of this era, Nguyen moved cautiously in attempting to organize his compatriots in Indochina: Marxist ideas were introduced only gradually into the League's weekly organ, *Youth*, and care was taken not to alienate possible allies among the more conservative wing of the nationalist movement.[80] The reason for the caution, it is evident, was Nguyen's own training in Moscow, during a period when the united front tactics were taking shape, and his later work with Borodin in Canton which had given force to these tactics in China.

The collapse of the Kuomintang-Communist alliance in China in mid-1927 brought to an abrupt end Nguyen's direction of the Youth League from a protected base in Canton. For the next two and a half years he was obliged to move frequently to avoid arrest, and the newly formed cadres in Vietnam were left largely to their own devices. In the meantime the recall of Varenne in 1927 and the more repressive policies put into force by his successor led to disillusion with the reformist approach within the Vietnamese nationalist movement. The growing deterioration of the Vietnamese economy fed this disillusion. Under these circumstances the revolutionary mood quickened in the colony and the Marxist movement grew. Some notice of these developments was taken by Communist observers outside Indochina. A Comintern handbook published in Moscow in 1928, for instance, remarked the existence in Indochina of "the embryo of a Communist Party and a labor movement."[81] A lengthy review of

[79] *Ibid.*, p. 52.
[80] See Professor Sacks' comments in Trager, *op. cit.*, p. 116.
[81] *Komintern: khoziaistvo, politika i rabochee dvizhenie v kapitalisticheskikh stranakh za 1924-1927 godu*, p. 1021.

Indochina published in *Pan Pacific Worker* in February 1928 observed that "the Chinese nationalist movement has had a very deep echo among the toiling masses of Indochina"; the Vietnamese movement, however, was seen as "very confused ideologically and organizationally weak and disunited."[82] The Annamese speaker at the Sixth Comintern Congress in August 1928 reminded his listeners that "the situation in Indochina is by no means so peaceful as Varenne made believe after the expiration of his mandate." He went on to chronicle in some detail the recent activities of nationalist and revolutionary organizations in the colony, especially those of Nguyen Ai Quoc's Vietnam Revolutionary Youth League.[83]

According to French colonial police records, an effort was made in May 1929 to bring some unity to the Vietnamese Marxist movement by convening a special conference for the purpose in Hong Kong.[84] Delegates from a number of Marxist organizations within the French colony are reported to have attended the conference, but no real unity was achieved. A Leftist faction, objecting to the continued efforts of the *émigré* leadership to bring about an alliance with non-Marxist groups, broke away and constituted itself as the Indochina Communist Party. The majority, claiming loyalty to Nguyen Ai Quoc (who was not present at the conference), reaffirmed the policies of the Youth League and petitioned the Comintern for assistance in the creation of an "authentic" Communist party.[85] By the end of the year, to coun-

[82] Maurice, "Indochina—the Far Eastern Stronghold of French Imperialism," *Pan Pacific Worker*, February 1, 1928, p. 13; this was one of the earliest items on Indochina to appear in the PPTUS journal.

[83] *Inprecor*, October 25, 1928, pp. 1357-9.

[84] An account of this meeting may be found in Trager, *op. cit.*, pp. 122-3, drawn from Gouvernement Général de l'Indochine, Directions des Affaires Politiques et de la Sûreté Générale, *Documents*, II. Reference to the Hong Kong meeting, described as the First Congress of the Vietnam Revolutionary Youth League, may also be found in the 1960 biography of Ho Chi Minh cited earlier; this source refers also to a Second Congress held later in the year in Macao, but no details of the latter have come to light.

[85] The petition is cited in an article by the North Vietnamese historian Min' Shan' (as transliterated from the Russian) in *Velikii Oktiabr' i narody Vostoka* (1957), p. 145.

teract inroads made into its organization in Indochina by the dissident faction, the Youth League felt obliged also to adopt the name Communist and accordingly became the Annam Communist Party. At this point there were three Marxist groups in Indochina calling themselves Communist: the two just referred to and a third organization called the Indochina Communist Alliance, which had replaced an organization known as the New Vietnam Revolutionary Party earlier in 1929.[86]

It required Nguyen Ai Quoc's intervention to unite the three factions. Early in 1930 he arrived in Hong Kong from Siam. By January 6, he had secured agreement from representatives of the three groups on the principle of a unified organization. By the end of February the merger was completed. The new party was initially called the Vietnam Communist Party, which was later changed to the Communist Party of Indochina (CPIC) to conform to normal Comintern practice. Its first secretary was Chan Fu;[87] Nguyen, though the initiator of the merger, remained in the background; considering himself as an agent of the International, he evidently disqualified himself even from membership on the first Central Committee.[88] Acknowledgment of the reorganization appeared promptly in the Comintern press,[89] and in April 1931 the CPIC was formally admitted into the Comintern.[90] It was mere coincidence, as we shall see in the next chapter, that the CPIC came into being on the eve of a great national crisis which opened unexpected opportunities for the Com-

[86] Min' Shan', in another article, acknowledges the existence of the three Communist organizations in 1929, placing them in North, Central, and South Vietnam, but mentions no rivalry between them; Min' Shan', "Revoliutsionnoe dvizhenie v V'etname," *Sovetskoe vostokovedenie*, No. 1, January-February 1956, p. 39.

[87] *Ibid.*, p. 39.

[88] According to an Indochinese informant interviewed by the writer in Saigon in February 1962.

[89] See A. N., "The Terror in Indochina and the Development of the Revolutionary Movement," *Inprecor*, January 16, 1930, p. 46.

[90] *Stenograficheskii otchet: XI plenum IKKI, vyp.* II, p. 246. According to French government records, the CPIC received from the ECCI at the time of its admission into the Comintern a monthly stipend of 5,000 francs (about $1,250); see Walter, *Histoire du parti communiste français*, p. 379.

munists but at the same time exposed their fragile organization to unusual strains.

PROTO-COMMUNISM IN THE PHILIPPINES

Revolutionary developments in the Philippines during the 1920's have often been overlooked by students of international Communism, probably because of the small number of direct contacts between Moscow and Filipino revolutionaries during these years and because the Philippines, which had no Communist party until 1930, was unrepresented in meetings of the Comintern. Moscow, however, kept abreast of events in the Philippines through channels other than the Comintern itself and found agents other than the Comintern's to transmit its instructions. In fact, there is evidence of a lively interest in this American colony on the part of international Communism, especially from 1927 on.

The Philippines provided fertile ground for Soviet revolutionary strategies. As a colony it was a potential target of Moscow's Eastern policy from the Second Comintern Congress forward, no less than other colonies; as an American colony—indeed the only significant American possession—it inevitably attracted attention when Moscow's anti-imperialist policies became directed as much against Washington as against London, Paris, and Amsterdam. The Profintern, enumerating its areas of priority emphasis in 1923, already recognized the Philippines as "an important strategic point in the Pacific Ocean."[91] The Philippines, moreover, possessed a labor movement dating from the early 1900's, the greater part of which was consolidated by World War I into a single labor organization, the *Congresso Obrero de Filipinas* (COF); there were, to be sure, occasional defections from the COF—such as the *Federacion del Trabajo* in 1917— but it remained nonetheless a significant force in Philippine political life during the 1920's. In 1924 the more radical labor leaders, led by Crisanto Evangelista, formed the first workers' party, the *Partido Obrero*. Similar activity among the peasantry

[91] *Inprecor*, October 6, 1923, p. 725; from a "Resolution on Work in the Far and Near East" passed by the Profintern's Central Council.

began soon after World War II; here the principal organization was (in its English translation) the National Confederation of Tenants and Farm Laborers and the most prominent peasant leader was Jacinto Manahan, a close ally of Evangelista.

The existence of these labor and peasant organizations, together with the political parties that had already come into being by the early 1920's, provided the means for much political intercourse in the Philippines. The Philippines were in effect one of the most politically conscious colonies in the Far East during the decade we are considering. The delay in forming a Communist party may have been due precisely to the opportunities for political expression already available to early Marxists.

The coming of Marxist ideas to the Philippines cannot be dated precisely. Some exposure to Marxism by Filipinos visiting the United States after World War I may easily be imagined, comparable to the exposure of Vietnamese in France. Evangelista, for instance, is known to have met Leftist American labor leaders in 1919 when he came to the United States as a member of the first Philippine independence mission.[92] Meanwhile the relative absence of censorship in the Philippines, both in the mails and in the press, meant that there was no serious barrier to the circulation of any Marxist ideas or literature that made its appearance in the colony. Until 1930 the annual reports of the Governor General showed little concern with a Communist problem.

Most histories of Philippine Communism trace the origins of the movement to visits by two foreign Communists in 1924 and 1925. The first was by the American Communist Harrison George, who came to Manila in May 1924, evidently with an introduction from responsible Philippine officials in Washington, and spent several days conferring with labor leaders. His mission, he said, was to invite a Filipino delegation to a conference of Pacific transport workers to be held in Canton the following month.[93] The second visit, which stretched with inter-

[92] Evidence of Evangelista's activities on this mission is cited in Hoeksema, *Communism in the Philippines*, p. 34.

[93] George's visit is described in a 1936 report by the Philippine Department of

ruptions over a two-year period, was by the Indonesian Tan Malaka, who, as we have seen, claimed to be the Comintern's agent in Southeast Asia. According to his own account of his stay in the Philippines, Tan Malaka arrived in Manila in June 1925, established contact with highly placed Filipinos, as well as with labor leaders, and traveled widely through the islands. He spent most of 1926 and the first half of 1927 in Malaya and Thailand, returning to Manila in mid-1927, when he was almost immediately arrested. His deportation, following lengthy proceedings, became a *cause célèbre* in the Philippines and brought many eminent Filipinos to his defense.[94]

There is no reason to doubt that the visits by Harrison George and Tan Malaka took place (although sources are contradictory on details). There are, however, grounds for doubting the impact these two foreign Communists are often said to have had on the incipient Marxist movement in the Philippines. Tan Malaka, by his own account, came to the Philippines chiefly for reasons of health, consorted mainly with Filipinos leaning to the *Nacionalista* Party rather than toward Communism, and had no sustained contact, as far as is known, with future Communist leaders such as Evangelista and Manahan. His autobiography, which is hardly a modest document, makes no claim of his having exercised great influence among the Filipinos and indeed shows that his major preoccupation during these years continued to be the revolutionary movement in Indonesia. Neither Soviet nor Comintern sources seen by this writer make refer-

---

Labor, cited in Hoeksema, *op. cit.*, pp. 40-1. Hoeksema also cites, as evidence of George's visit, his 1954 interview with a former Philippine Communist, Domingo Ponce, and an interview by Rev. Arthur A. Weiss with another ex-Communist, Cirilo Bognot; both Ponce and Bognot recall the 1924 meetings with Harrison George, who was using the alias "Girunas." The official party history written by José Lava in 1950, *Milestones in the History of the Communist Party of the Philippines*, makes no mention of the visit.

[94] For a summary of Tan Malaka's account of his Philippine visit, based on his autobiography entitled (in English translation) "From Jail to Jail," see American University Field Staff, Report WAH-1-'59 (by Willard A. Hanna), April 6, 1959, pp. 9-10. An account based in part on a stenographic report of Tan Malaka's deportation proceedings may be found in Scaff, *The Philippine Answer to Communism*, pp. 8-9.

ence to Tan Malaka's Philippine visit, at the time or subsequently; recent Philippine Communist sources refer to it only briefly.[95]

Nor should the impact of Harrison George's visit in 1924 be exaggerated. His stay was in the first place too brief to have left a lasting impression on any proto-Marxists he may have met. Moreover he was not immediately followed to the Philippines by other American Communists, who might have cemented any contacts he had made; the next visits to the Philippines by American Communists are reported only in 1927, when Earl Browder and Harrison George again came to Manila in behalf of the Pan Pacific Trade Union Secretariat (PPTUS).[96] The 1924 visit by George does, however, have historic significance in marking the beginning of a tie with American Communism which over the years was to influence profoundly the course of the revolutionary movement in the Philippines; we will have frequent occasion to discuss this influence.

The Filipinos responded to George's invitation in 1924 and sent a five-man delegation to the Conference of Transport Workers of the Pacific held in Canton in June. The tangible consequences of this maiden appearance of Filipinos in an international Communist gathering were modest. The conference was largely taken up with a doctrinal dispute between Kuomintang and Chinese Communist delegates on the proper form of the united front in China and in this the Filipinos were bystanders. Voitinsky, the Comintern's representative at the conference, noted their approval of the united front in principle, but added, with a suggestion of irony, that they chose to understand the united front "chiefly in the sense of the 'moral' struggle against the imperialists, extending it to all the elements of the oppressed na-

[95] José Lava, for instance, in *Milestones*, p. 13, remarks merely that Tan Malaka was sent by the Profintern to invite the *Congreso Obrero* to take part in a trade union conference to be held in Canton; it seems likely that Lava confuses Tan Malaka's mission with Harrison George's the preceding year—although his bearing a second such invitation is entirely possible.

[96] George's visit is referred to in a report on the work of the PPTUS made by Browder in 1929; see *Pan Pacific Monthly*, November 1929, p. 28. Evidence concerning Browder's visit is cited in Hoeksema, *op. cit.*, p. 52.

tionalities and ignoring the social and class differentiations within these nationalities."[97]

The attendance of Filipinos at the Canton conference does not
appear to have stimulated new Soviet interest in the Philippines.
Coverage of developments there in Soviet journals continued to
be meager.[98] The contacts initiated at Canton were not extended,
as far as is known (except by Tan Malaka). Meanwhile the
course of the revolutionary movement in the Philippines grew
sluggish; whether this was the cause or the effect of Moscow's
neglect is difficult to say. Evangelista's *Partido Obrero*, for instance, after a temporary success in the elections of 1925,[99] all
but disappeared. In short, during the better part of the three
years separating the Canton meeting from the next important
Moscow-sponsored gathering in the Far East, the Pan Pacific
Trade Union Conference in 1927, there is little to suggest that
Filipino radicals were launched on a course parallel or even
close to Moscow's—or, for that matter, that Moscow seriously
cared.

The Filipinos were not represented at the Pan Pacific Trade
Union Conference in May 1927, either because they were not
informed in time of the last-minute change in its location from
Canton to Hankow or because of a conflict with the approaching annual congress of the COF in Manila.[100] On June 30, however, the *Congresso Obrero*, on the basis of a reportedly "unanimous" decision at its Fifteenth Congress, requested affiliation
with the newly established Pan Pacific Secretariat (PPTUS) and

---

[97] G. Voitinsky, "First Congress of Transport Workers of the Pacific," *Inprecor*,
September 11, 1924, p. 705. An account of the Canton trip was given to Renze
Hoeksema in 1954 by the head of the Filipino delegation, Domingo Ponce; see
his *Communism in the Philippines*, pp. 40-4 *passim*.

[98] During 1925 and 1926, Soviet coverage of the Philippines was limited to
brief reports of annual peasant and labor congresses and reference to occasional
strikes: e.g., *Krasnyi internatsional profsoiuzov*, No. 7-8, 1925, pp. 126-9; *Mezhdunarodnoe rabochee dvizhenie*, No. 43, 1926, pp. 9-10; *Novyi Vostok*, No. 12,
1926, p. 104.

[99] At the Fourth Profintern Congress in 1928, Evangelista reported that the
Partido Obrero, soon after its founding, had polled 6,000 of the total 34,000 votes
cast in the 1925 elections; *IV Kongress Profinterna*, p. 270.

[100] Both reasons are given by Earl Browder in a subsequent report on the work
of the PPTUS; *Pan Pacific Monthly*, November 1929, p. 26.

117

the request was granted; later in the year the PPTUS also admitted the smaller "mutualist" labor organization, *Legionarios del Trabajo.*[101]

The affiliation of the two principal labor unions in the Philippines with the PPTUS marks a significant turning point in the history of the Philippine revolutionary movement. The very fact that affiliation was requested with an organization known to be close to Moscow testifies to a maturing radicalism already well advanced among leaders such as Evangelista, Manahan, Ponce, and Cirilo Bognot. The decision of the *Congresso Obrero* to affiliate was evidently not made easily, despite the claim of unanimity in the official PPTUS journal. According to José Lava, it was reached only "after a sharp ideological struggle"; he also notes that this was the first occasion when the "issue of Communism" was discussed at a Philippine labor conference.[102] What particular confluence of forces led the majority of the *Congresso Obrero* to follow Evangelista—or, for that matter, induced Evangelista himself to take the course he did—cannot be reconstructed with any precision at this distance from the event. Doubtless all of the considerations we have reviewed played a part in the process, including Evangelista's visit to the United States in 1919, the subsequent visits of Harrison George and Tan Malaka to the Philippines, and the sending of Ponce's delegation to Canton in 1924. The Hankow conference and especially the creation of a permanent Pan Pacific Secretariat, it may be imagined, also influenced the Filipinos. Now for the first time the possibility of an association with an international labor organization was offered them; moreover, it was an open association (despite the harassment of the PPTUS by the Kuomintang) where the

[101] The COF letter requesting affiliation, signed by its principal officers Evangelista and Francisco Varona, was printed in *Pan Pacific Worker*, July 15, 1927, pp. 3-4. Announcement of the admission of *Legionarios del Trabajo* was carried in *ibid.*, December 1, 1927, p. 3. In March 1928 Evangelista reported that there were 107,191 organized workers in the Philippines of a total labor force of approximately 300,000: 81,137 in the COF (including peasants); 3,268 in the *Legionarios del Trabajo*; and 22,786 in independent unions. See *IV Kongress Profinterna*, p. 267.

[102] Lava, *Milestones*, p. 13.

only prior association of this sort presumably open to the Filipinos—although there is no evidence that they made use of it—had been with the Comintern's clandestine *Dalburo* in Shanghai. If it is true that the Hankow conference and the establishment of the PPTUS prompted the more aggressive course of Philippine labor in 1927, this was of course precisely Moscow's intention in launching the Pan Pacific organization. In July 1927 the PPTUS could claim with some accuracy, in announcing the affiliation of the *Congresso Obrero*, that its activities were already "bearing fruit." Several years later Lozovsky claimed (with little tact) that "until the Secretariat came into being no one was aware that any trade union movement existed in the Philippines."[103]

Following the affiliation of the COF with the Pan Pacific Secretariat, Filipinos began to participate in increasing numbers in conferences abroad, which greatly enlarged their foreign contacts and provided further stimulation to the radical wing of the labor movement. In August 1927 the Filipinos were invited to send a delegation to a conference in Hankow in September sponsored by the Anti-Imperialist League.[104] In November a Philippine delegate was reported present at a special congress celebrating the tenth anniversary of the Bolshevik Revolution in Moscow.[105] In December 1927 a Filipino who described himself as "the first representative of the Philippine people to make a report in Europe on the struggle for independence going on there" attended the Second Congress of the Anti-Imperialist League in Brussels.[106]

[103] *Inprecor*, June 28, 1929, p. 669; see also a similar claim by Harrison George in *Pan Pacific Monthly*, August 1929, p. 11.

[104] Evidence of the invitation is cited in Hoeksema, *op. cit.*, p. 52; inasmuch as the alliance between Moscow and the Kuomintang collapsed entirely during the summer of 1927, it is unlikely the Hankow conference convened.

[105] *Inprecor*, December 1, 1927, p. 1540; there is no evidence who the Filipino was.

[106] *Ibid.*, December 22, 1927, p. 1634. Hoeksema believes that the Filipino, whose name was Alminiana, came from the United States, not the Philippines, and identifies him as a Filipino who returned to the Philippines in 1938 to work for the CPPI.

119

The most important foreign journey of Filipinos in this period was without doubt the visit of Evangelista, Manahan, and Bognot to Moscow early in 1928 to attend the Fourth Profintern Congress. Evangelista and Bognot, traveling under the auspices of the Pan Pacific Secretariat, stopped in Shanghai en route, where they attended the Second Plenum of the PPTUS[107] and reportedly met Chinese Communist leaders; they reached Moscow via Dairen and Harbin early in March. Manahan, traveling separately under arrangements made by the Peasant International (Krestintern), joined them there on the eve of the Congress. Evangelista, using the pseudonym "Juan Krisostomo," greeted the congress in behalf of the *Congresso Obrero* and told the delegates that, while formal affiliation with the Profintern was not yet possible, the COF was "ready to go shoulder to shoulder into battle with you against world imperialism." He also reported at some length on the Filipinos' struggle for independence —first against the Spaniards, then against the Americans—and described the new role of Philippine labor in this effort in the face of the betrayal of the bourgeois parties. Another address by "Dantes" (presumably Bognot) supplied details on the devious course of American capitalism in the Philippines and charged American labor, especially the AFL, with duplicity for championing Philippine independence on the one hand yet discriminating against Filipino laborers in California on the other. Both speakers urged closer ties between the Filipinos and the world trade union movement.[108]

At the close of the congress early in April Evangelista and Manahan spent another five or six weeks in the USSR, visiting Leningrad and Kiev, before returning to Manila in June. Bognot

[107] See "The Pan Pacific Secretariat Meeting," *Pan Pacific Worker*, March 1, 1928, p. 1. A later report of the Second Plenum describes it as "a turning point for the development of the Philippine trade unions, which, under the inspiration of their contact with the PPTUS, began a deep process of reorientation and reorganization"; *ibid.*, November 1929, p. 27.

[108] The texts of Evangelista's greeting and address are in *IV Kongress Profinterna*, p. 19 and pp. 265-70; "Dantes' " address is in *ibid.*, pp. 485-6. A reworked version of Evangelista's address appeared in *Far Eastern Monthly*, August 1928, pp. 36-42.

states that he remained in the Soviet Union more than a year, studying at Moscow University, and claims to have had an interview with Stalin before his departure; according to his account, he returned to the Philippines at the end of 1929 after attending the Second Congress of the Anti-Imperialist League held in Frankfurt in July.[109] Following their return Evangelista and Manahan soon put to use the lessons they had learned in Moscow. During 1928 Evangelista undertook a complete reorganization of the *Partido Obrero*, which had been largely inactive since the 1925 elections. Presumably this was in response to the current Comintern line that separate working-class parties were indispensable in all colonial movements; indeed Evangelista seems to have been aware of this even before leaving Moscow, to judge from his address at the Profintern Congress in which he emphasized the part the *Partido Obrero* was already playing "in stimulating the class struggle and class consciousness." The new *Partido Obrero* was to be the political arm of the *Congreso Obrero*. But it served an added purpose, we may imagine, in Evangelista's calculations: the annual congress of the COF, held during Evangelista's absence in Russia, had not reelected him secretary and had shown some evidence of conservative tendencies;[110] the *Partido Obrero*, accordingly, represented for Evangelista and his followers a separate base in the event they wholly lost control of the *Congreso Obrero*. This in fact was to take place, as we shall see, and Evangelista's party, whose aims according to José Lava were "Marxist in character and based on the principle of class struggle,"[111] became the nucleus of the Communist Party of the

110 The details of the Soviet visit by the three Filipinos vary slightly in different sources, but there is general agreement on the itinerary. Evangelista's report of the trip is in *ibid*., November 1928, pp. 12-8; Bognot's account, given in an interview with Rev. Arthur A. Weiss, is summarized in Hoeksema, *op. cit.*, pp. 60-2; brief mention of the journey is also made in Lava, *Milestones*, p. 17. There is some doubt as to the length of Bognot's stay in Europe inasmuch as he appears to have taken part in the critical congress of the COF in Manila in May 1929; Filipino representation at the Frankfurt Congress, however, is reported in *Pan Pacific Monthly*, September-October 1929, p. 23.
110 See Hoeksema, *op. cit.*, pp. 69-70.
111 Lava, *Milestones*, p. 19.

Philippines. Manahan, meanwhile, in a parallel effort among the peasants, in December 1928 transformed the existing peasant confederation into a more militant new combination called the Philippine Confederation of Peasants (or KPMP, after its name in Tagalog);[112] this organization affiliated with the Peasant International early in 1929.

The Pan Pacific Secretariat continued during 1928 and 1929 to strengthen its ties with the Filipinos. In October 1928 Manahan and Ponce attended the Third Plenum of the PPTUS in Shanghai, where Manahan delivered a lengthy report on the peasant movement. The plenum professed a wish to hold the next Pan Pacific Trade Union Conference in Manila, but was forestalled by lack of assurances that permission would be granted and so elected Vladivostok.[113] When the official call for the Vladivostok conference was released, the Filipinos were allotted five delegates, a number which was higher relative to total population than the allotment to other countries invited and which presumably reflects the increasing attention of the PPTUS to the Philippine movement.[114] Lozovsky, in an article prepared for the coming conference, devoted more attention to Philippine labor than to the movements in any other Pacific countries except China and Japan.[115] Browder reported to the conference in August that, during the preceding two years, the PPTUS had issued brochures in Tagalog, maintained a press service to the Philippines from Shanghai (and later San Francisco), arranged for distribution in the Philippines of the Profintern's English-language journal *Eastern and Colonial Bulletin*, and published numerous communications on developments in the Philippines in its own journals.[116] If there is any doubt that these "communications" served as directives to the Filipinos, not mere ex-

[112] Jacinto G. Manahan, "Philippine Peasants Draw up Militant Program of Action" (letter to the PPTUS), *Far Eastern Monthly*, January 1929, pp. 40-3.

[113] *Ibid.*, December 1928, p. 1.

[114] Indonesia, for instance, was allotted 3 delegates, Indochina 1; the Soviet Union was entitled to send 15, China 12, Japan 10, etc. See *Pan Pacific Monthly*, April 1929, p. 3.

[115] *Inprecor*, June 28, 1929, p. 669.

[116] *Pan Pacific Monthly*, November 1929, pp. 26ff.

pressions of opinion, the doubt should be erased by Lozovsky's observation that "many of the political and organizational directives given by the [Pan Pacific] secretariat to the Filipino comrades have brought the most gratifying results as regards the growth and development of the labor movement in the islands."[117] Evangelista also acknowledged on numerous occasions the guidance received from the PPTUS, as in a remark in mid-1928 that the reorganization efforts then in progress had as their goal the "realization of the program set forth by the PPTUS as regards trade union unity."[118]

There appears then to be little question that the PPTUS was the principal channel through which information on the Philippines reached Moscow as well as the channel through which any directives from Moscow, in pursuit of its varied objectives, might be transmitted to the Filipinos. We should now consider more particularly what these objectives were.

If we leave aside certain general objectives always present in Soviet colonial policies—such as the gaining of an additional voice to speak in defense of Moscow's interests, or the manipulation of a convenient lever against the "imperialism" of a major rival— the Kremlin's strategies in the Philippines in the 1920's, it may be argued, were aimed at the consolidation of Philippine labor against multiple future contingencies. Moscow was working in the Philippines not primarily with a nationalist movement, as elsewhere in East Asia, but with a labor and peasant movement. This did not mean that the Russians were less interested in Philippine independence than they were in Indonesian or Indochinese independence, as an ultimate objective, but it did mean that the forces they could summon to the struggle were more narrowly based than in other colonies. The participation of bourgeois elements in the struggle for independence was categorically rejected from the outset. "The Filipino bourgeoisie is not capable of a decisive struggle," one of the earliest Soviet

---

[117] *Inprecor*, June 28, 1929, p. 669.
[118] C. Evangelista, "Report on the Growth and Development of the Labor Movement of the Philippine Islands," *Far Eastern Monthly*, August 1928, p. 42.

commentaries on the Philippines proclaimed, "because it is tied to the American bourgeoisie. The islands will gain full independence only when the growing working class and the farmers take the matter of independence into their own hands."[119] The peasantry, Moscow presumably felt, posed no special problem in the Philippines so long as its close links with the labor movement were assured by the collaboration of Evangelista and Manahan.

The rejection of the Philippine bourgeoisie as a possible ally of the workers and peasants persists in Soviet commentaries throughout the 1920's, despite the fact that a large portion of the bourgeoisie was no less dedicated to independence than their counterparts in other Asian colonies. Possibly Moscow's hostility to bourgeois nationalist elements in the Philippines reflects the comparatively late date of a sustained Soviet interest in the colony, after earlier efforts to collaborate with national movements in other colonies had failed. It is equally possible that Moscow was enough impressed by the size of the labor establishment already in existence in the Philippines to imagine that here, for the first time, a genuine merger of the national revolutionary and proletarian movements might be brought about; if such a merger proved feasible, the two traditional stages in colonial revolutions—national liberation and seizure of power by the workers—could be telescoped into one. This was, of course, an entirely plausible objective in the context of Soviet Eastern policy during the 1920's; it would, however, be unwise to engage in too lively speculation on how far Moscow cared to pursue it in the Philippines. Little evidence suggests either sustained Soviet goals or sustained strategies in this colony during the 1920's, and, indeed, hardly any policy at all before 1927 or 1928.

By 1926 or 1927 it must have been apparent to Moscow that the Philippine labor movement was a more shadowy reality than its elaborate role of organized unions suggested. Harrison George, surely one of the most charitably disposed students of Philippine labor, wrote in a Profintern journal in November

[119] M. Galkovich, "Filippiny v bor'be za svoiu nezavisimost'," *Mirovoe khoziaistvo i mirovaia politika*, February 1926, p. 114.

1927 that the movement was weak and that the *Congresso Obrero* (already affiliated at the time with the PPTUS) was no better than a "possible future force" in the struggle for independence.[120] The Russian who reported to the Fourth Profintern Congress in March 1928 on labor movements in the colonies acknowledged that 100,000 organized workers in a country of only 12,000,000 represented a respectable accomplishment, but Philippine labor organization, he stated, had only "a formal character; it is dispersed, devoid of class content, without workers' cadres and during the entire twenty-five years of its existence it has been guided by bourgeois or petty-bourgeois intellectuals of the anarcho-syndicalist sect who have led the movement in the spirit of shop-unionism and the most primitive mutualism."[121] This was a harsher judgment of Philippine labor, of course, than can be found in the bland pronouncements of the Pan Pacific Secretariat, either before or after the Fourth Congress; but it doubtless represents a more authentic Soviet view. Neither Evangelista nor "Dantes" challenged the analysis, at least in their published interventions at the Profintern congress.

Under the circumstances, any serious effort by Philippine labor to undertake leadership of a national liberation movement was out of the question. The persistent discussion in Pan Pacific, Profintern, Comintern, and Soviet periodicals of the "betrayal" of the Philippine bourgeoisie and the urgency of a struggle against American imperialism based on the leadership of workers and peasants must be looked upon as *pro forma*, or at best as a reminder of objectives still some distance away.[122] The im-

---

[120] *Eastern and Colonial Bulletin*, November 1, 1927, pp. 6-8.

[121] *IV Kongress Profinterna*, p. 451; the report was delivered by Geller.

[122] It may be appropriate to indicate here the principal foreign Communist sources on the Philippine labor movement during the 1920's. By far the largest number of commentaries, as well as "official communications," letters, and other forms of directives, are carried in the PPTUS organ *Pan Pacific Worker* (also called *Far Eastern Monthly* and *Pan Pacific Monthly*; see Bibliography). Items on the Philippines appear in almost every issue of this journal from its founding in July 1927 to its closing early in the 1930's; a number of these items are cited in the present study and a great many more are cited in Hoeksema, *Communism in the Philippines*. The latter study also cites articles in American Communist organs such as *Labour Monthly* and *Workers Monthly* (sources not systematically

mediate problem was a more prosaic one: to galvanize the quarter-century old labor movement into a unified and disciplined force in Philippine political life. Only such an organization could respond effectively to Moscow's directives, whatever these might be; a labor movement without this capacity, it goes without saying, was not worth Moscow's trouble. The Fourth Profintern Congress accordingly set tasks for the Filipinos designed to overcome defects in organization. The tasks included the merger of parallel unions in the same industry; a more vigorous struggle against shop-unionism and mutualism and for industrial unions; the elimination of bourgeois leadership in the trade union movement; the creation of new unions among laborers still unorganized; above all, the establishment of a "united national trade union center."[123]

The Filipinos appear to have made tentative efforts toward trade union unity even before the Profintern congress, presumably at the request of the Pan Pacific Secretariat. In September 1927, for instance, *Congresso Obrero* leaders met with Joaquin Balmori, head of the independent *Federacion del Trabajo*, in a so-called "unity conference," but achieved little success. After the Fourth Congress, the PPTUS pressed the call for Philippine labor unity more vigorously, and new negotiations were opened between the *Congresso Obrero* and other labor organizations,

---

consulted by the present writer). The Profintern publications *Eastern and Colonial Bulletin*, *Mezhdunarodnoe rabochee dvizhenie* and *Krasnyi internatsional profsoiuzov* carry frequent articles on the Philippines from 1925 on, with a particularly heavy concentration in 1927 and 1928; many of these items are reprints or translations from the PPTUS organ. Similarly many articles on the Philippines in *Inprecor* are reprints from the *Pan Pacific Worker*, although occasional coverage of the Philippines may be found in *Inprecor* as early as 1925 (e.g., an article on the independence movement in the issue of October 15, 1925). Purely Soviet sources are few in number. The earliest article on the Philippines discovered by this writer is Galkovich's article in *Mirovoe khoziaistvo i mirovaia politika*, February 1926 (cited above). Other articles of interest by Soviet writers are F. Frankl, "Amerika i Filippinskie ostrova," *Novyi Vostok*, No. 12, 1926, pp. 89-104, and L. Geller, "Amerika i Filippiny," *Kommunisticheskii Internatsional*, August 1927, pp. 27-33. The Philippines are occasionally discussed in official publications released in Moscow, such as *IV Kongress Profinterna*, but no full length monograph on the Philippines was published in Moscow until A. Guber's *Filippiny* in 1937.

[123] *IV Kongress Profinterna*, p. 613; from the resolution on Geller's report.

but still with few gains.[124] The *Congresso Obrero* had more success in forging an alliance with Chinese workers in the Philippines than with non-affiliated Filipinos. In October 1928 Evangelista launched a campaign to bring the Philippine Chinese Laborers' Association into the *Congresso Obrero*, and in February 1929 a conference of representatives of the two organizations issued a joint resolution on unity and solidarity. The slogans included in the resolution clearly reflected Moscow's influence in the new alliance: "Hands off China!" "Long Live the PPTUS!" "Down with Imperialism!" and "Proletariat of the World, Unite!"[125]

The annual congress of the *Congresso Obrero* scheduled for May 1929 was to have taken a major step forward in the unification of the Philippine labor movement. The Pan Pacific Secretariat prepared an "official communication" for the occasion in which the congress' tasks were spelled out in detail, much as they had been enumerated by the Fourth Profintern Congress the year before. "The delegates should settle first," the communication emphasized, "that only the COF is recognized as the National Center for the Philippine trade union movement." The letter also stressed the danger of war against the Soviet Union, then a major item in Soviet propaganda, and indicated that the congress should shape its slogans accordingly: "The PPTUS would be negligent in its duty if it did not draw the attention of the congress to this growing war danger against the first Workers' and Peasants' Republic." The communication closed modestly enough: "The Secretariat offers to congress delegates the above suggestions which we hope will serve as a guide to your discussions."[126]

[124] These early efforts are described, *inter alia*, in G. Aguila, "The Philippines Toward Trade Union Unity," *Pan Pacific Worker*, May 1, 1928, p. 15, and Evangelista's article in *Far Eastern Monthly*, August 1928, pp. 40-2.

[125] On October 11, the anniversary of the Chinese Revolution, Evangelista addressed the Chinese Laborers' Association on the need of "solidarity between the Filipino and Chinese working classes"; *Far Eastern Monthly*, December 1928, pp. 43-8. The joint resolution of the February conference is given in *Pan Pacific Monthly*, July 1929, p. 28.

[126] The letter first appeared in *Inprecor*, May 3, 1929, pp. 463-4 (not, however,

The congress was not destined to carry out its tasks. Like the Second Congress of the Russian Social Democrats in 1903, which was also convened to bring unity, the May congress of the COF ended in a permanent division of the Philippine labor movement. Before the proceedings were underway, Evangelista and his supporters, numbering an estimated half of the delegates present, walked out of the congress on the grounds that it had been "packed" with conservative delegates. A few days later the dissidents, including all the Chinese delegates as well as the great majority of peasant delegates under Manahan, held a separate convention and formed a new labor organization, the *Congress Proletario di Filipinas* (or KAP, after its Tagalog title). Twenty-seven of the thirty-five unions in the *Congresso Obrero* were represented at this convention and by summer the KAP claimed a membership of 40,000 as against 8,000 in the old COF. An editorial in *Pan Pacific Monthly* in July commented that as a result of the division "the class struggle has been lifted to a higher plane. The COF (Proletariat) [that is, the KAP] is now the center of real trade unionism."[127] The PPTUS severed relations with the *Congresso Obrero* and henceforth dealt exclusively with the KAP; only the KAP, for instance, was represented at the Second Pan Pacific Trade Union Conference in August 1929.[128]

The causes of this fateful division in the Philippine labor movement were variously analyzed in the months following the May congress. One explanation, offered by a Filipino attending the Pan Pacific conference in Shanghai, was that the alliance earlier

---

labeled as an "official communication"); it was subsequently reprinted in *Pan Pacific Monthly*, June 1929, pp. 41-4.

[127] "The Split in the Philippine Labor Congress," *ibid.*, July 1929, p. 32. For other accounts of the split, see articles by Earl Browder in *Labour Monthly*, July 1929; by R. Alvarez in *Eastern and Colonial Bulletin*, June-July 1929; and by Evangelista in *Krasnyi internatsional profsoiuzov*, July 1929.

[128] Manahan was the only Filipino present at the main Pan Pacific conference in Vladivostok; several Filipinos, however, attended the "second section" of the conference held concurrently in Shanghai to accommodate delegates unable to reach Vladivostok. Accounts of the two meetings were carried in the November 1929 and December 1929-January 1930 issues of *Pan Pacific Monthly*.

in the year between the *Congresso Obrero* and the Philippine Chinese Laborers' Association proved unacceptable to conservative elements in the COF and led to their effort to pack the May congress; if the Chinese unions were expelled from the COF, the dissident faction would be willing to restore harmony.[129] Harrison George, on the other hand, considered that the split was caused by the intent of a conservative faction led by Ponce, Bognot, and Isabelo Tejada to sever the *Congresso Obrero*'s relations with the Pan Pacific Secretariat.[130] There were also indications that personal rivalries played a part in the crisis, especially the antagonism of the Ponce-Bognot faction toward Evangelista.[131]

It is likely, of course, that all these issues played a part in bringing on the crisis in the *Congresso Obrero*. The lines indeed must have been taking shape long before the congress convened. The persistent Leftward drift of the COF under Evangelista's radical leadership must have dismayed conservatives in the labor movement, no less than the conservatives' obstruction of measures such as the alliance with the Chinese unions frustrated the radicals. A clash was inevitable. The clash, moreover, was not unrelated to conflicting policies in the Philippines which traced their origins to Moscow itself. On one hand, Moscow, acting through its instruments in the Far East, had for some years been urging a unified labor movement in the Philippines, an objective which required patience and moderation given the acknowledged low level of class indoctrination on the part of all but a few Filipino labor leaders. On the other hand, after the affiliation of the *Congresso Obrero* to the PPTUS Moscow spoke increasingly of the "radicalization" and "revolutionizing" of the

[129] *Ibid.*, December 1929-January 1930, p. 34.

[130] Harrison George, "Tools of the Capitalists within the Filipino Labor Movement," *ibid.*, November 1929, pp. 59-60.

[131] George quotes letters the PPTUS received after the May congress from both Ponce and Bognot airing their grievances against Evangelista and expressing a wish (which George, of course, mistrusted) to remain affiliated with the PPTUS; *ibid.*, pp. 60-1. Bognot's defection, George indicates, was of brief duration and he was subsequently included in the KAP leadership as well as on the first Central Committee of the CPPI in 1930; see Hoeksema, *op. cit.*, p. 76, and Lava, *Milestones*, p. 21.

129

Philippine labor movement.[132] Moscow appeared to take it for granted that the *Congresso Obrero*, under Evangelista's guidance, was moving steadily and voluntarily along the course set forth by the Sixth Comintern Congress. There was too little guile in Moscow's approach. The radical policy was incompatible with the policy of unification, no less than Stalin's strategy of collaboration with the Kuomintang in China in 1927 had been in conflict with the effort to revolutionize the Chinese peasantry. The two policies in the Philippines accordingly moved on a collision course until the COF congress of May 1929 revealed how fragile the labor movement still was.

The role of American Communists in the foregoing developments in the Philippines merits brief consideration, particularly since the American contribution appears negligible on the surface. As early as the Second Comintern Congress, close links had been requested between national revolutionary movements in the colonies and Communist parties in the parent nation. At the Fifth Comintern Congress in 1924 reference was made specifically to the Americans' "duty" to assist the Filipinos.[133] There appears to have been some dissatisfaction, even within the CPUSA, about the way in which this "duty" was being fulfilled. In 1926, for instance, an American Communist berated American workers for not being "in the forefront of the struggle for Filipino liberty."[134] At the Sixth Comintern Congress in 1928, the same American demanded that the CPUSA "without further loss of time" send representatives to the Philippines to form Communist cadres. "Absolutely no effort has been made by our Political Committee to do this," he went on, "despite specific instructions from the Comintern."[135] American Communist records of the 1920's, meanwhile, show little more interest in the

[132] See, for instance, Geller's report at the Fourth Profintern Congress in March 1928; *IV Kongress Profinterna*, p. 451.

[133] See Sen Katayama's remarks in *Fifth Congress of the Communist International*, p. 198.

[134] Manuel Gomez, "The Crisis in Philippine Independence," *Workers Monthly*, October 1926, p. 540; cited in Hoeksema, *op. cit.*, p. 51.

[135] *Inprecor*, October 17, 1928, p. 1319.

Philippines than French Communist records show in Indochina. This negative evidence of significant ties between the American party, itself a fledgling organization and beset by its own internal problems, with the fledgling movement in the Philippines should not obscure the role played by individual Americans. Americans were the most active officials in the PPTUS; Browder was its head and Harrison George one of his principal aides. Inevitably they directed the attention of the Secretariat to the Philippines more than to other countries in the Far East, as the organs and records of this organization show. Not only were the Philippines a major focus of the Pan Pacific Secretariat during its early years but it may also be argued that the Secretariat registered its major accomplishments there. The split in the Philippine labor movement in 1929, while a temporary blow to Soviet designs for labor unity, should not obscure the considerable gains the PPTUS had already made in paving the way for a genuinely Communist movement in the Philippines. It is in this round-about sense that the importance of American Communists to the Philippine movement deserves notice, not for any success in establishing institutional ties between the CPUSA and the proto-Communist organizations of Evangelista and Manahan.

AN OPERATIONS CENTER IN SINGAPORE

Communism in Malaya in the 1920's was a minor offshoot of Communism in China and existed almost solely within the Chinese community in Singapore. The earliest Chinese Communist efforts to establish an organization in Singapore appear to date from the mid-1920's. According to Malayan government records, the Indonesian Alimin is quoted as having said agents from China were in Singapore as early as March 1924. The same source quotes Tan Malaka (who allegedly was designated the Comintern's agent for Southeast Asia in 1923)[136] as saying in 1925 that his Chinese representatives in Singapore were having little success with the Malays because they were "lazy and con-

[136] See above, p. 82n.

tented"; the chief hope, Tan Malaka felt, lay in cultivating the Singapore Chinese. The Kuomintang also played a part in early Communist activities in Malaya, according to these records, especially during the period of Kuomintang-Communist collaboration in China. Legal in Malaya until 1925, the Kuomintang served as a cloak for the Communists; after 1925 the Left Kuomintang created a secret Provisional Committee in Singapore, which was said to be under the direct supervision of the Central Committee of the Chinese Communist Party in Shanghai. The Soviet government is reported to have known of the existence of this center and to have felt that Moscow would not be compromised if it were discovered by the Singapore police; the Provisional Committee was in fact raided by the police and partially disabled early in 1926.[137]

Malayan Communist records confirm this account in its general outline and supply additional details. According to a document dated 1945 which appears to be an official Party history, the progenitor of the Malayan Communist Party, the South Seas (*Nanyang*) Communist Party (SSCP), was created in 1925 by "veteran comrades in China" and is described as "the overseas branch of the CCP." This organization held a Representatives' Conference in 1927, which set up a temporary committee, but due to the "inadequate knowledge" of its members and to "lack of leadership from the Comintern" little was accomplished. In

---

[137] The Malayan government records, although not yet made public, have been consulted by a number of students of Communism in Malaya (including the present writer) and constitute the principal evidence to date of the origins of the Malayan Communist movement: e.g., Brimmell, *Communism in South-East Asia*, pp. 88-96; Pye, *Guerrilla Communism in Malaya*, pp. 47-52; Thompson and Adloff, *The Left Wing in Southeast Asia*, pp. 123-5; Miller, *Menace in Malaya*, Chapter 1; Onraet, *Singapore—A Police Background*, Chapter 8; and Hanrahan, *Communist Struggle in Malaya*, Chapter 1. The latter study relies also on wartime Japanese materials, which appear, in turn, to have been based on the Malayan records. In the view of the present writer the Malayan documents, chief of which is a lengthy account composed in 1950 entitled "Basic Paper on the Malayan Communist Party," need to be treated with some caution since distinctions between hearsay and fact are not always sharply made. However, the account of Malayan Communism given in these records appears accurate on the whole and is corroborated by other materials.

1929, this document continues, directives to the SSCP from the Chinese Communists set forth the "basic lines of struggle."[138]

The Malayan Communists, presumably in response to general Comintern and Profintern instructions on organizing workers, created in May 1926 a parallel trade union organization called the South Seas (*Nanyang*) General Labor Union. The organization affiliated with the PPTUS after that body was established in 1927 and from time to time sent representatives to meetings of the Pan Pacific Secretariat in Shanghai.[139] Its effectiveness in Malaya, however, appears to have been minimal; apart from a major strike organized in March 1928, there is little record of the GLU's activities. A Malayan delegate at a PPTUS meeting in 1929 acknowledged that the union had been able to hold regular annual meetings only in 1926 and 1927 but that since early 1928 government repression had interrupted not only the regular meetings of the GLU but its organizational activities as well; unless help soon came from British workers and from the PPTUS, the GLU would languish.[140]

This meager record of the two principal Communist (or proto-Communist) organizations in Malaya in the 1920's indicates that Moscow's direct role in the *Nanyang* episode was negligible. The Comintern, in the meantime, engaged in no specific discussion of Malaya during the decade, and coverage of Singapore

[138] "History of the Malayan Communist Party," p. 12; also included in the Malayan government archives. A former Malayan Communist interviewed by the writer states that according to the party indoctrination he received after World War II, the date given for the founding of the SSCP was 1927, following the collapse of the united front in China and the arrival in Singapore of Communist refugees; interview with Gerald de Cruz, January 15, 1962. The Malayan government document "Basic Paper on the Malayan Communist Party" gives January 1928 as the founding of the SSCP following the arrival of five representatives from the Chinese Communist Party. Japanese sources also give early 1928 for the founding of the SSCP, adding that the Chinese cadres who came to Singapore to help organize the party were under orders of the Comintern; see Hanrahan, *Communist Struggle in Malaya*, p. 8.

[139] See Harrison George, "Two Years of the PPTUS," *Pan Pacific Monthly*, August 1929, p. 11.

[140] "Malay Labor Steps onto the World Arena," *ibid*, December 1929-January 1930, pp. 22-23.

133

and Malaya in Soviet publications was all but non-existent.[141] There is nonetheless evidence that Moscow was sufficiently aware of developments in Singapore by the end of the decade to feel some concern over the way Communist affairs were being managed there.

One problem, for instance, was the scope of the center's activities throughout Southeast Asia. Whether or not Tan Malaka, as the "Comintern representative" in Southeast Asia, had explicit instructions as early as 1923 or 1924 to coordinate revolutionary activities in the area—there is only his word to prove it—by the end of the decade it is clear that the *Nanyang* organizations did have such responsibilities. Both Communist and non-Communist sources refer to them. An item in the *Pan Pacific Monthly*, for instance, noted in 1929 that the *Nanyang* General Labor Union, "from its center in Singapore, federates the labor movement of Sumatra, Borneo, New Guinea, Celebes, the Malay Peninsula, Burma, Siam and Indo-China."[142] A British police officer who served in Singapore during this period states that the "South Seas Communist Group, controlled by the Chinese Communist Party, comprised the colonies of Great Britain, Holland and France, also Siam and Burma"—in short, all of Southeast Asia but the Philippines.[143] Comintern leaders, as they came to understand better the situation in Southeast Asia, may well have felt the assignment was too ambitious. A few years earlier exiled Indonesian leaders in Singapore had been unable to control even their own comrades a few miles away; how likely was it that the *Nanyang* center could effectively guide multi-national movements even farther away? Moreover increased police surveillance in Singapore in 1928 and 1929 made this port city less suitable as an operations center for Southeast Asia than it may have been a few years earlier. In the meantime the position taken by the Sixth Comintern Congress on the need for separate parties in

[141] The few listings for the 1920's in *Bibliografiia Iugo-vostochnoi Azii* include several items by Pavlovich on the significance of the Singapore naval base and a brief account of Malayan strikes in 1926-1928 (*Materialy po kitaiskomu voprosu*, No. 16, 1928).

[142] *Pan Pacific Monthly*, November 1929, p. 3.

[143] Onraet, *Singapore—A Police Background*, p. 112.

the colonies tended to make regional centers obsolete in Moscow's strategy.

A further problem was the predominantly Chinese orientation of the *Nanyang* organizations, which had a tendency to alienate other racial groups in the area. During the Second Pan Pacific Trade Union Congress in August 1929, and again early in 1930, the South Seas GLU was cautioned on its inattention to the needs of Indian workers in Malaya and asked to conduct special studies of the matter; trade unions in India were called on to send cadres to Malaya to organize the Indian laborers, presumably because the GLU had not done so.[144] At the time of the reorganization of the *Nanyang* groups in 1930 (see below), the PPTUS stated: "The main point to bear in mind is that the Malay worker must be reached and recruited to a greater degree than hitherto, the *Nanyang* Federation having been primarily a Chinese organization."[145] According to Malayan government sources, Nguyen Ai Quoc, said to be the Comintern representative in Singapore at the time of the reorganization, ascribed the failure of the *Nanyang* center to its inability to resolve the racial question.[146]

Apart from the Chinese orientation of the South Seas groups themselves, Moscow may also have felt uneasy about the extension of Chinese Communist influence in Southeast Asia via the Singapore center. It was one thing for Moscow to cite the Chinese revolution as a model for other Asians and to recommend to them the strategies being used in China, but it was quite a different matter to condone Chinese Communist supervision over revolutionary movements elsewhere. This jeopardized the Comintern's hegemony in the world revolution, if not immediately then at some future date. How acute any such rivalry had become in Singapore by 1930 it is impossible to say. The Malayan government sources, and most of the accounts

---

[144] "Indian Labor in Malaya," *Pan Pacific Monthly*, May 1930, pp. 6-7.

[145] *Ibid.*, September-October 1930, p. 40. According to one informant, in 1927 the Indonesian exiles in Singapore proposed that they undertake to organize the Malays while the Singapore Chinese be left to agents from China; the latter refused. Author's interview with Gerald de Cruz, January 1962.

[146] "Basic Paper on the Malayan Communist Party," Vol. 1, Part 2, p. 6.

based on them, lay great stress on this rivalry; no Communist sources, on the other hand—Soviet, Chinese, or Malayan—make reference to it. At best, the argument that Moscow intervened in the affairs of the Singapore center because of jealousy of the Chinese Communists is no more than a plausible hypothesis.

Whatever considerations led to the reorganization in Singapore, it is known that the two *Nanyang* groups ceased to exist in the spring of 1930. At the Third Representatives' Conference in April, the South Seas Communist Party was transformed into the Malayan Communist Party, henceforth to be responsible to the Comintern's Dalburo in Shanghai rather than to the CCP; a "Southern Bureau" of the latter, however, was to be established in Hong Kong to facilitate liaison with Southeast Asia. Separate parties were to be created—and were so before the end of the year—in Indochina and the Philippines, also responsible to the Dalburo. Communist movements in Indonesia, Thailand, and Burma were to be sub-departments of the MCP until they were strong enough to exist independently. Following the April conference, the *Nanyang* GLU was also reorganized as the Malayan General Labor Union (MGLU), its responsibilities now confined to Malaya. According to Malayan government records, the Comintern was represented on this occasion by Nguyen Ai Quoc, whose voice was said to have been decisive.[147]

CONCLUSIONS

What conclusions concerning Soviet policy in Southeast Asia during the 1920's may be drawn from the foregoing record? To put the question as it was put at the outset of this chapter, did Soviet efforts correspond to the promise of them in official pronouncements dating from Lenin's theses of 1920?

[147] The details of the reorganization are taken from *ibid.*, pp. 5-6. The party history notes merely the formation of the MCP at the Second Representatives' Conference (not the Third), but omits other organizational data and makes no reference to Nguyen Ai Quoc; "History of the Malayan Communist Party," p. 12. Nguyen's presence at Singapore is reported by French government sources as well as Malayan (see Gouvernement Général de l'Indochine, *Documents*, IV; cited in Trager, *Marxism in Southeast Asia*, p. 318) but is not mentioned in his official biography ("President Ho Chi Minh," Hanoi).

The "promise," of course, was never explicit. Nor is Soviet behavior in so delicate a matter as the inciting of revolution abroad susceptible of precise analysis. If one were to rely on the official records of British, Dutch, and French colonial administrations, one would conclude that Soviet activity in Southeast Asia was very real and very extensive; colonial officials seem to have taken it for granted that Moscow's open interest in the "Eastern question," expressed at meetings of the Third International and in the Soviet and Comintern press, was proof of an active program to subvert the colonies. By contrast, the student who bases his conclusions on Soviet documentation will be struck by the meager evidence to be found there of a Soviet program in Southeast Asia during these years, let alone of concrete steps to implement one. The tendency of colonial records thus being to expose Communist activity and of Soviet records to conceal it, a definitive judgment in this matter is not easily reached.

Without suggesting the existence of a Comintern network in Southeast Asia comparable to that claimed in Malayan records, it would be idle to take at face value Moscow's bland denials of clandestine ties with emerging Communist movements in the East. The role of the Comintern's Dalburo in Shanghai is illustrative. Its operations, all students of Soviet strategies in Asia agree, are disconcertingly obscure; yet references to this organization, in both Communist and non-Communist sources, are numerous enough to leave little doubt that it existed. If the Dalburo functioned at all as it was presumably designed to, one can readily imagine an accumulation of contacts over the years between authorized Comintern agents and Southeast Asian leaders which would have served to keep the latter informed of Moscow's views on a variety of questions, both local and international, and strengthened their loyalty to Moscow. The activities during this era of Nguyen Ai Quoc are also significant: in 1927, although Soviet records make no mention of it, there is reason to believe that he returned briefly to Moscow. What purpose could such a visit have had if not to give Nguyen an opportunity to review with Comintern leaders, conceivably even with Stalin himself, the course of events in Southeast Asia and to devise a coordinated strategy there? Upon his return, he played a major part in uniting rival factions in Indochina into a single Communist party; soon thereafter he is reported to have played a similar part in the Communist reorganization in Singapore. It would be capricious to deny that Moscow, through Nguyen Ai Quoc, had a hand in these events.

Meanwhile, dozens (if not hundreds) of native Southeast Asians returned home each year from special institutes and training centers throughout Russia—enthusiastic supporters, we may imagine, of Stalin's policies. Beyond the liaison provided through such devices as these, there were agencies such as the Pan Pacific Secretariat and Profintern whose activities further cemented links with the colonial East. Moscow, in short, was not without devices at its disposal to exert a certain influence in Southeast Asia. These devices are not necessarily revealed in Soviet documentation; on the other hand, the likelihood of their reality need not rest on evidence presented by colonial police officials.

When Moscow's engagement in Southeast Asia is viewed in its totality, however, and after due allowance is made for the possibility that more went on than met the eye, it is clear that Soviet efforts were pitched in a relatively low key—a lower key than Lenin's theses would have led one to expect, a lower key than the prospects for revolution in Southeast Asia warranted. It will be helpful to remind ourselves why this was so, although many of the reasons for Moscow's modest interest in Southeast Asia must now be apparent.

It may be noted, preliminarily, that recent Soviet accounts of developments in Southeast Asia in the 1920's provide few insights into the nature of Moscow's policies at that time. Contemporary ideology does not produce convincing history. Recent accounts imply, for instance, that events unfolded in Southeast Asia much as Soviet analysts, attentive to the wisdom of Marxism-Leninism, had always predicted they would. The Southeast Asian colonies in the 1920's, it is asserted, were living through an era not of class struggle itself but of *preparation* for the class struggle. Nationalist movements were emerging and held center-stage; class consciousness was only beginning to appear. Soviet strategy, it is now argued, was accordingly geared to these circumstances. Moscow's part was not agitator, and assuredly not conspirator, but honest patron of any genuinely popular movement against imperialism that needed moral encouragement.[148]

Such a reading of Soviet policy in Southeast Asia in the 1920's confuses hindsight with foresight and makes inaction part of a grand design. The Russians would not, if we judge from their behavior elsewhere, have refrained from a more vigorous role in Southeast Asia for doctrinal reasons alone, at least for the doctrinal reasons indicated in these contemporary histories. Their actions must be laid to more earthly considerations.

One such consideration was the lack of easy access to Southeast Asia. Not only were the political centers of the Southeast Asian colonies distant from Moscow but the growing efficiency of colonial police administrations and the coordination of their activities disrupted Communist networks and frustrated the Comintern's plans for improved liaison. The fact that no Comintern representative, for instance, is known to have been present in Indonesia during the 1920's testifies to the vigilance of the Dutch colonial police as readily as to Moscow's presumed lack of determination to send one. Having made this point, we should take care not to lay too great stress on it. The Comintern was not easily deterred, if we judge from its behavior in other parts of the world, where it felt a "revolutionary duty" involved. Networks shattered by frenzied imperialists could be repaired; agents thrown in jail were replaceable. It is not *frustration* but rather *absence* of program that in the main strikes the student of Soviet policy in Southeast Asia during these years.

The Russians were also comparatively ignorant about Southeast Asia, and this perhaps affected their policies more directly than lack of easy access to the area. The history of Southeast Asia was largely unknown to Russians; the complexities of its social, political, and economic structures remained for some years

---

[148] See, for instance, the chapters on Southeast Asia in *Velikii Oktiabr' i narody Vostoka*, a volume commemorating the fortieth anniversary of the Bolshevik Revolution.

beyond the grasp of those responsible for creating policy. Often all they knew of revolutionary prospects in the Southeast Asian colonies was what was passed on to them, second or third hand, by metropolitan Communists, whose judgments were not always above suspicion. Soviet scholars, meanwhile, were some years in breaking away from the traditional focus of Russian Oriental studies on China; although plans were announced in the mid-1920's, as we have seen, to channel the interest of certain Orientalists into studies of Southeast Asia, it was not until the 1930's that the first significant product of this new emphasis began to appear in Soviet publications.[149]

Still another reason for modest Soviet interest in Southeast Asia was the greater commitment elsewhere. There were not the resources, even if there had been the intent, to press revolutionary programs in all countries. In the East, the principal target was China; whatever talent and energy Stalin chose to devote to revolution in the East was channeled there. In the view of most Soviet and Comintern officials, we may imagine, this effort satisfied Lenin's request at the Second Congress that greater attention be given to the colonial world. The Chinese revolution was the pilot revolution in the East. Had it succeeded, there would, of course, have been no question of a general stimulation of revolutionary activity in Southeast Asia, and the Comintern would have been more attentive to it. The Chinese revolution, however, did not succeed. By the time its failure was acknowledged in Moscow, other events had intervened to deter a second effort of any consequence in East Asia. Moreover, the failure in China evidently seemed to Stalin to close off for the present the Eastern route to world Communism which had been discussed intermittently since 1917. No alternate prospects in the East were seriously considered.

A final reason for the meager attention devoted to Southeast Asia during the 1920's—a reason related to the limitation of the

---

[149] The quantitative difference in the focus of Russian Orientalists, as between Southeast Asia and China, is made clear in a comparison between *Bibliografiia Iugo-vostochnoi Azii*, which lists fewer than a dozen significant monographs on Southeast Asia before the Revolution and not many more from 1917 to 1930, and Skachkov, *Bibliografiia Kitaia*, which lists hundreds for both periods.

Comintern's resources—was the predominantly European cast of the International during its first decade. This is reflected in the scant and reluctant attention given to Eastern questions in the plenary and other meetings of the Comintern. It is also seen in the negligible assistance given the colonial movements by metropolitan parties, despite repeated requests by the ECCI that such assistance be provided. The PKI, an ex-Comintern official was later to write of the Indonesian party during its 1926-1927 uprising, was "Communist only in the vaguest sense of the word."[150] If this judgment of the oldest and for some years the largest Communist party in Asia accurately represents the Comintern's estimate at the time, it is easy to imagine that the International gave little serious thought to active support of such a party, let alone of haphazard Marxian and proto-Marxian movements where no Communist organization yet existed. Lenin and Stalin, it may be argued, opposed such an attitude within the International—Lenin because of a belief that developments in the East could truly hasten world revolution, Stalin because for some years he followed Lenin in this matter and because, tending to equate all revolutionary movements which were non-Russian, he was relatively free of prejudice as between East and West. Their detachment in this matter, however, seems not to have penetrated into the psychology and outlook of the International, whose focus remained riveted to Europe. Serrati's bias, for all the official abuse heaped upon it and upon him personally, remained dominant in the Comintern.

[150] Borkenau, *Communist International*, p. 288.

CHAPTER THREE

Eastern Strategies in Abeyance: 1930-1935

THE year 1930 marks a watershed in Soviet foreign policy.
It separates an era of policies affected by the NEP, by the
Rapallo association with Germany, and by internal uneasiness in
Russia following Lenin's death from an era of policies influenced by the First Five Year Plan, by the search for collective
security, and by Stalin's grasp of unchallenged control of the
USSR. It marks the end of a period when Soviet foreign policy,
in both its diplomatic and revolutionary manifestations, could
still be debated in Moscow with some freedom and the beginning of a period when the range of significant debate was sharply
curtailed by Stalin's ascendancy. The Comintern in particular
ceased to have reality as an international forum for the articulation of world revolutionary strategies. The records of its deliberations after 1930, if published at all, were now closely
edited to reflect Stalin's outlook; Comintern publications, except
in rare cases, ceased to convey explicit instructions to local Communist movements and increasingly took on the character of
mere commentaries on world affairs.

One should not, of course, insist on the year 1930 as the watershed between these two eras. A case could be made for a year,
or even two years, earlier or later; students of Soviet foreign
policy are not agreed on where best to set the dividing line. Nor
does it greatly matter. There is always an element of the arbitrary
in historical periodization. For our purposes, the establishment
of no fewer than three new Communist parties in Southeast
Asia during 1930, directly or indirectly inspired in Moscow, provides reason enough for the selection of that year as marking a
somewhat altered course of Communism in this sector of the
colonial world. Whether Soviet interest in Southeast Asia was
in any sense stimulated by the emergence of these new parties
we shall seek to discover.

Following the pattern used in this study so far, we will consider Moscow's colonial policy in general between the Sixth and

Seventh Comintern Congresses (but in less detail than in Chapter One since few new formulations appear) before taking up Soviet policies in Southeast Asia proper.

SOVIET POLICY BETWEEN THE SIXTH AND SEVENTH WORLD CONGRESSES

Readers of the Comintern press in the early 1930's must have detected little fundamental shift in Moscow's strategies. The formulations of the Sixth Comintern Congress of 1928—formulations which it has been remarked were more aggressive in tone than those of earlier congresses—continued in force. The mood of the Eleventh Plenum of the ECCI in March 1931 recalled the mood of the International soon after its formation a dozen years before. Manuilsky, reporting to the plenum, compared the current revolutionary upsurge throughout the world to the "first round" of revolutionary upheaval following the Bolshevik Revolution; it was distinguishable from the latter only "by the fact that it has not yet reached the full intensity of the upsurge of 1918-1919"; on the other hand, the growing strength of the USSR, the existence of Communist parties in many countries, the experience gained by workers during the preceding decade, and the growing "contradiction" in the capitalist world as the result of world depression were factors which made the revolutionary outlook especially promising.[1] The last two plenary meetings of the ECCI, the Twelfth in September 1932 and the Thirteenth in December 1933, reaffirmed this reading of revolutionary prospects throughout the world. The "end of capitalist stabilization" was repeatedly proclaimed at the Twelfth Plenum and "a new round of revolutions" said to be imminent; the theses of the Thirteenth Plenum stated that it would be "a Right Opportunist error . . . to fail to see now the objective tendencies of the accelerated maturing of a revolutionary crisis in the capitalist world."[2] The tactics the Comintern urged upon its sections

---

[1] Manuilsky, *The Communist Parties and the Crisis of Capitalism*, p. 44.

[2] *Theses and Decisions, Thirteenth Plenum of the ECCI*, p. 9. The full record of the Twelfth Plenum is contained in *XII plenum IKKI: stenograficheskii otchet*, 3 vols.; an abbreviated account in English may be found in *Guide to the XII Plenum ECCI* (New York, 1932).

to make the most of these alleged opportunities also remained largely unchanged between the Sixth and Seventh Congresses. They consisted in the main of the united front from below and implacable opposition to social democrats, reformists, and all who failed to adhere strictly to Moscow's line.

The colonial world did not engage the Comintern's attention appreciably more than it had during the preceding decade. Events in Europe, in the Comintern's view, continued to overshadow events in the East (except perhaps in China, which remained a focal point of Moscow's interest and where Soviet and Comintern writers continued, as best they could, to follow developments in the Chinese soviet areas).[3] None of the plenary sessions of the ECCI between 1928 and 1935 more than touched in passing on the "Eastern question." Comintern journals—although their coverage of developments in Southeast Asia constitutes the principal evidence of Moscow's policies there—devoted no more than five percent of their space to colonial affairs in general.

The Comintern's comparatively meager interest in the colonies contrasts with the increased activity of Russian Orientalists during these years. Several new Orientalist journals came into existence.[4] The first scholarly monographs of note—including several which dealt with Southeast Asia—began to appear. Orientalist conferences took up critical questions of colonial policy and set the tone for "instructions" forwarded through one channel or another to colonial parties. A meeting of Soviet Orientalists in mid-1934 discussed at some length the need for "proletarian hegemony" in colonial movements and established this as the "basic strategic objective" of Communist parties in the East.[5]

---

[3] The difficulties Soviet writers encountered in gaining accurate information on the Chinese soviet movement is suggested, for instance, in a published Comintern report of Mao Tse-tung's untimely death of consumption in 1930; *Inprecor*, March 13, 1930, p. 259. For Soviet and Comintern coverage of Chinese Communism during the early 1930's, see Skachkov, *Bibliografiia Kitaia*, 2nd ed., 1960.

[4] E.g., *Materialy po natsional'no-kolonial'nym problemam* (1931); *Kolonial'nye problemy* (1933, irregular); and *Tikhii okean* (1934). See Bibliography for fuller identification of these Orientalist journals.

[5] The keynote address at the conference, delivered by the former Comintern agent in China, Pavel' Mif, was published in *Bol'shevik*, No. 19-20, November 7, 1934, pp. 84-96; the remaining papers read at the month-long conference were published in *Kolonial'nye problemy*, sb. 3-4, 1935.

The activity of the Orientalists, then, adds a new dimension to Soviet colonial policy and lightens the task of the student of Russian affairs. One should not imagine, however, that Orientalist scholars replaced, or could replace, spokesmen for the Soviet government or for the Comintern; the contribution of these scholars to Soviet colonial policy was orderly and useful, but unofficial. The relative absence of sustained official interest in colonial affairs, except in China, remains the principal characteristic of Moscow's Eastern policy during the years between the Sixth and Seventh World Congresses. This is underscored by the fact that Stalin rarely commented on the Eastern question during this period.

Moscow's view of revolutionary prospects in the East paralleled the official view of revolutionary prospects elsewhere in the world. "The colonial East," an authoritative Soviet spokesman wrote in 1930, "is entering a new stage of revolutionary upsurge somewhat more intense than the tide of 1919-1922 and that which China experienced in 1925-1927."[6] This situation, he continued, required more vigorous organizational efforts: "The organization of the struggle for proletarian leadership of the colonial revolution and the organization of the proletarian-peasant revolutionary front from below are the necessary conditions for the further revolutionizing of the masses and for neutralizing the efforts of the bourgeois liberals to choke off revolutionary activity. . . . The key to the resolution of this question is obviously the formation of a Communist party in every country in the East."[7]

The chief task of the colonial peoples, the same author wrote a few months later, is "the struggle for the soviet dictatorship of workers and peasants."[8] Two years later, on the occasion of the fifteenth anniversary of the Bolshevik Revolution, another Soviet spokesman asserted that "the colonial world is entering a new October epoch."[9]

[6] G. Safarov, "Na fronte kolonial'noi revoliutsii," *Bol'shevik*, No. 15-16, August 31, 1930, p. 69.

[7] *Ibid.*, p. 85.

[8] G. Safarov, "Oktiabr' i kolonial'naia revoliutsiia," *Bol'shevik*, No. 19-20, October 31, 1930, p. 54.

[9] L. Geller, "Oktiabr'skaia revoliutsiia i ugnetennye narody kolonii," *Mirovoe*

Moscow's exuberance, it is clear in retrospect, was ill-founded. Although isolated instances of mutiny and insurrection occurred in Southeast Asia, at no time during the period under review was the general conflagration foreseen in the colonial world imminent in reality. Even in China, where Communist prospects were said to have been most promising, it was openly acknowledged in later years that the early 1930's represented the nadir of the revolutionary movement there.[10]

Official optimism in Moscow regarding revolutionary prospects in the East was not only unwarranted it was also misleading, for it implied a more vigorous Soviet engagement in colonial affairs than can be shown. We have already noted the relative lack of public interest in the East expressed by Soviet and Comintern spokesmen; the absence of operational ties with colonial movements is even more marked. A gradual withdrawal of the Comintern from direct participation in Eastern affairs between the Sixth and Seventh Congresses can be detected. In China, for instance, where Soviet and Comintern agents were particularly active during the 1920's, there appears to have been no significant Comintern representative with the Communists following the departure of Pavel' Mif early in 1931.[11] Nor is there known to have been sustained contact with Communist organizations in Japan, the Philippines, Indochina, Korea, Malaya, India, and in other Eastern countries, despite the fact that these organizations were normally based in cities where clandestine ties, had Moscow sought them, would have been possible. The Comintern's Dalburo in Shanghai, meanwhile, was shattered in 1931. This organization, we have seen, had been given responsibility the year before for coordinating Communist activities not only

---

khoziaistvo i mirovaia politika, No. 10, October, 1932, p. 83. See also McKenzie, *Comintern and World Revolution*, p. 138.

[10] A Chinese Communist historian, writing in 1950, refers to this era as the "low ebb" of his party's fortunes; Ch'ang Shao-wen, "Short History of the Labor Movement," *Ta Kung Pao* (Shanghai), November 1950-February 1951 (translated in *Current Background*, Hong Kong, No. 108).

[11] The question of Comintern representation in China in the 1930's is discussed in the author's *Soviet Policy and the Chinese Communists*, pp. 152-5.

in Northeast Asia but, via the Southern Bureau of the Chinese Communist Party in Hong Kong and the new Malayan Communist Party, in Southeast Asia as well. Its enlarged role was short-lived. According to Malayan government sources, a series of police raids and arrests brought to an end this elaborate Comintern network for the Far East: in December 1930 the Hong Kong police discovered and crushed the Southern Bureau of the CCP; in June 1931 an agent of the Pan Pacific Secretariat, Joseph Ducroix (Serge Lefranc), was arrested in Singapore; his revelations led to further exposure of the Dalburo's plans and to the arrest soon thereafter of Hilaire Noulens in Shanghai and Nguyen Ai Quoc in Hong Kong.[12] The Dalburo, always a shadowy organization, is believed not to have recovered from these blows. A successor organization, referred to as the "Comintern apparatus," is reported in Malayan police records to have been established in Shanghai two years later,[13] but if it functioned at all it did so on a far less ambitious plane.

Quite apart from the continued lower priority of the East as compared to the West in Moscow's calculations, there is, then, a significant discrepancy between what Moscow said of the colonial world and what it was prepared to, or could, do there. Revolutionary prospects were viewed as more favorable than during the preceding decade, but efforts to advance these prospects were more sparing. We will need in due course to consider in greater detail why this was so. For the present, we turn to Moscow's policies (such as they were) in Southeast Asia proper, against this background of a weakened Comintern posture in the East.

THE COURSE OF COMMUNISM IN INDOCHINA

The Communist Party of Indochina had been organized at a moment of national crisis: the mutiny in February 1930 of Vietnamese soldiers garrisoned at Enbay in Annam. The Communists

---

[12] "Basic Paper on the Malayan Communist Party," Vol. I, Part 2, pp. 6-7; see also Onraet, *Singapore—a Police Background*, p. 114, and T'ang Leang-li, *Suppressing Communist Banditry in China* (Shanghai, 1934), pp. 70-1.

[13] "Basic Paper on the Malayan Communist Party," Vol. I, Part 2, p. 9.

147

were not involved in the early phases of the disorders, and indeed denied, somewhat regretfully, any responsibility for the mutiny,[14] but they were in a sense the beneficiaries. "Communism in Indochina," the French Socialist leader Edouard Daladier observed, in response to rumors of Communist complicity in the rising, "is not the cause of the events at Enbay, but the consequence."[15] In the sense of a very great advantage accruing to the Communists in the aftermath of the insurrection, Daladier's observation was accurate.

The origins of the Enbay mutiny can be found in the rapid deterioration of the Indochinese economy under the impact of world depression. Foreign trade declined, investment fell off sharply, and living conditions throughout the colony had by 1930 reached the lowest point in many years. These circumstances, taken together with the repressive measures pursued by the French government following the relatively liberal regime of Varenne in 1925-1927, gave fresh impetus to the nationalist movement in the colony. The rising at Enbay was accordingly nationalist in inspiration, not Communist.

Moscow was not unaware of the tension building up in Indochina on the eve of the Enbay episode. According to one student of French Communism, in December 1929 Moscow directed the FCP to redouble its attention to Indochina because of the mounting crisis there.[16] A month before the insurrection, an article in *Inprecor* deplored the "unheard of terror" in Indochina and noted a marked increase in revolutionary activity.[17] When the Enbay garrison mutinied, although Moscow presumably knew that no Communists were involved, Soviet-controlled organiza-

[14] Jacques Doriot, for instance, the French Communist leader in closest touch at this time with developments in Indochina, wrote shortly after the outbreak of the mutiny: "We may be grateful that the Communist Party of Indochina is described as having played a role at Enbay which it did not in fact play—but which it soon will"; quoted in Dantsig, *Indokitai*, p. 110.

[15] *Ibid.*

[16] Walter, *Histoire du parti communiste français*, p. 377.

[17] A.N., "The Terror in Indochina and the Development of the Revolutionary Movement," *Inprecor*, January 16, 1930, p. 46; the article was reprinted in *Pan Pacific Monthly*, February 1930, pp. 34-5.

tions applauded the nationalist organizers of the revolt. On February 20, the International Secretariat of the Anti-Imperialist League in Berlin praised the uprising and called it "one of the signals of the coming storm in Indochina."[18] Throughout the spring Comintern and Profintern organs protested the trial of the "Indochinese patriots" responsible for the Enbay mutiny and appealed to the proletarians of the world to support the Vietnamese revolutionaries.[19]

The Vietnamese nationalists, however, did not succeed. The Enbay mutiny itself was suppressed within twenty-four hours and the related disorders elsewhere in the country within a fortnight. The leaders of the uprisings, for the most part members of the Vietnam Nationalist Party (known as the Vietnam Kuomintang), were arrested, tried, and many executed.[20] Leadership accordingly passed to the Communists, who were relatively untouched by the first round of trials in Saigon. By June Comintern journals were noting the extension of the Indochinese revolution under Communist control.[21] It was the latter circumstance, we may imagine, which led Stalin, in his report to the Sixteenth Party Congress in mid-1930, to commend the experience of the Indochinese revolutionaries to other Eastern peoples. When one recalls that Stalin rarely made direct reference to the Southeast Asian colonies, some significance may be attached to his singling out Indochina in this instance.[22]

It is doubtful whether the young Indochinese Communist Party was prepared for the role thrust upon it. Unified only on the eve of the Enbay episode, its leadership, according to a Comintern spokesman in June 1930, continued to exhibit "sec-

[18] *Inprecor*, February 20, 1930, pp. 164-5.

[19] E.g., *Pan Pacific Monthly*, April 1930, p. 48, and *Inprecor*, May 22, 1930, p. 437.

[20] According to one Russian account, based on French and Vietnamese sources, the trials of the nationalists in February and March 1930 led to 58 executions (22 by guillotine), 61 life imprisonments, and 42 prison sentences of varying length; another 576 lesser leaders were tried later in the year. See Dantsig, *Indokitai*, p. 107.

[21] J. Berlioz, "The Revolt in Indochina Is Spreading," *Inprecor*, June 12, 1930, p. 508.

[22] Stalin, *Sochineniia*, XII, pp. 250, 258, 318.

tarian tendencies."[23] Its initial manifesto, moreover, hardly provided guidance to a party engaged so soon after its formation in
a vigorous revolutionary effort. This document, allegedly authored by Nguyen Ai Quoc early in 1930, listed objectives which
were normal for all colonial Communist movements at this juncture—overthrow of imperialism, nationalization of banks and
syndicates, confiscation of land, eight-hour day, reduction of
rents, increased education, and so forth—but made no reference
either to armed uprising or to the formation of soviets.[24] Since
both armed uprising and soviets figured prominently in CPIC
activity during the latter part of 1930, it must be imagined that
the Vietnamese, either on their own initiative or on foreign advice, formally adopted these slogans during the late spring or
summer. The restless mood of the Indochinese population after
Enbay and perhaps some impact of the events at Changsha (in
South China) in July[25] must also have inspired a more vigorous strategy than the initial manifesto had called for. By mid-
summer local soviets were formed in sections of North Annam
and Cochin China.[26]

The Communist phase of the so-called Enbay era, although
longer than the nationalist phase, ultimately accomplished no
more. Comintern journals continued during the latter part of
1930 and through 1931 to speak of an unremitting revolutionary
surge in Indochina, but subsequent accounts make it clear that
the "climax" of the Communist effort was in September 1930

[23] Berlioz, *loc. cit.*

[24] The text of the 10-point 1930 manifesto is included in "President Ho Chi
Minh" (Hanoi, 1960).

[25] Changsha, capital of Hunan province, was the scene of a short-lived Communist *coup* late in July 1930; "soviet power" was proclaimed in the city but
lasted only three days.

[26] One Russian source gives August 1 as the date of the first soviet formed in
Indochina and claims that by September the greater part of the two northernmost provinces in Annam were under soviet control; *Materialy po natsional'no-
kolonial'nym problemam*, No. 1, 1931, p. 55. Another Russian source states that
the first soviets were formed "spontaneously," without the knowledge even of the
party Central Committee, but soon came under the leadership of local Communist
cells; *Kolonial'nye problemy*, *sb.* 3-4, p. 119.

and that the last soviets were crushed by January 1931.[27] Communist casualties were heavy, although evidently no more so than nationalist casualties after Enbay.[28] In 1933 a Vietnamese Communist is reported to have said that as a result of the government's actions "all the leading comrades are arrested and the party apparatus is destroyed in the center as well as locally."[29] In 1934 an authoritative Russian source acknowledged a sharp decline in Communist activity in Indochina following the collapse of the soviet movement of 1930.[30]

Post-mortems on the Enbay era reversed certain judgments that were made at the time. The nationalists, for instance, who as late as October 1930 had been praised in the Comintern press as "courageous patriots,"[31] were bitterly attacked in later years. A Soviet writer observed in 1932 that the Enbay episode marked the defection of bourgeois nationalist leadership in Indochina.[32] The 1932 "Program of Action" of the CPIC, which was published in Moscow and had the Comintern's endorsement, had this to say of the behavior of Vietnamese nationalists during the "immortal" days of Enbay: "The nationalist leadership, made up for the most part of petty officials, merchants and village elders, neither in its tactics nor in its programs attempted a resolu-

---

[27] Vasil'eva, *Indo-Kitai*, p. 201. Varying evidence is given of the duration of the Indochinese soviets. One Russian source indicates they lasted altogether five months (*Materialy po natsional'no-kolonial'nym problemam*, No. 1, 1931, p. 55); another gives four months (*Kolonial'nye problemy*, sb. 3-4, p. 119); and a Vietnamese source claims only two or three months (*Inprecor*, October 7, 1935, p. 1294).

[28] According to Soviet sources, 8 Communists were given the death penalty, 19 were sentenced to life imprisonment, and 79 to shorter terms during the Saigon trials of 1933 (as compared to 58, 61, and 42 nationalists, respectively, in the trials immediately after Enbay); Vasil'eva, *op. cit.*, p. 203. A total of 16,000 Indochinese, according to French sources cited by Vasil'eva, were imprisoned during 1930 and 1931; *ibid.*, p. 202.

[29] Orgwald, *Tactical and Organizational Questions of the Communist Parties of India and Indochina*, p. 74.

[30] *Programmnye dokumenty Kommunisticheskikh partii Vostoka*, p. 113.

[31] *Inprecor*, October 12, 1930, p. 982.

[32] L. Geller, "Oktiabr'skaia revoliutsiia i ugnetennye narody kolonii," *Mirovoe khoziaistvo i mirovaia politika*, No. 10, October 1932, p. 80.

151

tion of the basic tasks of the revolution, especially of the agrarian revolution. Isolated at all times from the masses, it persisted in following a petty bourgeois policy of compromise. Even during the Enbay affair itself nationalist leaders were seeking agreement with the imperialists on the condition of receiving certain insignificant concessions."[33]

If the nationalists, understandably, were made the scapegoats of the 1930-1931 failures, the Communists were not held blameless in Moscow's post-mortems. Inadequate policies regarding the agrarian question were laid also to the Communist leadership. One of the leading Soviet authorities on Indochina, V. Vasil'eva, argued in 1934 that this was a basic reason for the failure of the soviet movement of 1930: confiscation of land should have been far more extensive than it was (only holdings in excess of 100 hectares had been seized) and the land confiscated should have been redivided among the middle as well as poorer peasants. The attempt to collectivize, Vasil'eva continued, was "a huge error at the given juncture because it frustrated the peasant's struggle for land."[34] Another Soviet Orientalist argued that in over-emphasizing the struggle for independence the Communists ignored the "struggle of the peasants for land" and so lost their support at a critical juncture.[35]

The Vietnamese comrades were also charged in later years with having "underestimated the influence of national reformism among the masses."[36] It is not clear in the Indochinese context which elements were identified as "national reformists," but the charge doubtless relates to the persistent "sectarianism" which, according to Comintern accounts, troubled the CPIC. A Vietnamese delegate at the Seventh Comintern Congress in 1935 acknowledged that many comrades, both during and after the Enbay era, had exhibited "indescribable confusion in regard to the

[33] *Programmnye dokumenty Kommunisticheskikh partii Vostoka*, p. 119; see also the endorsement of this view in R. Minin, "Enbaiskoe vosstanie," *Revoliutsionnyi Vostok*, No. 3 (31), 1935, p. 89.

[34] *Kolonial'nye problemy*, sb. 3-4, 1935, p. 119.

[35] R. Minin, "Obzor kommunisticheskoi pechati Indokitaia," *Revoliutsionnyi Vostok*, No. 4 (32), 1935, p. 248.

[36] *Ibid.*, p. 248.

tasks and the stage of the revolution facing our country"; he explained this confusion by noting that many party members had brought "sectarian putschist ideas from the national reformist parties and the old [pre-1930] Communist groups."[37]

Criticism of the Vietnamese Communists after Enbay in no sense implied lack of sympathy for the revolutionary movement in Indochina. On the contrary, if the Enbay episode accomplished nothing else, it brought Indochina more firmly into Moscow's focus than it had been throughout the preceding decade. During the Enbay era, coverage of developments in Indochina in Soviet and Comintern publications was more intense than of any other events in Southeast Asia to date, including the 1926-1927 uprisings in Indonesia, and it continued so for some years.[38] Manuilsky, reporting to the Eleventh Plenum of the ECCI in March 1931, ranked Indochina after only China and India in his brief discussion of the colonial and semi-colonial world.[39] As late as 1934, when the revolutionary movement in the French colony was at a particularly low ebb, Indochina maintained the same rank in articles on the colonial question written by the influential Orientalist Pavel' Mif.[40] Whether or not this continued focus on Indochina was the consequence of the Enbay era it is difficult to say. Other considerations are also pertinent. For instance, revolutionary movements elsewhere in Southeast Asia which had appeared promising a few years earlier, such as in Indonesia and Malaya, were moribund early in the 1930's, giving some point to an emphasis on the one Southeast Asian colony where conditions were still thought to favor revolutionary upheaval. There was, moreover, the hope that as the soviet movement gained strength in South China it might link up with a parallel movement in the northern provinces of Indochina—a hope that was often expressed by Russian writers, as we shall see.

[37] *Inprecor*, October 7, 1935, p. 1295.

[38] See, for instance, the items listed in *Bibliografiia Iugo-vostochnoi Azii*, pp. 95-9.

[39] Manuilsky, *The Communist Parties and the Crisis of Capitalism*, pp. 60, 80, 102.

[40] See his articles in *Revoliutsionnyi Vostok*, No. 3 (25), 1934, pp. 5-14, and in *Bol'shevik*, No. 19-20, November 7, 1934, pp. 84-96.

Eastern Strategies in Abeyance: 1930-1935

Whatever considerations prompted Soviet attention to Indochina after the Enbay insurrection, it became apparent that Moscow was not indifferent to the course of events in this critical area.

Developments within the Communist Party of Indochina after the 1930-1931 uprisings are obscure. The present study is not directly concerned with these developments, but it may be useful to review briefly the fragmentary information available in order to comprehend more clearly the relationship of French, Chinese, and international Communism to the Indochinese movement.

The earliest Secretary of the CPIC, according to a Comintern source, was Li-Kwei, elected shortly after the unification of the party in 1930. Under his leadership the party was said to have become a "truly mass party" and to have adopted theses, authored by Li-Kwei, "which clearly proclaimed the principles of action and the tactics of the Bolsheviks." Li-Kwei's death in prison, following his arrest in Saigon in April 1931, was made the occasion for a flattering obituary in *Communist International*.[41] Sources seen by this writer do not indicate who succeeded Li-Kwei, but one student of Vietnamese Communism states that an underground apparatus was created early in 1933 by Tran Van Giau, a Vietnamese student recently returned from the Oriental University in Moscow.[42] Nguyen Ai Quoc evidently played a negligible role in intraparty affairs after his success in unifying the party in Hong Kong in February 1930. He was arrested in Hong Kong in June 1931, released two years later, and following a short sojourn in Shanghai evidently left for Moscow at the end of 1933; he remained there until 1935.[43] The present writer has discovered only one reference to Nguyen in

[41] *Communist International*, No. 8, May 1, 1932, pp. 289-90. A contemporary Vietnamese historian gives the name of the first Secretary General of the Indochinese party as Chan Fu, which may be a pseudonym of Li-Kwei; Min' Shan', "Revoliutsionnoe dvizhenie v V'etname," *Sovetskoe Vostokovedenie*, No. 1, 1956, p. 39.

[42] I. Milton Sacks, "Marxism in Viet Nam," in Trager, *Marxism in Southeast Asia*, p. 133; Professor Sacks gives no documentation for his statement.

[43] The Shanghai and Moscow visits of Nguyen Ai Quoc are mentioned, with few details, in "President Ho Chi Minh."

154

Comintern materials of the early 1930's: an appeal for international support of the "founder of the Communist Party of Indochina" following his release from jail in Hong Kong in mid-1933.[44]

The Indochinese party evidently held several plenary meetings and conferences during the early years of its existence, although what transpired at them is not clear. The Li-Kwei obituary refers to a First and Second Plenum, held respectively in November 1930 and April 1931, which adopted his political theses. There was presumably a conference during 1932 to approve the party's "Program of Action." In April 1933 a party conference is reported to have been held in Thailand, but without representation from all parts of Indochina.[45] The Central Committee was also reported to have been located in Thailand at that juncture and probably remained outside Indochina until after the First Party Congress, held in Macao in 1935. The fact that the Central Committee was called "provisional" during these years suggests the still tentative nature of the party's organization and leadership.[46]

The day-to-day activities of the Indochinese party are even more obscure than the constitution of its leadership and the location of its central organs. Most sources indicate that the major preoccupation of the cadres after the Enbay era was to evade arrest and maintain some kind of contact with each other. Only sporadically and from deep underground were the Vietnamese Communists able to coordinate their energies in a common effort. During the Saigon trials of 1933, for instance, they organized a campaign for the release of the imprisoned victims of the 1930-1931 uprisings. The same year the Communists participated in the election of the Saigon Municipal Council: a united front organization called *La Lutte*, including Trotskyists —then a powerful group in Indochina—and other revolution-

---

[44] *Inprecor*, June 16, 1933, p. 575.

[45] Trager, *op. cit.*, p. 133.

[46] Reference to the "provisional" Central Committee of the CPIC is made in several sources: e.g., XXX, "Vers le renforcement du parti communiste indochinois," *Cahiers du Communisme*, July 1, 1934, p. 799, and *Programmnye dokumenty Kommunisticheskikh partii Vostoka*, p. 114.

aries as well as Communists, put forth a "workers' list" of eight candidates, of whom two were elected. Their election, however, was subsequently annulled by the authorities on legal technicalities and the organization's newspaper, also called *La Lutte*, was suspended for a year and a half.[47] Early in 1935 the Communists again took part in an election, again in collaboration with Trotskyists and other revolutionary elements under the banner of *La Lutte*. On this occasion four of the "workers' opposition" slate of six were elected.[48] In both elections *La Lutte's* platform was moderate, stressing civil liberties and welfare measures and keeping clear of revolutionary slogans.

The Communists also maintained an underground press in Indochina. By 1935 there were as many as six Communist newspapers and periodicals appearing irregularly in Vietnamese. A detailed Soviet analysis of these publications in 1935 found that, while all but one (a theoretical journal entitled *Bolshevik*) were weak in Marxist formulations and "too abstract" in exposing Trotskyism and "national reformism," they had recently displayed a commendable expansion of their international coverage, including data on the Chinese soviet movement, on the Five Year Plans in Russia, and on developments in France, Spain, and Cuba.[49] The very existence of six clandestine Communist organs in 1935, of course, implies a measure of recovery from the low point of the party's fortunes in 1932 and 1933.

The Vietnamese Communists were guided during these years by the "Program of Action" adopted in 1932. The document, often cited in accounts of Indochinese Communism and endorsed by Moscow, bears inspection.[50] The first part of the program, entitled "Basic Tasks of the Indochinese Revolution," is a

[47] Trager, *op. cit.*, pp. 133-5.
[48] *Ibid.*, pp. 138-9; see also Gabriel Péri, "The Anti-Imperialist Front in the Elections to the Colonial Council in Indochina," *Inprecor*, March 23, 1935, p. 353.
[49] R. Minin, "Obzor kommunisticheskoi pechati Indokitaia," *Revoliutsionnyi Vostok*, No. 4 (32), 1935, pp. 247-55.
[50] It was published as a brochure in Annamese in 1932, in *L'Humanité* (in French) the same year, and translated into Russian in *Kommunisticheskii internatsional*, No. 34, 1932; the text used by the present writer is in *Programmnye dokumenty Kommunisticheskikh partii Vostoka*, pp. 114-30.

relatively sophisticated appraisal of recent developments in Indochina seen in an international context and bears the mark of foreign influence, probably French. France is seen as building Indochina into its Far Eastern "arsenal," from which it can more easily defend its imperialist interests in Asia and move against the Chinese soviets. The main purpose in suppressing the revolutionary movement in the colony, the program argues, is to give "French militarists a free hand in preparing intervention against the USSR." References to the Soviet Union and to the Chinese soviets abound throughout the document, and both are included prominently in the concluding hosannas. The French proletariat is considered the "closest ally" of the Vietnamese. "The struggle of the French workers is indissolubly linked with the struggle of the workers and toilers of Indochina against their common enemy, French imperialism."

The ten tasks listed in the program are in some respects similar to those of Nguyen Ai Quoc's ten-point manifesto of 1930, but go well beyond it. There is, for instance, a specific appeal for soviets and for a "revolutionary workers' and peasants' army." Self-determination is promised for the Laotians, Cambodians, and other national minorities in French Indochina. Above all, the 1932 program meets more bluntly than its predecessor the question of armed uprising: "Only through armed struggle can liberation be achieved." One of the terminal slogans put forward in the program is "Long live the revolutionary insurrection for independence and for land!"

The 1932 "Program of Action" of the Indochinese Communists, as much as any other document to come out of Southeast Asia during these years, testifies to the quickening tempo of the revolutionary movement in Asia—at least in the words and slogans it was prepared to use.

The relative indifference of foreign Communism, particularly French Communism, to developments in Indochina during the 1920's, we have seen, was one reason for the failure of Vietnamese Marxists to combine forces. This situation changed during the 1930's. Primary responsibility for the development of

157

Communism in Indochina remained with the French Communists, and there is evidence that they took this responsibility more seriously. The French Communist press, for instance, gave increased coverage to Indochinese affairs. Party leaders were more outspoken in their support of the Vietnamese comrades.

Maurice Thorez, in an impassioned speech before the Chamber of Deputies early in 1933, denounced the government's harsh treatment of Communists in the colony and in particular their exclusion from an amnesty bill then under consideration. He proclaimed the "complete solidarity of the French proletariat with the Communist Party of Indochina."[51] An Amnesty Committee in Defense of the Indochinese and Colonial Peoples was organized in France, and a call issued for mass demonstrations in behalf of the Vietnamese Communists and for protest telegrams to President Lebrun.[52]

In January 1934 a "workers' delegation" organized by the *Confédération Général du Travail* (CGT) was sent on a three-month tour of Indochina to investigate the crisis brought on by the Saigon trials. The delegation, the first of its kind to visit Indochina, included several Communists, who reported extensively to French workers when they returned. Although denied permission to travel in Annam and Tonking, the delegation made contact with Vietnamese Communists and claimed to have greatly raised their morale. A report on the visit by the Communist deputy Gabriel Péri asserted that, although the Indochinese party was harassed, it was not crippled. "After every bloody orgy of French imperialism, it has succeeded in mobilizing and organizing its forces to continue the struggle." Péri urged French workers to "support the toiling mass of Indochina and their Communist Party in their efforts to obtain independence."[53]

An anonymous article published shortly after Péri's report also asserted the revival of Indochinese Communism, contrary to "Trotskyist" claims, but expressed some criticism of the party

[51] *Inprecor*, March 31, 1933, p. 348.
[52] *Ibid.*, June 16, 1933, p. 575.
[53] Gabriel Péri, "The Workers' Delegation in Indochina," *ibid.*, June 8, 1934, pp. 884-5.

where Péri had given only praise. The greater part of the article was an attack on a "Leftist" element in the Vietnamese party on three counts: first, for urging the destruction of French troops in Indochina, instead of easing them out so that French soldiers could assist the revolutionary movement at home; second, for proposing self-determination for the minority peoples in Indochina, instead of seeking "a close union of the Annamites with the Cambodians, Laotians, and other nationalities . . . against imperialism and feudalism"; third, for misunderstanding the principles of "democratic centralism" in not accepting the decisions of the party's central bodies. The article concludes with a reminder of the importance "above all of the constant guidance of the Comintern."[54]

Although the article is obscure on some issues, taken as a whole it comes closer than any other statement published in France during these years to an official instruction to the Vietnamese comrades. There is implicit in the article a strong sense of French responsibility for the CPIC and a genuine concern over the influence of Trotskyism and sectarianism, especially among the newer cadres.

Fraternal advice also came to the Vietnamese from the Chinese Communists, or at least in their name. Shortly after the appearance of the anonymous article just cited, a letter purportedly written by the Central Committee of the CCP to the Indochinese Communists was carried in French Communist and Comintern organs. It was less severe on the Vietnamese than its French predecessor, but was no less concerned with the "possible rebirth of factional and sectarian tendencies" in the CPIC, tendencies which were seen as inherent in the Indochinese movement as a result of the years of Communist fragmentation before unification. Unity and discipline accordingly are stressed throughout the letter. The letter also expresses concern over the lethargy of the Indochinese movement following the setbacks of 1930-1931 and calls for "a more combative party." The 1932 "Program of Action," the letter asserts, must be put into force. In a concluding

---

[54] XXX, "Vers le renforcement du parti communiste indochinois," *Cahiers du Communisme*, July 1, 1934, pp. 766-800.

section entitled "Indochinese Communists! Prepare for new battles!" the authors urge the Vietnamese to follow the course of the Soviet Union and China, "a sure and proven path leading to victory. . . . The boundary between Kuomintang China and French Indochina will cease to divide our peoples. Soviet Indochina and Soviet China will unite in the World Federation of Soviet Republics."[55]

The authenticity of this letter remains in some doubt, at least as a communication from Mao's headquarters in Kiangsi province. Not only is there no reference to it in known Chinese Communist sources of this period but it is difficult to imagine through what channels the rather detailed information about Indochina reached the beleaguered Central Committee in South China, how its communication was transmitted to editorial offices in Paris and Moscow (when very meager first-hand information on the Chinese soviet movement itself was available to foreign Communist publications), and why, beset by multiple problems of their own, the Chinese Communists should attempt to resolve those of neighboring parties. It is more than likely that the "open letter" to the Indochinese comrades was composed in Europe— perhaps in Moscow—and made to appear as a communication from the Chinese in order to underscore the lessons to be learned from the Chinese soviet movement. It is also possible that Stalin, during a period when Soviet foreign policy was being conducted through more normal diplomatic channels, wished to deemphasize the use of the Comintern for the transmission of instructions of this nature which could be as easily transmitted through other agencies—such as the CCP.[56]

---

[55] "Lettre ouverte du Comité central du parti communiste de Chine aux membres du parti communiste de l'Indochine," *Cahiers du Bolschevisme*, August 15, 1934, pp. 957-68; the letter was also published in *Inprecor*, August 10, 1934, 1116-20, and in *Materialy po natsional'no-kolonial'nym problemam*, No. 9 (24), 1934, pp. 67-81.

[56] Two similar "open letters" to the Indian Communists about this time also appear to have been composed in Moscow, but made to appear as communications from fraternal parties; one, in 1932, is signed by the party Central Committees of China, England, and Germany, and a second, in June 1933, is signed by the Chinese Central Committee alone. See *Kommunisticheskii internatsional*, No. 16, 1932 and

Whether or not the letter in question is an authentic Chinese instrument, the impact of the Chinese soviet movement on the Vietnamese need not be doubted. Russians, French, and the Vietnamese themselves repeatedly refer to it and to the close fraternal ties allegedly linking the two parties. The Soviet Orientalist G. Safarov speaks of the CPIC as "the younger sister of the glorious Chinese Communist Party."[57] Péri closes his report on the visit of the French workers' delegation to Indochina with a striking testimony to the growing importance of the Chinese Communists, not only to the Vietnamese but to the entire colonial world: "The party [in Indochina] lives in close touch with the heroic Communist Party of China, whose glorious example serves as a beacon to the Communist parties of the East, like the Communist Party of the Soviet Union to the Communist parties of the West."[58] At the Seventh Comintern Congress in 1935 a Vietnamese delegate emphasized that "the victorious advance of the soviet movement in China played a tremendous role and had an enormous influence on the development of the revolutionary struggle in our country."[59]

Such assertions should not, of course, lead us to exaggerate concrete ties between the two parties. Chinese *influence*, based on the alleged successes of the soviet movement, was one thing; active *liaison* was something else again. There is in fact no evidence known to this writer that the activities of the Chinese and Indochinese parties were consciously coordinated during these years—except through such documents as have been cited.

Moscow's ties with the Vietnamese, finally, are no more demonstrable than Chinese. Soviet *interest* in Indochina, reflected in the greatly increased coverage of Indochinese affairs after Enbay, should not be mistaken for Soviet *intervention* in Vietnamese politics—although Russian commentaries undoubtedly influenced

---

No. 34-35, 1933, and *Programmnye dokumenty Kommunisticheskikh partii Vostoka*, pp. 257-90.

[57] Safarov, "Indo-Kitai i frantsuzskii imperialism," *Revoliutsionnyi Vostok*, No. 1 (17), 1933, p. 26.

[58] *Inprecor*, June 8, 1934, p. 885.

[59] *Ibid.*, October 7, 1935, p. 1294.

Eastern Strategies in Abeyance: 1930-1935

the content of special instructions to the Vietnamese included in such instruments as Péri's article in *Cahiers du Communisme* and the "open letter" from the Chinese Communists.[60] More direct "intervention" than this is found only irregularly and is often of doubtful authenticity. It is reported, for instance, that in May 1931 the Dalburo in Shanghai reprimanded Nguyen Ai Quoc for having taken insufficient precautions to ensure the safety of Vietnam cadres from the French police.[61] We have meanwhile noted the possible Russian authorship of the Chinese "open letter" of 1934—another conceivable instance of "intervention." The resolutions of Comintern-controlled organizations such as the Anti-Imperialist League and the Pan Pacific Trade Union Secretariat may also be read as political directives, of a sort, originating in Moscow.[62]

[60] Although a number of Soviet commentaries on Indochina between 1930 and 1935 have been referred to above, a general bibliographic note may be appropriate at this juncture. The most regular coverage of Indochina (other than in *Inprecor* and *Communist International*) is found in *Materialy po natsional'no-kolonial'nym problemam*, a publication of the Research Institute for the Study of National and Colonial Problems: see especially No. 2, 1932, pp. 41-54; No. 2, 1933, pp. 79-90; No. 7 (13), 1933, pp. 101-7; No. 1-2 (16-17), 1934, pp. 94-103; No. 4 (28), 1935, pp. 21-30. Another publication of the same institute, *Revoliutsionnyi Vostok*, includes additional material of interest: see especially No. 1 (17), 1933, pp. 18-28 (article by Safarov on French imperialism); No. 3 (31), 1936, pp. 87-96; and No. 4 (32), 1935, pp. 247-55 (two articles by Minin on the Enbay uprising and the Communist press in Indochina). The items in both of these scholarly Orientalist journals deal predominantly with economic rather than political questions. Other articles of more than routine interest are B. Dantsig, "Revoliutsionnoe dvizhenie v Indokitae," *Mirovoe khoziaistvo i mirovaia politika*, No. 1, 1931, pp. 81-7; K. Grant, "Revoliutsionnyi pod'em v Indokitae," *Krasnyi internatsional profsoiuzov*, No. 15, 1931, pp. 17-24; and Vasil'eva, "Bor'ba za gegemoniiu proletariata v Indokitae," *Kolonial'nye problemy*, sb. 3-4, 1935, pp. 117-22. The first serious book on Indochina by a Soviet scholar also appeared during these years: B. M. Dantsig, *Indokitai* (1931).

[61] According to Professor Sacks, the Dalburo letter is cited in Gouvernement de l'Indochine, Direction des Affaires Politiques et de la Sûreté Générale, *Documents*, IV, p. 108; Trager, *op. cit.*, p. 127.

[62] The Anti-Imperialist League's prompt approval of the Enbay insurrection, for instance, may be read as Moscow's signal to the Indochinese Communists to support the nationalists at the given juncture; the PPTUS call in June 1931 for an end to French atrocities in Indochina was a signal to the Vietnamese to organize a more vigorous protest against French "terror," which they proceeded to do. The resolutions, both cited above, may be found, respectively, in *Inprecor*, February 20, 1930, pp. 165-6, and June 11, 1931, pp. 563-4.

162

None of these communications, however, reveals Moscow's direct concern with the CPIC as vividly as a pamphlet entitled "Tactical and Organizational Questions of the Communist Parties of India and Indochina," which appeared in July 1933.[63] The author, using the pseudonym "Orgwald," was evidently a Comintern agent in the Far East and seems to have been thoroughly versed in Indochinese affairs; he appears to speak, moreover, with the full authority of Moscow.[64] The portion of the pamphlet dealing with Indochina consists of questions by a Vietnamese Communist and Orgwald's replies. He is optimistic about the future of Communism in Vietnam and feels that the present demoralization of the party, in the face of French terror, will soon pass; the "revolutionary revival" in evidence since 1930 will presently create more favorable conditions for the party's resurgence. The cadres, however, must work more strenuously to fashion a disciplined organization, especially an underground apparatus. Most of Orgwald's advice consists of practical, if elementary, steps to achieve this end: strict secrecy, silence when arrested, use of pseudonyms and codes, a foreign center to provide continuity of leadership (but a Central Committee located in Indochina), use of front organizations, and so forth.

Orgwald also discussed several policy questions of interest. In reply to a question why a slogan calling for the "overthrow of the bourgeoisie" might not be adopted, inasmuch as the bourgeoisie in Indochina was "counter-revolutionary," Orgwald answered that such a slogan would give satisfaction only to the workers, "an insignificant minority"; it would meanwhile alienate much of the peasantry, the urban petty-bourgeoisie, and the intellectuals. Instead, Orgwald advised the Vietnamese Communists to call for the independence of Indochina, an objective ap-

[63] The pamphlet appeared originally in English, under the imprint of the *Pan Pacific Worker*, and was subsequently translated into Russian in *Kommunisticheskii internatsional*, No. 29-30, 1933 (section on India), and No. 10, 1934, pp. 28-40 (section on Indochina); the portions quoted here are from the English original.

[64] Orgwald may have been Nguyen Ai Quoc, who was released from jail in Hong Kong about this time; this would explain Orgwald's detailed knowledge of Vietnamese affairs and the bluntness with which he answers certain questions.

pealing to all Vietnamese. Asked if a "united front" with the reviving nationalist parties, especially the Kuomintang (i.e., the Vietnam Nationalist Party), was appropriate, Orgwald answered that nothing was wrong with such an alliance per se, so long as it was conducted according to the principle: "fight together, but march apart."

Taken at face value, Orgwald's recommendations to the Vietnamese regarding a united front anticipated by nearly a year the evolution of these tactics in France and by more than two years the full articulation of the united front policy at the Seventh Comintern Congress in 1935. There was a discrepancy, of course, between these more moderate tactics and the militant "Program of Action" of 1932, which was nominally still in force. Since lip-service continued to be paid the latter for another year or more, both in Moscow and elsewhere, it must be imagined that Orgwald's counsels represented an exploratory—and presumably still tentative—search for alternate strategies in Indochina. Logic, however, favored the course Orgwald urged. A policy of expediency had much to recommend itself in Vietnam: from the Communist viewpoint, conditions in the colony continued to present excellent opportunities for a resumption of revolutionary activity; the CPIC, however, was far too weak to provide sole leadership of such activity; accordingly, an alliance with moderate nationalists (if not yet with "social reformists" and Trotsky-ites) was indicated.

As time passed, and especially as the united front became the major effort of French Communists, more and more was heard of the virtue of an anti-imperialist front in Indochina, much as Orgwald had urged it in mid-1933. Vasil'eva, for instance, closed a report to a panel of Soviet Orientalists in June 1934 with a call for a "united front against French imperialism composed of the most active revolutionary elements grouped around the Communist Party." Gabriel Péri applauded the activity of the Communist-led Workers' Opposition in the 1935 elections in Saigon as "a victory for the anti-imperialist front."[65] In May 1935, the

[65] Gabriel Péri, "The Anti-imperialist Front in the Elections to the Colonial Council in Indochina," *Inprecor*, March 23, 1935, p. 353.

Russian Orientalist Minin argued that "the central tactical problem" of the Vietnamese Communists, in view of the current revival of the nationalist parties, "is the creation of a united anti-imperialist front, and one of the principal immediate objectives is the winning over of the petty-bourgeoisie to the side of the Indochinese proletariat so that this element fights under the leadership of the Communist Party."[66] In Indochina, in short, the tactics of the united front appeared to be in force well before they were adopted for the international movement as a whole. The *implementation* of these tactics, however, was something else again.

DEBUT OF COMMUNISM IN THE PHILIPPINES

From time to time a digression into the internal affairs of local Communist parties in Southeast Asia will be useful, although this is not the central focus of the present study. Where party history is particularly complex or where general information about the evolution of a Communist movement is not widely available, such digression appears necessary in order to place Soviet policies in some intelligible perspective. Such is the case in the early development of the Communist Party of the Philippines.

In May 1929, the delegates who withdrew from the *Congresso Obrero de Filipinas* (COF) to form the *Congresso Proletario di Filipina* (KAP) determined among other things to create a new working-class party. The decision was carried out the following year. A five-man study committee, including Evangelista and Manahan, reported its recommendation to the KAP in July 1930, and on August 25 sixty representatives of various labor and peasant organizations assembled to form the Communist Party of the Philippines (CPP or CPPI).[67] A draft program was approved, and a thirty-five-man Central Committee and seven-man Politburo were elected.[68] The official launching of the party took

---

[66] *Revoliutsionnyi Vostok*, No. 3 (31), 1935, pp. 93-4.

[67] According to José Lava, the designation "Communist," proposed by Evangelista, was approved only after "lengthy discussion"; *Milestones*, p. 20.

[68] The members of the Politburo were: Evangelista, Manahan, Juan Feleo (a

place at a mass meeting in Manila attended by a reported 5,000-6,000 Filipinos on November 7, 1930, the anniversary of the Bolshevik Revolution. The agenda of the meeting included, appropriately, much discussion of Soviet achievements and of current threats to the USSR by world imperialism. The party's goals, listed in documents which were both circulated and read at the meeting, included: the immediate and complete independence of the Philippines from the United States; the overthrow of American imperialism and domestic capitalism; the establishment of a soviet government; and the adoption of Communism. It was repeatedly stated at the rally that the new party was "not reformist but revolutionary."[69]

The CPPI soon made it clear that the November pronouncements were not mere words. Demonstrations were organized by Communists during the months following the party's launching, and numerous Communist-led strikes took place, including a major strike of nearly one thousand employees of the Insular Lumber Company on the island of Negros.[70] In January 1931 the national offices of the CPPI opened in Manila and began publication of the party weekly *Titis* (*The Spark*, after Lenin's pre-Revolutionary publication *Iskra*); according to Soviet sources, the circulation of this organ reached 10,000 within a few weeks.[71] At the end of January a mass funeral for Antonio de Ora, a Polit-

---

peasant leader), Antonio de Ora (a lumberman), Felix Caguin (a printer), Urbano Arcega (a slipper-maker), and a Chinese representative; *ibid.*, pp. 20-1.

[69] Accounts of the founding of the CPPI in Communist and non-Communist sources vary only in minor details: see *ibid.*, pp. 19-22; Philippines (Republic), Congress, House of Representatives, Special Committee on Un-Filipino Activities (CUFA), *Report on the Illegality of the Communist Party of the Philippines*, pp. 17ff; *Inprecor*, April 23, 1931, pp. 406-7. For a more detailed account of the founding of the CPPI, see Hoeksema, *op. cit.*, pp. 85-92.

[70] Official Philippine sources list no fewer than 14 public meetings organized by the Communists in Manila alone during the last two months of 1930; CUFA, *Report*, p. 20. See also Harry Gannes, "A New Wave of Struggles in the Philippines," *Inprecor*, February 26, 1931, pp. 177-8. A discussion of the colony-wide repercussions of the Insular Lumber Company strike may be found in Levinson, *Filipinny mezhdu pervoi i vtoroi mirovoi voinami*, p. 78.

[71] *Kommunisticheskii internatsional pered VII vsemirnym kongressom*, p. 469; see also *Inprecor*, June 25, 1931, p. 603.

buro member killed in an automobile accident while under arrest for leading an illegal strike, allegedly drew the largest crowds of demonstrators ever seen in Manila.[72] Ceremonies in memory of de Ora, which continued for several days, were accompanied by the first wave of arrests of Communist agitators on charges of sedition. In February Evangelista and Manahan were arrested twice on this charge, according to published documents of the CPPI, but on each occasion were released on bail. These early efforts of the government to curb the CPPI, far from being effective, only provoked the Communists to press their campaign of protest more vigorously.

During March and April the see-saw struggle between the government and the Communists continued. The legal status of the party was still unsettled. No court had yet passed on its legality, but the government had issued decrees that public gatherings of Communists were in violation of existing statutes on sedition. Communist candidates in the coming election were accordingly refused permits by local authorities to hold political meetings. The Communists, quite naturally, argued that their civil liberties were being violated by the government's actions and continued to make propaganda over the issue. José Lava writes of this period:

> After the organization of the CPP, it launched a series of mass meetings, not only in the city of Manila but also in the neighboring provinces of Central and Southern Luzon. Because of the aggressiveness in its organizational and propaganda campaign, the Catholic Church, the bourgeois-owned newspapers and the government launched a counter-campaign against the CPP under the sponsorship of the reactionary landlords and capitalists. Meetings were disturbed and heckled by paid gangsters, and permits for many meetings refused. In many cases permits were canceled at the last minute. Invariably the Communist leaders went ahead, with or without permit, and their speeches were warmly applauded by the large audiences, notwithstanding the annoyance, persecutions, and threats of the government authorities and their agents.[73]

[72] *Ibid.*, February 26, 1931, p. 177; see also Hoeksema, *op. cit.*, p. 97.
[73] Lava, *Milestones*, p. 23.

167

Affairs came to a head in May. A permit to hold a parade on May 1 in Caloocan, outside Manila, was initially granted by the local authorities but subsequently revoked. An estimated 10,000 workers and peasants nonetheless gathered in Caloocan, where they were met by about one hundred police officers under orders to prevent the parade. Evangelista was requested by the officer in charge to ask the crowd to leave peaceably but, according to the official record of the incident, he addressed the gathering with inflammatory words which very nearly led to a pitched battle. He was immediately arrested, and the paraders in due course were dispersed.[74] Another May Day celebration in Manila proper, organized by the KAP, was also broken up by the police; sixty-four workers were reported arrested, including many Chinese.[75]

The decision to go underground appears to have been taken at about this time. Charges of sedition were now pending against virtually all of the party's leaders, several separate charges in the case of Evangelista and Manahan; it was only a question of time before the party would be outlawed by court order. It was therefore necessary to take precautions to preserve some continuity in the party organization. The First Congress, convened shortly after the events of May 1 and attended by forty delegates representing thirteen provinces, met in secrecy.[76] Its decisions, however, in no way reflected a party chastened by recent frustrations. The most important resolution, a "Manifesto to the Workers, Peasants and Toilers of the Philippines," stated that "the guiding principle of the party is the principle of class struggle, of irreconcilable, unyielding and unceasing class warfare." The manifesto reaffirmed the goals set in November—notably, independence and the establishment of a soviet government—and added new ones:

[74] An account of the May Day disorders, based in the main on Philippine government records, may be found in Hoeksema, *op. cit.*, p. 103; see also Lava, *Milestones*, pp. 24-5.

[75] S. Carpio, "May First in the Philippines," *Inprecor*, June 11, 1931, p. 565.

[76] There is conflicting evidence of the dates of the First Congress: an authoritative Soviet source, citing the text of one of the congress resolutions, gives May 2-3 (*Programmnye dokumenty Kommunisticheskikh partii Vostoka*, p. 131); an equally authoritative American Communist account gives May 9-10 (S. Carpio, "First Congress of the Communist Party of the Philippines," *Communist*, No. 8, 1931, p. 744).

civil rights for all, regardless of race or nationality;[77] a seven-hour day; nationalization of all imperialist enterprises; confiscation of large estates and Church lands and redistribution of land among the poorer peasants; and the organization of a workers' and peasants' army.[78] Four separate resolutions were passed on the four reports to the congress which concerned the party's tasks with regard to trade unions, peasant organizations, and youth groups and the party's immediate tasks in the light of the existing political situation in the Philippines. The resolution on the latter report, which was probably the second most important document to emerge from the congress, gave particular attention to ways of creating an "illegal apparatus."[79] The congress also sent warm greetings to the Russian Communist Party, "the model Bolshevik section in the CI, the most consistent and uncompromising fighter for Marxist-Leninist theory and practice . . . the only Fatherland of the international proletariat and of all oppressed peoples." An application for admission to the Comintern was forwarded to Moscow in which the CPPI "expresses its hope and desire that the CI will help the young CPPI with advice and guidance." Two additional resolutions concerning the party's relations with the American and Chinese parties were also adopted by the congress.[80]

The Communist Party of the Philippines, it is clear, began its

[77] Reference here was, of course, to the Chinese minority in the Philippines whose trade unions had been allied with the Communists since 1929. The provision for equal rights for the Chinese was particularly appropriate since the Chinese arrested in the May Day demonstrations, together with an estimated 500 Chinese affiliated with the KAP, were being threatened with deportation; see *Inprecor*, June 11, 1931, p. 564.

[78] The text of the manifesto is in *Programmnye dokumenty Kommunisticheskikh partii Vostoka*, pp. 131-9.

[79] *Ibid.*, pp. 143-4.

[80] For a more detailed account of the First Congress, drawn largely from two articles by S. Carpio in *Communist*, August 1931, pp. 744-54, and *Inprecor*, June 25, 1931, pp. 603-4, see Hoeksema, *op. cit.*, pp. 105-9. It is curious that Lava makes no reference to the First Congress in *Milestones*, although he refers to a KAP convention held later in May at which all of the 400 delegates were reportedly arrested. Other sources confirm the round-up of Communists on May 31, the largest raid carried out to that date in the Philippines; see Hoeksema, *op. cit.*, p. 110.

official existence with exceptional vigor, though with fewer advantages than the Indochinese party had enjoyed at its inception earlier in 1930.

It is not clear that Moscow had any direct hand in the surge of revolutionary activity in the Philippines in 1930 and 1931. The formation of Communist parties in all Eastern countries had been repeatedly urged in Moscow since the Sixth Comintern Congress, and it may be imagined that this counsel had some impact on the Filipinos. There is, however, no evidence of specific instructions from the Comintern in this matter. The Eleventh Plenum of the ECCI, meeting in March 1931 at the height of the crisis in the Philippines, all but ignored developments there.[81] The CPPI's request for admission to the Comintern was not acted on until the Seventh Congress in 1935, although favorable action had been taken promptly on a similar request by the Indochinese Communists. Coverage of Philippine affairs in Soviet (as distinct from Comintern) periodicals during 1930 and 1931 also contrasts sharply with coverage of developments in Indochina as well as in certain other Southeast Asian colonies during the same period.[82]

Moscow's observable interest in a given revolutionary movement, however, we now know is no accurate measure of Soviet influence upon it. In the 1920's the Soviet press was singularly inattentive to developments in the Philippines, yet a lively Soviet influence was maintained there by the Pan Pacific Secretariat, acting as Moscow's agent. The PPTUS continued during the early 1930's to serve as a link between Moscow and the Filipinos. Its official communications and its periodic analyses of Philippine

[81] The only mention of the Philippines discovered in the records of the plenum is a reference to de Ora's "murder" in January; *XI plenum IKKI: stenograficheskii otchet*, p. 366.

[82] For 1930-31, *Bibliografiia Iugo-vostochnoi Azii* lists fewer than half a dozen items on the Philippines in Soviet periodicals—chiefly concerning developments in the labor field—as contrasted with three dozen or more on Indochina, for instance, and slightly fewer on Indonesia.

affairs appeared irregularly in its own as well as in Comintern journals at least until early 1934.[83]

The PPTUS did not, however, play the same role in the Far East in the 1930's that it had earlier. The shift of its headquarters in 1930 from Shanghai to San Francisco, where it came under the control of the American Communist Party, removed the Secretariat from direct contact with Communist developments in East Asia; the discontinuation of its principal organ, *Pan Pacific Worker*, soon thereafter deprived the Secretariat of a regular voice in Asian affairs.[84] Another instrument of Soviet policy which survived for a time in the Philippines was the Philippine section of the Anti-Imperialist League, established in Manila early in 1930. Personal rivalry, however, between the leader of this organization, Cirolo Bognot, and Evangelista appears to have destroyed its usefulness and little is heard of it after the spring of 1931.[85]

Neither the Philippine section of the Anti-Imperialist League nor the PPTUS came close to equaling the role played by the CPUSA in the Philippines during the 1930's. At its Fifth Convention in June 1930, five months before the official launching of the CPPI, the American party voted the "adoption" of the Philippine Communist movement.[86] Soon after the formation of the party, according to José Lava, a representative from the American

[83] E.g., *Pan Pacific Worker*, April 1931, p. 5 (an appeal for public support of the Filipino party leaders awaiting trial for sedition); *Inprecor*, June 11, 1931, p. 564 (a call for mass protests throughout Asia in behalf of Chinese residents of the Philippines threatened with deportation in the wake of the May Day disorders); and *ibid.*, December 29, 1933, p. 1293, and February 23, 1934, p. 292 (political analyses of current events in the Philippines issued by the PPTUS).

[84] Occasional items were released under the imprint of the *Pan Pacific Worker* after the transfer of the PPTUS to San Francisco—e.g., Orgwald, *Tactical and Organizational Questions of the Communist Parties of India and Indochina*—but regular publication of the journal appears to have ended late in 1930.

[85] A lengthy appeal by the Philippine section of the Anti-Imperialist League, on the eve of a strike of High School Students in Manila in February 1930, is carried in *Pan Pacific Monthly*, May 1930, pp. 15-6; the section's "tasks" are spelled out in an article in *Inprecor*, March 12, 1931, p. 273. For a more detailed discussion of this obscure organization, see Hoeksema, *op. cit.*, pp. 80-3.

[86] *Communist*, No. 7, July 1932, p. 645.

171

party arrived in the Philippines and "through him the CPP was connected with the Communist Party of the United States."[87] American Communist writers in the meantime repeatedly emphasized the "duty" of the CPUSA to give "material and organizational assistance" to the CPPI.[88] The Filipinos, for their part, were no less desirous of help from the Americans. A letter from the Central Committee of the CPPI to the CPUSA in April 1931 stated that "close cooperation and concerted action" between the two parties was "an urgent need of the hour."[89] The political resolution of the First Congress of the CPPI closed with a demand for "the closest organizational ties with the Communist Party of the North American United States in order to guarantee aid and guidance from our brother party."[90] Such statements admit of little doubt that the CPUSA was to replace the Pan Pacific Secretariat as the principal agency of Moscow's policies.

How effectively did American Communists fulfill their obligations?

Institutional links between the American and Filipino parties, as might be expected, are not clearly documented. José Lava's assertion that the CPPI was "connected" with the CPUSA through an American representative in Manila is not convincing evidence that the connection was either close or effective. American Congressional investigations, supported by the testimony of such former American Communists as Whittaker Chambers, shed some light on organizational ties via San Francisco, where a "Philippine Committee" of the CPUSA was said to have existed in the mid-1930's under Harrison George.[91] These links, how-

[87] Lava, *Milestones*, p. 24.

[88] Tim Ryan, "The Revolutionary Upsurge in the Philippines," *Inprecor*, March 12, 1931, p. 273. Another American Communist, in his summary of the First Congress of the CPPI, urged that the CPUSA, as well as the Comintern, "devote especial attention and give tangible and practical guidance to this sector of the international revolutionary front"; S. Carpio in *ibid.*, June 25, 1931, p. 604.

[89] *Ibid.*, April 23, 1931, p. 406.

[90] *Programmnye dokumenty Kommunisticheskikh partii Vostoka*, p. 145.

[91] United States, Congress, House of Representatives, Hearings of the Special Committee on Un-American Activities, Vol. III (July 19, 1940), p. 1132; see also Whittaker Chambers, *Witness* (New York, 1952), p. 369. For a discussion of this evidence, see Hoeksema, *op. cit.*, pp. 148-51.

ever, remain shadowy at best and appear not to have created an intimate operational relationship between the two parties. American Communist leaders occasionally criticized the laxness of CPUSA in this regard. Earl Browder, for instance, in his report to the Eighth Convention of the CPUSA in April 1934, commented negatively on the role of the American party in the Philippines.[92] Harrison George, writing in 1935 of the CPUSA's failure to carry out plans for the organization of Filipino workers in the United States, charged party cadres with having ignored "their Bolshevik duty to the Philippines, the principal real colony of American imperialism. . . . Our duty to recruit and to train these workers for work in their homeland should devolve upon our Party as a first task."[93]

The guidance provided the Filipinos by American Communists, however, should not be minimized because of inadequate operational ties and because the CPUSA, in a spirit of self-criticism, occasionally felt it was doing less than it should. "Instructions" to the CPPI, in the form of articles by American Communists published in their own and in Comintern journals, were frequent during the early 1930's. In March 1931, for instance, Tim Ryan, one of the most prolific American writers on the Philippines, enumerated the immediate tasks of the CPPI, including among them several which had not been listed previously by the Filipinos themselves but which subsequently were to appear in their publications.[94] In November and December 1931 a five-part article by Ryan amplified his earlier remarks on the CPPI's tasks and spelled them out for the Filipinos in greater detail.[95] In July 1932, an article by another American Communist evaluated the deliberations of the First Plenum of the Philippine Central Commit-

[92] Earl Browder, *Communism in the United States* (New York, 1935), p. 86.

[93] Harrison George, "The Filipino Masses Enter the Stage of Armed Struggle for Freedom," *Communist*, June 1935, p. 509.

[94] One such task was support of the Chinese revolution—omitted from the draft party platform of November 7, 1930, but included in the May Day slogans and in the resolutions of the First Congress the following spring. Ryan's article appeared in *Inprecor*, March 12, 1931, p. 272.

[95] The article, entitled "The Imperialist Offensive Against the Revolutionary Movement in the Philippines and the Tasks of the CPPI," was carried in successive issues of *Inprecor* from November 12 to December 17, 1931.

tee in January 1932.[96] In October 1932, still another American Communist undertook both to praise and to reprimand the Filipinos for their conduct of a general strike in Nueva Ecija province.[97] In November 1932, S. Carpio, in a wholly new restatement of the CPPI's tasks, delivered the most detailed critique of the party's activities to that date.[98]

The very existence of articles such as these, with their strongly paternalistic tone, suggests the role the CPUSA sought to play in the Philippine movement. Moreover, the publication of most of the articles in Comintern organs implies Moscow's approval not only of the Americans' responsibility to instruct the Filipinos but also of the substance of the instructions. In the absence of any clearly articulated Soviet policy in the Philippines during these years, the American "instructions" to the CPPI constitute a reasonably complete record of what we may presume Moscow's policy to have been—much as the pronouncements of the Pan Pacific Secretariat provided a similar record of Soviet policies from 1927 to 1930.

The problem that American commentators felt to be most urgent, in the face of the presumed imminent sentencing of the party's leaders,[99] was the question of party organization. Two courses of action were recommended. Initially the emphasis was on mass tactics, presumably on the assumption that a broad "united front from below" represented the best chance of sur-

[96] William Simons, "The Philippine Islands in the War Area," *Communist*, July 1932, pp. 640-6.

[97] Paul Levin, "The Anti-Imperialist Struggle of the Filipino Peasants," *Inprecor*, October 13, 1932, p. 963.

[98] S. Carpio, "The Situation in the Philippines and the Tasks of the CPPI," *ibid.*, November 17, 1932, pp. 1109-12, and November 24, 1932, pp. 1126-7; also published in *Communist*, No. 12, December 1932, pp. 1120ff.

[99] The Court of First Instance in Manila on September 14, 1931, handed down fifteen convictions for sedition, with sentences ranging from four months to a year, and twenty convictions for illegal association (including Evangelista, Manahan, and most of the other members of the Politburo) with sentences of eight years; the sentences, however, were stayed pending appeal. As expected, the CPPI and KAP were officially pronounced illegal; see CUFA, *Report on the Illegality of the Communist Party of the Philippines*, pp. 17-52. For an American Communist account of the trial and of Evangelista's spirited and belligerent defense, see Paul Levin's article in *Inprecor*, September 22, 1932, p. 893.

vival during a period when party leadership was disrupted. Ryan stressed this policy in his listing of the CPPI's tasks in March 1931, urging not only a "mass party" but also the transformation of the KAP, the National Confederation of Peasants, and the Philippine Section of the Anti-Imperialist League into "mass organizations."[100] He underscored these tactics in his restatement of the party's tasks in November and December; the CPPI should take as its starting point, he wrote, "a mass united front movement around the specific issue of the sentencing of Evangelista, Manahan and the others."[101] The second course of action, also underscored in Ryan's article, was the establishment of an effective underground organization; while the CPPI should use every legal means to combat the sedition laws and should not go underground without a struggle, Ryan wrote, "the illegal apparatus should be put on a functioning basis."[102]

The Americans were dissatisfied with the Filipinos' compliance with these directives. Although the party leaders had not gone to jail, as expected, and were still at liberty to take part in modified political activity,[103] the progress of the CPPI during 1932 was judged insufficient. In November 1932 Carpio complained that the party had ignored warnings given it and had not used "to full advantage the extremely favorable conditions for its activities." It had not defended itself adequately when declared illegal; it had failed to resume publication of *Titis*, following its suppression in 1931; and it had not shown the vigor and resourcefulness appropriate to the "only revolutionary party" in the Philippines. The CPPI's explanation to the Comintern (Carpio does not specify how or when it was delivered) that its troubles stemmed from "the deep-rooted fear characteristic of the colonial and enslaved and oppressed masses" was summarily rejected. It was simply inertia, Carpio argued. The party had in effect gone

---

[100] *Ibid.*, March 12, 1931, pp. 272-3.

[101] *Ibid.*, December 10, 1931, p. 1142.

[102] *Ibid.*, December 17, 1931, p. 1157.

[103] The Supreme Court upheld the lower court's decision only on October 26, 1932 and the sentences did not begin until December 1933, nearly three years after the first arrests were made; during the greater part of this period, the party leaders were free on bail.

"so deeply underground that it could not be said to have functioned as a Communist party at all."[104] The present tasks of the CPPI, as Carpio saw them, continued therefore to be organizational: to consolidate the party apparatus through both legal and illegal means; to strengthen the revolutionary trade unions and peasant organizations which had been allowed to languish; and to reissue *Titis* immediately. To these Carpio added several new tasks: to adopt more specific programs, especially with respect to the exposure of "national reformism," in accordance with the recent directives of the Twelfth ECCI Plenum on the "concretization" of the class struggle; and finally—an obligatory task for any loyal Communist party—to react immediately to any anti-Soviet maneuvers of American imperialism.[105]

These counsels notwithstanding, the CPPI showed little recovery from 1932 to 1935. The Second Plenum in March 1933 reported a membership of only 845, which, though higher than Carpio's estimate of 500-600 the preceding November, was considerably below estimates of 2,000 or more in 1931.[106] In any event a membership of 845 represented a modest accomplishment for a Communist party in the third year of its existence. A congress of the KAP in November 1933, held simultaneously with a congress of the Communist-controlled National Confederation of Peasants, led to a brief wave of strikes and demonstrations at the end of the year. These were reported enthusiastically in the Comintern press, where they were seen as justification of the Thirteenth Plenum's forecast of a rising revolutionary wave;[107] but the gains appear to have been minimal. Similarly a "workers' and peasants' bloc," organized by the Communists in Feb-

104 *Inprecor*, November 17, 1932, pp. 1109-12.

105 *Ibid.*, November 24, 1932, p. 1127.

106 Ryan wrote at the end of 1931 that the CPPI had recruited 2,000 new members during the year and had polled 50,000 votes in the national elections during the autumn; *ibid.*, November 19, 1931, p. 1064. The source for the figure given at the Second Plenum is: Second Plenum of the CPP, "Resolution on Organization," March 12, 1933, cited in Hoeksema, *op. cit.*, p. 136.

107 G. Pedro, "The Philippine Masses in Counter-Attack," *Inprecor*, March 16, 1934, p. 433.

ruary 1934 for the forthcoming elections, was a short-lived and largely ineffective effort.[108]

There are several reasons for the meager showing of the Communists during these years. The government, more alert to the Communist danger, had devised more efficient ways of curbing illegal activities. Intraparty rivalry demoralized and divided the party membership. The long-awaited jailing of Evangelista and other leaders at the end of 1933 produced further demoralization and handicapped the CPPI's operations. Under these circumstances, it is perhaps not surprising that party strength declined rather than grew during the first half of the decade. José Lava, who devotes more space in his 1950 history of the CPPI to the activities of the Philippine Socialists during these years than to those of the Communists themselves, writes of the latter:

> There was no clear formulation of strategy and tactics. Organizational life was loose and inadequate, discipline was lax and educational work was very weak. . . . Leadership within the party and among the masses was personal rather than organizational. The party members and the masses followed the leadership of prominent Communist leaders like Comrades Evangelista, Capadocia, Abad Santos, Balgos, Castillo and Feleo and when lesser rank cadres go down to these party members and masses, they [*i.e.*, the party rank and file] were reluctant to follow the latter's leadership.
>
> . . . .
>
> During this period the party produced powerful agitators and orators without much foundation in Marxist and Leninist theory. This period can rightly be called the period of the party's infancy.[109]

Another criticism leveled at the Filipinos by American commentators concerned the question of forming soviets. The establishment of a soviet government, it has been noted, was included in the CPPI's long-range tasks both at the launching of the party in November 1930 and at the First Congress the following May. Reports of these two events by American Communist writers made no objection to the soviet slogan, and Ryan's list of the

[108] G. Pedro, "Progress in the Philippines," *ibid.*, June 8, 1934, p. 892.
[109] Lava, *Milestones*, pp. 44 and 48.

177

CPPI's tasks in November 1931 specifically included the establishment of soviets as the "future organization of the revolutionary dictatorship of the workers and peasants."[110] He clearly saw soviets as an *eventual* organization of state power, not an *immediate* objective. The Filipinos were therefore treading on risky ideological ground when they passed a resolution in the First Plenum (January 1932) which stated that of the party's current tasks "the most important of all is the immediate organization of local soviets in every town and rural district."[111] Carpio, in his critique of the First Plenum in November 1932, took sharp exception to this formulation. "There seems to be no clarity in the minds even of our leading comrades," he wrote, "as to the true significance and content of the slogan." He continued:

> To put up such a slogan for the "immediate organization of soviets" at a time when the Communist party has until now extremely little contact with the peasant movements in the most important rural districts, when our revolutionary trade unions can hardly be said to have rooted themselves among the proletarian masses in the shops, factories, transport enterprises, plantations, etc., when the Communist Party, Philippine Islands has not yet succeeded in securing a sound footing, and when the objective and subjective conditions in the Philippine Islands are not yet ripe for it—means simply to play with the slogan of establishing soviets.[112]

Carpio's comment (reminiscent of Stalin's famous admonition to the students at Sun Yat-sen University in 1927)[113] indicates that despite the successes of the soviet movement in China the Comintern still attached importance to the timing of any effort actually to create soviets. The time was not ripe in the Philippines, Carpio insisted, and the slogan, as an "immediate" task, appears to have been withdrawn in response to his objection. There continued to be confusion, however, even among the ortho-

[110] *Inprecor*, November 19, 1931, p. 1064.
[111] Cited in Carpio's article in *ibid.*, November 17, 1932, p. 1111.
[112] *Ibid.*
[113] The gist of Stalin's remarks was that the mere creation of soviets was not a difficult matter, but unless they could be used as genuine "organs of a new revolutionary power . . . they become an empty shell, a travesty on soviets"; Stalin, *Sochineniia*, IX, p. 268.

dox, on the soviet question: as late as 1935, although the Philippines were not directly at issue, an exchange of views between two writers in the American edition of *Communist International* revealed sharply conflicting estimates of the conditions necessary for creating soviets in colonial countries.[114] A Filipino reading these articles could be pardoned for wondering if Carpio's observations on soviets in the Philippines represented the last word on the matter.

There was less room for misunderstanding over another critical issue—the question of Philippine independence. From the outset immediate and full independence from the United States was urged in every article on the Philippines by American and other foreign Communists, often more vigorously than in pronouncements by the CPPI itself. Even visits by Philippine delegations to Washington to negotiate independence were rejected, inasmuch as the United States, it was asserted, "will never voluntarily fulfill her promise to give up the Philippines."[115] Carpio, in his 1932 critique of the CPPI, charged the Filipinos with emphasizing only Japanese imperialism and ignoring American; this, he argued, was simply "playing into the hands of the American imperialists and of the enemies of Philippine independence, who use the argument of 'Japanese danger' for their own imperialist purposes."[116] When the Hare-Hawes-Cutting bill was passed in January 1933, providing for independence after a transitional period of ten years, it was immediately condemned as a deception. Philippine leaders who supported the bill were excoriated and even Manuel Quezon, who opposed it, was said to have been forced to do so by public opinion, not, as he claimed, because of the formula which allowed American military and naval bases to continue after independence.[117] The American Bureau of the PPTUS charged Quezon with seeking to obstruct

[114] See the opposing views of V. Myro and Li in *Communist International* (U.S.), No. 4, February 20, 1935, pp. 151-9, and No. 5, March 5, 1935, pp. 222-39.

[115] *Pan Pacific Monthly,* May 1930, p. 18.

[116] *Inprecor,* November 17, 1932, p. 1110.

[117] A. G. Bosse (New York), "American Imperialism Grabs Philippine 'Independence,'" *ibid.,* February 16, 1933, p. 172.

Eastern Strategies in Abeyance: 1930-1935

approval of the bill in the Philippines simply to gain a political advantage over his rivals, Roxas and Osmeña. "The cause of Philippine national liberation will never triumph," the American Bureau stated, "unless and until the workers and peasant masses of the Philippines, by revolutionary actions, themselves take possession of the independence movement."[118]

The rejection by the Filipinos of the Hare-Hawes-Cutting bill at Quezon's instigation, and his success the following year in securing passage in Washington of the milder Tydings-McDuffie bill (which eliminated the provision for the retention of American military bases) occasioned no change in the Communists' attitude. One bill was as bad as the other. In April 1935 American Communist sources published with the party's blessings a strongly worded manifesto recently adopted by the CPPI which stated that the Tydings-McDuffie Act would make the Philippines "as 'free' as Manchukuo." The manifesto continued: "There is no salvation for us except by revolutionary struggle. . . . National independence will never be secured as a result of peaceful 'constitutional' methods."[119] Thus on the eve of the launching of a world-wide united front against fascism, a strategy that would require some modification of past policies, American and Philippine Communists continued their inflexible line on independence through violence—and only through violence.

The role of the peasantry in the Philippine revolutionary movement was another issue which engaged American Communist commentators. The principal peasant organizations, we have seen, had been linked with the Communists from the earliest days of the revolutionary movement. Manahan, who was at once the chief spokesman of the peasant organizations and a founder of the CPPI, cemented this link. Special attention accordingly was

[118] *Ibid.*, February 23, 1934, p. 292.
[119] *Communist*, April 1935, p. 372. This manifesto is also quoted approvingly in later Russian sources, as a policy appropriate to the given stage of Communist development in the Philippines; e.g., G. I. Levinson, "Kolonial'naia politika SShA i natsional'no-osvoboditel'noe dvizhenie na Filippinakh v period 'avtonomii' (1935-1941)," Akademiia nauk SSSR, Institut Vostokovedeniia, *Kratkie soobshcheniia, vyp.* VIII (1953), pp. 43-5, and Levinson, *Filippiny mezhdu pervoi i vtoroi mirovymi voinami*, p. 146.

180

directed to the peasant question during the First Congress of the CPPI, and in the months following, especially during 1932, peasant demonstrations organized by Communists were chronic throughout the Philippines.[120]

The National Confederation of Peasants, however, remained organizationally separate from the CPPI, and it was perhaps inevitable that some rivalry should arise between them, given the pre-eminent orientation of the latter to the problems of Philippine workers. During the First Party Plenum in January 1932, the Filipinos evidently discussed the peasant question with some candor and concluded, according to a subsequent account by Carpio, that the peasants were becoming "the hopeless rivals of the industrial workers." Carpio, as might be expected, sharply attacked this formulation in his general critique of the CPPI later in the year. "Not rivalry," he argued, "but a revolutionary alliance of workers and peasants" was the proper strategy at the given stage. He went on to criticize the CPPI for having shown too little interest in the peasantry and especially for having failed to provide guidance to the Peasants' Confederation. Why, he asked, had the Executive Committee of the confederation failed to meet during the last year? Why had the party's program on the agrarian question not been made known to the peasants? He stated that the recent wave of peasant risings throughout the Philippines had taken place "without the least initiative or leadership" of the CPPI. He thought it ironical that the Peasants' Confederation had published two pamphlets on religious questions during the preceding year but none on the peasant problem itself.[121]

The resolution of the "peasant question" in the Philippines, however, could not be simplified by a critique composed in San Francisco or Moscow. The issue had roots deep in the social

---

[120] See the generally sympathetic coverage of this peasant activity in two articles by Paul Levin in *Inprecor*, October 12, 1932, pp. 963-4, and December 29, 1932, p. 1254.

[121] Carpio's comments on the peasant issue are included in two sections of his five-part article; see *ibid.*, November 17, 1932, pp. 1110-2, and November 24, 1932, p. 1126.

181

structure of the country and continued to plague the CPPI leadership; ultimately the leadership divided over this issue. According to José Lava, the two peasant spokesmen on the Politburo, Manahan and Feleo, adopted the position that because of the agrarian-feudal character of the Philippine economy, the greater number of peasants over workers in the colony, and the richer revolutionary traditions of the peasants, the latter should in effect be said to constitute the proletariat. Evangelista and Capadocia argued the more orthodox Marxian view that, however small the number of workers, they were the most class-conscious; "the working class is a working class," Lava wrote, and no amount of verbalizing could change this fact. Lava stated that it was the "Chinese section" of the party which resolved the ideological dispute by pointing out that while the majority of the proletariat came from among the workers, as Evangelista contended, the ultimate determination of a proletarian depended upon his outlook irrespective of class origins.[122]

This formula did not settle the rivalry between Manahan and Evangelista, a rivalry which probably stemmed as much from a conflict of personal ambitions as from ideological differences. The Second Plenum in March 1933 charged Manahan with a variety of misdeeds—including cowardice, embezzlement of party funds, and negotiating with Quezon on Philippine independence—and dropped him from the Politburo and Central Committee.[123] He evidently quit the party at this juncture, and in September 1933 he was expelled from the Communist-controlled National Confederation of Peasants after attempting to create a rival peasant organization. The disposition of the Manahan case, which was the sharpest intra-party dispute to occur in the pre-war years, was handled by the Filipinos themselves, insofar as can be determined. The first reference to the case of the "renegade Manahan" in foreign Communist publications was not until December 1933,

[122] Lava, *Milestones*, pp. 44-5.
[123] CPPI, "A Direct Attack on Opportunism," March 11, 1933; cited in Hoeksema, *op. cit.*, pp. 139-40.

some months after his defection; on this occasion the source in question merely reported and approved the action taken.[124]

An issue arose in May 1935 that sharply tested American and Philippine Communist attitudes on the peasant question—the sudden rising of the *Sakdalistas*.[125] This movement, organized early in the 1930's and drawing its strength mainly from the peasantry, was dedicated to a single program: independence. It was therefore a vigorous opponent of both the Hare-Hawes-Cutting and Tydings-McDuffie bills, as were the Communists. The *Sakdal* movement attracted relatively little attention outside the Philippines until 1935 when, following the May Day celebrations, it organized peasant risings near Manila which led to 60 deaths, approximately 80 other casualties, and an estimated 500 arrests.

American Communists were of course obliged to take immediate notice of so formidable an insurrection. Early in June an American Communist, writing from New York, saw the rebellion as part of a growing crescendo of disorders in the Philippines inspired in the main by Communists; the cigar factory strikes in Manila the year before were part of the same revolutionary upsurge. He denied that the *Sakdalistas* had any special part in the preparation of the May rising; on the contrary, "it broke out in spite of them." He considered the *Sakdalistas* a "petty-bourgeois reformist party" and its leadership "a pawn in the hands of Japanese imperialism to offset the influence of Wall Street."[126] Harrison George, writing about the same time, also notes the reliance of the *Sakdal* movement on Japanese imperialism but gives a somewhat different view of the rebellion itself. Judging from the fact that the disorders took place in areas where the Communists were strong, he argued that "the young, illegal and heroic Communist Party of the Philippine Islands has taken

[124] *Inprecor*, December 29, 1933, p. 1293. Manahan began serving his sentence with the other Communist leaders at the end of 1933 and received a pardon in September 1935; thereafter he disappears as a leader of the Philippine revolutionary movement.

[125] The name comes from the Tagalog word "protest."

[126] Samuel Weinman (New York), "Revolutionary Upsurge in the Philippine Islands," *Inprecor*, June 8, 1935, pp. 633-4.

a hand in the uprising and is receiving its baptism of fire." He indicated that collaboration with at least a segment of the *Sakdalista* might be possible inasmuch as the "Left-wing" of the movement accepted the idea of armed insurrection.[127] Other American Communists rejected collaboration. Paul Levin, for instance, writing in August from Manila, called the *Sakdalista* "an outspoken bourgeois organization which opposes the workers' and peasants' power" and noted that the presence of the *Sakdal* leader in Tokyo following the rising was proof of the reliance of the movement on Japanese imperialism. The fact that the insurrection took place in areas of presumed Communist strength suggested to him that the *Sakdalistas* had made dangerous inroads into the Communists' following due to the party's weakness. "It is time," he wrote, "for the CPPI to win back these toiling masses into our own ranks."[128]

These somewhat divergent views on the *Sakdal* uprising, especially on the question of whether or not to collaborate with any portion of the *Sakdalista*, must have initially confounded the Filipinos. In due course they adopted a policy of non-collaboration. José Lava cites the Central Committee decision on the matter as follows: "Even if it is true that the *Sakdalista* revolt is anti-American imperialists [*sic*] in orientation, the *Sakdalistas* themselves are tools of Japanese imperialist militarists, and hence, while the party will continue its struggle against American imperialism, it will at the same time fight against the Japanese imperialists and their local instruments, in order not to confuse the Filipino people."[129] Since Lava fails to give the date of this decision, it is not clear whether it was inspired by the revised views on collaboration by such writers as Levin or vice versa. In any event, assuming the eventual identity of the American and Filipino attitudes on this question, it is interesting to note that on the

[127] Harrison George, "The Filipino Masses Enter the Stage of Armed Struggle for Freedom," *Communist*, June 1935, pp. 505-6; see also Helen Marcy (Manila), "The Situation in the Philippines," *Inprecor*, August 10, 1935, pp. 866-7.

[128] Paul Levin (Manila), "Mass Discontent and the *Sakdal* Uprising in the Philippines," *ibid.*, August 22, 1935, pp. 1006-7.

[129] Lava, *Milestones*, p. 46.

184

eve of the Seventh Comintern Congress both appear to have rejected collaboration with a predominantly peasant organization of unmistakably militant outlook. On a second count, then, Philippine Communism was likely to be jarred by policies presently to be announced in Moscow.

The foregoing represents an effort to piece together Moscow's policy in the Philippines, in the absence of definitive pronouncements by responsible Soviet or Comintern authorities, from other Communist sources—chiefly American. The publication, or republication, of most of the American "instructions" to the Filipinos in Comintern journals, it has been argued, is evidence of Moscow's approval of the course the CPUSA was recommending. It is perhaps not necessary to belabor this argument.

Soviet analysts were not wholly inattentive to developments in the Philippines during these years, however. While Moscow's interest in the Philippines was clearly less than in Indochina and in Indonesia, it was not negligible. Russian Orientalists were also gaining competence in Philippine affairs, and their articles appeared with growing frequency during these years in Orientalist and occasionally in more popular journals. As in the case of Indochina, this coverage of the Philippines was weighted heavily toward economics. The subjects treated by these emerging scholars included the impact on the Philippine economy of the Japanese occupation of Manchuria, mounting unemployment, rising inflation, and the strike movement.[130] Politics per se appears not greatly to have interested the Russian Orientalists. Where they dealt with purely political questions, they either confined their treatment to summaries of foreign press commentaries[131] or relied on the formulations of American Communists in the articles dis-

[130] E.g., "Otrazhenie iaponskoi interventsii v Kitae na Filipinnakh i v Indonezii," *Materialy po natsional'no-kolonial'nym problemam*, No. 3, 1932, pp. 130-44; "Filipinny," *ibid.*, No. 2, 1932, pp. 61-9; A. L. Gal'perin, "Filipinny: sotsial'no-ekonomicheskii ocherk," *Kolonial'nye problemy*, sb. 2, 1934, pp. 176-211; and O. Rykovskaia, "Stachka rabochikh sigarnykh fabrik na Filipinnakh, *Materialy po natsional'no-kolonial'nym problemam*, No. 1, 1935, pp. 114-24.

[131] "Filipinny: obzor pressy po Filippinam," *Materialy po natsional'no-kolonial'nym problemam*, No. 4-5, 1932, pp. 136-55, and S. Silesto, "Obzor anglo-amerikanskoi periodiki," *Tikhii okean*, No. 1, 1935, pp. 197-210.

cussed above. Thus the only serious discussion of Philippine Communism in the Soviet press of these years, contained in an obscure article published in 1933, is drawn almost wholly from Carpio's critique of the CPPI at the end of 1932; even the phrasing the author uses in his criticism of the Filipinos' position on soviets and on the peasant question is Carpio's.[132] An account of the *Sakdal* uprising of 1935, written some months after that event, is similarly based on American Communist accounts published at the time.[133]

Soviet commentaries, then, while they perhaps give some dimension to an understanding of social and economic conditions in the Philippines which fed popular discontents and which allegedly justified the militant policies urged on the CPPI, appear not to have contributed to the formulation of these policies by American Communists. Soviet analysts, moreover, appear to have been not only relatively uninterested in Philippine Communism but relatively unimpressed with its prospects. A Soviet writer at the end of 1932, for instance, spoke of the Philippine proletariat having gone for a decade or more "on rein behind the bourgeoisie."[134] An official Comintern appraisal of the CPPI on the eve of the Seventh Congress in 1935 was critical of the Filipinos' failure "to strengthen the underground apparatus and to win over a majority of toilers in city and country."[135] A leading Soviet Orientalist, Alexander Guber, dismissed the CPPI in a few sentences in a lengthy article on the Philippines early in 1936, arguing that inasmuch as the country was not yet industrialized the proletariat there was "too small to provide leadership of the national-revolutionary movement."[136] Philippine Communists, we

[132] S. Stol'iar, "Filippiny i amerikanskii imperializm," *Kolonial'nye problemy*, sb. 1, 1933, p. 95; in the English "Table of Contents" the author's name is given as "Stoller," which suggests that he may not have been a Russian contributor.

[133] O. I. Zabozlaeva, "Sakdalistskoe dvizhenie na Filippinskhikh ostrovakh," *Tikhii okean*, No. 1, 1936, pp. 153-60.

[134] L. Geller, "Oktiabr'skaia revoliutsiia i ugnetennye narody kolonii," *Mirovoe khoziaistvo i mirovaia politika*, No. 10, October 1932, p. 79.

[135] *Kommunisticheskii internatsional pered VII vsemirnym kongressom*, p. 471.

[136] A. Guber, "Amerikanskii imperializm i novaia konstitutsiia 'avtonomnykh' Filippin," *Materialy po natsional'no-kolonial'nym problemam*, No. 36, 1936, p. 27.

may imagine, could scarcely take heart from such judgments that Moscow was prepared to risk much in their behalf.

As far as direct liaison between Moscow and the Philippines is concerned, there is no evidence that Soviet agents visited Manila during these years, although some evidence exists of visits by Filipinos to Moscow. Non-Communist Philippine sources report that young Filipinos went yearly to the Soviet capital for political training and that foreign funds were provided for this purpose.[137] Even Communist sources refer to such a fund, although there is no indication whether it was actually used.[138] Whether or not such ties were significant in the development of Philippine Communism, it is worth recalling once again that the CPPI continued during these years to be deferential to Moscow and to applaud all important pronouncements issued by the Soviet government and the Comintern.

A word should be said, finally, on the impact of the Chinese revolution on developments in the Philippines. As in Indochina, there is no reason to doubt a general, unspecified influence of the Chinese soviet movement on Philippine Communism. Support of the Chinese soviets, we have seen, was a prominent slogan advanced by the Filipinos by May 1931—whether on their own initiative or at the urging of Americans—and was included in all important party statements from that time on. The First Congress, in its resolution of solidarity with the Chinese Communists, called the soviet movement in China "a mighty inspiration to the tens of millions of exploited toilers in all colonial and semi-colonial countries."[139] The 1935 manifesto of the CPPI called Chinese-type soviets "the future of the Philippines."[140]

---

[137] *Philippines Free Press*, September 8, 1934, cited in Hoeksema, *op. cit.*, p. 146; the same source states that Emilio Maclang, who became First Secretary of the CPPI when Evangelista was imprisoned, was one of the earliest Filipinos trained in Moscow.

[138] One of the charges against Manahan at the Second Plenum was that he had misappropriated funds set aside for the training of young Filipinos in Moscow; CPPI, "A Direct Attack on Opportunism," March 11, 1933, cited in Hoeksema, *op. cit.*, p. 139.

[139] *Communist*, August 1931, p. 752.

[140] *Ibid.*, April 1935, p. 375.

Greetings were meanwhile received from the Chinese comrades on the occasion of major party gatherings.[141] Within the CPPI, deference was shown to the local Chinese by the election of three Chinese representatives to the first Central Committee and one to the Politburo.[142] It was also the party's "Chinese section" which resolved the intra-party dispute over the peasant question in 1933.[143]

The influence of the Chinese revolution in the Philippines should not be exaggerated. At best, Chinese Communism must be regarded as a distant source of inspiration to the Filipinos, not as an active guiding force in their revolutionary efforts. If such a force existed during these years, all evidence indicates that it was provided by American Communists.

STAGNATION IN INDONESIA

During the years between the Sixth and Seventh Comintern Congresses, Moscow sought to keep alive the fiction that a Communist movement of some significance still existed in Indonesia. Who its local leaders were, however, or where they were located has never been made clear. The plan devised at the time of the Singapore reorganization in 1930 to return responsibility for Communist affairs in Indonesia from the MCP to the PKI whenever the latter was prepared to accept it was never formally carried out, insofar as is known. In all likelihood the only leadership the PKI had from 1930 to 1935 was that which Musso and his colleagues in Moscow could provide. It is doubtful if this was much.

Coverage of Indonesian developments in the Soviet and Comintern press, however, did not appreciably diminish during these

---

[141] Both the First Congress (which elected a Chinese Communist to honorary membership on the presidium of the Congress, along with Stalin, Ernest Thaelmann and William Z. Foster) and a party convention in June 1932 received greetings from the CCP; see Hoeksema, *op. cit.*, pp. 106, 122.

[142] Lava, *Milestones*, p. 21.

[143] *Ibid.*, p. 45. Lava's evidence on this point is interesting inasmuch as he has tended in recent years to minimize the role of the Chinese, both in the Philippines and abroad, in the course of Philippine Communism; interviews with the author in March 1961 and January 1962.

188

years. Musso himself was the most prolific contributor on Indonesia early in the 1930's. Eventually, however, the principal authority on Indonesia in Moscow came to be Alexander Guber, the first Russian Orientalist of note to develop a clear specialization in a single Southeast Asian country. Like his fellow Orientalists who followed events in Indochina and the Philippines, Guber's articles focused predominantly on economic affairs, but he was perhaps more alert than they to political developments as well. It is from such materials, at any event, that Moscow's view of Indonesia early in the 1930's ("policy" would be too strong a word) must be constructed.[144]

Commentaries on Indonesia, in keeping with the prevailing line of the International, expressed an unabashed optimism in the revolutionary prospects there. A Dutch writer, for instance, stated without equivocation early in 1930 that "the approaching revolt of the Indonesian masses under the leadership of the Communist Party of Indonesia will prove that Indonesia is not only ripe to take her fate into her own hands but is prepared to win."[145] No such revolt, of course, was to occur, although Moscow chose to see in the short-lived mutiny on the *Zeven Provincien* three years later the beginnings of the long-awaited upheaval. One writer saw the mutiny as "evidence that we are at the threshold of that revolutionary upsurge. . . . A rising of the PKI, with the genuinely Bolshevik help of the Communist Party of Holland, is more than ever the order of the day."[146] Guber also saw wide implications in the episode and called for "a revolutionary solution of the crisis, the overthrow of Dutch imperialist domination and national freedom"; he cited the resolutions of the recent

[144] Musso's and Guber's articles during this period, as well as those of other writers on Indonesia, are listed in *Bibliografiia Iugo-vostochnoi Azii*, pp. 150-1. Guber was also the author of a substantial monograph on Indonesia published in 1932: *Indoneziia: sotsial'no-ekonomicheskie ocherki* (380 pp.).

[145] Gerald Vanter, "Terror, Famine and Pestilence in Indonesia," *Inprecor*, January 9, 1930, p. 27.

[146] V. Resema, "Sobytiia v gollandskom flote v Indonezii," *Kolonial'nye problemy*, No. 1, 1933, p. 107. The mutiny involved the seizure of a Royal Dutch cruiser by its Indonesian crew, evidently angered over pay reductions; the crew held the ship for several days before being forced to surrender following the bombing of the vessel by the Dutch Air Force.

189

Thirteenth Plenum of the ECCI as the principal authority for this militant advisory to the PKI.[147]

The *Zeven Provincien* mutiny proved, however, to have been an isolated episode. The PKI, which was not involved in the planning of the mutiny, made no capital out of it. If Soviet and Comintern spokesmen seized so enthusiastically upon the incident as evidence of the Thirteenth Plenum's claim of a "revolutionary upsurge" in the colonies at this juncture,[148] we may imagine that this was precisely because there was no real upsurge in Indonesia on which they could focus attention. The claim of a leading Russian Orientalist in 1934 that "in Indonesia the struggle of tens of thousands of workers and peasants is progressing under the soviet banner"[149] appears to have been wholly without foundation.

The PKI during this period was under instructions, as most colonial parties were, to refrain from alliances with national movements in any form. Safarov, for instance, cautioned in 1930 that bourgeois-nationalist leaders in Indonesia had now "turned to full collaboration with Dutch imperialism."[150] Musso, who earlier had spoken with guarded respect for Sukarno's PNI (see above, p. 102), gave his amended view in 1932 that "the Sukarno group, the national reformist Left in Indonesia, is much more servile towards the imperialists than the Nehru clique in India

---

[147] A. Guber, "Vosstanie v indoneziiskom kolonial'nom flote i revoliutsionnoe dvizhenie v Indonezii," *Maierialy po natsional'no-kolonial'nym problemam*, No. 3, 1933, p. 57; another article by Guber on the episode, making the same point, appeared in the more widely read *Revoliutsionnyi Vostok*, No. 5, 1933, pp. 32-46.

[148] Attention to the episode in the Soviet press, beginning with coverage of it in *Pravda*, February 13, 1933, persisted for some months. In addition to the articles on the mutiny already cited, the following may be noted: K. Musso, "Vosstanie na gollandskom bronenostse 'De Tseven Provinsien,'" *Mezhdunarodnoe rabochee dvizhenie*, No. 2, 1933, p. 15; S. Rutgers, "Signal ostindskogo 'Potemkina,'" *Agrarnye problemy*, No. 9-10, 1933, pp. 211-9; "Uroki vosstaniia gollandskikh moriakov v Indonezii," *Kommunisticheskii internatsional*, No. 11, 1933, pp. 38-43; and N. Volchanskaia, *Vosstanie v voennom flote Gollandskoi Indii*, 1934 (32 pp.).

[149] Pavel' Mif, "Bor'ba za gegemoniiu proletariata v kolonial'noi revoliutsii," *Bol'shevik*, No. 19-20, November 7, 1934, p. 86.

[150] G. Safarov, "Na fronte kolonial'noi revoliutsii," *Bol'shevik*, No. 15-16, August 31, 1930, p. 72.

and the Wan Chin wei [Wang Ching-wei] crowd in China."[151] Guber, in an article ranging widely over the parties which had splintered off from the PNI since its founding, rendered the same verdict.[152] In 1934 a Comintern spokesman excoriated the entire nationalist leadership in Indonesia—Hatta for "grovelling before the Mikado," Sukarno for having "sold out" to the Dutch, others for sundry other sins—and considered that all were driven to distraction by "the effort to offer themselves to Dutch imperialism and the fear of selling themselves too cheaply."[153]

Without doubt this wholesale rejection of collaboration with the nationalist movement was shortsighted, especially in the Indonesian context. The nationalist parties enjoyed considerable prestige among Indonesians following the Communist debacle of 1926-1927. Although often frustrated in their political programs by the Dutch practice of arresting and summarily sentencing leaders as soon as they gained prominence, these organizations (the PNI, *Partindo*, and others) had legal existence, which the PKI did not, and so became the center of the continuing effort to overthrow Dutch rule.[154] They were the successors of *Sarekat Islam*[155] and the PKI; indeed so long as the PKI had dominated the more radical wing of the Indonesian nationalist movement, there had been no demand for these parties. Now, during the PKI's eclipse, former Communists, survivors of the 1926-1927 uprisings, joined the new nationalist parties in great numbers. Had Moscow's tactics in Indonesia been more flexible, ex-Communists might have been used to bring the nationalist

[151] Musso, "The Situation in Indonesia," *Inprecor*, January 14, 1932, p. 39.

[152] Guber, "Krizis i natsional'no-osvoboditel'noe dvizhenie v Indonezii," *Materialy po natsional'no-kolonial'nym problemam*, No. 4-5, 1932, pp. 105ff.

[153] K. R., "Concerning the 'New Era' in Indonesia," *Inprecor*, February 23, 1934, pp. 291-2; the author also attacks Maring, the founder of the Indonesian Communist movement, describing him as a "trusted friend of Mr. Trotsky" and linking him to the current nationalist leaders.

[154] Sukarno was under arrest from the end of 1929 to the end of 1931 and again from mid-1933 to the Japanese occupation; Hatta and Sjahrir were under arrest from early 1934 to 1942. For a detailed discussion of the nationalist organizations of the early 1930's, see Kahin, *Nationalism and Revolution in Indonesia*, pp. 87ff.

[155] *Sarekat Islam* was reorganized as the *Partai Sarekat Islam Indonesia* in 1929 but failed to recover its leading role in the nationalist movement.

parties into closer harmony with Soviet objectives. As it was, Communists gained prominence within the nationalist movement only in *Perhimpoenan Indonesia* (PI), the organization of Indonesian students in Holland; when Hatta, the organization's leader for a number of years, left Holland for Indonesia in 1932, PI fell more and more under the control of Communist-inclined members such as Setiadjit and Abdulmadjid.[156] By this time, however, PI was nearing the end of its role as the training school for future Indonesian leaders and its voice in affairs at home was limited.

Discouraged from playing a more constructive role in the overt nationalist organizations, the PKI was obliged to rely more and more on clandestine operations. Advice from Moscow stressed the need for training in underground work. "The absence of a Communist party experienced in illegal activity," Musso wrote in 1932, "is one of the main reasons why the proletariat and the broad masses of the poor peasants are unable to offer effective resistance to the ruthless attitude of the bourgeoisie."[157] The Indonesian delegate at the Thirteenth Plenum of the ECCI in December 1933 considered the party's first task "with the help of the Comintern . . . to accomplish as rapidly as possible the political and organizational strengthening of the illegal Communist party of Indonesia."[158] The phrase "Illegal PKI" was thus evidently in use within Comintern circles a year and a half before Musso was sent to Indonesia to give it substance.

Relations between the Dutch Communist Party and the PKI were evidently more cordial early in the 1930's than during the preceding decade, although not comparable to the close ties during this same period between French and Indochinese Communists or between American and Philippine. In December 1932 a resolution was passed at a Dutch party congress calling for a "united front of the toilers of Holland and Indonesia."[159] Subse-

---

[156] Kahin, *op. cit.*, pp. 88-9.

[157] Musso, "The Situation in Indonesia," *Inprecor*, January 14, 1932, p. 39.

[158] *Ibid.*, April 23, 1934, p. 638; the delegate, not readily identifiable, used the name "Arifin."

[159] *Kommunisticheskii internatsional*, February 10, 1933, p. 57.

quently it was held that gains in the Dutch Parliamentary elections in the spring of 1933 were due to this slogan, which the Communists used widely in their campaign; the Communists increased their seats from two to four, two of them won by Indonesians.[160] At the Thirteenth Plenum of the ECCI, the Indonesian delegate praised the Dutch party for its stand on Indonesian independence and asked for the help of the CPH in gaining the release of Indonesian revolutionaries still in jail.[161]

On the eve of the Seventh Comintern Congress in 1935 an official review of PKI activity since the Sixth Congress reflected a more sober appraisal of the party than is indicated in many of the interim reports cited above. The review found the Indonesian comrades guilty of many shortcomings. "They did not create a sufficiently durable illegal base for their organization; there were neither Communist factions nor groups of revolutionary trade union oppositionists within the reformist unions; the class content of the nationalist organizations was not understood." The PKI was also criticized for "lack of purposeful leadership and wavering" during the *Zeven Provincien* episode. Chinese Communists in Indonesia, by contrast, were singled out for praise.[162] The Dutch Communists were also praised, especially for their united front slogan during the 1933 elections. On balance, the Comintern report indicated, prospects were better for the PKI in 1935 than in 1928, but much remained to be done.[163] It is doubtful in retrospect whether even this more modest appraisal was justified; the PKI, as matters developed, was still a decade away from any significant revival.

COMMUNISM ELSEWHERE IN SOUTHEAST ASIA

Elsewhere in Southeast Asia the Communist movements were too ephemeral, or too obscure, to command Moscow's attention

---

[160] *Communist International*, July 1, 1933, p. 465.

[161] *Inprecor*, April 23, 1934, p. 639.

[162] This is the only mention in sources known to this writer of a Chinese Communist organization in Indonesia during the 1930's; if one existed, it is likely that it had little to do either with the PKI or with the CCP.

[163] The report is in *Kommunisticheskii internatsional pered VII vsemirnym kongressom*, pp. 486-90.

except at very great intervals. It will be useful, however, both to round out our study and to prepare for the time when these lesser movements assumed greater importance, to review briefly the salient facts of Communist experience in Burma, Siam, and Malaya prior to 1935 and to inspect briefly Moscow's random observations on the revolutionary process in these countries.

In *Burma* nothing resembling a Communist organization was created until the eve of World War II. There was, however, some exposure to Marxist and Comintern literature before this time. According to one early Burmese Marxist, a Burmese-language journal in Mandalay carried articles by a Marxist writing under the pseudonym "Atom" early in the 1920's; a decade later a small library founded on the proceeds of a book written by the leader of a 1930-1931 peasant uprising, Saya San, circulated Marxist and Leninist writings.[164] Burmans returning from Europe in the 1930's also brought Communist literature which circulated among students and intellectuals in Rangoon.[165] Direct contacts, however, between Burmese revolutionaries and the Comintern, or Comintern-oriented organizations, were virtually nonexistent. The Pan Pacific Trade Union Secretariat, for instance, is not known to have had contacts with the Burmese during the period when its headquarters was in Shanghai. Several Burmese in Europe evidently joined the Anti-Imperialist League early in the 1930's, but the connection appears to have been casual and no branch of this organization, insofar as is known, was established in Burma (as it was, for instance, in the Philippines).[166] Neither the *Nanyang* Group in Singapore nor its successor, the Malayan Communist Party, both of which had nominal responsi-

[164] Author's interview with Thein Pe Myint, January 1962.

[165] Interview with Dr. Ba Maw, February 1962; according to Ba Maw, he received miscellaneous Communist materials from Moscow on a regular basis for several years following his return to Burma from England in 1934.

[166] Ba Maw states that he joined the Anti-Imperialist League in Europe in 1933, but never attended its meetings. Another Burman, Thein Maung, also joined the League in London about the same time; see Trager, *Marxism in Southeast Asia*, p. 23.

bility for the revolutionary movement in Burma, appears to have
made contact with Burmese leaders.[167]

Marxism competed in Burma with revolutionary ideas from
all over the world. According to one student of Burmese Communism, the philosophies of Sun Yat-sen, Gandhi, Kemal Ata-
turk, the Sinn Fein, the Fabians, Nietzsche, and even Mussolini
and Hitler met in the incipient Burmese revolutionary movement in the early 1930's.[168] Marxism had no special recommendation. Moreover any philosophy, to hold a following in Burma,
needed to be reconciled with Burmese Buddhism. The cross-
fertilization of these divergent ideologies gave the Burmese nationalist movement a uniquely heterogeneous character which
survived for many years. Until World War II a single idea—
independence—was common to all and proved sufficient to unite
Burmese nationalists of all colors and persuasions. In 1931 the
Dohbama Asiayone ("We Burmans" Association) was formed;
known as the *Thakin* movement, it included in due course virtually all the future leaders of the Burmese nationalist movement,
whatever their social philosophy. Even many years later, when
the Burmese nationalist movement had broken up into separate
organizations corresponding to more sharply delineated ideologies, the members of the *Thakin* movement still sensed a bond
which non-Burmese were at pains to comprehend. The typical
Burmese engaged in the revolutionary movement through World
War II did not find it inconsistent to consider himself at once
Marxist, nationalist, and Buddhist.

The occasional Soviet commentaries concerning Burma early
in the 1930's, influenced as they were by the somewhat inflexible
attitude of the Comintern on "united front from below," accordingly bear little relationship to what was going on in the country.
The "heroic" Saya San rising of 1930-1931, for instance, despite
the fact that it was confined to the Tharawaddy district and had

[167] It is of some interest that Thein Pe Myint, who is associated with the
earliest development of Burmese Marxism, was particularly curious about the
author's evidence of this supposed early connection between the MCP and the
Burmese—since he himself had heard rumors but never discovered proof of it.
[168] See the remarks of J. S. Thomson in Trager, *op. cit.*, pp. 21-3.

no announced object other than a protest against the depressed living conditions in that region, is described in the Comintern press as signifying the profound desire of the masses for full independence.[169] The nationalist movement, by contrast, described in the Comintern press as composed of lawyers, well-to-do land-owners, and Buddhist priests, is said to be openly collaborating with British imperialism. This is evident, a Comintern writer noted in 1931, in the scheduled participation of nationalist leaders in the Round Table Conference in London to negotiate the separation of Burma from India.[170] When the conference was under-way, the Comintern press continued its attack on the nationalist leaders attending it and claimed they were wholly without support in Burma. "The only course open to the masses of peasants and workers along with the revolutionary youth of Burma is to learn the lessons of the struggle of other colonial and semi-colonial workers—to organize to smash British imperialism; to co-ordinate their struggle; build up trade unions among the oil workers, the mine workers, the transport workers; link up with the revolutionary movement of the peasants in a nation-wide struggle for independence."[171]

Moscow's formula for revolution in Burma, to judge from this advice, was singularly ill-suited to conditions there. On the basis of a local peasant rising in 1930 (led, incidentally, by a former monk and "dabbler in astronomy and astrology"),[172] Comintern writers persisted in believing that a vigorous peasant movement existed in Burma and that its alliance with an imaginary prole-tariat was a practical possibility. None of the articles cited, it should be noted, refer to the *Thakin* movement, which alone was capable of grasping Marxist ideas and of spreading them in

169 R. Bishop, "The Situation in Burma," *Inprecor*, August 27, 1931, p. 850. The rising lasted for nearly a year and continued intermittently even after the arrest and hanging of Saya San in 1931.

170 "Letter from Burma," *ibid.*, January 21, 1932, pp. 45-6.

171 A.G.E. "Burmah and the Round Table Conference," *ibid.*, December 8, 1933, p. 1235. The conference led to the Act of Burma of 1935, which gave the Burmese a certain measure of self-rule beginning in 1937.

172 This description of Saya San is given, for instance, in Maung Maung Pye, *Burma in the Crucible* (Rangoon, 1951), p. 28, cited in Trager, *op. cit.*, p. 21.

Burma. The only group singled out for praise (other than Saya San and his peasant followers) is a "Youth League of Burma," an organization which cannot be identified.

Given the ignorance of Burmese conditions reflected in these early Soviet commentaries, it is perhaps not surprising that the growth of Communism in Burma was as leisurely as it was.[173]

The Communist movement in *Siam*, like that in Burma, was also to have been directed by the Malayan Communists according to decisions reached at the time of the reorganization of the *Nanyang* groups in Singapore in 1930. No liaison, however, was established as far as is known. Nor did any contacts made with Thai leaders by Tan Malaka and Nguyen Ai Quoc, both of whom visited Bangkok in the 1920's, survive their departure. Although Bangkok was occasionally a haven for revolutionaries and reportedly a center, at intervals, for revolutionary work in Southeast Asia, Siamese Communism does not appear to have been greatly stimulated by this activity.

Such Communist influence as there was in Siam before 1935 was concentrated in the Chinese community in Bangkok. Politics in this community, as in all overseas Chinese communities in Southeast Asia, mirrored politics in China itself. During the alliance between the Kuomintang and the Chinese Communists in the mid-1920's, the "red flag flew freely in the streets of Bangkok," according to an early Comintern account of Siamese Communism; after the rupture in 1927, Communists in Bangkok were persecuted not only by the Siamese but by the Kuomintang as well.[174] To Siamese political leaders, however, *all* overseas Chinese were tainted with Communism. This became particularly evident after the anti-royalist revolution of 1932, as different Siamese factions competed in demonstrating their anti-Com-

[173] *Bibliografiia Iugo-vostochnoi Azii*, p. 75, lists eight or ten articles on Burma during the early 1930's, most of them concerning the Saya San rising and published in relatively obscure Soviet journals; the writer has not been able to consult these items.
[174] Musso, "The Economic Position and Communist Activities in Siam," *Inprecor*, February 13, 1930, p. 115; the same article, slightly revised, was also carried in *Pan Pacific Monthly*, April 1930, pp. 38-9.

munist postures. In consequence, the Chinese community as a whole suffered stern repression for several years: many were arrested on suspicion of being Communists; thousands were deported for alleged Communist sympathies; and immigration was virtually halted. In 1933 Communism was made illegal in Siam and remained so, despite several changes of government, until after World War II.

The severity toward Communism of the new "revolutionary" government in Bangkok of course affected Moscow's judgment of the 1932 revolution. A muddled appraisal appearing in *Inprecor* in 1934 asserted that it was not a revolution at all: Siam was still "one of the most characteristic kingdoms in the Orient"; the "so-called coup d'état" of 1932 had not altered the status of the Siamese king as "absolute ruler." The imperialist powers, moreover, especially Great Britain, would not have it otherwise, the author asserts. "Siam is in fact becoming the play-thing of the imperialist powers." With respect to Siamese Communism, the author acknowledges that the "Chinese inhabitants are the bearers of the Communist movement." He adds: "There is no doubt that the idea of soviets is beginning to take root in Siam, largely as a result of the victories of the soviet movement in China." The writer also comments on Pridi Phanomyong, the Leftist leader of the 1932 revolution who in 1933 was driven into exile for a year for having drafted a constitution labeled "socialist": Pridi is described, without great compassion, as "a Siamese prince who had studied in London and imbibed socialist ideas . . . and became known as the 'Stalin' of Siam." A revolt he organized against the new "constitutional" regime is said to have failed.[175] The most casual reading of Siamese history during these years reveals the compounded errors of this Comintern appraisal.

If we assume that the author relied, or sought to rely, on local Communist intelligence, his ignorance of developments in Siam may perhaps be excused. The identification of Siamese Communism with the Chinese community forced it for many years

[175] Ms, "The Revolutionary Ferment in Siam," *Inprecor*, May 4, 1934, pp. 693-4.

into a wholly clandestine existence. For this reason the origins of the movement are extremely obscure. Even the existence of a formal Communist organization in Siam prior to World War II must be considered as doubtful, although several students of Siamese Communism note one.[176] Soviet and Comintern sources, it is worth observing, note the existence only of a "Communist movement" in Siam in the 1930's and do not claim the existence of a Communist party as such.[177]

The most substantial Soviet commentary on Siam during the period under review was an article by the Orientalist A. Ivin carried in three successive issues of *Tikhii okean* in 1935. The focus of the article is not domestic political affairs but Japanese penetration into Southeast Asia via Siam. The author quotes the head of a recent Japanese "good will" mission to Bangkok as saying that "Siam is the door to British Malaya, British Burma, and French Indochina . . . and therefore serves as a valuable spring-board for Japanese racial policies in the South Seas area. The southward movement of Japan is its historic mission and in this respect the importance of an independent Siam is obvious." Ivin ridicules Japan's allegedly benign motives in Siam and considers Tokyo's object the subjugation of the country, much like her recent subjugation of Manchuria which threatens Eastern Siberia. The article also includes a lengthy and moderately well-researched account of the agrarian question in Siam, which concludes with the observation that the class struggle in the countryside has created a situation throughout the country "pregnant with revolutionary possibilities." Communism as such is touched on very briefly in the article, but Pridi, whose "communistic" con-

[176] Thompson and Adloff, for instance, speak of leaflets distributed in 1932 by the "Communist Party of Siam"; *Left Wing in Southeast Asia*, p. 54. Brimmell, evidently drawing on British intelligence reports, lists half a dozen Communist and Communist-front organizations allegedly existing in Siam in the 1930's; *Communism in Southeast Asia*, pp. 114-5. Neither of these accounts cites sources for its claims.

[177] Reference to a Siamese party organization is, however, made in a later British Communist account; it mentions "the small but influential Communist Party of Thailand (*sic*)" as one of the forces supporting the revolution of 1932 (a reversal, it may be noted, of the Comintern position of 1934, cited above). See *World News and Views*, December 20, 1941, p. 813.

stitution of 1933 is dealt with, receives sympathetic treatment; his "communism," however, is denied.[178]

Ivin's long article marks the beginning of a modest interest in Siam, especially within scholarly circles in Moscow, but does not reveal significant *political* preoccupation with Siamese affairs by the Kremlin's leaders. Siam no more than Burma had succeeded in exciting Moscow's concern by 1935.

In *Malaya*, meanwhile, the course of Communism in the first half of the 1930's, despite the earlier organization of the movement and the existence of a Communist party by 1930, is hardly less obscure than in Siam. The arrest of Ducroix in 1931, which led to the collapse of the Comintern's network in Southeast Asia, undoubtedly handicapped the Malayan party. For several years it appears to have been wholly without contact with the international movement, although not unaware of the direction of current Comintern policies. A meeting of the MCP in September 1932, for instance, adopted a twelve-point program which included most of the goals listed in other authoritative statements of Communist objectives in Southeast Asia at the time. According to a later Malayan Communist text of the 1932 program, British imperialism was to be overthrown; land was to be confiscated and redistributed; an eight-hour day, civil rights, and free education in the vernacular were to be guaranteed; above all, a "Malayan Workers' and Peasants' Soviet Republic" was to be established. The program concluded with the MCP's pledge to "defend and guard the Soviet Union; support the revolutions in China and India; and unite with the proletariat and the oppressed, weak and minor races throughout the world."[179] The similarity between the Malayan program and

[178] A. Ivin, "Chto proiskhodit v Siame?" *Tikhii okean*, Nos. 2, 3, and 4, 1935.
[179] "History of the Malayan Communist Party," p. 13. Another account of the 1932 meeting, also of Communist origin, gives a similar description of its principal resolution; see Wu Tien-wang, "The Communist Party of Malaya" (unpublished manuscript, 1947?), cited in Hanrahan, *The Communist Struggle in Malaya*, p. 17. The latter source refers to the conference as a Pan-Malayan Cadres' Meeting; the former describes it as the Third Representatives' Conference; a Malayan government source ("Basic Paper on the Malayan Communist Party," Vol.

such documents as the Indochinese "Program of Action" of 1932 and Carpio's "instruction" to the CPPI of the same year suggests that the MCP had discovered ways to keep abreast of developments in the international movement despite its isolation.

According to Malayan government sources, the MCP re-established contact with the international organization following the revival of the "Comintern apparatus" in Shanghai in August 1933. The Malayans were reportedly allotted a $300 (Malayan) monthly subsidy at this juncture;[180] in March 1934 a Comintern agent, a Cantonese named D. Ling, was sent to Malaya to help reorganize the party; in June a directive from the Shanghai apparatus (reportedly drafted by Earl Browder) instructed the MCP to create a mass party of all races, to organize strikes in the urban areas, and to devise slogans capable of exercising a wider appeal throughout the country.[181]

Whether or not in response to the directive from Shanghai, the Malayan Communists became particularly active during the latter part of 1934 and 1935. Branches of the party were reportedly established in all of the Malay states. Government sources place Communist strength at the end of 1934, including members of Communist-affiliated organizations, at 12,716.[182] Strikes, in the meantime, were widespread throughout Malaya during this period. In May 1935, again according to Malayan intelligence sources, the MCP reported enthusiastically to the "Shanghai apparatus" on its activities of the preceding year and requested closer liaison, more Comintern agents, and, of course, additional

---

I, Part 2, p. 8) lists the meeting as a full party congress, with appropriate reconstitution of the Central Committee. There is little doubt, however, that all three sources describe the same gathering.

[180] A previous subsidy for the Malayans, allegedly entrusted to Ducroix in 1930, was never received; see Onraet, *Singapore—A Police Background*, p. 113.

[181] "Basic Paper on the Malayan Communist Party," Vol. 1, Part 2, p. 10; this source notes some misgivings within the MCP on the receipt of the Shanghai directive, but indicates it was adopted in due course.

[182] The figure—which is doubtless an exaggeration—is seen as a substantial increase over Communist strength in 1932 and 1933 and slightly higher than the estimate of 11,000 for 1931 (allegedly based on captured Communist records); see *ibid.*, p. 7.

funds.[183] If this evidence of a resurgent militancy in the Malayan Communist movement may be credited, the MCP—like the CPPI—was ill-prepared to respond to the more moderate policies soon to be articulated at the Seventh Comintern Congress in Moscow.

The MCP had meanwhile adopted a constitution which, according to one available text, reveals the Malayans' intention of adhering as closely as possible to Moscow. The document, dated March 1934, describes the MCP as an "affiliate" of the Comintern and requires that any desiring admission must accept the Comintern's platform and Constitution as well as those of the MCP. The Comintern is given wide authority over party affairs, including the convening of party congresses. Indeed the entire constitution reads enough like the basic documents of the Russian Communist Party to leave little doubt that the latter served as its model.[184]

The deference paid to the Russians in the Malayan constitution, taken together with the MCP's apparent connection with a Comintern unit in Shanghai (although the reality of the latter must still be held in doubt), suggests that the orientation of the new Malayan leadership, in contrast to that of its predecessor in the *Nanyang* organization, was more toward Moscow than toward the Chinese Communists. This is, of course, possible and was allegedly the intent of the reorganization of the *Nanyang* groups in 1930, as we have seen. One should not, however, be misled by appearances. The membership of the Malayan party was still overwhelmingly Chinese; according to Malayan government sources (which accent the Soviet as distinct from Chinese Communist orientation of the MCP), the ratio of Chinese to Malays in Communist-front organizations during these years was approximately 15 to 1 and as high as 50 to 1 in the party itself.[185] So large a component of Chinese party members must

---

[183] *Ibid.*, pp. 9-11.

[184] The text of the MCP constitution, adopted at the Sixth Plenum of the party Central Committee in March 1934, is translated in full (from the Chinese original) in Hanrahan, *op. cit.*, pp. 87-101.

[185] "Basic Paper on the Malayan Communist Party," Vol. I, Part 2, p. 1.

have assured a continuing and instinctive allegiance to the CCP.

Moscow, in the meantime, was singularly inattentive to the Malayan Communists and to developments in Malaya during these years. The Comintern, to judge from the published records of its plenary meetings between the Sixth and Seventh Congresses, at no time discussed the Malayan situation. The few articles in the Soviet press touching on the colony were confined to the significance of the Singapore naval base and of Malaya's foreign trade in developing imperialist rivalries in the Far East.[186] Even the vigorous labor activity organized by the MCP after the middle of 1934 was acknowledged in the Soviet press only at the end of 1935.[187] In view of so modest a coverage of Malayan affairs, any effort to urge a growing Soviet influence in the Malaya Communist movement, at the expense of Chinese influence, must be considered premature.

CONCLUSIONS

The evidence reviewed in this chapter suggests an unmistakable increase in the tempo of revolutionary activity in Southeast Asia during the first half of the 1930's. It was not enough of an increase, perhaps, to give an impression of impending conflagration, as certain Soviet writers argued, but it marked a stirring worth Moscow's notice. In 1930 the insurrection at Enbay precipitated disorders which lasted a year or more in Indochina. The same year the Saya San uprising in Burma stimulated a peasant revolt which lasted nearly as long. In 1931 an era of chronic labor and peasant unrest began in the Philippines which lasted intermittently through the revolt of the *Sakdalista* in 1935. In 1933 the *Zeven Provincien* mutiny off Sumatra marked smoldering unrest even in Indonesia, where

---

[186] E.g., "Britanskaia Malaia kak rynok promyshlennogo oborudovaniia," *Vneshnaia torgovlia*, No. 25, 1932, p. 16; A. L. Gal'perin, "Singapurskaia baza i ee znachenie dlia strategicheskoi situatsii na Tikhom okeane," *Tikhii okean*, No. 3, 1935, pp. 90-104.

[187] See O. Rykovskaia, "Britanskaia Malaia," *Materialy po natsional'no-kolonial'nym problemam*, No. 5 (29), 1935, pp. 121-47. It is interesting to note that recent Soviet studies of this era of Malayan Communism rely almost exclusively on Western sources; e.g., Rudnev, *Ocherki noveishei istorii Malaii*, pp. 26ff.

revolutionary activity had been muted since the abortive insurrection of 1926-1927. In 1934 and 1935 labor disorders intensified perceptibly in Malaya. Only in Siam (which paradoxically experienced in the coup d'état of 1932 the only major *constitutional* upheaval during this period) was there no serious revolutionary activity of the sort likely to excite Moscow's interest. Three new Communist parties, meanwhile, came into existence in Southeast Asia during this era (in Indochina, Malaya, and the Philippines); older party organizations continued to exist, if not to flourish, in Indonesia and possibly Siam. Only in Burma (of the principal dependencies in Southeast Asia) was there no Communist movement by 1935.

The Russians took some note of these developments. An overall increase in coverage of Southeast Asian affairs in the Soviet and Comintern press can be shown, and a livelier attention to areas heretofore neglected is evident. The Enbay episode, for instance, stimulated an enduring new interest in the affairs of the Indochinese revolutionary movement which earlier Soviet commentators had overlooked. The formulations of the Comintern, meanwhile, stimulated the rebellious mood of Southeast Asian Communists and encouraged new ventures. The persistent claims of the ECCI that "capitalist stabilization" was at an end and that "a new round of revolutions" was at hand were not lost on activists in Indochina and the Philippines; the labeling of the "struggle for soviets" as a first task of colonial peoples everywhere finds expression in all major programs and resolutions adopted by the Southeast Asian parties after 1930. There was, however, minimal *operational* concern with Communist affairs in Southeast Asia. If we dismiss as doubtful reports of a "Comintern apparatus" re-established in Shanghai in 1933, all evidence suggests a distinct retreat of the Comintern from East Asia as an operational force. Since one judges Soviet behavior less by words than actions, the absence of a visible instrument for Moscow's strategies in Southeast Asia, comparable even to the modest instruments of the 1920's, is a consideration of some significance in weighing Soviet policy after 1930.

How is this "retreat" to be explained? Certain considerations which had limited the Comintern's effectiveness in the 1920's continued to affect Moscow's policies: the difficulty of access to the Southeast Asian movements, for instance, intensified during the 1930's as colonial police administrations became more vigilant; the Kuomintang's control over coastal ports in China which had previously served as operations centers for the Comintern frustrated Moscow's agents more after 1930 than before. The more modest role of the International, however, appears to have been due less to improved surveillance than to a deliberate decision in Moscow to curb its activities. Why? The reasons are germane to our discussion, for without consular and other diplomatic facilities in East Asia, through which "instructions" might be channeled, the Kremlin relied heavily upon the Comintern and its affiliates for any liaison it wished to maintain with the colonial movements; a restraint imposed upon the International meant a self-limitation on Stalin's designs in the East.

Stalin's decision to curb the International relates, above all, to the altered requirements of Soviet foreign policy early in the 1930's. Without attempting to catalogue the international events which led to this change, we may note that the need for a stronger security system was increasingly sensed in Moscow following the Japanese seizure of Manchuria in 1931 and the emergence of Nazi power in Germany soon thereafter. Soviet strategies were altered to meet these twin threats on the flanks of the USSR. In particular, it was imperative to seek allies among those nations also threatened by Japanese militarism or by Hitler and willing to collaborate in some measure with Russia. Diplomatic relations were accordingly restored with China in 1932; Soviet-American relations were normalized the next year; in 1934 the USSR entered the League of Nations. Clandestine activities conducted by the Comintern, notably in the colonies of the Western powers with which Moscow was seeking more cordial relations, were obviously inconsistent with the new commitments of Stalin's foreign policy and had to be forsworn. At the same time the urgent commitment to industrialization and collectivization, which accompanied the turn in Soviet foreign policy, had the effect of absorbing a large portion of Moscow's energies and of de-emphasizing risky revolutionary ventures in East Asia. It should be recalled, in seeking to explain Stalin's attitude toward the Comintern during these years, that he had never been a central figure in this organization, two of whose leaders in the 1920's—Zinoviev and Bukharin—had opposed his rise to power. It was therefore not a personal sacrifice of any consequence for him to relegate the International to a relatively inconspicuous role in Soviet foreign policy and to remain aloof from the operations still entrusted to it.

Stalin could, and indeed did, delegate responsibility for carrying out his colonial policies, such as they were, to the metropolitan parties. Where the relationship of the latter to the colonial movements was cordial, as in the case of Indochina and the Philippines, this device enjoyed some success. A delegated authority in so sensitive a matter as the implementation of a revolutionary strategy, however, could not be fully effective; it lacked the orchestrated offensive Moscow alone was capable of organizing. In the absence of a more lively role by the principal instrument of Moscow's revolutionary strategies, then, Soviet pronouncements on the colonial question, during these years, though no less clamorous than during the 1920's, have an air of unreality.

Why, then, if this reading of Stalin's foreign policy in the early 1930's is correct, did the aggressive line of the Sixth Comintern Congress continue to be asserted in East Asia? Call it a paradox of Soviet policy. It was not the first nor would it be the last instance of paradox. Soviet spokesmen continued by habit, as it were, to compose militant appraisals of revolutionary prospects in Southeast Asia and to call, as a matter of course, for appropriately aggressive strategies. This was justified by the directives of the Sixth Comintern Congress which had not been rescinded and which, indeed, were periodically reaffirmed by the ECCI. Until Stalin gave some sign that these formulations were no longer in force, Soviet and Comintern spokesmen alike continued to be bound by them in their commentaries on the colonial question. Moscow *spoke*, it has been suggested, according to one set of principles; it *acted* according to another. The paradox was not resolved until 1935, when the Comintern was brought into tune with policies Stalin had been pursuing for several years.

CHAPTER FOUR

United Front in Southeast Asia: 1935-1941

THE revolutionary feature of Soviet foreign policy, it was made clear in the last chapter, had been largely eclipsed by 1935. Diplomacy had replaced subversion and incitement as Moscow's chief strategy; the Foreign Office overshadowed the Comintern as the chief instrument for carrying it out. Burdened with directives shaped in a different era, the International grew increasingly estranged from the main thrust of Stalin's policies, and it is a measure of the lack of importance he attached to the International and its program of world revolution in the 1930's that he waited so long to bring it abreast of his plans. Once adopted by the Seventh Comintern Congress, the new directives for world Communism remained in force, with some modifications during the Nazi-Soviet era, until the end of World War II —and in some measure until the Autumn of 1947. The Seventh Congress, then, set a course for the world movement which was to survive for ten or a dozen years and outlive the Comintern itself.

SEVENTH COMINTERN CONGRESS: 1935

The Seventh Congress of the Third International, meeting in Moscow in July and August 1935, was a pale replica of its predecessors. The course of events during the seven-year interval between this and the Sixth Congress had drained the vitality of the International. It could, when summoned, make sounds, but its fury had passed. Stalin, who had attended no Comintern gatherings since 1928, insofar as is known, made only a brief appearance at the Seventh Congress, at its opening session, and did not speak. He was nonetheless fully in control of the proceedings in the Hall of Columns. Indeed, it is unimaginable that the Seventh Congress could have been held at all without his blessing. No speaker, needless to say, failed to render homage to Stalin's inspired leadership of the world Communist movement.

Under these circumstances, the Seventh Congress could hardly provide the forum earlier congresses had provided for debating and determining the course of Comintern strategies. Nor was it intended that it should. Stalin's design in summoning the Seventh (and last) Congress of the International was to gain a suitable platform from which a strategy already devised could be proclaimed. Occasional flourishes in behalf of ultimate world Communism notwithstanding, the sole purpose of the Seventh Congress was to outline to the 510 delegates assembled (representing 65 national parties) the virtues of the popular, or united, front.

Dimitrov, in his keynote address, gave the basic formulation of the new policy: "The first thing that must be done, the thing with which to begin, is to form a united front, to establish unity of action of the workers in every factory, in every district, in every region, in every country, all over the world. Unity of action of the proletariat on a national and international scale is the mighty weapon which renders the working class capable not only of successful defense but also of successful counter-attack against Fascism, against the class enemy."[1]

This message was repeated again and again throughout the month-long congress, with as much variation as doctrinal requirements and the imaginations of the 150 delegates who made interventions allowed. In due course it was incorporated in the congress' resolutions. The united, or popular, front was the principal tactical device for carrying out the main objective of defending the Soviet Union from Fascist aggression. As Ercoli, another major speaker at the Seventh Congress, put it: "Conscious of the deepest aspirations of the masses and the vital interests of all humanity, the Communist International puts itself at the head of the campaign for the defense of peace and the Soviet Union. The slogan of peace becomes our central slogan in the fight against war."[2] The united front, then, was to be an effort in behalf of "peace" and order, not social upheaval.

No one familiar with Moscow's strategies in the past will be

[1] *Seventh Congress of the Communist International*, p. 142.
[2] *Ibid.*, p. 415.

bewitched by a turn to "united front" tactics. This was the hardy perennial of Soviet revolutionary policy, both at home and abroad. In 1917 Lenin's "soldering" (*smychka*) of workers and peasants was a form of united front. In the 1920's the united front was broadened and applied with varying success to colonial revolutions—notably in China. The Sixth Congress, with its insistence on more lonely proletarian efforts, relegated the united front momentarily to the background, but by the early 1930's the "united front from below" emerged as a new variant of the old theme. Two features of the united front proclaimed in 1935 distinguish this latest model from its predecessors: first, it embraced a wider range of political allies for the proletarians than had heretofore been envisaged; second, it was given a focus in Soviet formulations no earlier united front had received. When one speaks of the "era of the United Front" in Soviet foreign policy, one refers to the years following the Seventh Congress. All significant activity of the Comintern during these years was directed at strengthening the anti-Fascist fronts ordered in 1935. No situation existed in the world in which the tactics of the united front were inapplicable: thus Communists supported Royalists in the Spanish Civil War, the Roosevelt administration in the United States, and Chiang Kai-shek in China—all in the name of a single world-wide slogan.

The Seventh Congress, preoccupied with its assignment to launch this far-reaching program, gave little attention to particular questions—such as the colonial question—which had engaged earlier congresses. There was no National and Colonial Commission, for instance. Where colonies, or semi-colonies, were discussed, it was normally in the context of establishing anti-Fascist fronts in the metropolitan. Thus Dimitrov reminded the European delegates that "the proletariat of the imperialist countries has possible allies not only in the working people of its own countries but also in the oppressed colonies and semi-colonies." He continued: "Every step in the direction of supporting the struggle for the liberation of the colonial peoples means transforming the colonies and semi-colonies into one of the most

209

important reserves of the world proletariat"—reserves, that is, to be used in the defense of peace and of the USSR.[3]

The Chinese delegate Wang Ming (Ch'en Shao-yü), responding to Dimitrov in behalf of the colonial world, also linked the revolutionary movement in the colonies to united front efforts in Europe. Noting the similar purpose of both, he said: "We have a common enemy—imperialism, we have a single program and the same aims of struggle for socialism, we have the same strategy and tactics of the world revolution, we have the same fortress of revolutionary struggle—the USSR, we have the same world party—the Communist International, and we have the same teacher and leader—the great Stalin!"[4]

Had the Seventh Congress been disposed to consider in greater detail the colonial question as such, it is not certain that the formulations of the Sixth Congress would have been appreciably altered. Wang Ming underscored the adequacy in all respects of the 1928 appraisal of revolutionary prospects in the colonies and considered it "beyond question even more convincing and well-founded today."[5] National liberation under Communist leadership, in short, remained the Comintern's stated objective for the colonies. The tactics of the "anti-imperialist united front" (the special term for the united front in the colonial world) in no way altered this objective, Wang Ming insisted; in fact, the united front rendered it more attainable: ". . . without the active participation of the Communists in the general people's and national struggle against imperialist oppression it is inconceivable that the Communist groups or the young, numerically small party can be transformed into a real mass party, and without this the hegemony of the proletariat and soviet power in their country is not to be thought of. Without a doubt imperialism is the principal and basic enemy of all the colonial peoples, and if Communists are unable to come out against imperialism in the

[3] *Ibid.*, p. 143.
[4] *Ibid.*, p. 312; Wang Ming's intervention, which was the principal review at the Seventh Congress of colonial developments since 1928, was published separately (*The Revolutionary Movement in the Colonial Countries*, London, 1935) and widely circulated in the following years.
[5] *Ibid.*, p. 284.

front ranks of the people, how can the people recognize in the party its vanguard and leader?"[6]

The final resolution on the Comintern's tasks also emphasized the continuing importance of the struggle for independence in the colonies. "It is the duty of Communists," the resolution stated, "actively to support the national liberation struggle of the oppressed peoples of the colonial and semi-colonial countries."[7]

The instruction of the Seventh Congress to colonial parties, to judge from these formulations, was to superimpose the tactics of the "anti-imperialist united front" upon the broadly militant strategies already in force. It was nowhere implied that these tactics required any slackening of the struggle for independence, for proletarian hegemony, or even for the establishment of soviets.

The experience of the Chinese Communists was cited repeatedly during the Seventh Congress as a model for all Eastern peoples. Wilhelm Pieck, in his report on the activities of the ECCI, called the creation of soviets in China "the outstanding event" since the Sixth Congress, "an event that has impressed its stamp on the entire colonial world in the post-war period." He continued: "The Chinese revolution provides the first model of a colonial revolution in which the ideological, and also, in its initial form, the state hegemony of the proletariat is realized. In the Chinese working class the colonial proletariat has proved in practice its ability to solve great historical problems, to maintain the complete economic and political independence of the country, to completely abolish feudal survivals, to put an end to large landed proprietorship, to cut out the cancer of usury, and to undertake revolutionary changes that clear the way for the victory of socialism."[8] Wang Ming made similar claims and added that one reason for Chinese Communist success was that "in recent years the Communist Party of China has applied and is applying the tactics of the anti-imperialist united front."[9]

One could well ask in what sense the experience of the Chinese Communists served as a useful model for the peoples of the East. Their alleged application of the "tactics of the anti-imperialist united front" was certainly not obvious during the Long

[6] *Ibid.*, p. 305.   [7] *Ibid.*, p. 593.   [8] *Ibid.*, pp. 50-1.   [9] *Ibid.*, p. 286.

March, which was still in progress while the Seventh Congress met; engaged as the Communists were in avoiding battle with Chiang Kai-shek's forces, alliance with the Kuomintang, we may imagine, was far from their minds in 1935. Moreover, the Seventh Congress itself made it clear that no early alliance with the Kuomintang was envisaged: the resolution on tasks commended the Chinese Communists specifically for "their struggle against the Japanese and other imperialists *and the Kuomintang*."[10] We must nonetheless take due note of the attention given to the alleged successes of the Chinese Communists, especially to their establishment of a soviet regime and the creation of an independent army. In the absence of a clearly enunciated instruction to the colonial parties, it must be imagined that the Seventh Congress was in reality urging them to follow the course of the Chinese soviet movement.

The interest the congress expressed in China was not matched by a parallel interest in Southeast Asia. Of the three major speakers at the congress, two—Pieck and Ercoli—made a single passing reference to Southeast Asia;[11] Wang Ming referred briefly to the 1930 risings in Indochina and to the mutiny of Indonesian seamen on the *Zeven Provincien,* but relied on developments elsewhere (mainly in China, India, and Brazil) to demonstrate the worldwide crisis in the colonies. Even delegates from the metropolitan parties overlooked the Southeast Asian colonies, an omission that casts some doubt on the permanency of ties established with colonial parties during the preceding years: no French delegate, for instance, mentioned Indochina; nor did Earl Browder, despite his recent long residence in the Far East, mention the Philippines. Brief interventions by a Vietnamese and an Indonesian provided the delegates with all the first-hand information they were to hear of the revolutionary movement in Southeast Asia.[12] For the first time in more than a decade, mean-

[10] *Ibid.,* p. 593; emphasis added.

[11] Pieck mentioned the peasant uprisings of 1931 in Indochina, and Ercoli referred to Japanese trade ascendancy in Indochina; *ibid.,* pp. 27 and 391.

[12] See Chajan's address in *Inprecor,* October 7, 1935, pp. 1294-5, and Roestan Effendi's in *ibid.,* December 2, 1935, pp. 1609-10.

while, no Southeast Asian was elected to the new ECCI, although several prospective candidates were then residing in Moscow.

The formulation given the united front by the Seventh Congress was altogether inconsistent as it applied to the colonies. The selection of China as the model for other colonies, quite apart from objections already noted, was inappropriate for a still more compelling reason: it overlooked the fact that China's antagonist was Japan, which was also Russia's, while the antagonist elsewhere in the colonial world was normally a Western power with which Moscow sought to join forces against Germany. This was universally the case among the colonies of Southeast Asia. Moscow had less to gain in promoting national liberation movements in Indonesia, Indochina, the Philippines, Burma, and Malaya than in building good will in Holland, France, the United States, and England by restraining these movements. To call attention, then, to "the duty of Communists actively to support the national liberation struggle of the oppressed peoples of the colonial and semi-colonial countries" was wholly incompatible with Stalin's broader purpose of creating popular anti-Fascist fronts in the major imperialist countries. No amount of rhetoric by speakers like Wang Ming could conjure away the incompatibility.

Whatever the reasons for this duality in the united front policy designed for the colonial world—whether it was due to oversight in Moscow or to subtle strategies we must eventually consider—the Comintern's simultaneous support of national liberation fronts in the colonies and anti-Fascist fronts in the imperialist countries could not last indefinitely. Stalin eventually had to decide between two courses: to continue support of the colonial movements or to remove the embarrassment to metropolitan parties—as well as the irritant to his own projects for a collective security alliance with European imperialist powers—by denying them. Cogent arguments favored the latter alternative, and in due course it prevailed. The Soviet decision led inevitably to a further slackening of interest in colonial affairs. This was particularly true of Southeast Asia, where coverage of local developments in the Soviet and Comintern press trailed off to virtual silence by the outbreak of World War II.[13]

The united front in Southeast Asia unfolded under these conditions. There were, as we shall see, many variations of the united front, both in timing and in content once adopted; there was further variation during the era of the Nazi-Soviet alliance in Europe, from August 1939 to June 1941. These variations will become apparent as we proceed. For the present, however, our task is to piece together the course of the united front in the Southeast Asian colonies from the fragmentary evidence available. Our principal object in this review is to discover how extensive Soviet influence could remain in an area which Moscow was neglecting and during an era when Stalin's strategies must inevitably disillusion local Communist leaders educated in class struggle and violence. Was the Communist base in Southeast Asia durable enough to withstand these strains on its loyalty to Moscow?

The course of the united front in four of the six Southeast Asian countries—Indochina, the Philippines, Indonesia, and Malaya—is germane to our purpose. Soviet policies in Siam and Burma, where Communist developments were still in embryo, we may conveniently leave to the following chapter.

COURSE OF THE UNITED FRONT: I

Indochina. By 1935, as we have seen, Vietnamese Communists, inspired by the People's Front in France, were already applying the tactics of "the anti-imperialist front."[14] They were thus well in advance of other Southeast Asian parties in anticipating Moscow's change in line. A Vietnamese delegate to the Seventh Con-

[13] Soviet bibliographies consulted by the author, such as *Zhurnal'naia letopis* and *Bibliografiia Iugo-vostochnoi Azii*, show a marked dropping off in articles on Southeast Asia published after 1935. Coverage in Comintern journals also declines noticeably after the Seventh Congress; *Inprecor*, for instance, which had annually carried as many as twenty-five or thirty items on Southeast Asia at the end of the 1920's and a dozen or more early in the 1930's, averaged fewer than half a dozen after 1935.

[14] E.g. Gabriel Péri, "The Anti-imperialist Front in the Election to the Colonial Council," *Inprecor*, March 23, 1935, p. 353.

214

gress pointed out the success the CPIC had had with these tactics, especially in the Saigon elections of May 1935. His party, he continued, "is fighting to carry out the program of the Communist International for the anti-imperialist and agrarian revolution and for the complete emancipation and the independence of Indochina."[15] If he laid greater stress on Indochinese independence and less on anti-Fascist fronts than a Russian official might have, his remarks were nonetheless in the spirit of other pronouncements on colonial affairs during the Seventh Congress —for instance, Wang Ming's. The Vietnamese, it might have been imagined, would encounter no great difficulty implementing Moscow's new line.

In fact, the CPIC did have trouble with the united front in Indochina. A party congress held in Macao in 1935 is said to have failed entirely in its efforts to formulate a united front program. A reference to this congress in a 1937 Comintern report on Indochina lays the failure to "sectarian" tendencies within the leadership which kept the party aloof from the masses.[16] If this charge, a recurrent one in appraisals of the CPIC, is ambiguous, the same source is more explicit in discussing the shortcomings of Vietnamese policies the following year. As late as May 1936, the Comintern report continues, the Vietnamese comrades were "still demanding of other groups and parties, as a condition for the formation of a united front, continued struggle for the immediate overthrow of imperialism and for the agrarian revolution."[17] Since the latter objectives were clearly authorized

[15] *Ibid.*, October 7, 1935, p. 1294. The name of the Vietnamese is given as Chajan in this account; another source gives Le Hong Phong as the Indochinese delegate at the Seventh Congress: "President Ho Chi Minh."

[16] I. Dun, "Narodnoe dvizhenie v Indo-Kitae posle pobedy frantsuzskogo narodnogo fronta," *Kommunisticheskii internatsional*, No. 2, February 1937, p. 36. There is some question as to the number and the date of the Macao congress: the source cited above calls it the First Congress and places it in March 1935—that is, before the Seventh Comintern Congress; Devillers, *Histoire du Viêt-Nam de 1940 à 1952*, p. 68, states the congress was held only after the Comintern congress. A Vietnamese Communist source, meanwhile, speaks of the 1935 meeting as the Second Party Congress, but does not attempt to date it precisely; see Chan Zan Then, *Rasskazy o zhizni i deiatel'nosti Prezidenta Kho Shi Mina*, p. 75.

[17] Dun, *loc. cit.*

215

by the Seventh Congress, the Comintern, it would seem, not the CPIC, should bear responsibility for shortcomings in the Vietnamese united front caused by conflicting policies in Moscow. This was not, however, Stalin's style—nor the Comintern's. Blame was laid squarely on the Vietnamese, and they were said to have purged themselves of their "sectarian errors" only at a party plenum held in South China in July 1936, "an historic date for the CPIC." On this occasion the "Comintern's political line" was explained and a suitable program for an anti-imperialist united front adopted.[18] According to a later North Vietnamese source, Nguyen Ai Quoc, who had recently returned from Moscow, directed the plenum in person. Its principal resolution argued that the slogan for the overthrow of French imperialism must be withdrawn; instead the Vietnamese Communists should create "anti-royalist revolutionary bases" for the overthrow of the feudal regime within the colony. It was this resolution, the North Vietnamese source claims, which made possible a "wide and open struggle" in Indochina.[19]

If the accounts of this meeting of the CPIC may be credited, the lines of the "Democratic United Front" in Indochina were thus set by the middle of 1936, two years before they were in the Philippines and three before they were in Malaya. National liberation was withdrawn as a Communist slogan in Indochina. Instead, the Comintern proposed a linking of the united fronts in France and Indochina "in order to help the Indochinese win first of all the elementary right of free organization"[20]—a modest objective, the Vietnamese comrades must have felt, when contrasted with their programs of earlier years. The French Communists set equally mild goals for their Vietnamese "brothers." French colonies, Thorez explained in 1937, of course have a right of self-determination, but they need not exercise it. He cited Lenin's famous dictum of 1914 to support his point: "the right to

---

[18] *Ibid.*

[19] "President Ho Chi Minh." A contemporary Soviet historian of Vietnam states that the CPIC reoriented its policies to Moscow's at a party conference in May, not July, 1936; see the chapter by S. A. Mkhitarian in *Demokraticheskaia respublika Vietnam, 1945-1960*, p. 38.

[20] Dun, *op. cit.*, p. 38.

216

separation does not signify the obligation to separate." The interests of French colonials, including the Indochinese, Thorez concluded, were best served by a "free, trusting, and paternal" union with France.[21]

The Communists' difficulties in Indochina during the era of the united front stemmed in large part from the mildness of these recommendations. The CPIC could not, forsaking national liberation, compete effectively for leadership of the Indochinese nationalist movement, whose objectives remained unaffected by the world situation and by Moscow's effort to forge a worldwide anti-Fascist front. In consequence, the Indochinese Trotskyites, who persisted in their opposition to French rule, gained in influence within the nationalist movement at the expense of the Stalinists. The struggle was carried on at various levels—in the pages of *La Lutte* (which continued to carry statements by both factions), in local organizations, and in electoral campaigns— and there is little reason to doubt that the bitterness of the rivalry took its toll of even the most dedicated Communists. Moscow would, of course, have wished to keep Trotskyites and Communists apart, and evidently made sporadic efforts to do so,[22] but the strange alliance was a necessary feature of the Democratic Front in Indochina. According to a Vietnamese Stalinist, writing in mid-1937, "in the particular situation in Indochina, unique in the world, . . . the breaking of our fighting front, the only one which can be built with Trotskyites and ourselves, will engender inextricable confusion among the masses and kill the combative ardor of our people. . . . Until some new pattern emerges, they [the Trotskyites] are still trustworthy anti-imperialist elements who deserve our support."[23] The alliance accordingly was sustained until the summer of 1939, although precarious and marked by growing rivalry between the two factions. In

---

[21] Walter, *Histoire du parti communiste français*, p. 377.

[22] A letter published under Trotskyist auspices in *La Lutte* on August 29, 1937, for instance, purported to be an instruction from the French Communists to the CPIC urging the latter to break the alliance with the Trotskyites; the inspiration for the instruction, it was alleged, came from Moscow. See Trager, *op. cit.*, p. 142.

[23] *La Lutte*, June 6, 1937, translated in Trager, *op. cit.*, pp. 321-2.

April 1939 a bitterly fought election in Cochinchina ended in a substantial victory for the Trotskyites, at Communist expense, and marked the high point of their influence in Vietnamese affairs.[24]

The Communists' efforts to maintain the Democratic United Front in Indochina ended abruptly with the signing of the Nazi-Soviet pact in August 1939. In September the CPIC, like the French Communist Party, was outlawed for supporting Moscow's "peace" policy now that France was at war. In November the Sixth Plenum of the Indochinese Central Committee, meeting in secrecy, passed a resolution which stated in part: "Nowadays, the situation has changed. At the present time, French imperialism has taken part in launching a world war. The domination imposed on colonies such as Indochina, which is clearly a Fascist militarist regime, and the scheme of compromising and surrendering to Japan have set a vital problem before the Indochinese people. *In the life and death struggle of the Indochinese nations there is no way out other than that of overthrowing French imperialism, opposing all foreign invaders, either white or yellow-skinned, in order to regain liberation and independence.*"[25]

This appraisal was entirely in tune with an article by a leading Russian student of Indochina which appeared at about the same time. The author, V. Vasil'eva, said little about the CPIC itself, except to note its persecution by the government, but was caustic in discussing French policies as they affected Indochina. "Invariably, in tense situations," she wrote, "the question comes up of strengthening 'Franco-Annamite co-operation' and the need of political reforms"—as during Varenne's administration in the 1920's and following the disorders of 1930-1931. Now, in 1939, Paris speaks again of "flexible" policies; but the Vietnamese, Vasil'eva asserts, are not interested. "The struggle for Indochina by French and Japanese imperialism is the struggle of two plun-

[24] For a more detailed summary of Stalinist-Trotskyite rivalry during the united front era, see the account of I. Milton Sacks in *ibid.*, pp. 140ff.

[25] Vo Nguyen Giap, *People's War, People's Army*, pp. 73-4 (emphasis in original); from an article first published in the Hanoi press in September 1961. Portions of this resolution, from a different source, are quoted in Devillers, *Histoire du Viêt-Nam de 1940 à 1952*, p. 79.

derers for booty. The Indochinese people do not wish to be the booty of either one or the other imperialist camp; they wish to create their *own* life independently and freely."[26]

This continued to be Moscow's view of Indochina during the era of the Nazi-Soviet pact, to judge from the few articles on the colony which appeared in the Soviet and Comintern press. Less and less attention, however, was devoted to domestic developments as Soviet observers concentrated on the diplomatic aspects of Japan's thrust southward and on the complicity of French imperialism with Japanese aggression; the activities of the CPIC were altogether ignored.[27] French Communists were more attentive to the Indochinese comrades, but powerless, it may be imagined, to provide them material assistance. The French Communist leader André Marty, for instance, wrote in 1940 of the leadership provided by the "fraternal, heroic and manly" CPIC in the struggle of the Vietnamese "for liberation from all imperialists." To demonstrate that not all Frenchmen were imperialists, he cited cases of French soldiers, sailors, and even officers befriending harassed Vietnamese revolutionaries.[28]

The CPIC, meanwhile, having regained leadership of the left wing of the nationalist movement as a result of the government's virtual annihilation of the Trotskyites, stepped up preparations for active rebellion. After the fall of France in June 1940, the Central Committee is reported to have resolved, "in view of the very critical internal situation in Indochina and of the imminent external danger which menaces the country, to prepare armed insurrection in order to install a republican government which will ally itself with the Resistance Front of the Chinese people, with the USSR, and with the world revolution."[29] According to

[26] V. Vasil'eva, "Indo-Kitai i polozhenie na Tikhom okeane," *Mirovoe khoziaistvo i mirovaia politika*, No. 11, November 1939, p. 168.
[27] E.g. Dan Khun, "Bor'ba za Frantsuzskii Indo-Kitai," *Kommunisticheskii internatsional*, No. 8, August 1940, pp. 90-4; V. I. Vasil'eva, "Indo-Kitai i obostrenie bor'by na Tikhom okeane," *Bol'shevik*, No. 19-20, October 1940, pp. 79-88; and V. I. Vasil'eva, "Bor'ba za frantsuzskie kolonii," *Mirovoe khoziaistvo i mirovaia politika*, No. 1, January 1941, pp. 77-87.
[28] André Marti, "Indokitaiskii narod i imperialisty," *Kommunisticheskii internatsional*, No. 10-11, October-November 1940, pp. 64-5.
[29] Devillers, *Histoire du Viêt-Nam de 1940 à 1952*, p. 79.

French police sources, Communist-inspired disorders occurred in the northern provinces of Tonking and in Cochinchina during the autumn of 1940. Nguyen Ai Quoc, heading an "external bureau" of the CPIC in Kunming province (in South China), was said to have opposed an early insurrection, but was unable to restrain his colleagues in Indochina, especially in Cochinchina. An insurrection was accordingly launched in Cochinchina at the end of the year, but was quickly put down by French troops. Following this effort, according to French colonial sources, a party gathering in January 1941 denounced the recent strategies and purged those responsible for them.[30]

Whatever the truth about the purging of party leaders responsible for the 1940 uprisings, the insurrectionary line was not entirely forsaken in 1941. In May the Eighth Party Plenum, summoned by Nguyen Ai Quoc,[31] reaffirmed this strategy, in general terms, and set the course of Indochinese Communism through the war years. The principal resolution adopted by the plenum read as follows, according to a recent Vietnamese text:

> At the present time the watchword of the party is first to liberate the Indochinese people from the Japanese and French yoke. For the fulfillment of these tasks, the forces of the whole of Indochina must be concentrated; those who love their country will unite together into a front and rally all their forces to fight for national independence and freedom, to smash the French and the Japanese invaders. The alliance of all forces of the classes and parties, the patriotic revolutionary groups, religious groups and all people fighting the Japanese, is the essential work of our party.[32]

[30] The foregoing is drawn from a report of the French *Sûreté* in Cochinchina summarized in Trager, *op. cit.*, pp. 144-5, as well as in other studies. Communist sources also refer to the insurrections of late 1940, but do not mention the reversal of the party's line after their failure; e.g. Min' Shan', "Revoliutsionnoe dvizhenie v V'etname," *Sovetskoe vostokovedenie*, No. 1, 1956, p. 40; *Le Viêtnam en lutte contre le fascisme*, p. 42.

[31] A recent North Vietnamese source states that the plenum was held in Indochina; "President Ho Chi Minh" (Hanoi, 1960). If so, this would have marked the first return of Nguyen Ai Quoc to Indochina in more than twenty years. Other sources, however, both Communist and non-Communist, state that the Eighth Plenum, like its predecessors, was held in South China; e.g. Mkhitarian, *Bor'ba v'etnamskogo naroda za natsional'nuiu nezavisimost', demokratiiu i mir*, p. 36, and Devillers, *op. cit.*, p. 97.

[32] Quoted in Vo Nguyen Giap, *People's War, People's Army*, p. 74.

This was, in short, a call for insurrection on a wider front than had heretofore been contemplated by Vietnamese Communists. Even the national bourgeoisie was to be attracted to the new program; the slogan for agrarian revolution, for instance, was "temporarily" withdrawn and a decision made not to confiscate the property of Vietnamese landowners, "in order," as a leading party official explained after the war, "to disunite the class of landowners and attract some of them to the anti-imperialist struggle."[33]

The CPIC, mindful of the failures of 1940 and anxious not to alarm the moderate Vietnamese nationalists it hoped to attract to the new united front, did not urge an immediate rising. This could occur, the resolution stated, only when the proper conditions existed—among them "the Chinese army's great triumph over the Japanese army, the outbreak of the French or Japanese revolution, the total victory of the democratic camp in the Pacific and in the Soviet Union, the revolutionary fermentation in the French and Japanese colonies, and particularly the landing of Chinese or British-American armies in Indochina."[34] The fact that in 1941 these conditions were still remote (and indeed were never completely fulfilled) should not cast doubt on the militancy of the Eighth Plenum resolution. On the ultimate goal the resolution did not mince words. "The revolution in Indochina," it asserted, "must be ended with an armed uprising." To this end the plenum called for a wide expansion of party work in both rural and urban areas; the creation of guerrilla bases; and, to coordinate the nation-wide program, the establishment of a new organization, the *Viet Nam Doc Lap Dong Minh Hoi* (Vietnam Independence League)—or, as it was subsequently known, the *Vietminh*.

More than a month before Russia became engaged in the war in Europe, then, and more than six months before the war spread to the Far East, the CPIC had devised not only its strategies but the principal vehicle for these strategies during the war and post-

[33] Truong Shin [Truong Chinh], *Avgustovskaia revoliutsiia vo V'etname*, p. 30, citing an article by Truong Chinh written in 1946.
[34] *Ibid.*, p. 82.

war years. Soviet influence in the adoption of these tactics may be discounted, and what Moscow thought of them is not known, since the Soviet and Comintern press had by this time ceased altogether its coverage of developments in Indochina.

COURSE OF THE UNITED FRONT: II

The Philippines. The Philippine Communists had adopted a militant and inflexible posture on the eve of the Seventh Comintern Congress, in marked contrast to Communists in Vietnam. A manifesto adopted by the CPPI early in 1935 distinguished "revolutionary struggle" as the only course for Philippine Communism; "peaceful 'constitutional' methods" were ruled out.[35] In May 1935 the party stood ostentatiously aloof from the *Sakdal* uprising near Manila, although sharing certain common goals with the *Sakdalista*—notably independence.

The intransigence of the CPPI is seen most clearly in its attitude toward the measures taken to implement the Tydings-Mc-Duffie Act and to prepare the Philippines for full independence. In September 1936, nearly a year after the colony had been made a self-governing Commonwealth and Manuel Quezon elected its first President, a Filipino wrote in *Inprecor* that the Philippines stood at the crossroads: "reaction *versus* revolution . . . dominion status *versus* independence." President Quezon, he argued, was an American puppet; the CPPI was "the only revolutionary and anti-imperialist working-class organization" in the country.[36] As late as September 1937, more than two years after the Seventh Congress, the CPPI demanded of a joint American-Philippine committee studying the affairs of the Commonwealth "complete and absolute" independence no later than July 4, 1939.[37]

This attitude was not in conflict with the views of Soviet Orientalists, who followed constitutional developments in the Philippines with some care during these years. O. Zabozlaeva, for in-

---

[35] *Communist*, April 1935, p. 372; see above, p. 180.

[36] "The Crisis in the Philippines," *Inprecor*, September 5, 1936, p. 1089; the article is unsigned but the author is said to be a Filipino.

[37] See the briefs prepared for the committee by the CPPI and by Communist-led trade unions on September 7, 1937, in Joint Preparatory Committee on Philippine Affairs, *Report* (Washington, May 20, 1938), Vol. 3, pp. 864, 888.

stance, wrote early in 1936 that American promises to the Filipinos were "a mask" to conceal Washington's true intentions.[38] Alexander Guber, in an analysis of the 1935 Constitution later in the year, found it full of loop-holes to guarantee American domination and the strengthening of the local ruling classes at the expense of workers and peasants.[39] Another article by Zabozlaeva in 1937 repeated these arguments.[40] So long as Moscow held these views, the CPPI was presumably under no pressure to modify its own in the interests of a broader anti-imperialist front.

The pace of the Philippine Communists toward a united front was accordingly slow. Although they knew of the Comintern's directives in this matter at least by June 1936, when materials of the Seventh Congress were published in Tagalog newspapers in Manila,[41] their isolation from the great majority of Filipinos over the question of independence prevented them from exercising effective leadership in any significant mass organization. The fact, moreover, that the CPPI was still illegal during these years, and its leaders in jail, further crippled Communist efforts. Mass tactics were nonetheless proclaimed and preliminary steps taken to apply them. In October Communists took part in the formation of the Popular Alliance, an uneasy union of Marxist and non-Marxist workers in Manila which later Soviet sources describe as the first effort to create a broad anti-Fascist front in the Philippines.[42] The Popular Alliance, however, had no distinctive program, exercised little influence in Philippine politics, and passed into oblivion long before the establishment of its successor, the *Frente Popular*. The conditions, in short, which fa-

[38] O. Zabozlaeva, "Sakdalistskoe dvizhenie na Filippinskikh ostrovakh," *Tikhii okean*, No. 1, 1936, pp. 156-7.

[39] A. A. Guber, "Amerikanskii imperializm i novaia konstitutsiia 'avtonomykh' Filippin," *Materialy po natsional'no-kolonial'nym problemam*, No. 36, 1936, pp. 27ff.

[40] O. Zabozlaeva, "SShA i Filippiny," *Tikhii okean*, No. 1, 1937, pp. 128-40; other articles on Philippine "autonomy" appearing in Soviet periodicals during this period are listed in *Bibliografiia Iugo-vostochnoi Azii*, p. 209.

[41] See Juan Tamarao, "The People's Front in the Philippine Islands," *Communist* (New York), No. 4, April 1937, p. 377; no Filipinos, it should be recalled, attended the Seventh Congress in Moscow.

[42] Levinson, *Filippiny mezhdu pervoi i vtoroi mirovymi voinami*, p. 165.

vored the adoption of vigorous united front tactics in Indochina by the middle of 1936 did not materialize so rapidly in the Philippines.

A change in the fortunes of the CPPI, however, was in the making. Late in 1936 or in 1937, thanks to the mediation of an American Communist, James Allen, the principal party leaders, including Evangelista, were granted conditional pardons by President Quezon and permitted to resume political activity.[43] Their release had the effect of restoring the party to legal status. It also led gradually to a change in Communist strategies. By early 1938, the tone of CPPI propaganda had moderated perceptibly, and Communists were freely collaborating with Socialists in various organizations. In May an alliance of Socialist and Communist-led trade unions was established, bringing under a single leadership an estimated 15,000 workers. At a congress of the new organization in June, Guillermo Capadocia, the Secretary-General of the CPPI, was elected Executive Secretary and a resolution was adopted which, among other things, pledged co-operation with the government in regulating labor disputes and offered qualified support of President Quezon's program of "Social Justice"; conspicuously absent in the resolution was any reference to the pace of Philippine independence.[44]

In August 1938 an extraordinary plenum of the Central Committee of the CPPI adopted a manifesto entitled "Mobilization of the Filipinos against Japanese Aggression," in which the party's new tactics were spelled out in some detail. Japanese aggression, the manifesto stated, was now "the greatest threat to our national

[43] There is uncertainty concerning the date of the pardon. Allen himself dates it at the end of 1937; James S. Allen, "Resurgent Democracy in the Philippines," *Inprecor*, April 1, 1939, p. 368. Other sources date it at the beginning of 1937 (Levinson, *op. cit.*, p. 221) or as early as December 1936 (Hoeksema, *op. cit.*, p. 178). Allen, for reasons not clear, fails to mention his part in obtaining the pardon, but Philippine Communists interviewed by the writer affirm it; interviews with José Lava and Luis Taruc. See also Lava, *Milestones*, p. 35.

[44] An account of the trade union congress, based on foreign sources, may be found in Levinson, *op. cit.*, p. 226. Quezon's program of "Social Justice" was launched in 1936, in an effort to broaden the basis of civil liberties in the Philippines, but up to this point had been derided by the Communists as "Quezonian socialism"; see Lava, *Milestones*, pp. 42ff.

integrity and the achievement of our independence." A slogan of "immediate independence at any cost" was accordingly meaningless and only played into the hands of the Japanese. "The right to separate from the United States," the manifesto stated, relying on Lenin's 1914 formula, "does not place upon us an obligation to separate." The manifesto continued: "The interests of the Philippine people demand unity with the democratic and progressive forces in the United States, not policies which will play into the hands of Fascists and lead Filipinos under the yoke of the Mikado. . . . At the present time the basic question is not a choice between gradual independence or some sort of continuing American sovereignty but between democracy and the preservation of our national integrity, on the one hand, and Fascism and military aggression on the other."

The manifesto then proposed a united front in the Philippines more embracing than any yet contemplated in Southeast Asia: "We are ready to cooperate with all parties, political groups, labor, peasant and fraternal organizations, no matter what our differences may be with regard to ultimate aims and programs, for the purpose of establishing a democratic front of the Filipino people which will be dedicated to the improvement of our living conditions, to the defense and extension of our democratic rights, to safeguarding our national autonomy and to furthering our cause of independence, peace and security. . . . We propose to President Quezon the immediate cooperation of our party, in order to secure mass support for the implementation of progressive and democratic legislation."[45]

The distance the CPPI had traveled in less than a year is evident in even a cursory comparison between this document and the brief (cited above) which the Communists presented to the joint American-Philippine commission the preceding September.

Socialists and Communists, meanwhile, were moving closer together, and the anticipated merger of the two parties took place during the Third Congress of the CPPI in October 1938. This congress, the first to be held openly, was attended by an estimated

[45] Translated from Levinson, *op. cit.*, pp. 230-2; an English translation of the manifesto may be found in *Communist* (New York), December 1938, pp. 1122-30.

5,000 delegates, observers, and guests.[46] Capadocia gave the key-note address, adhering closely to the August manifesto of the Central Committee. "The masses," he said, "should be wary of unprincipled advocates of independence right now, at all costs. . . . We offer President Quezon the support of our party for the realization of his program along the path of democracy. We stand ready to make possible the realization of our people's democratic unity." Pedro Abad Santos and Luis Taruc, representing the Socialists, spoke in similar vein. A representative of President Quezon is reported to have called the Communists' platform "the only constructive program" in the forthcoming elections. At the close of the congress, the delegates voted unanimously to unite the two parties into a single organization to be called "Communist Party of the Philippines (Merger of Socialist and Communist Parties)." Evangelista (who was ill in Europe at the time of the congress) was named National Chairman; Santos, Vice Chairman; and Capadocia, Secretary. The ten-man Politburo included seven Communists and three former Socialists (including Santos and Taruc). The resolutions adopted by the congress called for self-government in the Philippines, a united front against Japan, and collaboration with the peoples of China, the United States, Spain, and the Soviet Union; less conspicuously the resolutions also dealt with certain traditional demands relating to minimum pay, maximum hours, and social security.[47] In December, after the merger was completed, President Quezon removed the conditions on the pardons previously granted to Communist leaders and released the remaining Communists still in jail.

[46] According to one report of the congress, the Communists had 323 voting delegates, the Socialists had 57 representatives, and other organizations had a total of approximately 400 representatives; the remainder were "observers and guests." See *ibid.*, p. 1121.

[47] The fullest contemporaneous account of the Third Congress is in Helen Marcy, "Communist-Socialist Unity Answers Japanese Menace," *Inprecor*, December 24, 1938, pp. 1370-1. See also Lava, *Milestones*, pp. 35-7; Philippines, Republic of, Congress, House of Representatives, Special Committee on Un-Filipino Activities (CUFA), Report No. 3, Second Congress, Third Session (May 1952); and Hoeksema, *op. cit.*, pp. 179ff. The latter account is the most detailed seen by this writer.

The clamorous success of the Philippine Communists in launching their *Frente Popular* in 1938 was not entirely the consequence of their own strategies. It required, first of all, the compliance of the Socialists. The Socialists had been organized early in the 1930's by Pedro Abad Santos—some say as a legal cover for the outlawed Communists.[48] Whether or not this was so, the Socialists had preserved a separate entity during the intervening years and had not infrequently competed with Communists in labor organizations. They were, however, closer in spirit to Spanish and Mexican socialism than to European and accordingly in a political tradition less opposed to collaboration with Stalinists than were traditional Socialist parties in most countries. When, therefore, Moscow announced plans in 1935 for a broad anti-Fascist front, the Philippine Socialists were not averse to joining it; by 1938, indeed, they were eager to ally with Evangelista's Communists and did not count even the loss of their identity too high a price to pay for a broad alliance against Japanese aggression.[49]

Communist success was also due to the passive acquiescence of President Quezon. According to a Soviet analysis of the Philippines in mid-1938, Quezon's more tolerant attitude toward the Communists was forced upon him by mounting unemployment, growing Soviet influence throughout the world, and the unsettling impact in the Philippines of united front tactics in countries as distant as Spain and France.[50] Surely these claims of alleged Soviet successes reverberating in the Philippines are exaggerated. Social unrest, however, was real enough in the Commonwealth during these years to prompt Quezon to seek new ways of keeping order. His launching of a program of "Social Justice" in 1936, for instance, had had such a purpose; in 1938 his approval of the public merger of Socialists and Communists, on condition that they support his program, was presumably

---

[48] E.g. Lava, *Milestones*, p. 30.

[49] The foregoing is based in part on the author's interviews in 1961 and 1962 with Luis Taruc, the principal aide of Pedro Abad Santos prior to the 1938 merger.

[50] O. I. Zabozlaeva, "Sovremennoe polozhenie na Filippinskikh ostrovakh," *Mirovoe khoziaistvo i mirovaia politika*, No. 7-8, July-August 1938, p. 143.

based on the same considerations. It is in any event clear that had Quezon elected to oppose the merger, using the power of the government to do so, the *Frente Popular* would have died aborning.

The part played, finally, by James Allen—and therefore by the CPUSA, which he represented in the Philippines—must not be overlooked. Allen was the catalyst in the creation of the *Frente Popular*. Not only did he secure the release of the Communist leaders, who alone could give force and direction to the new policies, but according to José Lava, Allen personally conducted negotiations with Pedro Abad Santos for the merger of the two parties. He was also present at the Third Congress in October 1938 to deliver the greetings of the CPUSA on the historic occasion of the merger itself. Philippine government sources assert that Allen was acting throughout this period on instructions from Moscow transmitted through a "Philippines Commission of the Communist International" said to have been located in Los Angeles.[51] Whether or not this claim is credible, Moscow's endorsement of Allen's tactics may be taken for granted. By 1938 the Philippines were somewhat behind the timetable of united fronts in countries where it was possible to create them.

In this connection, the united front tactics in China undoubtedly had some impact on the Filipinos. By 1938 the Kuomintang-Communist alliance against Japan was in full force there. Allen probably cited its success in his arguments to both Socialists and Communists for similar strategies in the Philippines. China, in any event, was much in evidence during the deliberations of the Third Congress of the CPPI: a Kuomintang representative addressed the congress; a letter of greetings from Mme. Chiang Kai-shek was read aloud; and speakers repeatedly referred to the

[51] Philippines, Republic of, Congress, House of Representatives, Special Committee on Un-Filipino Activities (CUFA), *Report on the Illegality of the Communist Party of the Philippines*, p. 3; this report also claims that $4,000 was given to the CPPI in 1938 from an "international solidarity fund" of the CPUSA. Earl Browder made a similar claim during a Congressional hearing in 1939; United States, Congress, House of Representatives, Special Committee on Un-American Activities, *Hearings*, Vol. III (1939), p. 4319 (cited in Hoeksema, *op. cit.*, p. 197).

gallant resistance of the Chinese against Japan.[52] Following the congress, a "Friends of China" organization was created and a boycott of Japanese goods urged on the Philippine government.[53] Later Soviet sources are accordingly quite correct in singling out the united front in China as a major factor creating a climate of opinion in the Philippines favorable to the *Frente Popular.*[54] China, in Moscow's eyes, continued to be a model for the colonial world.

The course of the united front in the Philippines did not run smoothly. According to Luis Taruc, many Socialists opposed the adoption of the name "Communist" at the time of the merger, despite the approval of their leadership, and soon defected from the new organization.[55] The Communists for their part encountered numerous organizational and ideological difficulties working with Socialists. José Lava, reviewing the united front era a decade later, complained that the Socialists in the new party did not attend meetings, were lax in forming party nuclei, and ignored Marxist literature; Santos, he said, had a habit of issuing statements on his own authority without clearing them with the Politburo. Communists too committed errors, according to Lava, chief of which were a tendency to consider the *Frente Popular* "more as an oppositionist party than a united front against Fascism" and a "sectarian" inclination to denounce potential allies within the bourgeoisie.[56] In Central Luzon, wide-scale terrorism by both Socialists and Communists against local landlords was reported in 1939, despite Capadocia's repudiation of these tactics and his denunciation of "any reckless resolve to seize power through violence."[57]

There is no reason to doubt that these and other difficulties troubled the collaboration between Socialists and Communists.

[52] Helen Marcy, *loc. cit.*
[53] Lava, *Milestones*, pp. 40-1.
[54] E.g. Levinson, *op. cit.*, p. 220.
[55] Author's interview with Taruc in January 1962.
[56] Lava, *Milestones*, pp. 37-40.
[57] See Hoeksema, *op. cit.*, p. 215, citing *Manila Daily Bulletin*, December 19, 1939.

229

The threat from Japan had been enough to bring the two groups together, but since, from the Philippine viewpoint, it did not grow more menacing during 1939, it proved insufficient to preserve a strong alliance intact. Meanwhile, from Moscow's viewpoint, the conclusion of the Nazi-Soviet Pact less than a year after the merger of the two parties removed the urgency of united front strategies in the Philippines (although less emphatically than in Indochina since the United States, unlike France, was not yet at war with Germany, Stalin's new ally). The CPPI reverted to the tactics of "united front from below," which had the effect of disrupting the *Frente Popular* as such and ending Communist support of the government. Socialists and Communists grew further and further apart during the Nazi-Soviet era until in 1940 the alliance split into two groups—one, in which the Communists dominated, led by Santos; the other by Juan Sumulong. In 1941 the division became final when Sumulong ran in the Presidential elections against both Quezon and Santos.[58] The departure of Santos and his chief aides from what survived of the Socialist faction, needless to say, meant the ultimate eclipse of Philippine socialism during the war years.

The CPPI appears to have been left without foreign guidance after the formation of the *Frente Popular* and the departure of James Allen. The CPUSA, during its Eleventh National Convention in 1940, promised to mobilize its strength against the "predatory plans of Wall Street imperialism" in the Philippines and again reminded American Communists of their "duty" to aid the CPPI.[59] Little evidence of material aid, or even of ideological or other guidance, however, can be discovered. During the years prior to the Japanese assault on the Philippines in December 1941, the CPPI was largely left alone by its principal supervisor of the past.

If we discount as improbable reports of a Soviet effort to place

[58] Santos withdrew his candidacy before the elections when his party was denied adequate representation on the Ballot Inspection Commission; Levinson, *op. cit.*, p. 256. See also Hoeksema, *op. cit.*, p. 221.
[59] *Communist* (New York), No. 7, July 1940, pp. 621-2.

an agent in Manila in 1938,[60] there is little to suggest Soviet interest in the Philippines during the era of its united front. The Soviet press grew silent on the Philippines earlier than on Indochina. After two substantial articles on the eve of the *Frente Popular* by two leading Orientalist scholars, Zabozlaeva and V. Avarin,[61] coverage of developments in the Philippines is limited to a few insignificant notices—a routine article late in 1939, for instance, describing the Philippines as the victim of American imperialism (an expected shift during the era of the Nazi-Soviet Pact);[62] several items in agitational materials for party workers.[63] Moscow's growing preoccupation with developments in Europe after 1938 and the absence of a clearly defined policy toward the United States during the era of the Nazi-Soviet Pact rendered the Philippines negligible in Stalin's calculations.

COURSE OF THE UNITED FRONT: III

Indonesia. The united front in Indonesia (if one can be said to have existed there) was vexed by the same ambiguity that disturbed its course in the Philippines and to a slightly less degree in Indochina: *which* imperialists was the "anti-imperialist united front" meant to check—Japanese or those in the metropolitan? At the Seventh Congress the Indonesian delegate, Roestan Effendi, assumed it was the latter. "We are prepared," he said, "unconditionally to co-operate with each and any organization of Indonesian people whose object it is to fight against Dutch imperialism for the liberation of our country." He appeared to express relief that the crippling isolation imposed upon the PKI by the instructions of the Sixth Congress and the inter-

---

[60] See Hoeksema, *op. cit.*, pp. 197-9, citing United States, Congress, House of Representatives, Special Committee on Un-American Activities, *Hearings*, Vol. II (1940), p. 633.

[61] Zabozlaeva's article, cited above, appeared in *Mirovoe khoziastvo i mirovaia politika*, No. 7-8, July-August 1938, pp. 138-46; Avarin's, entitled "Iaponiia i bor'ba za Filippiny," appeared in the same journal, No. 10, October 1938, pp. 70-84.

[62] "Filipinny—koloniia amerikanskogo imperializma," *Internatsional'nyi maiak*, No. 19-20, 1939, pp. 15-6.

[63] See *Bibliografiia Iugo-vostochnoi Azii*, p. 201.

vening plenums of the ECCI had ended; the party was now free to seek allies within the more powerful nationalist movement for a vigorous struggle against the Dutch.[64]

Soviet commentaries on Indonesia for a year or more after the Seventh Congress, as in the case of the Philippines, supported this reading of the united front instruction. Primary emphasis continued to be on the anti-Dutch character of the united front, and Indonesian Communists were exhorted "to create a suitable leadership for this front by uniting and educating the present owning classes in Indonesia."[65] Japanese imperialism, however, was not neglected in these Soviet commentaries. Gradually, and especially after Japan's attack on China in mid-1937, Japanese imperialism in Indonesia overshadowed Dutch in Soviet publications.[66] During 1938 and 1939, complaints were periodically voiced concerning the pro-Japanese views of Dutch officials in the colony and the restrictions they placed on the anti-Japanese movement.[67]

Indonesian Communists in Holland responded promptly, if reluctantly, to Moscow's change of emphasis from Dutch to Japanese imperialism as the principal threat to Indonesia. In December 1937 Roestan Effendi (then an Indonesian deputy in the Dutch Parliament) stated in an interview that the Japanese attack on China had accented the urgent need of a strong anti-Japanese front in Indonesia and a boycott of Japanese goods.[68] The student organization *Perhimpoenan Indonesia* (which, as we have seen, had been under Communist control from the early 1930's) changed the name of its organ from *Indonesia Mer-*

[64] *Inprecor*, December 2, 1935, p. 1610.

[65] S. Rutgers, "Polozhenie v Indonezii i narodnyi anti-imperialisticheskii front," *Revoliutsionnyi Vostok*, No. 2-3, 1936, p. 261; see also I. Mil'gram, "Oblichitel'nyi dokument protiv gollandskogo imperializma," *Tikhii okean*, No. 2, 1936, pp. 189-91.

[66] E.g., "Niderlanskaia Indiia i Iaponiia," *Za rubezhom*, No. 19, October 1937, p. 441.

[67] Simon Krause, "Indonesia Also Menaced by Japan," *Inprecor*, February 19, 1938, p. 134; Jan Van Vliet, "The General Situation in Indonesia," *ibid.*, April 1, 1939, p. 369.

[68] "The War in China and the National Movement in Indonesia" (interview with Roestan Effendi), *ibid.*, December 11, 1937, pp. 1299-1300.

deķa (Free Indonesia) to *Indonesia* and criticized nationalist leaders, such as Sukarno and Mohammed Hatta, who persisted in their struggle for independence—albeit from jail.[69]

The response, meanwhile, of Communists in Indonesia to the Soviet shift must be left to the imagination. The latter half of the 1930's is a particularly obscure era in the history of the PKI. Outlawed since 1927, the PKI as such appears to have played no open part in united front activities in Indonesia. Nor did Moscow evidently expect it to; as one writer put it in 1936: "The illegal PKI exists deep in the underground and therefore has too weak ties with wide mass movements to lead these petty-bourgeois organizations to a more consistent mode of struggle."[70]

The "illegal [*nelegal'nyi*] PKI" referred to on occasion in Soviet commentaries is described in most accounts of Indonesian Communism as a more or less formal organization created by Musso in 1935. He is said to have returned secretly to Java before the Seventh Comintern Congress, presumably at the request of the International, and, according to recent PKI sources, "succeeded in drawing together again the cadres of the CPI [PKI] and building a new CPI Central Committee."[71] Dutch police surveillance, however, cut short his stay in Java—probably to less than a year[72]—and at his departure the organization he created appears to have suffered the same fate as the original PKI. There is, at any event, no record known to this writer of congresses or plenary meetings of party organs during these years (until after the war, in fact); no evidence of actions taken as a party; and only the most shadowy indication of who constituted the party leadership after Musso's departure.[73]

---

[69] See Kahin, *Nationalism and Revolution in Indonesia*, p. 89, and McVey, *The Development of the Indonesian Communist Party and Its Relations with the Soviet Union and the Chinese People's Republic*, p. 18; Miss McVey states that the Communists in *Perhimpoenan Indonesia* were under "instructions" from the Dutch Communist Party to alter their policies on independence.

[70] I. Mil'gram, "K voprosu o natsional'no-osvoboditel'nom dvizhenii v Indonezii," *Tikhii okean*, No. 3, July-September 1936, p. 112.

[71] Aidit, *The Birth and Growth of the Communist Party of Indonesia*, p. 19.

[72] See Kahin, *op. cit.*, pp. 86-7.

[73] According to McVey, *op. cit.*, p. 20, three Communists headed the Illegal PKI created by Musso—Kjokosudjono, Pamudji, and Achmad Sumadi; none of

If the PKI itself proved to be an inadequate vehicle for Moscow's policies, other organizations existed in Indonesia which could serve this purpose. One such organization was *Gerindo* (*Gerakan Rakjat Indonesia*, or Indonesian People's Movement), created in 1937 and representing the Left Wing of the nationalist movement prior to World War II. The *Gerindo*, while militantly nationalistic, adopted the view that the independence of Indonesia was contingent upon the outcome of the world imperialist struggle, especially the defeat of Japan, and that temporary collaboration with the Dutch was accordingly necessary. Since such views were entirely in tune with Moscow's after 1937, it was appropriate for Indonesian Communists to participate in this legal organization, and, according to recent PKI sources, individual party members did so.[74] It is also likely that Indonesian Communists influenced the policies of *Gerindo*. Amir Sjarifuddin, for instance, who later claimed to have been a PKI member from this period, was one of the leaders of the *Gerindo*, as well as the representative of the *Gerindo* in the leadership of the wider federation of nationalist organizations created in May 1939—the *Gapi* (*Gaboengon Politiek Indonesia*, or Federation of Indonesian Political Parties); this organization also muted demands for independence and called for solidarity between Indonesians and Dutch in an anti-Fascist front.[75]

Soviet commentaries, curiously, devoted little attention to the *Gerindo* and *Gapi* and appear to have considered neither the embodiment of the united front in Indonesia—comparable, for instance, to *La Lutte* in Indochina or to the Socialist-Communist merger in the Philippines. Greater coverage was given to the activities of the more moderate nationalist organization of these years, the *Parindra* (*Partai Indonesia Raja*, or Greater Indonesian Party). This organization, formed in 1935, sought self-govern-

these three, however, was to play a significant role in the PKI after the war. Miss McVey's forthcoming study of Indonesian Communism will doubtless shed light on this obscure era.

[74] Aidit, *op. cit.*, p. 19.

[75] See Kahin, *op. cit.*, p. 97. Sjarifuddin's claim of early membership in the PKI was made in 1948 and will be dealt with in a later chapter.

ment in Indonesia but not necessarily full independence. Moscow's attitude toward *Parindra* fluctuated during the united front period. In July 1937, for instance, an article in *Inprecor* (purportedly written in Java) reviewed favorably a recent *Parindra* congress which showed "a certain revival in the ranks of the Indonesian bourgeoisie." Although a "purely bourgeois reform party," the author wrote, "its political program contains a number of progressive items." Above all, *Parindra* showed "a perceptible tendency to bring about the unity of the national movement."[76] Concern over the possible pro-Japanese sympathies of the *Parindra* was expressed from time to time: following the visit of the party's leader, Dr. Raden Sutomo, to Tokyo in 1938, for instance, he was said to have fallen "greatly in sympathy with the Japanese."[77] By the following year, however, the *Parindra* appears to have purged itself of suspicion in Moscow's eyes and its annual congress in the spring of 1939 was reported in the Comintern press without hostility.[78] Whether Moscow's occasional interest in this organization stemmed from a hope that it might play a leading role in the creation of a united anti-Fascist front in Indonesia it is not possible to determine. The signing of the Nazi-Soviet Pact in August, at any event, ended for the time being Soviet interest in such a front in Indonesia, as it did elsewhere.

Following the outbreak of the war in Europe, Soviet commentaries reverted to the traditional and doctrinaire view of Indonesia as a Dutch imperial colony. Zabozlaeva, for instance, wrote in June 1940 that, with the defeat of the Dutch in Europe, England had replaced Holland as the master of Indonesia and the colony was becoming a pawn in a vast imperialist struggle involving the British, the Americans, and the Japanese.[79] Semaoen (who, though apparently still living in Moscow, had not appeared in Soviet or Comintern journals for a decade) also noted

[76] A__n, "The Congress of the 'Parindra'," *Inprecor*, July 24, 1937, p. 709.
[77] Simon Krause, *loc. cit.*
[78] Jan Van Vliet, *loc. cit.*
[79] O. Zabozlaeva, "Bor'ba derzhav za Gollandskuiu Indiiu," *Mirovoe khoziaistvo i mirovaia politika*, No. 6, June 1940, pp. 111-21.

this emerging pattern of imperialist rivalry. He argued, how-ever, that "the liberation struggle of the Indonesian people is growing. The people are striving more and more persistently and decisively for their full independence from all imperialists." He saw the *Parindra* (note: not *Gerindo*) as playing the major part in this effort and cited as evidence *Parindra*'s convoking in December 1939 the Indonesian People's Congress, "a united front of all political parties."[80] Semaoen quite possibly misrepresented the tone of this congress—which was less anti-Dutch than he im-plied[81]—but his reassertion of national liberation as the main objective in Indonesia is indicative of Moscow's policy at this juncture. In the spring of 1941 Zabozlaeva ridiculed belated Dutch offers of post-war reforms, which promised "the trans-formation of Indonesia from a colony to a semi-independent state," and predicted that the offers would be quickly forgotten when the war ended.[82]

These amended Soviet judgments—which Indonesian Com-munists presumably welcomed, as disillusion with the Dutch spread throughout the colony and the movement for independ-ence regained strength—had little impact on the fortunes of the PKI. By 1941 the party had become too impotent to be revived by a mere favorable turn in Moscow's ever-changing line. Mos-cow, in the meantime, could ill afford at this time to dispatch more Mussos to try their hand at artificial resuscitation. Indo-nesian Communism, in consequence, remained in a coma.

[80] R. Semaun, "Polozhenie v Gollandskoi Indii i bor'ba imperialistov za Indo-nezii," *Kommunisticheskii internatsional*, No. 6, June 1940, p. 82.

[81] According to Kahin, *op. cit.*, pp. 97-8, the congress approved the line of co-operation with the Dutch adopted by the leading nationalist parties in Indo-nesia at the outbreak of the war and considered that the best way to secure this co-operation was for the Dutch to grant more rights to the Indonesians, espe-cially self-government; the tone of the congress was thus strongly nationalistic (demanding, for instance, an official national language, a national flag, and a national anthem), but not necessarily anti-Dutch. (It is of some interest as a reflection on the confusion in Moscow concerning the nomenclature of the In-donesian nationalist organizations that the congress was convoked by the *Gapi*, not the *Parindra* as Semaoen indicates.)

[82] O. Zabozlaeva, "Gollandskaia Indiia posle okkupatsii Gollandi," *Mirovoe khoziaistvo i mirovaia politika*, No. 4, April 1941, p. 134.

COURSE OF THE UNITED FRONT: IV

Malaya. Malayan Communists responded less promptly than Communists elsewhere in Southeast Asia to the course set at the Seventh Comintern Congress of 1935. One reason for this was the comparative isolation of Malayan Communists from the international movement during the latter half of the 1930's. Although a force of some consequence in the political life of Malaya itself, Malayan Communism received little guidance from abroad. British Communists had never exercised significant influence within the MCP and did not begin to during this period. Chinese Communists were preoccupied for a year or more after their Long March with the establishment of a new base in Shensi and appear to have given no thought to Malaya at least until the end of 1936. Ties alleged to have existed since 1933 between the MCP and the so-called "Comintern apparatus" in Shanghai were allegedly severed with the dissolution of this apparatus in mid-1935;[83] no further ties between Moscow and the Malayans are reported (even by Malayan police officials, who are normally eager to claim them). The MCP meanwhile was unrepresented at the Seventh Comintern Congress and, to judge from the records of the Congress, Malaya was not discussed in any connection. Although describing itself in 1934 as an "affiliate" of the International, the Malayan party appears never to have been formally admitted to membership, as the Communist parties in Indonesia, Indochina, and the Philippines had been. The MCP, it is therefore easy to imagine, was less responsive than other Communist parties in Southeast Asia to the directives of the Seventh Congress.

Another factor affecting the response of the Malayans was the unusual success of the strike movement they had launched in 1934. This movement, which was the product of the Sixth Congress' evaluation of the colonial struggle rather than of the Seventh's (if, indeed, of either), gained momentum during 1935 and 1936 and reached a climax in a series of strikes at the Batu Arang coal mines early in 1937. According to a British police

[83] "Basic Paper on the Malayan Communist Party," Vol. 1, Part 2, p. 11.

official (who later described the episode as "the most serious crisis" in the colony's history), a "soviet" government was established at Batu Arang by Communist-led workers.[84] Since the Communists now controlled the principal labor organization in Malaya, the Malayan General Labor Union (MGLU), and thus had the means to implement their current policies, there was little incentive to seek a broader vehicle—although they reportedly paid lip-service to Moscow's "anti-imperialist united front" as soon as they learned of it.[85] Moscow, in the meantime, seems not to have been troubled by the policies followed by the MCP during this period. Soviet commentaries on the strike movement (among the few, incidentally, concerning Malaya during the latter half of the 1930's) continued to be favorably disposed toward it as late as mid-1937 and mentioned only the need to "organize stronger unions," without reference to a wider anti-Fascist front.[86]

Still another reason for the MCP's delay in implementing united front strategies may be discovered in the factional crisis that bedeviled the party leadership during 1935 and 1936. According to an official party history issued in 1940, an oppositionist element rejected the party's resolutions on the strike program and sought "to subjugate and tame the workers" by leading them away from open strikes. The issue was resolved, according to this account, at the Fifth Expanded Plenum (or Conference) of the Executive Committee in September 1936, when the party leadership held to the "battle spirit of Bolshevism" and purged the opposition; the meeting was said to have occasioned

[84] Onraet, *Singapore—A Police Background*, p. 116.

[85] A "Pan-Malayan Cadres' Meeting" is said to have been called soon after the Seventh Comintern Congress to adopt united front tactics and to make necessary changes in the party program; an extant account of the meeting, however, suggests that the Malayans did not grasp the significance of the new anti-Fascist line. See Wu Tien-wang, "The Communist Party of Malaya," p. 2, cited in Hanrahan, *Communist Struggle in Malaya*, p. 19.

[86] "Zabastovochnoe dvizhenie v Britanskoi Malaie," *Mirovoe khoziaistvo i mirovaia politika*, No. 6, June 1937, p. 127; see also O. Rykovskaia, "Promyshlennost' i rabochii klass Malaii," *Materialy po natsional'no-kolonial'nym problemam*, No. 33, 1936, pp. 84-104.

"the most serious changes in the history of the MCP so far."[87] Another Communist account of the crisis describes the opposition as militant "Left Opportunists" who demanded "the termination of strikes and the breaking up of militant workers into small underground groups . . . they advocated the policy of educating the militant workers secretly and striving for the establishment of soviet power."[88] A British Intelligence report also identifies the opposition as Leftist and relates the party crisis to a series of assassinations within the MCP during 1936, allegedly caused by suspicion of oppositionist betrayals which had led to the arrests in quick succession (in December 1935 and March 1936) of two party chairmen; this account also notes the resolution of the crisis at the Fifth Plenum, when the opposition was reportedly eliminated.[89] The lines of this dispute remain obscure; from the fragmentary accounts of it, it is not even possible to determine whether it involved serious doctrinal or merely factional differences. So long as it lasted, however—and the reality of the crisis does not seem to be in doubt—the question of establishing a united front in Malaya could hardly have engaged the party's leaders.

There were, then, a number of reasons why the Malayan Communists did not seriously consider united front strategies as early as other Communists in Southeast Asia. The emergence of an anti-Japanese movement in China during 1937 marks the beginning of a turn to united front tactics by the MCP. According to Malayan police records, seven Chinese Communists arrived in Singapore as early as October 1936 to press the Malayan Communists for a more vigorous anti-Japanese campaign.[90] Assuming that these Chinese agents established contact with the MCP, it is not unlikely that they stirred up anti-Japanese sentiment, but it is improbable that they offered significant advice on the

[87] "History of the Malayan Communist Party," p. 14.

[88] Wu Tien-wang, as cited in Hanrahan, *op. cit.*, p. 23.

[89] "Basic Paper on the Malayan Communist Party," Vol. I, Part 2, p. 12; the arrest of many Central Committee members in 1936 is also mentioned in a subsequent Malayan Communist source, "Statement of the Incident of Wright" (May 28, 1948).

[90] "Basic Paper on the Malayan Communist Party," Vol. I, Part 2, p. 13.

establishment of a broad anti-Japanese front inasmuch as the Chinese Communists themselves had not yet settled on this strategy. During the next twelve months, however, developments in China clarified the policies of the CCP and led, in September 1937, to the conclusion of a Communist-Kuomintang alliance against Japan. The MCP, whose membership was still predominantly Chinese, could not have been unaffected by this turn of events in China. Regular contact between the two parties had in the meantime been resumed, and a channel thus opened for closer Chinese supervision over the policies of the Malayan Communists.[91]

The anti-Japanese movement in Malaya centered initially in the Chinese community. In Singapore, for instance, an organization known as the Overseas Chinese Anti-Japanese National Salvation Association (SOCANSA) was formed in 1937 to encourage Chinese of all political persuasions to resist Japanese aggression in China. Another organization, the Anti-Enemy Backing-Up Society (AEBUS), operated more broadly throughout the colony; created from cadres of the Communist-dominated MGLU, this organization served as general fund-raiser for the anti-Japanese effort and as a vigilante committee to suppress any pro-Japanese sympathizers, especially among the overseas Chinese. By 1939 the membership of AEBUS was said to have reached nearly 40,000.[92]

There was still, however, no united front in Malaya outside the Chinese community. Moreover, the gains among the overseas Chinese which the Communists made during these years as a result of the anti-Japanese effort tended to have an opposite effect in the rival Malay and Indian communities. There Communist influence, never strong, declined still further, a circumstance that caused growing concern to party officials. An effort was accordingly made at the Sixth Enlarged Plenum in April 1939 to correct this situation by launching a nation-wide united

[91] *Ibid.*, p. 16; the contact was allegedly established in December 1936 with the Chinese Communists' so-called Southern Bureau in Hong Kong.

[92] *Ibid.*, p. 17; for a discussion of the activities of AEBUS during 1937-39, see Pye, *Guerrilla Communism in Malaya*, pp. 63-4.

front; the 1940 party history describes the plenum—the first important party meeting since 1936—as a "turning point" in the fortunes of the MCP inasmuch as it marked the beginning of the party's role in national (as distinct from labor and communal) affairs.[93] The party's principal task, set forth in a ten-point "Program of Struggle" adopted by the plenum, was the establishment of an "All-Races United Front to strive for a democratic system, to safeguard peace, and to implement action against the Japanese-German-Italian Fascist bloc." The program also urged party members to apply pressure on England to aid China and to join a collective security alliance with the Soviet Union, "the pillar that supports genuine peace." Other tasks included in the "Program of Struggle" concerned traditional objectives of the MCP: civil liberties, eight-hour working day, reduction of rents and interest rates, woman's rights (including abolition of "slave girls"), popular education in the vernacular, and so forth. Needless to say, there was no mention of soviets, of confiscation of estates, of overthrowing the sultans, or of immediate independence from Great Britain—all objectives of the party's 1932 program. Nor was there reference to the strike movement, which had been temporarily suspended in the interests of national harmony. The Sixth Plenum also established a new party leadership under the controversial Loi Tek, a Vietnamese (and, as it was later discovered, a British agent) who had joined the MCP several years earlier.[94]

[93] "History of the Malayan Communist Party," p. 20; this source contains the only detailed account of the Sixth Plenum known to the writer.

[94] The Loi Tek (or Lai Tech; alias, Comrade Wright) episode is discussed in the following chapter. It may be noted here, however, that he entered the Malayan party in the mid-1930's, evidently already a police informant passed on from the French *Securité* in Saigon to the Singapore Special Branch, and worked his way into the upper levels of the party hierarchy during the crisis of 1936. Sources differ on the date of his arrival in Malaya: he himself claims to have joined the MCP in 1934 (an interrogation with the Malayan police, March 16, 1947); an official party source dates his entry in the party in "late 1934 or 1935" ("Statement of the Incident of Wright"); a Malayan Communist, meanwhile, writes that Loi Tek was dispatched to Singapore by the Comintern in 1936 specifically to resolve the party crisis of that year, which he allegedly did during an intensive six-month "offensive against the opportunists" (Wu Tien-wang, as cited in Hanrahan, *op. cit.*, p. 23).

The Malayan Communists, then, gave concrete expression to united front tactics only during the Sixth Plenum of April 1939, an event comparable to the July 1936 plenum of the CPIC and the Third Congress of the CPPI in October 1938. They were moreover not only tardy in their turn to a united front but unorthodox as well, at least with respect to one significant feature of united front strategies then in force. By 1939, as we have seen, Communists in Indochina and the Philippines (presumably also in Indonesia) had adopted a line of at least partial collaboration with colonial administrations; the Malayans did not. The Sixth Plenum argued that party strength was "too inadequate for us to talk about co-operation with imperialism" and accordingly adopted a line of non-co-operation with the British in Malaya.[95] The Malayan Communists appear not to have altered this position during the few months remaining before the signing of the Nazi-Soviet Pact; the pact allowed them, with the full approval of the International, to reaffirm their customary anti-British posture.[96]

With the outbreak of the war in Europe, Communist-led strikes resumed in earnest, directed especially at British shipping in Singapore. The Communist organ *Emancipation News* and the organ of AEBUS, *Vanguard News*, meanwhile, carried intensive anti-British propaganda during the latter part of 1939 and the first half of 1940.[97] Simultaneously the anti-war movement was expanded "in order," as the party history of 1940 put it, "to smash the general offensive launched by British imperialism."[98] In February 1940 the Central Committee amended the "Program of Struggle" adopted the preceding April to eliminate the demand that England join collective security alliances. At the same time the party elaborated on its policies, still within the context of the "All-Races United Front" (now called the "Anti-Imperialist Racial United Front"): the Chinese in Malaya, the Central Committee said, should still consider their main

[95] "History of the Malayan Communist Party," p. 20.

[96] A party conference in July 1939 (said to be the Fourth) authorized co-operation "with all anti-Fascist forces," but seems not to have intended that this include the British; *ibid.*, p. 19.

[97] "Basic Paper on the Malayan Communist Party," Vol. 1, Part 2, p. 19.

[98] "History of the Malayan Communist Party," p. 22.

task "to assist the Motherland" (i.e., China); Malays should "carry on the Racial (National) Independence Movement"; Indians should struggle for the independence of India, as well as Malaya, from British imperialism. "These resolutions," the party history of 1940 asserted, "corrected the indiscriminate attitude with regard to the special demands of the various races which affected implementation of party work in the past."[99] The problem, however, was to continue.

The assault on Great Britain did not continue throughout the entire era of the Nazi-Soviet Pact. The Chinese Communists once again influenced the MCP to alter its policies, according to Malayan government records: an instruction received as early as July 1940 reportedly advised the MCP to call off its strikes and other anti-British agitation in view of Britain's current aid to China and the importance to Chungking of gaining London's intervention in the opening of the Burma Road; the MCP is said to have complied, at least in Singapore, where its control was firm.[100] The Seventh Enlarged Plenum of the Central Committee, held in Singapore in July 1941 (after Russia was at war), reaffirmed this more moderate line: since Great Britain was now aiding the USSR, as well as China, Malayan Communists should avoid friction with the British authorities. This was the party's overt position. Secretly, however, according to Malayan government records, a decision was taken at this time to expel the British from Malaya as soon as practicable; if Japan should invade Malaya, the Communists would continue to support an anti-Japanese front, but only as a means of extending Communist influence. This secret decision, it is reported, was made known only to the party leaders.[101]

What Moscow thought of these turns and twists in the policies of the MCP can only be conjectured. Apart from occasional articles relating to the British naval base at Singapore,[102] only a

[99] *Ibid.*, pp. 22-3.
[100] "Basic Paper on the Malayan Communist Party," Vol. I, Part 2, p. 19.
[101] *Ibid.*, p. 20.
[102] The importance of the Singapore base continued to engage the attention of Soviet writers during the latter part of the 1930's as it had earlier and was the subject of half a dozen or more articles between 1935 and 1939; see *Bibliografiia Iugo-vostochnoi Azii*, p. 184.

single Soviet article on domestic developments in Malaya from the climax of the strike movement in March 1937 to the outbreak of war in the Pacific at the end of 1941 has come to this writer's attention. This is a commentary by Zabozlaeva in July 1940 concerned chiefly with the strike movement then in progress throughout the country. The author's judgment is orthodox: "the frenzied growth of war profiteering by entrepreneurs, on the one hand, and the increasing exploitation of workers, on the other, lead more and more to open class conflict in Malaya."[103] Communists are said to be the principal organizers of the strikes, but no itemized treatment of their activities and no general appraisal of their policies are included in the commentary. The article hardly illuminates Moscow's attitude toward developments in Malaya during these years.

Malayan Communism, to judge from the foregoing, was left largely alone during the years of the united front. Apart from occasional advice reportedly received from the Chinese Communists (which must, of course, be held in some question), the Malayan party was free to work out its own response to and its own interpretation of Moscow's policies. In certain respects this was doubtless an advantage: the MCP was under little visible pressure to launch a united front before it was prepared to, and it was not overburdened by the requirement felt by other Southeast Asian parties to make some accommodation with metropolitan imperialism. Communist strength, meanwhile, grew astonishingly during the united front era; if British records are accurate, it more than quadrupled from 1934 to 1940—to an overall total, including Communist-affiliated organizations, of more than 50,000.[104] This provided the MCP with a very respectable base of support for its operations during the war.

[103] O. Zabozlaeva, "Britanskaia Malaia v obstanovke vtoroi imperialisticheskoi voiny," *Mirovoe khoziaistvo i mirovaia politika*, No. 7, July 1940, p. 118.

[104] The 1934 total was given as 12,716, including the MGLU and other Communist-led organizations; in May 1940 there were said to be 50,000 in the MGLU (20,000 in Singapore alone) and 1,700 in the MCP proper (700 in Singapore). *Ibid.*, p. 19.

United front strategies had two consequences, broadly speaking, as they applied to Communist movements in Southeast Asia. First, they released local Communists from the often crippling isolation imposed upon them by the harsh directives of the Sixth Comintern Congress of 1928 and subsequent plenums of the ECCI; this was a gain and led to more overt Communist activity and, as a result, to a strengthening of Communist organization in most countries. Secondly, as the central purpose of the united front became more clearly perceived, colonial parties were burdened by the need to deny national liberation in order to focus attention on German and especially Japanese aggression. Southeast Asians increasingly sought independence during these years; local Communists were increasingly restrained by the demands of Soviet foreign policy (until August 1939) from providing effective leadership to this end. The united front, then, yielded both profit and loss to the Southeast Asian parties.

The pattern of the united fronts in Southeast Asia, however, is so varied that it is not always easy to discover where and why a local party was helped or handicapped by Moscow's policies. The response of a local Southeast Asian party to Moscow's call for united front tactics was conditioned by many factors: its legal status, for instance, its strength, or its relationship to the metropolitan party. Philippine Communism, illegal until 1932, could not undertake the sustained efforts to create a united front that Indochinese Communism undertook two years earlier; the Indonesian Communists would have been incapable of carrying out Moscow's policies, even if all other circumstances favored it, as promptly as the better organized Indochinese and Malayans; the ties between French and Indochinese Communists and between American and Philippine were closer than between British and Malayans, which meant that the CPIC and the CPPI received clearer guidance from the metropolitan parties, normally more alert than colonial parties to Moscow's wishes. The prospects for independence and the relationship of Communists to local nationalist movements also influenced party strategies, whatever pressures there were from Moscow or elsewhere to create broader anti-imperialist fronts or to abandon national liberation. It was easier for Communists in the Philippines, where independence was already promised, than for Communists in Indonesia or Indochina, where it was not, to give up slogans of national liberation without damaging themselves in the eyes of their countrymen: in Indonesia—although the conjecture is necessarily hypothetical—the eclipse of the PKI during the united front era may have been due to its inability to survive with slogans that denied national liberation; in Indochina Communists appear to have waged a losing struggle with Trotskyites, until the signing of the Nazi-Soviet Pact, because of their more moderate position on independence.

We might indeed go further and ask whether Moscow in some measure *encouraged* diversity in the application of the united front formula in Southeast Asia. For instance, the initial instruction on the united front composed by the Seventh Congress was both ambiguous and contradictory as it applied to colonies. Was there design in Comintern spokesmen calling in one breath for anti-Fascist fronts and in the next encouraging colonial peoples to continue their struggle against the very partners Stalin sought so eagerly in his anti-Fascist campaign? Design is not impossible. If alliance with bourgeois parties in the colonies was seen as the *initial* step in creating any effective united front, Moscow may well have reasoned that Communists were obliged for a time to support national liberation; otherwise the bourgeois parties, which were strongly nationalistic, would have rejected any alliance with them. Let the real enemy of world Communism—German and Japanese aggressors—remain unspecified until these alliances were in operation. In due course they must be identified, to give some point to united front tactics, but in the meantime Moscow allowed itself, as well as Asian Communists, a certain latitude in determining the proper moment to redirect attention from British, Dutch, French, or American imperialism to Japanese. Thus it might be argued that in Indochina, where Communism was relatively strong, a turn to anti-Fascism was judged appropriate several years earlier than in the Philippines, where the Communists were weak.

Such imputation of design to Soviet colonial strategists is of course highly speculative and must on balance, I think, be rejected. It credits Soviet leaders, for one thing, with greater awareness of conditions in Southeast Asia and more foresight than there is reason to suppose they possessed. There is, indeed, more reason to think Soviet observers ignorant and indifferent than wise and devious where Southeast Asia was concerned. China was the focus of Moscow's attention in the colonial world. Chinese Communists, accordingly, would indicate the course for the colonial parties. Since an alliance between the CCP and the Kuomintang was considered out of the question in 1935, when united front strategies were being devised, no similar alliances were urged elsewhere in the East. After the Sian episode at the end of 1936[105] and the Japanese attack on China proper six months later, however, when a Communist-Kuomintang alliance was deemed feasible in China, such alliances became more urgent in other colonies and semi-colonies.

The tempo of united front activity in Southeast Asia, without any prompting from Moscow, in fact quickened perceptibly after the formation of the Communist-Kuomintang alliance in China in September 1937. China continued, in short, to serve as Moscow's model in the East. A direct Chinese role in Communist affairs in Southeast Asia (except, perhaps, in the case of the predominantly Chinese MCP) is not likely, to judge from evidence thus far available. The impact, however, of Chinese Communist policies and experience on the Southeast Asians may be discerned. Southeast Asian Communists were forming a habit, which Moscow would not easily set aside in later years, of shaping their policies to mirror those of the CCP.

[105] Early in December 1936 Chiang Kai-shek was kidnapped by rebellious Manchurian officers who opposed his policies of concentrating troops against the Communists instead of against the Japanese in Manchuria; his release was negotiated several weeks later, largely through the good offices of the Chinese Communists who by this time felt Chiang's leadership of the anti-Japanese united front a necessary prerequisite to its success.

United Front in Southeast Asia: 1935-1941

Communism in Southeast Asia, we may conclude, survived Moscow's neglect during the united front era. Except in Indonesia and Siam (where evidence does not allow us to judge either growth or decline of Communist strength) the Communist parties already in existence by 1935 were stronger at the end of this era than before. Perhaps this would have occurred in any case; perhaps the resourcefulness of local Communist leaders explains Communist gains. For our purposes, however, it is significant to note, in answer to a question posed earlier in the chapter, that the Communist base in Southeast Asia *was* durable enough to withstand any embarrassment caused by Soviet policies between 1935 and 1941 and that the loyalty of local party leaders to Moscow (though channeled in some measure through Yenan) was unimpaired. Southeast Asian Communism, indeed, stood on the threshold of its greatest gains as war in the Pacific approached.

CHAPTER FIVE

Southeast Asian Communism in Suspension: 1941-1947

SOVIET interest in the colonial world, already faint by the end of the Nazi-Soviet era, ceased almost entirely after Hitler's attack on the USSR in June 1940. For the next three and a half years Soviet energies were wholly absorbed by the war with Germany. No activity unrelated to the war effort was allowed. Soviet scholars, including the Orientalists, became war correspondents. World revolution was suspended. Even the Comintern was dissolved, an agency no longer with a purpose.

The Soviet press reflected the Kremlin's preoccupation with Europe. Coverage of Asian affairs, which was parsimonious compared to coverage of developments in Europe, was normally concerned with the progress of the war in the Pacific, seen as a minor offshoot of the European war. Even China was ignored.[1] A few writers reviewed the diplomatic background of the Pacific War, but without reference to the part played by local Communist movements or by Soviet strategies in the unfolding of pre-war politics in the Far East.[2] Standard reference works also ignored the role of Communism in East Asia and gave little clue as to future Soviet policies in the colonial East.[3] National liberation movements, meanwhile, were played down. When England rejected the demands for independence of Indian nationalists in 1942 because of wartime conditions, a Soviet writer showed himself entirely in sympathy with the British position. This was not

---

[1] Skachkov's comprehensive bibliography on China (*Bibliografiia Kitaia*, 1960) lists fewer than two dozen items on China appearing in Soviet publications from June 1941 to February 1945.

[2] E.g. G. Voitinskii, "Voina na Tikhom Okeane," *Istoricheskii zhurnal*, No. 3-4, 1942, pp. 68-81; Avarin, "Voina v Evrope i mezhdunarodnye otnosheniia na Dal'nem Vostoke v 1939-1941 gg.," *Mirovoe khoziaistvo i mirovaia politika*, No. 12, December 1944, pp. 58-71.

[3] For coverage of Southeast Asia in reference works published during the war, see, for instance, *Strany Tikhogo okeana* (1942), pp. 248-425; A. A. Guber, *Indoneziia i Indokitai* (1942); *Strany mira: ezhegodnik spravochnik* (1st ed., 1942), pp. 490-5, 546-55, 586-8; and *Britanskaia imperiia* (1943), pp. 262-87.

the moment for Indian independence, he wrote; "the war against Fascist aggression requires the maximum mobilization of all India's forces."[4]

Moscow's view of Southeast Asia does not vary from this pattern. Its remoteness, indeed, made it of even less interest in Moscow, once the Japanese had settled in there, than other parts of the colonial world. No Southeast Asian party, for instance, was listed as approving the decision in May 1943 to dissolve the Third International;[5] nor is there reliable evidence of any association with Moscow or with Soviet agents abroad while the war lasted. Our concern with Southeast Asia during the war is accordingly not so much to unearth Soviet strategies there as to discover what Moscow had to deal with once its attention was redirected to the area after the war.

After the Yalta conference in February 1945 Moscow's interest in the East began gradually to revive, although it was a year and a half before a positive policy crystallized for China and more than two and a half years for the rest of the colonial world. It is appropriate to review the slow evolution of these post-war strategies before turning to Communist experience in Southeast Asia during the years in question.

MOSCOW AND THE COLONIAL QUESTION AFTER THE WAR

The Soviet decision to enter the war in the Pacific inevitably redirected Moscow's attention to its objectives in the Far East and from there, ultimately, to a reconsideration of the long-neglected colonial question. The political objectives, spelled out during the conference at Yalta, reflected Russia's national interests at the time and showed no evidence of a concealed revolutionary purpose.[6] When the war ended, the Chinese Communists,

---

[4] S. Mel'man, "Polozhenie v Indii," *Mirovoe khoziaistvo i mirovaia politika*, No. 11-12, November-December 1942, pp. 46-7; see also I. Lemin, "Anglo-indiiskie otnosheniia i voina," *Mirovoe khoziaistvo i mirovaia politika*, No. 5-6, May-June 1942, pp. 76-84.

[5] The countries approving the decision are listed in *Bol'shevik*, No. 10, May 1943, p. 6.

[6] The Yalta protocol concerning Soviet entry into the war in the Pacific, within three months after the defeat of Germany in Europe, specified that Russia would

according to later reports, were specifically requested not to attempt a seizure of power through armed insurrection; Stalin advised them instead to disband their army, whose strength at the time Mao estimated at nearly 1,000,000, and to join a coalition government with the Kuomintang.[7] Stalin's reasons for this advice may be imagined: he did not believe the Chinese Communists strong enough at that juncture to challenge the Kuomintang, despite encouraging reports by foreign observers of their high morale; he wished to avoid provoking any large-scale American intervention in China which might jeopardize Soviet gains at Yalta or obstruct any further projects, such as the dismantling of Japanese factories in Manchuria; moreover, by the end of the war it must already have been determined in Moscow that the principal post-war efforts were to be made in the West, not the East. Stalin's objectives in the Far East at the end of the war, and for some months thereafter, were accordingly limited to the achievement of a few specific goals in Northeast Asia. It is worth noting that he achieved them all.

The colonial question had meanwhile been broached in the Soviet press. In March 1945, a month after the Yalta conference, E. Zhukov—who was to emerge as the principal Soviet spokesman on colonial affairs after the war—underscored in *Voina i rabochii klass* the urgency of resolving the colonial question once and for all. The urgency, he argued, arose from two considerations: first, colonialism had been a perennial cause of international conflicts and wars; second, the actual political and economic transformations in the colonies during the present war demanded a change in their status. The change should correspond

---

gain in return a leasehold on Port Arthur, a guarantee of its "preeminent interests" in Manchuria, and a guarantee of the status quo in Outer Mongolia; Russia would also acquire the southern half of Sakhalin and the Kurile Islands. The Russians pretended to look on these gains as a recovery of their losses during the Russo-Japanese War of 1905.

[7] See Vladimir Dedijer, *Tito* (Simon and Schuster, 1953), p. 322, and Milovan Djilas, *Conversations with Stalin* (Harcourt, Brace, 1962), p. 182. Though both reports of Stalin's advice to the Chinese Communists in 1945 were made by Jugoslavs who had fallen out with Stalin, they are now credited as authentic by most students of Soviet affairs.

to the "spirit of the Atlantic Charter," but the latter, Zhukov pointed out, was interpreted differently by the Western powers. The United States, for instance, proposed changes which would have turned the colonies "into a sphere of unobstructed investment for American capital and a market for American goods." The European powers, by contrast, sought to keep a preferred position in their colonies, as before the war. India was singled out as a colony where the differences between the American and European views were particularly evident. Various proposals, such as regional commissions to co-ordinate foreign investment and local economic development, had been advanced to resolve these differences, Zhukov noted, but all had foundered thus far on the question of where, in the last analysis, administrative responsibility for the colonies should lie. The European colonial authorities, the British in particular, insisted that ultimate responsibility must lie with the metropolitan power concerned—at least in the immediate aftermath of war. Zhukov quoted approvingly liberal opinion, both British and American, on the colonial question; but he also noted, and deplored, the tenacity in many quarters of "a racist, overbearing and colonizing attitude toward the peoples of backward and dependent countries." He concluded: "There can be no doubt that these forces will stubbornly resist all steps to end or even to modify the colonial yoke. At the same time, however, it is obvious that a system of keeping hundreds of millions of people in colonial enslavement is an extremely dangerous obstacle to general progress and a stronghold of reactionary tendencies throughout the world. The elimination of this obstacle is a necessary condition for the inclusion of the Great Powers and of their population in the general stream of economic, political and cultural advancement."[8] In short, the granting of independence to the colonies would not only benefit the suppressed millions but would also have a purifying effect on the imperialists themselves.

Zhukov's article sounded many of the themes that were to be heard again and again in the Soviet press during the next two

[8] E. Zhukov, "Kolonial'nyi vopros na sovremennom etape," *Voina i rabochii klass*, No. 6, March 15, 1945, p. 9.

252

and a half years. As a pioneering analysis of the colonial question after the war, its forthright tone should be noted. The article was not, however, sharply critical of the Western powers per se, as distinct from certain forces in them agitating for the *status quo ante bellum*. Zhukov's diagnosis, moreover, remained in the area of generalities and dwelt on no particular colonial situation other than the Indian. India was separately discussed during the last months of the war by another Orientalist, A. Diakhov, who emphasized even more pointedly than Zhukov India's urgent desire for independence. In an article on April 1, Diakhov wrote that "only the most reactionary elements, those with a very narrow base—*rajahs* and rich landowners—support the present colonial regime, while the basic strata of Indian society are uniting more and more in the struggle for independence."[9]

These articles, written before the Japanese surrender, would lead one to expect more vigorous support of the emerging independence movements throughout the colonial world once the war was over. This was not the case. Zhukov's next important article on the colonial question, which appeared in December, showed little change in his thinking. He noted some initial successes in Indochina and Indonesia, where "the efforts of colonial administrations to restrain the national liberation movements failed from the outset," but he cautioned against premature rejoicing over the "independence" won by Vietnamese and Indonesian patriots. "A recognition of formal sovereignty," he warned twice in the article, "is no guarantee of actual independence." Still no mention was made of a need for colonial subjects to take to arms to win their freedom; Zhukov appeared to rely instead, although with misgivings, on United Nations trusteeships "to accelerate the progressive development of complete independence for the colonies."[10] There is also no discussion in the article of

[9] A. Diakhov, "K politicheskomu polozheniiu v Indii," *Voina i rabochii klass*, No. 7, April 1, 1945, p. 13; see also Diakhov's articles in *ibid.*, No. 2, January 15, 1945, and No. 15, August 15, 1945.

[10] E. Zhukov, "Porazhenie iaponskogo imperializma i natsional'no-osvoboditel'naia bor'ba narodov Vostochnoi Azii," *Bol'shevik*, No. 23-4, December 1945, p. 86; see also E. Zhukov, "The Trusteeship Question," *New Times*, No. 13 (23), December 15, 1945, pp. 3-6.

the role Communists were playing, or should be playing, in the national liberation movements, despite the fact that Communist parties were legalized in most Asian colonies immediately after the war. This moderate tone struck by Zhukov, in the first general article on the colonial question to appear in the Soviet press after the war, was also adopted by Diakhov in his articles on India during the following months[11] and, as we shall see, in the earliest post-war commentaries on Southeast Asia.

The reason for Moscow's moderation in dealing with the colonial question may be related to Soviet policies in China after the Japanese defeat. During their eight-month occupation of Manchuria, the Russians continued to pay lip-service to the idea of a Communist-Kuomintang coalition, as did the Americans. They did, it is true, render valuable assistance to the Chinese Communists by offering them a protected base of operations in Manchuria and by allowing them to take possession of much surrendered Japanese equipment, but they gave no signal for a general rising. It was not until July 1946, after Japanese equipment valued at approximately a billion U.S. dollars had been removed from Manchuria as "war booty" and the last Russians had withdrawn, that Moscow became resigned to—or possibly encouraged—civil war between the Communists and the Kuomintang. Moscow's views became apparent, on the one hand, in increasingly sharp attacks in the Soviet press on Chiang Kai-shek, the Nationalist government, and General Marshall, under whose auspices the Communists and Nationalists had been negotiating—and continued to negotiate—the terms of the hapless coalition; and, on the other, in growing acknowledgment and praise of Communist leadership of the "democratic" forces opposing Chinese reaction.[12]

These events, widely reviewed by students of Soviet foreign policy, bear on our discussion of Soviet post-war strategies in the colonial world because of the importance Moscow had always,

[11] These articles, appearing in *Bol'shevik*, February 1946, and in *New Times*, January 15 and March 1, 1946, are reviewed in Overstreet and Windmiller, *Communism in India*, pp. 226-8.

[12] For a more detailed review of the Soviet occupation of Manchuria and Moscow's policies vis-à-vis the Chinese Communists after the war, see, *inter alia*, the author's *Soviet Policy and the Chinese Communists*, Chapter 5.

and still, attached to China as a model for the East. So long as Soviet policy in China remained moderate, whatever the reasons for moderation, it was not likely that more vigorous policies would be urged elsewhere in the colonial East. When, however, Moscow's view of China altered, in mid-1946, it was a signal for a reappraisal of developments in other Eastern countries.

In fact, a firmer note can be detected in Soviet commentaries on colonial matters after the middle of 1946. In September, an article on developments in India charged the British with fomenting religious strife in order to make the new interim government under Nehru less able to rule and in consequence more dependent on England. The author also doubted that a government formed from the Indian Congress, which Soviet writers had appeared previously to support, was capable of bringing India closer to independence; true independence could be achieved only through a broader coalition and the "unity of the masses."[13] In October 1946 Zhukov viewed the national liberation movements in the colonial world as a major consequence of the war and offered the Bolshevik Revolution in Russia as the surest guide for colonial peoples. He also, now that the rupture with the United States over policies in China and elsewhere was a reality, noted that American imperialism competed with European, especially British and Dutch, as the chief obstacle to aspirations for independence.[14] In May 1947, Vasil'eva, in the course of giving a new formulation of the relationship between revolution in the East and West, spoke for the first time of armed uprisings in the colonies. "If during World War I," she wrote, citing Lenin as her authority, "the fate of the colonies was decided by war on the continent [i.e., in Europe], now the situation is basically reversed. As a result of World War II the colonial peoples themselves, *often with guns in their hands*, are

---

[13] V. Bushevich, "Bor'ba Indii za nezavisimost'," *Mirovoe khoziaistvo i mirovaia politika*, No. 9, September 1946, p. 52.

[14] E. M. Zhukov, "Velikaia Oktiabr'skaia sotsialisticheskaia revoliutsiia i kolonial'nyi Vostok," *Bol'shevik*, No. 20, October 1946, pp. 38-47. French imperialism, it should be noted, was being treated more circumspectly by Soviet writers at this juncture in order not to embarrass Communists in the French coalition government.

determining the fate of their countries."[15] In June a conference of Soviet specialists on India led by Zhukov (who had just returned from a short visit there) reappraised past Soviet support of the Indian Congress and of Nehru and now condemned both. Inasmuch as this was the first important conference of Soviet Orientalists since the war, its deliberations, though marked by minor differences in interpreting the alignment of class forces in India, inevitably influenced subsequent appraisals of the colonial question.[16]

Many of these emerging themes were reflected in an important article by Zhukov which appeared in *Pravda* on August 7, 1947. The colonial question, he wrote, was one of the most critical unsolved problems of the post-war era. He noted the war-inspired independence movements in the Arab world, the intensified struggle against British imperialism in India and Burma, and the national liberation movements which had sprung from the "armed partisan struggle" during the war by anti-imperialists in Indochina, Malaya, Indonesia, and the Philippines. Nowhere, however, had the colonial peoples yet succeeded in throwing off imperialism entirely. In essence, this was because of the "more flexible and disguised forms of domination" devised by the imperialists, especially by the Americans, who had now replaced the British as the major exploiters of colonial peoples. Once again Zhukov warned: "The grant of formal independence to the colonies by no means guarantees their actual independence." The Soviet Union alone could help the colonies and ex-colonies escape the new yoke of "dollar servitude."

> Only Leninism offers a solution of the national-colonial problem.
> . . . Marxism-Leninism calls all the oppressed peoples to the struggle for their complete liberation, binding the national liberation move-

---

[15] V. Vasil'eva, "Ekonomicheskoe razvitie kolonii v godu vtoroi mirovoi voiny," *Mirovoe khoziaistvo i mirovaia politika*, No. 5, May 1947, p. 64 (emphasis added).

[16] Zhukov's paper was published in *Mirovoe khoziaistvo i mirovaia politika*, No. 7, July 1947, pp. 3-14; other papers were published two years later in Akademiia nauk SSSR, Tikhookeanskii institut, *Uchenye zapiski*, Vol. ii (*Indiiskii sbornik*), pp. 5-66. For a discussion of the conference, see Kautsky, *Moscow and the Communist Party of India*, pp. 24-6.

ment of the oppressed peoples of the colonies and dependent countries with the revolutionary struggle of the proletariat. The great teachers —Lenin and Stalin—revealed profoundly and exhaustively in their works the existence of the national colonial question, and worked out the theoretical methods of its solution. Leninist-Stalinist nationality policy found complete fulfillment in the USSR, where the problem of cooperation of nations and the national question were solved better than in any other state. The brotherhood of peoples seems to be the wellspring of power of the Soviet state.[17]

Zhukov had moved some distance in this article, which links colonial freedom with over-all Soviet objectives, from his first formulations on the Eastern question at the end of the war. At the very least, the *Pravda* article served notice that Moscow planned to use emergent nationalism in the colonies as a lever in its struggle with the West, with the United States in particular. The article should not, however, be read as an exhortation to the colonial peoples to turn to violence in defense of their rights. The tone of the article is still restrained; Zhukov leaves more unsaid than said regarding ultimate strategies. A warning, for instance, not to be deceived by a formal grant of independence does not suggest how colonial subjects should respond when such an offer is actually made. A caution that they should mistrust imperialism told them nothing they did not know. Should they resort to armed uprising to seize independence, as in Indochina, they had no assurance from Zhukov that Moscow would support their cause, except in words. Meanwhile the traditional distinction made by pre-war Soviet and Comintern writers between bourgeois and popular leadership of national liberation movements is curiously muted here, as though the distinction no longer mattered. The part Communists should be playing in these movements is overlooked entirely. Zhukov's article, in short, was a lively reminder to any who cared to note it that Moscow's interest in the colonial question was very present; it was *not* an instruction to colonial leaders, Communist and non-Communist,

[17] E. Zhukov, "Kolonial'nyi vopros posle vtoroi voiny," *Pravda*, August 7, 1947; translated in Alvin Z. Rubinstein, *The Foreign Policy of the Soviet Union* (Random House, 1960), pp. 389-90.

who might have been looking to Moscow for guidance and support at a time when their efforts to gain independence were encountering growing opposition. Such an instruction was yet to come.

Before we turn to the course of events in Southeast Asia proper, it is appropriate to consider briefly what instruments Moscow devised after the war for carrying out its policies with regard to the world Communist movement. The Comintern was not restored, for reasons we will later inspect. If, however, world Communism was to retain its cohesion, new means for achieving this had to be discovered; articles such as Zhukov's appearing in *Pravda* and *Bol'shevik* were hardly enough to give force to Stalin's policies on a global scale. Moscow's authority was accordingly delegated. On major doctrinal issues, the leading parties abroad often provided guidance which Soviet leaders felt it imprudent to offer themselves. A case in point is the stern rebuke administered by the French Communist Party to the Americans in April 1945 over the issue of Browderism,[18] an episode which was to have repercussions in Burma. With respect to colonial policy, authority was normally delegated to (or perhaps simply assumed by) the metropolitan parties. The Vietnamese, for instance, received some guidance from French Communists both in Indochina and in France. Indian Communist policy was directly influenced, for better or worse, by the British Communist R. Palme Dutt, who spent four months in India in the spring and summer of 1946.[19]

A more ambitious effort to provide guidance to colonial movements in the post-war era was the Conference of Communist

[18] Earl Browder, the wartime leader of the CPUSA, had dissolved the party in 1944 and reorganized it as the Communist Political Association, a body designed to bring pressure on the Roosevelt administration but not fundamentally to obstruct it; following the French attack, appearing in an article by Jacques Duclos in *Cahiers du Communisme*, April 1945, Browder was repudiated and the CPUSA restored. For a discussion of the episode, see the author's *Soviet Policy and the Chinese Communists*, pp. 186-7.

[19] For a discussion of Dutt's visit and his part in shaping the policies of the CPI, see Overstreet and Windmiller, *op. cit.*, pp. 237-42.

Parties of the British Commonwealth, which, after several post-ponements, met in London in February 1947. Twelve parties (including the Burmese and Malayan from Southeast Asia) were represented. The conference mirrored Moscow's current views on national liberation and appears to have stimulated the independence movements in all British colonies. The principal resolution passed by the conference demanded "the immediate and unqualified independence of India, Burma, and Ceylon"; greeted "with enthusiasm the unprecedented upsurge of the colonial and subject peoples"; and considered "the immediate advance of the peoples of subject countries to national independence now the order of the day."[20] The fact that no Soviet source, insofar as this writer is aware, made reference to the London conference, at the time or subsequently, does not mean that it was a less effective instrument for projecting Moscow's policies into an important segment of the colonial world.

Liaison with the colonial movements was also achieved through the Moscow-inspired world youth and labor organizations after the war. The World Federation of Trade Unions (WFTU), founded in the autumn of 1945, enrolled many labor organizations from the colonies and passed frequent resolutions on colonial problems. The International Union of Students (IUS) was created at a large International Youth Congress held in Prague in August 1946. Delegates from the colonies, including several in Southeast Asia, attended the periodic meetings of these organizations and so gained an opportunity to meet Soviet representatives and, presumably, to discuss colonial strategies with them. Until the end of 1947, however, most of these world organizations included as many non-Communists as Communists,

[20] John Gollan, "Strengthening the Fight for Peace," *World News and Views*, March 15, 1947, p. 98; see also a brief reference to the conference in the published report of its successor in 1954, *Allies for Freedom: Report of the Second Conference of Communist and Workers' Parties of Countries within the Sphere of British Imperialism*, p. 6. Malayan government materials indicate that invitations to the conference were issued as early as the end of 1945 and that the conference was at one point to have been held in India; it was eventually shifted to England on the strength of the argument of the Secretary of the CPGB (Harry Pollitt) that "quite frankly the political importance of the conference will not be as great if held in any other country."

259

despite the Communist character of their leadership, and so could serve as a channel for only the most general instructions to colonial movements. In no sense did they replace, in the constellation of instrumentalities for world communism, such pre-war organizations as the Profintern, the Pan Pacific Trade Union Secretariat (PPTUS), or the Comintern itself.

Within Southeast Asia, meanwhile, there is some evidence of contact between the local Communist parties on a regional level. Malayan Communists were periodically in touch with the PKI; Indochinese Communists are reported to have been in contact with Thai Communists—though reports of a so-called League of Southeast Asian Communist Parties in Bangkok are doubtless exaggerated.[21] Of greater consequence than such local liaison were the occasional contacts with Indian and Chinese Communists; in Burma and Malaya in particular, the CPI and CCP, who were doubtless more alert to changes in Soviet strategies than party leaders in Southeast Asia, exercised significant influence at critical junctures. Finally, the possibility that infrequent Soviet travelers in Southeast Asia were able to meet with Communist leaders should not be ignored, although there is no evidence of their having influenced local strategies.[22]

We are now ready to turn again to our country-by-country analysis, beginning with the colony where Communism registered the greatest success in the post-war era.

[21] According to the Laotian Rightist leader, Phoumi Nosavan, the league was established early in 1947 under the auspices of Pridi Phanomyong, then the dominant political figure in Thailand; the Laotian representative was said to be Prince Souphanouvong. Interview with author, February 9, 1962. Another Laotian Rightist reports a meeting in Oudorn, Thailand, in September 1947, presided over by Souphanouvong and attended by representatives of the Burmese, Indonesian, Malayan and Thai Communist Parties, the Vietminh, the *Lao Issara* and the *Khmer Issarak*; Sisouk Na Champassak, *Tempête sur le Laos*, pp. 21-2. It seems likely that both Phoumi and Sisouk confuse these alleged Communist organizations with a League of Southeast Asia States sponsored by Pridi after the war in which Souphanouvong but, so far as is known, no other Southeast Asian Communist leaders took part; see Rebrikova, *Ocherki noveishei istorii Tailanda*, pp. 124-5.

[22] A Russian member of a World Federation of Democratic Youth (WFDY) delegation, for instance, visited Malaya, Indonesia, and Burma in the spring of 1957; her travel notes appeared in *New Times*, No. 31, July 30, and No. 34, August 20, 1947.

The formation of the Vietminh at the Eighth Party Plenum in May 1941 proved to be a decisive step in the fortunes of Indo-chinese Communism. Its moderate domestic program, coupled with a determination to drive both French and Japanese from the country and to establish an independent democratic republic, guaranteed a wide appeal throughout Vietnam. Although the principal Vietminh cadres and leadership were openly Communist from the outset, rank and file support came from trade unions, youth groups, peasant organizations, and, in due course, nationalist organizations composed of middle-class elements. The Vietminh, in short, had the virtue, from the Communist viewpoint, of exercising the appeal of a "united front from above" while organized as a "united front from below."

The Vietminh was not the only organization resisting the French and Japanese in Indochina during the war. Various nationalist groups dating from the pre-war era competed not only for local support within Indochina but for Chinese Nationalist support, without which, it was generally agreed, no resistance in Vietnam could be effective. Initially the nationalist organizations fared better than the Vietminh in competing for the Kuomintang's favor. This was to be expected, since the Kuomintang, embittered over its long experience with the followers of Mao Tse-tung, was not likely to be charitable where Communism was concerned. Chinese authorities in Kwangsi province accordingly arrested Nguyen Ai Quoc sometime in 1942, during a mission to China in search of Kuomintang support, and held him prisoner for more than a year. In October 1942 the Chinese governor of Kwangsi, Chang Fa-kwei, convened a congress of representatives of all Vietnamese political groups in South China, including the Vietminh, at which a new organization was created—the Vietnam Revolutionary League (in English translation). The League, with Chang's support, was to establish an espionage network in Vietnam for the Chinese military. The League's efforts, however, did not meet with much success, and in February 1943 Nguyen was able to negotiate his release on a promise of providing better intelligence for the Chinese authorities through his superior underground organization within Vietnam. It was at this juncture that Nguyen changed his name to Ho Chi Minh (He Who Is Enlightened) in order, as one student of Vietnamese Communism puts it, "to dispel the aura of his Communist past."[23]

Chang Fa-kwei continued to be uneasy about the Communist character of the Vietminh and in March 1944 returned control of the Vietnam Revolutionary League to nationalist leaders. The Vietminh continued nominal membership in the League but increasingly gave its attention to organization within Indochina rather than to *émigré* politics in Kwangsi. By 1944 most of the resistance groups in Vietnam had been absorbed into the Vietminh, and the ground was thus prepared for a strike at the appropriate moment against the Japanese, or the French, or both.

Indochinese Communist strategies during the war continued to center on the struggle for independence. When General de Gaulle in December 1943 promised political reforms after the war, amounting to Indochinese autonomy within a larger French association, the Vietnamese Communists reacted negatively. "The Algiers Liberation Committee [de Gaulle's government-in-exile] is mistaken in believing that the Indochinese people will content themselves with flatteries, assurances, and promises," read a CPIC statement in June 1944. "We want complete liberty." The statement went on to ridicule the Gaullist hope that Allied intervention in Indochina would salvage French control over the colony. "The Allied powers who denoted themselves as 'liberators' at Teheran," the Communist statement read, "do not have

---

[23] I. Milton Sacks in Trager, *Marxism in Southeast Asia*, p. 147. There is some discrepancy in accounts of Nguyen's imprisonment in China. The source cited by Sacks (Le Tranh Khoi, *Le Viêt-Nam: Histoire et Civilisation*, Paris, 1955, p. 458) indicates an imprisonment of thirteen months, from January 1942 to February 1943. A recent North Vietnamese source, on the other hand (which, incidentally, describes Nguyen's mission to China in 1942 as seeking liaison with the Chinese Communists, not the Kuomintang), states that he was imprisoned for two years, from mid-1942 to mid-1944; "President Ho Chi Minh" (Hanoi, 1960). Both accounts indicate that Nguyen was able to remain active politically while in prison and to maintain contact with his chief lieutenants in Indochina, Vo Nguyen Giap and Pham Van Dong.

the right to impose any kind of yoke on other people, even when the yoke is 'humanized' and sweetened by the partisans of de Gaulle."[24] The latter remark, to be sure, is puzzling, inasmuch as the Teheran "liberators" included the Russians (who elsewhere in the CPIC document are singled out as leaders of the "freedom offensive"), but the statement as a whole indicates the determination of the Indochinese Communists to press for full independence and to be satisfied with no half-measures.[25]

The problem of selecting the proper moment for an uprising preoccupied the Vietminh leadership during the last year or so of the war and led to some disagreement. As early as the Eighth Plenum of the CPIC in 1941, the question of timing an insurrection had been discussed in some detail and the ideal conditions for it set forth (see above, p. 221). In May 1944 a Vietminh instruction on "preparations for the insurrection" again cautioned that an uprising must not be undertaken prematurely. "If we launch the insurrection at the right time," the instruction read, according to Vo Nguyen Giap's version of it many years later, "our revolution for national liberation will certainly triumph. We must always be on the alert to feel the pulse of the movement and know the mood of the masses, estimate clearly the world situation and the situation in each period in order to seize the right opportunity and lead the masses of the people to rise up in time."[26] Despite such cautions (which Giap, of course, may exaggerate years after the event for reasons of his own) an insurrection was evidently planned for September 1944, following the harvest, and was canceled only at the last minute by Ho Chi Minh's veto; Ho, it is reported, favored a war of attrition against the Jap-

[24] The text of the statement, entitled "For the Complete Independence of Indochina" (June 4, 1944), is in *Témoinages et documents français relatif à la colonization française au Viêt Nam* (Hanoi, 1945), pp. V5ff.; cited in Trager, *op. cit.*, p. 148.

[25] The Vietminh, as distinct from the CPIC, appears to have taken a more moderate view of the Gaullists in 1944; see, for instance, a Vietminh leaflet addressed "To the French Soldiers and Legionnaires, To the Patriots and Anti-Fascist French in Indochina" (September 5, 1944), also reproduced in *Témoinages . . .* , pp. V3ff., and cited in Trager, *op. cit.*, p. 149.

[26] Vo Nguyen Giap, *People's War, People's Army*, p. 83.

anese and Vichy French over a direct assault.[27] The Vietminh was meanwhile developing armed units which in December 1944 were formally organized into the Vietnam Liberation Army.

In March 1945, the political situation in Indochina changed dramatically with the arrest by Japanese occupation authorities of the Vichy officials throughout the colony and, immediately thereafter, the proclamation of Vietnamese independence, with Japanese approval, by the Annamese Emperor Bao Dai. The Vietminh responded promptly, declaring the new regime "a puppet government which deceives the people on behalf of its Nipponese masters."[28] A general uprising, however, was still considered premature. An instruction of the Party Central Committee dated March 12, 1945, stated that "conditions for the insurrection are not yet ripe" and would be only when Allied troops landed in Indochina, a supposition held by the Vietminh leaders throughout the war. The instruction continued, according to a later text: "If revolution breaks out and people's revolutionary power is set up in Japan, or if Japan is occupied as was France in 1940, then even if the Allied forces have not yet arrived in our country, our general insurrection can be launched and win victory."[29] The Vietnamese appear to have weighed all contingencies except the one that was finally to make a declaration of independence possible—the simple collapse of the Japanese war machine at home without revolution, occupation, or even serious demoralization of Japanese troops overseas.

Events moved rapidly in Vietnam from March to August 1945. By June Vietminh forces had "liberated" many sections of the country, especially in the north (Tonking), and set up "people's

[27] Ho's blocking of the 1944 uprising is mentioned in a number of Vietnamese and Soviet sources: e.g. *Vietnam's Fight Against Fascism* (an official release by the Democratic Republic of Vietnam, 1948), pp. 6-7; A. Guber, "V'etnamskii narod v bor'be za svoiu nezavisimost' i demokratiiu," *Voprosy istorii*, No. 10, October 1949, p. 41; "President Ho Chi Minh" (Hanoi, 1960).

[28] From a Vietminh appeal to the people dated March 15, 1945; cited in Trager, *op. cit.*, p. 150, from *Factual Records of the Vietnam August Revolution* (Hanoi, 1946), pp. 19ff.

[29] Vo Nguyen Giap, *op. cit.*, p. 83.

264

revolutionary committees."[30] According to a Vietminh statement dated July 1, 1945, Japanese- and French-owned property in these areas was being seized and distributed to the poor; taxes had been abolished; working hours were shortened; and various other reforms were being put into effect. The statement went on to charge Gaullist elements with "attempting to stage a comeback and to re-establish the French colonial yoke in our country."[31] The Vietminh, however, was playing a double game with the Gaullists. According to other accounts of this period, the Vietminh was negotiating with Gaullist agents in China for some sort of agreement with the new regime in Paris.[32] A Vietminh memorandum to the Gaullists about this time—which has every appearance of being authentic—restricted its demands to modified self-rule through a popularly elected parliament; independence "in a minimum of five years and a maximum of ten"; the return of Vietnam's natural resources to the inhabitants "after a just compensation of the present holders"; a guarantee of liberties proclaimed in the United Nations Charter; and a prohibition on the sale of opium.[33] The discrepancy between the tone of the July statement and that of the memorandum to the French is puzzling, but, if the accuracy of both can be accepted, they would suggest that the Vietminh leaders were determined to keep all courses open, revolutionary and otherwise, which could ensure their independence.

The Vietminh continued to move cautiously as the Japanese surrender neared. On August 13 the newly created Military Committee of the Vietnam Liberation Army called for a "general insurrection," but little fighting was necessary. The Japanese authorities remained aloof, pending instructions; such

[30] Soviet sources subsequently referred to these committees as "people's soviets"; e.g. S. A. Mkhitarian, "Rabochii klass v narodno-demokraticheskom gosudarstve V'etnam," *Sovetskoe vostokovedenie*, No. 5, September-October 1958, p. 45. No such claim was made at the time.

[31] "Factual Records . . . ," pp. 21-3, cited in Trager, *op. cit.*, p. 151.

[32] See Hammer, *The Struggle for Indochina*, pp. 99, 129.

[33] The text of the memorandum is in Devillers, *Histoire du Viêt-Nam de 1940 à 1952*, p. 134.

French as were not still in jail were too demoralized to act. On August 16 a "congress" called by the Vietminh met secretly and appointed a People's National Liberation Committee. Ho Chi Minh was elected its president. Ho was evidently ready, even in the midst of what was later called the "August Revolution," to work for the present within the framework of a constitutional monarchy under Bao Dai rather than jeopardize independence. The public clamor for Bao Dai's abdication, however, grew daily, apparently from pressures beyond the Vietminh's control, and on August 24 his abdication was accepted by the People's National Liberation Committee. On September 2, 1945, the Provisional Government of the Democratic Republic of Vietnam (DRV) was sworn in in Hanoi and solemnly proclaimed the independence of Vietnam from France, several weeks before the first Allied forces entered Indochina.

All factors, it seemed, conspired to favor the Indochinese Communists: the unexpected early surrender of Japan; the fact that no Allied forces were immediately available to accept the Japanese surrender in Indochina; the sudden surge of nationalism within the country; and the parallel demand to terminate the Annamese monarchy. The Vietminh, well organized and long prepared for these developments (if not precisely for the way in which they unfolded), had merely to reap the benefits.

Moscow, which had taken scant notice of Indochina during the war, took no immediate notice of these events at the end of the war.[34] Nor has reliable evidence subsequently come to light showing Soviet involvement in any way in the wartime strategies of the Vietminh or in Communist tactics during the August

[34] Apart from general reference studies on Indochina, such as Guber, *Indoneziia i Indokitai*, 1942, the only wartime coverage of Indochina seen by this writer—though there must be other references—occurs in an article on Japanese-occupied countries published in 1944. It treats Indochina as a typical Asian colony exploited by Japan, the more readily because of Vichy's acquiescence; no mention is made of a resistance movement. K. Popov, "Iaponiia i okkupirovannye strany Vostochnoi Azii," *Voina i rabochii klass*, No. 12, June 15, 1944, p. 19. The Soviet bibliography on Southeast Asia, *Bibliografiia Iugo-vostochnoi Azii*, lists no items on Indochina during the period of the war in the Pacific.

uprising. There is, on the other hand, evidence of early interest by French Communists in Vietnamese developments after the war. An official statement by the FCP on September 20, for instance, condemned the warlike movements of the French military with respect to Indochina and considered a proposal by the Algiers Committee the preceding March for "self-government" in Indochina a "regrettable retreat" from de Gaulle's plan of October 1944, which had promised "autonomy"; the statement insisted that equal rights and self-determination be guaranteed to the Indochinese, in accordance with the principles of the Atlantic Charter.[35] Articles in *L'Humanité* early in October expressed growing concern with the intentions of the Paris government as the French prepared to return to the colony.[36] French Communists appear nonetheless to have urged caution on the Vietnamese comrades. A secret instruction reported to have been delivered to the CPIC by a French Communist unit in Saigon, dated September 25, requested the Vietnamese to be sure that their struggle "meets the requirements of Soviet policy" and to await the outcome of the election in France scheduled for October; the instructions also advised the CPIC to send representatives both to Paris, to contact the FCP, and to Moscow.[37]

Whether because of such advice from the French or because of their own reading of the situation in Vietnam, the Indochinese Communists continued to proceed cautiously during the first six months of the new regime. From its inception, the new government pleaded for moderation and derided the efforts of Trotskyists to arouse the populace to armed insurrection against Japanese forces still in Indochina. A Vietminh leaflet dated Sep-

[35] The statement, released in *L'Humanité*, September 21, 1945, is cited in V. Vasil'eva, "Porazhenie Iaponii i sobytiia v Indo-Kitae," *Mirovoe khoziaistvo i mirovaia politika*, No. 12, December 1945, p. 56.

[36] These articles are reviewed in A. C., "Indo-china and Indonesia," *World News and Views*, October 13, 1945, p. 320.

[37] Harold Isaacs, *No Peace for Asia* (New York, 1948), pp. 173-4; Isaacs claims to have seen the French instruction. Liaison between the French and Indochinese parties after the war (although not as early as September 1945) is also reported by Vietnamese informants who claim that it was maintained through French correspondents such as Leo Figuère and Michele Bosquet; author's interview in Saigon with Dang Duc Khoi and others, February 1962.

267

tember 7 pointed out that the Japanese were obliged by international agreement to keep order in the country pending arrival of Allied troops and urged compliance with their decrees. "In the interests of our country," the leaflet read, "we call on all to have confidence in us and not let themselves be led by people [i.e., Trotskyites] who betray our country. It is only in this spirit that we can facilitate our relations with the Allied representatives."[38] When Allied troops entered Vietnam in mid-September—the British south of the sixteenth parallel, the Chinese north of it, and the French following in the wake of each as best they could—the Vietminh, true to its word, behaved moderately, despite the rude manner in which the government was ejected from Saigon and the rough treatment accorded Vietnamese citizens by a few aroused French colonials. In October a "live and let live" agreement was reached between the Vietminh and the leaders of the Vietnam Revolutionary League, who by now had returned from wartime exile in Kunming and Kwangsi. In November the CPIC formally dissolved itself "in order," as its Central Committee said in a final communiqué, "to destroy all misunderstandings, domestic and foreign, which can hinder the liberation of our country."[39] In January 1946, the Vietminh allowed popular elections, in response to demands of oppositionist nationalist leaders for a broadening of the government coalition. On March 6 Ho Chi Minh, who had withdrawn to the north as the French administration widened its control over the south, signed an agreement with Jean Sainteny, the French Commissioner, allowing French troops to enter North Vietnam to replace the Chinese (who were as troublesome to the French as to the Vietminh) on condition that Paris recognize the DRV as a "free state . . . belonging to the Indochinese Federation and the French Union."[40]

[38] Quoted in Trager, *op. cit.*, p. 155.
[39] The communiqué, dated November 11, 1945, is quoted in *ibid.*, p. 158, from a text in *La République* (Hanoi), November 18, 1948. The decision evidently encountered some opposition from Communists in South Vietnam, where the party organization was strong and the Vietminh weak; Trager, p. 327.
[40] An English text of the March 6 agreement may be found in Cole, *Conflict in Indochina and International Repercussions*, pp. 40-2. For more detailed cover-

Vietminh restraint during the first six months of the DRV's existence, with respect both to domestic and foreign affairs, should not lead one to suppose that the Vietnamese leadership was paralyzed by its sudden and unexpectedly easy assumption of power. Subsequent events were to reveal that behind the moderate façade the Communist element within the Vietminh made good use of the confused conditions in Vietnam during this period; not only was the government successful in building a solid base of support throughout the countryside and in keeping alive a profound mistrust of the French but the Communists were able successively to neutralize their most formidable rivals, especially the Trotskyists and Vietnam Revolutionary League, so that Communist leadership of the Vietminh and the DRV was not subsequently threatened. The Vietnamese Communists, in short, awaiting a more definitive instruction from Moscow, or from some authoritative source within the international movement, had weathered the transition from war to peace far better than most Communists not directly in the line of advancing Soviet troops.

By the time of the Ho-Sainteny agreement the first Soviet press commentaries on the situation in Indochina had appeared. In the November 1 issue of *New Times,* for instance, A. Guber had reviewed post-war developments in Indochina and Indonesia. Although limited in his information—as indicated by certain errors in dates and sequence of events—Guber sets forth with little editorializing what had been taking place in Indochina: he notes the collaboration of French colonial officials during the war; their arrest in March 1945 after their refusal to continue collaboration with the Japanese when the outcome of the war became apparent; the Japanese-sponsored declaration of "independence" by Bao Dai and its rejection by the Vietminh; the Vietminh's successful exercise of control over all Vietnam and the establishment of the DRV in August, weeks before the

age of events in Indochina leading to the Ho-Sainteny agreement, see Devillers, *Histoire du Viêt-Nam de 1940 à 1952,* Chapters viii-xii, and Hammer, *The Struggle for Indochina,* Chapters 5 and 6.

269

appearance of Allied troops; and the disillusioning behavior of British troops when they arrived and of the French authorities who assumed power, under British protection, in Saigon. Guber notes the hope of the Vietminh that American and Chinese assistance will soon arrive. He closes: "The threat to restore colonial rule in its previous forms, which are unacceptable to the peoples of Indonesia and Indochina, is meeting with growing resistance. The sympathies of progressive forces all over the world are entirely with the masses who are striving for freedom and who have a right to be free."[41]

Apart from noting the Communist Party as one of the parties uniting to form the Vietminh in 1941, there is no other reference to Vietnamese Communism. Nor is there mention of Ho Chi Minh. Zhukov, in his article in the December issue of *Bol'shevik*, does mention Ho, but adds no fresh details or interpretation of the situation in Indochina.

An article by Vasil'eva which appeared in February 1946 gives fuller coverage of the events in Indochina and suggests more forthright Soviet support of the Vietminh. Vasil'eva makes much, for instance, of French surrender of its sovereignty in Indochina even before the Japanese occupation, through such actions as the granting of tariff autonomy to the colony. The final abdication of French authority in March 1945 was thus merely the culmination of a long process of French withdrawal from Indochina. The DRV's claim to independence was accordingly a strong one, Vasil'eva argued. The Hanoi government, meanwhile (which Vasil'eva described as "provisional"), sought peaceful ties with France, not violence and bloodshed, as was clearly set forth in its declarations to the French people and to the French government.[42]

Another article by Vasil'eva approximately a year later shows the Soviet line in Indochina still moderate. By this time the

[41] A. Guber, "What's Happening in Indonesia and Indochina?" *New Times*, No. 11, November 1, 1945, p. 13.

[42] V. Vasil'eva, "Porazhenie Iaponii i sobytiia v Indo-Kitae," *Mirovoe khoziaistvo i mirovaia politika*, No. 12, December 1945, pp. 49-50 (the issue went to press only on February 18, 1946).

agreement of March 6, 1946, had been generally discredited and the climax of the "peaceful" phase of French-Vietnamese negotiations had been reached in the frustrations of the Fontainebleau Conference during the summer of 1946. Vasil'eva took a mild view of Fontainebleau. Ho was quoted as saying on September 16, after the negotiations had terminated with a few paltry agreements: "After a three month visit in France I take away with me a 'modus vivendi.' Am I satisfied with this? Yes and No. It is too little, but it is better than nothing." Vasil'eva, clearly relying on the emergence of a "new France" (that is, with Communists in power), places the Vietnamese question in this context. According to her account, so does Ho. "We do not lose hope," she quotes him as saying on his return to Saigon. "I personally am an optimist. I believe in the 'new France'." Vasil'eva concludes her article: "The further development of Vietnam depends to a significant degree on its ties with democratic France, whose progressive forces have always spoken forth in support of colonial liberation."[43]

It is apparent from these early post-war commentaries on Indochina that Moscow's views were closely in tune with the Vietminh's behavior and perhaps helped to shape it. Until the outcome of the Communist struggle for power in France was known, a clear-cut policy in Indochina was blocked. No Communist, respecting Stalin's interest in a Communist France, could urge the revolutionary course which the situation in Vietnam appeared to warrant. All councils were accordingly moderate. French Communists, for instance, were if anything more restrained than Russian regarding Indochina. "Are we," a spokesman for the FCP asked in July 1946, during the Fontainebleau Conference, "after having lost Syria and Lebanon yesterday, to lose Indochina tomorrow?"[44] In September a Communist deputy

[43] V. Vasil'eva, "V'etnam—indokitaiskaia demokraticheskaia respublika," *Mirovoe khoziaistvo i mirovaia politika*, No. 12, December 1946, p. 89. Vasil'eva's articles on Indochina were made the basis for her volume *Indo-Kitai*, which went to press in December 1946—the first full length study of a Southeast Asian country (275 pp.) to appear in Russia after the war.

[44] *L'Humanité*, July 24, 1946, cited in Hammer, *The Struggle for Indochina*, p. 190.

said in the National Assembly that while the proposed French Union must be founded "on the confident, fraternal and, above all, democratic collaboration of all the peoples and races who compose it, . . . Communists are as much as the next person for the greatness of the country."[45] British Communist opinion seconded French: a review of Indochina in August 1946, drawing largely on articles in *L'Humanité*, asserted that "far from Ho Chi Minh wanting to break away from the French Union" it was the French government which was forcing him out of it.[46] The Vietminh, meanwhile, continued to speak mildly despite all frustrations. Ho's address to the second session of the DRV National Assembly in October, for instance, following his return from France, was a model of moderation: he spoke chiefly of "people's rights" and "people's well-being," urged campaigns against illiteracy and gambling and asked for an increase in production; there was no mention of revolution or of the impasse in talks with the French.[47] As late as December 10, less than a fortnight before the civil war was to erupt in Indochina, Ho reaffirmed "the sincere desire of the Vietnamese government and people to collaborate fraternally with the French people . . . and to be part of the French Union."[48]

There is no need to doubt that these public pronouncements on Vietnam throughout the Communist world were genuine. It was one thing, however, to desire and proclaim a peaceful course in Indochina and quite another to pursue it. The Vietminh was increasingly caught between the need to give lip service to moderate policies, in order not to give offense to world Communist leaders, and popular pressure at home for more decisive action. By the end of 1946 the time for moderation was running out in Vietnam. As Vo Nguyen Giap had explained earlier in the year, in justifying the Ho-Sainteny accord, there were at that juncture

[45] *Ibid.*, citing Assemblée Nationale, *Journal Officiel*, September 19, 1946, p. 3844.

[46] Peggoty Freeman, "Vietnam," *World News and Views*, August 9, 1947, p. 354.

[47] A text of the address is included in *Vietnam: A New Stage in Her History* (released by Vietnam News in Bangkok, June 1947).

[48] Hammer, *op. cit.*, p. 185, citing *Le Monde*, December 10, 1946.

three courses open to the Vietminh: a prolonged struggle to achieve complete freedom, a limited war to secure a better settlement with the French, or negotiation. In March, he considered the third superior—and cited the Bolsheviks' signing of the Treaty of Brest-Litovsk in 1918 as an historic parallel to the Ho-Sainteny agreement.[49] By December it was doubtful if the Vietminh leadership could hold to these views whatever "directives" it was in possession of from Paris or from Moscow.

The outbreak of open hostilities between France and the DRV on December 19 marked the beginning of a civil war which was to last seven and a half years. Whatever the immediate causes of the war—the intransigence of the French authorities in Indochina, notably the High Commissioner D'Argenlieu, or a decision by the DRV that it had exhausted the possibilities of negotiation—all prospects for a peaceful solution of the affair soon vanished. Despite occasional new appeals for negotiations, the DRV leadership remained underground from this time forward. It maintained the fiction for several years of leading a broad nationalist movement against French imperialism, unassociated with international Communism, but gradually it shaped its policies and strategies in the image of other great Communist insurrections such as Mao Tse-tung's.

The French Communists, still in the French coalition at the time of the outbreak, considered it inappropriate to support the Vietnamese rebels and so remained aloof for the present; after their ejection from the coalition in the spring of 1947, they gradually voiced their full support of the Vietminh, but did not, so far as is known, exercise appreciable influence over Ho's strategies. Moscow, meanwhile, responded to the civil war in Indochina with anguish and blamed it on "influential French reactionary circles" and on British imperialist maneuvers. The government of Leon Blum, so long as French Communists were in it, was not held directly responsible.[50] When the FCP had left the coalition, Soviet writers were less circumspect. An item in

---

[49] Devillers, *op. cit.*, citing the text of a speech by Vo Nguyen Giap in a contemporary Vietnamese newspaper.

[50] "Events in Viet-Nham," *New Times*, No. 3, January 16, 1947, pp. 15-6.

New Times in April, for instance, insisted that the Paris government must bear full responsibility for the military action against the DRV and for efforts to sabotage the regime by negotiating with anti-Vietminh Annamese leaders in exile. The DRV, in the meantime, was said to be issuing periodic appeals for a peaceful resolution of the crisis, but on condition that its independence and the unity of the country be respected. "If France counts on re-establishing a colonial regime in Vietnam," Ho is quoted as having said in March, "we shall continue to fight." *New Times* was confident the DRV's struggle would succeed.[51] In a public lecture delivered in July, a leading Soviet Orientalist called the DRV's struggle "a just war of national liberation" and noted that, of the political parties of the Left in France, only the Communists sought a "fair regularization" of the civil strife.[52] The same month Zhukov singled out for special praise the Vietnamese, along with the Indonesians, for "carrying the banner of freedom and independence into the heart of Asia."[53]

Moscow's response to the civil war in Indochina, to judge from these early commentaries, was appropriately sympathetic to the Vietminh's cause but noncommittal concerning any specific assistance the Vietnamese might expect. There were, for instance, no appeals for worldwide demonstrations in support of the DRV, as there had been in similar episodes before the war and would be subsequently. One gains, indeed, the impression of a certain detachment on Moscow's part, the more remarkable when one considers that the civil war in Indochina was the first conflict between colonial subjects and imperialism in a major Asian colony and one which would affect profoundly the course of events throughout the East. Stalin, it appears, was unprepared for colonial revolutions in such timetables as he kept. He evidently felt that his hand was not yet fully played out in Europe and until it was, a civil war in Indochina—which in its early stages at-

51 "En Indochine," *Temps Nouveaux*, No. 15, April 11, 1947, pp. 18-9.
52 V. A. Avarin, *Politicheskie izmeneniia na Tikhom okeane posle vtoroi mirovoi voiny*, p. 14.
53 E. M. Zhukov, "K polozheniiu v Indii," *Mirovoe khoziaistvo i mirovaia politika*, No. 7, July 1947, p. 3.

tracted more worldwide attention than the smoldering struggle in China—served no good purpose. It was not until 1948 or 1949, after the Soviet concept of colonial revolution had undergone a total reappraisal, that Ho's struggle in Vietnam gained Moscow's unequivocal approval and became the model for Communists in neighboring countries.

French Indochina as such ceased to exist after the war, with the separation of Cambodia and Laos from the other three parts of the colony (Cochinchina, Tonking, and Annam) that joined to make up Vietnam. In consequence three nations must be considered in discussing post-war Soviet policies in this area. Prior to 1945, infrequent references to Cambodia and Laos in Soviet publications had described them as hinterland kingdoms of little consequence in the life of Indochina; occasionally they were mentioned as areas where harassed Vietnamese revolutionaries could regroup comparatively free of police surveillance.[54] No indigenous nationalist or Communist movements in Cambodia or Laos had been identified.

Cambodian independence was initially proclaimed by King Norodom Sihanouk on March 13, 1945, immediately after Bao Dai's proclamation of the independence of Vietnam. The Cambodians, however, were compelled to come to terms with the French after the war following the unopposed return of the latter to Phnom Penh in the company of British troops. In January 1946 an agreement was signed which returned the French to effective control over the Khmer kingdom on a promise of regaining for Cambodia the western provinces seized by Thailand in 1941. A national liberation movement had meanwhile come into being, the *Khmer Issarak* (or Free Cambodians), which opposed the policies of Sihanouk and insisted on a greater measure of Cambodian autonomy. The *Khmer Issarak* con-

[54] An article in *Kommunisticheskii internatsional*, No. 8, August 1940, p. 91, for instance, noted that the survivors of the Enbay uprising had been able to keep alive a revolutionary spirit in the country by transferring their activities to Cambodia and Laos. See also *Bol'shaia sovetskaia entsiklopediia*, Vol. 31 (1937), pp. 13-6 (Cambodia), and Vol. 35 (1937), pp. 750-1 (Laos).

trolled for a time the area surrounding Siem Reap, in north-western Cambodia, but it was unable to gather sufficient strength for an assault on Phnom Penh. Its leaders, alternately under Thai (during Pridi's ascendancy) and Vietnamese influence, were disunited and the movement gradually dissolved, some joining the Vietminh, others accepting the amnesty offered them by Sihanouk.

The experience of the Laotians paralleled in certain respects that of the Cambodians. Laos too declared its independence following the Japanese coup of March 1945 and was obliged, in due course, to come to terms with the French. The principal difference between the Laotian and Cambodian experiences lay in the more determined resistance shown by Laotian nationalists to the return of the French. The nationalist organization, the *Lao Issara*, formed like the *Khmer Issarak* during the closing months of the war, seized power in Vientiane in October 1945 and abolished the monarchy. The *Lao Issara* at this juncture included Laotians of varying political outlook who united—like the various factions in the Anti-Fascist People's Freedom League (AFPFL) in Burma—solely to ensure independence. The most radical element in the *Lao Issara* from the outset centered on Prince Souphanouvong, a member of the junior branch of the royal family at Luang Prabang, who was married to a Vietnamese Communist and had spent the war years in Hanoi in close touch with the Vietminh. He is reported to have returned to Laos after the war with Vietnamese cadres and with funds from Ho Chi Minh to pursue the struggle for Laotian independence.[55] Souphanouvong served as Foreign Minister in the short-lived *Lao Issara* government and was largely responsible for the attempted defense of the country against the French in the spring of 1946. Following its defeat and the re-establishment of the monarchy, the *Lao Issara* withdrew to Thailand, where it sought, under

[55] Interview with Nhouy Abahy in February 1962; many details concerning the origins of the *Lao Issara* were given to the writer in a series of interviews in Vientiane with early members of the organization, including—in addition to Nhouy Abahy—Phoumi Nosavan and Oun Sananikone. Their accounts tally on most details, but not always on interpretation.

Pridi Phanomyong's protection, to organize a counterattack against the French-imposed regime. Rivalries within the organization, however, reflecting political differences as well as ancient feuds between the various princely families of Laos, frustrated its plans. By 1949 the majority of the *Lao Issara* leaders had returned to Laos under amnesty terms offered by the government; many of them, like Souvanna Phouma and Phoumi Nosavan, were subsequently to play major roles in the succession of governments in Vientiane. Only Souphanouvong, of the original leadership of the *Lao Issara*, rejected the amnesty. He withdrew with his followers to the northern section of Laos where, as we shall see, his new organization, the *Pathet Lao*, became increasingly dependent upon the Vietminh.[56]

Soviet commentaries noted briefly developments in Cambodia and Laos after the war but showed some confusion over the actual course of events there. Vasil'eva, for instance, in her article in the December 1945 issue of *Mirovoe khoziaistvo i mirovaia politika*, quoted contradictory sources on the fate of the regimes established at the end of the war. Relying on an Australian report of October 29, 1945, that Laos and Cambodia had both fallen under French control, Vasil'eva concluded that this was because the Laotians and Cambodians had always had close ties with "the reactionary French administration." She quotes a Vietminh broadcast of October 30, on the other hand, which asserted that the independent regimes in Cambodia and Laos would in due course decide by popular vote whether or not to unite with the DRV. According to Vasil'eva, the broadcast also announced that if King Sisavang Vong in Laos did not step down, as requested by the new Provisional Government (of the *Lao Issara*), a "soviet of the Laotian people" would be created. Vasil'eva meanwhile failed to identify Souphanouvong as the leader of pro-

[56] Fragmentary accounts of the *Khmer Issarak* and *Lao Issara*, whose history has been very imperfectly explored by competent scholars, may be found, *inter alia*, in Hammer, *op. cit.*, pp. 134, 156-7, 254-62 and in George M. Kahin (ed.), *Governments and Politics of Southeast Asia*, 2nd ed. (Cornell 1964), pp. 535-7 and 608-9. For the *Lao Issara*, see also Sisouk Na Champassak, *Tempête sur le Laos*, Chap. 2, and Reference Division, Central Office of Information (London), *Laos*, p. 4.

277

Communist elements in Laos, which he was: she cites, in fact, an appeal by his wife for support of the independence movements in Indochina as evidence that "even among monarchist elements" there was no agreement on the course to follow.[57] Vasil'eva touches again on Cambodia and Laos in an article a year later. She now sees little hope for the two kingdoms. Their rulers, she writes, "always had close ties with the French administration" and this facilitated the reassertion of French control. She makes no mention on this occasion of the nationalist movements in exile or of their leaders.[58] Thereafter Soviet observers remained largely silent on events in Cambodia and Laos until 1951, when the course of the civil war in Vietnam again directed Moscow's attention to the two interior kingdoms.

INDONESIAN COMMUNISM MARKS TIME

During the war the nationalist movement in Indonesia expressed itself in two forms. One, the best known, was open collaboration with the Japanese. Those who took this course, under the leadership of Sukarno and Hatta, whom the Japanese released at the outset of the occupation, were active in Japanese-sponsored organizations such as *Poetera* (*Poesat Tenaya Rarjat*, or Center of People's Power) and maintained close ties with the Japanese-organized Indonesian Army. Their goal was consistently the independence of Indonesia, not collaboration for the sake of collaboration, and even the sharpest critics of Sukarno and Hatta acknowledged their integrity where the chief objective was concerned. This branch of the nationalist movement came particularly into prominence during the last year of the occupation after Tokyo had decided on preparations for independence.

The other branch of the nationalist movement was anti-Japanese and operated mainly underground, as in Indochina. Sjarifuddin organized the first resistance movement in 1942 and is said to have had Dutch funds for the purpose. Following his

[57] V. Vasil'eva, "Porazhenie Iaponii i sobytiia v Indokitae," *Mirovoe khoziaistvo i mirovaia politika*, No. 12, December 1945, pp. 58-9.
[58] V. Vasil'eva, "V'etnam—indokitaiskaia demokraticheskaia respublika," *ibid.*, No. 12, December 1946, p. 88.

278

arrest early in 1943, the principal resistance against the Japanese was led by Soetan Sjahrir. Neither movement had significant engagements with the Japanese, but the existence of both anti-Japanese and collaborationist factions in Indonesia assured some continuity in the nationalist movement whatever the outcome of the war. There was evidently liaison between the two and mutual recognition of the value of the alternate effort; when Sjarifuddin, for instance, was sentenced to death in 1943, Sukarno's intervention with the Japanese authorities secured a reduction of his sentence to life imprisonment. The course taken by individual Indonesians, however, appears to have been a matter of personal choice, not the result of any allocation of roles. Subsequent claims of a common grand strategy on the part of the nationalist movement during the Japanese occupation may on the whole be dismissed.[59]

Indonesian Communists were restrained by Soviet anti-Fascist policies during the war from open collaboration with the Japanese and so were active—if at all—only in the underground movement. Many joined Sjarifuddin's movement in 1942 and reportedly attended his lectures on Marxism in Jogjakarta.[60] The PKI as such, insofar as is known, played no part in Sjarifuddin's underground and certainly none in Sjahrir's, which succeeded it. As a separate force in the resistance movement, the PKI—in contrast to Ho Chi Minh's organization in Indochina—appears to have been singularly ineffective.

The only other "Communist" movement reported during the war was a curious Japanese-sponsored effort in 1944 and 1945 which consisted of a school to indoctrinate semi-educated Indonesians in Marxian principles and an ostensibly anti-Japanese

[59] Accounts of the nationalist movement during the war may be found, *inter alia*, in Kahin, *Nationalism and Revolution in Indonesia*, Chapter Four, and Anderson, *Some Aspects of Indonesian Politics under the Japanese Occupation*. These accounts are supported by evidence given the author during interviews in March 1961 with such wartime nationalist leaders as Mohammed Hatta and Iwa Kusumasumantri, as well as with lesser figures in the nationalist movement.

[60] A non-Communist Indonesian who attended these lectures states that the program had barely begun when Sjarifuddin was arrested; interview with Soedjatmoko, March 1961.

underground for its graduates; the school was headed by an Indonesian believed to have been an active Communist at the time, Wikana, and the underground organization by a former Communist named Achmad Subardjo.[61] Sources disagree on the number of students who graduated from the school, as well as on Japanese motives in sponsoring it and in condoning the underground organization,[62] but the Subardjo movement had gained sufficient strength by the end of the war to be a factor of some consequence in political developments attending independence. There is no reason to believe, at any event, that this "Communist" activity was in any way related to PKI strategies, despite the fact that several of Subardjo's associates were subsequently to emerge as leaders of the revived PKI after the war.

Soviet sources took no notice of the Subardjo movement. Nor was there discussion of the nationalist or resistance movements except in the most general way. As in the case of other Southeast Asian countries, Soviet wartime coverage of Indonesia was confined to surveys of the pre-war period, studies of local geog-

---

[61] Wikana had been a leader of the Communist-dominated *Gerindo* before the war and after the war was active in the *Pesindo*, also Communist-oriented; he was also one of the open Communist leaders of the Madiun uprising of September 1948. Subardjo had been a leader of the *Perhimpoenan Indonesia* (PI) in Holland early in the 1920's and subsequently is reported to have spent a year in Moscow; by the 1930's he is believed to have left the PKI and during the war worked for the Japanese in their naval headquarters in Java. See Kahin, *op. cit.*, p. 115.

[62] Among the possible explanations of Japanese motives offered by Professor Kahin, based on interviews with Indonesian leaders after the war, are: a Japanese aim to subvert the Communist underground and turn it against England and the United States, should the latter invade Indonesia in the course of the war; a more modest effort merely to split the Communists by holding before them a more orthodox, international Marxian alternative to Stalinism; a maneuver on the part of the Japanese naval officers involved in the effort, whose leanings to Marxism were genuine, to hasten Indonesian independence in an "extremely progressive manner" (Hatta's words); and an attempt to turn to Japanese purposes the popular appeal of Tan Malaka, who was known to have close ties with Subardjo and whose anti-Western, pan-Asian views had long been apparent. Kahin, *op. cit.*, pp. 117-9; see also Anderson, *op. cit.*, pp. 50-1. Kahin states that several hundred graduated from the Japanese-sponsored schools; Anderson indicates only 25 or 30.

raphy, and, at rare intervals, descriptions of naval battles in the vicinity.[63]

The absence of a significant Communist underground in Indonesia during the war meant that the PKI played no part in the dramatic events leading to the establishment of the Indonesian Republic after the war. These events, competently reviewed elsewhere,[64] are too complex to unravel in the present study and need concern us only where they bear on the re-emergence of the Indonesian Communist movement during the post-war era and on Moscow's views of the Indonesian revolution.

The disorder within Indonesian Communism in 1945 is reflected in the fact that there were at least three separate centers of Communist activity during the early months of the republic. The Subardjo group was initially the best organized, and its leaders played a major part in the initial declaration of independence (August 17, 1945) and in the establishment of a government; Subardjo himself served as Minister of Foreign Affairs in the first cabinet, which held office from August 31 to November 14. His faction, however, suffered from widespread, and justifiable, suspicion of its Japanese origins. With the reintroduction of a multi-party system in October, Subardjo's party —which had in any case dropped its wartime "Communist" label —soon disappeared from the political scene, although Subardjo and a number of his associates remained active in other organizations.

A second "Communist" effort centered on Tan Malaka, who by 1945 was widely regarded in Indonesia as a legend—the "hero" of the Communist uprising of 1926-1927. He had spent the intervening years, according to his own account, avoiding the police in Tokyo, Shanghai, Hong Kong, Singapore, and elsewhere, an outcast from the Comintern and the author of a native brand of pan-Asian and militantly anti-Western Marxism. In

[63] The section on Indonesia in *Bibliografiia Iugo-vostochnoi Azii* lists ten or a dozen such items; see also A. Guber's small volume published in 1942, *Indoneziia i Indokitai*.

[64] Notably in Kahin, *op. cit.*, Chapters v and vi.

1942 he evidently returned to Java, but kept his identity secret until August 1945, when he immediately became a force for Sukarno and other Indonesian leaders to contend with.[65] Tan Malaka's ambition to lead the Indonesian revolution was unbounded and caused him during the first year of the republic to seek alliances successively with nearly all of the nationalist leaders in an effort to overthrow Sukarno. Repeated frustrations led him to attempt a coup d'état against Sukarno and Hatta in mid-1946, relying on his mass organization *Persatuan Perdjuongan* (Fighting Front). The failure of the coup and Tan Malaka's arrest terminated his stormy career in Indonesian politics—except for a brief, and final, appearance during the Madiun rising of September 1948. His large following, which was in any case no more Communist than Subardjo's in the normal use of the word, quickly dissolved with his removal from the scene.

The Indonesian Communists with whom we have properly to deal, those able and likely to respond to Moscow's guidance should any be forthcoming, were the members, open and clandestine, of the new PKI. The PKI was re-established legally, on November 7, 1945, following the decision to institute a multiparty system in Indonesia. The leader of the new formation was Mohammed Jusuf, a former member of Subardjo's movement but with no known connection with the pre-war PKI. The PKI's attitude toward the Sukarno regime was evidently hostile from the outset of Jusuf's leadership. It is not clear whether Jusuf adopted this view on his own initiative or in response to the initial hostility toward the republic of certain European Communists,[66] but his policies were in direct conflict with Moscow's

[65] Tan Malaka's account of his travels during this period is reviewed in American Universities Field Staff, WAH-1-'59 (April 6, 1959), a report by Willard A. Hanna.

[66] A British Communist organ, for instance, in an editorial at the end of September, spoke of a fake "independence" in Indonesia under former Japanese collaborators; a week later, however, the same journal corrected its position and noted that "the important fact in the situation" was the support of the new government by the anti-Japanese resistance, which therefore meant that "it must command the sympathy of the democrats." See *World News and Views*, September 29, 1945, p. 297, and October 6, 1945, p. 306. Dutch Communists made a similar reversal of their views about the same time; see McVey, *The Develop-*

by the time the new PKI was launched. His arrest in February 1946, following a Communist-inspired attack on a government police barracks, was accordingly followed by a full review and repudiation of his policies at a party meeting in March. In April Sardjono, a former chairman of the PKI before the 1926-1927 uprising and recently returned from a twenty-year exile in Boven Digul concentration camp and in Australia, was made party chairman. A manifesto adopted at this time described the new regime as "a democratic government which embraces all classes and parties, unifying all the progressive forces of the people"; ultimately, the manifesto said, the objective was a Communist society, but, "as a first step in achieving this goal, the PKI joins in the defense of the Republic of Indonesia."[67] In August, Alimin returned to Java, also following an absence of twenty years, and shared power with Sardjono;[68] for the first time since 1927 (except perhaps during Musso's brief return to Java in 1935) it was possible to identify a Communist leadership within Indonesia which might be expected to respond to international directives.

The reorganization of the party leadership in the spring of 1946 did not lead to any appreciable growth of the PKI. One reason for this may have been that many known and suspected Communists, some of them members of the pre-war PKI, failed to join the party after the war. Sjarifuddin, for instance, who was later to claim party membership as early as the mid-1930's and who was known to Malayans as a Communist at least by January 1947,[69] chose to lead the Socialist Party with Sjahrir. Of

---

ment of the Indonesian Communist Party and its Relations with the Soviet Union and the Chinese People's Republic, p. 27.

[67] *World News and Views*, July 13, 1946, p. 218; an accompanying item on Sardjono's election makes special note of the fact that Tan Malaka was not a member of the PKI, nor had he been since 1927.

[68] Following more than fifteen years spent in Moscow, Alimin left for Java in 1941, according to Malayan sources, but was delayed in Yenan by the war. He reached Singapore in June 1946 and spent several weeks contacting Communists in Malaya before returning to Indonesia; interrogation of Loi Tek by Singapore police officers in January 1947.

[69] This information also comes from Loi Tek; see n. 68 above.

the Communist leaders of *Perhimpoenan Indonesia* in Holland who returned to Indonesia after the war, only Maruto Darusman joined the PKI; his two principal associates, Abdulmadjid and Setiadjit, associated themselves, respectively, with the Socialist and Labor Parties.[70] Doubtless there were tactical considerations in this bypassing of the PKI by returning Communists. Until the PKI had created a broad base of support, the opportunities for wielding influence were doubtless judged greater in powerful organizations such as the Socialist Party than in the PKI. Moreover, the prospects for subverting other Leftist parties and bringing them closer to the Communists were enhanced if no affiliation with the PKI were made known. In 1948, as we shall see, a large part of the Socialist Party, following Sjarifuddin, as well as the entire Labor Party and the *Pesindo* (a para-military youth organization led by Wikana), did in fact join the PKI; in 1945 and 1946, however, the towering personality of Tan Malaka in Indonesian politics meant that Communism in the republic was likely to be associated with him in the public mind, despite all efforts of the PKI to disclaim him. Whatever considerations led Communists and Communist sympathizers in the national leadership to remain aloof from the PKI, the consequence of their non-participation was that the party was denied the prestige which might have attached to their open membership and so enjoyed less growth during the post-war years than might otherwise have been possible.

A further reason for the PKI's failure to emerge as a strong and independent political force in Indonesia before 1948 may have been its close identification with the government, especially with respect to the Linggadjati agreement of March 1947.[71] In

[70] Kahin, *op. cit.*, p. 161; both Abdulmadjid and Setiadjit, like Sjarifuddin, were later to claim long-standing membership in the PKI.

[71] The Linggadjati agreement, the first signed between the Dutch and Indonesians since the war, was—like the Ho-Sainteny protocol of the previous March in Indochina—an interim agreement to pave the way for subsequent negotiations on the precise relationship between the two countries; it called for "cooperation" of the two governments to establish a Netherlands-Indonesian Union, the Indonesian portion to consist of three states—the existing Republic (whose authority was to be limited to Java and Sumatra), Borneo, and the Great Eastern State (embracing the remainder of Indonesia and to be ruled by the Dutch).

November of the preceding year, when the agreement was under discussion, the PKI offered Sukarno its prompt support on the issue. Sukarno, grateful for any support of the difficult concessions he felt it necessary to make to the Dutch to avoid bloodshed, rewarded the PKI by increasing its membership in the Indonesian "parliament" from two to thirty-five. This raised the PKI to an official status in the legislature equal to the Socialists and behind only the PNI and *Masjumi* (the principal Muslim party); the Leftist coalition, the *Sajap Kiri*, in which the PKI played a major role, now held as many votes in the Indonesian legislature as were reserved for the dominant PNI-*Masjumi* alliance (the *Benteng Republik*, or Republican Fortress). The parliamentary gain, however, was doubtful compensation for the loss of mass support the PKI suffered in approving the generally unpopular, if necessary, Linggadjati accord. The PKI was still without a firm base in labor, peasant, or other elements in Indonesian society; moreover its new role in the "parliament," whose power was in any case small compared to Sukarno's,[72] distracted the party leadership from building such a base. In later years this was the principal charge laid to the PKI leadership during the Sardjono-Alimin era: its failure to build a stronger party organization. "The weaknesses of the Party in the political, ideological, and organizational spheres," the Fifth PKI Congress charged in 1954, reviewing the post-war years, "made it incapable of providing leadership to the objective situation [*sic*] which was, at that time, very favorable."[73]

Whatever criticism was later heaped on the Sardjono-Alimin leadership, the PKI's actions under their guidance do not appear to have been in conflict with Moscow's views of the Indonesian situation at the time. Guber, in 1945, had indicated Soviet approval of the establishment of the Indonesian Republic. He noted

---

[72] The "parliament" was called the Indonesian National Committee (or KNIP) and functioned more as an advisory group to the government than as a genuine legislature.

[73] Quoted in Aidit, *The Birth and Growth of the Communist Party of Indonesia*, p. 25. Similar charges are also made by I. Steklov, "Imperialist Aggression in Indonesia," *New Times*, No. 47, November 16, 1949, p. 4, and by Vasil'eva, *Natsional'no-osvoboditel'naia bor'ba v stranakh Iugo-vostochnoi Azii*, p. 20.

a difference between the Vietnamese and Indonesian revolutions —that the former was led by anti-Japanese nationalists, the latter by collaborators with the Japanese—but he dismissed as "absurd and injudicious" Dutch charges that the independence movement in Java was "inspired by the Japanese." Sukarno was treated dispassionately and was pictured as favoring "non-violent methods of achieving independence" in contrast to Hatta, "an old fighter in the anti-imperialist struggle" (a judgment inspired, no doubt, by Hatta's brief membership in the League Against Imperialism in the 1920's). The motives of the British and Dutch troops in Java were of course subjected to much caustic innuendo.[74]

In February 1946 Guber wrote again of Indonesia, noting that the passing of the fifth month of the new Republic on January 17 "should be regarded as a definite landmark"; British and Dutch efforts to restore colonial rule had thus far been checked. The author explained the success of the revolution to date as due not necessarily to the leadership, which was still treated with some circumspection, but to the "absence of a strong and influential feudal-landlord class characteristic of most colonies"; this, Guber argued, "greatly reduces the reactionary base of the colonizers within the country." Reference was made to the first Soviet (or Ukrainian) effort in the United Nations in behalf of Indonesia, a proposal to send a commission of enquiry to Java consisting of representatives of England, the United States, China, Holland, and the USSR. The proposal, Guber wrote, was received with great warmth in Indonesia and he quoted Sjahrir (then the premier) as having said of it: "The Soviet Union is the major power with the least direct interest in Indonesia and is therefore better able to present the case as a moral issue."[75] Early in March *New Times* reproduced the text of an Indonesian resolution which charged the Dutch with overlooking three pertinent facts in the present impasse between the two countries: the change of sovereignty in Indonesia that occurred when the

[74] A. Guber, "What's Happening in Indonesia and Indo-China," *New Times*, No. 11, November 1, 1945, pp. 10-3.

[75] A. Guber, "The Situation in Indonesia," *New Times*, No. 4, February 15, 1946, p. 10.

Dutch surrendered unconditionally to the Japanese in 1942; the proclamation of Indonesian independence on August 12, 1945; and the de facto existence of the Indonesian government. "The three facts enumerated in this resolution," the editors commented, "are indisputably true. It is difficult to take any exception to them and still adhere to the principle of the sovereign equality of great and small nations proclaimed by the Charter of the United Nations Organization."[76]

These early Soviet comments leave no doubt of Moscow's wholehearted approval of the republic, at least from November 1, 1945, on (the date of Guber's first article on Indonesia). The PKI could not continue to ignore this approval and so altered its policies at meetings in March and April 1946. Jusuf, already under arrest, was a convenient scapegoat for the party's tactical errors from November to March and was duly chastised in the international Communist press.[77]

In April an article by Vasil'eva appeared in the Soviet press which gave a fuller analysis of the events in Indonesia and discussed, for the first time, the activities of the PKI. The wartime record of Communists in the Indonesian underground was mentioned and the legalization of the PKI in November 1945 noted; the PKI was described, along with the PNI and the *Masjumi*, as one of the major parties in the new republic. A recommendation to Sukarno by an independent Indonesian group that the government be broadened to include these parties was reported sympathetically. Vasil'eva refers many times to Sukarno throughout the article, never with hostility. She does, however, note that his career has been "one typical of a petty-bourgeois nationalist"; as in earlier articles, charges of his wartime collaboration are dismissed.[78]

[76] "The Situation in Indonesia" (from the section on "International Life"), *New Times*, No. 5, March 1, 1946, p. 15.

[77] In August 1946, for instance, a British Communist described Jusuf as a "Dutch agent" and linked him with Tan Malaka and Subardjo (the latter identified as a former member of the "Japanese secret service"); Arthur Clegg, "The Indonesian Republic Lives," *World News and Views*, August 3, 1946, p. 243.

[78] V. Vasil'eva, "Sobytiia v Indonezii," *Mirovoe khoziaistvo i mirovaia politika*, No. 1-2, January-February 1946, p. 91; the issue went to press only on April 2.

The Soviet attitude toward the Indonesian revolution did not change appreciably for the next two or two and a half years, to judge from periodic commentaries in the Russian press. The PKI was not discussed again during 1946 and 1947, insofar as this writer has discovered, though some attention was given to labor organizations in which Communists were active.[79] Sukarno and other government leaders continued to be mentioned neutrally, but less conspicuously than during the first six months of the revolution; Sjarifuddin was singled out and quoted on one occasion—but as Defense Minister, without any suggestion that his views differed from Sukarno's or from those of other members of the government.[80] Notice was taken of the signing in March 1947, after long Dutch procrastination, of the Linggadjati agreement. The Dutch, *New Times* editorialized, were forced to sign the agreement, having failed to pacify the Indonesians through force, but their intention of disregarding it was immediately indicated by their ordering a resumption of the offensive on several fronts.[81] The Dutch, supported by the British, were pictured as seeking by every means to destroy the republic and to reassert their authority throughout the former colony. In addition to outright military action, the Dutch, *New Times* charged in May, were applying British "divide and rule" tactics, especially in the Eastern islands where puppet states and Quisling regimes were being established; this maneuver too would fail.[82]

When the first Dutch "police action"—a determined effort by the Dutch to crush the republic once and for all—opened on July 20, 1947, the Soviet reaction was immediate and bitter. A lead editorial in *New Times* placed the blame less on Holland than on the United States and England. "Every right-minded

[79] The first congress of the Indonesian Federation of Trade Unions (known as SOBSI), for instance, was reported in *New Times*, No. 22, May 30, 1947, p. 18; see also *Professional'nye soiuzy*, No. 6, 1947, pp. 42-3. The Communists were subsequently to gain a dominant position in SOBSI.

[80] I. Kopylov, "The Events in Indonesia," *New Times*, No. 19, October 1, 1946, p. 12.

[81] See *ibid.*, No. 14, April 4, 1947, pp. 25-6, and No. 16, April 18, 1947, pp. 17-8.

[82] "Divide and Rule—Dutch Style," *ibid.*, No. 20, May 16, 1947, p. 17.

person understands," the editorial stated, "that little Holland, which only recently was subjected to occupation by Hitler's armies, would never have embarked on a new colonial venture were not its ruling circles solidly backed by the United States— American dollars and the Truman doctrine—and by British financial and industrial magnates, only too pleased by any chance to avail themselves of the colonial riches that are not their own." The "regrets" expressed by American and British spokesmen concerning the new turn of events in Indonesia were therefore "outright hypocrisy." The Indonesian leadership was meanwhile fully exonerated of any responsibility for the outbreak, and its "patience and readiness to make concessions" in recent negotiations were noted. The closing paragraph of the editorial, which placed the Indonesian crisis in the context of general world politics, should be read as a preview of Zhukov's important article in the August 7 issue of *Pravda* (see above, p. 256), as well as of Andrei Zhdanov's address in September at the founding of the Cominform:

> The prolonged conflict between Holland and the Republic of Indonesia is of more than local importance. It represents a clash of old and new tendencies in international life. The attempts of the imperialist colonizers to preserve the old system and simply reshape the colonial map to harmonize with the new balance of power are faced with an increasing desire on the part of peoples of dependent and colonial countries to achieve national liberation and embark on the path of democratic development. With every passing day it becomes increasingly clear that these imperialist tendencies are fraught with danger to peace and to the security of nations. It is in the interests of universal peace that the legitimate rights of the colonial peoples to liberty and independence be realized.[83]

As the fighting progressed, Soviet reports claimed, on very doubtful evidence, that initial Dutch gains were offset by Indonesian counterattacks.[84] In fact, by the time the Dutch called

---

[83] "The War in Indonesia," *ibid.*, No. 31, July 30, 1947, pp. 1-2.
[84] "Colonial Blitzkrieg in Indonesia," *ibid.*, No. 32, August 6, 1947, p. 10; see also A. A. Guber, "Imperialisty—dushiteli svobody i nezavisimosti narodov," *Bol'shevik*, No. 19, October 1, 1947, pp. 50-61, and Guber, *Voina v Indonezii* (1947).

a halt to their offensive, on August 4, most of their immediate objectives had been achieved and the military position of the republic was greatly weaker than before.

Within the United Nations, meanwhile, the Russians vigorously supported the Indonesian side of the argument. When debate began in the Security Council ten days after the surprise attack, Gromyko insisted that, prior to any negotiations, Dutch troops withdraw to the positions from which the attack had been launched; the American delegation, on the other hand, called for a cease-fire along the actual battle-line and a settlement through arbitration. In mid-August, when Sjahrir, the Indonesian representative in the United Nations, asked that the Security Council itself supervise the cease-fire, the Russians supported his request and put it into a formal proposal. This, however, was vetoed by France, and the Russians abstained from voting on the final compromise worked out by the United States —a three-power "Committee of Good Offices" composed of members of the Security Council, two to be selected by the parties to the dispute and the third to be chosen by the first two. The reason given for the Russian abstention was that the compromise proposal did not protect the interests of the Indonesians.[85] In October, as the debate on Indonesia continued, Russia again proposed that Dutch troops be ordered to withdraw to their positions prior to July 20, but the proposal, as a later Soviet source put it, was rejected by the "American voting machine" in the Security Council.[86]

Soviet sources, even after Moscow had grown hostile toward the republic, were to make much of Russian support of Indonesia after the war, particularly during the crisis brought on by

[85] The members of the committee eventually selected were Belgium (chosen by Holland), Australia (Indonesia's choice), and the United States as the third member; the committee began its investigations in Indonesia only at the end of October.

[86] I. Steklov, "Imperialist Aggression in Indonesia," *New Times*, No. 48, November 23, 1949, pp. 13-5. For a more detailed discussion of Soviet policy on the Indonesian issue at the United Nations, see Alistair M. Taylor, *Indonesian Independence and the United Nations* (London, 1960), pp. 51-3 and 384-9.

the Dutch "police action" in 1947. This support was cited as evidence of Moscow's consistent encouragement of national liberation movements. Soviet policies during this period did in fact tend to alter the balance of opinion in Indonesia vis-à-vis the United States and Russia: the United States became increasingly identified as a supporter of the Dutch and of pre-war colonialism —which was, of course, what Moscow by mid-1947 was persistently arguing—while Russia was emerging as a disinterested party in the colonial struggle whose sympathy could be depended upon and whose renowned revolutionary objectives were not, at least in Indonesia, in conflict with the objectives of the republic itself. As one student of Soviet policy in Indonesia has stated: "Russia thus found in the Indonesian question an excellent tool with which to pry away the rather prevalent Asian faith in the United States as an anti-colonial power."[87] So long as the Russians were making progress in this direction, a more lively revolutionary program in Indonesia, they may have felt, could wait.

Moscow's interest in Indonesia, it is apparent, was primarily in the external affairs of the republic rather than its internal politics. Curiously, however, Soviet commentators overlooked the cabinet crisis on the eve of the first Dutch police action which led to the formation of a government headed by Sjarifuddin. The PKI, through its dominant role in the *Sajap Kiri*, was directly involved in this crisis. During the spring of 1947 the Sjahrir cabinet had steadily lost support over the issue of what concessions, if any, to make to the Dutch in the negotiations following the signing of the Linggadjati agreement. In June the *Sajap Kiri*, largely at the instigation of Sjarifuddin (a co-leader of the Socialist Party with Sjahrir, it will be recalled), joined the opposition and Sjahrir resigned. The *Sajap Kiri* reversed its position almost immediately and asked Sjahrir to continue in office, but he declined. One explanation of the *Sajap Kiri's* abrupt *volte-face*—which bears directly on our inspection of Soviet strategies in Indonesia—is that the PKI leaders in the alliance, on instructions from Moscow, brought it about. The instructions were allegedly delivered to the PKI by Setiadjit, who returned to

[87] McVey, *op. cit.*, p. 31; see also Kahin, *op. cit.*, p. 215.

Indonesia from a conference of the WFTU in Prague in the midst of the political crisis; Setiadjit would not, it is argued, have been able to bring about so prompt a switch in the PKI's tactics without an explicit Soviet directive.[88]

Whether or not this explanation of the episode is plausible, Sjahrir's refusal to continue in office led, on July 3, to the formation of a new cabinet under Sjarifuddin—an event which the Soviet press apparently failed to note at the time.[89] Sjarifuddin's government, which included a representative of the PKI as Minister of State, lasted for six months and marked the climax of Soviet-Indonesian cordiality. It coincided with the first major crisis, as we have seen, in Indonesian-Dutch relations—the police action of July 1947; it also coincided with a shift in Soviet policies which was to affect Moscow's behavior throughout the colonial world for the next five or six years.

WAR AND INDEPENDENCE IN THE PHILIPPINES

Communist experience in the Philippines during the war may be compared with that in Indochina. In both countries Communist leaders of the pre-war anti-Fascist movements moved promptly, and naturally, into the leadership of the anti-Japanese underground. The CPPI's plans for guerrilla activity were reportedly laid as early as October 1941, two months before the Japanese attacked.[90] In December, after the Japanese attack began, the Communists issued a twelve-point appeal to General MacArthur, President Quezon, and the American High Commissioner Francis B. Sayre calling for the arming of Filipinos to assist regular forces in repelling the invasion, the creation of guerrilla bases in the event the Japanese could not be driven out, and the establishment of a broad anti-Japanese united front of

[88] See McVey, *op. cit.*, p. 48. Miss McVey comments: "This was the first instance of direct Soviet intervention into postwar PKI affairs."

[89] A note on the formation of the new cabinet does, however, appear in the British Communist organ, *World News and Views*, July 12, 1947, p. 303.

[90] See Taruc, *Born of the People*, p. 115, and G. I. Levinson, "Kolonial'naia politika SShA i osvoboditel'noe dvizhenie na Filippinakh v period 'avtonomii' (1935-1941)," Akademiia nauk SSSR, Institut vostokovedeniia, *Kratkie soobshcheniia, vyp.* VIII, 1953, p. 45.

Filipinos regardless of political, economic, and social differences; the CPPI, the appeal stated, "pledges its loyalty to the governments of the Philippines and the United States."[91] Quezon is reported to have acknowledged the appeal and welcomed Communist co-operation.[92] In February 1942 the united front was formally launched with a five-point program, according to a post-war Russian source: ejection of the Japanese, co-operation with the United Nations, "full independence," guarantee of minimum living standards, and the liquidation of traitors.[93]

In March the Communists established their guerrilla organization, the *Hukbong Bayan Laban Sa Hapon* (People's Anti-Japanese Army)—normally known as the *Hukbalahap*, or simply the *Huks*. Like the Vietminh, created a year earlier in Indochina, the *Hukbalahap* served as the basis of Communist power during and after the war. Luis Taruc, the former Socialist now wholly in the Communist camp, was the field commander of the *Hukbalahap* during the war. By 1945 its strength was estimated at more than 50,000.[94]

The *Hukbalahap*, despite its strength and undoubted prestige during the war, did not play the part in Filipino politics after the war that the Vietminh did in Indochina. One reason for this was that independence had already been promised to the Filipinos and American officials periodically reaffirmed this promise during the war.[95] The opportunity of leading a vigorous national liberation movement accordingly did not present itself

[91] Taruc, *op. cit.*, p. 53; see also Lava, *Milestones*, p. 49.

[92] *World News and Views*, December 27, 1941, p. 819, cited in Hoeksema, *Communism in the Philippines*, p. 239.

[93] V. F. Vasil'ev, G. I. Levinson, V. S. Rudnev, "Iz istorii osvoboditel'noi voiny narodov Iugo-vostochnoi Azii v 1941-1945 godakh," *Voprosy istorii*, No. 10, October 1955, pp. 55-6.

[94] A later Soviet estimate was 60,000; see the paper by O. Zabozlaeva in Akademiia nauk SSSR, *Vestnik*, No. 1, 1948, p. 44. An American estimate indicates 20,000 regulars and 50,000 reserves; see B. Seeman and Lawrence Salisbury, *Cross Currents in the Philippines* (IPR Pamphlet No. 46, New York, 1946), cited in Hoeksema, *op. cit.*, p. 273.

[95] British Communists in 1944 noted statements to this effect by President Roosevelt and General MacArthur and contrasted ther.. with the absence of any similar promise to the Malayans and Burmese; see *World News and Views*, October 28, 1944, p. 349.

293

to the Philippine Communists as it did to the Vietnamese. The CPPI's efforts after the war had of necessity to be directed toward the more difficult task of surpassing the entrenched Philippine middle class, either by force or by the subversion of this class through some sort of coalition, the strategy initially contemplated in China.

Another reason for the relative ineffectiveness of the *Hukbalahap* after the war was the weakness of its national organization. The *Huks* shared with the Indonesian resistance movement the problem of constructing under wartime conditions an effective guerrilla force throughout a widely scattered archipelago, a problem that troubled Communist underground movements on the mainland far less. According to José Lava, a false sense of *Huk* strength, based on a comparatively strong position in Central Luzon, discouraged adequate efforts to organize the movement elsewhere;[96] as a result, the *Hukbalahap* was less prepared to play a significant part in national politics after the war than its prestige would have led one to expect.

A third, and perhaps more significant, reason for the frustrations of Philippine Communism after the war was the confusion within higher echelons of the party, which was in turn the consequence of the need to reconstruct an entirely new leadership of the CPPI. In January 1942 the pre-war leadership had been eliminated in one stroke with the arrest of Evangelista, Pedro Abad Santos, and Capadocia by the Japanese, then in control of the entire Philippines except Corregidor and the Bataan peninsula.[97] A "second front" leadership emerged under Vincente Lava (known as Vy), the oldest of the Lava brothers with whom the course of Philippine Communism was to be closely identified for the next twenty years.[98] Disputes over military tactics

[96] See Lava, *Milestones*, pp. 55-6.

[97] Evangelista died in prison and Santos in January 1945, soon after his release. Capadocia, also released before the end of the war, evidently attempted to construct "a united front with the Japanese against the feudal landlords." This effort, however, was mistrusted by the party and Capadocia was expelled in 1944; he was reinstated only in 1948. See *ibid.*, pp. 51-2.

[98] According to Hoeksema, *op. cit.*, p. 243, Vincente Lava was educated before the war at Columbia University and Oberlin. At his death in September 1947,

arose almost immediately. During the first year of the Occupation the prevailing strategy was "continuous attacks" against the Japanese. This strategy, which José Lava later called "adventurist," provoked a surprise Japanese attack on the *Huk* bases in March 1943 causing much disruption and demoralization. The party shifted to a strategy of "retreat for defense," evidently over the objections of Taruc and a vigorous minority; José Lava later considered the new policy equally in error in an opposite sense inasmuch as it was based on the "dubious formulation that there was an ebb in the tide of the revolutionary struggle necessitating such tactics." This policy was in turn canceled at a Central Committee meeting in September 1944, shortly after the first American bombings in the Philippines preliminary to invasion; on this occasion the Politburo was reorganized, only Vincente Lava remaining from the previous leadership, and the post of Secretary-General gave way to a three-man Secretariat.[99]

These wartime disputes were only a foretaste of the rivalries that paralyzed the party leadership after the war. The principal differences among the party leaders, as was the case in other Southeast Asian Communist parties, centered on the question of whether to pursue a militant policy, relying on the strength of the *Hukbalahap*, or to adopt a more conciliatory line, in accordance with the tactics of the united front presumably still in force insofar as the international movement was concerned. The question was central to the two immediate tactical problems facing the CPPI at the end of the war: the attitude to be taken toward the returning Americans and the government-in-exile of Osmeña,[100] and the strategy to be followed in the first post-war elections, scheduled for the spring of 1946. The opposing groups

---

José Lava emerged as a major figure in the CPPI; following José's arrest in 1950, Jesus Lava led the party until his arrest in the spring of 1964.

[99] This account of Communist rivalries during the Occupation is based—as are most Philippine Intelligence accounts—on Lava, *Milestones*, Chapter Three. Taruc's account of this period, given to the author during interviews in 1961 and 1962, largely corroborates Lava's; see also Taruc's published account in *Born of the People*, pp. 6off.

[100] Sergio Osmeña assumed the Presidency of the government-in-exile in Washington following Quezon's death in 1944.

within the party crystallized into two more or less distinct factions; one was known as the "majority PB" (Politburo), led by Pedro Castro (who became the new Secretary-General when this post was restored late in 1945), Lacuesta, and Jorge; the other, the "minority PB," was allied with the Orgburo and the *Hukbalahap* and was led by the Lava brothers and Luis Taruc.

The attitude of the CPPI toward MacArthur and American Army officials in the Philippines was complicated by several considerations. In the first place, the *Hukbalahap* had never put itself under the aegis of the USAFFE (United States Armed Forces in the Far East) and so did not constitute, in the eyes of the Americans, an official resistance movement. When *Huk* assistance was offered early in 1945, it was accordingly rejected— at least officially, although there is evidence of some liaison between American and *Huk* units.[101] A *Huk* delegation did, however, take part in liberation ceremonies in Manila in March 1945. In Central Luzon, meanwhile, the *Hukbalahap* greatly alienated any American good will by taking affairs there largely into its own hands, appointing Communist governors, setting up local governments, and dispensing rough justice to collaborators and suspected collaborators. These terroristic activities led to the arrest of Taruc[102] and several other Communist leaders in April; MacArthur's release about the same time of Manuel Roxas, whom the Communists had persistently (and with good reason) condemned as a collaborator, hardly served to improve American-*Huk* relations.

These developments intensified differences between the "majority" and "minority" factions on party policy but did not immediately lead to a change in line. In June, for instance, party spokesmen denied that the CPPI sought civil war and insisted that its aims, like those of the American army itself, were to remove collaborators and place in office those with a record of loyalty "to our Commonwealth and to America."[103] Luis Taruc,

---

[101] See Hoeksema, *op. cit.*, p. 271.

[102] Taruc himself describes with some candor *Huk* activities in Central Luzon in the spring of 1945; see his *Born of the People*, p. 209.

[103] See Hoeksema, *op. cit.*, p. 291.

after his release from jail in September, described the CPPI as a movement "which can fairly compare with the Labour Party of Britain or the Popular Front of France."[104] Moderation was also the posture of the CPPI in its strategies for the forthcoming elections, although these strategies occasioned the sharpest dispute within the party leadership thus far. The "majority" faction, confident of Communist strength, wished to present an independent slate of candidates for the newly created Communist front organization, the Democratic Alliance; the "minority" sought, for tactical reasons, an electoral coalition between the Democratic Alliance and the Osmeña wing of the *Nacionalista*. The issue was bitterly fought out at a party conference in January 1946, and the "majority PB" was checked, according to Taruc, only by the threat of a *Huk* defection. The program of the Democratic Alliance, which was accepted by Osmeña in February, demanded full independence on July 4, as promised; the removal from power of all collaborators and the punishment of traitors; the institution of democratic practices in all areas of Philippine life; and a guarantee of minimum living standards for all. The program also stated that, "after the defeat of Fascist reaction in the coming elections, a coalition government will be created to ensure final victory over Fascism."[105] Taruc referred to the coming coalition as a "peacetime continuation of a united front against Fascism and reaction."[106]

The Communists' tactics in the April elections did not succeed. The Liberals, Roxas' party, won by a comfortable margin, gaining the Presidency, nearly three-quarters of the seats in the House of Representatives, and more than one-half in the Senate. The Democratic Alliance, thanks to the Communists, showed strength only in Central Luzon, where six seats were won, two of them by Taruc and Jesus Lava; both, however, were barred from taking their seats on legal arguments pressed by the new

[104] *Ibid.*, p. 294, citing *Manila Post*, October 3, 1945.

[105] The five-point program of the Alliance is summarized in an article by O. I. Zabozlaeva in *Krizis kolonial'noi sistemy*, pp. 230-1.

[106] Hoeksema, *op. cit.*, p. 309, citing *Daily Standard* (Manila), February 8, 1946.

government. The election and the denial of their seats to Taruc and Lava marked the end of serious Communist efforts toward collaboration with the parliamentary regime. "Minority" leaders withdrew to Central Luzon, where *Huk* strength remained intact. Taruc for a time appeared to be on the verge of serious negotiations with the government concerning the disarming and demobilization of *Huk* units (an issue which had continued unresolved since the Japanese surrender), but by August 1946 it was apparent that no negotiations would be held for the present.[107] Despite periodic statements by the Communists on the conditions they would consider minimal for a truce,[108] relations between the *Huks* and the government deteriorated steadily to a state of de facto, if undeclared, civil war; the sporadic fighting, however, was confined to Central Luzon.

The struggle within the party leadership, meanwhile, continued without appreciable let-up after the elections. The "majority PB," according to José Lava's undoubtedly colored account, now sought to pacify the victorious Liberals by proposing a partial surrender of arms held by the *Hukbalahap*. The "minority," which despite its open united front tactics in the electoral campaign had always been more inclined to a militant course, ignored the official leadership and pursued its own intransigent course in Central Luzon. A meeting of the Politburo in January 1947, to which the Lava brothers were evidently not invited, failed to resolve the impasse despite a reorganization of the party leadership under Jorge. A statement of the party's policy by Jorge six months later indicates the distance that still separated the "majority" faction from the "minority," by then in open defiance of the government: Jorge saw the opposing forces in the Philippines as imperialists and landlords *versus* workers, peasants, and "the democratic bourgeoisie"; he argued that respect for an "orderly process of change," not force, determines the party's behavior; he denied that the CPPI favored the abolition of private property, rather the "development of capitalism"

---

[107] See the discussion of correspondence on this question between President Roxas and Taruc in Hoeksema, *op. cit.*, pp. 324-6.

[108] See Taruc, *op. cit.*, p. 254, and Levinson, *Filipiny: vchera i segodnia*, p. 145.

and, with respect to peasants, the distribution of land.[109] A party leadership still embracing such moderate principles as late as August 1947 could not forever co-exist with the militant leadership of the *Hukbalahap* in the field. The crisis, however, continued to paralyze the CPPI until the spring of 1948.

We must, of course, make some allowance for inaccuracies in the reporting of the intra-party dispute by two of the principals involved in it.[110] The reality of the dispute, however, may be taken for granted and, more important than this for our purposes, its impact on the fortunes of the CPPI need not be doubted. Philippine Communists could not, for instance, pursue the parliamentary course, as Indonesian Communists did, so long as a segment of the party was in open revolt; nor could they mount a nation-wide rebellion, like the Vietminh, so long as the "majority PB" remained in Manila asserting its peaceful aims and making gains in the Philippine labor movement.[111] More than any other party in Southeast Asia after the war, the CPPI was prevented by its own deep divisions from devising any consistent strategy offering some hope of success.

How attentive to the foregoing developments, both within the CPPI and in the Philippines generally, were the foreign parties most likely to be concerned—the American, the Chinese, and the Russian?

As far as American Communists are concerned, the curtain that was drawn over the Commonwealth early in 1942—for them as for other Americans—terminated not only their influence but also any sustained interest in the CPPI. A student of Philippine

[109] From a letter by Jorge in *Philippines Free Press*, August 16, 1947, cited in Hoeksema, *op. cit.*, pp. 333-4.

[110] Most evidence of the dispute comes from José Lava and Luis Taruc, in both their written accounts (*Milestones* and *Born of the People*, respectively) and in their oral testimony to the writer during interviews in 1961 and 1962; with respect to the latter, it is worth noting that though Taruc and Lava were at odds with one another at the time of these interviews, their accounts tally on all significant details.

[111] Hoeksema, *op. cit.*, p. 338 cites figures from the *Philippines Free Press* (May 3, 1947) showing gains in the Communist-controlled Committee on Labor Organizations (CLO) from 10,000 to 50,000 between May 1, 1946, and May 1, 1947.

Communism who has been attentive to the relations between the two parties over the years discovers little evidence of an American Communist *presence* in the Philippines during and immediately following the war. Early in the war James Allen, the architect of the Communist-Socialist merger of 1938, noted that Philippine Communists were leading the "war of national liberation" (against Japan, that is), but gave no significant details.[112] As late as January 1945, after American troops had already landed in the Philippines, the CPUSA appears to have had only the cloudiest idea of the resistance movement: an item in the New York *Daily Worker*, for instance, made reference to the *"Kukbalahap"* and surmised that this was "undoubtedly" composed of the same elements which had constituted the pre-war united front.[113]

Infrequently after the war American Communists sought to assist the CPPI—as in the publication of a letter purportedly signed by 600 American soldiers in Manila who demanded immediate demobilization in order to forestall U.S. Army interference in the 1946 elections[114]—but such intervention was rare. The few American Communist commentaries on the Philippines that can be found show little sensitivity to developments there and make no reference to the rivalries that were frustrating a more purposeful CPPI program.[115] Clearly so desultory an interest in Philippine affairs by the CPUSA can neither have inspired nor instructed the beleaguered Filipinos. We must rather imagine that the American party was itself perplexed by the course of events in the Philippines, assuming it made some effort to study them, and unable to compose a relevant directive to the CPPI.

[112] James S. Allen, "The Far Eastern Front in the War Against the Axis," *Communist*, No. 2, March 1942, pp. 142-62; cited in Hoeksema, *op. cit.*, p. 238.

[113] *Daily Worker*, January 28, 1948, quoted in *World News and Views*, March 31, 1945, p. 103.

[114] The letter, addressed to the United Auto Workers of America (CIO), was carried in the *Daily Worker*, January 10, 1946, cited in Hoeksema, *op. cit.*, p. 305.

[115] See James Allen, "Enlightened American Imperialism in the Philippines," *Political Affairs*, No. 6, June 1946, p. 527, and Alexander Bittelman, "Problems of Peace, Democracy and National Independence," *Political Affairs*, No. 6, June 1947, p. 511 (cited in Hoeksema, *op. cit.*, pp. 294, 322).

The inattention of the Chinese Communists to the Philippines occasions less surprise since they had never ventured to play a part there, although their experience had occasionally been a source of inspiration to the CPPI before the war. Soon after the outbreak of war in the Pacific the Chinese Communists called for a broad anti-Japanese alliance of the peoples of the Far East, including the Filipinos, and urged the overseas Chinese to play a leading role in this alliance.[116] It was quite possibly in response to this appeal that the Philippine Chinese organized their own resistance movement, known as Squadron 48; the unit is said to have had representatives from the Chinese Communists' Fourth and Eighth Route Armies.[117] Relations were established between Squadron 48 and the *Hukbalahap* but, according to Philippine Communist sources, grew strained during the war. José Lava, for instance, charges the Chinese with major responsibility for the adoption of the "continuous attacks" strategy which led to the crippling Japanese counter-attack in 1943.[118] At the party meeting in September 1944 a number of Filipinos were dropped from leading party organs on charges of having followed Chinese Communist experience too "mechanistically."[119] By this time the Chinese squadron had withdrawn to one of the southern islands of the archipelago and, according to Taruc and José Lava, had no further contact with the *Hukbalahap*. The "Chinese section," which existed within the CPPI during the 1930's and on occasion played an important part in the party's decisions (see p. 182), was evidently not restored after the war. The influence of Chinese Communism accordingly was confined, as it was before the war, to whatever inspiration the Filipinos could derive from the success of Mao's strategies as they unfolded.

The Russians, in the meantime, were no more attentive to Philippine affairs than were Chinese and American Communists. The few articles in Soviet periodicals touching on the wartime

[116] The statement is carried in the *Sunday Worker* (London), January 2, 1942, cited in Hoeksema, *op. cit.*, p. 239.

[117] See Hoeksema, *op. cit.*, p. 256.

[118] Lava, *Milestones*, p. 56.

[119] Hoeksema, *op. cit.*, p. 268, citing his interview with a former Philippine Communist.

experience of the Filipinos single out the collaboration of such leaders as Laurel and Vargas, but make no mention of either the CPPI or the *Hukbalahap*.[120] After the war a modest revival of Moscow's interest in the Philippines can be detected, centering principally on the ephemeral "independence" the Filipinos were gaining from the United States. Zhukov, for instance, cited the Philippines as the principal example of his thesis that "a recognition of formal sovereignty is no guarantee of actual independence."[121] In April 1946 a brief item in *New Times* noted the recent American seizure of hemp plantations formerly belonging to Japanese owners and offered this as evidence that "the nominal independence granted to the Philippines happily combines with complete American domination of the country's economy."[122] In October, after independence had been formally conferred on the Philippines, *Pravda* editorialized that it was a "fiction."[123] In December another item in *New Times* called attention to the persecution of loyal patriots, branded "bandits" and "extremists," while known collaborators were elevated to positions of trust. "How is it," the item approvingly quotes Harold Ickes (a former member of President Roosevelt's cabinet) "that collaborators who occupied positions of public trust under the Japanese, and who would have ruled the Philippines had the Japanese won, are still in power despite the victory of the United States?"[124] In a public lecture in July 1947 Avarin reiterated the same points with greater bitterness: as a consequence of "pro-Fascist" tendencies in the Philippines, spurred by the Americans, "thousands of democrats have been thrown into jail, tortured, and slaughtered."[125]

[120] E.g., V. Avarin, "Amerikanskie pozitsii na Tikhom okeane," *Mirovoe khoziaistvo i mirovaia politika*, No. 1-2, January-February 1942, pp. 61ff; a book review by Avarin in *ibid.*, No. 6, June 1944, pp. 87-8; and K. Popov, "Iaponiia i okkupirovannye strany Vostochnoi Azii," *Voina i rabochii klass*, No. 12, June 15, 1944, p. 19.

[121] *Bol'shevik*, No. 23-4, December 1945, p. 86.

[122] *New Times*, April 15, 1946, p. 19.

[123] *Pravda*, October 10, 1946, p. 3.

[124] *New Times*, December 1, 1946, p. 16.

[125] V. A. Avarin, *Politicheskie izmeneniia na Tikhom okeane posle vtoroi mirovoi voiny*, p. 17.

The Soviet Union, needless to say, made no moves to recognize the new regime.

If these comments were more forthright than those which can be discovered in the American Communist press of these years, they provided no more explicit advice to the CPPI and the *Hukbalahap* on what course to pursue. Neither are mentioned in Soviet commentaries and any division within the "democratic" camp is of course overlooked. Several years later, after the intra-party dispute was resolved, O. Zabozlaeva blandly labeled the party's tactics during the post-war era as entirely "correct," without seeking to sort out the conflicting positions of the "majority" and "minority" factions.[126] Whether she was ignorant of the substance of the dispute or simply careless in setting the record straight once the leadership issue had been resolved, her slighting of the episode suggests what both José Lava and Taruc persistently claim—Moscow's indifference to the course of Philippine Communism in the post-war era.

LOST OPPORTUNITIES IN MALAYA

Malayan Communism, like Vietnamese and Philippine, also experienced unusual growth during the war as a result of its dominant role in the anti-Japanese underground. The MCP, we have seen, modified its rigorous anti-British position before the close of the Nazi-Soviet era, in preparation for collaboration with local British authorities in the event of a Japanese attack on the colony. In the summer of 1941, following the German attack on the USSR, the Malayan Communists are reported to have offered their assistance to the colonial administration, but the offer was for the moment rejected. In December, however, as the Japanese began their swift march down the Malayan peninsula, following the attack on Pearl Harbor, the British agreed to collaborate. Political prisoners were released in mid-December; immediately thereafter a meeting was held in Singapore between British officers and representatives of the MCP, including Loi Tek, and agreement reached on the training of Communist-selected cadres

[126] *Krizis kolonial'noi sistemy,* p. 231.

303

at special guerrilla schools.[127] During the next few weeks, before Malaya and Singapore were overrun by the Japanese, an estimated 165 Malayans were graduated from these schools. They became the nucleus of the Malayan People's Anti-Japanese Army (MPAJA), which the MCP formally created in March 1942— about the same time that the *Hukbalahap* was created in the Philippines. Loi Tek stated in an interview during this period that 10,000 guerrillas were to be trained for the MPAJA, and he pledged its co-operation with the British government.[128]

The party program had in the meantime been brought into line with these new policies. On December 21, shortly after the agreement with the British officers, a four-point resolution was adopted which focused attention on immediate tasks. These included: unification of the Malayan peoples in the resistance effort, in co-operation with the British; the arming of all party members for the anti-Japanese campaign; the elimination of Fifth Columnists, enemy agents, and traitors; and sustained resistance to Japanese occupation (should it occur) "through the formation of clandestine guerrilla bands and planned terror."[129] Fourteen months later a plenum of the Central Committee expanded on these tasks in a new nine-point program. This combined certain traditional Communist objectives—such as a guarantee of civil liberties, free education in the vernacular, and abolition of high taxes—with those relating to the resistance effort. The final point called on Malayans to "unite with Soviet Russia and China to support the independence of the weak and small races in the Far East and to aid the people of Japan in their anti-Fascist struggle."[130] This program served as an official statement of MCP policies until 1945.

[127] Chapman, *The Jungle is Neutral*, pp. 29-31; Chapman, a British major, was present at the meeting and subsequently served as Deputy Commandant of the "101" Special Training Schools.

[128] *World News and Views*, April 4, 1942, p. 191. A detailed account of the formation and wartime activities of the MPAJA was published by the MCP in 1945; see Hanrahan, *Communist Struggle in Malaya*, pp. 33ff.

[129] *Ibid.*, p. 32, citing a Japanese source entitled (in English translation) *Military Government in the Southern Regions* (Tokyo, 1944).

[130] Quoted in a Malayan Communist pamphlet entitled "MCP Proclamation Regarding the Present Situation in Commemoration of the 28th Anniversary of

Claims of Communist strength and successes during the occupation have been greatly exaggerated in subsequent accounts. A Soviet source, for instance, places the strength of both the MPAJA and the MCP at 10,000 by 1945;[131] another Soviet writer asserts 10,000 Japanese troops were killed by Communist guerrillas.[132] The figure for the MPAJA may not be too inaccurate—inasmuch as Malayan government sources acknowledge a force of no fewer than 6,500 trained guerrillas[133]—but the same figure for MCP membership is very unlikely; Loi Tek, during interrogations by British officials after the war, claimed no more than 2,000 party members at the end of 1946, representing only a slight increase over pre-war estimates.[134] The assertion that 10,000 Japanese were the victims of Communist resistance conflicts sharply with a Japanese estimate of 2,300 fatalities in Malaya during the entire war, including the initial drive on Singapore.[135] In reality, there appear to have been few significant engagements between the MPAJA and the Japanese. In 1943 liaison was established between the MPAJA and Force 136, a British unit responsible for clandestine military operations in Malaya, and by the end of 1944 supplies and Allied personnel were being parachuted into the guerrilla bases.[136] However, before the MPAJA and the Allied teams were prepared to go into action against the Japanese the war had ended. The judgment of most serious stu-

---

the Red October Revolution" (November 7, 1945); a translation of this document, issued in Chinese, is in Malayan government files.

[131] A. I. Levkovskii, *Natsional'no-osvoboditel'naia bor'ba narodov Malaii za svoiu svobodu i nezavisimost'*, pp. 12-3.

[132] V. S. Rudnev, *Ocherki noveishei istorii Malaii*, p. 48.

[133] "Basic Paper on the Malayan Communist Party," Vol. 1, Part 2, p. 25.

[134] The claim of a party of 10,000 members, however, persisted. This was the figure, for instance, given at the Nineteenth Congress of the CPGB in February 1947; *World News and Views*, March 22, 1947, p. 119.

[135] See Hanrahan, *op. cit.*, p. 44; Hanrahan observes that the Japanese figure is lower than the number of *Malayans* the MCP admits to having killed for collaboration.

[136] A first-hand account of the ties between Force 136 and the MPAJA is given in Chapman, *op. cit.*, pp. 248ff. It is estimated that over 500 liaison personnel and more than a million and a half pounds of equipment were flown into Malaya during the last eight months of the war.

dents of Malayan Communism is that the MCP was careful to husband its strength during the war for whatever contingencies might arise after the Japanese defeat.[137]

Malayan government sources claim that the Communists prepared themselves for a direct and early confrontation with the British after the war. In January 1945, it is claimed, a secret memorandum circulated by the MCP argued that inasmuch as British policy toward Malaya remained unchanged, independence could be gained only through a "bitter and bloody struggle"; in the spring a directive from the Central Committee, also secret, allegedly called for open and secret MPAJA units, the latter to be made up of trusted party members, incognito, whose responsibility it was to gather and hide arms.[138] It is doubtful whether these documents are authentic. The party's official line, at any event, continued to be moderate. An eight-point program released by the MCP in the spring or summer of 1945 listed goals not likely to offend even the most determined British colonial. The program directed Malayan Communists "to uphold the alliance of Russia, China, Great Britain, and the United States and to support the United Nations."[139] In November, after the British had re-established their control over all of Malaya, the Communists were still outwardly conciliatory. "We still believe," the MCP proclaimed on the anniversary of the Bolshevik Revolution, "in the good things which the British government has promised us." The statement went on to make six specific demands on the British including, along with the usual requests for civil liberties and so forth, financial assistance in the rehabilitation of the country's economy and London's promise to "stop military intervention in Indochina and Indonesia in connection with

---

[137] See Pye, *Guerrilla Communism in Malaya*, pp. 69-70, and Hanrahan, *op. cit.*, p. 45.

[138] The two documents are described in "Basic Paper on the Malayan Communist Party," Vol. 1, Part 2, pp. 26-7.

[139] The eight-point program called the "Eight Great Postulates," is included in "MCP Proclamation Regarding the Present Situation. . . ." The date of the program given in this source is March 1945; a slightly different version of the program in "Basic Paper on the Malayan Communist Party," Vol. 1, Part 2, p. 27, is dated August 27, 1945.

their independence movements." *Malayan* independence is not specifically urged in the November proclamation, although it is touched on in a final passage which argues that so long as the situation in Malaya remains "fundamentally unchanged," the party's "revolutionary task of thorough racial (national) liberation" remains unfulfilled; it was the duty of the MCP, the statement read, ultimately to relieve the Malayan people from "the atrocious rule of capitalism." The comparatively moderate policies reflected in the six demands and the eight-point program appear, in retrospect, to have influenced the MCP's course after the war more decisively than any secret circulars such as those described above. This was so at least through 1947.

The MPAJA was officially dissolved by the government in December 1945—without, as in the Philippines, any formal protest by the Communist leadership. Not all weapons, however, were surrendered. Sources differ on the number of guerrillas who failed to turn in their arms and receive the mustering-out pay of 350 Malayan dollars, but it became evident, during the course of the rebellion in 1948, that the Communists had a considerable arsenal of wartime weapons at their disposal.[140] The secret MPAJA allegedly ordered by the Communists in the spring of 1945 appears not to have existed.[141] The MCP moved immediately to fill the gap left by the dissolution of the MPAJA by creating a variety of front organizations. An MPAJA Ex-Service Comrades Association was formed to maintain contact with former guerrillas. The New Democratic Youth League, with branches throughout the country, was organized to attract Malayans too young to have served in the resistance movement during the war but anxious not to be left out of post-war developments stemming from it. In the labor field, the traditional source of Malayan Communist strength, the MCP quickly re-

[140] Malayan government sources estimate that as many as 4,000 failed to surrender their arms; "Basic Paper on the Malayan Communist Party," Vol. 1, Part 2, p. 28. Hanrahan, *op. cit.*, p. 51, gives the number as fewer than 500. During interrogations in October 1946, Loi Tek stated that an estimated 2,400 assorted rifles, revolvers, tommy-guns and so forth were cached throughout Malaya.

[141] Loi Tek also said that no such force existed but that 2,000 Communist guerrillas could be mustered if necessary.

captured its pre-war pre-eminence. A general strike in January 1946 paralyzed the country for two days and drove home to the government the power at the disposal of the MCP.

The party leadership, however, showed no disposition to alter the policies it had been advocating—at least in public—by using this newly found power toward more frankly revolutionary ends. The Eighth Plenum of the Central Committee meeting in January 1946, the first since 1941, reaffirmed the moderate course. Loi Tek, who was re-elected Secretary-General at the plenum, presented the arguments for moderation. "The colonial problem," he told the plenum, "can be resolved in two ways: liberation through a bloody revolutionary struggle (as in the case of Vietnam and Indonesia) or through the strength of a national united front." Conditions in Malaya were not favorable for the first alternative, Loi Tek argued; accordingly the party's tasks were "to preserve a peaceful front, determinedly to protect world peace, to carry out the Charter of the United Nations, to annihilate the remnants of Fascism, and to counter the imperialist policy of colonial exploitation." Again, nothing was said specifically of independence as an immediate objective.[142] These modest formulations, periodically reaffirmed in fresh pronouncements,[143] remained the official policy of the MCP for the next two years.

How are the moderate post-war policies of the MCP to be explained? In Indochina, moderation after the war was a temporary tactical maneuver the Vietminh could risk because its armed strength remained intact. In Indonesia moderation was forced on the PKI, after a brief essay at militancy, because of its relatively weak position in the national movement and because many

[142] Portions of the published text of Loi Tek's speech are translated from the Chinese in Hanrahan, *op. cit.*, pp. 51-2.

[143] In May 1946, for instance, a new nine-point program was issued which summarized and amplified the principal objectives and tasks listed in earlier post-war programs; at the end of 1946 the MPAJA Ex-Service Comrades Association offered proposals for the new Malayan Constitution which also reflected the party's moderate line during this period. The texts of both documents may be found in *ibid.*, pp. 52-4.

known Communists identified themselves with other parties. In the Philippines, moderation was the policy of only one faction of the CPPI and gradually yielded to insurgency under the pressure of events. What considerations account for moderation in Malaya—and why did it survive for nearly three years after the Japanese occupation ended?

We may note at the outset that the moderate course coincided with the last years of Loi Tek's rule over the MCP and must therefore be associated with the personality and career of this figure, one of the most bizarre in the annals of world Communism.

From the time of his entry into the MCP in the mid-1930's and during his rise to leadership of the party by 1939, Loi Tek served as an occasional informant for the Singapore Special Branch (see p. 241, above). During the occupation, he performed similar services for the Japanese, using the wide powers conferred upon him by his party colleagues in December 1941 to enhance his personal fortunes. He was, for instance, one of the few Communist leaders to escape arrest during a Japanese raid on a party meeting at Batu Caves in September 1942—a raid which, according to government sources, he himself arranged to eliminate rivals in the party hierarchy.[144] He is also said to have given information to the Japanese leading to the arrest of all major party leaders in Singapore, where Loi Tek made his headquarters.[145] Whether or not these allegations are true, Loi Tek appears to have been the only high-ranking Communist who could move more or less freely about the country during the occupation.

---

[144] "Basic Paper on the Malayan Communist Party," Vol. 1, Part 2, p. 36; Loi Tek is said to have informed the Japanese of the time and place of the meeting and then to have arranged his own "inadvertent" delay in arrival in order to avoid both his own arrest and the suspicion of his colleagues. Malayan Communist sources published after Loi Tek's expulsion from the party, it should be noted, do *not* charge him with responsibility for the Batu Caves episode (a very serious blow to the wartime party organization), although they of course would have had it been suspected; see "Statement of the Incident of Wright [Loi Tek]" (May 28, 1948) and "Seven Years After the September 1st Episode" (Singapore, 1949, cited in Hanrahan, *op. cit.*, pp. 38-9).

[145] Miller, *The Communist Menace in Malaya*, p. 68.

Southeast Asian Communism in Suspension: 1941-1947

Immediately after the war, charges of collaboration with the Japanese were raised against Loi Tek but dismissed, in part because they came from Malayans who had themselves collaborated with the Japanese, in part because of Loi Tek's wide prestige at this juncture as a hero of the *résistance*.[146] By mid-1946, however, rumors of Loi Tek's irregular behavior, both past and present, were too persistent to ignore and led to a full investigation.[147] Chen Peng, Loi Tek's chief aide during the war, led the investigation and by March 1947 had succeeded in gathering sufficient evidence of Loi Tek's treachery to confront him with it. Loi Tek, in the meantime, was discovering his position in the party increasingly jeopardized: not only were his past connections with British and Japanese agents under suspicion, as he knew, but through Vietnamese Communists in Singapore his own complex personal life (he maintained two families and engaged in private business in Singapore) was in danger of being revealed. Accordingly he disappeared from view on the eve of the meeting called by Chen Peng in March at which the confrontation was to take place. In August Loi Tek left Singapore for Hong Kong, assisted by British authorities with whom he had again been in contact since early 1946; his "deportation" was pre-dated March 10 so that, should the opportunity ever arise, he might prove his involuntary absence from the March meeting and re-establish himself in the MCP. His subsequent whereabouts are unknown.[148]

[146] One such charge was published in a Penang newspaper in September 1945; "Basic Paper on the Malayan Communist Party," Vol. 1, Part 1, pp. 29-30. Loi Tek himself, in subsequent interrogations by British officials, noted that letters exposing him were sent to the Central Committee about the same time by two former Communist collaborators, but were disbelieved.

[147] According to a Malayan who was a party member during this period, a Vietnamese waiter in Singapore recognized Loi Tek at a party gathering after the war as a frequent guest of Japanese officials he had served during the occupation; his report of this to party officials led to the investigation. Interviews with Gerald de Cruz in March 1961 and January 1962. De Cruz also notes the great pains Loi Tek took to conceal his identity, even after the MCP had been legalized: during a six- or eight-month assignment at party headquarters in Kuala Lumpur in 1946, de Cruz says, he was never certain which of the officials he dealt with was Loi Tek.

[148] The principal details of Loi Tek's final break with the MCP are drawn

310

In May 1947 Loi Tek was formally expelled from the party at the Ninth Plenum and Chen Peng named as his successor as Secretary-General. A full report on the episode was delayed more than a year, following Chen Peng's visit to China in the summer of 1947 in search of evidence of Loi Tek's past connections with the international movement, and when released was limited to circulation within the party. According to a text of the report which has subsequently come to light, the charges raised against Loi Tek covered a wide range of misconduct and treachery. His claims of having studied in the USSR, having served with a branch of the Chinese Communist Party in Shanghai, and having been a founder of the CPIC were all fraudulent, the report stated; "he had no international connections whatsoever." His wartime associations with the Japanese were reviewed, but his pre-war connections with the British were left vague. "We are not in a position to investigate his pre-war activities," the statement read, "but according to estimates there is a great possibility of his collaboration with imperialism." His post-war collaboration with the British was evidently not suspected. The report also exposed the irregularities of his personal life. He was moreover charged with embezzling 350,000 Malayan dollars from party funds. Finally—and more germane to our purposes—he was charged with pressing for policies "which could not be carried out," thereby serving as "a running dog and traitor of the revolution."[149]

We may dismiss the latter charge as central to the party's case against Loi Tek—it was made, in any case, at a time when the MCP had forsaken moderation and was seeking a scapegoat for

from interrogations carried on at the time by British police officials. Malayan records trace Loi Tek to Hong Kong and thence to Bangkok, but thereafter lose sight of him. According to rumors prevalent in Malayan Communist circles, Loi Tek was murdered by Communist agents in Hong Hong early in 1948; interview with Gerald de Cruz. For other accounts of the Loi Tek episode, see Miller, *op. cit.*, pp. 65ff; Hanrahan, *op. cit.*, pp. 59-60; and Pye, *op. cit.*, pp. 83-5.

[149] "Statement of the Incident of Wright [Loi Tek]," a letter to party members (in Chinese) dated May 28, 1948; the portions quoted here are from a Malayan government translation. A somewhat different version of the letter is given in Miller, *op. cit.*, p. 67.

its past failures—but we should not overlook the possibility that Loi Tek, for personal reasons, encouraged mild strategies after the war. If the evidence of his having served again as a British informant after the war is accepted (and there is, in this writer's view, little doubt of its authenticity), the emoluments he presumably received for his revelations and on which he had evidently come to depend were more assured if the course of Malayan Communism continued to be moderate. Certainly his account of party policies to British officials who periodically interrogated him during 1946 and 1947 was calculated to remove any fears they may have had of Communist intransigence: he denied that the MCP sought immediate independence for Malaya; he spoke of alliance with the Kuomintang in Malaya to protect the interests of overseas Chinese; the party, he argued, felt that peaceful pressure on the government rather than intimidation was the best way to achieve specific goals such as price reductions and wage increases; he also affirmed that the MCP looked favorably on the Labor government in England, from which it expected significant economic and social reform in the colony. So devious a figure as Loi Tek can be expected, of course, to have told British police officials what they most wished to hear, but it is also true that the policies he described, which were the same as those set forth in official party pronouncements, were precisely the ones best designed to protect his own interests. He was perhaps unable wholly to curb the activities of the Malayan labor movement, which reverted during most of 1936 to its traditional form of protest in a vigorous wave of strikes,[150] but so long as he maintained his control over the party, he could—and did—restrain Communist activity in all other respects.

The drama of the Loi Tek episode should not overshadow other considerations which explain the moderation of Malayan Communism after the war. The Malayans may have been simply responding on their own initiative to what they thought to be the international line, which they found totally appropriate in

---

[150] The British Communist organ *World News and Views* (December 14, 1946, p. 410) reported 3,000 strikes in Malaya since the end of the war; see also Hanrahan, *op. cit.*, pp. 55ff.

Malaya: their prestige was considerable after the war, even if predominantly in the Chinese community; England had been too discredited in 1941 and 1942 to prolong its control over the colony; when Indian independence was granted, that of other Southeast Asian colonies could not long be withheld, in particular by a Labor government. Time therefore played into the Communists' hands and it was a sufficient policy merely to keep Communist forces on the alert and ready for all contingencies. Such a reading of Malayan Communist motives need not apply only to Loi Tek, though he appeared as the principal spokesman of such policies at the Eighth Plenum early in 1946; inasmuch as the moderate line continued in force for ten months after his expulsion, and more than a year and a half after his leadership first came under review, it is reasonable to imagine that the majority of the party leaders favored this course—at least until developments at home or abroad signaled a better alternative.

Such advice as the MCP received from the Chinese and British parties after the war tended to support these policies. Contact with the Chinese, according to Loi Tek, was established soon after the war when a representative of the CCP who had been in Malaya during the occupation returned to Yenan to provide liaison between the two parties. During 1946 Loi Tek himself visited China—twice, according to government reports[151]—and in December brought back with him an instruction from the South China Bureau of the CCP in Hong Kong. According to his own version of this instruction, which was passed on to his colleagues at a party meeting in Kuala Lumpur in January 1947 (evidently one of the last he attended), the MCP was directed to refrain from armed insurrection, rely on united front tactics, limit its demands to self-government so long as the Labor Party was in office, and look to the CPGB for both aid and tactical guidance.[152]

[151] "Basic Paper on the Malayan Communist Party," Vol. 1, Part 2, pp. 31ff; the first visit was allegedly to attend a conference of Communist representatives from Thailand, Burma, the Philippines, Vietnam, and China—a conference that is otherwise unmentioned in sources known to the writer.

[152] If Loi Tek's account to British officials of his visit to Hong Kong is ac-

British Communist views of Malaya both during and after the war seconded this counsel. A commentary on a Parliamentary debate on colonial policy at the end of 1942 did not go beyond demands for "self-government" in Malaya.[153] A fuller treatment of the colonial question by the CPGB later in the war reaffirmed "self-government," not independence, as the present objective in most of England's colonies, including Malaya, and stated that the MCP's policies should be directed toward social and economic reforms and a unification of the three racial communities *prior to* independence.[154] The attitude of the CPGB on Malaya did not change appreciably after the war. In September 1945 the English Communist press noted with approval British co-operation with the "anti-Fascist underground" in Malaya[155] and a few months later approved the program of the Communist-led Democratic Union which accented as its chief objective "the self-government of Malaya within the British Commonwealth."[156] Some concern was expressed in March 1946 over the trials of former guerrillas charged with assassinating collaborators during the war;[157] there was also periodic coverage, and approval, of the strike movement during 1946.[158] There was not, however, any explicit retreat from the policy of "self-government," as distinct from independence, for Malaya. Nor was there any suggestion that the MCP needed to adopt a more vigorous program. The resolution of the Commonwealth Conference of Communist Parties in February and March—which took a relatively forthright stand on the colonial question in general—omitted Malaya from its list of colonies scheduled for "immediate and unquali-

---

curate, the Chinese Communists evidently did not know of Chen Peng's investigation, which by December 1946 had been in progress for several months.

[153] "Colonial Policy," *World News and Views*, December 12, 1942, p. 477.

[154] *The Colonies: The Way Forward: a Memorandum issued by the Executive Committee of the CPGB* (November 1944), pp. 49-58.

[155] See *World News and Views*, September 15, 1945, p. 279, and September 29, 1945, p. 297.

[156] *Ibid.*, February 9, 1946, p. 47.

[157] *Ibid.*, March 23, 1946, p. 94.

[158] E.g., *ibid.*, May 4, 1946, p. 143; July 20, 1946, p. 228; and December 14, 1946, p. 410.

fied independence." The Malayan spokesman at the conference, Wu Tien Wang, seems to have accepted the limited objectives for Malaya set forth in the resolution: although he complained of the "semi-legal conditions" under which the MCP was obliged to operate, he asked the conference only for an expression of support regarding the legalization of parties and trade unions and the adoption of a democratic constitution; the demand even for "self-government," let alone full independence, is muted in his report.[159]

Soviet influence on Malayan policies may in the meantime be counted as negligible—unless one attaches significance to occasional meetings between Russian and Malayan delegates abroad.[160] Coverage of Malayan developments in the Russian press was as meager after the war as during it. In May 1946 a note in *New Times* described as "scandalous" the efforts of the MacMichael mission to cajole the sultans into surrendering their authority to a new Malayan Union. Protests both in Malaya and England against MacMichael's high-handed tactics were being ignored, *New Times* said. The item went on to quote Mr. Creech-Jones, Under Secretary for the Colonies, as saying in Parliament: "It is not imperialism, but an effort to carry out faithfully our economic liabilities." *New Times* responded: "*Qui s'excuse, s'accuse.*"[161] In June 1947 an article in *Mirovoe khoziaistvo i mirovaia*

[159] *Ibid.*, March 15, 1947, pp. 163-4. The other Malayan delegates at the London conference were Abdul Rashid bin Maidin (a Malay) and Balan (an Indian); the latter is said to have stopped in India en route home in order to make contact with the CPI. Malayan government sources claim that the MCP representatives returned unimpressed with British Communist leadership and disillusioned in the prospects of receiving aid from the CPGB; "Basic Paper on the Malayan Communist Party," Vol. 1, Part 2, p. 36. This disenchantment was also described to the writer by Gerald de Cruz during an interview in 1962.

[160] Three Malayans attended the WFTU meeting in Paris in 1946 and two the WFDY congress in Prague the following summer; "Basic Paper on the Malayan Communist Party," Vol. 1, Part 2, p. 36.

[161] "The Malayan Union," *New Times*, No. 9, May 1, 1946, p. 21. Sir Harold MacMichael made a rapid trip through Malaya at the end of 1945 and did indeed apply extraordinary pressures on the sultans of the nine Malayan states to accept the British plan for a single administration of the entire country; his actions, widely resented at the time by all classes of Malayans, were subsequently repudiated by the British government itself and the proposed Malayan Union gave way in 1948 to a federation, constructed more or less along pre-war lines.

politika touched on recent Malayan events: the switch in British tactics from union to federation was noted; an increase in labor unrest was remarked, as exploitation resumed. There was, however, no mention of independence or of a national liberation struggle comparable to that noted in Burma.[162]

The Russians, then, were no more helpful than the British and Chinese in suggesting an alternative to the policies which Loi Tek set after the war and which Chen Peng allowed to continue in force until early 1948.

COMMUNIST TAKE-OFF IN BURMA

In Burma—whose revolutionary movements we have discussed only up to 1935—a full-fledged Communist movement did not emerge until the war. There had been some exposure to Marxist ideas prior to 1935, but Marxism had made no perceptible impact on the nationalist movement as a whole.

During the latter part of the 1930's Marxist study groups sprang up among students and former students of Rangoon University. Indian Communists were particularly active in the formation of these groups. According to Thein Pe Myint (one of the earliest Burmese Marxists), his first contact with Communists was in Calcutta where he spent two years following his graduation from Rangoon University in 1935; a Bengalese Communist named Dat returned with him to Rangoon in 1938 and helped organize the first Marxist study group in Burma. Although the group evidently stayed intact only a few months, it brought together several of the later leaders of the nationalist movement including, in addition to Thein Pe Myint (then known as *Tet Pongyi*, after the title of a book he had written in Calcutta on monastic reform), Bo Let Ya and Aung San. Aung San served as secretary of the group. About the same time another Marxist study group was organized in Rangoon by Ghoshal, an Indian graduate of Rangoon University who had also just returned from India. In 1939 Ghoshal attempted—but evidently failed—to unite

[162] I. Lemin, "Sovremennye problemy Britanskoi imperii," *Mirovoe khoziaistvo i mirovaia politika*, No. 6, June 1947, p. 3.

a number of these Rangoon groups into a single Communist organization.[163]

Indians thus played an important role in early Burmese Marxism, setting a precedent which was to last for more than a decade. The material studied by these groups, according to participants, included such literature as they could obtain in English, since nothing, of course, was available in Burmese. Stalin's principal writings, for instance, were known to them. Attention was also given to the *History of the Communist Party of the Soviet Union (Short Course)*; *New Age*, the publication of the Indian Communists; Edgar Snow's *Red Star Over China*; and Dimitrov's speeches in the Comintern. There was evidently some familiarity with the decisions of the Seventh Comintern Congress of 1935, but little concept of how to apply united front tactics in Burma. It was only after the signing of the Nazi-Soviet Pact that a united front against British imperialism was seriously discussed among Burmese Marxists; Bo Let Ya, for instance, speaks of a 1940 symposium on this subject in which he, Thein Pe Myint, and Thakin Nu participated.

All participants in these early study groups interviewed by the author stress the identity of the Marxists' goals with those of the *Thakins*, the more radical element of the nationalist movement growing out of the *Dohbama Asiayone* (We Burmans Association). As Bo Let Ya states it, the Aung San study group thought of itself as the "prime mover" of the *Thakins*, and he makes much of the fact that Aung San was at the time secretary both of the group organized by Dat and of the *Thakins*. The diversity of the careers later pursued by members of these groups also testifies to the fact that Marxism continued to appeal to the Burmese during the pre-war years primarily as a panacea for independence, not as a distinctive social and political philosophy; they accepted as much of it as suited their purposes and ignored the rest.

---

[163] The activities of these early Marxist study groups in Rangoon were described to the author during interviews in January 1962 with several participants, including Thein Pe Myint, Bo Let Ya, and Thakin Kyaw Sein, the leader of still another such group.

There was no direct contact whatsoever, insofar as is known, between Burmese Marxists and the Comintern. Moscow's attention to Burma, after the brief interest expressed in the peasant uprisings early in the 1930's, was negligible until the very end of the decade. In December 1939 an article in *Mirovoe khoziaistvo i mirovaia politika* called attention to Burma as a critical British possession in the East now that England had been excluded from China by the Japanese. The article noted the "low level of political consciousness" within the colony, which gave Japanese agents a fertile field for intrigue. A few rudimentary labor and peasant organizations are mentioned, as well as several political parties and secret societies, but no reference is made to the *Thakins*—and of course none to the Marxists.[164] An article in a party journal in June 1940 was elementary and displayed little familiarity with commonly known facts about recent developments in Burma (which the author insisted was properly pronounced "Barma").[165] Other items on Burma appearing in Soviet periodicals during the Nazi-Soviet era were concerned primarily with the strategic importance of the Burma Road, which the British closed as a supply line to China in July 1940.[166]

After war broke out in Europe the *Thakins*, both Marxist and non-Marxist, used England's preoccupation with the war to press more vigorously than before their demands for independence. At the end of September 1939, for instance, they put forth a three-point program which in effect demanded England's recognition of Burma's right to be independent, preparations for a Constituent Assembly, and immediate self-government; the program became the basis for the formation of the so-called "Freedom Bloc," an alliance of the *Dohbama Asiayone* and the Poor Man's (*Sinyetha*) Party of Dr. Ba Maw, the first Burmese premier under the 1936 Constitution.[167] The Freedom Bloc sought

[164] V. Bushevich and A. D'iakov, "Obostrenie imperialisticheskikh protivorechii na Dal'nem Vostoke i Birma," *Mirovoe khoziaistvo i mirovaia politika*, No. 12, December 1939, pp. 119-26.

[165] D. Gol'dberg, "Birma," *Propaganda i agitatsiia*, No. 21, June 1940, pp. 60-1.

[166] E.g., "Doroga Birma-Kitai," *Sputnik agitatora*, No. 20, 1940, pp. 43-4; other items are listed in *Bibliografiia Iugo-vostochnoi Azii*, p. 75.

[167] The three-point program was printed in *New Burma* (Rangoon), October 6, 1939; see Cady, *A History of Modern Burma*, p. 416.

318

to extend its contacts abroad. In addition to liaison already established with the Congress Party in India, a good will mission was sent to China at the end of 1939 to establish relations with the Kuomintang; Thakin Nu, who was a member of this mission, reported on the success of the mission following its return. Bo Let Ya led a similar mission to Bangkok, but evidently without success. Contacts with the Japanese, which were conducted at various levels, proved in the long run to be more fruitful. Ba Maw, for instance, as early as the autumn of 1937 established personal ties with officials in Tokyo which helped to ensure Japanese support of the national movement after the fall of Burma. Left-leaning *Thakins* within the Freedom Bloc also made contacts with Japanese agents, more furtively. Aung San and Bo Let Ya were secretly in touch with Japanese army officers in Rangoon during 1940. At the end of 1940, Aung San, reportedly on a mission to the Chinese Communists bearing a letter of introduction from the CPI, was arrested by the Japanese in Amoy and released on condition that he collaborate with Japan. He returned secretly to Burma in 1941, with the help of the Japanese military attaché in Rangoon, and was able to recruit a number of *Thakins* for military training by the Japanese on Hainan. This group, limited to thirty by the *Thakins* themselves (and thus known as the "Thirty Comrades"), returned to Burma in the wake of Japanese troops in 1942 and became the nucleus of the Burma Independence Army (BIA).[168]

Not all *Thakins*, it should be noted, approved of ties with the Japanese. The more orthodox Marxists such as Thein Pe Myint and Thakin Soe, for instance, attentive to the anti-Japanese line which prevailed in Moscow during the first year or more of the Nazi-Soviet Pact, appear to have resisted the trend

[168] Many details of the Freedom Bloc's foreign contacts during 1939 and 1940 were revealed in a speech delivered by Aung San in Rangoon in August 1945; an English translation of his speech, entitled "The Resistance Movement," was loaned to the author by Professor John H. Badgley. Additional details were given to the author by Bo Let Ya, a close associate of Aung San, and by Dr. Ba Maw during interviews in Rangoon in 1961 and 1962. Their evidence is corroborated by other accounts of this era based on different sources: e.g., Cady, *op. cit.*, pp. 418, 428-9.

of Aung San's strategies; it was their opposition in all likelihood which limited the number of Burmese to be trained in Hainan to thirty. At any event, the flirtation with Tokyo, in 1940 and 1941, led to the first signs of division within the *Thakin* movement—albeit still of a minor nature—and, since it was the Japanese who were to prevail in Burma, to a lessening of orthodox Marxist influence in the nationalist movement as a whole.

The British, in the meantime, responded to these maneuvers by Burmese nationalists with increased vigilance. In July 1940 a number of *Thakin* leaders were arrested, including Thakin Nu, Thakin Soe, and Than Tun, the two latter subsequently to emerge as leaders of the Burmese Communist Party. In August Dr. Ba Maw was arrested and, amidst manifestations of general public indignation, sentenced to a year's imprisonment; this was extended indefinitely a year later by the new premier U Saw, less for considerations of state than for reasons of personal political rivalry. Warrants were also issued during 1940 and 1941 for the arrest of other *Thakin* leaders—including, of course, Aung San, Thein Pe Myint, and Bo Let Ya—but many escaped detection.

The withdrawal of the British before Japanese forces in the spring of 1942 immediately altered the prospects for the nationalist movement in Burma. The imprisoned leaders were released. Ba Maw headed a pro-Japanese government which included a curious (in retrospect) assortment of future Socialist, Communist, and resistance leaders: Aung San served both as Minister of Defense and Commander of the newly created Burma Independence Army (later in the occupation called the Burma National Army); Thakin Nu was Foreign Minister; Than Tun was Minister of Agriculture. In 1943, after Japan granted "independence" to Burma, the Ba Maw cabinet became the first government of an allegedly sovereign nation. From the outset of the occupation, however, differences intensified within the Freedom Bloc, and especially among the *Thakins*, concerning collaboration with the Japanese. Initially the prevailing view, inspired by the experience of the "Thirty Comrades," was in favor of collaboration as the quickest route to independence. How-

ever, as disillusion with the Japanese grew, a resistance movement gradually developed throughout the country under the
leadership of Thakin Soe. As in Indonesia, there was some co-
ordination between the collaborationist and underground leaders
and there were instances—similar to Sukarno's intervention in
behalf of Sjarifuddin in 1943—of government officials protecting
members of the underground: in 1942, for instance, Bo Let Ya,
who was Aung San's deputy in the Ba Maw government, shielded
Thein Pe Myint from arrest by Japanese occupation authorities.

The co-ordination during the first year or more of the occupation, however, should not be exaggerated; in general, the two
leaderships went their separate ways awaiting a clearer delinea-
tion of the political forces at work in Burma before linking
their fortunes. Ideology, it should be emphasized once again,
was not yet at issue. Different views on the question of relations
with the Japanese did not reflect significant ideological differences within the *Thakin* movement. All, excluding only Ba Maw
and his immediate followers, considered themselves Marxists in
one degree or another. Socialists and Communists by 1943 were
perhaps more clearly distinguishable than before the war—Aung
San, U Ba Swe, Bo Let Ya, among others, now stood forth as
Socialists; Thakin Soe, Thein Pe Myint, and Than Tun, as
Communists—but serious rivalry between the two groups did
not appear until the closing months of the war. The two above-
ground leaders of the so-called Socialist and Communist factions,
Aung San and Than Tun, were both friends and allies and
linked to one another by marriage to sisters. It is accordingly
inappropriate to seek correlation in Burma between Socialists
and collaboration, on the one hand, and Communists and non-
collaboration, on the other. In this sense there was less distinction between collaboration and non-collaboration in Burma than
in Indonesia.[169]

---

[169] The events of the wartime period are again drawn in large part from the
author's interviews with Burmese who took part in them, notably Ba Maw,
Thein Pe Myint, and Bo Let Ya, and from Aung San's address in August 1945
(see above). While some discrepancies occur in their accounts, especially in the
interpretation put on different episodes, to the extent that the evidence of these
Burmese leaders has been used here, it does not conflict with the more detailed

Southeast Asian Communism in Suspension: 1941-1947

The Burmese Communist Party was officially launched at a "congress" called by Thakin Soe in 1942 or 1943. Fewer than ten, it is reported, attended. Thakin Soe was elected Secretary; Than Tun, who was evidently present at the secret meeting though a member of the Ba Maw government, was named his deputy.[170] In March 1944 an agreement was reached between the Socialists (organized since 1941 as the People's Revolutionary Party) and the Communists to collaborate in a resistance movement against the Japanese. An instruction explaining the agreement to both Communist and Socialist cadres called for the organization of a unified resistance movement within two months, after which a date would be set for the commencement of organized operations. The instruction continued: "We must regard the Fascist Japanese forces as our first and worst enemy. . . . We must seek friendship of Soviet Russia and the Allied Forces. After we have driven out the Fascist Japanese we must form organizations along democratic lines and start talks for independence. We will fight any foreign power which presents itself as detrimental to the rights of the Burmese people."[171]

In August 1944 nine Socialists, Communists, and Army leaders—all but two of them members of the Ba Maw government—met at the Rangoon home of Thakin Nu (who was then politically neutral) and launched the organization subsequently to be known as the Anti-Fascist People's Freedom League, or AFPFL. Aung San was named President of the organization and Than Tun Secretary-General.[172]

and generally accepted accounts of Burmese wartime politics in such studies as Cady, *op. cit.*, Chapter XIII; Trager, *Marxism in Southeast Asia*, pp. 28-31; and Tinker, *The Union of Burma*, pp. 9-18.

[170] The date of the founding of the BCP is disputed. Thein Pe Myint gives the date as sometime during 1942, Bo Let Ya as sometime during 1943; neither, however, was present at the "congress."

[171] The full text of the seven-point instruction is given in Trager, *op. cit.*, p. 30; it is translated from a 1952 Burmese Communist pamphlet entitled "Who is Right, The AFPFL or the Communist Party?" in the possession of Frank N. Trager.

[172] The meeting is described in an article by Maung Maung in *The Guardian* (Rangoon), II, 16, March 1955; cited in Trager, *op. cit.*, p. 30. Among those present were Thakin Soe and Than Tun (Communists); Kyaw Nyein, Thakin

The Communists thus played a major role in the AFPFL from its inception. If their following was less numerous than Aung San's—it is estimated that there were 3,000 members of the BCP in 1945 as against 10,000 in the Burma National Army led by Aung San[173]—their superior underground organization and their leading role in the resistance movement prior to 1944 somewhat compensated for the handicap. Moreover, through Thein Pe Myint, the *Thakins'* representative in India since 1942 (and unofficially the Burmese Communists' link with the CPI after the formation of the BCP), the Communists maintained the principal liaison with the Allied forces under Admiral Mountbatten, with whom the AFPFL was now to collaborate. After the formation of the AFPFL Thein Pe appealed to Force 136 for aid to the Burmese underground and after some hesitation on the part of British officers secured a promise of it.[174]

The AFPFL opened its revolt in March 1945 when Aung San, sent by the Japanese into North Burma to attack a British force, turned instead against the Japanese; simultaneously, according to Bo Let Ya, a Burmese unit under his command in the Irrawaddy delta turned against the Japanese there. British

Mya and U Ba Swe (Socialists); and Aung San and Ne Win (Army). According to one account, based on British Intelligence sources, the name AFPFL derived from the merger of two resistance organizations known as the Anti-Fascist Organization and the People's Freedom League, founded, respectively, by the Communists and by Aung San during 1943; Brimmell, *Communism in Southeast Asia*, p. 186. The same author's assertion, however, that at the time of the formation of the AFPFL the three constituencies (Socialist, Communist, and military leaders) united to form an enlarged Burmese Communist Party, with Aung San as a member of the Central Committee, appears very doubtful.

[173] The estimate of Communist strength in 1945 was given to the author by a former Communist, U Than Maung, during an interview in Mandalay in January 1962; U Than Maung, now a journalist, was formerly a member of the BCP. The estimate of the size of Aung San's forces is one generally accepted by students of Burma during these years; see, for example, Cady, *op. cit.*, p. 483.

[174] For a discussion of the conflicting views on Burma held by Force 136 officers and British civil officials, see Donnison, *British Military Administration in the Far East, 1943-1946*, pp. 346ff. Thein Pe's reception in India was affected by this rivalry: according to his own account, he was initially detained by British authorities following his arrival in India in 1942 and gained access to Force 136 officials only after a visit to Chungking in 1943, where he sought—without success—support from the Kuomintang.

troops in the meantime had launched attacks on Burma at various points, according to a long-delayed plan, and by May occupied Rangoon. Liaison between the British and the AFPFL was understandably irregular during these few months of intense fighting, but was maintained where possible through Force 136 operatives parachuted into Burma after November 1944; the British view, of course, was that the AFPFL was fighting the Japanese under the general command of Admiral Mountbatten.[175]

The first significant differences between the Socialist and Communist factions within the AFPFL arose over the question of relations with the returning British. Most Socialists, including Aung San, initially favored retaining the Burmese National Army as an independent force until assurances of independence were received. The Communists argued for the disbandment of the army—at least as an independent force—and for temporary co-operation with the British. According to Bo Let Ya, Aung San, following his first meeting with the British in mid-May, was persuaded by Thakin Soe and Than Tun that their course was the proper one; in June Aung San, Than Tun, and other Burmese leaders met with Admiral Mountbatten and placed the Burma National Army (now the Patriotic Burmese Forces) under his command.[176] Disbandment and re-registration in a regular Burmese army under British control began soon thereafter.

There are several explanations of Communist strategy during this episode. One is that the party leadership, especially Thakin Soe, who was less intimately associated with Aung San than was Than Tun, doubted the use Communists might make of an armed force so thoroughly under the influence of Aung San; nor would Thakin Soe, who was excessively self-centered according

[175] An account of British-AFPFL relations during this period may be found in Donnison, *op. cit.*, pp. 351ff.

[176] Burmese sources indicate that the meeting took place at Admiral Mountbatten's headquarters in Kandy, Ceylon: e.g., interview with Bo Let Ya and Ba Thein Tin's speech at the London conference of Communist parties of the British Empire, *World News and Views*, March 15, 1947, p. 103. British sources state that the meeting was held in Rangoon: e.g., Cady, *op. cit.*, p. 515, and Donnison, *op. cit.*, p. 358.

to those who knew him during this period, have welcomed the
widely acclaimed Aung San within the party leadership, assuming Aung San had any inclination to join it. Accordingly, the
wisest course was to dissolve the army and thereby curb Aung
San's authority. Another explanation, which finds support in
subsequent debates within the BCP, is that the Burmese leadership during this period was afflicted by what was to be called
"Browderism"—a tendency, as we have seen,[177] to rely less on
traditional oppositionist tactics than on co-operation with Western democratic forces allied with Russia during the war (in
this case, the British government). Thein Pe Myint later acknowledged that the materials he sent into Burma from India
during this period, both those he transmitted from foreign
sources and those he composed himself, consciously reflected the
Browderist line. If reports are true that Thakin Soe secretly
visited India in the spring of 1945, to consult with Indian Communists, and that Ghoshal returned to Burma soon thereafter
after spending the war years in India, both would have brought
back similar counsels, since the CPI at this juncture was also
following a "Browderist" line.[178]

If the adoption of "Browderism" by Burmese Communists was
a consequence of influences from outside the country, the cure
of the malady appears to have been related to personal rivalries
within the party. During the party's Second Congress, held in
the summer of 1945, Thakin Soe, though he had been widely
acknowledged even by non-Communists as the real leader of the
resistance movement,[179] was sharply criticized by his colleagues

[177] See above, p. 258.

[178] Thakin Soe's alleged visit to India, with the assistance of Communist RAF
officers, was mentioned to the author by two Burmese journalists—U Than Maung
and U Thaung Myine—during separate interviews in January and February 1962;
Ghoshal's return to Burma in 1945 is mentioned in Brimmell, *op. cit.*, p. 189. For
Indian Communist policy during the latter part of the war, see Overstreet and
Windmiller, *Communism in India*, pp. 218-22; the line consisted of an attempt,
largely futile, to support the British war effort without alienating the militantly
anti-British Congress leaders.

[179] Evidence of this is provided, for instance, by Bo Let Ya (a close associate,
it will be recalled, of Aung San) who states that Aung San freely acknowledged
Thakin Soe's leadership of the resistance movement during his first meeting with

for moral misdemeanors. He was removed from leadership, including membership on the Politburo; Thein Pe Myint was named party secretary and Than Tun chairman of the Politburo.[180]

Thein Pe, who was still in India at the time of the Second Congress, returned to Rangoon in the autumn, according to his account, and assumed leadership of the party. His return assured continuation of the moderate line for the present, despite a reported message from the Chinese Communists about this time to prepare for "armed struggle."[181] Than Tun, whose principal activity during this period was with the AFPFL, of which he continued to serve as Secretary-General, appears fully to have supported Thein Pe's policies.

Thakin Soe, meanwhile, took his demotion badly. He evidently felt that he had been dismissed from leadership on irrelevant charges and that his wartime role in the underground entitled him to greater recognition—within the party at least, if not within the AFPFL. He accordingly seized upon the issue of "Browderism," which by the end of 1945 had been everywhere rejected in the Communist world, and launched a sharp attack on Thein Pe Myint and Than Tun for continuing the moderate line. At a meeting of the Central Committee in late February 1946 he succeeded in forcing from Thein Pe what the latter

---

the British in May 1945 and insisted on consulting with him before negotiating further; as a result of this consultation, we have seen, the agreement with Admiral Mountbatten was reached in June.

[180] According to a subsequent report by Thein Pe Myint, the principal charge against Thakin Soe involved an affair he had had with a young Burmese girl attending his indoctrination lectures during the war; a copy of the report, delivered to the Politburo in April 1945, is in the possession of U Thaung Myine and was translated by him for this writer in February 1962.

[181] The origin of the Chinese message, referred to as the "Teng-fa letter," is obscure. Thein Pe Myint, in discussing the letter with the author, described it as a "suggestion" not an "instruction" and felt that the Burmese were in no way bound by it; U Than Maung, whose description of the message parallels Thein Pe's, notes that no notice was taken of the Chinese advice. The author knows of no discussion of the letter in published sources. Teng-fa was a Chinese labor leader who represented the CCP at a congress of the CPGB in London in November 1945; his speech on this occasion, which is not marked by its militancy, is printed in *World News and Views*, December 8, 1945, p. 398.

himself describes as a "confession of guilt" on the issue of Browderism, but he failed, by a vote of 29 to 8, to oust his two rivals.[182]

On the issue of leadership Thakin Soe split the Burmese Communist Party. In March he founded his own party, the Communist Party (Burma)—or "Red Flag" Communists, as they came to be known. The CPI promptly sent off a telegram to the Burmese leaders warning them that "the public airing of party differences must be stopped . . . both sides should strive to achieve unity."[183] The gesture, however, was to no avail; the division between "Red Flag" and "White Flag" Communists was final.

The troubles of the Burmese Communists did not end here. Within the "White Flag" faction—which was the most numerous and has generally been considered the orthodox branch of the movement—a further change in leadership came in July when Than Tun replaced Thein Pe Myint as Secretary; Thein Pe himself describes the charge against him as one of "weak leadership." Than Tun, meanwhile, was forced about the same time to give up his position as Secretary-General of the AFPFL due to differences with the majority, including Aung San, on the question of political activities allowable outside the AFPFL.[184] Thein Pe was defeated by one vote in the election of Than Tun's successor as Secretary-General and control of the AFPFL now passed wholly to the Socialists.[185] Relations between the BCP and the AFPFL thereafter deteriorated rapidly. Aung San offered the Communists only one seat instead of the two they demanded in the Executive Council formed after the arrival of

[182] The vote on the leadership question was given to the author by Thein Pe; a reference to his "confession of guilt" appears in Thein Pe's report to the Politburo in April 1946, cited above. See also *Burma and the Insurrections* (an official publication of the Burmese government), p. 2.

[183] The telegram, which was signed by Joshi, is quoted in Thein Pe's report to the Politburo in April.

[184] The exact issue forcing Than Tun's resignation is obscure but appears to have centered on the question of declaring the "Red Flag" Communists illegal—a move which Than Tun protested and Aung San upheld; see Cady, *op. cit.*, pp. 534-5 and Trager, *op. cit.*, p. 34.

[185] Cady, *op. cit.*, p. 535; the vote was 53 to 52 in favor of the Socialist candidate Thakin Kyaw Nyein.

the new Governor, Sir Hubert Rance; the seat moreover was offered to Thein Pe rather than to Than Tun, as the latter had expected—a maneuver presumably calculated to exacerbate rivalries within the BCP. In November 1946 the BCP was finally expelled altogether from the ruling AFPFL for having condoned strikes against the government. Thein Pe was simultaneously dropped from the Executive Council, where he had served for only three weeks; he subsequently drifted away from the party until he broke with it entirely in March 1948 on the eve of the insurrection.

Following their expulsion from the AFPFL the "White Flag" Communists appear to have steadily lost political influence, despite some gains in the labor and peasant unions.[186] They were now isolated from leadership of the nationalist movement and so played no part in the negotiations for independence which began in London in January 1947. At the same time they had no alternative to put before the country. "Browderism" was dead but no clear policy had been devised to replace it. There was, for instance, no all-out attack on the Aung San government comparable to that which the "Red Flag" Communists had directed against it since quitting the AFPFL in March 1946. The elections to the Constitutional Assembly in April 1947, in which the "White Flag" Communists hesitantly participated, should have removed any doubt that Communist influence had declined sharply: of the 29 seats which they contested, the Communists carried only seven, as contrasted with more than 170 won by the AFPFL.[187]

[186] The Communists had organized the All Burma Trade Union Congress as early as July 1945, some months before the Socialists had taken comparable steps in the labor field. Among wide segments of the peasantry, meanwhile, the postwar Communist slogans "no rent, no taxes," although essentially irresponsible and sharply protested by the Socialists, also gained the Communists support. According to a Burmese Communist who attended the conference of Communist parties of the British Empire in February 1947, the Communist-controlled labor unions at the end of 1946 included 35,000 workers; 300,000 peasants were in Communist-led peasant organizations; and the BCP itself (i.e., "White Flag") had 6,000 members. See Ba Thein Tin's speech at the conference in *World News and Views*, March 15, 1947, p. 103.

[187] See Cady, *op. cit.*, p. 551.

The Burmese Communists had in the meantime extended their international contacts beyond the CPI. Reports of liaison with Communists in the British armed forces during the spring of 1945 may be exaggerated,[188] but once travel between Europe and Asia returned to normal, contact was established with the international movement. Two Burmese delegates, for instance, attended the conference of Communist parties of the British Empire in London in February 1947 and one of them reported on developments in Burma.[189] Burmese delegates also attended meetings of the WFDY and WFTU in Europe during 1947.[190] On these occasions they inevitably came into contact with Soviet representatives; however, there is no evidence that these early contacts with Russians abroad, or with occasional Soviet visitors to Burma,[191] specifically influenced Burmese Communist policies. There is also no evidence of Chinese Communist influence in Burma after the war—other than the so-called "Tengfa letter," whose origin, we have seen, is obscure; the CCP, it may be imagined, was too preoccupied with its own affairs in North China at this juncture to give to developments in Burma the attention they were later to receive.

The Russian press, both during and after the war, provides only those very general clues to Moscow's intentions in Burma which we have discovered in the case of other Southeast countries. It is useful, however, to review these commentaries for

---

[188] U Than Maung and U Thaung Myine both mentioned such contacts to the author, during interviews in January and February 1962, but could supply no details—other than the alleged visit of Thakin Soe to India with the help of Communist officers in the RAF, referred to above.

[189] The two delegates were Aung Gyi (not to be confused with Brigadier Aung Gyi, later an aide of General Ne Win) and Ba Thein Tin; the latter's report to the conference, discussed below, was published in *World News and Views*, March 15, 1947, p. 103. Thakin Soe was evidently invited to attend the conference, as representative of the dissident "Red Flag" faction, but is reported to have rejected the invitation charging that the meeting was the "opening of a lunatic asylum"; interview with U Than Maung.

[190] U Than Maung states that he and several other Burmese Communists (or sympathizers) attended international conferences in Belgrade, Prague, and London between May and October 1947.

[191] A brief report on a visit to Burma by the Soviet correspondent O. Chechetkina appears in *New Times*, August 20, 1947, pp. 23-7.

what little they reveal; it is also useful, and more instructive, to review simultaneously commentaries by the CPGB and its organs, since, in the absence of a clearly perceived Soviet line, the British Communist attitude toward Burma can perhaps be taken as an authentic reflection of Moscow's.

At the outset of the war in the Far East, Soviet attention to Burma continued to focus on the question of a supply line to China now that the Burma Road was sealed off entirely by the Japanese occupation.[192] A few articles probed more deeply into political developments, but with little apparent grasp of Burmese realities. An article in the spring of 1942, for instance, spoke of the centuries-old ties between Burma and Siam, an assertion most historians would challenge; the author's review of the governmental structure under the 1936 Act of Burma omitted reference to the nationalist movement.[193] A short pamphlet by Vasil'-eva at the end of 1942 was also elementary but did—evidently for the first time—take cognizance of the *Thakins*; none, however, were mentioned by name, and their activities since the beginning of the Japanese occupation were overlooked.[194] In 1944 an article in *War and the Working Class* on Japanese occupation policies in East Asia considered the "puppet" government of Ba Maw no better than the Roxas and Wang Ching-wei regimes in the Philippines and China; Burmese "independence," the author concluded, was "a farce."[195]

British Communists took more notice than Russian of the independence movement in Burma. In April 1942, for instance, *World News and Views* noted the stimulation given Burmese nationalism by the Cripps mission to India.[196] During the next

<hr/>

[192] Several items on this theme in *Sputnik agitatora* and *Ogonek* during 1942 and 1943 are listed in *Bibliografiia Iugo-vostochnoi Azii*, p. 75.

[193] N. Lazarev, "Birma," *Mirovoe khoziaistvo i mirovaia politika*, No. 1-2, January-February 1942, pp. 121-8. The author, who wrote a number of other articles for the same journal on South America, was evidently not a specialist on Burma.

[194] Vasil'eva, *Birma*, pp. 25ff.

[195] K. Popov, "Iaponiia i okkupirovannye strany Vostochnoi Azii," *Voina i rabochii klass*, No. 12, June 15, 1944, p. 18.

[196] *World News and Views*, April 25, 1942, p. 211.

two years British Communist attention to the colonial question was riveted almost exclusively on India, but late in 1944 a policy regarding Burma began gradually to emerge. In October 1944, we have noted, approval was expressed of General MacArthur's promise of independence to the Philippines and the British government criticized for being "still unable to make a statement of this kind to the people of Burma and Malaya."[197] In November the memorandum on the colonial question issued by the Executive Committee of the CPGB urged the government to give a firm pledge of independence to Burmese patriots rather than a promise merely to restore the 1935 constitution.[198] In December another article, commenting on the recent discussion of Burma in the House of Commons (which, it was observed, was the first in more than a decade), noted that there was little awareness in Parliament of Burmese "realities." The "realities," the author stated, were three. First, Burmese guerrillas were actively taking part in the struggle against the Japanese; they should accordingly be armed, as Americans were said to be arming guerrillas in the Philippines. Second, the Burmese people wanted independence and "their own representative government"; a promise of Dominion status was not enough. Third, the just desire of the Burmese for a higher standard of living could not be satisfied simply by settling accounts with Indian moneylenders; a more ambitious program of economic recovery was necessary to repay the Burmese for decades of British and Indian exploitation.[199] The CPGB, it should be noted, was directing its efforts through 1944 mainly at the policies of the London government; as yet there was no clear indication of an attitude toward the various factions in Burma itself, although the Communists were occasionally singled out as active in the resistance movement.

When the AFPFL launched its attack on the Japanese in March, British Communists responded immediately. At the end

[197] *Ibid.*, October 28, 1944, p. 349.
[198] *The Colonies: The Way Forward*, p. 47.
[199] A.C., "Burma—Present and Future," *World News and Views*, December 23, 1944, p. 412.

of the month *World News and Views* expressed concern over the government's failure to give its blessing to the AFPFL's action.[200] In May, the official, if belated, recognition of the AFPFL was duly approved and the next step was said to be the establishment of local governments, and eventually a national government, made up of guerrilla leaders.[201] The same argument was used again in June in a sharp critique of the recently published White Paper on Burma which proposed to delay national elections and self-government for three years.[202] By the end of the war in the Far East, then, the CPGB appears to have adopted a relatively explicit and forthright line in Burma: the alliance between the Communists and the AFPFL was openly acknowledged; the past collaboration of certain AFPFL leaders was recognized and forgiven; and the independence of Burma under the leadership of the AFPFL was set forth as the immediate post-war objective. We can only conjecture that Moscow shared these views.

Following the Japanese surrender, British Communists continued to serve as the principal interpreters of Burmese affairs in the international movement, Soviet observers remaining silent. In September an article in *World News and Views* for the first time discussed the Burmese Communist Party, as one of the major parties constituting the AFPFL, but showed some ignorance of the origins of the party and of recent intra-party developments: the BCP was said, for instance, to have been very small at the time of the Japanese invasion and only subsequently to have grown (as we have seen, the BCP did not exist as such until late 1942 or 1943); the head of the party was said to be Thakin Soe (although, if evidence presented earlier is correct, he was removed from the leadership several months before this article appeared).[203] Later in September an editorial in the same

---

[200] Michael Carritt, "Burma Reconstruction," *World News and Views*, March 31, 1945, p. 103.

[201] *World News and Views*, May 19, 1945, p. 147.

[202] *Ibid.*, June 2, 1945, p. 164.

[203] *Ibid.*, September 15, 1945, p. 282; the article lists Than Tun and Thein Pe Myint as the chief Communist collaborators with Aung San in the AFPFL.

paper cited continuing collaboration with anti-Fascist forces in Burma as the correct policy for the new Labour government to follow, in contrast to the support given pro-Fascist elements in Indochina and Indonesia by the French and Dutch.[204] In November, however, the Labour government's good intentions in Burma were doubted: the rejection of what were described as the AFPFL's moderate proposals to shorten the timetable for self-government put forward in the White Paper was seen as a return to "imperialism with a vengeance."[205]

At this juncture there is an interruption in British Communist attention to developments in Burma, possibly because of the intra-party disputes over the post-war leadership. Whether this issue was resolved to the satisfaction of the CPGB it is impossible to say since there is no subsequent reference to it in British Communist sources known to this writer; in fact, the BCP itself attracted little attention in commentaries on Burma once they were resumed. *World News and Views* at the end of September 1946 reaffirms support of the AFPFL but makes no mention of the Communists.[206] In December, after the Communists were expelled from the AFPFL, their British comrades still showed no sign of withdrawing support from the AFPFL leadership. A resolution on the colonial question passed by the Executive Committee of the CPGB says of Burma, in one of the most forthright policy statements to this time: "Give real executive responsibility in all departments of government, including External Affairs, to the Executive Council [which, it will be recalled, was at this juncture entirely made up of AFPFL leaders, without Communist representation] unfettered by the Governor's special powers and vetoes. Withdraw the unpopular and undemocratic White Paper proposals for the future and permit a Constituent Assembly to be called in 1947 to decide freely, without political or economic interference, Burma's future status and constitution."[207]

[204] *Ibid.*, September 29, 1945, p. 297.
[205] *Ibid.*, November 3, 1945, p. 340.
[206] Geoffrey Parsons, "Last Chance in Burma," *ibid.*, September 28, 1946, p. 308.
[207] *Ibid.*, December 7, 1946, p. 396.

The first doubts about the AFPFL leadership openly expressed by British Communists came only at the beginning of 1947 as negotiations opened in London between the Burmese delegation led by Aung San and British colonial authorities. In accepting his post in the Executive Council without a full guarantee of demands previously put forth by the AFPFL, a British Communist writer argued, Aung San "went against the nationalist principles of the progressive independence movement." He was unsuccessful, the writer continued, "in his attempt to use a violent anti-Communist campaign as a means of diverting the attention of the Burmese people from the fact that, although their national hero was now Deputy Chairman of the Executive Council, Burma was no nearer to independence."[208] When a preliminary agreement was reached in London, the same author doubted that rank and file AFPFL members in Burma would accept it since one of the three conditions for undertaking the negotiations—a promise of independence by January 1948—had not been met by the British.[209]

It was only now that the Soviet press broke silence on Burma.[210] In February 1947 an item in *New Times*, on the occasion of the preliminary agreement signed between the Burmese and the British in London, took Aung San to task for his part in the negotiations. Aung San, the item recalled, had joined the anti-Fascist movement during the war only when it was evident that the Japanese would be defeated; since the war he had sought "to divide the AFPFL and to isolate and destroy the forces struggling for independence." *New Times* noted, and appeared to approve, opposition to the agreement within the Burmese

[208] Geoffrey Parsons, "Burma Talks," *ibid.*, January 4, 1947, p. 6.

[209] *Ibid.*, February 8, 1947, p. 64. The other two conditions put forward by the Burmese leaders prior to the talks—conditions which were met by the English —were: the transformation of the Executive Council into an interim government pending general elections and a pledge of elections for a constituent assembly during the spring of 1947.

[210] Burma had of course been touched on in a few articles appearing in the Soviet press since the war—such as a review of Alexander Campbell's *It's Your Empire* (Victor Gollancz Ltd., 1945) in *New Times*, No. 22, November 15, 1946, p. 28—but had been the subject of no sustained comment, insofar as this writer has been able to discover.

delegation led by U Saw (soon to be held responsible for Aung San's assassination).[211] An article in the following issue also criticized the agreement and mentioned the "cruel suppression" of Communists in Burma by the British and their allies in the AFPFL.[212] By June the Soviet view on the AFPFL leadership had stiffened perceptibly. Another article noted a "sharp and complete struggle" going on within the AFPFL, brought on by clever British strategy, and lamented the gradual elimination from the movement of all "progressive" elements.[213] *New Times* used less equivocal language: "The leaders of the Anti-Fascist League and the government have no intention to demand [*sic*] the country's independence"; Aung San's gesture of publishing a draft constitution which would proclaim Burma's full independence was declared "demagogic."[214] The country in the meantime, *New Times* went on, was sinking into chaos: guerrillas were said to be in control of extensive areas and had even established their own governmental bodies. The item does not identify the guerrillas, but since the "Red Flag" Communists of Thakin Soe were the principal group in open rebellion at this juncture it would appear that Moscow was acknowledging—and perhaps even giving inadvertent support to—this dissident faction of the Communist movement.

Aung San's assassination on July 19[215] led to reappraisals of

---

[211] *Temps nouveaux*, No. 6, February 7, 1947, pp. 16-7.

[212] N. Chtcherbinovski [Shcherbinovskii], "La Birmanie," *Temps nouveaux*, No. 7, February 14, 1947, p. 30.

[213] I. Lemin, "Sovremennye problemy Britanskoi imperii," *Mirovoe khoziaistvo i mirovaia politika*, No. 6, June 1947, pp. 12-3.

[214] *New Times*, No. 24, June 13, 1947, pp. 24-5. It is of some interest that Aung San, despite the negative view of him in the Soviet press, still held the counsel of world Communist leaders in high regard where revolutionary strategy was concerned; in a speech delivered in Rangoon on May 23, he defended AFPFL moderation on the grounds that precisely such a course was recommended in the teachings of Stalin and Mao Tse-tung. "Taking these lessons to heart," he asserted, "one realizes that only as a part of a general revolutionary movement all over Southeast Asia can the revolution in Burma have a fair chance of complete success"; Aung San, "Burma's Challenge," p. 30 (loaned to the author by Professor John H. Badgley).

[215] Aung San and six close associates in the AFPFL were murdered in Rangoon by gunmen allegedly hired by the pre-war politician (and former premier) U Saw.

335

the Burmese scene by both British and Russian Communists. The British were the first to respond. A week after the assassination, *World News and Views*, while noting the decline of the AFPFL under Aung San's leadership, argued that since the April elections a "campaign for unity" had progressed in Burma which had led to new conversations between Communist and AFPFL leaders; Aung San's last public speech a week before the assassination, it was recalled, had shown a tendency to move closer to the Communists' position regarding full independence.[216] The implication of the commentary, although the identity of the assassins had not yet been revealed, was that the British had arranged Aung San's murder to forestall a reunification of the "White Flag" Communists and the AFPFL. Soviet comment, a few days later, also suggested British complicity in the assassination but emphasized fear of Aung San's rejection of the January agreement rather than of a Communist-AFPFL rapprochement as the principal reason for it. "We are not thinking of dominion status," Aung San is quoted as having said on July 13. "All that is mere speculation in the press and the malicious talk spread by enemies of the Freedom League." In marked contrast to this view, the Soviet comment remarked, was the outlook of Thakin Nu who was said to have reported enthusiastically on the "large measure of agreement" reached in his current negotiations with the British in London; it was implied that the prompt appointment of Thakin Nu as Aung San's successor was designed "to make Burma's colonial status permanent."[217]

Of the two slightly different explanations of the episode at the time, the British—with its stress on the approaching reunification of Communists and AFPFL—has become the more generally accepted one in Communist literature. This interpretation has made it possible for Communists to argue in later years that but for

U Saw's attempted coup—if such it was—was frustrated by the prompt naming of Thakin Nu as Aung San's successor and the formation of a new cabinet; U Saw and his accomplices were tried and executed later in the year.

216 *World News and Views*, July 26, 1947, p. 336.

217 "The Burma Murders," *New Times*, No. 31, July 30, 1947, pp. 13-4; see also I. A. Vasil'eva, "Polozhenie v Birme," *Mirovoe khoziaistvo i mirovaia politika*, No. 9, September 1947, pp. 111-24.

British treachery in July 1947 the long drawn-out civil war in Burma might never have occurred: Aung San's assassination removed the last good chance for a Communist-AFPFL rapprochement, which alone could stabilize the country and guarantee independence.[218]

There is some evidence that the views of British and Russian Communists influenced the attitudes and formulations of Burmese Communists, especially during 1947. The Burmese delegate who spoke at the Commonwealth conference of Communist parties in February 1947, for instance, reflected views about Aung San and the January agreement which were then current in Soviet and British Communist journals. He held Aung San responsible, in retrospect, for having agreed to disband the armed forces in 1945—a decision which meant that "the mass upsurge released by the anti-Fascist rising was temporaily decimated." (It apparently made no difference to the Burmese delegate that the decision, if evidence presented above is accurate, was pressed upon Aung San by the Communists themselves.) The January agreement, meanwhile, was considered a "national humiliation" because it fell so far short of the minimum conditions previously set by the AFPFL, when the Communists had still been in it.[219] There is also some correlation between Burmese Communist policies proclaimed after Aung San's assassination and the views expressed at this juncture by Russian and British Communists, especially in the more markedly hostile attitude toward England. A resolution adopted by the Burmese Central Committee on July 30 read in part:

> The form of power which imperialism was compelled to concede to the national movement, if correctly implemented, offers us greater opportunity today for greater mobilization of our country to prepare for a national war against British imperialism. Under the circumstances, the existing Provisional Government and the Constituent Assembly become strategic weapons in the hands of the national united front [with which] to implement its program. At the same time the Provisional Government can be made to play a progressive role in

[218] See, for instance, *Birmanskii soiuz* (1958), p. 111.
[219] Speech by Ba Thein Tin in *World News and Views*, March 15, 1947, p. 103.

alliance with other progressive forces of the world against the menace of American imperialism and its junior partner, British imperialism.[220]

The July 30 resolution, however, parallels British and Russian Communist views only in part inasmuch as it clearly continues the effort at reconciliation with the AFPFL at a time when Communist opinion abroad indicated misgivings about the direction of League policies under Thakin Nu. Possibly the Burmese Communists felt they knew better than the British and Russians the prospects for collaboration with Thakin Nu;[221] at any event, it is unlikely that they could have received specific instructions from abroad during the short interval between the assassination and the July 30 resolution, and so they simply continued the policy of reconciliation in force since April. The time had not yet come, the White Flag leadership appears to have felt, for a complete break with the AFPFL. This would not occur for another eight months and less as a consequence of advice from Moscow or from the CPGB than as a consequence of advice once again from the Indians.

MYSTERIOUS WAYS OF COMMUNISM IN SIAM

Our occasional focus on Siamese Communism and on Soviet policy toward it may be considered an exercise in speculation since

[220] Quoted from Ba Tin [Ghoshal], "On the Present Political Situation in Burma and our Tasks" (January 1948), p. 11; a translation of this document, known as the Ghoshal Thesis, was given to the author by U Thaung Myine.

[221] Contrary to the impression British and especially Russian Communists had of Thakin Nu at this juncture, he appears not to have been hostile to a reconciliation with the Communists. In November 1946, for instance, at the time of the Communists' expulsion from the AFPFL, he is quoted as having said: "May the real Communist movement in Burma be successful and may the leadership be un-scrupulous people who are misusing the name of Communism . . . be quickly destroyed"; from the pamphlet *Who is Right, the AFPFL or the Communist Party?* quoted in Trager, *op. cit.*, p. 33. The remark is, to be sure, ambiguous, especially as it might apply to the White Flag leadership, but indicates Thakin Nu's tolerant attitude toward Communism per se. In a speech delivered in November 1947 Thakin Nu stated that White Flag leaders had met with him immediately after Aung San's assassination to discuss the possibility of a reconciliation; *Towards Peace and Democracy* (Rangoon, 1947), p. 20, cited in Johnstone, *Burma's Foreign Policy*, p. 31.

next to nothing is known of either—at least in comparison with the relatively abundant, if uneven, sources of information on Communism and Soviet policies elsewhere in Southeast Asia. The effort to set forth what can be discovered, however, is not wasted if it sheds light on Moscow's resourcefulness, or lack of it, in devising revolutionary strategies under conditions very different from those in surrounding colonies.

During the dozen years reviewed in the present chapter (1935-1947) there appears to have been little stirring by Siamese Communists. The 1933 act banning Communism remained in force through the war and its enforcement was evidently vigorous enough to discourage any significant activity by organizations willing to admit to being Communist or pro-Communist. There was no anti-Fascist front in the latter part of the 1930's, as in most other Southeast Asian countries; nor was there a native guerrilla movement in Siam during the war.

Siam was not, however, more ignored by the Soviet and international Communist press than other Southeast Asian countries. The long survey of Siamese politics and economics in *Tikhii okean* in 1935 (see p. 199) was followed by other discussion of Siamese affairs. In the pre-war years the principal topic of interest in these commentaries was the growing Japanese penetration of the country. In July 1936, for instance, an American Communist asserted: "There can be no doubt that when in the opinion of the Japanese military specialists the Siamese military base is sufficiently prepared, a new 'Manchurian incident' will break out . . . it will have more serious consequences than in 1931-32."[222] The governments of the late 1930's are seen as increasingly receptive to Japan's role in Siam, despite some restraining influence by Pridi Phanomyong; Pridi is treated sympathetically in most accounts, but not as a Communist.[223]

[222] J. Berry, "The Southern Direction of Japanese Aggression," *Communist International* (US), No. 7, July 1936, p. 876.
[223] E.g., E. Alin, "Siam - novyi platsdarm iaponskogo imperializma," *Tikhii okean*, No. 1, 1937, pp. 157-9; W. Damnus, "Reaction in Siam," *Inprecor*, July 10, 1937, p. 656; "Siam i derzhavy," *Tikhii okean*, No. 1, 1938, pp. 118-9; "Iaponiia i Siam," *Mirovoe khoziaistvo i mirovaia politika*, No. 8, August 1938, p. 125.

Communism receives occasional mention. *Inprecor* at the end of 1936, for instance, notes that despite penalties of ten years in prison for the mere possession of Communist literature, the country is "inundated" with it on the occasion of each new crime committed by the government.[224] Moscow appears, however, to have been in some doubt as to the party leadership in Siam: a later version of the *Inprecor* article mentions as head of the party one Naiam (then under arrest), although in the original version Naiam is said to have been the leader of a nationalist organization seeking to ally with the Communists.[225] No explanation is given of the discrepancy. The Soviet press occasionally emphasized the kinship between radical elements in Siam—who, as in Malaya, were predominantly Chinese—and the revolutionaries in China. A letter allegedly written by political prisoners in Siam expressing their solidarity with the Chinese anti-Fascist movement is carried in a Soviet periodical in 1938.[226] In 1939 Zabozlaeva notes the role of the Chinese in Siam, who are said to constitute 90 percent of the proletariat, in spreading the ideas of the Chinese revolution: "under the revolutionary influence of the struggle of the Chinese people," she writes, "the demand for democratic rights and freedoms in Thailand is strengthening."[227]

By 1940 Japan was seen as wholly in control of Thailand, formerly a "semi-colony of England," as the result of England's preoccupation with the war in Europe and Japanese ascendancy in Indochina.[228] Japan was thus the prime mover in Thailand's seizure of portions of Cambodia and Laos in 1941, according to Soviet press notices of the short Thai-Indochinese war in January

---

[224] Veradti, "The Struggle Against the Feudal Military Dictatorship," *Inprecor*, December 5, 1936, p. 1445; the article was datelined Bangkok.

[225] *Ibid.*, May 15, 1937, p. 497.

[226] "Iz siamskoi tiurmy: pis'mo politzakliuchennykh Siama boitsam kitaiskogo naroda," *Internatsional'nyi maiak*, No. 19, 1938, p. 3; the letter is translated from a Chinese Communist newspaper.

[227] O. Zabozlaeva, "Tai (Siam) i derzhavy," *Mirovoe khoziaistvo i mirovaia politika*, No. 9, September 1939, p. 228; Siam was renamed Thailand in June 1939.

[228] O. Z. "Ekonomicheskoe polozhenie Tai," *ibid.*, No. 10, October 1940, pp. 88-90.

and February of that year.[229] Moscow, however, moving now toward a rapprochement with Japan as relations with the Nazi bloc (which included the Vichy government in Indochina) deteriorated, adopted a neutral position toward the Thai-Indochinese war. Diplomatic and trade relations were established with Bangkok on March 12, 1941, a day after Indochina had been forced under Japanese pressure to accede to the Thai seizures in Cambodia and Laos.[230]

During the war only scattered references to Thailand may be found in Soviet publications. A brief discussion of the country in a Soviet reference book in 1942 is critical of the government of Pibulsonggram and, in effect, dismisses Thailand as little more than a Japanese colony.[231] In 1944, a book on pre-war Thailand by an American author, who can hardly be considered sympathetic to Pibulsonggram, is criticized as an "apology" for his pro-Japanese regime.[232] These infrequent notices, needless to say, give no clues as to Soviet intentions regarding Thailand after the war.

Following the Japanese defeat, Thai Communism enjoyed a brief period of legal, or semi-legal, existence. This was due in large measure to the need to restore Thailand's prestige in the eyes of the victors with whom the kingdom had been nominally at war; a gesture of respect for political liberties was considered a minimum step to this end. Even before the 1933 act outlawing Communism had been officially repealed, in October 1946, several pro-Communist organizations had appeared. In November 1945, for instance, a so-called Proletarian Party was organized; in 1946 a Central Labour Union was created which, according to later Soviet sources, numbered 50,000 workers by the end of the following year.[233] Soviet sources also mention "armed uprisings" in the

---

[229] E.g., "K konfliktu mezhdu Tai i Frantsuzskim Indo-Kitaem," *Sputnik agitatora*, No. 9, 1941, pp. 43-4; Iu. Savel'eva, "Na reke Mekong," *Ogonek*, No. 2, 1941, pp. 14-5; "Podpisanie mirnogo dogovora mezhdu Frantsiei i Tai," *Mirovoe khoziaistvo i mirovaia politika*, No. 6, June 1940, pp. 120-1.

[230] The exchange of notes is given in *ibid.*, No. 4, April 1940, p. 193.

[231] *Strany Tikhogo okeana*, p. 259.

[232] *Mirovoe khoziaistvo i mirovaia politika*, No. 5, May 1944, pp. 90-1; the review, written by Avarin, is of Virginia Thompson, *Thailand: The New Siam* (Macmillan, 1941).

[233] Rebrikova, *Ocherki noveishei istorii Tailanda*, p. 127. A history of the

341

countryside after the war during which demobilized peasants, evidently under Communist influence, seized land and drove out both the landowners and government officials.[234] In another country these worker and peasant formations might be considered Communist-front organizations, but in Thailand (or Siam, as it was once again called after the war) the Communist organization itself was so weak that if a "front" did in fact exist there was little behind it. It was not until January 1, 1947, that the Communist Party of Siam came into the open, during a public rally in Bangkok allegedly attended by 50,000 Chinese and Thai workers. Nai Prasert Sapsunthorn, a member of Parliament elected in 1946 on the Proletarian Party ticket and a recent convert to the CPS, addressed the rally. The party's five slogans were read forth and repeated in mass by those present:

1. Progress and unity of all workers' unions!
2. Unity of the workers is the powerful force!
3. Unity and cooperation between Siamese and Chinese Workers!
4. Prosperity and Progress of Siam!
5. Long live Siam![235]

For the next six or eight months the CPS showed fitful signs of life. It published a weekly newspaper in Thai, *Masses Weekly News*. It sent appeals abroad for Communist literature to translate into Thai and Chinese.[236] It maintained its own publishing

---

Thai labor movement written in the 1950's by a Thai Communist, Supachi, exists (in English translation) in government police files in Bangkok and was used in evidence during Supachi's trial in 1959; the author was able to consult this document briefly in 1961, but unfortunately not long enough to record any details. For another account of the Thai labor movement after the war, based on research carried on in Thailand in 1947, see Thompson and Adloff, *Left Wing in Southeast Asia*, pp. 58ff.

[234] Rebrikova, *op. cit.*, p. 116.

[235] *World News and Views*, March 15, 1947, p. 107; the report of the rally is signed by Udam Sisuvarn, "Labour Editor, *Masses Weekly News*, published by the Communist Party of Siam." Another account, presumably based on British Intelligence records, dates the official launching of the party on December 6, 1946 and states that Prasert Sapsunthorn (or Prasad Sabsunthorn) was elected Secretary-General; Brimmell, *Communism in Southeast Asia*, p. 242.

[236] See, for instance, a letter signed by the Communist Party of Siam in *World News and Views*, June 14, 1947, p. 263.

house in Bangkok, called *Mahachon*, and circulated Communist leaflets and pamphlets throughout Siam. One of the latter, entitled (in English translation) "What the Thai Communists Will Do Now," includes a ten-point program; since it is the only Thai Communist program known to this writer—and may be the only one they ever devised—it is worth giving in some detail:

1. Support of democratic principles and co-operation with any political party which upholds democracy.
2. Direct election of members of Parliament and the extension of popular government to the local level.
3. Right to vote and to be candidates to all Thai nationals over 18, regardless of sex, property qualifications, and education.
4. Recognition by local governments of the equality of national minorities and their right to self-government.
5. A guarantee of freedom of assembly, speech, press, religion, demonstration, and political association.
6. Improvement of workers' living standards through higher wages, eight-hour day, increased social insurance, relief from unemployment and abolition of unfair treatment of apprentices; promotion of higher morality, as well as higher living standards, for soldiers, police and minor officials; protection of cooperatives and those with independent occupations.
7. Abolition of heavy taxes; tax collection to be based on social justice and to protect national industries; guarantee to foreign nationals of "equal and reasonable" opportunities for investment.
8. Promotion of agriculture and reduction of farm rentals and interest; support of farmers' associations and cooperatives; poor farmers to receive implements and paddy seed without charge.
9. Improvement of teachers' living standards; promotion of universal primary education, with emphasis on social studies, and of vocational training; preparation of textbooks "following democratic and scientific principles."
10. Closer relations with foreign nations, especially Russia, China, England and the United States; support of the United Nations and world peace; punishment of war criminals and suppression of Fascists; guarantee of rights to foreigners.[237]

[237] The ten points are paraphrased here from the translation by David A. Wilson in Trager, *Marxism in Southeast Asia*, pp. 92-3. Professor Wilson gives the

The Siamese party program, though designed in part to support the rights of the Chinese minority in Siam (e.g., points 4 and 7), is enough like the programs of other Communist parties in Southeast Asia to suggest that the Siamese were not entirely isolated from the international movement. What channels of communication they had with foreign Communists—other than correspondence by mail—are not known. Since Siam was not a colony, the CPS had no natural sponsor as other Southeast Asian parties had. The early efforts of Malayan Communists to help the Siamese were evidently without success.[238] If there was foreign influence in the CPS, or supervision over it, it presumably came from China, inasmuch as Siamese Communism, like Malayan, was predominantly Chinese; there is indeed some question as to whether there may not have been two separate parties at this point, as there are known to have been some years later—a Siamese Communist Party and a Chinese Communist Party of Siam.[239] Whether this was the case or not, Chinese influence in the Siamese Communist movement was persistently argued by Pibulsonggram after his return to power, on a strongly anti-Communist platform, at the end of 1947. The subsequent flight to Communist China not only of Prasert but also of Pridi Phanomyong of course gave plausibility to Pibulsonggram's claim of a Communist threat to Thailand operating through its Chinese community.[240]

---

date of publication of "What the Thai Communists Will Do Now" as 1945, but the pamphlet was evidently not circulated until December 1946; see Thompson and Adloff, *op. cit.*, p. 61, citing *Bangkok Post*, December 7, 1946. Among other information given in the pamphlet are the assertions that a Siamese Communist organization had existed since 1925, although not unified as a party until 1935, and that between 1935 and 1945 more than 500 party members had been imprisoned by the government.

[238] Loi Tek described to British officials in Malaya after the war his attempt to reach Bangkok in 1946, in response to a request for Malayan aid from the Siamese Communists; his trip was blocked, he said, by Siamese border guards.

[239] An interview by two Americans with a Chinese Communist in Siam, in May 1947, for instance, clearly indicated the existence of two parties, which moreover had no connection with each other; Thompson and Adloff, *op. cit.*, p. 60. A Thai police official, Col. Chat, whom the author interviewed in Bangkok in March 1961, also thought two separate parties existed at this time.

[240] In Pridi's case the self-imposed exile in China in the 1950's was doubtless

Following Phibun's coup d'état in November 1947, Siamese Communism once again receded into the shadows—unlamented, be it noted, by the Russians. This writer has discovered no expression of Soviet interest in Thailand during the two and a half years following the war, other than a brief mention of Siam's request in December 1946 for a resumption of diplomatic relations between the two countries;[241] the request, which was related to Siam's application for admission to the United Nations, was granted by the Soviet Union and the exchange of ambassadors took place in May 1948.[242] Subsequent Soviet accounts of Thailand during the post-war era, it is interesting to note, rely almost exclusively on English, American, and French sources.[243]

CONCLUSIONS

Generalization of Communist experience in Southeast Asia grows increasingly difficult. The political forces at work become almost too numerous to keep in mind. Diversity in Communist behavior is more to be remarked than parallels.

If, nonetheless, we seek somehow to generalize the heterogeneous experience reviewed in the present chapter, leaving aside Soviet strategies for the moment, two very elementary propositions may be put forth. First, where Communists were able, during the war, to identify themselves with the anti-Japanese movement—as in Indochina, the Philippines, Malaya, and, ultimately, in Burma—their fortunes rose and they were in a position to influence the course of events in their countries after the war; to the extent that they failed to achieve this identification—as in

---

an afterthought, to judge from his remarks on Siamese Communism in 1946. "I have studied enough economics," he is quoted in an interview in May of that year, "to be in a position to say that Communism can never happen in this country and that we have nothing to fear about that. I wish to make this point clear because I was once branded as a Communist"; Thompson and Adloff, *op. cit.*, p. 71, citing *Siam Daily*, May 4, 1946.

241 *Izvestiia*, January 7, 1947.

242 For a discussion of Soviet efforts first to block Siam's admission into the United Nations and then acceptance of the application, following Bangkok's request for diplomatic relations, see Rebrikova, *op. cit.*, p. 126.

243 E.g., *ibid.*, Ch. VI, and Rebrikova, *Amerikanskaia politika v Tailande*, Ch. I.

Indonesia—their growth was arrested and their prospects for playing a significant role in post-war politics accordingly reduced.
This was, of course, the consequence of Japan's defeat and occasions no surprise. To be able to identify with the victors inevitably meant a gain in stature, at least during the first flush of
victory itself; the closer the identification, the greater the gain.
There was, however, a liability in this identification, for it meant
claiming kinship with the colonial powers, who were also victors,
and placed Communists in conflict with local nationalist elements determined to resist the re-establishment of colonial regimes. Communists, therefore, were faced with the task of selecting with a very particular precision the right moment to alter
their identification. Our second proposition, then, concerns the
timing of the Communists' re-identification with the forces of
national liberation: where this was accomplished promptly and
decisively, the use that Communists could make of their wartime prestige was greatly enhanced; where their behavior was
sluggish and devious, their advantage was soon lost. The Vietminh, obviously, presents the best record in this regard; and it is
of more than passing significance that the Southeast Asian country where Communism enjoyed the least post-war success was
Siam, where independence was not an issue which Communists
could exploit.

We may for the moment let these two propositions stand, passing over the many qualifications that a meticulous reading of
political developments in Southeast Asia must impose on them—
such as the different consequences of collaboration with the Japanese, the different speeds with which the Southeast Asian colonies approached independence, the different relationships with
metropolitan parties, and so forth.

A single obsession seems central to all Soviet strategies in Southeast Asia after the war (it is a futile exercise, surely, to seek a reconstruction of them during the war): Moscow's mounting hostility toward her wartime allies, most of whom held colonies in
this area. The Soviet attitude toward national liberation in any
given instance was accordingly determined not by Communist
strength in the movement seeking it or by the imminence of

346

independence, but by the irritation the national liberation movement, Communist or non-Communist, was capable of producing in the metropolitan. Thus national liberation movements in Indochina, where Communists prevailed, and in Indonesia, where they did not, both won Moscow's endorsement because of their lively opposition to European imperialism; similar movements in Burma and the Philippines, by contrast, did not command Moscow's respect because the Kremlin judged their anti-imperialist posture unconvincing. In short, independence per se interested the Russians less than the worry it caused Moscow's rivals in Europe; Russia's policy in Southeast Asia was once again secondary to its policies in the West. Local Communists, though Moscow said little to them directly, were expected to play their proper part in allying with or opposing the forces Moscow designated as friend or foe: thus the PKI was expected to associate with Sukarno—and did—however PKI leaders might have judged the advantages of another course; Burmese Communists were expected (after some initial wavering) to repudiate Aung San—and did—although arguments favoring a continued effort through the AFPFL must surely have occurred to them. We cannot, of course, be sure that specific strategies originated in all cases in Moscow, but there is enough similarity between the formulations of Russian, metropolitan, and local Communists to take for granted agreement within the Communist movement as a whole—except, of course, in the case of such deviations as Tan Malaka's in Indonesia or Thakin Soe's in Burma.

If this reading of Russia's basic post-war objectives is accepted, the apparent inconsistency in Moscow's response to certain episodes and situations in Southeast Asia is more readily explained. Wartime collaboration in Indonesia and Burma, for instance, was forgiven more promptly than in the Philippines because Indonesian and Burmese collaborators, in Moscow's judgment, were quick to adopt an anti-imperialist posture where Filipinos like Roxas were not; the denunciation of Aung San in Burma, and the belated recollection of his wartime collaboration, occurred only after his negotiations with the British were judged too amicable. Independence was urged more vigorously in Burma than in Malaya, we may imagine, because Moscow felt the Burmese, nationalist *or* Communist, more capable than Malayans of worrying the British. The greater attention given to Indonesia than to Indochina, meanwhile, despite the unusually strong position of the Vietminh and the fact that its leadership was unmistakably Communist, must be related to Stalin's policies in France, where French Communists would be handicapped by too overt Soviet interest in France's principal colony in Asia; no such consideration restrained Moscow's support of Sukarno. This consideration was not, we must assume, urgent enough to recommend calling a halt to Ho Chi Minh's efforts—assuming Stalin could have done so—but it did serve to discourage exuberance regarding the Vietminh's prospects and, generally, to keep Soviet observations *sotto voce*.

This diversity in Soviet commentaries on Southeast Asia suggests that Moscow was perhaps better informed about the area, and therefore able to respond to developments there with greater subtlety and finesse, than before the war. It should not suggest a more vigorous Soviet engagement. The most impassioned Soviet remarks relating to Southeast Asia during the years under review were not on national liberation as such, still less on socialist revolution, but on the evils of imperialism. Even where these remarks were most acid, as after the first Dutch police action in Indonesia in 1947, there is no threat of Soviet reprisal or counter-action in behalf of the colonial movements, the only course that might significantly have raised Soviet influence in Southeast Asia. There was not, in short, a thrust to Soviet policies in Southeast Asia, less indeed than during certain periods in the past. Moscow responded to situations, often with a sophistication and flexibility not found in her pre-war responses, but offered no serious leadership. The fact that articles by Zhukov, Guber, Zabozlaeva, Vasil'eva, and other Orientalists reflect a progressive stiffening of Moscow's attitude toward the problem of colonialism from the spring of 1945 to the summer of 1947 is of interest, to be sure, but it should not obscure another fact: the burden of formulating Soviet policy fell on a small band of virtually unknown and politically insignificant scholars—as though the articulation of British or French colonial policy were entrusted to Orientalists at Oxford and the Sorbonne. Neither Stalin nor any other important Soviet leader spoke forth on the colonial issue during these years (except as it related to China).

Two considerations, we may imagine, in the last analysis determined the course of Soviet policy in Southeast Asia after the war. The first is related to Stalin's apparent reluctance to restore the pre-war image of the Soviet Union as the militant leader of world Communism and world revolution. The war had changed many things, not the least of them being Russia's position in world affairs. The strategies and institutions (like the Comintern) appropriate to an era of Soviet isolation and weakness were no longer necessary. Meanwhile, Stalin's concept of Soviet responsibility as a Great Power and co-founder of the United Nations doubtless strengthened his conviction that Moscow's pre-war role as custodian of the world revolutionary movement was now inexpedient. Since the situation in Southeast Asia was potentially revolutionary, any decisive action there inspired by Russians—any action, that is, likely to be tempting to Stalin—would only arouse fresh fears among his erstwhile allies and so revive precisely the image he was seeking to obliterate. For what? For very uncertain prospects of success, he must have felt, in a distant sector of the colonial world. Stalin's reluctance to reactivate the revolutionary feature of Soviet foreign policy was temporary; it also was not compelling enough to dissuade him from launching a bitter attack on the imperialist powers soon after the war. It did, however, set certain limits to Communist behavior in Southeast Asia: any strategies devised must be moderate enough to avoid giving the impression of an imminent and general Communist uprising, there or elsewhere; responsibility for guiding the colonial movements must be delegated to metropolitan parties, or other suitable vehicles of Communist policy; and Moscow, it was to be understood, would remain aloof in the event of any inadvertent outbreak of Communist violence.

The second consideration, which cuts across the first, relates to the two principal alternatives facing Stalin at the end of the war with respect to the extension of Soviet influence: a drive into

Western Europe, past the farthest limits reached by the Red Army (behind which Soviet influence and Communist consolidation were assured); or Soviet sponsorship of revolutions in the East, which, according to the formulation of the early post-Revolutionary years, could be expected to hasten revolution in Europe. Stalin chose the first alternative for what must by now be obvious reasons: the prize of a Communist France or Italy or Germany—not inconceivable goals in 1945—too far outweighed the prize of a Communist Indonesia, Indochina, or even China to encourage a vigorous activity in the East; the Communist parties in Europe, especially in France and Italy, were more disciplined and far better equipped to rule should they be called upon to do so—through victory at the polls or carefully staged coup d'état; moreover, nothing had changed since Lenin's time to alter the persistent notion of Marxism-Leninism that revolutions are best able to occur successfully in advanced industrialized countries. All rational arguments, then, led Stalin once again to look westward after World War II; a parallel effort in the colonial East was out of the question until Russia had recovered from the exhaustion of war and until the United States stood less prepared, through demobilization, to thwart his designs.

Having made his decision to face west, Stalin hardly paused to take a backward glance until the autumn of 1947. His policy was at least consistent in this respect, if fruitless. Even the Chinese Communists were left to shift for themselves; what Mao did, he did himself, once Russian troops had facilitated the establishment of a Chinese Communist base in Manchuria (the very least Stalin could do, we must conclude in retrospect). Communists in the East, in short, were obliged to await the outcome of Stalin's venture in Europe.

CHAPTER SIX

Engagement and Disengagement in Southeast Asia: 1948-1954

To MOST students of Soviet foreign policy, Andrei Zhdanov's speech on the occasion of the founding of the Cominform in September 1947 marks a watershed in Moscow's post-war strategies. In the following months the speech was widely reproduced and translated into many foreign languages;[1] its significance was pondered in Communist as well as in non-Communist journals throughout the world. It also inaugurated an era of increased tension in Soviet relations with the West which lasted without appreciable let-up for the next four or five years.

It may be questioned whether Zhdanov's speech and the establishment of the Cominform marked as much of a "watershed" in Soviet foreign policy as other episodes before and since—the turn from preoccupation with revolutionary "troughs" and "crests" to the tactics of the United Front in the mid-1930's, for instance; the conclusion of the Nazi-Soviet Pact in 1939; or the gradual shift to "peaceful co-existence" which spanned the years immediately before and after Stalin's death. These latter episodes (if they may be so designated) *redirected* the course of Soviet policy. Zhdanov in 1947 *affirmed* a course already set. He did, it is true, put Communist activity throughout the world into a steeper incline, but did not fundamentally alter the direction Stalin's foreign policy had taken since shortly after the wartime conference at Yalta.

Be that as it may, Zhdanov's speech in September 1947, more than any other single event, set the tone of international relations during the era known as the Cold War. It is therefore a suitable point of departure for the present chapter, which con-

---

[1] The official English translation of the speech, from which the excerpts quoted below are taken, was published in the first issue of the Cominform Journal, *For a Lasting Peace, for a People's Democracy!* (November 10, 1947), and later issued in Moscow as a separate pamphlet: Andrei Zhdanov, *The International Situation,* 1947.

351

cerns Soviet strategies in Southeast Asia during a period of engagement, then of disengagement.

MOSCOW AGAIN FACES EAST

Zhdanov's famous speech at Wiliza Gora (Poland) on September 22, 1947, would have attracted world-wide attention whatever his message. Few comparable statements covering the entire range of world affairs had been made by leading Soviet spokesmen since the war. Stalin's only significant public comment on the international situation, which accented growing rivalry among capitalist states, had been made in February 1946, twenty months earlier.[2] Official statements by Foreign Minister Molotov had been frequent enough but were normally confined to events of contemporary interest; he had not attempted to render a comprehensive prospectus of Soviet foreign policy.[3] No Party congress or Central Committee plenum, occasions when significant pronouncements on foreign policy might have been expected, had been held since the war. Accordingly, the observations of a Soviet spokesman as highly placed as Zhdanov—he was widely considered, until his death in 1948, to have been Stalin's heir-apparent—were certain to be studied with interest. Their significance was heightened by the fact that they were made on the occasion of what was generally believed to be the re-incarnation of the Communist International.

Zhdanov opened his speech by noting the changes in international affairs brought on by the war, notably the increased importance of the Soviet Union and the virtual elimination of three of the six major capitalist powers in the pre-war world (Germany, Italy, and Japan). He also remarked—although he did not dwell on the question at length—the intense aggravation of the "crisis of the colonial system" since 1945. This, he said, relying on a formulation that went back many years, "has placed the rear of the capitalist system in jeopardy." He con-

[2] This was a "campaign" speech delivered on February 9, 1946; an English text is in Rubinstein, *The Foreign Policy of the Soviet Union*, pp. 221-3.

[3] See V. N. Molotov, *Problems of Foreign Policy: Speeches and Statements, April 1945-November 1948* (Moscow, 1949).

tinued: "The peoples of the colonies no longer wish to live in the old way. The ruling classes of the metropolitan countries can no longer govern the colonies on the old lines." Two camps, Zhdanov went on, increasingly emerged as the war receded into the past: an "imperialist and anti-democratic" camp, headed by the United States and including the capitalist world; and a "democratic and anti-imperialist" camp led by Russia and including the people's democracies of Eastern Europe, countries which "have broken with imperialism" (such as Finland) and certain colonies well on their way to independence; he singled out Vietnam and Indonesia as former colonies "associated" with the anti-imperialist camp and noted the "sympathy" toward it of India, Egypt, and Syria. In theory, Zhdanov asserted, the two camps could co-exist and Soviet policy, indeed, was founded on this assumption. He left no doubt, however, that in Moscow's view the likelihood of an amicable co-existence was negligible due to the course of Western policies, and American policies in particular, since 1945. It was this consideration which led him to the point of his address and to the purpose of the gathering at Wiliza Gora: the Communist parties, which had everywhere grown in size and influence since the dissolution of the Comintern in 1943, must now reunite in their own interests and in the interests of a new international solidarity. He concluded:

The chief danger to the working class at this present juncture lies in underrating its own strength and overrating the strength of the enemy. Just as in the past the Munich policy untied the hands of the Nazi aggressors, so today concessions to the new course of the United States and the imperialist camp may encourage its inspirers to be even more insolent and aggressive. The Communist parties must therefore head the resistance to the plans of imperialist expansion and aggression along every line—state, economic and ideological; they must rally their ranks and unite their efforts on the basis of a common anti-imperialist and democratic platform, and gather around them all the democratic and patriotic forces of the people.

If Zhdanov's speech is read as one of ten or a dozen critical statements on Soviet foreign policy, spanning a period of forty-odd years, its militancy will of course stand forth. If, on the

353

other hand, it is read in the context of authoritative, but less publicized, statements concerning Soviet foreign policy during the preceding five or six months—for instance, E. Zhukov's article in *Pravda* on August 7 (see above, pp. 256-57)—the message is less remarkable. Much of what he said could have been predicted by an alert student of Soviet affairs. What could not perhaps have been predicted, on the basis of official Soviet discussion of international affairs prior to September 1947, was Zhdanov's candid appeal to foreign Communists to assume a larger role in world affairs and in developments within their respective countries. Stalin had for various reasons been reluctant to speak directly to the foreign parties or to allow Moscow openly to assume leadership of the world Communist movement. Now this caution was set aside. Communists abroad were explicitly encouraged to devise more energetic ways of advancing the common goal.

The East—that is, the colonial and recently colonial world—was not represented at the founding of the Cominform.[4] Since Zhdanov's message, however, was clearly intended for Communists everywhere, ways had to be discovered to project it to the Eastern peoples. This was not accomplished overnight. Old habits linger. An Orientalist conference held in mid-November, although reflecting certain features of the new line (Zhukov, for instance, acknowledged in his keynote address the need for a more vigorous role for Communist parties in the colonies), was characterized more by pre-Zhdanov than by post-Zhdanov thinking on the Eastern question. Possibly this was because the topic of the conference, the impact of the Bolshevik Revolution in the East, was too contrived and too remote from present realities to stimulate new formulations. The fragmentary record of the conference, at any event, does not suggest a vigorous new approach to the colonial world, and the fact that the papers prepared for the occasion were never published, as orig-

---

[4] The nine signatories of the declaration establishing the Communist Information Bureau were the USSR, Jugoslavia, Bulgaria, Hungary, Rumania, Poland, France, Czechoslovakia, and Italy; other European parties were later associated with the Cominform but none formally from Asia, Africa, or the Americas.

inally intended, suggests that Soviet authorities were quite aware of this.[5]

Zhukov, in an article which appeared in *Bol'shevik* in December, made a more systematic effort to apply Zhdanov's theses to the East and in the course of his analysis touched on a number of issues which had clouded Soviet policies in recent years.[6] An alliance with "parts of the bourgeoisie, mainly the petty and middle sectors," for instance, is authorized so long as it is understood that Communists constitute the "main force of the anti-imperialist struggle." He appears to draw some guidance in this matter from the Chinese Communists, whose recent program he cites approvingly: the first tactical objective, according to the program, was "a union of workers, peasants, soldiers, students, commercial elements, all democratic parties and organizations, and all national minorities for the establishment of a united national front." Since, however, Zhukov uses interchangeably during the greater part of his article "bourgeoisie," "national bourgeoisie," and "big national bourgeoisie"—condemning them all—it is apparent that the precise line to be drawn between acceptable and non-acceptable bourgeois elements had still not been fixed; nor does his linking of Indonesia with China, Vietnam, and North Korea as countries where Communists have properly taken over leadership of the "united national front" clarify Moscow's intent. The lack of clarity on this point was to trouble many colonial parties in the years ahead—perhaps none as intensely as the Communist Party of India.[7]

[5] The two accounts of the conference seen by this writer are: "Velikaia oktiabr'skaia revoliutsiia i strany Vostoka," Akademiia nauk SSSR, *Vestnik*, No. 1, January 1948, pp. 39-46 (translated in *Soviet Press Translations*, III, 9, pp. 272-7) and B. Kremortat, "Sessiia Tikhookeanskogo instituta Akademii nauk SSSR," *Voprosy istorii*, No. 4, April 1958, pp. 151-7. Both articles summarized Zhukov's opening address and the dozen papers read at the conference, which dealt with China, India, Korea, Japan, Outer Mongolia, South America, and—in Southeast Asia—Indonesia and the Philippines. It was stated that many more papers than could be heard had been prepared and that all reports would be published in the Pacific Institute's *Uchenye zapiski*; subsequent issues of this irregular periodical contain no such reports.

[6] E. Zhukov, "Obostrenie krizisa kolonial'noi sistemy," *Bol'shevik*, No. 23, December 15, 1947, pp. 51-64; the issue went to press on December 29.

[7] The CPI's dilemma over this question is discussed in some detail in Kautsky,

Engagement & Disengagement: 1948-1954

Zhukov is less ambiguous on the question of neutralism in the colonial world, the "so-called theory of a third force." "According to this 'theory,'" Zhukov writes, "the countries of the East are to preserve a strict 'neutrality' in the struggle between Communism and imperialism." This is an "imperialist device," he argues, "to slander the USSR by placing it on the same level with American imperialism." The device should of course be exposed since the Soviet Union is not a force separate from the national liberation movements but in the same camp with them. This position, which grew directly from Zhdanov's two-camp thesis several months earlier, although not explicitly stated by him, was to remain a hallmark of Soviet policy in the colonial world during Stalin's lifetime.

Zhukov was again ambiguous, however, on a third tactical question, one which was soon to be of critical importance in the East: the question of armed struggle. He acknowledged the success of armed struggle in China and Vietnam, and included non-Communist Indonesia in the anti-imperialist camp because of the armed struggle there, yet nowhere did he imply that Communists elsewhere in the East should rise in arms against either foreign imperialism or a local bourgeois regime. Zealots in the colonies were left to draw what conclusions they could from the curious mixture of doctrine, folklore, and faith with which Zhukov closes his article: "The old mole of history burrows well. And inasmuch as an objective scientific analysis of the development of society leads to the irrefutable conclusion that 'all roads lead to Communism,' these roads will not be blocked; nor will the half of mankind in the colonial world, which imperialism has shackled and deprived of its most elementary rights, be checked in its efforts to achieve liberation."

Despite its ambiguities and inconsistencies, Zhukov's article

Moscow and the Communist Party of India, pp. 29ff. Kautsky considers that Zhukov's article in *Bol'shevik* was "neo-Maoist" with respect to the issue of alliance with the lower and middle bourgeoisie—that is, condoning such an alliance, in contrast to the "Leftist" line adopted by the CPI at this juncture and maintained until 1949.

represents a significant departure in Moscow's formulations on the colonial question. The implications of Zhdanovism in the East had not yet been fully analyzed, but an imminent change in Soviet views is forecast here.

If Zhukov's article in *Bol'shevik* was an effort to *apply* the doctrines of Zhdanovism to the East, a more active *projection* of these doctrines into the strategies of colonial parties occurred at the Southeast Asian Youth Conference in Calcutta in February 1948. Because of the Communist insurrections that broke out in Southeast Asia following this conference, a special significance has always attached to it. We need now to relate the Calcutta conference to Moscow's emerging strategies both in the colonial world at large and in Southeast Asia in particular.[8]

The conference, which was conceived as early as March 1947 (at an informal gathering of Communists and non-Communists in New Delhi), was originally to have been held in Indonesia in November but had to be postponed because of the first Dutch "police action." It was then rescheduled for Calcutta and met there from February 19 to 25, 1948, immediately preceding the Third Congress of the CPI. Invitations were issued by the co-sponsors of the conference, the World Federation of Democratic Youth (WFDY) and the International Union of Students (IUS), to youth groups in each of the Southeast Asian countries as well as in India, Pakistan, Ceylon, and Nepal. Thirty-nine organizations are reported to have sent delegations, representing all of the countries to which invitations had been sent except Thailand. A six-man Chinese Communist delegation was given full voting status at the opening of the conference. Observers and guests were present from Korea, Mongolia, Australia, Jugoslavia,

---

[8] The present writer, like all students of Communism in Southeast Asia, is much indebted to Ruth McVey for her detailed analysis of the meeting in Calcutta in *The Calcutta Conference and the Southeast Asian Uprisings* (1958). Miss McVey had access in her research to two accounts of the conference which are unfortunately not widely available: *Hands Off Southeast Asia!* (a Special Bulletin of the Colonial Bureau of the International Union of Students, published in Prague in April 1948) and *La jeunesse combat le colonialisme*, No. 1, 1948 (organ of the Colonial Bureau of the WFDY).

357

France, Canada, Czechoslovakia, and the USSR—the latter consisting solely of Central Asians.[9]

The records of the Calcutta conference reveal the militancy which had spread through the world Communist movement since Zhdanov's address at Wiliza Gora five months earlier. The "two-camp" doctrine penetrated all discussion. Asian regimes were judged by the vigor of their resistance to the "imperialist, anti-democratic" camp: thus Burma and India were criticized for having negotiated their independence from England and for maintaining allegedly cordial relations with London; Indochina and Indonesia, by contrast, were praised for their resistance, respectively, to the French and Dutch. The principal resolutions adopted by the conference violently attacked foreign imperialism of all sorts, especially American. The question of whether a resort to arms against imperialism was now appropriate was handled obliquely. No general endorsement of the tactics of "armed struggle" was given, yet the persistent praise of military successes in China, Indochina, and Indonesia must surely have suggested to the conferees the virtue of this course. The twin question of alliance with portions of the national bourgeoisie, meanwhile, was treated more forthrightly and resolved in favor of non-alliance. The national bourgeoisie, as an entity, was consigned to the "imperialist, anti-democratic camp"; the only united front condoned was "from below." The fact that deference was paid throughout the conference to the Chinese delegates, who were known to hold more moderate views on this subject, underscores the still tentative nature of Zhdanovist formulations as they applied to the East. The resolutions are a reminder that the natural tendency of Communists during a period of militancy, in the absence of directives to the contrary, is to adopt tactics traditionally identified as Leftist; alliance with any portion of the bourgeoisie is not such a tactic.

[9] Reports of the composition of the conference vary slightly; see McVey, *op. cit.*, pp. 7-9. The representatives from Southeast Asia appear to have included the following: seven from Vietnam (all Army officers); six from Indonesia; twelve from Burma (representing different organizations and including five observers); and two from Malaya. The size and status of the Philippine delegation are unclear.

358

Moscow's relationship to the Calcutta conference has been much discussed by students of world Communism. Some have felt that the conference conveyed an "instruction" to the Southeast Asian parties. The coincidence of so many Communist-led uprisings, it is argued, cannot otherwise be explained. If we assume that this argument refers to Moscow's *use* of the Calcutta meeting to pass on some general directive regarding armed insurrection—since the initial planning for the conference predated by many months Moscow's change of line—there are still objections to the hypothesis. For one, the composition of the conference did not make it a suitable vehicle for a revolutionary instruction. The delegates were for the most part non-Communist, nor was it ever intended they should be otherwise. The special role of the IUS and the WFDY in Soviet foreign policy after the war was to project Moscow's ideas on world affairs to Communist sympathizers and Leftists, but not necessarily to Communists themselves, precisely through such meetings as the Southeast Asian Youth Conference; they were not entrusted with a revolutionary function comparable to that formerly held by the Comintern and now, presumably, by the Cominform. Meanwhile, among the known Communists from Southeast Asia who did attend the conference only one—Than Tun of Burma—was a recognized party leader at the time. There is also the question of who might reasonably be supposed to have been the bearer of the alleged Soviet "instruction." Certainly not Vladimir Dedijer of Jugoslavia, at the moment of rupture between the Russian and Jugoslav parties;[10] nor, in all likelihood, Lawrence Sharkey of Australia, a controversial figure in the international movement engaged at this juncture in a bitter feud with the British Communist Party.[11] The Soviet Central Asians, in the meantime, none of whom held high rank in

[10] The first serious confrontation of Russian and Jugoslav party officials had taken place in Moscow in January 1948, a month and a half before the Calcutta conference; see Milovan Djilas, *Conversations with Stalin* (New York, 1962), pp. 133ff.

[11] A British Communist account of this dispute, which evidently dated back at least to the beginning of 1948, may be found in *World News and Views*, August 7, 1948, pp. 332ff.

359

the CPSU, appear to have played a negligible part in the proceedings of the conference. If weight is given to the thesis that the Calcutta conference was the occasion for passing some "instruction" to the Southeast Asians, the question of who might have carried it and to whom it might safely have been revealed remains puzzling. It will also become clear that the insurrections in Southeast Asia had their own logic and need not be explained solely in terms of Moscow's strategies or of some secret Soviet "instruction."

Denying that Moscow used the Calcutta conference to pass on a specific directive to the Southeast Asian parties, however, does not mean that the conference failed to serve a useful purpose in Soviet strategies. Zhdanovism was actively projected into Asia at Calcutta. If the conference was more agitational than operational, stressing "action rather than method," as Ruth McVey puts it,[12] it nonetheless quickened perceptibly the tempo of all revolutionary movements in Southeast Asia. Moscow cannot but have been pleased by the militant anti-imperialism of speaker after speaker at Calcutta (although the Soviet press, for reasons that are not clear, gave no coverage of the conference). It is another question, however, whether the course taken by Southeast Asian Communists after Calcutta, in part because of what transpired there, was the one Moscow intended. Certainly Moscow assumed that any aggressive instincts unleashed at Calcutta would be directed primarily against imperialism, and only incidentally against local bourgeois regimes—yet of the four major Communist uprisings subsequently to break out in Southeast Asia (in Burma, Malaya, Indonesia, and the Philippines) only one, the Malayan, fitted this description.

Soviet response to the ensuing rebellions in Southeast Asia followed no fixed pattern. Nor was there at the outset any effort to draw significant conclusions from Communist experience there which might be applied to the rest of the colonial world. The strategy of "armed struggle," for instance, was not proclaimed as the proper course for colonial parties, although the

[12] McVey, *op. cit.*, p. 15.

resort to arms by Communists was general throughout most of
Southeast Asia by the autumn of 1948; nor was there a clearer
formulation on the question of alliance with the national bourgeoisie, or any portion of it, than Zhukov had given in his article
in *Bol'shevik* the preceding December. A leading editorial which
appeared in August 1948 in *New Times* (the Soviet journal most
likely to come to the attention of colonial peoples) may be considered typical of Moscow's views during the period when the
Southeast Asian parties were everywhere turning to violence to
achieve their goals: the tendency of the world to divide itself
into two camps is reaffirmed; the inevitable failure of the imperialists' maneuvers is foreseen with the usual optimism of
Soviet commentators; Russia is said to serve as "a majestic
beacon . . . [which] illumines the path of oppressed humanity."
But the "illumination" Russia provides is no more explicit than
before Zhdanov's speech and Calcutta, as the next sentence indicates: "The sympathy displayed by the Soviet Union and by
the entire democratic camp inspires the enslaved peoples staunchly to resist all plans to perpetuate the moribund colonial system
of violence and oppression."[13] Moscow, despite its more truculent
pose in world affairs, still had only "sympathy" to offer to colonial revolutionaries; at least the Russian press would reveal
no more.

Soviet Orientalists, stung by charges of "bourgeois cosmopolitanism" in their studies,[14] made a more serious effort during a
conference in June 1949 to translate Moscow's obvious "sympathy" toward the colonial world into certain broad formulas

---

[13] "The Struggle of the Colonial Peoples," *New Times*, August 4, 1948, p. 3.

[14] The charges—current in all fields of Soviet scholarship during this era—
were made at a joint meeting of the Pacific Institute and the Oriental Institute of
the Academy of Sciences in March and were amplified in an editorial in the April
issue of *Voprosy istorii*. The editorial called attention to the "major part played
by the East in the current struggle between the forces of socialism and democracy
and the forces of imperialism and reaction" and asked why it was that so few
studies of the contemporary East were available; the leading Orientalist journal,
Sovetskoe Vostokovedenie, it was said, "has yet to discover the Twentieth Century."
See *Voprosy istorii*, No. 4, April 1949, pp. 3-8; a note on the March meeting,
when the charges were initially made, may be found in the same journal, No. 3,
March 1949, p. 155.

for action. Zhukov, evidently untouched by the recent criticism, was once again the keynote speaker. He touched on many of the topics he had treated in his article in *Bol'shevik* a year and a half earlier, but with a noticeably firmer hand. The armed struggle in a growing number of Eastern countries, he asserted, attests "not only to the increased scope of the national liberation struggle but also to a heightening of its qualitative level." He considered the armed risings specifically in China, Vietnam, Burma, Malaya, India, and Indonesia as "vivid testimony to the fact that the national liberation movement has entered upon a new higher stage of its development."[15] Another principal speaker at the conference, V. Maslennikov, referring to the same armed uprisings, noted that they "are not fortuitous, spontaneous outbursts but an organized class conscious struggle of the masses . . . led by the Communist Party [and directed] against the imperialists and internal reaction."[16] If such observations did not quite constitute a general instruction to all colonial Communist parties to proceed to armed insurrection, they came closer to it than any previously published commentaries on the colonial crisis.

A somewhat clearer distinction was made between the "national bourgeoisie" and the "petty and middle bourgeoisie" than had previously been drawn. The former was roundly condemned in its entirety and to its ranks were now added—along with all Kemalists, Gandhiists, pan-Arabists, and Zionists—such colonial leaders as Nehru and U Nu, who until this time had not incurred Moscow's full wrath. Zhukov's attack on Nehru, for instance, shows the distance Moscow had traveled since the Orientalist conference two years earlier when the projected alliance of the CPI with the Indian Congress had first been questioned; the defection of the national bourgeoisie, Zhukov asserts, is no-

[15] E. Zhukov, "Voprosy, natsional'no-kolonial'naia bor'ba posle vtoroi mirovoi voiny," *Voprosy ekonomiki*, No. 9, September 1949, p. 54; an English translation of the article (from which the excerpts here are taken) may be found in *Current Digest of the Soviet Press*, I, 49, pp. 3-6.

[16] V. Maslennikov, "O rukovodiashchei roli rabochego klassa v natsional'no-osvoboditel'nom dvizhenii kolonial'nykh narodov," *Voprosy ekonomiki*, No. 9, September 1949, p. 75; see also *Current Digest of the Soviet Press*, I, 49, pp. 6-7.

where more clearly seen than in the "metamorphosis of Nehru, who has turned from a Left-wing Congressite and exposer of imperialism into a nimble servant of two masters, Britain and the USA, and an ally of the Indian princes and landowners, a bloody strangler of the progressive forces of India." The "urban petty bourgeoisie," on the other hand, and "even a certain section of the middle bourgeoisie interested in being delivered from the imperialist yoke" are capable, it is said, of uniting with workers, peasants, and the intelligentsia in the struggle for national liberation. New categories, then, are added to differentiate between acceptable and non-acceptable bourgeois colonials, but the margin for error, we may imagine, was not significantly reduced.

Zhukov reaffirms, meanwhile, his earlier views on the "rotten little idea" of a third course between Communism and imperialism. He states: "The national reformists in the colonial and semi-colonial countries mendaciously insist upon their desire to 'remain aside' from the struggle of the two camps, upon their 'neutrality' in the 'ideological conflict,' as they put it, between the USSR and the USA, while in reality, acting in bloc with the reactionary bourgeoisie, they slander the USSR and actively aid the imperialists." Neutralism, which within three or four years was to become the hallmark of Soviet policy in the East, was still buried far beneath the Zhdanovist strategies.

One new theme is introduced in Zhukov's address to the Orientalists—the character of "people's democracy" in the colonies, which he sees as the ultimate objective of the national liberation movements. In the new "people's democracies" of the East, when they are formed, "the timing of the transition to the solution of socialist tasks, to building a socialist economy," Zhukov cautions, "may prove more protracted than in other countries of people's democracy which were not colonies." In respects other than the "tempo" of transition to socialism, however, the "people's democracies" in the East are (or will be) no different from those in Eastern Europe. It is clear from this linking of national liberation in the East to "people's democracy" in the Soviet sphere that Zhukov was groping toward a more explicit formu-

363

lation of the relationship of colonial revolution to the world revolution than had heretofore been attempted. Meanwhile, Zhukov's discussion of the rebellions in the East less as instruments of anti-imperialism than as vehicles for bringing "people's democracies" into existence indicates a shift in Moscow's attitude toward the colonial world. The Russians were at last taking an interest in the East for itself, not merely as a stepping-stone to revolution in Europe.[17]

The Orientalist conference of June 1949 in Moscow was the last occasion—or very nearly the last occasion—when Russians could speak forth as the unchallenged interpreters of revolutions in the East. As the Chinese Communists neared their goal of driving the nationalist government from the mainland, inevitably their voice in colonial affairs carried more and more weight; this was especially true in neighboring Southeast Asia, where the colonial struggle continued to be fiercest.

As early as November 1948 Liu Shao-chi had delivered the Chinese Communist view on the colonial question. The subject is not treated systematically in Liu's article—which was prompted by Jugoslavia's expulsion from the Cominform the previous June, an episode Liu treats much as Soviet commentators were treating it at the time—but his scattered references to the colonial question reveal at least one departure from views then current in Moscow. This concerned the tactical use to be made of a broad anti-imperialist front, a major feature of Chinese strategy at this juncture and now emphatically urged on neigh-

[17] A summary of other papers prepared for the Orientalist conference of June 1949 (including reports by Vasil'eva on Indochina, Guber on Indonesia, Zabozlaeva on the Philippines, and Bondarevskii on Malaya) may be found in *Voprosy ekonomiki*, No. 10, October 1949, pp. 74-93. An Indian volume, *Colonial People's Struggle for Liberation* (Bombay, 1949), also summarizes most of the reports read at the conference. Revised texts of eight reports, in most cases updated to include developments in China through October 1949, were published at the end of the year (with a new introductory chapter by Zhukov) in *Krizis kolonial'noi sistemy: natsional'no-osvoboditel'naia bor'ba narodov Vostochnoi Azii*; this volume was later published in English as *Crisis of the Colonial System: National-Liberation Struggle of the Peoples of East Asia* (Bombay, 1951). Papers read at the conference dealing with Southeast Asian countries are discussed later in the chapter.

boring colonial movements. Referring specifically to India, Burma, Siam, the Philippines, Indonesia, Vietnam, and South Korea, Liu wrote: "The Communists must establish anti-imperialist collaboration with the national bourgeoisie which is still opposing imperialism and which is not opposing the anti-imperialist struggle of the masses. If the Communists do not take such collaboration seriously and, on the contrary, oppose it or reject it, they are committing an exceptionally great mistake. Such collaboration must be established, even though it is temporary, unstable, and unreliable."[18]

Liu's view on this question and the view, say, of Zhukov (both in his December 1947 article in *Bol'shevik* and in his address to the Orientalist conference in June 1949) are not necessarily irreconcilable; in the context of doctrinal formulations on such matters, however, where a change of phrasing can imply profound distinctions, the difference between the two views is striking.

After the Chinese Communists had come to power, Liu Shao-chi spoke again on the colonial question in no less equivocal language. "The path chosen by the Chinese people," he told delegates attending a WFTU conference in Peking in November 1949, "is the path which must be followed by the peoples of many colonial and semi-colonial countries in their struggle to win national independence and a people's democracy." This path was expressed in four terms, Liu said. The first was a union of the working class "with all those classes, parties, groups, organizations, and individuals who wish to oppose the oppression of imperialism and its minions and to create a broad united front on a nation-wide scale"—a front, then, considerably broader than any proposed by Soviet spokesmen since 1947 and even than that indicated by Liu himself a year earlier. The second and third points concerned the dominant role of the working class in the united front and the need for a strong Communist Party to lead the masses—traditional strategies. The fourth, and most

[18] "Internationalism and Nationalism," *Pravda*, June 7-9, 1949; an English translation, from which this excerpt is quoted, may be found in *Soviet Press Translations*, IV, 14, pp. 423-39.

crucial, was the need "to create, wherever and whenever possible, strong people's armies of liberation . . . and supporting bases for the operation of these armies." Liu continued: "Armed struggle is the main form of struggle in the national liberation struggle in many colonies and semi-colonies. This is the main path followed in China by the Chinese people in winning their victory. This path is the path of Mao Tse-tung. It can also become the main path of the peoples of other colonial and semi-colonial countries for winning emancipation where similar conditions prevail."[19]

This was not, to be sure, the first time Chinese Communist spokesmen had spoken of armed struggle so unambiguously as the "main form" of struggle in the colonies.[20] Liu's statement of the new formula at the WFTU conference, however—a formula more compelling than Zhukov's and Maslennikov's in June—gave added weight to the virtue of armed struggle and made it virtually mandatory in the colonial world where conditions allowed it. The fact that Liu's speech was printed in the Cominform journal at the end of December and in *Pravda* several days later (January 4, 1950) indicates Moscow's acceptance of the Chinese formulation. A lead editorial in the Cominform journal on January 27, 1950, gave further approval to Peking's views on the colonial question: calling attention to Liu's speech and to the relevance of the Chinese experience to all colonial parties, the editorial emphasized again the virtue of the broadest possible "nation-wide united front" and the importance of armed struggle, "the main form of the national liberation movement in many colonial and dependent countries."[21] The Chinese and Cominform statements remove all doubt that, except in a few colonies,

[19] *For a Lasting Peace, for a People's Democracy!*, December 30, 1949, p. 2.

[20] E.g., Sha Ping, "The Lessons of Events in Indonesia," *World News and Views*, May 7, 1949, p. 228, translated from a Chinese Communist newspaper in "liberated China" in March; the author writes that "the main form of the national liberation struggle must be the armed struggle."

[21] "Mighty Advance of the National Liberation Movement in the Colonial and Dependent Countries," *For a Lasting Peace, for a People's Democracy!*, January 27, 1950, p. 1. Many of the same points were reiterated in a lead editorial entitled "China's Revolution and the Struggle Against Colonialism" which appeared in *People's China* on February 16, 1950 (pp. 3-5).

the optimum form of struggle is henceforth to be the armed struggle, the ultimate goal is to be "people's democracy," and the tactics to be used include a united front with portions of the national bourgeoisie. These formulations remained officially in force until Stalin's death.

To place Soviet colonial strategies in perspective, it is useful to distinguish between two separate developments in Moscow's foreign policy during this period, from late 1947 to early 1950. The first, in point of time, was the shift from the relatively moderate strategies of 1945-1947—reflected, for instance, in the parliamentary struggle of the French and Italian Communist parties —to the more militant line articulated by Zhdanov in September 1947 and reaching a crescendo in Liu Shao-chi's address in Peking in November 1949 and Moscow's explicit endorsement of his views the following January. The second development was a shift of Moscow's focus from Europe to Asia, at least insofar as immediate revolutionary objectives were concerned; this began about the time of the Calcutta conference in February 1948 and grew more pronounced as the Southeast Asian rebellions gathered momentum and as the victory of the Chinese Communists neared. While the reasons underlying these two developments in Soviet foreign policy are not unrelated, it should be noted that a shift to more aggressive tactics did not necessarily imply a turn to the East, or vice versa. It is therefore appropriate to consider separately the causes of these two developments, especially since Soviet interest in the East was to remain undiminished when the militant line gave way to moderation in the 1950's.

The shift from moderation to militancy in 1947—which has been described as an affirmation and intensification of a course already decided upon rather than a fundamental turn in Moscow's policies—may best be explained by the frustrations the Kremlin encountered in Europe in applying a basically non-revolutionary line. These frustrations multiplied during the first half of 1947. In France and Italy the legal, parliamentary efforts by Communists to expand their influence came to an end with their exclusion from the post-war coalition cabinets in each country. Another Foreign Ministers' Conference, this one in Moscow, collapsed over the question of Soviet claims for reparations. In March President Truman offered generous aid to Greece and Turkey to bolster their economies and make them less vulnerable to Communist threats, whether overt or covert. In June Secretary of State George C. Marshall proposed a plan for large-scale economic aid to all of Europe which ultimately was to serve the same purpose. It made no difference that these programs were designed to "contain" Communism, not necessarily to destroy it where it existed; to Moscow, intent on its own goals, the American policies were threatening and made obsolete tactics which for two years had held forth some promise of success. New strategies had to be devised if the forward momentum of Communism, which Stalin obviously believed in as well as desired, were to be sustained. It was this consideration which led to Zhdanov's speech at Wiliza Gora and to the creation of the Cominform. The significance of these events was soon manifested in a bitter sequence of Communist-led strikes in France and Italy at the end of the year and by the overthrow of the parliamentary regime in Czechoslovakia early in 1948.

The turn to the East also may be explained in part by Moscow's frustrations in Europe, especially by the singular failure of Communism to expand beyond the range of Russian armies. History repeated itself. In much the same way that Lenin had directed attention to the East following the setbacks to revolutionary movements in Europe after World War I, Stalin, following new setbacks in Europe after World War II, sought more fertile fields for revolution in Asia. The circumstances were of course different. Colonies were not in the same sense the "weakest links in the chain of imperialism," as they had been said to be after World War I; the "road to London" in 1947 did not as assuredly lie "through Hindustan" as Moscow professed to believe in 1920. There were, however, no less compelling reasons for Moscow's attention to the East in the late 1940's. For one, the restlessness of the colonial world was a reality. The national liberation struggles which Moscow was supporting in Indochina and Indonesia, and had briefly supported in India and Burma, were inevitably due to extend during the next decade throughout the rest of Asia and Africa. To have delayed too long the formulation of a clear policy for Communists affiliated with these movements would have been to allow leadership of them to pass by default to non-Communist elements; to have remained too long detached from the colonial struggle would have been to yield an advantage to the United States in future relations with the emerging nations—for Stalin must have appreciated that whatever Soviet propaganda said of American "imperialism" the American claim of friendship towards these nations was no weaker than Moscow's.

The turn to the East from 1947 on, then, may be seen as the result of these considerations. Zhukov's elaboration of Zhdanov's Cominform address, in December 1947, was in this sense not simply an effort to apply Zhdanov's theses to the colonial world but a reminder that Moscow was not indifferent to developments in the East; the Calcutta conference provided a convenient forum at which to drive this point home to Asians. These early beginnings of a new attention to the East should not be obscured by the fact that it was several years before Moscow successfully divorced its interest in the colonial question from continuing goals in the West, nor by the fact that Soviet preoccupation with the East never matched (and still does not match) its concern with Europe and the West. In the very relative and sliding scale of Soviet priorities in foreign affairs, especially in foreign revolutionary movements, a significant post-war concern for the East may be dated from 1947. It was to prove a shift in Soviet policy more enduring and of far greater importance in the long run than the militant course indicated by Zhdanov in September 1947.

Before turning to the Southeast Asian rebellions proper, we should finally relate Moscow's developing interest in the colonial question during 1948 and 1949 to events in China during these years. It is not clear when the Russians became convinced that the Chinese Communists would succeed in gaining power in

369

China,[22] but when they did, two conclusions doubtless followed from their appraisal. First, a Communist victory in China would obviously enlarge the prospects of Communist victories elsewhere in Asia. Moscow could hardly ignore these prospects. If the initial interest in the East cannot, with any precision, be related to developments in China, as time passed Chinese Communist successes bore a particular relevance to Soviet strategies. The Russians accordingly devoted increasing attention to East Asia and in the process made much of Chinese Communist experience. For a number of years they held it conspicuously forth as the model for other Asians; there is nothing in official commentaries to suggest they did so with misgivings.

Yet we would be short-sighted to imagine that there were no misgivings—which suggests the second conclusion Moscow may have reached as the Chinese Communists neared success. A Communist regime in China would exercise a powerful, if not decisive, influence over other Communist movements in East Asia, and perhaps eventually in other parts of the colonial world. Moscow's supremacy in doctrinal matters could become blurred; the Kremlin's authority in revolutionary strategy could be weakened; the strategies themselves could be obscured by being filtered through Peking. If the Russians could hardly express these possibilities aloud in 1948 and 1949, they were still real enough to stimulate new thinking about Moscow's colonial strategies. The surest way for Moscow to assure its continued prestige in the revolutionary East was to assume for itself greater initiative in providing guidance to the colonial movements. This may, for instance, explain the charges of "bourgeois cosmopolitanism" leveled at Soviet Orientalists in the spring of 1949 and the more militant posture of the latter in June—at a time when Soviet policy in Europe was absorbed in the Peace Movement and in seeking alternatives to Zhdanovism. What, in short, is suggested

[22] The present writer, in another study, concluded that Soviet policy turned decisively in favor of Mao's effort to seize power by force, on the assumption that he would ultimately succeed, as early as mid-1946; *Soviet Policy and the Chinese Communists*, pp. 255ff. Other students of Soviet policy in China date Moscow's belief in Chinese Communist success as late as the spring of 1949; see Beloff, *Soviet Policy in the Far East*, p. 64.

here is that Moscow, having found reasons of its own to turn its attention to the East in 1947 and 1948, applied itself with special vigor to the Eastern question during 1949 (and thereafter) in order to avoid seeing Peking become sole arbiter of Communist strategies in East Asia.

If the foregoing policy pre-dates by some years a demonstrable Sino-Soviet hostility, the writer can only suggest that one need not assume rivalry between China and Russia, or even significant lack of good will, to understand why Soviet leaders would have wished to ensure the continuity of Moscow's control over all aspects of world Communism. If the hypothesis set forth here is valid, we must of course consider at the proper time why Moscow retreated from a militant line in colonial affairs in the first half of the 1950's when Chinese Communist capabilities of providing vigorous leadership of Asian revolutionary movements was, if anything, greater than in 1949. This question may be discussed more fruitfully after we have traced the course of the revolutionary movements in Southeast Asia after 1947 and Moscow's response to them.

COMMUNIST INSURRECTION IN BURMA

Early in 1948 a document prepared by the Indian H. N. Ghoshal, who, as we have seen, played a significant part in the founding of Marxist groups in Rangoon before the war, profoundly affected the future course of Burmese Communist strategies. The document, known as the "Ghoshal Thesis,"[23] was clearly inspired by two events: Zhdanov's speech at Wiliza Gora, which is quoted at several points in the lengthy text, and a plenary meeting of the CPI in December 1947, which, also under

---

[23] A mimeographed translation in the author's possession is entitled Ba Tin [Ghoshal], *On the Present Political Situation in Burma and Our Tasks* (27 pp.). It appears to this writer to be an authentic document, although some uncertainty naturally attaches to the question inasmuch as the Burmese Communists have never published the paper. There is, however, frequent enough reference to the Ghoshal Thesis in other studies of Burmese Communism to admit of little doubt that such a document existed: see, for instance, *Burma and the Insurrections*, p. 4 (which refers to the document as "The Revolutionary Possibilities for 1948"); Thuriya Than Maung, *Burma and the Red State*, p. 5; and Trager, *Marxism in Southeast Asia*, p. 38.

the influence of Zhdanovism, adopted a sharply Leftist policy that was to guide the Indians for the next two years. Ghoshal attended this meeting and shortly thereafter drafted the thesis, either immediately before or following his return to Rangoon.[24] It was discussed by the Burmese Central Committee in February and adopted.

The Ghoshal Thesis is essentially a denunciation of the moderate policy adopted by the BCP in its resolution of July 30, 1947 (see above, pp. 337-38), in the wake of Aung San's assassination. This policy was now considered "opportunist," "reformist," and "tailist": its supporters, Ghoshal argued, wholly misunderstood the tenor of the era. "We are in a period of acute revolutionary crisis in the colonies," the thesis proclaimed, "where the national revolutionary movements headed by the working class and Communist Parties which play a decisive role in them today stand on the threshold of overthrowing the imperialist feudal order." The strategy which this situation indicated for the Burmese is summed up in the new slogans Ghoshal proposed (cited here as he set them forth):

No support to the present government—but its exposure—as a government of collaborationists—carrying out the dictates of Anglo-American imperialists—Burmese capitalists and landlords—betraying the fighting traditions of AFPFL-CP unity—betraying the January 1946 program of the AFPFL.[25]

National rising to tear up the treaty of slavery and assert real independence—take over British monopolies—land to the tiller—repudiate debts—smash imperialists—bureaucratic machinery.

Set up a people's government—based on AFPFL-CP unity—to carry through the democratic revolution.

Alliance and Co-operation with democratic China, fighting Vietnam and Indonesia, and all democratic countries and movements which are resisting Anglo-American imperialist domination.

[24] A reference in the text to "six months" having lapsed since the assassination of Aung San (July 19, 1947) suggests that the document was prepared during the latter half of January 1948.

[25] The AFPFL resolution of January 1946, adopted before the Communists had been expelled from the organization, had taken a strong stand on Burmese independence without concessions to the British.

That Ghoshal considered the adoption of these slogans a matter of some urgency is indicated by another passage in the thesis:

The fate of the Burmese Revolution and also of the revolutionary movements in India and other Southeast Asiatic countries are closely linked together. *The present situation places great responsibility on our shoulders. We could be the initiators of a new revolutionary upsurge and an uprising which is bound to lead to similar developments in the neighboring countries.* Much therefore depends upon how quickly we uproot this disease of reformism which is eating away the vitals of our Party and *swing our forces into action in the coming months.*[26]

It may be questioned whether the Ghoshal Thesis called for armed rebellion against the Nu government itself or solely against British imperialism, represented by British forces still in Burma under the terms of the Nu-Attlee Treaty.[27] U Nu is roundly denounced throughout the document as a "collaborator," "compromiser," and "hypocrite." Ghoshal writes, in attacking the "reformist illusion" of the July 30 resolution that Communists could achieve power by isolating U Nu through collaboration with his government: *"We totally forgot the Leninist principle that the imperialist bureaucracy and State machine cannot be taken over and run in the interest of the people; on the contrary, it has to be smashed."* Such remarks surely imply an intention to attack the government as well as British imperialism; a close reading of the Ghoshal Thesis, however, shows that the emphasis is predominantly on armed struggle against the latter and only incidentally against the former. It appears to have been Ghoshal's rather naïve idea that through leadership of a "national rising" against the Nu-Attlee Treaty the Communists would somehow come to power without having to undertake civil war. Circumstances, however, made civil war inevitable,

[26] The emphasis is as indicated in the copy of the Ghoshal Thesis in the author's possession.

[27] A military agreement, signed in August 1947 and included in the Nu-Attlee Treaty of October 17, provided that England would maintain certain bases and troops in Burma for the country's defense for a period of at least three years; see Cady, *A History of Modern Burma*, pp. 567-8.

and the Communists were obliged from the outset to direct their attacks almost exclusively at the Nu government, which defended itself with vigor; British forces were involved in the civil struggle only peripherally.

Following the adoption of the Ghoshal Thesis, Than Tun led a Burmese delegation to the Southeast Asian Youth Conference and the Second Congress of the CPI in Calcutta. One need not doubt the impression made upon the Burmese leader by the two meetings, especially the latter, which reaffirmed the Leftist line adopted at the December plenum of the CPI.[28] In his greetings to the Indian congress, it is reported, Than Tun indicated the intention of the BCP to overthrow the Rangoon government, if possible without fighting; should it be necessary to resort to arms, Than Tun said, the Communists were prepared to do so in order to "smash the imperialist-feudal-bourgeois combine, establish real independence, a people's democracy, and lasting peace."[29]

The Burmese returned to Rangoon early in March, accompanied by foreign observers (including Vladimir Dedijer and other Jugoslavs) who had attended the two recent conferences in Calcutta. All, it appears in retrospect, were greatly exhilarated. Communist-led strikes were ordered in Rangoon. On March 18 a giant peasant rally took place in Pyinmina (in Central Burma) attended by 75,000, according to Burmese government sources. Speeches by Ghoshal, Than Tun, and others were warmly applauded. Resolutions passed by the rally acclaimed minority groups, such as the Arakanese, who had successively fought the Japanese, the British, and the AFPFL to secure their independence; approved forceful seizure of lands previously leased for peasant cultivation, "whether or not the landlords acquiesce"; supported strikes currently in progress in Rangoon;

[28] For a discussion of the critical Second Congress of the CPI, see Kautsky, *Moscow and the Communist Party of India*, pp. 46-52.

[29] Trager, *Marxism in Southeast Asia*, pp. 38-9, citing a mimeographed text of Than Tun's greetings to the CPI on February 28, 1948. A British Communist account of the CPI's Second Congress makes no mention of Than Tun's speech, but notes the presence of a ten-man Burmese delegation led by him; *World News and Views*, April 3, 1948, p. 135.

and vowed a determination to "smash Fascism (AFPFL) by all possible means."[30]

The unexpectedly enthusiastic response at Pyinmina, which appears to have impressed the foreign observers (especially the Jugoslavs) no less than the Burmese themselves, was a decisive factor in the future course of the BCP.[31] On March 27, eight days after the Pyinmina meeting, Than Tun is reported to have delivered an inflammatory speech at a public rally in Rangoon calling for an open revolt against the AFPFL and for "the blood of the socialists." The next day, according to official Burmese sources, the Communist leaders went underground and issued orders for a general uprising against the government.[32] At the time of writing (1965) the insurrection of the Burmese Communists has still not been formally called off.

A detailed chronology of the Communist insurrection in Burma (assuming one could be composed) is beyond the scope of the present study. It is useful, however, before analyzing Soviet and other foreign Communist reactions to the rebellion to make several observations concerning its origins and the way it developed.

No single episode brought the Burmese Communists to the point of openly defying the Nu government. It was rather a chain of circumstances and events, each adding a new dimension to the restlessness of the BCP leaders and contributing to their

[30] *Burma and the Insurrections*, p. 41; the identity of "Fascism" and the AFPFL is explicit, according to the text of the resolutions in this official government report. It should be noted that the government's explanation of the large attendance as well as of the expansive mood at Pyinmina was that the harvest had just been completed and the peasants, with ready cash in their pockets, were in a jubilant frame of mind; "they had not had such mass fun during all the five years preceding" (*ibid.*, p. 16).

[31] Several sources call attention to the part played by the Jugoslavs in goading the Burmese leaders on to more vigorous action after the Pyinmina meeting: e.g., Cady, *op. cit.*, p. 583, and Thuriya Than Maung, *op. cit.*, p. 6. The latter writer told the author that later in 1948 (after the Jugoslavs' break with Moscow) spokesmen in Belgrade acknowledged to visiting Burmese Socialists some measure of Jugoslav responsibility for the rebellion of the White Flag Communists; interview in Mandalay in January 1962.

[32] *Burma and the Insurrections*, pp. 17-8. U Than Maung, in his interview with the author, stated that the order for the rising was given only after the government had issued a warrant for the arrest of the BCP leaders on March 28.

resolution to take to arms: the adoption of a Leftist course by the Indians in December, Ghoshal's vigorous application of this policy to Burma in January, the two exuberant conferences at Calcutta in February, the successes of strikes in Rangoon and the peasant rally at Pyinmina in March. Whether, if less congenial incidents had occurred to dampen the enthusiasm induced by these developments, there would still have been insurrection at the end of March, it is not possible to say. No exclusive significance, at any event, attaches to the Southeast Asian Youth Conference as the source of the Burmese rising—an argument made by those who look upon the Calcutta conference as the occasion for a Soviet "instruction" to the Southeast Asian parties; the Burmese Communists might well have taken to arms when they did had there been no Youth Conference at Calcutta, or no Burmese delegation present at it.

It should also be noted that the disorders in Burma in 1948 and thereafter were not solely of Communist origin. Although the first open revolt against the Rangoon government (other than the relatively inconsequential revolt of the Red Flag Communists under Thakin Soe, which had been in progress since 1946) was led by White Flag Communists, within four or five months the People's Volunteer Organization (PVO), Karen and Mon nationalist organizations, and even sections of the army had turned against the government and gone underground. Co-ordination between the activities of these various groups was irregular and temporary, a principal factor in the survival of the Nu regime. Personal rivalries and ambitions as much as, if not more than, significant ideological differences kept the rebels apart.[33] As a result, by the early 1950's the separate insurgent forces had been reduced to a state of little more than dacoity, a condition endemic in Burmese rural life.

The government, in addition to its military campaigns to isolate and wipe out the insurgent pockets, sought various peaceful means of bringing the insurrection under control. As early as July 1948, a conference of Communist and Socialist leaders

[33] See Trager, *op. cit.*, p. 40, and Cady, *op. cit.*, p. 595.

376

was called in Rangoon to unite the warring Marxists: the Socialists—all above ground—attended, as well as several Communist
leaders released from jail for the occasion; but no guerrilla leaders appeared.[34] The government also issued periodic amnesty
decrees, extending them frequently, and offered liberal terms to
any who made use of them.[35] In 1950, in an effort to give the
Communists an opportunity to express their views legally and
thus, it was hoped, remove the necessity for their continuing the
rebellion, the government authorized the formation of two pro-
Communist organizations, the Burma Workers and Peasants
Party (BWPP) and the Trade Union Council (Burma)—or
TUC (B); both were affiliated with the WFTU.[36] Steps were
also taken, as in Malaya and the Philippines, to rehabilitate captured Communists by teaching them useful trades and giving
them reindoctrination lectures. These measures blunted the impact of the Communist revolt but did not break the determination of the White Flag leaders to continue their insurgency.

Developments within the BCP are obscure during the early
years of the insurrection. According to a former guerrilla who
served as a regional leader for the Communists from 1949 to
1954, the party's strategies shifted erratically during this period.
In 1948 and 1949 the strategy was said to be "total war," and
such agrarian policies as the BCP pursued were directed against
well-to-do peasants as much as against the landlords. In 1950,
however, under the influence of the Chinese Communists, the
military strategy shifted to "peace and unity"—unity, that is,

[34] Thein Pe Myint, who had left the BCP by this time, attended this conference and described it to the author during an interview in January 1962; the
principal Communist representative was Aung Min, who rejoined the guerrillas
after the failure of the conference and remained underground for a dozen years
before making use of an amnesty offer in 1961.

[35] The first amnesty offer was made in July 1950 and was repeated at intervals
during the next decade; see Cady, *op. cit.*, p. 595.

[36] Neither of these organizations were admitted into the AFPFL, however, and
so were excluded from any effective role in the government. Within the AFPFL
the most radical position was held by U Ba Swe, who acknowledged his Marxist
views but denied the relevance of Soviet, Chinese, or other foreign Communist
experience to Burmese Marxism; his speeches and writings during the early years
of the insurrection are included in U Ba Swe, *The Burmese Revolution* (Rangoon,
1952).

with other insurgents, including the Red Flag Communists; the party's agrarian policies were similarly modified to secure an alliance with the rich peasants against the landlord class. By 1954, it is said, the BCP was calling for an end to the civil war; as in Malaya, however, the Communists were willing to negotiate only on the basis of the government's acknowledgment of their strength—a strength which was by then largely illusory.

Than Tun's leadership, in the meantime, was challenged on several occasions early in the 1950's. In 1953, for instance, it is reported that a meeting of guerrilla commanders at Pyinmina adopted a resolution of "no confidence" in the Party Secretary; the resolution, however, did not reach the Central Committee, where Than Tun's control was firm (supported by Ghoshal, Ba Thein Tin, Thakin Zin, and others). A similar protest of regional leaders in Upper Burma in December 1954 also failed to weaken Than Tun's position. Thereafter the opposition gradually disintegrated, most of its leaders (including the author's informant for the foregoing information) taking advantage of the government's most recent offer of amnesty.[37]

If these scraps of information about the internal affairs of the BCP are too meager to allow us to reconstruct a reliable history of the Burmese movement during the early phase of the rebellion, they can at least remind us that a party organization continued to exist, facing its own leadership and policy problems—as do political formations everywhere.

There was no immediate response in the Soviet press to the uprising in Burma. Three months after it began, a brief commentary in *New Times* reviewed recent events in Burma and

---

[37] The ex-guerrilla in question is U Than Maung, now a journalist in Mandalay. The two published accounts of his experience with the BCP—in translation, *No Man, Lawyer or Doctor, Is Infallible* and *Burma and the Red Star* (see Bibliography)—are written in highly emotional vein, soon after his defection from the BCP, and would normally disqualify U Than Maung as a reliable informant for our purposes; the author's lengthy interviews with U Than Maung in Mandalay in January 1962, however, were reassuring and showed him capable of detached analysis of Burmese Communist developments. The evidence presented above is drawn from the interviews rather than the published works but still must be accepted with great caution.

criticized the government for its "draconic measures against the popular movement" and for outlawing the Communist Party on the grounds that the disorders were due to " 'Communist incitement.' " The item did not, however, show unstinting approval of the rebellion and was surprisingly moderate with regard even to U Nu. Commenting on U Nu's recent announcement of a program for nationalization, the author stated: "The future will show whether the Premier of Burma really intends to satisfy the hopes and desires of the people, or whether the British press is right in estimating his statement as a 'propaganda stroke' " —a reference to speculation in certain British newspapers that U Nu's threat of nationalization was merely to attract greater domestic support. In all of this there was little acknowledgment of a serious insurrection underway in Burma led by Communists.[38] A British Communist commentary about the same time was more attentive to the BCP and more critical of U Nu. He was attacked for having rejected a rapprochement with the Communists proposed by the PVO (this was before the PVO had joined the rebellion); his hypocrisy in November 1946 was recalled, when he had expelled the Communists from the AFPFL while shouting "Long Live Communism!" Burmese workers and peasants, the British Communist writer asserted, were more and more turning to the combined PVO-BCP leadership to combat "Nu-ism."[39]

By September the Soviet press indicated that U Nu had justified Moscow's worst fears. A Soviet commentator wrote in *Izvestiia* that the premier's promise of nationalization was rank deception "inasmuch as the provocative tone of this declaration merely helped the English and American press to open a slanderous campaign regarding the 'Communist menace' in Southeast Asia"; this, in turn, would hasten the dispatch of "imperialist" troops to Burma who would in the end support the Nu government—exactly as U Nu had foreseen. Further evidence of his betrayal of the country is seen in his declaration of martial law

---

[38] "Burma Unvanquished," *New Times*, July 7, 1948, pp. 17-8.

[39] Geoffrey Parson, "What's Brewing in Burma?" *World News and Views*, July 10, 1948, p. 282; see above, p. 338n., for Thakin Nu's remarks on Communism in November 1946.

in August and his willingness to accept British assistance in crushing the national liberation movement. The Communists, meanwhile, are nowhere mentioned as such in the article; the insurrection is described as having begun, not as a result of any overt decision by the BCP or its allies, but in the wake of strikes in British-owned oil fields during March.[40] In October a more detailed review of Burmese developments in *New Times* implied, for the first time, that Communists were leading the insurgency; the uprising was said to have extended to nearly one-third of the country and to have resulted in the formation of "popular governments" which were already undertaking radical social and economic reforms.[41]

Soviet comment on Burma continued in this vein during 1949. Primary responsibility for the insurrection was now placed more squarely on the Nu government: repressive acts by the government dating from the end of 1947, it was said, had provoked the strikes in March 1948 which led to the uprising.[42] Soviet writers, it appears, wished at this juncture to conceal the initiative of Burmese Communists by arguing that their action was defensive, presumably to guard against the risk of failure; should they succeed, there would be time to place the decision to take up arms in a proper Communist perspective. The Soviet press also referred during this period to American support of the Nu regime, though with no evidence to sustain the claim.[43] The progress of the insurrection, meanwhile, is reported favorably. One-half of the country was said to be under rebel control by the spring of 1949 and popular governments were noted in the "liberated" areas. "A united committee representing all progressive forces

---

[40] I. Plyshevskii, "Polozhenie v Birme," *Izvestiia*, September 12, 1948; a translation of this article may be found in *Soviet Press Translations*, III, 19, pp. 586-8.

[41] I. Alexandrov, "Events in Burma," *New Times*, October 6, 1948, pp. 9-13.

[42] E.g., A. Leonidov, "Labour Imperialism's Colonial Strategy in Burma," *ibid.*, February 9, 1949, p. 10.

[43] E.g., *Pravda*, May 21, 1949, p. 3, citing a report from Delhi. No formal offer of American aid, insofar as is known, was made to the Nu government until the spring of 1950; this led to a technical aid agreement in September 1950 which lasted for two years when, as we shall see, it was denounced in Rangoon.

in Burma," an observer wrote in May, "has taken over government functions," and he went on to enumerate them.[44]

The implication of Soviet references to a rival regime in Burma
by mid-1949 is that Moscow was considering formal recognition of
this regime, as it extended formal recognition to Ho Chi Minh's
government in Vietnam early the following year. This was the
moment of truth, we may imagine, in Moscow's relationship to
the Burmese uprising, coinciding with the realization that Communist success in China was now virtually assured. Had the Russians recognized a clandestine government led by Than Tun, the
course of the rebellion and certainly of future Soviet-Burmese
relations would have been very different. Moscow did not recognize such a government. Indeed a perceptible decline in Soviet
interest in the Burmese insurrection may be detected after the
spring of 1949. No paper on Burma, for instance, was prepared
for the important conference of Soviet Orientalists in June 1949,
although reports were delivered on all other Southeast Asian
countries. Nor was there a chapter on Burma in the critical
volume *Krizis kolonial'noi sistemy* published at the end of 1949.
The important editorial in *For a Lasting Peace, for a People's
Democracy!* on January 27, 1950, while it mentions the Burmese revolt in passing, singles out other rebellions—notably in
China, Vietnam, and Malaya—to illustrate the success of the
strategy of armed struggle.

A number of reasons may explain Moscow's declining interest
in the Burmese rising; indeed, its interest from the outset had
never matched that in Communist uprisings elsewhere in Southeast Asia. One perhaps obvious reason was a sense that the course
of events in Burma could not affect Soviet interests as critically
as events in Indochina, Indonesia, or India; Moscow seems not,
in short, to have shared Ghoshal's view, expressed before the rebellion broke out, that the Burmese rising could be pivotal in the
revolutionary course of Southeast Asia. The Burmese rebellion,
meanwhile, was less satisfactory than the rising in Malaya, with

[44] N. Pakhomov, "Sobytiia v Birme," *Izvestiia*, June 25, 1949, p. 2; see also
Pravda, May 27, 1949, p. 3.

which it is most readily compared, because it was directed less against imperialism than against the local nationalist leadership—however Soviet spokesmen sought to conceal this fact. So long as Soviet policy continued to emphasize the assault on imperialism, especially American, a colonial rebellion not directly serving this end must ultimately lose Moscow's attention. The Russians must also have had misgivings about the divided leadership of Burmese Communism and the undisciplined nature of what passed as Burmese Marxism. In this connection it is significant that the Soviet press rarely mentioned Than Tun by name, although his control over the brand of Burmese Communism most loyal to Moscow admits of little doubt.[45] With respect to the prospects of ultimate Communist success in Burma, Moscow would have had good grounds, despite gains reported in the Soviet press, for doubting the strength of the BCP—especially when compared with that of the Malayan party, with its strong roots in the labor movement, or of the Philippine and Vietnamese parties, with their armies still intact from World War II. Finally, there was an alternative to revolution in Burma that was not everywhere present in Southeast Asia, an alternative to which the Russians eventually turned, as we shall in due course discover.

The Burmese insurrection, then, seems to have been something of an ugly duckling in Soviet eyes. It deserved acknowledgment, and this was given, but it warranted no unusual enthusiasm. As time passed, though it is premature to speak of this as early as 1950, the Burmese rebellion was allowed to slip into obscurity and insignificance. Neither the errors of Burmese Communists nor their sacrifices were deemed worthy of notice.

Contacts between the Burmese Communists and foreign parties after the outbreak of the insurrection are, needless to say, difficult to trace. The British Communists appear to have lost interest in Burma after its independence and its decision to remain outside

---

[45] The only mention of Than Tun in the Soviet or Cominform press during the Burmese insurrection noted by this writer is in a letter from a Burmese Communist published in *For a Lasting Peace, for a People's Democracy!* September 17, 1951, p. 4; the letter quotes from a speech Than Tun had recently made to members of the People's Army.

the Commonwealth. Far less attention was given in the British Communist press to the Burmese insurrection, for instance, than to the Malayan.[46] The British, moreover, appear to have been quite out of touch with the BCP by the spring of 1948, to judge from a reference in *World News and Views* to Thein Pe Myint, who by this time had broken with the party, as a "Communist member of the Provisional Government."[47] The Indian Communists, whose policies had influenced the BCP at most critical junctures in its history, also appear to have lost contact with the Burmese as the insurrection proceeded. A former Burmese Communist speaks of ties with the CPI through 1948 but states that thereafter they ended;[48] students of Indian Communism note no significant contacts between the Indian and Burmese parties after the Second Congress of the CPI in February 1948. Liaison with the Russians was impossible during an era of martial law in Burma and when Moscow would in any case have been circumspect in its behavior in order to counteract the wide-spread belief that the Burmese insurrection was part of a larger Soviet plot to subvert all of Southeast Asia. By the time the first Russian diplomatic mission reached Rangoon in 1951, Moscow's policies had shifted and any effort to contact the BCP was presumably out of the question.[49]

The Chinese Communists, it appears, maintained a closer relationship to the Burmese insurgents than British, Indian, or Russian. By the end of 1949, when the Chinese Red Army had overrun all of South China, direct liaison with the Burmese guerrillas

[46] The last item on the Burmese rebellion discovered in *World News and Views* is in the issue of September 25, 1948 (p. 414); coverage of the Malayan Emergency continued until 1950.

[47] *World News and Views*, April 3, 1948, pp. 133-5; the reference precedes the text of an address delivered by Thein Pe on January 1, 1948.

[48] Interview with U Than Maung.

[49] Some years later, according to a former Soviet diplomat who defected to the West in Rangoon in 1959, a secret meeting was held at the Soviet Embassy between a high Russian official and a representative of the BCP; this meeting, the purpose of which was allegedly to reassure the BCP of Soviet sympathy toward it despite Moscow's cordial relations with the Burmese government, was said to have been the first direct contact with the Burmese Communists in many years. Interview with Alexander Kaznacheev, March 1960; Kaznacheev served as interpreter at the meeting, which took place during 1958.

was possible, and there are numerous reports of intercourse between the two parties during the following years. Chinese military advisers are said to have been active with the insurgents and to have provided both arms and training to Communist units;[50] hundreds of Burmese guerrillas are reported to have received training in China from early 1950 on;[51] after the establishment of diplomatic relations between Burma and China in 1950, the Chinese Embassy in Rangoon is alleged to have been the principal channel for instructions to Burmese Communists both above ground and in the jungle.[52] While these reports, based on non-Communist sources, are obviously difficult to verify in Communist documentation, there is no good reason to doubt Chinese influence in the Burmese movement after 1949. Burma, it may be imagined, presented to the new regime in Peking a situation analogous to that in North Vietnam, a ready-made armed insurrection which could be used as a vehicle for extending Chinese Communist influence into Southeast Asia. It is worth noting in this connection that Liu Shao-chi, in his address at the WFTU conference in Peking in November 1949, gave a higher priority to the Burmese insurrection than Soviet publications did at this juncture: twice in his address he mentioned the Burmese rebellion immediately after the Vietnamese, and ahead of the anti-imperialist struggles in Malaya, the Philippines, Indonesia, and elsewhere. According to the former Burmese guerrilla cited previously, the purpose of Chinese strategy in 1950 and 1951 was to

[50] Declassified Intelligence reports in Malayan government files occasionally refer to interrogations of captured Burmese guerrillas who testify to the presence of Chinese officers in North Burma; U Than Maung, both in his published studies and to a lesser degree in his interviews with the author, also reports the activities of Chinese military advisers in the North.

[51] For a detailed summary of these reports in the Burmese press, see Johnstone, *Burma's Foreign Policy*, pp. 180-4.

[52] Burma was the first non-Communist nation to recognize the Peking government, in December 1949; ambassadors were exchanged, after some delay, in June 1950. Kaznacheev (the former Soviet diplomat in Rangoon) reports that the Chinese Embassy assumed responsibility for Burmese Communist strategies from the outset and, even after the establishment of the Soviet Embassy in Rangoon the following year, continued to guide the BCP without consultation with the Russians.

shift the base of guerrilla operations to North Burma, precisely in order to facilitate Chinese liaison.[53]

Peking's failure to press its advantage in Burma as vigorously as in Vietnam must be attributed to considerations other than the matter of access to the BCP and the latter's receptivity to Chinese aid. Many of the considerations which deterred Soviet interest in Burma deterred Peking less, we may imagine, but the Chinese like the Russians found an alternative in Burma which had the effect of muffling, if not extinguishing, their interest in the revolutionary course.

THE MALAYAN EMERGENCY

The Fourth Plenum of the Malayan Communist Party, which met in Singapore from March 17 to 21, 1948, marked a turning point in the strategies of Malayan Communism comparable to the adoption of the Ghoshal Thesis in Burma six weeks earlier. It met after the conferences in Calcutta at the end of February and was influenced by them more than any other local party meeting in Southeast Asia. The dominant figure at the Fourth Plenum was the Australian Communist leader Lawrence Sharkey, who had stopped over in Singapore en route home from Calcutta. He is said to have delivered a scathing criticism of the MCP's past policies, especially the decision to dissolve the MPAJA after the war, and to have conveyed to the Malayans the significance of the new international line which had evolved since Zhdanov's Cominform speech six months earlier.[54] Sharkey, whose views on

---

[53] Interview with U Than Maung; the maneuver, according to U Than Maung, met some opposition within the BCP, which was reluctant to give up its base in central Burma, but was frustrated in the last analysis by the government's suspicion of just such a move and its tightening of the ring around the Pyinmina area.

[54] "Basic Paper on the Malayan Communist Party," Vol. I, Part 2, pp. 43-4. Sharkey's activities in Singapore have never been fully detailed, insofar as this writer is aware, but are mentioned in several accounts of Malayan Communism: e.g., Brimmell, *Communism in Southeast Asia*, p. 255, and Pye, *Guerrilla Communism in Malaya*, p. 84. The latter account cites as follows the evidence of a former Australian Communist: "Sharkey told us, too, how he had been commissioned by the Comintern [*sic*] representatives at the Indian Congress to convey decisions to the Malayan Communists"; *The Great Decision: The Autobiography of an Ex-Communist Leader* [Cecil H. Sharpley] (London, 1952), p.

world affairs at this time are known to have been radical,[55] evidently served as a catalyst to the Malayans: stunned as they were by the revelations of the Loi Tek episode, which was now generally known throughout the party, leaders and rank and file alike were receptive to strategies that would have taken them as far as possible from Loi Tek's course.

The Fourth Plenum passed three resolutions, according to Malayan sources. The first was a political analysis of the situation in Malaya which concluded that inasmuch as the Labour government in London had shown itself no different from its predecessors in protecting Britain's imperialist interests, the struggle for independence must ultimately take the form of a "people's revolutionary war"; the MCP stood ready to provide leadership in "this most glorious task." The second resolution, regarding political strategies, set two tasks before the party: reversal of the former "ostrich policy" of "surrenderism" (manifested in the dissolution of the MPAJA, the acceptance of self-rule instead of full independence, and the party's retirement behind front organizations); and preparation of the masses for an uncompromising struggle for independence, without regard to considerations of legality. The third resolution stressed the need to restore party discipline, after the laxness of the Loi Tek era. The resolutions did not, then, specifically call for an uprising, although as internal party documents they might well have done so had it been the intention of the leadership to proceed immediately to armed insurrection. They stressed the urgency of *preparing* for rebellion, not yet of precipitating one. The national liberation movement in Malaya at the present stage is described as "a democratic revolution of a bourgeois nature," including the petty bourgeoisie and national capitalists along with workers and peasants; the former

---

111. The only Malayan delegate known to have been present at the Calcutta conferences—Li Sung, representing the Democratic Youth League—is said to have returned via Rangoon and was evidently not present at the Fourth Plenum; "Basic Paper on the Malayan Communist Party," Vol. 1, Part 2, p. 43.

55 Sharkey's sharp opposition at this time to the mildness of British Communist policies has been referred to above (see p. 359). While in Singapore in March he published an attack on the CPGB in a "theoretical journal" of the MCP; see *World News and Views*, August 7, 1948, p. 332.

will ultimately defect, the second resolution asserts, and it is this which accents the need to strengthen proletarian leadership of the liberation movement.[56]

The Fifth Plenum, which convened on May 10, moved the Malayan Communists closer to open rebellion. The short interval between the two plenary meetings, the party leaders explained, was due to the government's growing suppression of legal Communist activities. A vigorous twelve-point "plan of struggle" was adopted to counter the government's program. According to a text subsequently recovered by the Malayan government, the "plan of struggle" emphasized the primacy henceforth of illegal work; urged that trade unions be used as vehicles of anti-British propaganda; called for strikes specifically aimed at the disruption of the Malayan economy; demanded a more vigorous assault on the democratic parties and on the national bourgeoisie (including Chinese elements sympathetic to the Kuomintang); and proposed measures to attract intellectuals and peasants to the Communist cause.

The government's restrictions on Communist activity increased throughout the spring, especially in the labor field. On May 31 the government banned any federation of labor unions except by trade and decreed that Trade Union officials must have a minimum of three years' experience in labor organizations. The measures effectively crippled overt Communist influence in the labor movement since Communist strength had been greatest in the Pan Malayan Federation of Trade Unions (PMFTU), which was now illegal, and since most Communists had served in the MPAJA until the end of 1945 and so were ineligible for election as Trade Union officials. About the same time the government began systematically to use its powers of banishment and deported many undesirable Chinese, most of them suspected Communists, who did not hold citizenship. The Communists re-

---

[56] Translations of the three resolutions of the Fourth Plenum, as well as of the "plan of struggle" adopted by the Fifth Plenum (discussed below), are in Malayan government archives; they have not been published in full, insofar as the author is aware, although quotations from them appear in various Malayan publications on the Emergency.

sponded to these steps by initiating a wave of assassinations and public terror. On June 16 the murder of three British planters in Perak led to a declaration of a state of emergency—first in Perak and presently throughout the country. The "Emergency" was to remain officially in force for the next dozen years.

Where responsibility for the Emergency should properly be placed has engaged students of Malayan Communism for many years. The Communists have argued persistently that they were provoked into rebellion by the crippling restrictions placed upon them by the British during the spring of 1948; even during periods of maximum success in their jungle warfare, they were not moved to acknowledge any initiative on their part in bringing on the civil strife. Infrequently—and, of course, inadvertently—British sources have given some support to the Communist claim: a government pamphlet issued in 1949, for instance, mentions the decrees of May 31 as giving the *"coup de grace"* to Communist hopes and refers to the deportations as "hastening" the MCP's change of tactics. The Communists, this pamphlet states, "raced against time" to consolidate their strength in the labor movement before the government could transform it into a source of loyal support; when the Communists lost this race, they turned to open revolt.[57] The usual British view, however, is that the uprising was a calculated move on the part of the MCP, inspired by the Southeast Asian Youth Conference at Calcutta and by Sharkey's visit to Singapore immediately following it.[58] The British argument, indeed, is the principal stimulus to the widely held view of the importance of the Calcutta meeting in post-war Soviet strategies in the colonial world.

However one may weigh the evidence of British "provocation" *versus* the evidence of a calculated strategy by the party leadership, the mood of the Malayan Communists in the spring of 1948 was such that an insurrection not very different from the

[57] *Communist Banditry in Malaya: The Emergency, June 1948-December 1949,* pp. 1-2.

[58] See, for instance, *The Fight Against Communist Terrorism in Malaya* (1951; 2nd ed., 1953), pp. 6-7; *The Danger and Where It Lies* (1957), pp. 13-4; and *The Communist Threat to the Federation of Malaya* (1959), p. 16. All are official government publications relating to the Emergency.

one that broke out in June would doubtless have developed before the end of the year. The Fourth and Fifth Plenums had advanced the Malayan Communists too far along the road to insurrection to permit retreat—short of a major shift in world Communist strategy, which of course was nowhere in sight during this period. British "provocation," it may be argued, did no more than hasten a step the Malayan Communists had already determined to take.

The course of the Malayan insurrection does not directly concern us, any more than the course of that in Burma. The MCP's concept of its insurrection, however, and the general strategies it devised during the early years of the Emergency are of significance. It is useful, before we turn to Moscow's view of the insurrection, to piece these together from Malayan Communist documents which have recently come to light.

Six months after the Emergency was proclaimed in Malaya the MCP issued a lengthy analysis of the civil war which was to serve as the basic instruction to party cadres for the next five or six years. It was entitled "Strategic Problems of the Malayan Revolutionary War"—after Mao Tse-tung's "Strategic Problems of China's Revolutionary War," written in 1936. Mao is quoted extensively in the document and the influence of Chinese Communism on the Malayans is apparent in many ways. The struggle for liberation in Malaya, the document asserts, has the character of a "new democratic revolution." A coalition of forces is engaged in the struggle: primarily, workers (Chinese and Indians) and peasants (Malays); secondarily, the urban petty bourgeoisie, junior civil servants, and the intelligentsia. The national bourgeoisie "also forms an integral part of this spirit," despite its "fixed and narrow" revolutionary nature which places its ultimate reliability in some doubt. The Malayan revolution is especially favored, the document continues, by prospects of Communist success in China; it is handicapped by the grip of British imperialism on Malaya and by the absence of bases, rear areas, local government and foreign aid. Because of these handicaps, the party's tactics must be flexible. Precisely the flexibility in Chinese tactics

389

must be the Malayans' model, and Mao is quoted at some length to illustrate the essence of flexibility and maneuverability in a protracted war. Chinese tactics per se, the document cautions, are for the most part inapplicable in Malaya, "a small, sparsely populated country governed by direct British rule"; an effort, for instance, to seize power immediately, as in China, would lead only to disaster. Not until the Malayans had covered the ground already covered by Chinese Communism would it be appropriate to speak of "a strategic counter-offensive." In the meantime the Malayans must construct an army, create bases and rear areas, maintain the initiative even though the basic strategy is defensive—and be patient.[59]

The striking reliance of this basic Malayan document on Chinese doctrine and experience inevitably raises a question as to whether Malayan Communist behavior in 1948 is not, after all, traced most plausibly to the Chinese Communists rather than, as normally supposed, to Moscow via Zhdanov, Calcutta, and Sharkey. It is a question to which we will return.

A month after the appearance of "Strategic Problems" the MCP issued an eight-point program for the Malayan People's Democratic Republic—a regime that was not yet in existence, but which it was anticipated soon would be. The goal, according to the preamble to the program, was:

> to unite and mobilize the strength of all the people throughout Malaya to eject British imperialism and thoroughly and completely to annihilate the military, political and economic forces of British imperialism and its feudal running dogs in order to establish a completely independent Malayan People's Democratic Republic in which there shall be racial equality and democracy for the people and which unites Singapore with the rest of Malaya.

The program went on to enumerate the principles which would govern the new republic. Education was to be in the vernacular and citizenship open to all races—traditional goals dating from

---

[59] A translation of "Strategic Problems of the Malayan Revolutionary War," from which the quotations here have been taken, may be found in Hanrahan, *op. cit.*, pp. 101-16; the translation is made from a Chinese text published in 1950.

the 1930's. Major industries were to be nationalized through expropriation, but certain enterprises (notably mining) would be left in private hands and would receive government subsidies. Trade unions would play a major role in running nationalized industries; a planning board would adjust markets. The political organization of the republic was described as "a dictatorship of a coalition of the revolutionary classes of the various races." A Central People's Council would run the country, including Singapore, and would be composed of representatives of the various races proportionate to population. The foreign relations of the republic were to be based on friendship with all countries. Foreign investment, under conditions safeguarding the national economy, would be welcomed.[60]

The MCP, to judge from this program, was again more attracted by the Chinese than by the Soviet model. The new republic was to be a mixed regime, as in China, designed to appeal to the national bourgeoisie and intellectuals as well as to workers and peasants. The document shows that even at a time when the party leadership was of necessity preoccupied with questions of jungle warfare and terror, it sought to project an image of itself as a moderate and constructive force in Malaya. It was doubtless this consideration which led to the omission of any reference in the program to Russia or China, a device to dissociate Malayan Communism in the public mind from the international movement.

The problem of the predominantly Chinese character of the rebellion greatly concerned the party leadership and did, in effect reduce the prospects of Communist success. Various measures were taken to surmount this traditional handicap, now magnified by adroit British propaganda. In February 1949, for instance, the Communists created the Malayan Races Liberation Army (MRLA), to accent the multi-racial nature of the revolt. In June, announcement was made of the formation of an all-Malay regiment—evidence, it was said, of the growing "political con-

[60] A translation of the program, which is dated January 25, 1949, is in Malayan government archives.

sciousness" of the Malays.[61] A year later the Central Committee advised all party members, in and out of the jungle: "The Malays now realize that the party will help them to win their independence; now is the time to win them over to the MCP."[62] Progress was slow, however, in recruiting Malays into the party and the MRLA. If government casualty figures are to be credited, the Chinese component of the MRLA remained constant at something over 90 percent; Indians, it is believed, made up the majority of the remainder.[63]

Another problem that troubled the leaders of the rebellion was the steady decline in Communist morale as months, and eventually years, passed without significant victories. Party documents during 1949 and 1950 reflect this concern. The resolution adopted by the Politburo in June 1949 acknowledged the superiority of government forces and demanded more aggressive tactics to restore confidence. In November the MCP developed this argument in greater detail in its "Supplementary views on 'Strategic Problems of the Malayan Revolutionary War.'" The disadvantageous factors in the struggle were indeed formidable, this document acknowledged, perhaps even greater than a year earlier (at the time "Strategic Problems" was issued), but so were the factors advantageous to the Communists: the establishment of the Chinese People's Republic; Liu Shao-chi's enunciation of the doctrine of "armed struggle" at the WFTU conference in Peking; the growth of the civilian organization, the *Min Yuen*,[64] in support of the guerrilla effort; and so forth. Party members must not, therefore, be discouraged. The MRLA's tactics must be "stra-

---

[61] Cited from a Politburo resolution of June 1949 in the Malayan archives.

[62] "An Open Letter addressed to the entire body of comrades from the Central Committee on the commemoration of the second anniversary of the June 20th [*sic*] incident"; a translation of the letter, made by the Singapore Special Branch, is at the Hoover Library at Stanford.

[63] Casualty figures through 1950, 1952, and 1955 may be found, respectively, in *The Fight Against Communist Terrorism in Malaya* (1951 edition), p. 9; same, 1953 edition, p. 9; and Pye, *Guerrilla Communism in Malaya*, p. 109.

[64] The *Min Yuen*, or People's Movement, was organized early in the Emergency to supply the MRLA in the field. By 1950 it is estimated that the *Min Yuen* numbered 10,000, or twice the estimated strength of the MRLA; see Pye, *op. cit.*, p. 98.

392

tegically defensive, tactically offensive"; only by faithfully adhering to these tactics could the Communists prevail in a struggle described as "gradual, protracted and bitter." "Any foolish thoughts of short-cuts must be dismissed" the party again cautioned its cadres. "All colonial and semi-colonial revolutionary wars have such common hardships."[65] Morale continued to decline, however, to judge from a rash of pamphlets issued during 1950 bearing such titles as "Clarification of Doubts Arising Out of Shaken Confidence" and "Strengthening Confidence in the Communist Undertaking."[66]

There was, in effect, no remedy for a problem of "shaken confidence" arising from the frustrations of guerrilla warfare against overwhelming odds. In retrospect, the Communists appear to have enjoyed their greatest success precisely during the period when the party leadership was complaining of low morale. From mid-1950 on Communist fortunes declined. By the end of 1950 the government forces fighting the Communists numbered approximately 100,000, or nearly twenty times the strength of the MRLA.[67] In 1951 the Briggs Plan was introduced, resettling Chinese "squatters" on the edge of the jungle in fortified villages and thereby choking off the supply line to the guerrillas set up by the *Min Yuen*. When at the end of 1951 the MCP sought to modify its strategies, reverting to underground work and infiltration in the cities, its civilian base had collapsed; any good will toward the Communists that had survived the first thrust of the rebellion had been dissipated by three and a half years of disrupting and largely futile terror. The Communists had no recourse but to remain indefinitely in the jungle—or surrender on the government's terms.

[65] "Supplementary Views" was issued on November 12, 1949, and published secretly in Singapore in December 1950; a translation may be found in Hanrahan, *op. cit.*, pp. 117-30.

[66] A collection of translations of these materials, made by the Singapore Special Branch from a Communist publication called "Emancipation Series," is at the Hoover Library.

[67] "Supplementary Views" places the size of government forces at 100,000 as of November 1949. Official sources do not indicate that this figure was reached until sometime during 1950; of these the majority were Malays. See Pye, *op. cit.*, p. 97.

Engagement & Disengagement: 1948-1954

Coverage of the Malayan Emergency in the Soviet press began within six weeks of its declaration and remained fairly constant for the next four or five years. At the end of July 1948, *New Times* carried an item which ridiculed the British charge of a "Communist plot" in Malaya and considered the declaration of an Emergency as further proof that British policy in Malaya was bankrupt.[68] In August, *Pravda*, citing London news sources, charged British atrocities in Malaya in the use of head-hunting tribesmen from Sarawak to put down the insurrection, a charge that was to be repeated many times in Soviet dispatches during the succeeding years.[69] In November an analysis of the origins of the Emergency stated categorically that the government's suppression of labor the previous spring and the outlawing of the PMFTU on May 31 were the direct causes of the flight of Malayan citizens to the jungle;[70] this too became a thesis persistently argued in Soviet accounts. In December the Orientalist A. Guber described the struggle there as "a protracted colonial war"—a description similar to that used in the MCP's "Strategic Problems" issued about the same time; Guber also called attention to American participation in Malayan affairs, which he said was "increasing steadily."[71]

The comprehensive report on Malaya prepared by G. L. Bondarevskii for the conference of Soviet Orientalists in June 1949 (which was somewhat amplified for publication in *Krizis kolonial'noi sistemy* in November) repeated most of these arguments and added new ones. Additional "evidence" was brought forth to demonstrate American pressure on England as early as the spring of 1948 to crush the Malayan Communists: a meeting of the Joint Chiefs of Staff in Washington in June was said to have "demanded from the British the defeat of the democratic forces of

[68] "Colonial War in Malaya," *New Times*, July 28, 1948, pp. 16-7.
[69] *Pravda*, August 20, 1948, p. 4. See also *New Times*, April 27, 1949, p. 18; September 7, 1949, pp. 15-7; and *For a Lasting Peace, for a People's Democracy!* April 21, 1950, p. 4.
[70] *Trud*, November 2, 1948; a translation of this article by S. Pavlov, entitled "The Truth about Events in Malaya," may be found in *Soviet Press Translations*, IV, 2, p. 38.
[71] A. Guber, "Malaya," *New Times*, December 8, 1948, pp. 19-25.

Malaya, the restoration of 'order' there and the re-occupation of the country by a sufficient number of British forces." The British dutifully responded, Bondarevskii argued, by transferring its Far Eastern naval squadron from Hong Kong to Singapore and raising in the London press "a heart-rending wail about the 'Communist' menace in Malaya." Bondarevskii cites, with qualified approval, the judgment of the Far Eastern correspondent of the *London Times*, Ian Morrison: "An incontestable conviction is growing that the Malayan Communists were compelled to undertake military operations sooner than they were ready for them; that is, they were forced into revolution . . . the murder of the three British planters [on June 16, 1948] was not part of the plans of the Communist leadership, but an accident."[72] Bondarevskii pretends to discover the real purpose of Anglo-American strategy in Malaya in a *London Times* editorial of August 7 which is quoted as follows: "The crushing of the Communist forces in Malaya would be a powerful blow against Communism throughout Southeast Asia. . . . This would clear the way for the economic and political rehabilitation of these countries, in collaboration with the Western Powers who expect help from this part of the world in balancing their budgets." Bondarevskii comments:

It is difficult to set forth more explicitly the aims of the British monopolists. It turns out that the question is not of the mythical menace of Communism but the desire once again to subjugate the peoples of Southeast Asia, to convert this area into a vast reserve of raw materials and dollars for the Marshallized countries of Western Europe.[73]

Once driven to revolution, Bondarevskii continues, the Malayan Communists gave a good account of themselves: by November 1949 they controlled 40 percent of the colony and had 20,000 men in arms against a British force of 75,000 (British estimates for 1950, it will be noted, were respectively 5,000 and 100,000). The

---

[72] Morrison is quoted correctly, though slightly out of context, from an article in *Far Eastern Survey*, December 22, 1948, p. 285; the phrasing used here is retranslated from the Russian, to reflect more accurately Bondarevskii's emphasis. See *Krizis kolonial'noi sistemy*, pp. 198-200.

[73] *Ibid.*, p. 204.

author also calls attention to the MCP's success in "uniting for the first time in the history of Malaya the Chinese, Malay, and Indian peoples."

The victory of the Chinese Communists in the autumn of 1949 stimulated Soviet interest in the Malayan Communists. Articles on Malaya in Soviet journals struck an even more optimistic and belligerent note than during the first year and a half of the Emergency. The editorial in the Cominform journal of January 27, 1950, listed Malaya after only China and Vietnam as an example of a country where the tactics of the "armed struggle" were being correctly applied. A long article by V. Vasil'ev in *Pravda* in April noted that even the British now acknowledged the existence of a full-scale civil war in Malaya, not merely a struggle against "a handful of rebels."[74] In the April issue of *Voprosy istorii* Bondarevskii claimed that the ratio of government to guerrilla losses in battle was 5 to 1.[75] In May the Cominform journal vigorously denied claims that the Malayan rebellion was predominantly Chinese and cited letters to foreign newspapers showing that British atrocities against Malays were as brutal as against Chinese; the first victim of the Emergency, it was said, had been a Malay.[76] *New Times*, in a summary of the first two years of fighting, asserted that the British had "failed ignominiously" despite a commitment of more than 100,000 troops and 2,754 air sorties against the guerrillas in the past year alone.[77] In November, a writer in *Bol'shevik* put British losses at 12,000 and claimed that Great Britain was spending 100,000,000 pounds yearly to suppress the insurrection.[78] Early in 1951, *TASS* quoted a

[74] *Pravda*, April 10, 1950, p. 4.

[75] G. Bondarevskii, "Natsional'no-osvoboditel'naia bor'ba narodov Malaii posle vtoroi mirovoi voiny," *Voprosy istorii*, No. 4, April 1950, p. 82; the article is much like his piece in *Krizis kolonial'noi sistemy* the previous November, with some updating.

[76] "Failure of British Military Adventure in Malaya," *For a Lasting Peace, for a People's Democracy!*, May 19, 1950, p. 3.

[77] Orestov, "Two Years of War in Malaya," *New Times*, July 5, 1950, p. 16; Communist estimates of British forces in use at this juncture varied between 100,000 and 125,000.

[78] *Bol'shevik*, No. 22, November 15, 1950; translated in *Soviet Press Translations*, VI, 3, pp. 82-5.

high British official in Southeast Asia, Malcolm MacDonald, as acknowledging that 75 percent of Malaya was in Communist hands and that the government was "in no position to win any victories."[79]

Soviet comment on Malaya continued in this vein during 1951 and 1952. The themes stressed in the Soviet press remained relatively constant: British responsibility for the outbreak of hostilities in 1948; the multi-racial character of the Communist forces; British atrocities (for a time the picture of a beheaded Malay which had appeared in the London *Daily Worker* was featured in the Soviet and Cominform press;[80] the herding of half a million defenseless Chinese, during the era of the Briggs Plan, into "concentration camps"; the growing unpopularity of the war among rank-and-file British citizens; the mounting rivalry between England and the United States over the conduct of the war; and, above all, the steady successes of the MRLA, whether or not there was any basis for the claims. As late as the autumn of 1952, nearly two years after the Soviet press had grown silent on the rebellion in Burma, a Soviet student of Malaya continued to speak of the armed revolt there as "the basic and highest form of struggle." "Under the banner of the MCP," the author asserted, 35,000 armed Malayans in the MRLA "are carrying on to the finish the business of liberating their country from the imperialist and colonial yoke."[81]

[79] *Pravda*, February 21, 1951, p. 4; see also *For a Lasting Peace, for a People's Democracy!*, August 3, 1951, p. 2.

[80] E.g., *ibid.*, May 9, 1952, p. 4, and *Pravda*, June 17, 1952, p. 4; the picture, allegedly submitted by a returning British soldier, was carried in the *Daily Worker* on April 28, 1952.

[81] Levkovskii, *Natsional'no-osvoboditel'naia bor'ba narodov Malaii za svoiu svobodu i nezavisimost'*, p. 32; the pamphlet went to press in September 1952. Items of note on Malaya appearing in the Soviet press during 1951-52 may be found in: *Pravda*, April 3, December 3, and December 29, 1951, and June 17 and November 17, 1952; *Izvestiia*, February 13 and June 27, 1952; *Trud*, March 12, 1952; and *Krasnaia zvezda*, April 30, 1952. (Many of the above items are translated in *Soviet Press Translations*.) Additional items from Soviet periodicals during these years are listed in *Bibliografiia Iugo-vostochnoi Azii*, pp. 185-6. For Cominform coverage of Malaya, see *For a Lasting Peace, for a People's Democracy!* June 29 and August 3, 1951 and February 15, February 29 and May 2, 1952.

There is little doubt, to judge from Soviet press coverage of events in Malaya, that Moscow's interest in the Malayan insurrection was both more profound and more sustained than in the case of other upheavals in Southeast Asia, excluding only the civil war in Indochina. There are, moreover, enough parallels between the content of Soviet commentaries and Malayan Communist documents—concerning the origins of the Emergency, the allegedly multi-racial character of the MRLA, the proper strategies to be used, British atrocities and so forth—to indicate more than a casual relationship between the Malayan and the international movements. How the relationship was maintained it is not easy to determine. Moscow appears initially to have kept abreast of developments in Malaya through the British Communists.[82] The latter, however, did not retain an intense interest in the Malayan Emergency, to judge from the attention given to it in the British Communist press, and Moscow came to rely more and more on data culled from non-Communist publications which Soviet commentators fitted to their purposes; occasionally Malayan Communist documents came to Moscow's attention and were duly cited in the Soviet press.[83] No Soviet or Cominform agents, insofar as is known, visited Malaya during the Emergency;[84] nor is there evidence, after Sharkey's visit to Singapore in March 1948, of any activity in Malaya by representatives of the CPGB or of other Commonwealth parties. Occasional Malayans who attended pro-Communist international conferences in Europe, it is perhaps safe to assume, were residing in Europe, or at least too far out of

[82] British Communist publications gave detailed attention to Malaya at the outset of the Emergency: e.g., *Daily Worker*, June 14, June 19, June 22, July 17, July 26, August 6, September 23, and November 22, 1948, and *World News and Views*, August 7, 1948. Later Soviet studies of Malaya rely heavily on these articles for developments early in the Emergency; see, for instance, Rudnev, *Ocherki noveishei istorii Malaii* (1959), pp. 72-6.

[83] E.g., *Pravda*, January 20, 1950 (citing a manifesto of the MRLA); *New Times*, July 5, 1950, p. 19 and *For a Lasting Peace, for a People's Democracy!*, August 3, 1951, p. 2 (citing the 1949 program).

[84] Ruth McVey notes the presence of a Soviet Trade Commissioner in Singapore from early 1947, but does not indicate whether he remained there after the outbreak of the insurrection; McVey, *The Calcutta Conference and the Southeast Asian Uprisings*, p. 1.

touch with the Communist leadership in Malaya to provide effective liaison.[85] We must conclude, therefore, with respect to the relationship between the Malayan and international Communist movements, that the coincidence of views reflected in Soviet commentaries and in documents issued by the MCP does not of itself indicate Russian supervision of the Malayan Communists, either directly or through the CPGB; that Soviet interest in the Malayan insurrection was a natural consequence of Moscow's attitude during this period toward the colonial question; and that the interest would—and did—last as long as the Malayan struggle satisfied Soviet concepts of national liberation in East Asia.

The relationship between Malayan and Chinese Communism was more direct. We have already noted the deference to Mao and to Chinese Communist strategies in the principal Malayan Communist documents issued during these years: in "Strategic Problems of the Malayan Revolutionary War" at the end of 1948, in the "supplementary views" on this statement a year later, and, to a lesser degree, in the program for the Malayan People's Democratic Republic early in 1949. Malayan Communist newspapers also show an orientation toward the Chinese Communists. Much attention, for instance, is given in these clandestine local organs to developments in China. World news, even where it originates from Soviet and Cominform sources, is given from monitored dispatches of the New China News Agency. Chinese sources are sometimes cited even for evidence of gains by the MRLA in Malaya.[86]

---

[85] According to a Communist newspaper published in Singapore, a Malayan named Sama (not identifiable) attended a youth conference in Prague in August 1950; *Student News*, December 1, 1950. Another report in a Malayan Communist organ of a representative of the MCP attending Stalin's funeral in 1953 must be held unreliable: after noting that the representative reached Moscow from Malaya in three days, the report goes on to explain that the reason for the long delay in reporting the event (eleven months) was "poor communications"; *Truth*, February 1, 1954.

[86] E.g., *Combatant News*, July 1, 1950, citing an NCNA cable dispatch of March 14. Scattered copies of this newspaper (published in Chinese in South Pahang)—as well as of *Freedom News* (Chinese, Singapore), *Student News* (Chinese, Singapore), and *Truth* (English, Penang, and Kedah)—are at the Hoover Library and in Malayan archives; the Chinese organs have been translated by the Singapore Special Branch.

Engagement & Disengagement: 1948-1954

Malayan attention to China, however, does not necessarily mean Chinese attention to Malaya. Contacts between the two parties were evidently infrequent.[87] Coverage of Malayan developments in the Chinese press appears to have been minimal during the early 1950's—notably less, for instance, than in the Russian and Cominform press.[88] Where Peking did give attention to Malayan affairs, it concerned treatment of the overseas Chinese, not the Communist rebellion. In December 1950, for instance, a Chinese spokesman expressed outrage that 35,000 Chinese had been deported from Malaya since the beginning of the Emergency. "The 475,000,000 free Chinese people," he said, "will not tolerate the persecution of our brethren abroad."[89] A few days later the Chinese Foreign Office issued a lengthy formal statement protesting England's behavior and demanded that a delegation from Peking be admitted to Malaya to inspect the condition of the Chinese there.[90] When after several months no reply had been received to the request for visas, Peking responded in a threatening tone. "The persecution of the Chinese community in Malaya," an editorial in People's China stated, "is part of the futile attempt of the imperialists to suppress the national liberation movement which is now surging through Southeast Asia. . . . The British government must bear the full consequences of persisting in its frantic policy of bloody suppression [of the Chinese community] in Malaya."[91] What the "con-

[87] An unauthenticated report of twenty Chinese Communist agents arriving in Singapore in November 1948 appears in a British Intelligence Report (now declassified) in the Malayan archives; their mission was allegedly part of a Chinese Communist project "to build up and develop all the Communist parties of the South Seas." After the Chinese Communists came to power, Malayans occasionally attended conferences in the CPR: a Malayan delegate, for instance, is reported to have been present at the Asian Women's Representative Conference held in Peking in December 1949; Combatant News, July 1, 1950.

[88] This judgment, whose tentative nature should be emphasized, is based on the author's analysis of People's China from 1950 to 1953; People's China, which may be compared to the Soviet organ New Times, was the only foreign language periodical published in Peking during these years dealing with international affairs.

[89] Pravda, December 26, 1950, p. 4, citing a TASS dispatch from Peking.

[90] Pravda and Izvestiia, December 31, 1950, p. 4.

[91] "Fascist Police Rule in Malaya," People's China, No. 7, April 1, 1951, p. 4.

400

sequences" might be was not indicated. However, the possibility exists that Peking was at this juncture considering a more active role in Malaya (and perhaps in other Southeast Asian countries where similar charges were being made) on the pretext of defending the overseas Chinese. If this was for a time Peking's intent, nothing came of it. Active Chinese assistance to the Malayans during the period of their greatest need does not emerge in retrospect as significant, although the continued psychological impact of Chinese Communist successes on Malayan Communism may be taken for granted.

INSURRECTION FAILS AGAIN IN INDONESIA

The crest of Moscow's benevolence toward the Republic of Indonesia after the war occurred during the government of Amir Sjarifuddin (July 3, 1947 to January 23, 1948). There is a paradox in the fact that this was precisely the period when Soviet policy was undergoing a general shift to the Left, a shift not easily reconciled with the course in Indonesia. The Kremlin was faced with two alternatives: should it continue to accept the Indonesian Republic as constituted, not only under Sjarifuddin (whom the Russians may or may not have thought to be a Communist at this juncture) but equally under Sukarno, Hatta, and other decidedly non-Communist nationalist leaders? Or should Moscow turn against the nationalist leadership, as it was doing in India, Burma, and elsewhere in the colonial world where the situation was comparable, in favor of a more vigorous effort by Communists to seize power in their own right?

So long as Sjarifuddin remained in office the choice between these alternatives was not urgent; the interests of the PKI as well as Moscow's continuing attachment to the anti-imperialist struggle, still the cornerstone of Stalin's foreign policy, were both served by his administration. Zhdanov accordingly, in his Cominform address in September, listed Indonesia among the countries "associated" with the anti-imperialist camp led by the USSR; Indonesia, it is worth noting, was one of two non-Communist countries (along with Finland) so listed. Guber, in an article pub-

401

lished in October, had kind words not only for Sjarifuddin but for Nationalists, Socialists, and even representatives of the *Masjumi* in his cabinet.[92] Zhukov, writing in December, linked Indonesia and Vietnam as former colonies where the struggle against imperialism was proceeding as it should—"under the leadership of the Communist party."[93] In January 1948, before the fall of the Sjarifuddin cabinet, Vasil'eva spoke of Indonesia as a "people's democratic republic," a term normally reserved for Soviet satellites in Eastern Europe.[94]

Sjarifuddin fell in the wake of the Renville agreement of January 17, 1948, which had repercussions on the domestic political scene in Indonesia not unlike those which had followed the signing of the Linggadjati agreement a year before.[95] Sjarifuddin, who had been a powerful force in Indonesian politics for several years, failed to gain a seat in the succeeding cabinet of Mohammed Hatta due to pressure from the *Masjumi*, the PNI, and Hatta's other supporters. He thus became the principal leader in the opposition, which in February was reorganized as the People's Democratic Front (*Front Demokrasi Rakjat*, or FDR) replacing the former Left coalition, *Sajap Kiri*; the PKI, needless to say, assumed a major role in the new formation.

One might expect a change in Moscow's attitude toward Indonesia now that the Communists were out of the government and in open opposition to the new cabinet. This did not, however, occur. In March, for instance, an editorial in *New Times*

[92] A. Guber, "Imperialisty—dushiteli svobody i nezavisimosti narodov," *Bol'shevik*, No. 19, October 15, 1947, p. 57.

[93] E. Zhukov, "Obostrenie krizisa kolonial'noi sistemy," *ibid.*, No. 23, December 15, 1947, p. 57.

[94] V. I. Vasil'eva, "Bor'ba za demokraticheskoe razvitie Indoneziiskoi respubliki," *Voprosy ekonomiki*, No. 1, January 1948, p. 71.

[95] The Renville agreement, signed aboard the American naval vessel of that name after several months of delicate negotiations between the Dutch, the Indonesians, and the Committee of Good Offices, brought formally to an end the Dutch police action of the preceding July and set forth the conditions for an eventual Dutch-Indonesian federation. The agreement, however, was opposed by Sjahrir, the *Masjumi*, and other elements who combined to force the resignation of the Sjarifuddin government. See Kahin, *Nationalism and Revolution in Indonesia*, pp. 228-9.

402

affirmed Moscow's continuing support of Indonesia in the United Nations Security Council as though no change of government had taken place in Java.[96] In May the Soviet government ratified a consular agreement with Indonesia which had been negotiated in January, while Sjarifuddin was still in office; a commentary on the agreement in *Pravda* early in June acclaimed it as a blow to American-Dutch efforts to deny to the Indonesians, by invoking the Renville agreement, their right to maintain independent foreign relations.[97] Throughout the summer—the summer, be it noted, when the rebellions in Burma and Malaya were gathering momentum—Soviet commentaries continued to focus attention on Dutch imperialism and had little to say of the Hatta government. Early in August Hatta was quoted in *Izvestiia*, with no innuendo of criticism, on the intransigence of the Dutch during the current stage of negotiations.[98] For the first year, then, following the pronouncement of what was everywhere taken to be a significant shift in Soviet strategies, Moscow's views on Indonesia remained comparatively unchanged, to judge from comments appearing in the Russian press.

The strategies followed by the pro-Communist Left in Indonesia—the *Sajah Kiri* and its successor, the FDR—were not always attuned to Soviet policy during these months. In January, for instance, Sjarifuddin (who, Communist or not, was the principal spokesman of the Indonesian Left) is reported to have op-

---

[96] "The Indonesian Question in the Security Council," *New Times*, No. 11, March 10, 1948, pp. 1-2. See also Alastair M. Taylor, *Indonesian Independence and the United Nations* (London, 1960), pp. 386-7.

[97] *Pravda*, June 8, 1948; the article, written by I. Viktorov, is translated in *Soviet Press Translations*, III, 14, pp. 425-8. The consular agreement was worked out in Prague between the Soviet ambassador and Suripno, who had been sent to Europe during the Dutch police action the previous summer to gain diplomatic support wherever possible; although it was not widely known at the time, Suripno was a Communist—a factor which doubtless facilitated his negotiations with the Russian ambassador. There is some uncertainty whether Suripno exceeded his authority in initialing the agreement. The Indonesians, at any event, did not immediately ratify it and the formal status of Soviet-Indonesian relations remained ambiguous for some years; an exchange of representation occurred only in 1954.

[98] I. Plyshevskii, "Polozhenie v Indonezii," *Izvestiia*, August 7, 1948, p. 4; see also the lead editorial in *New Times*, August 4, 1948, pp. 1-2.

403

posed consular relations with the USSR on the grounds that this would jeopardize negotiations with the Dutch leading to the Renville agreement;[99] Moscow, it has been indicated, responded eagerly to Suripno's proposal in Prague and hastened the initialing of a consular protocol. With respect to the Renville agreement itself, Sjarifuddin and the PKI fully supported it when it was signed; Moscow, to judge from the persistent hostility to the Committee of Good Offices reflected in the Soviet press, did not. The Russian view was also reflected, we may imagine, in resolutions passed by the Calcutta Youth Conference bitterly condemning the Dutch-Indonesian agreement.[100] Meanwhile, the Soviet press ignored entirely, during the months following Sjarifuddin's fall, the emergence of a powerful Leftist opposition to the Hatta government, the most formidable opposition in which the PKI and its allies had engaged since the war.

From this evidence it appears that Moscow and the Indonesian Communists were working somewhat at cross purposes. The Russians continued to be interested in Indonesia primarily as a "lever" against American prestige in East Asia. They were therefore concerned with the *image* of the Indonesian Republic, its integrity against actual and alleged imperialist designs upon it; who ruled in Indonesia was a less crucial matter. In this sense Zhdanovism had relevance in Java, at least until September 1948, principally as a device to harden Indonesian resistance to the Dutch. The PKI, on the other hand, could not be so detached about domestic politics. Even if Indonesian Communists had fully grasped the aim of Soviet policies during this era (which is doubtful), they could not have avoided being drawn into the vortex of a political crisis brought on by Sjarifuddin's personal ambitions. Having linked their fortunes with Sjarifuddin and accepted him as their spokesman, the Communists

---

[99] Kahin, *op. cit.*, p. 268.

[100] See McVey, *The Calcutta Conference and the Southeast Asian Uprisings*, p. 12. This view was presumably conveyed back to Java by the Indonesian delegates attending the Calcutta conference; it is likely, however, that by the time they arrived the Left (including the PKI) had already altered its view of Renville as a result of having moved into open opposition against Mohammed Hatta, who now supported the controversial agreement.

were unable to escape involvement in the direct confrontation with the Sukarno-Hatta leadership which Sjarifuddin was contemplating.

It was into this highly charged political situation that Musso stepped in August 1948, returning to Java after a residence of more than two decades in Moscow (broken, insofar as is known, only by his brief return to Java in 1935 to establish the illegal PKI). He was immediately, upon making known his identity, acknowledged as the leader of the PKI—evidence of the regard Indonesian Communists held for Moscow's authority, which they believed vested in him.[101] Musso's return must be seen against the background of two recent developments in Indonesia, in addition to those already discussed. The first was a growing disillusionment with American policy, which seemed to favor the Dutch, and a consequent inclination on the part of many Indonesians to look more favorably toward Communist leadership, which offered a hope of Soviet support.[102] The second was Sjarifuddin's failure after persistent efforts to gain a seat in the Hatta cabinet which caused the FDR to look for other ways to gain power.

As early as mid-July the FDR leadership had drafted a plan which envisaged a two-stage assault on the Hatta government: one through "parliamentary means"; the second, in the event the first failed, through "non-parliamentary means"—that is, through a military rising. The latter course was not unrealistic. The loyalty of a large segment of the army to Hatta was in doubt, thanks to Sjarifuddin's personal popularity in the armed forces following his long tenure as Minister of Defense; the FDR quite naturally expected to increase its influence in the army during the months ahead. Should the second course prove necessary, the FDR planned to "cut off all relations with the govern-

[101] Musso returned disguised as Suripno's "secretary" early in August; he revealed his identity at a party meeting in Jogjakarta on about August 15 and was elected Secretary of the PKI in place of Sardjono. See Kahin, *op. cit.*, p. 272.

[102] The FDR made extravagant claims of promised Russian support, once consular relations were established. In reality, the Russians promised no more than trade relations, according to the evidence of Suripno himself; see Kahin, *op. cit.*, p. 268, citing an interview with Suripno following his return to Indonesia.

ment and continue our struggle either as a rebellion or as a separate government."[103]

The PKI, then, and this becomes significant in any assessment of Musso's role in the rebellion at Madiun in September, had determined to undertake armed struggle, if all else failed, a month *before* Musso appeared in Jogjakarta. Musso became the principal instrument of this strategy; he was not its initiator. His principal activity during the month following his arrival concerned the reorganization and strengthening of the PKI. At the end of August the Labor Party, the Sjarifuddin Socialists (the Socialist Party had split earlier in the year into majority and minority factions, led, respectively, by Sjarifuddin and Sjahrir) and other groups identified with the FDR were absorbed into an enlarged Communist Party. Sjarifuddin announced at this time that he had been a Communist since 1935; within several days Setiadjit, Abdulmadjid (both former leaders of the *Perhimpoenan Indonesia* in Holland), and others followed suit.

Musso's tactics were not at this juncture openly militant— considerably less so, for instance, than those of the Burmese and Malayan Communists on the eves of their respective revolts. He described his strategy as the "Gottwald Plan," accenting the legal aspect of a Communist seizure of power, as in Czechoslovakia, rather than the resort to armed force which appears to have been the dominant message of the FDR program in July. A resolution adopted at his recommendation at the time of the merger emphasized the need for a broad national front. "The CPI [PKI] is convinced," the resolution read, according to a recent text, "that at the present time, the party of the working class cannot possibly complete the bourgeois democratic revolution on its own and that is why the CPI must cooperate with other parties."[104] Early in September Musso accordingly pro-

---

[103] This document, entitled (in translation) "Stepping to the New Stage of Military Struggle," is cited at some length in Kahin, *op. cit.*, pp. 269-71. The document came to light only after the Madiun uprising, but Professor Kahin appears not to doubt its authenticity.

[104] Quoted in Aidit, *The Birth and Growth of the Communist Party of Indonesia*, p. 29; the resolution is entitled "The New Road for the Republic of Indonesia."

posed a conference of PKI, PNI, *Masjumi,* and other nationalist leaders to create a national front and a new "national cabinet." Although the proposal was turned down, Musso gave no sign of turning to the "second course." On September 7, Musso, Sjarifuddin, and other party leaders left Jogjakarta for what was to have been a fortnight's speaking tour throughout Java, designed to publicize the PKI program (the portions of it that could be openly discussed) and to gain adherents to the Communist cause. It is unlikely, needless to say, that they would have planned so extensive a tour had they foreseen a Communist rebellion midway through it.

Events caught up with Musso and his companions on September 17, when Madiun was seized by local Communist elements, evidently on their own initiative. The PKI leaders hastened to Madiun, a day's drive from the last stop on their itinerary, and promptly supported the rising. Sukarno, in a dramatic appeal to the country on September 19, closed off all escape routes for the Communist leaders by asking Indonesians to choose between "following Musso and his Communist Party, who will obstruct the attainment of an independent Indonesia, or following Sukarno-Hatta, who, with the Almighty's help, will lead our Republic of Indonesia to become an independent Indonesia which is not subjected to any other country whatsoever." Musso replied by calling for the overthrow of the Sukarno-Hatta regime throughout the country. "The happenings in Madiun," he said, "are a signal to the whole people to wrest the powers of the state into their own hands." In the following days the PKI leaders made a belated attempt to limit the scale of the insurrection by arguing that the government established at Madiun was "a regional popular administration and . . . part of the democratic Republic of Indonesia." These disclaimers, however, were ignored by the government. Martial law was declared and supreme authority vested in Sukarno for three months. Well before that time ran out the government, cautiously withdrawing troops from the truce line between the Dutch and Indonesian armies, had put down the Communist insurrection. Musso was killed in a skirmish at the end of October. Sjarifuddin, Suripno, Sardjono,

Harjono, Darusman, and five lesser leaders were captured and, on December 19, shot.[105]

The fact that the Madiun rising, according to all evidence, was inadvertent[106] does not mean that the PKI would not have made a similar effort at some later date, a consideration we have also raised with regard to the Malayan insurgency the previous June. PKI documents and behavior too clearly indicate this intention to encourage quibbling over ultimate Communist aims. When a revolutionary movement prepares for a national rising—as the Bolsheviks, for instance, did in 1917 and the PKI in 1948—it assumes a risk that the rising may be premature. The Bolsheviks were very nearly forced into revolution in July 1917, a development which could have given a very different turn to events in Russia; the PKI in September 1948 *was* forced into revolution—or, what comes to the same thing, its leaders elected to launch a revolution on the basis of action already taken at Madiun—and the prospects of a more orderly effort at a later date were never tested. The Indonesian revolution did not reach its "October"; it foundered in "July."

The larger question for our purposes, however, is not whether insurrection was premature in Indonesia but whether, and to what degree, Moscow can be said to have been responsible for it. The principal argument advanced to "prove" Soviet involvement is Musso's arrival in Java, after long residence in Moscow, on the eve of the most formidable Communist effort in Indonesia in more than twenty years. It is unimaginable, some argue,

[105] Students of Indonesian Communism are more than usually indebted to George Kahin for his treatment of the Madiun episode in *Nationalism and Revolution in Indonesia*, pp. 256-303. Professor Kahin was in Java before and during the uprising and was in contact with many of the principals involved, including Sjarifuddin, Suripno, Hatta, and others. The foregoing brief account of the episode is drawn largely from his detailed study; the passages quoted are taken from contemporary Indonesian sources which he cites.

[106] As further evidence of the unplanned nature of the Madiun rising, it may be noted that PKI leaders arrested at party headquarters in Jogjakarta immediately after the outbreak appeared to know nothing of the events at Madiun; elsewhere in Java local party officials denounced the Madiun insurgents as "Trotskyites" even after Musso had assumed direction of the insurrection. See Kahin, *op. cit.*, pp. 294, 301.

408

that he could have returned without an explicit instruction from Moscow. This is a hypothesis. It could equally be argued, since nothing is known of Musso's activities prior to his departure for Indonesia or of his relations with Russian leaders able to instruct him in so delicate a matter as armed insurrection, that he returned of his own volition, uninstructed, and responded to the situation in Indonesia entirely on his own initiative. We do know, assuming a Communist seizure of power to have been his intent, that he found PKI strategies already geared to that end. Perhaps Moscow had had a hand in shaping these strategies as well, through some "instruction" inspiring the FDR's two-stage plan of July (a plan, we should note, comparable to the Ghoshal Thesis in Burma in January or the resolutions of the Malayan Fourth Plenum in March). Hypothesis is now built upon hypothesis. But are we any wiser?

The most that can be reasonably said of Soviet involvement in the Madiun affair, in this writer's view, is that Moscow perhaps bore some *general* responsibility for the PKI's strategies through its more truculent posture in world affairs since Zhdanov's speech in Poland a year earlier. Whether or not Zhdanovism was devised with Indonesia in mind, and it would appear on balance not to have been, Moscow's repeated calls for a division of the world into two camps, its persistent doubts concerning the reliability of the colonial bourgeoisie, and its incessant appeals for a more vigorous effort by Communists everywhere could not fail, eventually, to find their mark within the PKI. Since no instruction arrived to restrain the party leaders, they moved inevitably toward their final (and premature) confrontation with the republican leadership. If the Russians opposed this course, they failed to make their opposition clear. Emphasis, then, attaches more properly to the likely *absence* of Soviet directives, which might have restrained the Indonesians, than to the probability that any existed to goad them on.

The Soviet press ignored the Communist uprising in Indonesia while it was proceeding and for another month or more after it was put down.[107] This was not because Moscow had ceased suddenly to concern itself with developments in Indonesia. An item in *New Times* six days after the insurrection broke out reiterated the usual charges against the Committee of Good Offices, asserted the "bankruptcy of the Dutch colonial imperialists in face of the growing liberation movement of the Indonesian people," but made no mention of Madiun.[108] In November a long article in the same journal by a recent Russian traveler to Indonesia took note of Communist developments on the eve of Madiun—the reorganization of the PKI at the end of August, for instance, and the party's call early in September for "a new and truly national government"—but still made no reference to the rebellion.[109] Moscow's lack of concern with the fate of the PKI might be laid to ignorance of developments in Indonesia were it not for the fact that the course of the rising was amply covered in the world press, including foreign Communist organs. A British Communist organ discussed the Madiun revolt on October 2, before its outcome was certain, and argued that Hatta's capitulation to the United States had

[107] Evidence presented by Kahin concerning an early Soviet broadcast supporting the uprising must, in this writer's view, be rejected. The broadcast, said to have been monitored by a member of the Committee of Good Offices on September 19, a few hours after Musso's open defiance of Sukarno and Hatta, is given as follows (in translation):

> There has been a People's Government set up in Madiun and People's Committees are being established in other leading towns. This was a popular uprising against the government of the Fascist Japanese Quislings, Sukarno and Hatta. (See Kahin, *op. cit.*, p. 294.)

The reasons for doubting the authenticity of the broadcast are these: it is wholly uncharacteristic of Soviet news media to respond so promptly to revolutionary developments of this nature; if past Soviet coverage of events in Indonesia is any indication of the time-lag necessary for Moscow to be sufficiently apprised of developments to react, a week to ten days was minimum during this period; the charges raised in the broadcast against Sukarno and Hatta had not been made prior to Madiun and were not made for some time after it—several months in the case of Hatta, a full year in the case of Sukarno.

[108] *New Times*, September 22, 1948, p. 20.

[109] G. Afrin, "In Indonesia," *ibid.*, November 3, 1948, pp. 27-32; the item is date-lined The Hague, October 1948. The author does not indicate the purpose of his trip but he traveled quite extensively throughout the country, in both Dutch and Indonesian-held areas and was often transported on a Committee of Good Offices plane.

caused it.[110] Early in December the CPGB passed a resolution holding Hatta responsible for the safety of Communist leaders arrested during the rebellion.[111] About the same time Dutch Communists denied categorically that the PKI had had any part in the Madiun uprising, since its leaders had been elsewhere at the time; the episode was seen as an instance of government terror directed against the Communists at American instigation.[112] Since Moscow could hardly have been unaware of these positions taken by other Communists abroad, the failure of the Soviet press to offer some explanation of the Madiun episode, or even to discuss it, must be taken as evidence that Moscow did not wish to jeopardize its relations with the republic by showing concern over a domestic political crisis.

The first clear reference to Madiun in Soviet periodicals seen by this writer occurs in a lengthy article on Indonesian affairs (largely foreign affairs) which appeared early in 1949. The author of the article charged that "the Hatta government provoked a rebellion at Madiun with the purpose of beheading the progressive movement and crushing the democratic organizations, especially the trade unions"; the American representative on the Committee of Good Offices, he asserted, had provided arms and instructors for the venture.[113] This remained the official Soviet interpretation of the episode, supplemented from time to time by new data as they became available. In August, for instance, when the execution of the PKI leaders was made known, *New Times* deplored the "brutality with which Hatta ended the lives of such outstanding leaders of the Indonesian working class as Amir Sjarifuddin, Musso, Darusman, Sardjono, Suripno, and others."[114] In September a writer in *Pravda* charged Hatta with having "received $65,000,000 from the Americans for the staging

[110] *World News and Views*, October 2, 1948, pp. 428-9.

[111] *Ibid.*, December 4, 1948, p. 544.

[112] *Ibid.*, December 11, 1948, p. 548, citing the Dutch Communist organ *De Waarheid* (Amsterdam).

[113] V. Berezhkov, "Colonial War in Indonesia," *New Times*, January 5, 1949, p. 9.

[114] *Ibid.*, August 31, 1949, p. 22.

and execution of the provocation."[115] Subsequent references to Madiun added little to these details and offered no new interpretations of the episode; it was a chapter Moscow wished stricken from the record.[116]

Moscow's profession of interest in the integrity of the republic, meanwhile, did not immediately slacken after Madiun. When the second Dutch "police action" began on December 19, 1948, Soviet representatives at the United Nations immediately called for a cease-fire, the withdrawal of Dutch forces to positions held before hostilities began, and the replacement of the Committee of Good Offices (Belgium, Australia, and the United States) by a committee composed of representatives of the nations currently on the Security Council. The Russians refrained from voting on the compromise resolution, after their own proposal was rejected, and were bitter when the Dutch ignored even this milder restraining order. On December 26 a writer in *Pravda* charged that the attack had been long planned by the Dutch and Americans and termed American protestations of disapproval "hypocritical."[117] Gromyko, addressing the Security Council on December 29, accused the "Anglo-American majority" of encouraging the Dutch to ignore the cease-fire order.[118] On January 1, 1949, a Soviet commentator stated that American demands for an "investigation" to determine where responsibility lay made a mockery of the principles of the United Nations since it was altogether obvious which party was the aggressor.[119]

Early Russian reaction to the Dutch attack, then, gave no sign of a deterioration in Soviet-Indonesian relations. When Sukarno was arrested by the Dutch at the outset of hostilities, the Russians duly protested. Despite Madiun, the Russians continued to

[115] *Pravda*, September 19, 1949; the article, written by O. Chechetkina, is translated in *Soviet Press Translations*, IV, 19, pp. 616-8.

[116] The official PKI view of the Madiun rising, which amplifies Moscow's, was delivered by Aidit in February 1955; see *Aidit Accuses Madiun Affair* (Djakarta, 1955).

[117] *Pravda*, December 26, 1948; the article, written by I. Viktorov, is in *Soviet Press Translations*, IV, 2, pp. 35-8.

[118] See Kahin, *op. cit.*, p. 343.

[119] *New Times*, January 1, 1959, pp. 13-4.

present themselves as the staunch and unyielding defenders of the republic; who held power in Jogjakarta appeared to be a matter of no official concern in Moscow.

On January 5, 1949, the first overt attack on Hatta, but not yet Sukarno, appeared in the Soviet press. His "open pro-American sympathies," it was stated, had long been obvious, as evidenced by the fact that American investments in Indonesia now totaled $1,000,000,000 thanks to Hatta's help; his treachery at Madiun had "paved the way"—and not unintentionally, it was implied—for the second Dutch "police action" in December.[120] Mounting hostility toward Hatta and his "'so-called' government" was amply reflected in the Soviet press through the first half of 1949. It did not, however, affect Moscow's attitude toward the republic as such. Hatta was one thing; the republic was another. The Russians accordingly continued to support Indonesia in the United Nations and to argue that Indonesia was the victim of Dutch-American aggression. The imperialists' goal, *Pravda* commented in May, was to "make Indonesia into a base for the struggle against the national liberation movement of the peoples of Asia"; a special urgency attached to this goal now that the fall of Nationalist China was imminent.[121] Soviet spokesmen appear to have been persuaded, or wished at least to give the impression of being persuaded, that the Indonesian masses would somehow defend the republic against both Dutch-American aggression and Hatta's treachery. A broad mobilization of Indonesians was asserted; guerrilla activity was reported as widespread throughout Java.[122] Hatta might bargain away Indonesia's independence at the conference table, as it was claimed he did in the Batavia agreements of May 7 which formally ended the second Dutch "police action," but he did not represent the Indonesian people. "The people," according to an item in *New Times* at the end of May, "are upholding their independence *arms in hand*."[123] Zhukov, in his report to the Orientalist con-

---

[120] *New Times*, January 5, 1949, p. 9; this article by V. Berezhkov, the first in which reference was made to the Madiun uprising, was cited above.

[121] *Pravda*, May 16, 1949, p. 4.

[122] See *New Times*, March 30, 1949, pp. 15-6.

[123] *Ibid.*, May 25, 1949, p. 19; emphasis added.

ference in June, makes reference to the "armed struggle" in Indonesia (which he rates ahead of the "armed struggle" in Burma
and Malaya) and leaves open the question whether it is directed
more against the Dutch than the Hatta government.[124]

Sukarno had thus far escaped attack in the Soviet press, presumably because during his detainment by the Dutch he was
more than ever the symbol of Indonesia's integrity that Moscow
was so persistently upholding. Zhukov, for instance, made no
reference to Sukarno in his June address, concentrating his
venom instead on the Socialist leader Sutan Sjahrir. After Sukarno's release in the summer, Soviet spokesmen no longer felt
a need to restrain themselves concerning him. In September,
accordingly, Sukarno was linked in the Soviet press with Hatta
as a "quibbler" and "deceiver of the people."[125] Zhukov, in his
introductory chapter in *Krizis kolonial'noi sistemy* (published in
November), made the charges against Sukarno retroactive: he,
like Hatta, had "from the beginning oriented himself toward
the attainment of a 'decent' compromise with imperialism" and
sought as his goal "the conversion of Indonesia into an ordinary
bourgeois republic, as dependent on the United States—politically, economically, and militarily—as the 'independent' Philippines."[126] Vasil'eva, in December, cited Sukarno's wartime collaboration with the Japanese as proof that the Indonesian leader
had always been ready to collaborate with imperialism.[127]

The end of 1949 was the nadir in Soviet-Indonesian relations
as well as in Moscow's prospects of shaping events in the republic to its liking. By this time the Russians were left with

[124] E. Zhukov, "Problemy natsional'no-kolonial'noi bor'by posle vtoroi mirovoi
voiny," *Voprosy ekonomiki*, No. 9, September 1949, pp. 55-7.

[125] *Pravda*, September 19, 1949, p. 4 (article by O. Chechetkina). An Indonesian delegate attending a meeting of the WFTU in Paris at the end of June
had linked Sukarno and Hatta as "hirelings of Dutch imperialists and their Anglo-
American masters"; *Report of Proceedings of the Second World Trade Union
Congress* (June 29-July 9, 1949), p. 521. Chechetkina's attack on Sukarno, however, is the first seen by the writer in the *Soviet* press.

[126] *Krizis kolonial'noi sistemy*, pp. 16-7; Guber, writing in the same volume,
also links Sukarno with Hatta, but still places primary responsibility for the
treachery of the republican leadership on the latter (see p. 173).

[127] *Trud*, December 9, 1949; translated in *Soviet Press Translations*, v, 4, p.
119. See also Plyshevskii's article in *Izvestiia*, December 8, 1949.

little to fall back on in their Indonesian policy. One by one Moscow had turned from the nationalist leaders on whom it had originally depended in its campaign against American imperialism. It had seen a Communist insurrection languish at the end of 1948. A year later it watched the republic reach a formal settlement with the Dutch during the Round Table talks at The Hague, bringing to an end for the present the troublesome Indonesian question.[128] From Moscow's viewpoint the outlook in Indonesia was not encouraging, and, in fact, references to Indonesia as an ex-colony in the throes of revolution were soon discarded: the editorial in *For a Lasting Peace, for a People's Democracy!* on January 27, 1950, for instance, did not attempt, as Zhukov had attempted the previous June, to link the Indonesian revolution to those in Indochina, Burma, and Malaya, let alone China. A wan hope, to be sure, was occasionally expressed that "armed struggle"—now everywhere accepted as the "highest form of struggle" in the colonial world—*would* develop in Indonesia; but the tense was future, not present. Thus an editorial in *Izvestiia* in mid-January, making no claim that a significant struggle was currently in progress in Indonesia, argued the urgent necessity of "*intensifying* armed struggle against the so-called Hatta government."[129] Now, fifteen months after the event, Moscow appears to have been ready for Madiun.

Chinese Communist influence within the PKI, it is believed, replaced Russian early in the 1950's. The Chinese were perhaps better equipped than Moscow to guide the Indonesians. Peking was less preoccupied than Moscow during these years with the global implications of the struggle against American "imperialism" and therefore better able to consider the fine points of strategy in an emerging nation such as Indonesia. The CCP's more flexible concept of united front tactics, for instance, made

[128] The settlement, reached in November 1949, transferred full sovereignty over the Dutch East Indies to the Indonesians except for West Irian; the disposition of the latter was to be arranged by negotiation during the following year, but was finally resolved only in 1963. A Netherlands-Indonesian Union was also created at The Hague but was dissolved by Sukarno a few years later.

[129] *Izvestiia*, January 15, 1950, p. 4.

its advice more relevant to Indonesian Communists at a time when they desperately needed to reroot themselves in the masses, after the losses at Madiun. The closer racial kinship of Indonesians and Chinese, moreover, gave the latter easier access to the PKI leaders. Aidit and Lukman, who established a new party leadership in 1951, had both spent some time in China after the Madiun rising and while there had doubtless absorbed much of Mao's thinking on revolutionary strategy.[130]

The Chinese Communist view of the Indonesian revolution did not in all respects parallel Moscow's, at least after the Madiun rebellion. In November 1948, before the outcome of the rebellion was known to the Chinese, Liu Shao-chi—like the Russians at this juncture—still ranked Indonesia among the Eastern countries where the national liberation struggle was proceeding satisfactorily and included its "liberated" population among the half billion already freed "from the imperialist yoke."[131] The following spring, however, some months *before* any fundamental shift in view was evident in Soviet commentaries, the Chinese Communist press was contrasting the failure of the Indonesian revolution with the success of China's: the chief difficulties facing the PKI, it was said, were the absence of a revolutionary army and the lack of a sufficiently broad base of support among the Indonesian people.[132] The Chinese, unlike the Russians, appear not to have subsequently singled out Indonesia as an example of a colonial country correctly meeting the imperialist challenge.

Diplomatic relations were nonetheless established between Indonesia and the CPR soon after the formation of the Peking regime, and a Chinese embassy was operating in Djakarta by

[130] The nominal leader of the PKI until 1953 was Alimin, who, though arrested during the Madiun uprising, had escaped punishment and was soon released; the Politburo, however, is said to have been under the control of the Aidit-Lukman faction from January 1951 on. See McVey, *The Development of the Indonesian Communist Party and Its Relations with the Soviet Union and the Chinese People's Republic*, p. 76.

[131] See Liu's "Internationalism and Nationalism," translated in *Pravda*, June 7, 1949, p. 3.

[132] Sha Ping, "The Lessons of Events in Indonesia," *World News and Views*, May 7, 1949, p. 228; the article is said to have been translated from a "leading newspaper" appearing in liberated China in March.

August 1950—some years before the Russians opened an embassy there. The Chinese embassy, in addition to its announced mission of protecting the interests of the 2,000,000 overseas Chinese in Indonesia (four were elected as delegates to the Chinese People's Congress on the grounds that they had no citizenship in Indonesia), also engaged in extensive propaganda activities and maintained liaison with the PKI. It is said that Chinese-language publications distributed throughout Indonesia were more numerous by the end of 1950 than those in any other foreign language. In August 1951, during a wave of new arrests of PKI leaders, Alimin briefly took refuge in the Chinese embassy.[133]

This Chinese activity in Indonesia, if we may credit the slender evidence of it, suggests Peking's growing concern with the course of Indonesian Communism. It is interesting to note that it comes at a time when the Russians had ceased to show interest in the affairs of the PKI (apart from carrying occasional PKI releases in the Soviet and Cominform press)[134] and appeared indifferent even to developments in Indonesia itself.

HUK RISING IN THE PHILIPPINES

In the Philippines the Communists turned to armed struggle only at the end of 1949, over a year later than in Burma, Malaya, and Indonesia, not to mention Indochina. The delay is the more striking since the Communists possessed, in the *Hukbalahap*, a force capable of sustaining civil war earlier. In this respect the Philippine Communists were more fortunate than their comrades in Malaya and Burma, where by 1948 the Communist-led guerrilla organizations created during the war had fallen into disrepair, or in Indonesia, where there had been none. The excuse for armed struggle in the Philippines, on the other hand, was less compelling than in Malaya, Burma, and Indonesia, or so the CPPI judged it. They therefore chose the time and place

---

[133] For a fuller discussion of Chinese activities in Indonesia during this period, see McVey, *op. cit.*, pp. 66ff.

[134] E.g., *Pravda*, December 31, 1949, p. 4 (a PKI resolution attacking the Round Table talks); *For a Lasting Peace, for a People's Democracy!*, July 21, 1950, p. 2 (a routine communiqué from the Central Committee criticizing the Hatta government).

417

of their rebellion more deliberately than party leaders elsewhere.

It is not known when Zhdanov's message to world Communism in September 1947 first came to the attention of the Philippine Communists. Since the CPPI leaders are known to have been alert to world affairs, it is likely that they knew of the Cominform address and had grasped its implications before the end of the year. The Calcutta conference perhaps also helped to project Zhdanovism to the Philippines (although the Filipinos attending this conference were not Communists and reportedly denounced its resolutions on their return to Manila).[135] The party leadership at any event appears to have been fully cognizant of the new international line at a critical meeting of the Central Committee held in May.

Political developments in the Philippines immediately preceding the May plenum bore a direct relationship to its deliberations. On March 6 President Roxas, frustrated by his repeated failures to disarm the *Hukbalahap*, outlawed the organization together with its affiliate, the National Peasant Union.[136] Had Roxas lived, he would doubtless have carried his campaign against the Communists to its logical conclusion, the outlawing of the CPPI itself, and so driven them to open rebellion; the Communists were indeed preparing for it. Roxas' sudden death in mid-April, however, led to a reversal of the government's policy toward the *Huks*. By early May Roxas' successor, Elpidio Quirino, using his brother as intermediary, had established contact with Luis Taruc and opened negotiations which it was hoped would lead

---

[135] See McVey, *The Calcutta Conference and the Southeast Asian Uprisings*, p. 9; Miss McVey cites WFDY sources for the presence of a Philippine delegation at Calcutta but gives no source for its later denunciation of the conference. Both José Lava and Luis Taruc, in interviews with the writer in 1962, claimed to have known nothing of the Calcutta conference at the time and doubted if any Philippine Communists attended it. (It should be noted, of course, in evaluating their evidence, that both were at the time awaiting appeal on convictions involving CPPI contacts with international Communism and so would have been careful to conceal any knowledge of such contacts.)

[136] The National Peasant Union, a civilian organization which stood in the same relationship to the *Huks* as the *Min Yuen* stood to the MCP's Liberation Army (that is, its provisioner), was said to have numbered 200,000 by the spring of 1947; see Hoeksema, *Communism in the Philippines*, p. 338, citing *Philippines Free Press*, May 3, 1947.

418

to the end of the intermittent and undeclared civil war with the *Hukbalahap*. These negotiations were in progress when the party conference convened.[137]

The response of the May conference to these developments was in part a reflection of Zhdanovism, in part a reflection of the hesitations which had characterized party policy since the end of the war. The basic formulation set forth by the conference, according to José Lava, was that "the main form of struggle is the armed struggle." Lava, writing of the conference two years later, noted that there was "less clarity of thought" on this question than on certain others inasmuch as the conference could not agree whether a "revolutionary situation" existed at the time warranting a resort to arms. The conference specifically rejected, according to Lava, "a 'Leftist' proposal by Lacuesta that the Party and the *Huks* should openly declare their aims of overthrowing the rule of American imperialism and its puppets through armed struggle." On the other hand, it gave no indication when or under what conditions such a declaration might be appropriate. There was also ambiguity in the resolutions on other issues. It was asserted, for instance, that "the main blow of the proletariat" should be directed at the *Nacionalista* rather than the Liberals (a deference to the latter presumably arising from the negotiations currently in progress with the Quirino government); the Liberals, however, were in the last analysis no better than "instruments of the main enemy, American imperialism," and should be treated accordingly (an attitude not likely to facilitate the amnesty talks). One issue at least was resolved without ambiguity at the May conference, the long smoldering rivalry between the "majority" and "minority" factions: Jorge (Frienza), Castro and Lacuesta (the "majority" leaders) were suspended for "conscious appeasement"; a new party secretary, Balgos, was elected; and the "minority PB," led by the Lavas and Luis Taruc, was ascendant in the new Central Committee.[138]

[137] Both Communist and non-Communist sources affirm the initiative of the Quirino government in opening negotiations with the *Hukbalahap*; see Lava, *Milestones*, pp. 88-9, and Scaff, *The Philippine Answer to Communism*, p. 30.

[138] The only detailed account of the May 1948 conference known to the writer is in Lava, *Milestones*, pp. 89-95.

Engagement & Disengagement: 1948-1954

Since the Central Committee reached no decision in May on the "peace" negotiations with Quirino, the new party leadership was left to devise its own course in the matter. It elected to continue the talks and with one dissenting vote (presumably on the Politburo) agreed to allow Taruc to proceed to Manila in June to conclude the terms of an amnesty. José Lava subsequently described the decision as a "tactical maneuver," designed to recapture the "political initiative which we held at the time of Roxas' death, but which Quirino was trying to seize through his offer to negotiate."[139] Whether or not this was the attitude of the party leadership at the time, Taruc did go to Manila and regained the seat in Congress, with back pay, which he had been denied by the Roxas government following the elections of 1946. An amnesty was proclaimed on June 21. The *Huks* were given to July 15 to register their fire-arms and the deadline was twice extended. Of an estimated 5,000-10,000 in the *Hukbalahap*, fewer than one hundred, it is said, reported for registration[140]— a number not likely to persuade the Quirino administration that it had come closer than its predecessor to finding a solution to the *Huk* problem. On August 29 Taruc returned to the jungle as abruptly as he had left it two months earlier. In a letter explaining his action, he said that he had left, not because of threats on his life (though he implied these existed), but as a protest against the course the Quirino government was taking. There could be no "democratic peace" in the Philippines, Taruc stated, until American imperialism ended; "legal, constitutional, parliamentary methods of struggle alone cannot achieve democratic peace."[141]

Thus ended the brief interlude of Communist-Liberal negotiations over the *Huk* question. These negotiations occurred at a curious juncture in the course of Communism in Southeast Asia: in Burma and Malaya the insurrections were gathering

[139] Lava, *Milestones*, p. 96.

[140] Hoeksema, *op. cit.*, p. 356, citing Manila news accounts.

[141] Taruc, *Born of the People*, p. 263. Taruc's account of the letter squares with a report of it published at the time in the Manila press; see Hoeksema, *op. cit.*, p. 357.

420

momentum; in Indonesia preparations were being made for rebellion (not necessarily in September, when rebellion inadvertently broke out, but on some not too distant date); the Filipinos themselves, in May, had given a formulation to the question of "armed struggle" which was in advance of anything yet heard from Moscow. The CPPI's behavior, in short, was a great deal more moderate than its own words and the behavior of other Communist movements in Southeast Asia would have led one to expect.

One explanation of the CPPI's moderation is José Lava's suggestion that the CPPI was engaged in a "tactical maneuver" in its negotiations with the Liberals. "Maneuver" is always a plausible explanation of Communist behavior and was especially relevant to the CPPI's prospects during the summer of 1949: should the negotiations go in their favor and restore the *Hukbalahap* to legal status, the re-entry of Communists into Philippine political life would have been greatly facilitated. Divisions within the party, meanwhile, persisting after the reorganization in May, rendered the Communist movement as a whole too disunited to encourage party leaders to urge a strategy of "armed struggle."

Such considerations undoubtedly deterred the CPPI from armed rebellion through August. It proved impossible, however, to continue negotiations with the government *and* hold the *Hukbalahap* intact for future contingencies. The party leadership had to choose between a legal and semi-legal existence, and elected the latter. Taruc's return to the jungle at the end of August dramatized the party's turn from the moderate course; it represented an effort to bring CPPI policies in line with those of the world Communist movement, which Taruc had perhaps come to appreciate more fully during his two months in Manila.

The CPPI did not, however, turn to open rebellion after Taruc's return. If the "tactical maneuver" was now played out, armed neutrality was a minimum program so long as divisions persisted in the Communist movement. These in fact multiplied during the autumn of 1948. According to José Lava, two of the former "majority PB," Castro and Lacuesta, after failing to reverse the decisions of the May conference, established their own

421

Politburo and sought to rally around it rank-and-file party members in Manila. For this they were in due course expelled altogether from the CPPI, but not before they had succeeded in dividing the Congress of Labor Organizations (CLO) where formerly Communist strength had been virtually unchallenged; although the CLO grew by mid-1949 to an estimated 100,000,[142] it was lost to the CPPI after the Castro-Lacuesta defection as an agency capable of rendering effective support to the *Hukbalahap*.

The approach of the presidential elections of 1949, meanwhile, absorbed the attention of the new party leadership and provided a further reason for postponing the decision to take to arms. Philippine Communists were attracted, as by a magnet, to the bi-annual elections. They took part, with some success as we have seen, in the first post-war elections in 1946; in 1948, under the Jorge leadership, they supported four Liberal candidates in the Senatorial elections; now they were prepared, under new leadership, to test their strength again at the polls.[143] At a Central Committee conference early in 1949 the party leadership, reversing the position of the Central Committee the preceding May, decided in a divided vote to support the *Nacionalista*. The reason for this decision, according to Lava, was that José Laurel, the *Nacionalista* candidate, had given early pledges to *Huk* representatives that he would campaign on a strongly anti-imperialist platform and support agrarian reform. As the campaign progressed, however, and growing popular dissatisfaction with the Quirino administration became apparent, Laurel spurned Communist and *Huk* support. He made Liberal corruption his chief campaign issue and left the question of American "imperialism" largely aside. The CPPI continued nonetheless to support him, at one juncture even offering him "armed support to assure the integrity of the election." This too was rejected.[144]

---

[142] See Hoeksema, *op. cit.*, p. 370, citing figures announced by the CLO at its Fourth Convention in July 1949.

[143] It is significant that José Lava, in his interview with this writer in January 1962, placed much emphasis on these post-war elections; he related the major developments in the CPPI and the principal changes in policy and leadership to the electoral alliances the party devised during the campaigns.

[144] See Lava, *Milestones*, p. 110.

The narrow defeat of the *Nacionalista* in November, amid widespread (and justifiable) charges of Liberal corruption at the polls, marked the turning point in Communist strategies. The party leadership now went entirely underground and called openly "for the armed overthrow of the Liberal Party puppets of American imperialism."[145] An enlarged meeting of the Politburo on January 18, 1950, affirmed the order in a resolution on the existing political situation and the party's current tasks. The mounting economic crisis, election frauds, the demoralization of the Army, and widespread unemployment, the resolution stated, had brought on an intense national crisis. "The beginnings of a revolutionary situation already exist," the document continued; the party must undertake "total mobilization." American policy, it was anticipated, would be to bring about unity between the Liberals and *Nacionalista*, healing the wounds opened at the recent election, in order to establish an anti-Communist front; both parties, it was expected, would respond sympathetically to this effort. Under these circumstances the CPPI's course was clear: without giving up entirely its legal opposition through Communist-front organizations still in existence, the slogan for the masses must now be "Armed Overthrow of the Quirino Liberal Administration and the Imperialist-Feudalist Domination of Our Country!" The CPPI must undertake "active preparations for such armed overthrow on a national scale."[146] At this point the *Huk* rebellion began in earnest.[147]

Soviet commentaries on the Philippines from the autumn of 1947 to the outbreak of the *Huk* uprising at the end of 1949 continued to reflect some indifference concerning developments there. The most comprehensive report on the Philippines since the end of the war was Zabozlaeva's at the Orientalist confer-

[145] *Ibid.*, p. 111.

[146] Hoeksema, *op. cit.*, pp. 375-9, citing "Analysis of the Developing Situation and Our Tasks" (January 18, 1950), introduced as evidence in the trial of José Lava in November 1950.

[147] The *Hukbalahap* (Anti-Japanese People's Army) was formally renamed the *Hukbong Magpalayang Bayan*, or HMB (People's Liberation Army) at the end of 1949; the abbreviated name *"Huk,"* however, continued in use.

ence in November 1947 (the conference commemorating thirty years of Bolshevik impact on the East). Devoting her attention largely to events before the war, Zabozlaeva noted that the independence struggle in the Philippines was different from those in other colonies because of the existence there of a nationalist movement totally dependent on and loyal to the United States; because of the close economic ties of the Philippine bourgeoisie to American imperialists, the latter "allowed themselves the luxury of encouraging a landowning nationalism." The CPPI's task was accordingly to "gain a leading role in the national liberation movement of Filipino workers and peasants and wean them away from the influence of the bourgeois 'National Party' and conservative Trade Union leaders."[148] Zabozlaeva's grasp of postwar developments in the Philippines appears to be quite elementary: reference is made to only one political party, presumably the *Nacionalista*—although the Liberals were in power at the time; no mention is made of the 1946 elections, in which the Communists played a major part; nor does the author indicate the disposition of the 60,000 reportedly left in the *Hukbalahap* at the end of the war, an issue which preoccupied both government and the CPPI during these years.

Where Soviet interests were affected, Moscow showed a more lively interest in current affairs. In March 1948, for instance, *Pravda* promptly repudiated Roxas' charge, as he outlawed the *Hukbalahap* and the *National Peasant Union*, that their dependence on the USSR "through the Chinese Communists" made his action necessary; it was one further proof, the author of this more than usually immoderate article commented, of the efforts of this "Philippine liar" to do Wall Street's bidding.[149] An item in *New Times* at about the same time called Roxas'

---

[148] B. Kremortat, "Sessiia Tikhookeanskogo instituta Akademii nauk SSSR," *Voprosy istorii*, No. 4, April 1948, p. 155; this article includes a summary of Zabozlaeva's report, as does another account of the conference in Akademiia nauk SSSR, *Vestnik*, No. 1, 1948, p. 44 (translated in *Soviet Press Translations*, III, 8, pp. 275-6).

[149] *Pravda*, March 14, 1948; the article, written by V. Maevskii, is translated in *Soviet Press Translations*, III, 10, pp. 303-4.

charges of Soviet support of the *Hukbalahap* "wild ravings" and considered the outlawing of the two organizations "an outrageous violation of elementary democratic liberties."[150] From these commentaries one gains the impression that Moscow was more concerned with a denial of any Soviet involvement in the Philippines than it was troubled over the fate of the *Hukbalahap* and its affiliate.

The Soviet press, insofar as this writer has been able to discover, remained unaccountably silent on events in the Philippines during the next eight months—months which we have seen were critical for the CPPI. When the silence was broken in November, Moscow's view of developments in the Philippines was greatly altered. A writer in *Izvestiia*, evidently influenced by the growing intensity of the insurrections in Burma and Malaya (and perhaps also in nearby Indonesia, where the outcome of the Madiun rising was not yet known), argued that a state of civil war not only existed presently in the Philippines but had been in progress for two years—that is, from the autumn of 1946; the *Hukbalahap*, it was said, had increased its strength fourfold during this period.[151]

A similar interpretation was given by Zabozlaeva in her report to the Orientalists' conference in June 1949. According to a revised text of her report, published later in the year, she explained the Communists' turn to armed struggle as follows:

In the period immediately after the war, when illusions of parliamentarianism had not yet been destroyed, the national liberation struggle against American imperialism was still carried on in the form of demonstrations against the naming of collaborators to administrative posts and demands for immediate independence. After the achievement of "independence" and especially after the passing of American laws and agreements concerning bases, however, the leaders of the national liberation struggle became more and more con-

---

[150] N - - v, "Fabrications of a Philippine Quisling," *New Times*, March 17, 1948, pp. 27-8.

[151] *Izvestiia*, November 4, 1948, p. 4; a review of Ernando J. Abaya, *Betrayal in the Philippines* (Moscow, 1947) by F. Shakhmagonov (translated in *Soviet Press Translations*, IV, 5, pp. 152-3).

vinced that without an armed struggle against American imperialism itself, victory over internal reaction was impossible.[152]

When this view crystallized in the Philippines Zabozlaeva does not indicate, but she implies that it was prior to the amnesty talks the preceding year: describing that period as an "armed truce," she quotes Taruc as having said quite openly at the outset of the talks that, if the achievement of their goals "through peaceful means" proved impossible, the Communists would revert to their "revolutionary course." Zabozlaeva notes the party's open defiance of the government at the end of August after the negotiations had failed. She cites Taruc's view, in his letter of August 29, that "the USSR is the ally of the Philippine people" and that in the event of war between Russia and the United States "it would not be necessary, in order to be a good Filipino, to risk one's life defending American bases." Balgos' view was even more explicit, according to Zabozlaeva: "In the event of war the Philippine Communists will be on the side of the Soviet Union."[153]

Moscow, to judge from Zabozlaeva's report, had a better understanding of the Philippines in 1949 than several years earlier, but still was unable to fit all developments there into a coherent scheme. The assertion, for instance, that a state of civil war existed in the Philippines, at least since Taruc's return to the jungle in August 1948, was plausible in the sense that the *Hukbalahap* was intact and occasional encounters with government forces had occurred; it did not, however, account for the fact that many party leaders, including First Secretary Balgos, continued to operate more or less openly in Manila. Above all, it failed to explain the CPPI's efforts to form a new electoral alliance with the *Nacionalista* in the presidential campaign of 1949.

[152] *Krizis kolonial'noi sistemy*, pp. 245-6; a summary of the report as originally presented (including this passage) is in *Colonial People's Struggle for Liberation* (Bombay, 1949), p. 78.

[153] *Krizis kolonial'noi sistemy*, p. 247. Balgos, who was present at the rally Taruc was to have attended on August 29, is reported to have made such a statement in response to a question from the crowd; see Hoeksema, *op. cit.*, p. 358, citing *Philippines Free Press*, September 4, 1948.

Possibly Moscow disapproved of the CPPI's tactics as being too great a diversion of energy from the revolutionary course which was now everywhere prescribed for the colonial world. If so, the only way Moscow could indicate its disapproval, in the absence of some liaison with the Filipinos, was to ignore the Communists' part in the election. This the Soviet press did, but found little else to say in its stead. There was occasional reference to government "terrorism" against the *Huks*—the nearest thing to coverage of a "civil war" in the Philippines;[154] there was also some discussion of the Philippines in the context of Moscow's continuing concern with American "imperialist" influence in the Far East.[155] But the course of Philippine Communism as such was ignored. If it is true, as occasionally reported in the Manila press, that the *Huks* expected aid from the USSR during 1949,[156] the reason for their confidence cannot be discovered in published Soviet commentaries.

Once the *Huk* uprising developed in earnest, in the spring of 1950, the Russians took more explicit notice of it. In July (a month after the outbreak of the Korean war) the Soviet press reported extensive *Huk* gains despite desperate efforts by the government, with the help of American military advisers, armored cars, and weapons of various sorts, to put down the rising.[157] In August 60 percent of the four central provinces of Luzon was said to be under *Huk* control.[158] A long article in *Pravda* the following April found the *Huks'* position still more advantageous and the rebellion extended to Mindanao, despite a vigorous offensive by the Quirino forces in the autumn of 1950;

---

[154] E.g., *Izvestiia*, May 5, 1949, p. 4, citing foreign dispatches on government "atrocities" against the *Huks*.

[155] See *Trud*, April 8, 1949, and *Literaturnaia gazeta*, August 31, 1949; translated in *Soviet Press Translations*, iv, 11, pp. 328-9, and iv, 20, pp. 621-2. Both articles deal with President Quirino's proposal for a "Pacific Pact," Washington's version (it was alleged) of a Far Eastern NATO; Moscow's preoccupation with this proposal will be discussed later in the chapter.

[156] E.g., *Philippine Herald*, July 19 and August 4, 1949; cited in Hoeksema, *op. cit.*, p. 375.

[157] V. Danilov, "Bor'ba filippinskogo naroda protiv imperialistov," *Trud*, July 25, 1950; translated in *Soviet Press Translations*, v, 16, pp. 505-7.

[158] I. Lapitsky, "The Philippine Scene," *New Times*, August 2, 1950, pp. 12-5.

American military aid for the suppression of the rising, it was said, now totaled more than one and a half billion dollars.[159] Another lengthy review of the Philippine insurrection, in August, considered the present phase of the struggle (since March 1950) as merely a continuation of the civil war which broke out in 1945. The *Huks*, the author stated, "will not lay down their arms until the American imperialists are expelled from the country"; he admitted no doubt that the *Huks* could accomplish this.[160] In November an article in *Izvestiia* referred to a recent military alliance concluded between the Philippines and the United States as "another step on the road to dragging the country into the aggressive ventures of the American military." The author argued that *Huk* successes were due precisely to these maneuvers of American imperialism and to the corruption of Philippine politicians.[161]

There was thus no suggestion in the Soviet press through 1951 that the Philippine Communists had suffered reverses. Yet they had. From the autumn of 1950, soon after Magsaysay was appointed Secretary of Defense, the Communist position began gradually to deteriorate. On October 18, 1950, the party's organization in Manila (referred to as the "Politburo In"—that is, in Manila, as distinct from the "Politburo Out," in the jungle) was destroyed in a series of raids by the security police; 105 Communist leaders, among them José Lava, were arrested on this occasion and sentenced to long terms of imprisonment.[162] Other Party leaders in Manila were arrested in the following months.[163] In December Magsaysay created a special organization, the Economic Development Corps (EDCOR), to deal with the prob-

---

[159] *Pravda*, April 2, 1951, p. 3.

[160] Manuel Cruz, "The Truth about the Philippines," *New Times*, August 1, 1951, pp. 12-6.

[161] *Izvestiia*, November 13, 1951, p. 4.

[162] Lava, we have noted, was sentenced to life imprisonment; other terms varied in length.

[163] Among these was an American, William Pomeroy, who had been close to the CPPI since serving in the U.S. Army in the Philippines at the end of the war; he returned to study in Manila in 1948, married a Filipino (a Communist) and joined the *Huk* rebellion in April 1950. See Hoeksema, *op. cit.*, p. 411. Pomeroy was released from jail and deported in January 1962.

lem of rehabilitating captured and surrendered *Huks*. It began
work early in 1951, reclaiming land for new settlements on Mindanao, and by the end of the year its progress was affecting the
morale of the usually landless *Huks*. American aid in the meantime made a difference in the effectiveness of government military operations during 1951: according to official sources, *Huk*
losses in 1951 were 2,000 killed and 2,500 captured, as compared
to 1,286 killed and 550 captured in 1950.[164] Among the dead was
Guillermo Capadocia, who since his reinstatement in the party
in 1948 had served as an effective and evidently popular leader.
Finally, the Army's supervision of the bi-annual elections in November 1951 and the absence of appreciable corruption at the polls
destroyed one of the principal propaganda advantages the CPPI
had had after the 1949 elections.

A party conference in December 1951 took sober note of these
developments. According to the report of a *Huk* commander who
surrendered soon after the conference, Taruc in particular was
pessimistic about the prospects of the rebellion: the raid on the
Politburo, Capadocia's death, the clean elections had all, he felt,
dealt the *Huks* a heavy blow.[165] A "Political Transmission" issued
at the time of the conference acknowledged that the "revolutionary current has abated" and cautioned party members to prepare
themselves for a "long, protracted struggle"; more attention, in
particular, should be given to work in the trade unions and
amongst students.[166] The next "Political Transmission," issued in
July 1952, discussed with some candor the causes of the troubles
besetting the party: inadequate indoctrination of the cadres, an
erroneous estimate of the effectiveness of American aid to the
government, and problems of leadership.[167] The latter issue was

[164] Hoeksema, *op. cit.*, p. 408, citing figures released by the Philippine Department of Defense.
[165] Hoeksema, *op. cit.*, p. 417, citing a report in *Philippines Free Press*, February 2, 1952.
[166] "Political Transmission," No. 2, December 22, 1951, p. 14. These party
statements (known as PTs) were issued once or twice a year beginning in July
1951; they consisted normally of detailed analyses of both international and
domestic developments and enumerated current tasks.
[167] "Political Transmission," No. 3, July 1952, pp. 14-8.

not dealt with in detail, but may have reflected the difficulties party leaders were having at this juncture with Luis Taruc, who grew more and more estranged from the CPPI and was eventually expelled for violating "democratic centralism."[168] At the end of 1952 another "Political Transmission" stressed the party's antiwar policy and gave little attention to the insurrection. The CPPI was ready, the document said, "to co-operate with any party, group or individual who will hold the line against war, although they [may] have been enemies in the past. . . . This policy does not mean that we are abandoning the class struggle. On the contrary, at the period when the danger of war is growing, the antiwar policy is the highest form of class strategy, since war is what our class all over the world is avoiding most."[169] The "class struggle" as represented by the *Huk* rebellion does, however, appear to have been curtailed (if not "abandoned") during 1952. Far fewer *Huk* raids were reported in 1952 than the year before, as the party's emphasis shifted from recruitment for the HMB to penetration of open organizations; Communist fatalities, according to official sources, fell from 2,000 to 1,335, despite the greater effectiveness of government forces.[170]

Soviet commentaries after 1951—which were fewer than during the first two years of the rebellion—reflected very imperfectly

[168] The date of Taruc's expulsion from the party is in doubt. According to a later "Political Transmission" (No. 7, June 1954), he was suspended from membership in July 1953 and expelled the following January. Taruc himself states that he was formally voted out of the *Huk* leadership as early as August 1950, for opposing the decisions of the party conference of the previous January, and claims to have had nothing further to do with the *Huks* or the CPPI (other than his own personal following) once he was informed of this vote; interview with Taruc, January 1962. This evidence conflicts, of course, with the report of his presence at the party meeting of December 1951, noted above. It should be observed, in connection with Taruc's alleged intransigence, that since his voluntary surrender in May 1954 he has persistently emphasized his independence at all times from the leadership of the CPPI; it was his desire to remain independent, he argues, that led him to reject the party leadership when it was offered to him in 1946.

[169] "Political Transmission," No. 4, December 1952 (from a translation in the writer's possession). For a more detailed discussion of these early PTs, see José M. Cristol, "Communist Propaganda in the Philippines, 1950-1953," *Philippine Studies*, 1, Nos. 3-4, December 1953.

[170] See Hoeksema, *op. cit.*, p. 419.

these modifications of CPPI tactics. An article in *Trud* in March 1952 continued to make exaggerated claims of *Huk* successes; the author saw in a sequence of recent American visitors to Manila (Vice President Barkley, William Bullitt, Admiral Collins, and others) a last-ditch effort by Washington to shore up the tottering Quirino regime.[171] If it is true that the party leadership was having troubles with Luis Taruc, Moscow was evidently unaware of it as late as January 1953: a small volume on the Philippines that went to press that month continued to identify Taruc as the leader of the *Huks* and quoted him sympathetically on various matters.[172] In July 1953 the synopsis of a recent dissertation on the Philippines by a Soviet Orientalist opened with a reference to the "wonderful revolutionary events" unfolding in the Philippines and to the virtues of the vigorous struggle waged by the Filipinos, "led by Communists and arms in hand."[173] Since Moscow's encouragement of colonial insurrection was not usually so outspoken as late as mid-1953, we will need later in this chapter to consider why this was the case in the Philippines. For the present it is enough to note some irony in the fact that Moscow appears to have been growing less and less sensitive to developments in the Philippines (or less interested in them) at a time when the CPPI, to judge from the "Political Transmissions," was growing more attentive to world affairs and more conscious of the need to co-ordinate its strategies with those of the world Communist movement.[174]

If Russian Communists were inattentive to the Philippines, on balance, American and Chinese were equally so. Speakers at the Fifteenth Convention of the CPUSA in 1951 referred sympathetically to the "heroic liberation struggle of the Philippine peo-

---

[171] *Trud*, March 12, 1952, p. 3.

[172] Levinson, *Filippiny*, pp. 57-8.

[173] G. I. Levinson, "Kolonial'naia politika SShA i natsional'no-osvoboditel'noe dvizhenie na Filippinakh . . . ," Akademiia nauk, Institut Vostokovedeniia, *Kratkie soobshcheniia*, VIII, 1953, p. 36.

[174] A point is made in "Political Transmission" No. 3, July 1952, for instance, that an urgent need exists to co-ordinate Communist strategies in Asia and Europe.

ple" but acknowledged far too little support from workers in the United States.[175] A search of American Communist journals and other materials published during the period under review confirms the modest interest shown in the Philippines by the CPUSA.[176] Liaison between the two parties, meanwhile, appears to have been irregular, to judge from an exchange of letters between José Lava and William Pomeroy in 1950 on the occasion of the latter's application for membership in the CPPI: Lava appears quite uncertain, and seeks Pomeroy's advice, as to how an "official transfer" from one party to the other might be effected.[177] As far as the Chinese Communists are concerned, finally, this writer has discovered no evidence of a link between the CCP and the CPPI or of Peking's interest in the *Huk* rebellion once it began in earnest—despite a remark reportedly made by Luis Taruc in 1948 that "the Philippines will go the same road as China";[178] reference to the remark in a 1953 Soviet source suggests Moscow's willingness to recognize some Chinese supervision over the CPPI, but it was an option Mao evidently did not take up.

WAR IN INDOCHINA

Moscow's reluctance to indicate full approval of Ho Chi Minh's course in Indochina did not dissipate until the spring of 1948, nearly a year and a half after the outbreak of civil war there. Even Zhdanov's Cominform address, marking a signal shift in Soviet policies, changed nothing: a solitary item in the Soviet press, insofar as this writer has discovered, represents Moscow's interest in Vietnam during the six months following the Wiliza Gora meeting.[179]

[175] *Political Affairs*, No. 5, May 1951, p. 67, cited in Hoeksema, *op. cit.*, pp. 410-11.

[176] The author's search has been less exhaustive than Hoeksema's; the latter, in his comprehensive *Communism in the Philippines*, shows few American Communist commentaries on the Philippines after 1949.

[177] The letters, included in the large volume of Communist materials recovered by the Philippine government during the raids of October 1950, are discussed in Hoeksema, *op. cit.*, p. 411.

[178] Levinson, *op. cit.*, p. 58.

[179] The item—sympathetic, of course, to the Vietminh—is a review of two recent Vietnamese publications: *Vietnam: A New Stage in Her History* (Bangkok,

The Calcutta conference of February 1948 appears to have initiated a livelier Soviet interest in Vietnam. The seven-man Vietminh delegation, all army officers, played a major part in the proceedings, and the report on Vietnam was said to be the "keynote message of the conference."[180] It emphasized, not surprisingly, the virtues of armed struggle and cited both Indochina and Indonesia as countries where guerrilla strategies had been particularly successful. This view was not challenged at the conference, although it was a more forthright statement on the use of force in the colonial world than had yet been made by Soviet spokesmen. The official resolutions of the conference, we have seen, did not specifically include a recommendation in this matter. Vietnamese experience was not unanimously endorsed at Calcutta. A Jugoslav observer, for instance, is reported to have criticized the Vietminh for having placed national interests above party interests—a reference, presumably, to Ho Chi Minh's liquidation of the CPIC in 1945. The criticism appears, however, to have been made solely on the Jugoslavs' initiative. Soviet commentaries never took Ho Chi Minh to task for this move; the fact, moreover, that this was in essence the offense Stalin was presently to lay to the Jugoslavs themselves lends a note of irony to the charge.[181]

Soon after the Calcutta conference, the first detailed account of the Indochinese war to appear in the Soviet press in many months was carried in *New Times*. Fifteen thousand German Nazis, it stated, were fighting for the French in Vietnam; most French administrators were former Vichyites; French losses, according to North Vietnamese estimates, were 60,000 killed and wounded since the fighting began; a large scale French offensive in February and March was said to have been repulsed. American intervention in the civil war on France's side, it was reported, had greatly increased in recent months, as reflected in the frenzied efforts of William C. Bullitt to restore Bao Dai as Emperor of

---

1947), and Vo Nguyen Giap, *One Year of Revolutionary Achievement* (Bangkok, 1946); see *New Times*, October 1, 1947, p. 28.

[180] McVey, *The Calcutta Conference and the Southeast Asian Uprisings*, p. 15.
[181] See Ruth McVey's comment on this point; *ibid.*, p. 15.

433

Vietnam.[182] By July 95 percent of Vietnam was said to be under Vietminh control, and French casualties were placed at 53,000 killed and 45,000 wounded. The establishment by the French of a "central government" in May under Nguyen Van Xuan (described as a wartime collaborator) and their agreement with Bao Dai in June promising Vietnam its "independence" were regarded as desperate and futile maneuvers.[183] In October Vasil'-eva, commenting on the proposal of a French journalist for a cease-fire and the conclusion of a "dignified peace" with the DRV, wrote: "But for this France would need a truly democratic and really French government, conducting its own policy independent of the American monopolies." Since she sees no such government in the offing, she implies that the war in Indochina will, and *should*, continue.[184] This was, of course, consistent with Moscow's attitude at this juncture toward the rebellions in Malaya and Burma, now in full swing. For the present, Southeast Asian Communism had passed the point of no return.

During the first half of 1949 Soviet attention focused on French and American efforts to arrange Bao Dai's return to Vietnam as Emperor. His apparent reluctance to quit the certain comforts of the French Riviera for an uncertain throne in Saigon was recorded in February.[185] The agreement reached between Bao Dai and the French early in March, allegedly establishing Vietnam's "independence," was described as a transparent deception on the part of the Paris government—evidenced by the latter's simultaneous dispatch of ten new French battalions to fight the Vietminh.[186] The installation of the Emperor in Saigon in June was viewed as proof of the growing dependence of the French government on the United States, said to be Bao Dai's principal supporter.[187]

[182] I. Podgurov, "Reportazh iz V'etnama," *Novoe vremiia*, April 21, 1948, pp. 29-31.
[183] "V'etnamskaia avantiura 'dvukhsot semeistv,' " *ibid.*, July 7, 1948, p. 18.
[184] *New Times*, October 20, 1948, pp. 29-31.
[185] *Ibid.*, February 2, 1949, p. 20.
[186] I. I. Podkopaev, "V'etnam v bor'be za nezavisimost'," *Novoe vremiia*, April 13, 1949, p. 12.
[187] "Imperator na verevochke," *ibid.*, June 30, 1949, p. 17.

The attention given to the Bao Dai issue, and especially to the alleged American role in his restoration, must be seen in the context of Moscow's views at this juncture on the war in China and its relationship to developments in Vietnam. The civil war in Indochina was no longer an isolated colonial upheaval; it was now—or presently would be—linked with China's great revolution. There were two ways of looking at this prospect. It could be heralded as a mighty setback for imperialism. This, for instance, was the view expressed by Zhukov at the Orientalist conference in June: "The imperialists are mortally afraid of the perspective [i.e., prospect] of direct contact being established between liberated China and Vietnam, Indonesia, Malaya and Burma."[188] But there was equally the possibility that the imperialists might seek to use Vietnam as a base *against* China. The increasing attention to American intervention in Indochina, in the Bao Dai and in other episodes, reflects Soviet concern with this problem. In August it was argued that the French objective in Indochina was "to convert that country into an operational base for the American military, who are embarking on a new campaign against the democratic movement in Asia and, above all, against People's democratic China."[189] However cheerful the Soviet press appeared to be about Ho's successes, it is clear that for a time in 1949 Moscow was uneasy about a possible escalation of the war in Vietnam.

The victory of the Chinese Communists and the establishment of the Chinese People's Republic in October, without any "escalation" of the Indochinese war initiated by France and the United States, greatly enhanced Ho's prospects of ultimate victory. This was immediately reflected in Soviet commentaries on Indochina, which now became more numerous and more detailed. A long and well-researched article by Alexander Guber in the October issue of *Voprosy istorii*, for instance, made much of Chinese Communist influence within the Vietminh and accented the new prospects of success in Vietnam:

[188] *Colonial People's Struggle for Liberation*, p. 5.
[189] *New Times*, August 24, 1949, p. 18.

The world-wide historic victories of the Chinese people assumed an extremely important significance in the struggle of Vietnam for independence and democracy. They not only influenced the Vietnamese to heroic struggle against the aggressors, but imbued them with confidence that the most difficult period of their resistance to the imperialistic invaders is coming to an end, that along with the growth in reinforcement of the internal forces of the Republic it will have, in place of the hostile Kuomintang rear, the friendly, neighborly, Chinese people's democratic republic.[190]

Vasil'eva concluded her chapter on Indochina in *Krizis kolonial'noi sistemy* (published in November) with the observation that while difficulties still faced the young Vietnamese republic, these were greatly lightened by (note the order she uses) "the success of the Chinese people, the development of the people's struggle in Southeast Asia, and the support of the republic of Vietnam by progressive forces throughout the world led by the Soviet Union."[191]

In January 1950, Moscow formally recognized the DRV. The initiative was taken by Ho Chi Minh in an invitation on January 14 to all countries to exchange ambassadors with his government; Peking responded on January 16, Moscow on January 30.[192] An editorial in *New Times* explained the action by pointing out that only 2,000,000 of the 20,000,000 in Vietnam lived in French-occupied territory, that the USSR was a consistent opponent of colonial enslavement and that the DRV had a constitution and was the "legal" government of the country; nothing, accordingly, was "more natural" than Soviet recognition.[193] The editorial leaves unexplained, of course, why Moscow had not recognized the DRV earlier, inasmuch as all the conditions now offered as a justification for recognition had allegedly existed for several years (including the Vietminh's effective control over most of the country). Moscow has never subsequently explained

---

[190] A. Guber, "V'etnamskii narod v bor'be za svoiu nezavisimost' i demo-kratiiu," *Voprosy istorii*, No. 10, October 1949, p. 60; the translation used here is taken from *Soviet Press Translations*, IV, 6, 206.

[191] *Krizis kolonial'noi sistemy*, p. 194.

[192] *Pravda*, January 31, 1950, p. 1.

[193] *New Times*, February 6, 1950, p. 1.

its delay, but it presumably related to Communist efforts in China which the Russians did not wish to jeopardize by premature—and perhaps unnecessary—action in Vietnam; if it is true, as argued above, that the Russians were concerned that the Indochinese war not escalate to a general Far Eastern war, a delay in according formal recognition to Ho's government served this end by not giving additional cause for concern to the Western powers.[194] At any event, after recognition Moscow could treat the war in Indochina not as an insurgency or revolutionary war but as a sovereign nation's legitimate defense of its integrity against foreign imperialist aggression. Needless to say, Soviet commentators made the most of this new circumstance.

Coverage of Vietnamese developments in the Russian and Cominform press after recognition was continuous and extensive. For the first time in the Soviet era a Southeast Asian country became a focal point of Moscow's attention. Domestic as well as foreign affairs were treated in Soviet commentaries, but, as before, the course of the civil war continued to be the principal topic of discussion.[195]

The outbreak of the Korean war in June 1950 stimulated interest in the war in Indochina since the two were related in the Soviet view: both were seen as manifestations of American aggression. In December, *Pravda* endorsed a recent editorial in *Jen Min Jih Pao* which argued that the American attack on North Korea was part of a "three-pronged invasion" of mainland China —the other two prongs directed from Formosa and Vietnam.[196] If Moscow's reading of American aggression in the Far East appeared to make the Vietminh's efforts subordinate to the de-

---

[194] In this connection, it should be noted that the DRV also adopted cautious foreign policies until the end of 1949—seeking, for instance, to dissociate itself from the international Communist movement and to maintain friendly relations with non-Communist neighbors such as Thailand and even the Nationalist government in China; see Trager, *Marxism in Southeast Asia*, p. 163.

[195] Soviet bibliographies show a sharp rise in coverage of Vietnam during the early 1950's, making discussion of the DRV in some portion of the Russian press almost a daily occurrence; see, for instance, *Bibliografiia Iugo-vostochnoi Azii*, pp. 102ff.

[196] *Pravda*, December 12, 1950, p. 3.

fense of China, this in no way lessened Soviet enthusiasm over Ho Chi Minh's success. Repeated Vietminh victories were reported in the Soviet press throughout the Korean war.[197]

The United States' replacement of France in Indochina, meanwhile, was increasingly emphasized in Soviet commentaries. *Pravda*, commenting in October 1951 on General de Lattre's recent mission to Washington, noted growing rivalry between the two powers and forecast early American supremacy; the American ambassador in Paris was quoted as saying: "Indochina is no longer of interest to France."[198] In May 1952, *Izvestiia* cited the view of Joseph and Stewart Alsop that the "loss" of Indochina would be a serious blow to American prestige in the Cold War as proof that Washington was preparing to assume active leadership of the "imperialist" forces in Vietnam.[199] By the summer of 1953 Soviet commentators were explaining French *malaise* as the consequence of a growing realization that Vietnam must be lost by France whatever happened, either to the Vietminh or to the United States.

The most arresting feature of the Soviet commentaries on Indochina during these years, seen in the context of Soviet comments on other Southeast Asian countries (or, for that matter, on world affairs in general), is the continuing endorsement of the Vietminh's militant course, a course that was being set aside nearly everywhere else. So long as active fighting continued in Korea, an aggressive line remained appropriate in Indochina, given Moscow's linking of the "anti-imperialist" struggle in the two countries. When, however, fighting in Korea gave way to truce talks in July 1951 and during the lengthy negotiations at Panmunjom, one might have anticipated some parallel consideration of truce in Indochina. No sign of such consideration is reflected in Soviet commentaries, at least none leading to proposals that might be listened to in Paris (or Washington). Even

---

[197] E.g., *Trud*, December 1, 1950, p. 4; *Izvestiia*, September 1, 1951, p. 4; *Izvestiia*, February 13, 1952, p. 3; *Pravda*, October 25, 1952, p. 4; *Izvestiia*, November 5, 1952, p. 44—among many others.

[198] *Pravda*, October 18, 1951, p. 4; see also, on the de Lattre mission to Washington, *Trud*, November 1, 1951, p. 3.

[199] See *Pravda*, July 27, 1953, p. 4.

after a final settlement was reached in Korea, in June 1953, there was no immediate shift in Soviet and Vietnamese attitudes toward the war in Indochina. Questions, to be sure, were raised why no peace was yet possible in Vietnam, but they were asked—and answered—in a way not likely to spur negotiations leading to a truce. *New Times*, for instance, argued early in August that the reason no cease-fire was possible in Indochina was that American investments there required the continuation of the war.[200] A writer observed in *Pravda* later in the month that "the ink was no sooner dry" on the Korean truce agreement than Secretary of State Dulles pledged one billion dollars to end the war in Indochina in eighteen months; Washington promised, according to this account, "even to send military forces if necessary." A sharp attack on President Eisenhower followed, stemming from a remark he allegedly made earlier in the month: "the situation [in Indochina] is fraught with most ominous consequences for the United States since, if we lose everything, how can the free world (i.e., the USA—O.C. [the Russian author]) hold the rich empire (?!) of Indonesia?"[201] These were not comments, even if the charges in them were creditable, which normally precede a serious invitation to negotiate. In September the Cominform journal—undoubtedly with Moscow's full approval—carried a long article by the Vietnamese premier, Pham Van Dong, in which he described the DRV's goal as "total victory" and the regime's gravest handicap the absence of a "material base solid enough for a resistance of long duration."[202] Clearly the end was not yet in sight in Indochina, six months after Stalin's death and slightly more than six months before the opening of the Geneva conference.

We may reasonably assume the existence of direct liaison between Moscow and the DRV, but public reference to it is rare. From time to time Soviet correspondents reported interviews with various Vietnamese personalities, both in Vietnam and at

[200] A. Kurov, "Why There is no Cease-Fire in Indochina," *New Times*, August 5, 1953, pp. 14-6.
[201] *Pravda*, August 31, 1953, p. 4.
[202] *For a Lasting Peace, for a People's Democracy!*, September 11, 1953, p. 4.

international conferences;[203] diplomatic exchanges between the two governments, however, are not mentioned in Soviet publications, insofar as this writer has discovered. Nor was there announcement of any Soviet aid to the DRV. Indeed, as late as the spring of 1953 Moscow went to some pains to *deny* a report of a recent aid agreement between Russia, China, and North Vietnam.[204] Not until after the Geneva conference of 1954 were formal cultural and other exchanges between the two countries discussed in the Soviet press.

French Communist influence in North Vietnam, we may note in passing, steadily declined during the Indochinese war for the very good reason that communication with the Vietminh, at war with France, was all but impossible. The FCP did, however, make some effort at home in behalf of the Vietnamese. In December 1949 the French Central Committee adopted a resolution giving the highest priority to efforts to secure "the immediate withdrawal of the expeditionary force in Indochina."[205] In response to this instruction Communist-led dockers in Marseille systematically disrupted shipments of war materials to the Far East during the following months.[206] As the war dragged on, the FCP periodically passed resolutions demanding an end to the *"sâle guerre,"* the withdrawal of French troops and a normalization of relations between the two countries.[207] Beyond these gestures there was little French Communists could do about Vietnam.

Chinese Communist influence, it is clear, replaced French (and in some measure limited Moscow's) in North Vietnam

---

[203] E.g., *Novoe vremiia*, November 30, 1949, pp. 21-2; *Ogonek*, No. 32, 1951, pp. 10-1; *Sovetskaia zhenshchina*, No. 4, 1953, p. 11.

[204] *Pravda*, May 9, 1953, p. 2; the report was made by Wellington Koo, Chinese Nationalist representative at the United Nations, in an interview with the New York *Herald Tribune* on May 7.

[205] The resolution is given in a long article by A. Marty, Secretary of the FCP, in the French edition of *For a Lasting Peace, for a People's Democracy!*, February 24, 1950, p. 2.

[206] *Ibid.*, p. 2; *New Times*, March 8, 1950, pp. 10-2.

[207] See, for instance, the article by Leo Figuères in *For a Lasting Peace, for a People's Democracy!*, March 14, 1952, p. 3.

after 1949. In April 1950 Ho Chi Minh is reported to have visited Peking, although he made no such pilgrimage to Moscow until the mid-1950's, and to have concluded with the Chinese a military agreement which initiated a large-scale build-up of Vietminh strength.[208] By the end of 1950, when the Vietminh occupied the northernmost provinces of the country, they were in direct contact with Chinese forces and thus in a position to receive any assistance Peking was willing to offer.

Students of Vietnamese Communism have puzzled over the question of Chinese aid to North Vietnam, the existence of which both countries persistently denied. There appears, however, to be little serious doubt of it. Former officers in the Vietminh report such aid;[209] foreign Communists have mentioned it;[210] Western observers purport to have detailed knowledge of it;[211] and even official North Vietnamese sources have inadvertently made reference to it.[212] The question, then, would appear to be not *whether* there was Chinese aid to the Vietnamese,

[208] See Hinton, *China's Relations with Burma and Vietnam*, p. 18, citing a report by the French correspondent Robert Guillain.

[209] A former major in the Vietminh (an informant of unquestioned integrity in the writer's opinion) reports that both Russian and Chinese advisers were present in North Vietnam by the end of 1950, the latter far more numerous than the former; supplies, mostly of Russian manufacture, reached the Vietminh over a truck route maintained by the Chinese. Interview with Pham Ngoc Thao, February 1962 (Colonel Thao was at the time a provincial chief in the Mekong delta area); the author's interviews with other former Vietminh officers in Saigon confirm this evidence.

[210] A Philippine Communist document released in 1953 reported that 10,000 Chinese troops were at the time in North Vietnam "helping in the liberation of the country"; "Political Transmission," No. 3, July 1952, p. 4.

[211] E.g., Fall, *Le Viet-minh: La République Démocratique du Viêt-Nam, 1945-1960*, p. 120; Robert Guillain, *La Fin des illusions* (Paris, 1954), pp. 39-42 (cited in Hinton, *op. cit.*, p. 27).

[212] A monitored DRV broadcast of April 20, 1953, for instance, is said to have stated: "China will grant facilities to its brother fighters who are able to ask for aid, such as *the aid given to the fighting forces in Vietnam*"; cited in Hinton, *op. cit.*, p. 18. A remark in 1951 by a ranking Vietminh army officer is more guarded, but still revealing: China, he asserts, has provided the Vietnamese with "a complete system of military thought and a strategy and tactics suitable for colonial and semi-colonial countries"; *Ta Kung Pao*, December 22-24, 1951 (translated in *Soviet Press Translations*, VII, 6, 170).

but whether the aid they received was decisive in their final victory at Dienbienphu. Most students of Vietnamese Communism, it is worth noting, conclude that it was.

There is some evidence that Peking for a time contemplated open intervention in Indochina. In December 1950 the Chinese protested French air and ground violations of the South China frontier dating from the previous May.[213] During the next eighteen months such protests were periodically repeated, often accompanied by warnings of retaliatory action if the violations did not cease. In April 1951, for instance, a Chinese correspondent wrote: "We warned the French imperialists that if they repeat their provocative actions, our border troops will trade blow for blow and the French imperialists will bear full responsibility for the consequences."[214] These warnings must be seen as providing a *casus belli* in the event Peking decided to intervene in Indochina. The Chinese, however, did not intervene—presumably because their engagement in Korea after October 1950 prevented it and because, when that no longer deterred them, the international climate had changed sufficiently to discourage such a venture. As matters turned out, Chinese intervention (which, it may be imagined, was never a popular idea in Moscow) proved unnecessary.

We need not doubt, finally, the gratitude of the North Vietnamese for Peking's assistance at a critical period in their struggle against the French. The close relations which have evolved between the two nations in recent years, despite a traditional hostility between them, are founded on this timely support. It should, however, be noted that Chinese Marxism did not in any sense replace Russian Marxism in the Vietminh during the period we have reviewed. The DRV's successes, Ho remarked in 1951, are based on "the *doctrines* of Marx, Engels, Lenin, and Stalin, and on the *thought* of Mao Tse-tung"[215]—a distinction,

[213] *Pravda*, December 9, 1950, p. 4, citing a release by the Chinese news agency *Hsinhua*.
[214] *Pravda*, April 14, 1951, p. 4; see also *ibid.*, June 8, 1952, p. 4.
[215] *For a Lasting Peace, for a People's Democracy!*, April 4, 1952, p. 5—a letter from Vietnam, citing a speech by Ho Chi Minh in March 1951 (emphasis added).

perhaps, without a difference, but setting Maoism somewhat below Stalinism in the scale of Marxist orthodoxy.

Laos and Cambodia, after the collapse of their short-lived national liberation movements following the war, did not seriously
engage Moscow's attention until 1951. Russian commentaries on
Indochina made no more than passing reference to the two kingdoms. Alexander Guber, for instance, mentioned them once in
a long article on Indochina in the autumn of 1949, noting that
the reactionary leadership in each was only too eager to escape
the necessity of undertaking democratic reforms by making an
agreement with French imperialism.[216] Vasil'eva, in her chapter
in *Krizis kolonial'noi sistemy* (November 1949), wrote of the
two countries:

> The French imperialists applied all their strength to destroy the
> Laotian and Cambodian republics after the war and to restore the
> "kingdoms," fully dependent on French imperialism. This was sim-
> plified by the fact that monarchical and semi-feudal elements, which
> constitute a significant force in Laos and Cambodia, have always
> been closely tied to the French administration and have faithfully
> carried out its wishes. Now, however, a partisan struggle is beginning
> to encompass even Laos and Cambodia, where the French imperialists
> have up to the present considered their position eternal and secure.[217]

No details of the "partisan struggle" are given.

Soviet interest in the two kingdoms accelerated in 1951, evidently because of fresh fears that French troops stationed there
posed a threat to both the Chinese and the Vietminh. An editorial in *New Times* in February commented: "The treachery
of the feudal aristocracy of Cambodia, headed by King Norodom
Sihanouk, is playing into the hands of the imperialists, who want

---

[216] A. Guber, "V'etnamskii narod v bor'be za svoiu nezavisimost' i demokratiiu," *Voprosy istorii*, No. 10, October 1949, p. 37.

[217] *Krizis kolonial'noi sistemy*, p. 194. In 1949 France signed agreements with
both Laos and Cambodia which gave each a limited degree of autonomy; full
independence was conferred on the two kingdoms only in 1953. For a detailed
discussion of the background to Laotian and Cambodian independence, see the
chapters by Roger M. Smith in George M. Kahin (ed.), *Governments and Politics
of Southeast Asia*, 2nd ed. (Cornell 1964), pp. 534ff. and 606ff.

Engagement & Disengagement: 1948-1954

to make Cambodia a bridgehead against the Chinese People's Republic and the Democratic Republic of Vietnam."[218] The same month a substantial article on Laos and Cambodia by Vasil'eva, apparently the first ever to appear in the Soviet press, was carried in *New Times*. Although the two kingdoms have remained "the colonies they were . . . under the yoke of French imperialism," she writes, national liberation movements are now active. In Cambodia a National Unity Front is said to have been organized in May 1950 and by the end of the year its armed forces had "liberated" a third of the country; a similar organization in Laos, also with armed units, was created in August. Both had indicated their intention to maintain close relations with the Vietminh. "It is now quite certain," Vasil'eva asserted, "that the French imperialists cannot rely on Laos and Cambodia as support bases in their war against the DRV."[219]

Following the reorganization of the Vietminh in March 1951, and the reincarnation of the CPIC as the *Lao Dong* (Workers' Party), the alliance between the North Vietnamese and the national liberation movements in Laos and Cambodia was increasingly acclaimed in Soviet and Cominform journals. "Indochina consists of three states but it has a single battlefield," a Vietnamese spokesman wrote in the Cominform journal in April. "We cannot suppose that Vietnamese resistance has definitely triumphed until the French aggressors are chased from Laos and Cambodia."[220] By the spring of 1952 it was claimed that Cambodian "patriots," with help from the DRV, controlled virtually all of eight of the ten provinces in the country, and similar gains were reported in Laos.[221] Such gains were largely illusory.

[218] *New Times*, February 7, 1951, p. 1.
[219] V. Vasil'eva, "People's Liberation Struggle in Laos and Cambodia," *New Times*, February 28, 1951, p. 12; Vasil'eva does not specifically mention the Pathet Lao, although this organization is believed to have been founded as early as 1949 by Prince Souphanouvong following his return from exile in Bangkok.
[220] *For a Lasting Peace, for a People's Democracy!*, April 6, 1951, p. 3; see also *ibid.*, July 20, 1951, p. 4.
[221] *Ibid.*, May 23, 1952, p. 3; a slightly more modest claim—a third of each country under partisan control—is made by V. Avarin in *Voprosy ekonomiki*, No. 7, July 1952, p. 110.

444

In the spring of 1953 Soviet attention was drawn especially to Laos in connection with the DRV's probe into, and abrupt withdrawal from, the *Plaine des Jarres*—a maneuver that has never been satisfactorily explained. The action, a Soviet observer wrote in April, had been initiated entirely by the Laotian patriots; the refusal of the French to acknowledge this was a "shallow device" to justify their claim of North Vietnamese aggression. "This only testifies," the author concluded, "to the impotent fury of the imperialists in the face of the United National Front of the Vietnamese, Pathet Lao, and Khmer."[222]

It is apparent from these scattered references to Laos and Cambodia in the Soviet and Cominform press that from 1951 on there was some intention of extending the Communist drive in North Vietnam into the two kingdoms to the west. Had the war developed differently, both Laos and Cambodia might have become more directly involved. In Cambodia, where the partisan forces were dissolved after the Geneva conference, there were few after-effects of the "national liberation" episode inspired by the North Vietnamese. In Laos, however, the stimulus given the Pathet Lao by its association with the Vietminh early in the 1950's was enough to keep the movement intact after the Geneva conference and to project it into a major role in Laotian politics later in the decade.

DOLDRUMS OF THAI COMMUNISM

The failure of Thai Communists to organize—or, so far as is known, even to contemplate—armed insurrection during the period under review places the movement somewhat outside our discussion in the present chapter. The occasional Soviet commentaries on Thailand that can be discovered show in consequence a fitful character.

There was, to begin with, very sparse coverage of Thai affairs in the Soviet press, insofar as this writer is aware, during the three years following Zhdanov's address inaugurating the Com-

[222] I. Podkopaev, "The Events in Pathet Lao," *New Times*, April 29, 1953, p. 15; see also *Izvestiia*, May 7, 1953, p. 4.

inform, years when the rest of Southeast Asia was plunged into Communist-inspired disorders of one sort or another. In August 1948 *New Times* carried brief "travel notes" by a Soviet journalist that did little more than remind readers of the existence of the Siamese kingdom.[223] A year later a passing Soviet visitor in Bangkok gave a fuller report, accenting especially the strike movement during 1947 and early 1948 (in which, it was said, fifty-seven out of sixty-seven strikes ended in victory for the workers); the Communist Party in Siam was mentioned as underground, but active.[224] Early in 1950 another Soviet traveler in Thailand (the country had by now been renamed once again) closed his remarks on current development with the observation that "Thailand's democratic forces, led by the working class . . . have a big future before them."[225] It is doubtful that the past or present warranted his confidence.

Two topics predominated in the more numerous Russian commentaries on Thailand during the last two or three years of Stalin's life. The principal topic, not surprisingly, was the degradation imposed upon the country by American imperialists following the conclusion of economic and military aid agreements in September and October 1950. Thailand, a writer observed in *Izvestiia*, "is tied hand and foot."[226] By the spring of 1953 American domination of the Thai economy was said to be total, down to control of the nation's soft drink industry by the Coca-Cola Company.[227] The government of Pibulsonggram, according to Soviet accounts, had from the outset abetted American penetration of Thailand. The government's charge of a "Communist menace" in the country, it was observed shortly after the conclusion of the economic and military agreements, was "a camou-

---

[223] V. Tsvetkov, "V Siame," *Novoe vremiia*, No. 35, 1948, pp. 20-3.

[224] A. Belsky, "Siam: a Journalist's Notes," *New Times*, September 14, 1949, pp. 23-8.

[225] L. Alarin, "Travel Notes on Thailand," *New Times*, February 15, 1950, p. 26.

[226] I. Kozhevnikova, "Ianki [Yankees] v Tailande," *Izvestiia*, April 15, 1951, p. 5; see also K. T., "United States Transforms Thailand into a Colony and Military Base," *For a Lasting Peace, for a People's Democracy!*, August 3, 1951, p. 4.

[227] O. Orestove, "V Tailande," *Pravda*, May 28, 1952, p. 4.

flage to mask the activities of imperialists who are busily con-
verting Thailand into a base of operations against the Asian
people's movement for national liberation."[228] In August 1951
Phibun was quoted as having declared in Parliament, allegedly
under American pressure, that "all funds, to the last *satang*,
must go for military needs."[229]

Thailand's foreign policies, meanwhile, reflected this virtually
total dependence on the United States, according to Soviet observers. The Phibun government had initially welcomed some
50,000 Vietnamese refugees from French "terror" in Indochina,
one observer noted, but following recognition "on Washington's orders" of the French-imposed Bao Dai government in
Vietnam, Bangkok had turned against these refugees, subject-
ing them to searches and deportation.[230] By contrast, the Kuomintang troops forced to flee into northern Thailand at the end
of 1949 were given a safe haven there, it was said, and Bangkok
became, again on American orders, a "recruiting center" to
gather fresh volunteers for these Chinese irregulars so that they
could be turned against the CPR and North Vietnam.[231] On
only one occasion did the Soviet press suggest resistance by the
Thai government to Washington's demands: in reporting the
Honolulu conference of August 1952, when the signing of a
"Pacific Pact" (the precursor of SEATO) was first discussed,
a writer in *Pravda* linked Thailand with India, Indonesia, Burma,
and Malaya as opposed to this American project.[232] Since, however, nothing came of Bangkok's "opposition," the episode was
soon forgotten.

The second issue treated with some persistence in Soviet commentaries was the strength of the "peace" movement in Thailand despite the capitulation of the Pibulsonggram government
to American "imperialism." In April 1951 the Stockholm Peace
Appeal was said to have gained 138,000 signatures in Thailand

228 *New Times*, January 17, 1951, p. 20.
229 A. Bel'skii, "Bor'ba taiskogo naroda," *Trud*, August 22, 1951, p. 4.
230 See the article by S. Pogosov in *Trud*, December 8, 1950, p. 3.
231 See *Pravda*, June 26, 1951, p. 4 and December 28, 1951, p. 4.
232 *Pravda*, August 11, 1952, p. 11.

and the election of three Thai to the executive of the World Peace Council was noted.[233] A year later the number of signatures was reported as having risen to 150,000, despite growing government resistance to the movement and the denial of visas to its officials.[234] So long as the "peace" movement could legally exist in Thailand, it provided Moscow with ammunition for its thesis that even in the most backward countries[235] wholly subjected to foreign imperialism there was hope for the oppressed masses. The movement, however, was crushed at the end of 1952 with the arrest of more than a hundred of its leaders, who were subsequently tried for conspiring against Phibun's regime.[236] Their arrest and trial appear to have gone unnoticed in the Soviet press.

The affairs of the Thai Communist Party received scant attention in Russian commentaries, although reference to the party was frequent enough to leave little doubt that Moscow took its existence for granted. In December 1950 the Cominform journal reported an appeal by Thai Communists for a "national democratic united front" to combat the recent military agreements concluded with the United States.[237] In mid-1952 the same journal noted the recently held "Second Congress" of the CPT: a report by the party's General Secretary, Prasong Vong-Vivat, is said to have attacked both Leftist and Rightist factions who opposed the united front tactics; a new party program as well as new statutes are reported to have been adopted, but neither is described.[238]

[233] Kozhevnikova, *loc. cit.*, p. 5.

[234] *New Times*, March 5, 1952, p. 31; see also *ibid.*, August 21, 1952, pp. 24-7.

[235] Thailand was described by a Soviet economist in 1952 as "the most industrially backward country in Southeast Asia"; see the article by V. Avarin in *Voprosy ekonomiki*, No. 7, July 1952, translated in *Soviet Press Translations*, VII, No. 7.

[236] See Trager, *Marxism in Southeast Asia*, p. 94.

[237] *For a Lasting Peace, for a People's Democracy!*, December 1, 1950, p. 2.

[238] *Ibid.*, June 27, 1952, p. 3. According to Malayan Intelligence sources consulted by the author, the Secretary of the CPT in 1949 was Nai Thianthai, also said to have been head of the Communist-controlled Central Labour Union (CLU); at the end of 1950, according to the same sources, the CPT was reported to have had a membership of 40,000 (most unlikely) and to have published two newspapers.

Peking's interest in the Thai Communists after 1949 may be assumed, since the CPT—like the Malayan Communist Party—is known to have been made up largely of overseas Chinese; there is indeed some speculation that two Communist parties existed in Thailand—a Thai and a Chinese.[239] Peking's relations, however, with either or both of these organizations are obscure. A Thai delegate attended the WFTU conference in Peking in November 1949,[240] but no evidence is known to this writer of subsequent contacts with the Chinese Communists until the mid-1950's. Peking's official concern with Thailand, as with most other Southeast Asian countries, was confined for the most part to the treatment given the overseas Chinese, whose interests the Chinese government made it its business to protect. Thus the closing of three Chinese schools in Bangkok was made the occasion for a protest by Peking in March 1951;[241] in September a "credentials check" recently ordered in Thailand was similarly protested because it was said to discriminate against the Chinese community.[242]

If these findings cast no very clear light on Communist strategies in Thailand, they at least round out our story. We should in good conscience be able to lay Communism in Thailand to rest for the purpose of the present study.

DISENGAGEMENT

The gestation period of a major shift in the foreign policy of a nation the size of Russia is measured in years, not months or weeks. We should accordingly not expect to find Zhdanovism yielding to peaceful co-existence as the consequence of a single broad stroke by Stalin. Much evidence exists to show that Moscow

[239] A Thai security official who specializes in Communist affairs told the author that inter-racial rivalry in 1949-50 led to the creation of two separate parties; they were merged only in the mid-1950's. Interview with Col. Chat of the Thai Criminal Investigation Division, March 1961.

[240] His report on the Thai labor movement was subsequently carried in the WFTU organ published in Paris: Vas Sunderashamara, "Doklad o polozhenii profsoiuzov v Siame," *Vsemirnoe profsoiuznoe dvizhenie*, No. 8, 1949, p. 39.

[241] *People's China*, March 16, 1951, p. 28.

[242] *Pravda*, September 28, 1951, p. 4, citing a report by the CPR Committee on the Affairs of the Overseas Chinese.

followed conflicting policies during Stalin's last years: the Soviet thrust in Korea, for instance, was in marked contrast to the Peace Movement then in progress in Europe. Both were genuine manifestations of Stalin's foreign policy in 1950; both, in the last analysis, served the same goal of extending Soviet influence and power. One, let us say, was a late resort to militancy, the other an early essay in moderation.

Soviet policy in Southeast Asia during the last years of Stalin's life presents a striking example of the overlapping of militancy and moderation. On the one hand, there were the Communist insurrections still in progress in Burma, Malaya, the Philippines, and, above all, in Indochina that Moscow could not conveniently disown; on the other, there was growing evidence that the Russians were seeking a less turbulent course in Southeast Asia. In the present section we shall attempt to catalogue some of this evidence, in an effort to demonstrate Moscow's disengagement from the Zhdanov line in the East; in the final section of the chapter we shall endeavor to explain the shift.

Before studying Moscow's changing attitudes toward the Southeast Asian regimes—attitudes that constitute the principal evidence, for our purposes, of Soviet disengagement in Southeast Asia—it is useful to consider several more general indications of the impending policy shift in the East. An early sign that Soviet policies were not irrevocably wedded to the notion of a world divided into two camps may be found in the way in which Russian analysts reported Asian response to the so-called "Pacific Pact." The first references in the Soviet press to this proposal, said to have been made by Secretary of State Dean Acheson in August 1949, did not mention Asian reaction,[243] but Russian accounts of a conference called the following May to discuss the proposal noted unexpected opposition. Three delegations attending the meeting—the Indian, the Ceylonese, and the Indonesian— were said to have rejected the "anti-Communist" slogans put forward by the conference; they were also reported to have denied

[243] See *New Times*, August 24, 1949, pp. 17-8, and *Literaturnaia gazeta*, August 31, 1949, p. 3.

their competence to discuss a security alliance involving the United States. A writer in *Izvestiia* hardly flattered these delegates in explaining *why* they resisted such an alliance: "they did not dare, at least openly, to put on the harness of American imperialism."[244] Acknowledgment of their opposition, however, may be considered early recognition of the independent course Asian countries heretofore consigned to the "imperialist, anti-democratic" camp were capable of pursuing. As time passed the resistance to American pressure by the legally constituted governments of other Asian nations was remarked. Burma, for instance, was added to the opponents of the "Pacific Pact" in May 1951[245] and Malaya and—quite incomprehensibly—Thailand in August 1952.[246] The mounting resistance to a "Pacific Pact," one Soviet writer explained, was due to the strength of the national liberation movements throughout East Asia: "It is this which explains the significant fact that the Asian states are reluctant to join the American organized variant of the North Atlantic alliance."[247] The opposition of various Asian powers to the American-sponsored Japanese Peace Conference in San Francisco in 1951 had meanwhile been noted in the Soviet press. The refusal of India and Burma to take any part in the conference was of course singled out as particularly praiseworthy conduct; the "negative attitude" toward the conference of Indonesia, Pakistan, and the Philippines was treated with respect.[248]

It is not necessary to question whether Soviet commentators correctly reported the resistance of these Asian nations to the United States, let alone correctly interpreted their motives, to grasp the significance of Moscow's *assertion* of some independence

[244] *Izvestiia*, June 6, 1950, p. 3. The conference was held in Baguio (Philippines) in May and was attended by delegations from the Philippines, India, Pakistan, Thailand, Indonesia, Ceylon, and Australia; the United States was not a formal participant.

[245] *New Times*, May 23, 1951, p. 5.

[246] *Pravda*, August 11, 1952, p. 11.

[247] *Izvestiia*, August 7, 1952, p. 4; the author of this article, V. Kudriavtsev, was reviewing the failure of a recent conference at Honolulu, called to bring the long-delayed "Pacific Pact" into existence.

[248] *Ibid.*, October 6, 1951, p. 3 (article by Kudriavtsev on the national liberation movements).

on their part. It foreshadowed Soviet acknowledgment of a broad band of neutral states through Asia which were perhaps not yet ready for affiliation with the Socialist bloc but which might at least be weaned from their dependence, or alleged dependence, on the United States. It was, in short, a departure from earlier Soviet attitudes regarding the "rotten little idea" of a third force (see p. 356, above).

A turn in the strategies of the Indian Communists in 1951, reflecting an altered view of the relevance of Chinese Communist experience in the colonial world, further reveals an impending shift in Soviet Eastern policies. The importance of the turn is heightened by the fact that the CPI leaders had visited Moscow shortly before adopting their new course. The CPI, it should be recalled, although it had been one of the first Asian parties to adopt a radical line after Zhdanov's Cominform speech of 1947, had not succeeded in organizing a significant rebellion in India— comparable, for instance, to those in Burma, Malaya, Indochina, and the Philippines. India was therefore a logical proving ground, Moscow appears to have felt, for more moderate strategies. The Indian turn originated in a secret party directive late in 1950 which first questioned the suitability of the Chinese model in India, especially the reliance on partisan warfare in the countryside. In a country where no Communist-controlled army exists (as in China) and where there is no near neighbor like the USSR to stand behind armed insurrection, the directive asserted, "partisan war alone cannot ensure victory. It has to be combined with the other major weapons, that of strikes of the working class, general strikes, and uprisings in the cities led by armed detachments of the working class."[249]

The significance of the directive does not, obviously, lie in any retreat from the strategy of armed struggle per se, but in the explicit rejection of the Chinese formula for armed struggle. In effect, calling the Chinese model into question soon led the CPI wholly away from the militant course it had been following since 1947 and which since 1949 had been linked to the Chinese Com-

[249] *Communist Conspiracy at Madurai*, p. 37.

munists. A published "Statement of Policy" in April 1951 openly divorced Indian Communist policies from Chinese, at least with respect to the armed struggle, and endorsed a moderate course in domestic affairs; in May the "moderates" in the CPI, led by Ajoy Ghosh, replaced the militant Andhra faction which had dominated the party since 1947.[250] Soviet writers in due course indicated full approval of these developments.[251]

The relevance of the Chinese model to revolutions elsewhere in Asia was openly discussed by the Russians themselves at an Orientalist conference in November 1951. Zhukov, once again the keynote speaker, asserted that, while the "fruitful influence" of the Chinese revolution could be detected in the colonial movements, "it is risky to regard the Chinese revolution as some kind of 'stereotype' for people's democratic revolutions in other countries of Asia." Too mechanical an imitation of Chinese experience, he went on, violated Lenin's thesis that each colonial revolution was distinctive and had to be considered in its own particular environment; "people's liberation armies," for instance, did not exist in all Eastern countries. Accordingly full independence, let alone socialist revolution, could not be considered a "near prospect" everywhere in Asia. Asian Communists had to gird themselves for a longer struggle. Some exception was taken during the conference to these formulations on China, especially with respect to the apparent down-grading of the strategy of "armed struggle,"[252] but Zhukov's very great influence among Soviet Orientalists, both before and after this critical conference, leaves little doubt that his views represented official Soviet policy at this juncture. He returned to the subject of the Chinese model in his summary of the deliberations and cautioned against making the

[250] The CPI shift (which is more complex than is indicated here inasmuch as it involved a rejection of only the militant feature of Chinese experience while preserving the more moderate, "neo-Maoist" four-class alliance) is discussed in some detail in Kautsky, *Moscow and the Communist Party of India*, pp. 140-7.

[251] E.g., *Voprosy ekonomiki*, No. 1, January 1952, pp. 73-89, and *Bol'shevik*, No. 5, March 1, 1952; both are cited in Kautsky, *op. cit.*, p. 148.

[252] Two respondents in particular—V. N. Nikiforov and G. I. Levinson—objected to Zhukov's argument on the grounds that he failed to note the strong probability of Chinese experience *stimulating* the formation of "people's liberation armies" and thus making "armed struggle" more likely and more appropriate.

Chinese revolution "into a fetish by viewing it as universally applicable to all situations which may arise in the various countries of Asia."[253] The conference as a whole, and Zhukov's remarks in particular, appear to have signaled more clearly than heretofore a turn to more flexible strategies in the East.

It would be an error to imagine, because of questions raised in Moscow concerning the relevance of Chinese experience to revolutions currently in progress in Asia, that the Chinese Communists themselves were inflexible in their approach to revolutionary tactics in Asia. Although by the end of 1950 their own principal foreign commitment was in Korea, an effort that surely accented rather than minimized the virtue of armed struggle, there is evidence that Peking too was prepared to explore alternate strategies. In September 1950, for instance, the new Chinese ambassador in Rangoon called attention to the parallel routes Burma and China had taken to independence and affirmed the strong ties between the two nations.[254] In January 1951 Mao appeared in a conciliatory and cordial mood at a reception given by the Indian ambassador in Peking and emphasized the ancient ties that bound the two countries together;[255] this was a year or more, it should be noted, before similar gestures of friendliness toward Nehru's India were displayed in Moscow. In June the Chinese press featured Mme. Sun Yat-sen's plea for "peaceful co-existence," which she saw as the principal objective of the Peace Movement. "Not only is it possible for the nations of the earth to exist and compete peacefully side by side," she wrote in *People's China*, "but it is also possible for them to construct an era of great co-operation."[256] At the end of 1951 the first official Chinese cultural delegation to go abroad visited Burma and India and reported enthusiastically on its mission.[257] These early gestures toward

[253] A summary of the meeting was carried in Akademiia nauk SSSR, *Izvestiia*, Seriia istorii i filosofii, No. 1, 1952, pp. 80-7; the summary is translated in full in *Current Digest of the Soviet Press*, IV, 20, pp. 3-7, 43.

[254] See Johnstone, *Burma's Foreign Policy*, p. 161, citing *The Nation* (Rangoon), September 9, 1950.

[255] *Pravda*, January 27, 1951, p. 4, citing a Chinese news release.

[256] Soong Ching Ling, "On Peaceful Coexistence," *People's China*, June 1, 1951, pp. 5-6.

[257] *Ibid.*, February 16, 1952, p. 29.

moderation indicate that whatever emphasis was being placed on the armed struggle, in certain contexts Peking no less than Moscow—and perhaps in response to Moscow's urging—was willing to show a different face; it is well to bear this in mind when assessing the relative strength of moderation and militancy in Moscow and Peking during the ensuing decade.

These, then, were some of the early indications of an impending shift of Communist policy in the East. A clearer indication of the shift from Zhdanovism may be found in Moscow's attitude toward developments in Southeast Asia proper during the years of gestation. To this we now turn, briefly and for the last time.

Indonesia, whose nationalist leadership was the last in Southeast Asia to draw Moscow's fire during the Zhdanov era (Sukarno was not under attack, it will be recalled, until the autumn of 1949), was one of the first non-Communist nations in this area to gain favorable notice in the post-Zhdanov years. The shift in Soviet policy was neither abrupt nor, at the outset, decisive. For some months while it was in progress Russian commentators blew alternately hot and cold on developments in Indonesia. At the beginning of 1951, for instance, firm support of the Indonesian claim to West Irian as "an inalienable part of its national territory"[258] was accompanied by assertions that the new Natsyr government (formed in September 1950) was a "puppet" of the United States, that Sukarno and Hatta were as dependent as ever on American imperialism and that democratic forces in the country led by the PKI "were regrouping and preparing for decisive struggles ahead."[259] During the spring the militant program of the PKI, now fully legalized, continued to be applauded in Cominform journals,[260] although this was a time when Indo-

---

[258] See *Izvestiia*, January 7, 1951, p. 4 and February 2, 1951, p. 4.

[259] N. Ch., "Les impérialistes américains n'asserviront point l'Indonésie," *For a Lasting Peace, for a People's Democracy!* (French edition), January 5, 1951, p. 4.

[260] E.g., *For a Lasting Peace, for a People's Democracy!*, March 16, 1951, p. 4 (noting the republication of the PKI's theoretical journal, *Bintang Merah*); April 6, 1951, p. 3 (an article by a Dutch Communist applauding the revival of the PKI after Hatta's "brutal massacre" at Madiun); and June 22, 1951, p. 2 (Aidit's

nesia's opposition to alleged American maneuvers in the Far East was gaining favorable notice in the Russian press (see p. 451).

A new government assault on the PKI in the summer of 1951 appears to mark a watershed in Soviet policies in Indonesia. The action, which led to the arrest of an estimated 2,000 Communists in August, was carried out by the Sukiman (*Masjumi*) government and was evidently prompted by Communist activities in the trade unions. The first Soviet response was sharp. "The reign of terror is mounting in Indonesia," *New Times* declared and indicated that Sukarno no less than the *Masjumi* cabinet was responsible for it.[261] The early release of the Communists, however, softened Moscow's attitude toward the episode and no further reference to it appears in the Soviet press. The event seems to have cleared the air in Indonesia, insofar as Moscow was concerned, to judge from the more sympathetic Soviet commentaries on Indonesian affairs from this time on. By the end of 1951 it was possible for Russian observers to mention Sukarno and Hatta for the first time in more than two years without any innuendo of disapproval.[262]

The prolonged cabinet crisis early in 1952 gave Moscow an opportunity to develop its new attitude toward Indonesia. The crisis, Soviet press sources indicated, was brought on by American efforts to force its aid on Indonesia. The dismissal of Foreign Minister Subardjo in February for having signed an aid agreement with the United States was seen as evidence of a growing firmness on the part of the government;[263] Sukiman's resignation soon thereafter was the consequence of a growing popular protest against American imperialism when news of the "secret deal" leaked out.[264] In April *Pravda* carried, and presumably approved, the PKI's offer to support the new Wilopo cabinet on condition

---

address on the occasion of the thirty-first anniversary of the founding of the PKI). The government's decision to allow the PKI again to take part in political activity was reached in March 1951.

[261] *New Times*, August 29, 1951, p. 18; see also Tass reports of the episode in *Pravda*, August 18, 1951, p. 4.

[262] See, for instance, *New Times*, December 12, 1951, p. 20.

[263] *Pravda*, February 22, 1952, p. 4.

[264] *New Times*, March 5, 1952, pp. 18-9.

that it "pursues an independent national policy"; specifically this included, according to the PKI statement, a refusal to take part in any American-sponsored negotiations leading to a Japanese Peace Treaty and a refusal to accept American aid.[265] The implication was that any Indonesian government—the Wilopo cabinet was a coalition of the Nationalist, *Masjumi*, and Socialist parties, all past rivals of Indonesian Communists—which pursued a neutralist foreign policy would have the PKI's, as well as Moscow's, support. In May the PKI launched a broad National Unity Front which within a year or two would restore the party to its pre-Madiun role as a major political force in the country.

It is apparent, then, that by mid-1952 a decided change had come over Soviet views of Indonesia. Moscow had reverted, in some measure, to its pre-1950 support of the republic. Indonesia was no longer, of course, a member of the "anti-imperialist, democratic" camp as it had once been; even diplomatic relations between the two countries were still two years away, a tardy sequel to Suripno's consular agreement of 1948. The future course of Soviet-Indonesian relations, however, was clear, founded on Moscow's respect for Indonesian neutrality and non-alignment. There was no significant retreat from this revised view of Indonesia during the balance of Stalin's life or during the years following his death.

The shift in Moscow's attitude toward Burma paralleled the shift in Indonesia but was affected, negatively and positively, by two circumstances not relevant in Indonesia: the continuation of the White Flag insurrection, which made it impossible for Burmese Communists to play the supporting role played by the PKI; and the early establishment of diplomatic relations between Moscow and Rangoon, which allowed normal intercourse between the two countries several years before this was possible in Indonesia. The exchange of ambassadors in February and May 1951[266] led

---

[265] *Pravda*, April 24, 1952, p. 3; the PKI statement was dated the day before.
[266] The Burmese ambassador presented his credentials in Moscow in February, the Russian his in Rangoon in May; Beloff, *Soviet Policy in the Far East, 1945-1951*, p. 238. The assertion in a later Soviet source that diplomatic relations be-

to renewed Soviet interest in Burma after several years of virtual silence on developments there. In May, the Soviet press noted Burma's opposition to the "Pacific Pact"; the same month *Izvestiia* noted respectfully Burma's abstention from the United Nations vote imposing an embargo on China.[267] In October the Soviet press saw in Burma's refusal to attend the San Francisco peace conference additional proof of the nation's progress toward an independent foreign policy.[268] The Soviet press meanwhile supported Rangoon's early protests on the presence of Kuomintang forces in North Burma, doubting only whether these protests were presented vigorously enough.[269] By early 1952 Moscow appears to have been satisfied that the protests were genuine and noted approvingly the announcement of the dispatch of a Burmese expeditionary force to drive the intruders from the country; *Pravda* linked Burma and China as innocent victims of American imperialism, said to be behind the Kuomintang venture.[270] Thereafter, although the episode was not to be closed for many years, periodic protests by the Rangoon government were treated sympathetically in the Soviet press.[271]

The question of American aid also was touched on frequently in Soviet commentaries on Burma. Early in the Korean war the Burmese, evidently fearing a Chinese invasion of Burma, had concluded a technical assistance agreement with the United States and invited an American military mission to visit Rangoon.[272] Opposition to this association, however, was strong in the country,

---

tween the two countries were established in February 1948 is in error, though some communication between the two capitals could have taken place at that time; see *Birmanskii soiuz*, p. 155.

[267] *New Times*, May 23, 1951, p. 5; *Izvestiia*, May 25, 1951, p. 4 (article by V. Kudriavtsev); for a detailed discussion of Burma's attitude toward China's role in the Korean war, see Johnstone, *op. cit.*, pp. 209ff.

[268] *Izvestiia*, October 6, 1951, p. 3 (also by Kudriavtsev).

[269] E.g., *Pravda*, June 26, 1951, p. 4; *New Times*, July 11, 1951, pp. 19-20; *Pravda*, December 28, 1951, p. 4.

[270] *Ibid.*, February 6, 1952, p. 4; the article is by a *Pravda* staff writer, Ia. Viktorov.

[271] E.g., *New Times*, February 20, 1952, pp. 19-20; *Pravda*, October 4, 1952, p. 4. For a fuller discussion of this issue, see Johnstone, *op. cit.*, pp. 225ff.

[272] See Cady, *A History of Modern Burma*, p. 608.

on the grounds that it jeopardized Burma's neutrality, and by early 1952 U Nu felt constrained to denounce American aid in principle, without immediately suspending current assistance. The Soviet press took joyful note of U Nu's announcement—the first specifically favorable notice of U Nu, incidentally, since before Aung San's assassination four and a half years earlier.[273] During the following months, demonstrations in Rangoon against the acceptance of American aid were noted as popular manifestations of support for the government's position.[274] It was the government's "mature reflection," a Soviet editorial writer observed, which led to the cancellation of *all* American aid programs in March 1953.[275] "Mature reflection," needless to say, was a new quality for Moscow to attach to the Burmese leaders.

If Moscow was embarrassed by the insurgency, the Soviet press revealed it through silence. A single item on the course of the rebellion was all this writer could discover in Soviet and Cominform sources dated after the establishment of diplomatic relations. This was a letter, purportedly by a Burmese Communist official, carried in the Cominform journal in September 1951; the author openly applauded the rebellion against the Burmese "puppet government" and cited an optimistic appraisal of Communist prospects by Than Tun.[276] The party itself, meanwhile, was referred to only infrequently in Soviet publications after 1951 and never as an organization engaged in open revolt against the government.[277]

The turn in Soviet policies in Burma, then, was no less definite than the turn in Indonesia and, due to the early exchange of ambassadors, led to an even more intense and sustained rela-

---

[273] *Pravda*, January 28, 1952, p. 4.

[274] E.g., *ibid.*, February 19, 1952, p. 4, and *New Times*, April 23, 1952, p. 22.

[275] "Aid to Underdeveloped Countries," *ibid.*, August 5, 1953, p. 2.

[276] S.P.H., "Le Peuple de Birmanie triomphera," *For a Lasting Peace, for a People's Democracy!* (French edition), September 7, 1951, p. 4.

[277] The BCP is reported, for instance, to have sent fraternal greetings to the Nineteenth Congress of the CPSU in 1952; *Pravda*, October 15, 1952. A volume on the colonial question published shortly after Stalin's death refers to Burmese Communists as "emerging as the political leaders of the liberation struggle"—but does not specify how they are doing this; Maslennikov, *Uglublenie krizisa kolonial'noi sistemy imperializma posle vtoroi mirovoi voiny*, p. 363.

tionship. It came as no surprise, after high-ranking Burmese officials had been visiting Moscow at intervals since early 1952,[278] that Khrushchev should include Burma on the itinerary of his first Asian visit in 1955.

In Malaya and the Philippines, Soviet disengagement—if, indeed, there had ever been "engagement"—came later than in Indonesia and Burma. Soviet hostility toward the regimes in both countries persisted without appreciable let-up through 1952; if on rare occasions Russian writers pretended to see a glimmer of hope in these regimes, as in the references to Manila's "negative attitude" toward the San Francisco conference in 1951 or to Malaya's opposition to the "Pacific Pact" in 1952, this was not the prevailing attitude of Soviet analysts. The more normal view was scorn for the failure of the bourgeois nationalist leadership in the two countries to resist British and American imperialism and praise for the noble and selfless struggle of partisans in the jungle. No alternative to armed struggle appears to have presented itself to Soviet writers.[279]

Disengagement in Malaya and the Philippines, accordingly, took the form of silence, as in Burma. Coverage of the Malayan Emergency reached a peak during 1952 and fell off sharply in 1953; the same was true of Soviet coverage of developments in the Philippines. Silence did not initially mean a change of attitude. On the rare occasions during 1953 when an estimate of the national liberation struggle in the two countries was given in Soviet commentaries no basic shift in policy was indicated. In June, for instance, a Soviet writer contrasted the struggle in Malaya and the Philippines with that in China, North Korea, and North Vietnam: while in all five nations "the wars being waged today spring from an effort on the part of imperialism to crush the national liberation struggle," the significant difference was

---

[278] A Burmese delegation, headed by a cabinet officer, attended the Moscow Economic Conference of April 1952; another cabinet officer led a delegation of Burmese on an extended tour of China and the USSR in the autumn of the same year. See Cady, *A History of Modern Burma*, p. 623.

[279] Soviet commentaries on Malaya and the Philippines early in the 1950's are discussed above, pp. 396ff. and 428ff.

that the latter three had "succeeded in winning their national independence" where Malaya and the Philippines had not.[280] In July a Soviet Orientalist asserted that the liberation struggle in the Malayan jungles was making new gains "under the leadership of the heroic Communist Party of Malaya," and he quoted approvingly from an MCP declaration (which though released several years earlier was still in force): "The era of the constitutional struggle has given way to an era of armed struggle which alone can smash British imperialism. Force must be met with force; this is the only way to freedom for our people."[281] An article on the Philippines published at the same time opened with words which have been quoted earlier but which bear repeating in this context: "Wonderful revolutionary events are unfolding in the Philippines. The people, led by the Communist Party, are carrying on their struggle against American imperialism arms in hand."[282] Another Soviet writer, commenting on the forthcoming Presidential elections in the Philippines, in which three parties were competing (the Liberals under Quirino, the *Nacionalista* under Magsaysay, and the Democrats under Romulo), commented: "It is obvious that no matter which of the three bourgeois parties gains the upper hand in the elections, the fate of the Filipino people will be unaltered."[283]

It is apparent from these continuing negative attitudes toward the Malayan and Philippine regimes that, although the growing silence in the Soviet press regarding developments in the two nations perhaps *foreshadowed* a shift in Moscow's policies, no perceptible change actually occurred during the months following Stalin's death. In the case of the Philippines—to look for a moment beyond the scope of the present study—the first tentative suggestion of a more moderate Soviet attitude, comparable to the early indications of moderation in Indonesia and Burma

[280] V. Avarin, "Disintegration of the Colonial System," *New Times*, June 10, 1953, p. 3.

[281] V. S. Rudnev, "Proval angliiskoi politiki 'razdeliai i vlastvui' v Malaie," *Kratkie soobshcheniia* Instituta Vostokovedeniia, No. VIII, 1953, p. 20; the declaration is dated 1949.

[282] See p. 431, above.

[283] *Pravda*, July 21, 1953, p. 4; see also *New Times*, July 22, 1953, pp. 27-31.

in 1951, appears only in 1954 on the eve of the Geneva conference on Indochina: noting with approval President Magsaysay's firm rejection of Syngman Rhee's call for a conference of anti-Communist states in East Asia, a *Pravda* commentator remarked that "even in the Philippines an understanding is growing [in government circles] of what catastrophic consequences U.S. foreign policy holds for the countries which go along with this policy. Everywhere understanding is spreading of the truth that peace and security can be safeguarded not through forging aggressive blocs, but through businesslike co-operation among all peoples."[284]

In Malaya, meanwhile, the silence in the Soviet press apparently became total during 1954; when attention to Malayan affairs resumed, in 1955, it was related to the efforts of the Malayan Communists to initiate peace talks with the government—talks which took place, but failed to end the Emergency.[285] The fact that the Soviet government was unable in subsequent years to cultivate better relations with Malaya and the Philippines is less significant for our purposes than the fact that even in these staunchly anti-Communist countries Moscow looked for what advantages it could find. The Communist rebellions, which continued in both countries, as in Burma, for several more years (and even at the time of writing, in 1965, are not wholly extinguished), did not again engage Moscow's attention.

Vietnam presented a wholly different problem to Soviet policy-makers. There the Communist and nationalist leaderships were identical, apart from a relatively insignificant element in Saigon whose influence throughout the country was sharply circumscribed by continuing French rule and by the nature of the civil war itself. There was accordingly no Communist rebellion which had to be disowned, as elsewhere in Southeast Asia, in order to

[284] *Pravda*, March 23, 1954, p. 4.

[285] See *New Times*, July 17, 1955, pp. 15-6, and *Mezhdunarodnaia zhizn'*, No. 10, October 1955, pp. 123-4. The talks, which took place at Baling in Central Malaya, broke down over the insistence of the Communists that they be restored to all their pre-Emergency rights and privileges.

gain the confidence of a nationalist leadership and bend it toward neutralism; neutralism was not an issue in Vietnam, a substantial portion of which was for all practical purposes already counted in the Communist bloc. The only questions were when and under what conditions to abandon the armed struggle and seek a settlement through negotiation. Since either course held forth a promise of advantage to Vietnamese Communists, the decision was not likely to produce the misgivings it presumably did elsewhere; on the other hand, given the general trend of Soviet foreign policy early in the 1950's, the importance Moscow attached to the Indochinese war and the favorable outlook in that war, the decision was not an easy one.

The Korean truce in July 1953, we have seen, although it prompted some discussion of a truce in Indochina, did not immediately lead to Soviet moves for negotiations; this was evident in the tone of Soviet commentaries on Indochina following the Panmunjom agreement and in the appearance of an important article by the Vietnamese premier in the Cominform journal as late as September accenting the expected "long duration" of the Indochinese war (see above, p. 439). In October the Soviet-dominated WFTU congress in Vienna proclaimed December 19, the seventh anniversary of the outbreak of the civil war, an "international day of active solidarity with the Vietnamese people" —a gesture designed to dramatize support of the armed struggle, not of peace.[286]

The first open move for a cease-fire was made by Ho Chi Minh late in November. In an interview with a Swedish correspondent, he indicated that the DRV was now ready and willing to negotiate, and it was immediately clear that his offer was not similar to those made periodically in the past which were contingent on French withdrawal from Vietnam. The United States, Ho argued, was now responsible for the continuation of the war in Indochina (an argument Soviet observers had also been urging in recent months); the American objective, he said, was not merely to replace French influence in Indochina but to weaken French

[286] *World Trade Union Movement*, No. 21-2, December 1, 1953, p. 12.

prestige in Europe in order to force France into an American-dominated European defense alliance including a remilitarized Germany.[287] German rearmament—which is again related to American goals in Indochina in Soviet commentaries on Ho's interview[288]—is a concern so obviously of greater importance to the Russians than the Vietnamese, that its introduction into an offer of peace talks suggests Soviet inspiration of the move. Whether this was the case or not, the course to Geneva had been set. If Ho Chi Minh had doubts about the wisdom of this course on the eve of the great thrust toward Dienbienphu, he kept them to himself. He referred again to his willingness to negotiate with the French in a statement on December 19 (the anniversary of the civil war).[289] Other Vietnamese spokesmen followed suit.[290]

The Russians, meanwhile, grew restrained in their commentaries on Vietnam. Coverage of the war was reduced as the Geneva conference approached. The principal concern of Soviet observers was that the Americans, not the French, might at the last minute hinder the cease-fire. The way in which the Soviet press treated even the spectacular Vietnamese victory at Dienbienphu in April was a study in *sang-froid*, quite obviously to avoid any risk to the Geneva talks.[291] At Geneva Russian disengagement from the Zhdanov course in Southeast Asia was completed, six years after this course was launched. For better or worse, the lanes were now open for peaceful co-existence.

REASONS FOR DISENGAGEMENT

Why did Moscow turn from the Zhdanovist line in Southeast Asia? The turn must be seen, first of all, in the context of a general

---

[287] *Pravda*, December 1, 1953, p. 4.

[288] E.g., *Izvestiia*, December 5, 1953, p. 3.

[289] *Pravda*, December 19, 1953, p. 4.

[290] E.g., Hoang Quoc Viet, "We are Ready to Negotiate an Armistice," *World Trade Union Movement*, No. 3, February 1, 1954, pp. 16-9.

[291] For a sampling of Soviet commentaries on Indochina during the months preceding the Geneva conference, see *New Times*, February 27, 1954, p. 21; March 10, 1954, pp. 8-11; March 24, 1954, pp. 11-4; April 7, 1954, pp. 13-7; April 21, 1954, pp. 15-7.

shift in Stalin's foreign policy which dates from 1949 or even the latter part of 1948. During the last years of Stalin's life the pressing reality of the Cold War, the continued bitterness toward the United States, the intense campaign for conformity within the Soviet Union, and the growing paucity of information on Soviet affairs had the effect of obscuring from students interested in the USSR (American students in particular) the steps which Moscow had already begun to take in search of an alternative to Zhdanovism. Recent studies of this era place Soviet strategies in a new perspective.[292] Stalin, it now seems clear, far from gloating over the successes of his militant course as official Soviet pronouncements pretended, was in reality much frustrated by the West's response to Zhdanovism. The Berlin blockade was rendered ineffective by the air-lift; Marshall Plan aid in Europe weaned from the Communists' cause many marginal supporters; the growing strength of NATO neutralized the threat of Soviet divisions in Eastern Europe and accented the mounting weapons gap between East and West, despite the preponderance of ground forces at Moscow's disposal. As time passed, moreover, the capacity of the Soviet Union to build and test atomic weapons raised questions in the Kremlin about the suitability of policies which risked nuclear war. Stalin, accordingly, grew more attentive to other ways of advancing Soviet influence in world affairs. The massive Peace Movement launched in 1949 was one device to create a new image abroad of the Soviet Union and to create a broader front against the Western Powers. After the Czech *coup* of February 1948 Communist efforts in Europe relied less and less on the tactics of direct assault.

Since the confrontation of the Soviet Union and its principal Western antagonist, the United States, was sharpest in Europe, and the risk of war greatest there, Stalin's "moderation" was first evident in the West. Parallel strategies in the East were initially blocked by the success of certain ventures there directly inspired, or stimulated, by Zhdanovism. The rebellions in Burma and Malaya, for instance, reached their crest only in late 1949 and 1950;

[292] E.g., Marshall D. Shulman, *Stalin's Foreign Policy Reappraised* (Harvard, 1963).

the *Huk* uprising in the Philippines was not underway in earnest until early 1950. In China, meanwhile, the fruition of armed struggle came only at the end of 1949 and the impact of Mao's success on other Asian Communists, we may imagine, had the effect of muting moderate counsels from Moscow; in Indochina, for instance, the validity of armed struggle could not be properly tested until after 1949 when victory in China assured the Vietnamese a protected rear, as the Chinese themselves had had a protected rear since 1946 in Manchuria. The yield from Zhdanovism, in short, was too rich in East Asia, at least until 1950, to encourage serious consideration of more moderate strategies.

The Communists' thrust in Korea in 1950—whose inspiration we may reasonably trace to Moscow, despite Russian disclaimers—marked the climax of Soviet militancy in the East. In conception and in purpose this action should be viewed as a sequel to the rebellions in Southeast Asia, with which the Korean war was in fact often linked in Soviet commentaries. The assault on South Korea was indeed a more deliberate venture on Moscow's part than the Southeast Asian risings inasmuch as the Russians were better able here to influence both the timing of the attack and the broad strategies to be followed as the fighting progressed. The outcome of the venture accordingly was more likely to affect Soviet policies in the East. Had the Korean effort succeeded, the strategy of armed struggle, we may imagine, would have been vindicated in Soviet eyes and would have been more widely urged throughout the East than heretofore. The ensuing chapter in Moscow's Eastern policy would have been very different. The Korean venture did not, however, succeed. If Moscow's objective in Korea is seen as an extension of Communist influence by force in an area where foreign intervention to contain it was judged unlikely, the action fell well short of this goal. Leaving aside the purely military outcome of the conflict, which at least preserved the *status quo ante bellum* and showed an encouraging resourcefulness on the part of Communist forces, the disadvantages to Moscow arising from the Korean episode cannot but have had a sobering impact on Soviet policy-makers. Much neutralist opinion in the world was alienated (it was the Korean war, for instance,

that caused neutralist Burma initially to accept American aid);
the United Nations was unexpectedly galvanized into action, due
to Moscow's imprudence in not regaining its Security Council
seat in time to veto intervention; above all, the Korean war
thoroughly alarmed and mobilized the United States in East Asia.
Washington made use of the Korean crisis to conclude a peace
treaty with Japan which assured the presence of American forces
in the North Pacific for the foreseeable future. At the same time
the United States advanced its concept of armed security in the
Pacific by concluding alliances with Formosa, the Philippines,
New Zealand, and Australia. The attention which Soviet spokesmen early in the 1950's gave to the projected "Pacific Pact" reveal,
however much they rejoiced at the repeated failures of the pact
to materialize, the concern with which Moscow viewed the prospects of its success. The combined force of the United States, the
United Kingdom, and half a dozen Asian countries could well
frustrate for decades any further Communist gains in East Asia
and could threaten, if not China itself, gains already made in
Vietnam; the fact that the "Pacific Pact," when it eventually
materialized in 1955 as SEATO, proved to be a less formidable
threat to Soviet interests than anticipated should not obscure Moscow's uneasiness over the alliance before it came into force.

The Russians' failure, then, to gain their initial objective in
Korea and the new American posture in the Far East which was
a direct consequence of the Korean war were further considerations leading Stalin to seek alternate strategies in Southeast Asia
after 1950.

Two additional considerations deserve our attention, though
both are perhaps more speculative than those presented thus far.
One concerns Soviet economic prospects early in the 1950's. By
1950 much attention was being given to the recovery of pre-war
levels through wide sectors of the Russian economy, accompanied
by forecasts of rapid economic growth during the years ahead;
these predictions multiplied as the years passed and not infrequently took the form of claims that Soviet output would exceed
that of one or another capitalist nation, including the United
States, by such and such a date. Such persistent forecasts undoubt-

edly influenced the thinking of Soviet officials concerned with policies in the underdeveloped world: if a planned economy could one day be demonstrably shown as superior to a capitalist economy in such areas as growth rates, rapid industrialization and full employment, underdeveloped nations could perhaps be expected to regard the USSR with increasing favor as a model for their own faltering economies. Countries such as India and Indonesia, for instance, might turn toward Russia first in economics, then in politics. The end result, Moscow may well have felt, would be the same. Local Communist parties might have to be bypassed for a decade or more, but their prospects for ultimate ascendancy would be advanced; as far as that goes, did it greatly matter whether the future leadership of a socialist India or Indonesia, attentive to Moscow's guidance in economic, political, and ultimately in ideological affairs, be labeled "Communist"? We need not explore here all the ramifications of this argument—the accuracy of the Soviet forecasts in the first place; the validity of the thesis that underdeveloped nations would necessarily be attracted by Soviet economic successes to a closer association with the USSR—to acknowledge that it may have had some force in Moscow and led Russian policy-makers to adopt a more moderate course in the East. We know only that a more moderate course *was* in fact adopted at this juncture; we suggest here a possible relationship between this course and forecasts of rapid economic growth.

The final consideration in Soviet disengagement in Southeast Asia was China—or, more particularly, Moscow's evaluation of the impact of the Chinese revolution in the East. Earlier in this chapter it was argued, quite tentatively, that one reason for Moscow's turning to more aggressive tactics in East Asia in the late 1940's may have been the challenge posed by Chinese Communist militancy: the Russians, in short, felt constrained to *match* this militancy or default in their leadership of the revolutionary East. Now the opposite is suggested, that it was precisely the challenge of Chinese militancy in the early 1950's that led Stalin to a measure of moderation in his policies in Southeast Asia. Is our logic too inconsistent?

The momentum of the Chinese revolution after Mao's victory in 1949 needed no pointing up in Moscow. It was altogether evident in the manner, for instance, in which Liu Shao-chi took up the cry of armed struggle at the WFTU conference in Peking in November, in the abandon with which Chinese "volunteers" launched themselves into the fighting in Korea, and in certain other irrepressible activities of the new regime. When the Korean war ended—and it is possible that Moscow used its influence to prolong the truce talks precisely to delay the prospect—large numbers of Chinese troops would be released for new ventures elsewhere. A campaign against Taiwan, the most compelling target for Peking, was for the present blocked by the American Seventh Fleet. The logical direction of any Chinese thrust was accordingly southward, in support of Ho's forces in Vietnam, of the insurrections in Burma and Malaya, or of any new rebellions which might break out in Southeast Asia. Various factors favored Peking in this area: large numbers of overseas Chinese could be depended upon to facilitate an expansion of Peking's influence; the prestige of the Chinese Communists, whatever the local sentiment toward Communism *per se*, was undeniably great after their stunning victory over the Kuomintang and their having held at bay for some months the combined forces of the United Nations under American leadership; moreover the factor of a common Asian identity gave the Chinese an advantage in Southeast Asia over all non-Asians, including Russians.

Soviet leaders, it may be surmised, could not consider without misgivings the prospect of a massive Chinese penetration of Southeast Asia. It would inevitably have foreclosed any distinctive Soviet influence in this area, except as filtered through Peking. It might result in an extension of China's authority as far westward as India. It would, in short, have greatly reduced Russian maneuverability in a critical sector of the East which had only recently entered the stage of world politics. Beyond this, it placed too squarely on the line the future of world Communism. Were a Chinese thrust into Southeast Asia to succeed and actually to deny to imperialism its "inexhaustible rear," quite possibly Western capitalism would be delivered a crippling blow, much as

469

Engagement & Disengagement: 1948-1954

Lenin had foretold thirty-odd years earlier. But should the enterprise fail, even if war with the Western powers could be avoided, Communism would suffer a loss of prestige more serious than any caused by setbacks in Korea. Moscow, we may imagine, sensed its responsibility to guide the world Communist movement along lines that offered more certain, if more leisurely, prospects of success—lines that the Chinese Communists, in their infancy, could not be depended upon to follow with discretion, even assuming the best will on their part to do so.

Students of Southeast Asian Communism have debated the likelihood of a division of responsibility between Russia and China in Southeast Asia during this period.[293] Possibly this occurred, though the nature of such a division has never been revealed. There was, however, a better solution from Moscow's viewpoint, the one they in fact adopted: the cultivation of friendly relations with Southeast Asian regimes willing to divorce themselves from dependency on the West, in particular the United States, and the ensuring of their neutrality through cultural exchange, profitable trade, and economic assistance. In the latter category, if not necessarily the former, Moscow enjoyed a distinct advantage over Peking; the new policy served to cancel China's advantage in other respects should the two nations, consciously or unconsciously, compete with one another in Southeast Asia. Surely one need not imagine at this stage implacable rivalry between Moscow and Peking—a heritage from the era when Stalin disparaged the Chinese Communists as "agrarian reformers" or a first harbinger of the "dialogue" that was to emerge at the end of the 1950's—to recognize that Russians and Chinese had at times opposing interests in Southeast Asia and, thus, opposing strategies. At this juncture, in any case, the Chinese yielded to Moscow's desires. This is evident in their supporting pronouncements on Southeast Asia and, above all, in their enthusiastic

[293] One such "student"—hardly known for his detached outlook in these matters—developed at some length to this writer his views on a very explicit division of responsibilities between Russians and Chinese in North Vietnam dating from the early 1950's: the Russians, he asserted, were chiefly responsible for ideological guidance and for supplies, the Chinese for tactical guidance, both political and military. Interview with the late Ngo Dinh Nhu in Saigon, February 1961.

470

support of the decisions reached at Geneva in 1954, an event which closed an era of Soviet militancy in the East.

It remains only to explain why a general policy shift in Southeast Asia, as we have analyzed it, should have taken effect at different times in different countries. The reasons are perhaps obvious by now, yet might profitably be reviewed.

The earlier change in Indonesia and Burma must be related to the fact that in each, as in India, there existed a national leadership by no means wholly opposed to the existence of a legal Communist movement, willing to establish normal relations with the USSR and China, and, above all, increasingly doubtful about the wisdom of giving any priority to cordial relations with the United States. In some measure this outlook stemmed from the character of the nationalist movement as it had developed over the years in each country—the persistent Marxist influence on the Burmese leaders, for instance; the frequent collaboration, both during and after the war, between the PKI and Indonesian nationalists. In some degree it sprang from a sense of vulnerability to possible Communist expansion and a desire to keep this in check by meeting Communism half-way. In some measure too it derived from an especially virulent hostility to foreign imperialism, which led to a ready identification of the United States with lingering Dutch and British interests in Southeast Asia and, in consequence, to a willingness—if not an eagerness—to cultivate friendly relations with the Socialist camp as an expression of non-alignment. In Indonesia a special consideration favored Soviet strategies: the brevity of the 1948 rising of the PKI which by the early 1950's had been conveniently forgotten, or was at least ignored. The expected receptivity, then, of Indonesia and Burma to Soviet approaches from 1951 on was a factor which prompted Moscow to make them. Neutralism in Indonesia and Burma, in short, was as much a cause as a consequence of Stalin's shift.

In Malaya and the Philippines different considerations prevailed. In neither was there a leadership which the Russians believed would respond to any approaches they might make. Malaya was not independent; such national leadership as existed, which was Malay, was generally in agreement with British policies regarding the Communist insurrection, which was Chinese. Being anti-Chinese and therefore anti-Communist, Malayan nationalists were *ipso facto* anti-Russian. In the Philippines the national leadership had from the outset, long before independence, been drawn predominantly from conservative, middle-class elements which had little sympathy with the objectives of the *Hukbalahap* and the CPPI. Independence, moreover, though leaving much to be desired as a full expression of Philippine sovereignty, was still genuine enough to most Filipinos to destroy the effectiveness of Communist slogans calling for an end to "American imperialism." Neither Malaya nor the Philippines, then, was in the least receptive to fresh approaches from Moscow, and the Russians were accordingly without an effective alternative to their earlier strategies in these two countries. The Soviet press limited itself after 1950 to perfunctory coverage of the fading rebellions in each—showing perhaps greater enthusiasm in the case of the Malayan Emergency, since the Communists' opponents there were at least foreign—until by 1953 there seemed little point in prolonging even this desultory notice of Philippine and Malayan affairs.

Vietnam, finally, was a special case. Two circumstances here bore directly on Soviet strategies: the growing rather than diminishing prospects of Communist success as years passed; and the fact that the Vietminh's effort was more directly aimed at foreign imperialism than any comparable effort by Communists in Southeast Asia. Since Moscow, moreover, was able with some success to argue that the war in Indochina was directed as much against American as French imperialism, the war served a principal objective of Soviet foreign policy during these years, harassment in one way or another of the United States. These considerations made Soviet strategies in Indochina an exception to the general trend of Stalin's foreign policy during his last years. By 1953, however, the exception became an obstacle to Soviet designs. With the end of the Korean episode, an advance to peaceful co-existence, along the lines indicated above, was blocked by continued fighting in Indochina. It was an irritant to normal diplomatic intercourse in Southeast Asia, which Moscow now desired; it also gave the Eisenhower administration, which Moscow appears initially to have regarded with more alarm than its predecessor, an excuse to adopt strong counter-measures against Communist and Soviet influence in the Far East. The Geneva solution was a risk. It pitted possible victory through arms within a relatively short period against the more distant (and still uncertain) gains anticipated from peaceful co-existence. It was, however, a decision that the new Soviet leadership evidently felt could no longer be delayed. The Vietnamese were expendable, if it came to that; they were the sacrificial lambs of a basic turn in Soviet foreign policy that had been under active consideration for some years and now was consummated.

Epilogue

ONE purpose of the present study, it was suggested at the outset, was to seek in Soviet behavior—in a particular sector of the colonial world—clues to Moscow's strategies in the East as a whole. The time has come to consider whether such clues have in fact been discovered. Does the particular in this instance significantly illuminate the general?

Any judgment must depend upon what is expected of such a study. If the reader imagines that Soviet colonial strategies, through some magic, will now suddenly be revealed in a clear and unambiguous light, these concluding remarks will surely be a disappointment. The handicaps under which the student of Southeast Asian Communism labors are too apparent to gloss over here. The story of Moscow's efforts in Southeast Asia, let us confess it, is only half-told—if, indeed, it is reasonable to claim so much. The evidence is dispersed; records are incomplete; the authenticity of such documentation as exists is often in doubt due to distortions in translation and to the bias of authorship. The heterogeneous circumstances, meanwhile, in which Communism developed in Southeast Asia discourage generalizations that might apply to the colonial world at large; it is difficult enough, indeed, to generalize with confidence on Communist behavior within Southeast Asia. No two Southeast Asian parties were alike in any significant degree; they shared no common experience, other than colonialism (which assumed many different forms, whatever Moscow said of the matter); their leaders were for the most part unknown to each other; the few efforts to co-ordinate Communist activity in Southeast Asia failed. Whether or not future students of these affairs will have an easier time of it, these considerations constitute a present barrier to any definitive study of Lenin's and Stalin's policies in the East. The reader, then, will find the following observations useful only if he is prepared to acknowledge, with the author, the more modest aim of this undertaking: to cast *tangential* light on Moscow's Eastern strategies by studying Soviet resourcefulness (or lack of it) in a

475

peripheral colonial area where it could be foreseen that Moscow's engagement would be erratic. We would not, of course, have selected Southeast Asia as the proving ground of Lenin's and Stalin's Eastern policies had it been the purpose of this study to fix these policies with any finality.

It is appropriate, before sorting out our conclusions, to underscore an observation made at the outset of this study regarding the detection of Soviet policies in an area as neglected as Southeast Asia. What, in the last analysis, constitutes Soviet "policy"? If leading Soviet spokesmen articulate an attitude toward a given situation, if official resolutions confirm this attitude, and if some implementation of the resolutions can be discovered, there need be little doubt that a policy is in force (subject, as always, to the consideration that the policy in question may have as its purpose the concealment of another policy which the Kremlin chooses for the moment not to make known). Where no such statements and resolutions exist, one is compelled to fall back on less clear evidence of Soviet intentions. Often such evidence is found in the Soviet press, whose controlled nature serves in this case as an aid to students since all, or virtually all, published material in the USSR reflects an "official" attitude at a given time. Where the Soviet press is silent, the evidence of foreign Communist spokesmen and publications, especially in the metropolitan country, serves as a plausible substitute for more authoritative Russian evidence; during certain eras Moscow indeed delegated to foreign parties responsibility for working out policies in the colonial world and, insofar as it could, remained intentionally aloof from them. Where evidence is lacking, finally, in foreign Communist sources, there is occasionally evidence of strategies actually in force in the colonies concerned which may be assumed to have Moscow's approval if neither Moscow nor the metropolitan party has given indication to the contrary. Soviet policy in the East during our period of enquiry emerges, then, as a mosaic of Communist activity at different levels: local, metropolitan, Chinese (especially after World War II), and Russian, the latter at times quite incidental.

476

The difficulty of deciding when, from this welter of evidence, an authentic Soviet policy may be said to have been in force needs no elaboration here; it is a rash student of Russian affairs who claims he has overcome this dilemma. As a general rule, however—since it is desirable to have at least one fixed point of reference—the Russians may be said to have pursued a given policy in the East (although not necessarily with vigor) if it can be detected through any one of the devices described; in the case of detection in non-Russian sources, the rule holds of course only if no explicit or implicit rejection of the policy in question is indicated within a reasonable period of time in authoritative Soviet pronouncements. Moscow's silence, then, so often frustrating to students of Soviet affairs, need not mean indifference or absence of policy at a given juncture. It may signify tacit confirmation of a strategy already in force.

A few examples may serve to drive this point home. During the era of the Nazi-Soviet Pact, the Russians, preoccupied with events in Europe, were generally silent on the colonial question. The Southeast Asian parties, attentive to the demands of Soviet foreign policy as they interpreted it, revised their united front strategies to reflect the hostility to the Western Powers implicit in Stalin's alliance with Hitler; when the alliance collapsed, the Southeast Asian parties reversed their strategies and created, in most countries, anti-Fascist fronts which supported Russia's war effort. In neither case is there evidence of Soviet directives, and only very uncertain evidence of metropolitan or Chinese Communist directives, to prompt these turns; yet the new strategies as they evolved may be considered as authentic a manifestation of *Soviet* policies as if Stalin himself had ordered them. Proof of this may be discovered in the fact that Soviet spokesmen neither at the time nor subsequently found fault with the Southeast Asian parties on this ground. Another example may be found in developments in Southeast Asia immediately after the war. Again the Soviet government, absorbed by events in Europe, largely ignored the East. Most Communist leaders in Southeast Asia would undoubtedly have welcomed a militant instruction from Moscow, yet they restrained themselves in response to Stalin's apparent opposition to

477

aggressive tactics at that time, manifested in the meager attention devoted to the East in the Soviet press and in Moscow's unwillingness to alter the formula of wartime united fronts; even the Vietnamese, it should be recalled, resorted to insurrection only when all other routes were closed. Moderation was surely the substance of Stalin's post-war policy in Southeast Asia, though local Communist leaders elected this course without prompting from Moscow insofar as is known.

These preliminaries aside, we may venture a few observations on Moscow's Eastern policies as revealed in the present study of strategies in Southeast Asia.

An initial observation, again underscoring a thesis put forth at the outset, is that Moscow's interest in the Eastern question has been more persistent than generally acknowledged. What struck certain foreign observers as a meddlesome intervention in the affairs of the colonial, or former colonial, world in the mid-1950's was in reality the more active implementation of strategies that had been worked over for thirty-five years. Quite apart from traditional *Russian* interests in the East—in the border regions of China and in China itself—the Bolsheviks entertained specific revolutionary ambitions in the East which date back to the early years of their regime. This interest did not derive from the Marxian heritage before 1917. Marx's occasional references to revolutions in colonial Ireland or semi-colonial China triggering revolutions in Europe were not compelling enough to fix this idea in the arguments of his immediate heirs; Marxists in Europe, for the most part orthodox, held to the view that proletarian revolutions would be self-starting and ignored the possibility that colonial upheavals might significantly hasten the overthrow of capitalism. The pre-1917 Bolsheviks shared this view. Thus Lenin, in his 1916 study of imperialism, overlooked the role of overseas colonies in the revolutionary process. Once in power and seeking all ways to expand the world revolution, the Bolsheviks recalled Marx's argument concerning China and Ireland and occasionally applied it to the colonial world at large. They appear to have done so, however, more to stir up revolutionary-minded Muslims and Asians against the English than because the idea was already a part of Marxist-Leninist doctrine. As late as 1920 Stalin, the most Eastern-oriented of the Bolshevik leaders, assumed that the "Eastern Question" on the agenda of the forthcoming Second Comintern Congress still referred chiefly to the Balkans (as it had, though with certain differences, throughout the nineteenth century). At Lenin's insistence, however, the Second Congress took up the colonial question in some detail and set forth most of the issues which were to remain central to Soviet Eastern policy for the next three or four decades: the relationship of colonial revolutions to revolutions in Europe; the proper attitude to adopt toward indigenous nationalist movements not yet under Communist control (and in most cases not likely to be); the degree of co-operation, or non-co-operation, with such movements it was appropriate for local Communists to seek under different conditions; the responsibility of metropolitan parties toward Communist or proto-Communist formations in the colonies; the critical question of choosing the right moment to revolt; and so forth. Not all judgments of the Second Congress stood the test of time; fewer indeed survived than were overturned. The issues, however, were fixed. The efforts of succeeding generations of Soviet Orientalists, both within and without the official hierarchy, to find the proper formulations on these questions constitute the principal evidence of Moscow's Eastern policy.

If we may consider the persistence of Moscow's doctrinal interest in the East sufficiently established, we must note simultaneously the low priority Soviet leaders assigned to operations in the colonial world. Soviet efforts in the colonies, despite repeated reminders to the international movement that more vigorous activity was needed there, were on the whole parsimonious. This is nowhere clearer than in Southeast Asia. Time and again the guidance Southeast Asian revolutionaries awaited from Moscow, guidance that would have cost little to give, was not forthcoming: in Indonesia in 1926 timely advice from the Comintern might have brought rival factions of the PKI together long enough to give some common purpose to their scheduled rising; in the early 1930's the militant tactics articulated for the colonial parties at the Sixth Comintern Congress were allowed to remain in force long past the time when they offered any prospect of success and when, in fact, they were in conflict with the general trend of Soviet strategies elsewhere; during the era of the united front, Communists in Southeast Asia were again left largely to themselves to work out their relations with nationalist movements, when more explicit guidance from Moscow might have hastened and coordinated alliances beneficial to Stalin's aims.

Soviet directives were no more explicit after the war than before. The Kremlin's delay until 1948 in providing guidance to colonial parties was very nearly catastrophic in Southeast Asia. Communists there, fresh from their struggle against the Japanese, were never more poised for a significant strike than they were at the end of 1945. Their strength was impressive; their morale was high. They awaited only a sign from Moscow. When none came, the wartime movements languished (except in Indochina where on its own initiative the Vietminh, following the example of the Chinese Communists, elected to fight rather than see its advantage eroded away through inaction). The belated shift to Zhdanovism, meanwhile, did not mean more explicit guidance to Southeast Asian Communists, who were left, as before, to work out local strategies as best they could. In consequence, the Burmese, Malayans, Indonesians, and Filipinos successively stumbled into insurrection unprepared and only half-aware of the consequences of their actions. Nor did they receive useful hints from Moscow, let alone material assistance, once in arms. When Soviet policies shifted early in the 1950's, no effort was made, except eventually in Vietnam, to co-ordinate local Communist strategies in Southeast Asia with Moscow's growing preference for moderation over militancy.

Drift and indecision, then, characterize Soviet Eastern policy during most of Stalin's rule and one might well ask what purpose a *doctrinal* interest in the East served if so little thought was given to an *operational* program supporting it. The modest efforts in the East can, of course, be explained. The Comintern, for instance, dominated by Europeans, never succeeded in ridding itself of a bias in favor of Europe and felt its obligation to the East, as well as to Lenin's reminder of the obligation, satisfied in the adoption of occasional (and usually only theoretical) formulations. Improbable revolutions in Germany or France were more real to the leaders of the International than present upheavals in India or Indonesia; the failure in China in 1927 doubtless fortified them in their conviction that the West was the proper place for revolution, not the East. Stalin, meanwhile, though not sharing this bias, was sufficiently chastened by the outcome of his venture in China to pass up similar ventures elsewhere in the colonial world. Moreover his preoccupation with domestic affairs and with Soviet security during the 1930's further dissuaded him from any significant engagement in the East. Revolutionary activity was everywhere curtailed during the war, as a matter of course, and after the war Stalin elected to concentrate his energies first in Europe, where he judged revolutionary prospects more promising than in Asia. By the time Soviet leaders were ready to redirect their attention to the East, in 1948, the configuration of world politics was such that an operation on the scale of the 1925-1927 effort in China was no longer practicable.

Reasons for modest Soviet efforts in the East do not, however, conceal the reality of a sharp discrepancy between words and actions. No student of Soviet colonial policy can escape the conclusion that the Russians articulated a more abrasive strategy in the East than they were able or willing to carry out. In Southeast Asia the price of Stalin's stewardship over the Communist movement was the virtual extinction, by 1953, of all but two of the parties constructed to serve as the instruments of his policies there: one survived by virtue of its own timely initiative, the other by the luck of having its premature insurrection in 1948 promptly crushed.

We should say a word, finally, of the impact of events in China on Soviet strategies. The Chinese revolution intersects the course of Soviet policies in Southeast Asia at too many critical junctures to permit a detailed review here of its total impact. One episode, however, which more than any other affected Moscow's course, may usefully be singled out for comment. This was Stalin's effort in China in 1925-1927. The episode had three significant consequences. First, while it lasted, the energies expended in China

481

exhausted Moscow's slender reserves for parallel efforts in other colonial and semi-colonial areas where the prospects, and perhaps even the rewards, were not significantly less than in China—for instance, India, Indonesia, or Egypt. Second, the defeat in China discouraged further engagements of this nature, with the inevitable result that Communist movements in the East, which during the years of the Depression still had some hope of success, failed to experience the growth they otherwise might have had. In this sense the thesis of the Second Comintern Congress that colonial upheavals might hasten revolution in Europe was never tested, since Moscow's efforts did not extend appreciably beyond China. Parenthetically, it may be questioned whether China was ever the best testing ground for the thesis since it was neither a colony, whose loss might cripple some metropolitan power, nor after a decade of civil disorder so rich a semi-colony that any imperialist nation would be gravely shaken by its collapse. The third and perhaps most important consequence of the 1927 debacle in China was that the Chinese Communists emerged from it in a better position ultimately to influence the colonial world than would have been the case had they come to power through Stalin's efforts. Dependent on Moscow, they would have served as Stalin's mouthpiece in Asia; their regime would have been fashioned in the image of the USSR, as the regimes in Eastern Europe were after World War II, and undoubtedly they would have been no more capable than the latter of attracting adherents to the world Communist movement. Left to their own devices, the Chinese Communists developed perforce a distinctive brand of Marxism-Leninism that, as time passed, had a wider appeal to colonial parties than the opportunistic strategies devised, and occasionally implemented, by Stalin. The fact that Moscow during the 1930's (and more guardedly after the war) approved the Chinese experience as a model for other colonial and semi-colonial parties in no way lessens the distinctiveness of Maoism; indeed this approval merely accelerated the inevitable gravitation of these parties to Chinese leadership. In this respect the confrontation of Chinese and Russian Communism in the early 1960's, which is based in large part on divergent attitudes toward revolution in the

482

"East," may be said to have had its origins in Stalin's failure in China three and a half decades earlier. Stalin's Eastern policy never fully recovered from the setback of 1927.

The foregoing discussion calls into question Stalin's conduct of Soviet foreign policy, especially that feature relating to revolutionary movements abroad. For all the talk of revolution in Stalin's time, he does not emerge as an effective or even very attentive leader of world Communism. He neither understood the East, Asiatic though he was by birth, nor does he appear to have grasped, as Lenin did, the enormous approaching significance of the East in world affairs. Stalin's single full-fledged venture in Asia, marred by misjudgments and a Byzantine devotion to intrigue, was a disaster from which recovery was possible only in the avoidance of similar ventures in the future. If Communism in the East was nonetheless a force to be reckoned with at Stalin's death, this was the consequence of Russia's having become a formidable world power during his rule, not of any skill he displayed in guiding the world movement. Khrushchev, it is clear, did more in a single decade to extend Soviet influence and prestige in the East, despite his rivalry with the Chinese Communists, than Stalin had done in three. It remains to be seen whether Khrushchev's heirs, or theirs, can do as well.

Short Biographies

COMINTERN AGENTS AND RUSSIAN ORIENTALISTS CONCERNED WITH
SOUTHEAST ASIA

AVARIN, V. A. Prominent Soviet writer on international politics in
the Far East preceding, during, and following World War II.

BONDAREVSKII, G. L. Post-war Orientalist specializing on Malayan
affairs, especially during Emergency.

BROWDER, EARL (b. 1891). American Communist active in the Far
East during 1920's; head of Pan Pacific Trade Union Secretariat in Hankow, 1927-29; General-Secretary of CPUSA from
1930 to 1945, when he was reprimanded for having dissolved
party during war (charge of "Browderism"); expelled from
CPUSA but remained independent Communist.

CHECHETKINA, O. Soviet correspondent after World War II; visited
Burma in 1947.

DANTSIG, A. Soviet Orientalist, author of first significant monograph
on Indochina published in USSR, 1931.

DIAKHOV, A. M. Principal Russian specialist on Indian affairs after
World War II; his views influenced Soviet interpretations of
Southeast Asia.

DUCROIX, JOSEPH (alias Serge Lefrance). Allegedly an agent of Pan
Pacific Trade Union Secretariat in Singapore, 1930-31; his
arrest and revelations in June 1931 led to break-up of Dalburo
in Hong Kong and Shanghai.

GUBER, A. A. (b. 1902). Leading Soviet academician and authority
on Southeast Asia since early 1930's; a student of Indonesia in
particular.

HO CHI MINH. *See* below under Indochina.

IVIN, A. Soviet Orientalist in 1930's; wrote, *inter alia*, on Thailand.

LEVINSON, G. I. Soviet Orientalist in post-war era specializing on the
Philippines; at Orientalist conference in 1951, opposed E. M.
Zhukov's modification of "armed struggle" strategy.

LEVKOVSKII, A. I. Soviet writer on Malaya in post-war period.

MARING. *See* below under Indonesia.

MASLENNIKOV, V. A. Soviet Orientalist specializing on the colonial
question after World War II.

MIF, PAVEL'. Comintern agent in China during 1920's; subsequently a
leading Soviet spokesman and writer on Far Eastern affairs,
until World War II.

485

Short Biographies

PAVLOVICH-VOLONTER, M. P. (also called Veltman, M. P.). Senior Soviet Orientalist in 1920's; director of first Soviet Center of Oriental Studies, founded in 1921.

ROY, M. N. (b. 1899). Indian Communist, asked by Lenin in 1920 to draft "supplementary theses" on the colonial question for Second Comintern Congress; until mid-1920's remained principal spokesman in Comintern for Asian revolutionary movements; sent as Comintern agent to China early 1927; broke with Moscow following year.

RUDNEV, V. S. Soviet Orientalist after World War II; specialist on Malaya.

SAFAROV, G. Prolific Soviet writer on Eastern question in 1920's, early 1930's.

TAN MALAKA. *See* below under Indonesia.

VASIL'EV, V. F. Post-war Orientalist, student of Burma.

VASIL'EVA, V. Prominent Soviet Orientalist from early 1930's to mid-1950's; specialized on Indochina.

VOITINSKY, G. Comintern agent in Far East during 1920's, in contact with Southeast Asian Communists; subsequently acknowledged as a leading authority on Far East, through World War II.

ZABOZLAEVA, O. Orientalist and journalist, specializing on the Philippines, Thailand and Indonesia; active since mid-1930's.

ZHUKOV, E. M. (b. 1907). Principal Soviet academician and spokesman on Eastern affairs after World War II; Director of Pacific Institute of Academy of Sciences, 1943-50; visited India in 1946; key-note speaker at Orientalist conference in Moscow in June 1949, when more vigorous support given to Southeast Asian rebellions; again key-note speaker at Orientalist conference in November 1951, when Soviet line was moderated.

INDONESIA

Indigenous Communist Leaders

ABDULMADJID. One of pro-Communist leaders of Indonesian student organization in Holland, *Perhimpoenan Indonesia*, in 1930's; after World War II associated with Socialists until 1948; acknowledged long association with PKI in August 1948, on eve of Madiun uprising.

AIDIT, D. N. (b. 1923). One of leaders of People's Democratic Front in 1948; following Madiun rising, fled to China; with Lukman,

486

constituted new PKI leadership in 1951; elected party Secretary in 1954.

ALIMIN PRAWIRODIRDJO. With Musso, guided PKI in 1924-25, during preparations for 1926 uprising; fled to Singapore in 1925; reportedly went to Moscow in 1926 (with Musso) to gain approval of uprising; arrested on return to Singapore in December; on release, returned to Moscow, where he attended Sixth Comintern Congress in 1928; remained in exile (reportedly during World War II in Yenan) until 1946, when he came back to Java and shared party leadership with Sardjono; arrested during Madiun uprising, but escaped punishment, and on release headed PKI until 1951.

DARSONO. Elected Vice-President of PKI at its founding in 1920; attended Third Comintern Congress in Moscow, 1921; assumed leadership of PKI in 1923 on departure of Semaoen; reportedly arrested in 1925, but escaped to Singapore the following year; attended Sixth Comintern Congress in Moscow, 1928, and elected alternate member of ECCI; apparently broke with Comintern soon thereafter.

JUSUF, MOHAMMED. Associated with Subardjo's "Communist" organization during World War II; led reorganized PKI from November 1945 to March 1946, when he was repudiated by party Central Committee for anti-government policies.

MUSSO, MANOVAR (b. 1898). PKI leader from early 1920's; active in preparations for 1926 rising until exile at end of 1925; with Alimin, reportedly went to Moscow in 1926 to win Soviet approval of insurrection; arrested on return to Singapore in December; replaced Semaoen as principal PKI spokesman in Moscow after Sixth Comintern Congress; returned briefly to Java in 1935 to organize "Illegal PKI"; returned secretly to Indonesia in August 1948 and replaced Sardjono as Secretary to PKI; assumed leadership of Madiun uprising in September; killed in fighting in October.

SARDJONO. Early leader of PKI in 1920's; imprisoned after 1926 rising on Java and returned to Indonesia, from Australia, only in 1946; elected Secretary of PKI in March 1946, on repudiation of Jusuf; replaced by Musso in August 1948; arrested during Madiun rising and shot in December.

SEMAOEN (or Semaun; b. about 1897). First President of PKI, at founding in 1920; attended Congress of Toilers of the Far East in Petrograd, 1922; exiled from Java in 1923 and resided thereafter in France and Russia, representing the PKI at numerous congresses of the Third International and other organizations; elected to the ECCI at Fifth Congress, 1924; overshadowed by Musso after Sixth Comintern Congress in 1928 and played minor role in PKI affairs thereafter.

SETIADJIT. A pro-Communist leader of *Perhimpoenan Indonesia* in 1930's, with Abdulmadjid; on return to Java after war, active in Labor Party and served in several governments until 1948; acknowledged long association with PKI on eve of Madiun rising but disappeared from view soon thereafter.

SJARIFUDDIN, AMIR (b. 1907). Active in *Gerindo* and other revolutionary organizations in late 1930's; led anti-Japanese movement until arrest in 1943; after war identified with Socialists until 1948; served as Minister of Defense in several post-war governments and as Prime Minister from July 1947 to February 1948; on demission, led oppositionist People's Democratic Front, which he merged with PKI in August; at this time he acknowledged membership in PKI since late 1930's; with Musso, led PKI during Madiun uprising; arrested and executed in December 1948.

SUBARDJO, ACHMED. Early leader of *Perhimpoenan Indonesia* in Holland; reportedly spent year in Moscow in 1930's; during World War II led allegedly Japanese-sponsored "Communist" organization in Indonesia; served in several post-war governments, but not associated with PKI.

SURIPNO. Communist diplomat entrusted by Sjarifuddin with consular negotiations with USSR, early 1948; returned to Indonesia with Musso in August; arrested during Madiun rising and shot in December.

TAN MALAKA (b. 1893). Represented PKI at Fourth Comintern Congress in Moscow, 1922; exiled from Java in 1923 and allegedly served as Comintern representative in Southeast Asia from 1924 to 1927; opposed 1926 rising in Java; arrested in Manila in 1927 and deported; clashed with Bukharin at Sixth Comintern Congress in 1928 and labeled Trotskyite; broke with Comintern after 1928 and carried on independent Communist work in Southeast Asia and Japan during 1930's; returned secretly to Java during World War II and played role in independence movement in 1945; arrested for opposition to Sukarno and

Sjahrir in 1946; released in 1948, during Madiun rising, but disappeared from view soon thereafter—presumably killed.

WIKANA. Active in pre-war *Gerindo* and possibly in "Illegal PKI"; reportedly headed Japanese-organized "Communist" school in World War II; led Communist-oriented *Pesindo* after war; apparently took part in Madiun rising and disappeared from view thereafter.

Dutch Communists

BERGSMA. Elected Secretary of PKI at founding congress in 1920; following exile from Java in 1923, wrote on Indonesian affairs in Comintern journals.

MARING (Hendrik Sneevliet). Founder of Indies Social Democratic Association in Java 1914; principal figure in proto-Communist movement in Java until exiled in 1920; represented PKI at several Comintern congresses early in 1920's; in 1922 served as Comintern agent with Chinese Communist Party; broke with Comintern in mid-1920's.

PHILIPPINES

Indigenous Communist Leaders

BALGOS, MARIANO. Active in CPPI from 1930's; elected Secretary-General of CPPI in May 1948, on defeat of "majority PB"; later killed during Huk rebellion.

BOGNOT, CIRILO. Attended Fourth Profintern Congress in Moscow, 1928, under auspices of Pan Pacific Trade Union Secretariat, and reportedly remained a year in USSR; opposed Evangelista during split of *Congresso Obrero* in 1929, but rejoined Communists in 1930 and was member of first party Central Committee; clashed again with Evangelista early in 1930's over policies of Anti-Imperialist League in Philippines.

CAPADOCIA, GUILLERMO. Early CPPI leader, sentenced along with Evangelista and others in 1933; Secretary-General of CPPI prior to merger with Socialists in 1938 and continued as Secretary of enlarged party; arrested by Japanese in 1942, but released during war to form united front against Filipino land-owners; in 1941 expelled from CPPI for collaboration with Japanese; reinstated in 1948 and played active role in Huk rebellion; killed during fighting in 1951.

489

Short Biographies

CASTRO, PEDRO. Emerged in CPPI leadership during World War II and elected Secretary-General in 1945; headed "majority PB" until May 1948, when Lava brothers and Luis Taruc gained upper hand in party; expelled from CPPI in 1949 for oppositionist tactics in Congress of Labor Organizations.

DE ORA, ANTONIO. Member of First Politburo of CPPI; his death in January 1931, while under arrest, was *cause célèbre* of CPPI.

EVANGELISTA, CRISANTO. Pre-World War I trade union organizer; in 1924, formed *Partido Obrero*, precursor of CPPI; attended Fourth Profintern Congress in Moscow, 1928; organized CPPI in 1930, after split in *Congresso Obrero*; arrested several times in 1930, finally sentenced in 1933; released in 1937 and elected Chairman of reorganized CPPI in 1938 (though absent abroad) following merger with Socialists; arrested by Japanese in 1942 and died in prison during war.

FELEO, JUAN. Early peasant leader in CPPI and member of first Politburo, 1930; joined Manahan in opposition to Evangelista early in 1930's, but subsequently identified with Hukbalahap; apparently killed in 1946 or 1947.

JORGE. A leader of "majority PB" faction, 1945-48, in opposition to Lava brothers and Luis Taruc; elected Secretary of CPPI after reorganization of January 1947; replaced by Balgos in May 1948.

LACUESTA. Member of "majority PB," 1945-48; expelled from CPPI, with Castro, for opposing new party leadership after reorganization of May 1948.

LAVA, JESUS. Youngest of Lava brothers active in CPPI during and after World War II; elected to Congress in 1946, but barred from seat; succeeded José Lava as CPPI leader after latter's arrest in 1950; led Huk rebellion during 1950's and arrested, finally, in Spring 1964.

LAVA, JOSÉ (b. 1912). Second of Lava brothers in CPPI; dominant figure in CPPI after defeat of "majority PB" in 1948; arrested in October 1950 and sentenced to life imprisonment.

LAVA, VINCENTE (alias Vy). Oldest of Lava brothers in CPPI, educated in the United States; led party during World War II after arrest of Evangelista and Santos; lost leadership to Castro–Jorge–Lacuesta faction in 1945; died in 1947 before his supporters, the "minority PB," regained power.

MANAHAN, JACINTO. Peasant leader during 1920's, associated with Evangelista; attended Fourth Profintern Congress in Moscow, 1928, under auspices of Krestintern; member of First Politburo of CPPI, 1930; arrested and sentenced in 1933; expelled from CPPI for alleged misdemeanors in March 1933.

SANTOS, PEDRO ABAD. Founder of Socialist Party, early 1930's; elected Vice-Chairman of reorganized CPPI after merger of Communists and Socialists in October 1938; Communist candidate for President in 1939, but withdrew candidacy due to split in *Frente Popular*; arrested by Japanese in 1942 and died shortly after release in 1945.

TARUC, LUIS. Close associate of Santos during 1930's in Socialist Party; became CPPI member on merger of Communists and Socialists in 1938; field commander of Hukbalahap during World War II and after; associated with Lava brothers in "minority PB"; jailed by Americans for terrorism, April–September 1945; elected to Congress in 1946, but barred from seat; negotiated amnesty with Quirino government in June 1948 and took seat in Congress; returned to jungle and Huk leadership in September; led Huks in open revolt against government after 1949 elections, but grew increasingly estranged from CPPI leadership; surrendered to government in 1954, after expulsion from CPPI, and sentenced.

American Communists

ALLEN, JAMES. Negotiated freedom of Evangelista and other CPPI leaders in 1936 (or 1937); instrumental in bringing about merger of Communists and Socialists in October 1938.

BROWDER, EARL. *See* above under Comintern Agents.

CARPIO, S. American Communist, perhaps of Filipino origin, who wrote definitive articles on CPPI tactics early in 1930's.

GEORGE, HARRISON. In 1924 visited Manila to invite Philippine labor delegation to Canton conference of transport workers of Pacific; subsequently aide to Earl Browder in PPTUS; said to have headed "Philippine" section of CPUSA in San Francisco, early 1930's.

RYAN, TIM. Author of articles on Philippines and CPPI in 1930's.

Short Biographies

Indigenous Communist Leaders

CHAN FU. According to one source, first Secretary of CPIC, 1930.

LI-KWEI. Also listed as first Secretary of CPIC; died in prison, 1931.

HO CHI MINH (until 1943 known as Nguyen Ai Quoc; b. 1892?).
Present at founding of French Communist Party at Tours,
1920; attended Third Profintern Congress and Fourth Comin-
tern Congress in Moscow, 1924; attached to Borodin's staff in
Canton, 1925-27; in 1926 founded Vietnam Revolutionary
Youth League, precursor of CPIC; reportedly returned to
Moscow briefly in 1926; in February 1930 played major role in
uniting rival Vietnamese factions into CPIC, in Hong Kong;
reportedly in Singapore in 1930 for reorganization of Nanyang
Communists as Malayan Communist Party; arrested in 1931, in
Hong Kong, and jailed for two years; on release, allegedly
returned again to Moscow; in May 1941 organized Vietminh
(while in Kunming) to oppose both French and Japanese;
jailed in China by Kuomintang in 1942 and released following
year; led Vietminh during independence struggle in 1945 and
elected first President of Democratic Republic of Vietnam in
August; negotiated *modus vivendi* with French at Fontainebleau in September 1946; led DRV during Indochinese Civil
War, 1946-54, and after.

PHAM VAN DONG. Close associate of Ho Chi Minh during World
War II and Indochinese Civil War; later Premier of Democratic Republic of Vietnam.

SOUPHANONVONG, PRINCE. Prince of junior branch of royal Laotian
family; spent war years in Hanoi and married a Vietnamese
Communist; returned to Laos in 1945 and played leading role
in *Lao Issara*; on dissolution of the latter, withdrew to northern
Laos and with help from the Vietminh organized the Pathet
Lao, about 1950.

TRUONG CHINH (b. 1913). Elected Secretary-General of Lao Dong
(revived CPIC) in 1951.

VO NGUYEN GIAP (b. 1912). Active in Popular Front in Indochina
in late 1930's; reportedly in Yenan during early years of
World War II; in 1944 named Commander-in-Chief of newly
formed Vietnamese Liberation Army; Minister of Defense in
DRV and principal military leader in Vietminh during Civil
War and after.

492

French Communists

DORIOT, JACQUES. In 1920's considered principal authority on Far Eastern affairs in French Communist Party; attended Pan Pacific Trade Union Conference in Hankow, 1927; broke with FCP in 1930's.

PÉRI, GABRIEL. Headed delegation of French workers to Indochina in 1934; later wrote on Indochinese affairs in French Communist journals.

BURMA

Socialist and Communist Leaders

AUNG SAN (b. 1915). Student activist at University of Rangoon and member of early Marxist study groups, late 1930's, said to be secretary of one of them; following clandestine contacts with Japanese agents in 1941, arranged military training of "thirty comrades" as anti-British nucleus in Burma; during occupation served as Minister of Defense in collaborationist government of Dr. Ba Maw; linked to Communist leader Than Tun by marriage; in August 1944 became President of secret Anti-Fascist Peoples Freedom League, created by Communist, Socialist, and Army leaders; led anti-Japanese rising in March 1945 and conducted independence negotiations with the British during 1946 and early 1947, though growing more and more estranged from Communists; assassinated on August 19, 1947.

GHOSHAL (Thakin Ba Tin; b. about 1920). Burmese-Indian, educated in Rangoon and organizer of early Marxist study group, 1939; after wartime residence in India, returned to Rangoon early in 1948 with "Ghoshal Thesis," containing recommendation of more militant policy for BCP; active in BCP leadership during rebellion against government after March 1948.

THAKIN NU (U Nu; b. 1907). Like many Thakins, associated with early Marxist study groups in Rangoon and later associated with Communists in AFPFL from 1944 to the autumn of 1946, but never a member of BCP; succeeded Aung San as head of AFPFL and Prime Minister in August 1947.

THAKIN SOE (b. about 1913). Active in Marxist study groups, late 1930's; arrested by British, 1940; reportedly called conference in 1942 (or 1943) at which BCP formally launched; elected Secretary and acknowledged during war as leader of anti-

Japanese resistance, though in contact with other nationalists in the Ba Baw government; instrumental in AFPFL negotiations with the British in 1945; removed from party leadership in summer 1945 for "moral misdemeanors"; in February 1946 attacked "Browderism" of his successor, Thein Pe Myint, but failed to unseat him; in March broke with BCP and formed independent CP (Red Flag), which has since been in intermittent state of insurrection against the central government.

THAN TUN (b. 1911). Member of Thakin and Marxist groups in Rangoon, 1930's; arrested by British in July 1940 following visit to India; served in wartime cabinet of Dr. Ba Maw; a founder, with Thakin Soe, of BCP in 1942 (or 1943) and deputy to latter; elected Secretary-General of AFPFL at its founding in August 1944; succeeded Thein Pe Myint as Secretary of BCP in July 1946, but forced to yield post in AFPFL in autumn; led BCP delegation to Southeast Asian Youth Conference and Third Congress of CPI in Calcutta, February 1948; in March led BCP (White Flag) in insurrection against government and remained leader of rebellion during following years.

THEIN PE MYINT (b. 1916). Organized earliest Marxist study group in Rangoon, 1938, following two post-graduate years in Calcutta; returned to India in 1942, following Japanese invasion, and during war served as liaison between Thakins and British authorities in India, as well as between BCP and CPI; named Secretary of BCP in summer 1945, though still in India, following removal of Thakin Soe; after accusations of "Browderism" in 1946 yielded party leadership to Than Tun and gradually ceased active role in BCP.

U BA SWE. Socialist leader since World War II, associated with Communists only in AFPFL from 1944 to autumn of 1946.

MALAYA

Local Communist Leaders

CHEN PENG. Chief aide of Loi Tek during World War II; in 1946, led party investigation of Loi Tek's suspected war-time collaboration with Japanese; succeeded Loi Tek as MCP Secretary on latter's flight in 1947; led party in insurrection during Emergency.

LOI TEK (or Lai Teck; alias Comrade Wright). Vietnamese who joined MCP in mid-1930's, possibly already an informant for

494

British intelligence passed on from French *Securité* in Indochina; elected party Secretary in 1939; cooperated with British military in 1941 to train anti-Japanese guerrillas, but during occupation collaborated with Japanese; re-elected party Secretary in 1946 on moderate program; in 1947, anticipating exposure, fled Malaya and was reportedly assassinated in Hong Kong later in year.

Foreign Agent

SHARKEY, LAWRENCE. Australian Communist present at Southeast Asian Youth Conference in Calcutta, February 1948; en route home, stopped in Singapore, where he urged more militant line at Fourth MCP Plenum.

THAILAND

Indigenous Communist Leaders

NAI PRASERT SAPSUNTHORN (b. 1915). Elected to Parliament on Proletarian Party ticket in 1946; led brief public revival of CPT in January 1947; subsequently fled to China.

NAI THIANTHAI. Listed as Secretary of CPT in 1949.

PRASONG VONG-VIVAT. Described as Secretary-General of CPT in 1952.

Chronology

ABBREVIATIONS

BCP	Burmese Communist Party (white flag)	FDR	*Front Demokrasi Rakjat*
		GLU	General Labor Union
CPC	Communist Party of China	Ho	Ho Chi Minh, or
CPI	Communist Party of India		Nguyen Ai Quoc
CPR	Chinese People's Republic	KAP	*Congresso Proletario di*
CPT	Communist Party of Thailand (or Siam)		*Filipinas*
		KMT	Kuomintang
CPIC	Communist Party of Indochina	MCP	Malayan Communist Party
CPPI	Communist Party of the Philippines	PB	Politburo
		PKI	Communist Party of Indonesia
DRV	Democratic Republic of Vietnam	PPTUS	Pan Pacific Trade Union Secretariat
ECCI	Executive Committee of the Communist International	WFTU	World Federation of Trade Unions

NOTE: Unless otherwise indicated all international meetings listed in column one convened in Moscow.

Outside SE Asia	Indonesia	Indochina	Philippines	Malaya	Burma	Siam
1917						
November Bolshevik Revolution						
1918						
November I Congress of Muslim Communists	Maring exiled from Java					
1919						
March I Comintern Congress						
November II Congress of Muslim Communists						
1920	*May* Founding of PKI					
July-August II Comintern Congress						
September Congress of Toilers of East, Baku		*December* Ho at founding of French CP, Tours				
1921	Darsono at Comintern congress					
April Founding of Communist Academy of Toilers of East						
June-July III Comintern Congress						

OUTSIDE SE ASIA	INDONESIA	INDOCHINA	PHILIPPINES	MALAYA	BURMA	SIAM
1921						
July Founding of CPC, **Shanghai** I Profintern Congress		*December* Ho at I Congress of French CP				
1922						
January-February Congress of Toilers of Far East, Leningrad	Semaoen at Leningrad congress					
November IV Comintern Congress	Tan Malaka at Comintern congress					
November II Profintern Congress						
1923						
January Sun-Joffe agreement, Shanghai	*Spring* Founding of *Sarekat Rakjat*	Ho at Krestintern congress				
June 3rd ECCI plenum						
October Founding of Krestintern						
Fall Borodin arrives in Canton						
1924						
January Death of Lenin						

Outside SE Asia	Indonesia	Indochina	Philippines	Malaya	Burma	Siam
1924						
June Conference of Transport Workers of Pacific, Canton	Javan delegation at Canton conference		*May* Harrison George in Manila Filipino delegation at Canton conference			
June-July V Comintern Congress; 4th ECCI plenum	Semaoen at Comintern congress	Ho at Comintern congress				
July III Profintern Congress		Ho at Profintern congress	Founding of *Partido Obrero*			
	December PKI conference at Jogjakarta					
1925						
March 5th ECCI plenum				Reported founding of *Nanyang* CP		
May Rioting in Shanghai		*June* Formation of Vietnam Rev. Youth League, Canton	*June* Tan Malaka arrives in Manila			
	October PKI conference at Prambanan plans uprising					

OUTSIDE SE ASIA	INDONESIA	INDOCHINA	PHILIPPINES	MALAYA	BURMA	SIAM
1926						
February-March 6th ECCI plenum						
July Beginning of Northern Expedition of KMT and CPC	*July* Alimin and Musso seek Moscow's approval of planned rebellion			Founding of *Nanyang* GLU		
November-December 7th ECCI plenum	*November-December* Rising on Java					
1927						
	January Rising on Sumatra; PKI outlawed					
February I Congress of Anti-Imperialist League, Brussels			Filipinos at Brussels congress			
May 8th ECCI plenum						
May I Pan Pacific Trade Union Conference, Hankow; PPTUS founded	Alimin at Hankow conference	Ho reported at Hankow conference				

	Outside SE Asia	Indonesia	Indochina	Philippines	Malaya	Burma	Siam
1927							
				June *Congresso Obrero* affiliates with PPTUS			
				July Trial and deportation of Tan Malaka			
July	Break up of CPC-KMT alliance; Borodin leaves China						
October	XV CPSU Congress; Left Opposition routed						
December	CPC rising in Canton fails		Ho visit to Moscow reported				
1928							
February	9th ECCI plenum						
March	IV Profintern Congress			Evangelista and Manahan at Profintern Congress			
July-September	VI Comintern Congress	PKI delegates report at Comintern congress	Vietnam delegate reports at Comintern congress				
October	PPTUS conference, Shanghai			Manahan at Shanghai conference			

Outside SE Asia	Indonesia	Indochina	Philippines	Malaya	Burma	Siam
1929						
		May Conference of Vietnam Rev. Youth League, Hong Kong	*May* Split in *Congresso Obrero*; formation of KAP			Ho reported in Bangkok
July 10th ECCI plenum	Musso at ECCI plenum					
July II Congress of Anti-Imperialist League, Frankfurt						
August II Pan Pacific Trade Union Conference, Vladivostok and Shanghai			Manahan at Vladivostok conference	*Nanyang* delegate at Shanghai conference		
1930						
PPTUS transferred to San Francisco		*January-February* Merger of Vietnamese Marxists in CPIC, Hong Kong *February* Mutiny at Enbay		*April* *Nanyang* CP and GLU reorganized as MCP and MGLU		

Outside SE Asia	Indonesia	Indochina	Philippines	Malaya	Burma	Siam
1930						
July CPC revolt at Changsha fails						
August V Profintern Congress		*Fall* "Soviets" formed in No. Annam				
		November 1st CPIC plenum	*November* Founding of CPPI			
1931						
			January Evangelista, Manahan arrested			
March 11th ECCI plenum					*Formation of Dohbama Asiayone*	
		April 2nd CPIC plenum reported				
			May I CPPI Congress			
		June Ho arrested in Hong Kong, imprisoned 2 years		*June* Arrest of Ducroix; Comintern network destroyed in SE Asia		

Outside SE Asia	Indonesia	Indochina	Philippines	Malaya	Burma	Siam
1931						
					Summer Beginning of Saya San rising	
November Chinese "soviet" republic proclaimed by Mao Tse-tung			*September* Trial of CPPI leaders			
1932						
	Hatta returns to Java; *Perhimpoenan Indonesia* comes under Communist control	CPIC "Program of Action" affirms militant line				*June* Anti-royalist revolution
September 12th ECCI plenum			*November* 1st CPPI plenum	*September* MCP adopts party program		

OUTSIDE SE ASIA	INDONESIA	INDOCHINA	PHILIPPINES	MALAYA	BURMA	SIAM
1933						
	January Mutiny on Zeven Provincien					Communism outlawed by new regime Pridi exiled as "Communist"
			March 2nd CPPI plenum; Manahan expelled			
		April CPIC conference reported in Siam *May* CPIC allies with Trotskyites in Saigon election				
August Comintern "apparatus" reported in Shanghai						
		Fall Ho visit to Moscow reported	*Fall* CPPI leaders begin sentences after appeal fails			
December 13th ECCI plenum	PKI delegate reports at ECCI plenum					

	OUTSIDE SE ASIA	INDONESIA	INDOCHINA	PHILIPPINES	MALAYA	BURMA	SIAM
1934			*January-March* French workers' delegation visits Indochina				
					March 6th MCP plenum; adopts constitution	Round Table talks in London on new constitution	
	June Orientalist conference urges "proletarian hegemony"						
	October CPC begins Long March to Northeast				*Fall* Strike activity by MCP increases		
1935	*January* Mao Tse-tung assumes leadership of CPC		*March?* I CPIC Congress, Macao			Burma granted limited self-government	

	Outside SE Asia	Indonesia	Indochina	Philippines	Malaya	Burma	Siam
1935			*March* CPIC supports coalition in national election				
		Spring Musso returns from Moscow to form "illegal PKI"					
				May *Sakdal* rising			
	July-August VII Comintern Congress	PKI delegate reports at Comintern congress	CPIC delegate reports at Comintern congress				
				October Philippines become self-governing			
1936			*July* CPIC plenum in China; united front tactics adopted				
					September 6th MCP plenum; intra-party dispute resolved		

Outside SE Asia	Indonesia	Indochina	Philippines	Malaya	Burma	Siam
1936						
December Capture of Chiang Kai-shek at Sian; released with help of CPC			*October* CPPI takes part in Popular Alliance			
1937						
	PKI collaborates with *Gerindo*		CPPI leaders released, due to efforts of James Allen	*Winter* "Soviet" reported established during strike at Batu Arang		
June Japan attacks China						
August Sino-Soviet Non-aggression Pact						
September CPC and KMT form united front						
1938						
			May Merger of Communist and Socialist trade unions	MCP supports anti-Japanese organizations in Chinese community	First Marxist study groups in Rangoon	

OUTSIDE SE ASIA	INDONESIA	INDOCHINA	PHILIPPINES	MALAYA	BURMA	SIAM
1938						
			August CPPI manifesto calls for united front			
			October III CPPI Congress; merger of Communist and Socialist parties (*Frente Popular*)			
1939						
		April Trotskyites surpass CPIC in Cochinchina election		*April* 6th MCP plenum calls for united front; Loi Tek named party leader		
August Nazi-Soviet Pact						
September World War II begins in Europe		*September* CPIC outlawed			*September* Burmese Marxists join nationalists in Freedom Bloc	
		November 6th CPIC plenum abandons united front				

Outside SE Asia	Indonesia	Indochina	Philippines	Malaya	Burma	Siam
1940						
June Fall of France		*July* Japanese occupy Indochina				
		Fall Communist disorders in Annam and Cochinchina			*Fall* Aung San and "30 comrades" trained by Japanese	
1941						
		January CPIC conference reportedly condemns 1940 disorders				
April Soviet-Japanese Non-aggression Pact		*May* 8th CPIC plenum; founding of Vietminh				
June Hitler opens attack on USSR				*July* 8th MCP plenum supports British war effort		

Outside SE Asia	Indonesia	Indochina	Philippines	Malaya	Burma	Siam
1941						
December Japanese attack on Pearl Harbor			*Fall* Split in *Frente Popular*	*December* British officers and MCP set up guerrilla schools		*December* Japanese occupy Thailand
1942						
		Ho arrested in China	*January* Japanese take Manila; Evangelista, Santos arrested	*February* Fall of Singapore		
	March Dutch surrender to Japanese		*March* Formation of *Hukbalahap*	*March* Formation of MPAJA		
	PKI supports Sjarifuddin's resistance movement				*May* British withdraw from Burma	
	Tan Malaka returns to Java, incognito				Aung San, other *Thakins* in pro-Japanese government of Ba Maw	

Outside SE Asia	Indonesia	Indochina	Philippines	Malaya	Burma	Siam
1942						
					Thein Pe Myint flees to India	
				September Arrest of MCP leaders at Batu Caves	*Founding of BCP under Thakin Soe (date unknown)	
1943 *Winter* Battle of Stalingrad	*Winter* Sjarifuddin arrested; resistance leadership passes to Sjahrir	*February* Ho released; changes name		*February* MCP conference elaborates on war aims		
			March Japanese disrupt *Huk* bases			
May Comintern dissolved			*October* Philippine "independence" proclaimed under Laurel		*August* Burmese "independence" proclaimed	
				MCP contacts with Force 136	BCP contacts with Force 136 via Thein Pe Myint	

Outside SE Asia	Indonesia	Indochina	Philippines	Malaya	Burma	Siam
1944	Japanese launch "Communist" organization under Subardjo					Pibulsonggram overthrown by Pridi
					March Socialists, Communists ally in AFPFL under Aung San and Than Tun	
		September Planned rising of Vietminh canceled *December* Formation of Vietnam Liberation Army	*September* Reorganization of CPPI leadership *October* MacArthur lands in Philippines			
1945 *February* Yalta conference; USSR agrees to enter war in Far East		*March* Japanese arrest Vichy officials; Vietminh rejects "independent" regime of Bao Dai				
April "Browderism" rebuked in French CP journal			*April* Taruc arrested for *Huk* disorders			

OUTSIDE SE ASIA	INDONESIA	INDOCHINA	PHILIPPINES	MALAYA	BURMA	SIAM
1945						
		Spring Formation of *Khmer Issarak, Lao-Issara* in Cambodia, Laos				
					May AFPFL revolts against Japanese *Summer* II BCP Congress; Thakin Soe relieved, Thein Pe Myint elected Secretary	
August Sino-Soviet Treaty; Russians attack Manchuria; Japanese surrender	*August* Republic of Indonesia proclaimed	*August* Vietminh rebels; Ho named President of Nat'l Liberation Committee				
		September DRV proclaimed	*September* Taruc released			
		October Lao Issara seizes power in Vientiane		*October* Democratic Youth League formed		
	November PKI reestablished under Jusuf	*November* CPIC "dissolved"				

	Outside SE Asia	Indonesia	Indochina	Philippines	Malaya	Burma	Siam
1945		*November* Tan Malaka forms Fighting Front			*December* MPAJA "dissolved"		
1946	*February* Founding of WFTU, London	*February* Jusuf arrested after PKI disorders	*March* Ho-Sainteny accord; DRV in French Union	*January* CPPI conference fails to end factional dispute	*January* 2-day general strike led by MCP *January* 8th MCP plenum sets moderate course; reelects Loi Tek	*February* Thakin Soe attacks Thein Pe Myint for "Browderism"; fails to unseat him	
		March-April PKI repudiates Jusuf; names Sardjono leader			Visits by Loi Tek to China reported	*March* Thakin Soe launches "Red Flag" party	

Outside SE Asia	Indonesia	Indochina	Philippines	Malaya	Burma	Siam
			April CPPI supports Osmeña in national election; Taruc, Jesus Lava denied seats			
		Spring Lao Issara withdraws to Bangkok after defeat by French				
		Summer French-DRV talks at Fontainebleau: *modus vivendi*				
	June Tan Malaka arrested after abortive coup					
			July Philippines become independent		*July* Than Tun replaces Thein Pe Myint as BCP leader	
August Founding of International Union of Students, Prague	*August* Alimin returns; shares PKI leadership					
					September Than Tun forced out as Sec'y of AFPFL	

1946

OUTSIDE SE ASIA	INDONESIA	INDOCHINA	PHILIPPINES	MALAYA	BURMA	SIAM
1946						
						October Communist organizations legalized
					November BCP expelled from AFPFL	
		December Civil War begins				
1947						
			January Leadership of CPPI reorganized under Jorge; PB rivalry continues			*January* CPT in open at New Year's Day rally
February Conference of CPs of British Commonwealth, London; demands independence of India, Burma				MCP delegates at London conference	BCP delegates at London conference	
	March Linggadjati agreement			*March* Loi Tek disappears on eve of denunciation; Chen Peng succeeds		
Spring E. Zhukov visits India						

Outside SE Asia	Indonesia	Indochina	Philippines	Malaya	Burma	Siam
1947						
June Orientalist conference on India attacks Congress Party						
	July Sjarifuddin cabinet formed				*July* Aung San assassinated; U Nu succeeds as premier	
	First Dutch "police action" begins					
August India becomes independent						
September Cominform founded; Zhdanov address on "two camps"						
					October Nu-Attlee agreement	
November Orientalist conference on Russian Revolution and the East						*November* Pibulsonggram seizes power; Pridi flees

OUTSIDE SE ASIA	INDONESIA	INDOCHINA	PHILIPPINES	MALAYA	BURMA	SIAM
1947						
December CPI plenum adopts Leftist line					Ghoshal at CPI plenum	CPT again underground
1948					*January* Burma becomes independent	
	January Suripno negotiates consular treaty with USSR					
	Renville agreement ends Dutch "police action"					
	February Sjarifuddin cabinet falls; he heads FDR				*February* BCP adopts "Ghoshal Thesis"	
February Conference of SE Asia Youth, Calcutta; III CPI Congress	Indonesian delegates at Calcutta	Vietminh officers at Calcutta	"Observers" at Calcutta	MCP delegation at Calcutta	BCP delegation at Calcutta	
			March Roxas outlaws *Hukbalahap*	*March* 4th MCP plenum; Sharkey attends	*March* Pyinmina rally; strikes in Rangoon; MCP insurrection begins (March 28)	
			April Roxas dies; Quirino succeeds			

Outside SE Asia	Indonesia	Indochina	Philippines	Malaya	Burma	Siam
1948						
	May USSR ratifies consular treaty		*May* CPPI conference endorses "armed struggle" in principle; "minority PB" in power	*May* 5th MCP plenum		*May* USSR and Siam exchange ambassadors
			June Temporary amnesty for *Huks*	*June* Emergency declared		
	July FDR adopts militant course					
			August Taruc returns to jungle		*Summer* Rebellion widened	
	August Musso returns to Java; merger of PKI, Socialists and FDR					
	September Madiun uprising					
	December Second Dutch "police action" begins Execution of PKI leaders					

Outside SE Asia	Indonesia	Indochina	Philippines	Malaya	Burma	Siam
1949						
	January USSR supports Indonesia in UN	*Lao Issara* disbanded; formation of *Pathet Lao*				
			Winter CPPI conference votes support of *Nacionalista* in coming election	*February* Creation of Malayan Races Liberation Army (MRLA)		
June Orientalist conference reveals firmer line		*July* French-Laotian accord on self-government				
	August-November Round Table talks, The Hague					
October Formation of Chinese People's Republic						

OUTSIDE SE ASIA	INDONESIA	INDOCHINA	PHILIPPINES	MALAYA	BURMA	SIAM
1949						
		November Cambodian constitution ratified	*November* Nacionalista defeated; CPPI goes underground			
November WFTU conference, Peking				Malay delegates at Peking		Thai delegates at Peking
	December Indonesia becomes independent				*December* Burma recognizes CPR	
1950						
		January CPR, USSR recognize DRV	*January* PB orders armed insurrection		Legal Communist front organizations created	
		April Ho visits CPR; reported aid agreement				
		May Khmer People's Party formed				
May Conference of "Pacific Pact" powers, Baguio						

OUTSIDE SE ASIA	INDONESIA	INDOCHINA	PHILIPPINES	MALAYA	BURMA	SIAM
1950						
June Korean War begins						
	August CPR opens diplomatic relations with Indonesia					
			September Magsaysay named Min. of Defense; opens active campaign against *Huks*			
					September CPR Embassy opens in Rangoon; reported aid to BCP guerrillas	
October Chinese enter Korean War			*October* José Lava, other PB members arrested			
1951		*March* CPIC revived as *Lao Dong*; union with *Pathet Lao* and Khmer People's Party		Briggs resettlement plan checks MCP guerrillas		

Outside SE Asia	Indonesia	Indochina	Philippines	Malaya	Burma	Siam
1951						
April CPI rejects militant line						
			Capadocia killed		*May* Soviet Embassy opens in Rangoon	
July Truce talks open in Korea						
	August Sukarno arrests 2000 PKI; Alimin takes refuge in CPR Embassy					
November Orientalist conference questions Chinese "model"			*December* CPPI conference acknowledges set-backs		*December* CPR cultural mission visits Burma	
1952						
	April PKI offers support to Wilipo cabinet					
	May PKI launches Nat'l Unity Front					
October XIX CPSU Congress						

Outside SE Asia	Indonesia	Indochina	Philippines	Malaya	Burma	Siam
1953						
March Death of Stalin					Than Tun leadership reported challenged within BCP	
		Spring Vietminh invades Laos; withdraws				
			July Taruc reported suspended from CPPI			
June Korean War ends						
	October Aidit replaces Alimin as PKI leader					
		Fall Cambodian independence				
		November Ho proposes peace talks				
1954						
		April Vietminh victory at Dienbienphu				
		May Geneva conference on Indochina opens				

Bibliography

THE BIBLIOGRAPHY is organized in four sections. The *first* includes official materials relating to the congresses, plenary meetings, and activities of the Communist International, the Profintern and several other affiliated organizations; these materials are listed chronologically. The *second*, and main, section of the Bibliography lists alphabetically all other works, both Russian and non-Russian, used in this study; the list, it should be noted, is not exhaustive but includes all items the author consulted and found in one way or another useful. In order to facilitate for readers the location of materials relating to a particular Southeast Asian country, the following symbols (preceding each entry) are used:

In   Indonesia
IC   Indochina (including Laos and Cambodia)
PI   Philippines
M   Malaya
B   Burma
T   Thailand (or Siam)
Gen   Southeast Asia as a whole; countries outside Southeast Asia (e.g., India and China); Communist or Soviet Eastern strategies in general

The *third* section of the Bibliography includes Russian and foreign Communist periodicals consulted in this study. The *fourth* and final section lists the principal interviews conducted by the author in Southeast Asia during 1961 and 1962, together with a brief description of the topics discussed.

OFFICIAL RECORDS OF THE COMINTERN, PROFINTERN, AND RELATED ORGANIZATIONS

FIRST COMINTERN CONGRESS

Pervyi kongress Kommunisticheskogo Internatsionala: protokoly. Moscow, 1933.

SECOND TO THIRD COMINTERN CONGRESS

Vtoroi kongress Kommunisticheskogo Internatsionala; stenograficheskii otchet. Petrograd, 1921; reprinted in 1934 under the title *Vtoroi kongress Kominterna.*

527

Bibliography

Second Congress of the Communist International; proceedings of Petrograd session of July 17 and of Moscow session of July 19 - August 7, 1920. New York, 1921. Abridged report of Second Congress.

Pervyi s"ezd narodov Vostoka; stenograficheskii otchet. Moscow, 1921. Report of Congress of Toilers of the East at Baku, September 1920.

THIRD TO FOURTH COMINTERN CONGRESS

Tretii vsemirnyi kongress Kommunisticheskogo Internatsionala; stenograficheskii otchet. Moscow, 1922.

Pervyi s"ezd revoliutsionnykh organizatsii Dal'nego Vostoka; sbornik. Petrograd, 1922. Record of the Congress of the Toilers of the Far East, January-February, 1922.

First Congress of the Toilers of the Far East. Petrograd, 1922. An abridged translation of the preceding item.

FOURTH TO FIFTH COMINTERN CONGRESS

IV vsemirnyi kongress Kommunisticheskogo Internatsionala (5 noiabria - 3 dekabria, 1922 g); izbrannye doklady, rechi i rezoliutsii. Moscow, 1923.

Fourth Congress of the Communist International; abridged report of meetings held at Petrograd and Moscow, Nov. 7-Dec. 3, 1922.

Rasshirennyi plenum Ispolnitel'nogo komiteta Kommunisticheskogo Internatsionala (12-23 iunia, 1923 goda). Moscow, 1923. Stenogram of the Third ECCI Plenum.

FIFTH TO SIXTH COMINTERN CONGRESS

Piatyi vsemirnyi kongress Kommunisticheskogo Internatsionala, 17 iunia - 8 iulia, 1924 g.; stenograficheskii otchet, 2 vols. Moscow, 1925.

Fifth Congress of the Communist International; abridged report of meetings held at Moscow, June 17 to July 8, 1924. London, 1924.

Third World Congress of the Red International of Trade Unions: resolutions and decisions. Moscow, 1924?

III kongress Krasnogo Internatsionala profsoiuzov; otchet. Moscow, 1924. Report of Third Profintern Congress, July 8-22, 1924.

Rasshirennyi plenum Ispolkoma Kommunisticheskogo Internatsionala, protokoly zasedanii; stenograficheskii otchet. Moscow, 1925. Stenogram of the Fifth ECCI Plenum, March 21-April 16, 1925.

528

Otchet Ispolkoma Kominterna (aprel' 1925 g - ianvar' 1926 g); sostavlem sekretariatom IKKI. Moscow, 1926. Materials for Sixth ECCI Plenum, February-March, 1926.

Shestoi rasshirennyi plenum Ispolkoma Kominterna (15 fev. - 15 marta, 1926 g); stenograficheskii otchet. Moscow, 1927.

Puti mirovoi revoliutsii: sed'moi rasshirennyi plenum Ispolnitel'nogo komiteta Kommunisticheskogo Internatsionala (22 noiabria - 16 dekabria, 1926); stenograficheskii otchet, 2 vols. Moscow, 1927.

VIII plenum Ispolnitel'nogo komiteta Kommunisticheskogo Internatsionala, 18-30 maia, 1927 goda: tezisy, rezoliutsii i vozzvaniia. Moscow, 1927. The only report of the Eighth ECCI Plenum, pocket size; no stenogram was published.

Resolutions and Decisions of the Pan Pacific Trade Union Conference; bulletin of proceedings. Hankow, 1927.

SIXTH TO SEVENTH COMINTERN CONGRESS

Kommunisticheskii Internatsional pered Shestym vsemirnym kongressom; obzor deiatel'nosti IKKI i sektsii Kominterna mezhdu V i VI kongressami. Moscow, 1928.

The Communist International Between the Fifth and the Sixth World Congresses, 1924-1928: a report on the position in all sections of the World Communist Party. London, 1928. English edition of preceding item.

Shestoi kongress Kominterna: stenograficheskii otchet, 6 vols. Moscow, 1929.

The Revolutionary Movement in the Colonies: thesis adopted at the Sixth World Congress of the Communist International, 1928. New York: Workers' Library Publishers, 1929.

IV kongress Profinterna: stenograficheskii otchet, 3 vols. Moscow, 1928. Stenogram of congress which ran from March 17 to April 3, 1925.

Mezhdunarodnoe profdvizhenie za 1924-27 gg.; otchet Ispolbiuro IV kongressy Profinterna. Moscow, 1928.

X plenum Ispolkoma Kominterna, 3 vols. Moscow, 1929.

XI plenum IKKI, stenograficheskii otchet, 2 vols. Moscow, 1931-32.

Manuilsky, D. Z. *The Communist Parties and the Crisis of Capitalism.* New York: International Publishers, 1931. Principal report to the XI ECCI Plenum, March 1931.

Bibliography

XII plenum IKKI: stenograficheskii otchet, 3 vols. Moscow, 1933.
Guide to the XII Plenum ECCI. New York: International Publishers, 1932.

Kuusinen, Otto. *Fascism, the Danger of War and the Tasks of the Communist Parties.* New York: International Publishers, 1934. Kuusinen's report to the XIII ECCI Plenum, December 1933.

Communist International, Executive Committee, XIII Plenum. *Theses and Decisions.* Moscow, 1934.

SEVENTH COMINTERN CONGRESS

Kommunisticheskii Internatsional pered VII vsemirnym kongressom: materialy. Moscow, 1935.

VII Congress of the Communist International: stenographic report of proceedings. Moscow, 1939. Also translated into French and German; no Russian edition exists.

Wang Ming [Ch'en Shao-yü]. *The Revolutionary Movement in the Colonial Countries.* New York: International Publishers, 1935. Report on the colonial question at the Seventh Comintern Congress.

OTHER COMINTERN MATERIALS

Kommunisticheskii Internatsional v dokumentakh; resheniia, tezisy, i vozzvaniia kongressov KI i plenumov IKKI, 1919-1932. Moscow, 1933. Edited by Bela Kun; a collection of most Comintern resolutions through 1932.

> *Note*: For additional materials relating to Comintern activity, see in next section under Agol, Borkenau, Degras, Eudin and North, McKenzie, Pavlovich-Volonter, *Second Congress of the Communist International* . . . , Varga, and Zamyslova.

GENERAL WORKS

Gen Agol, Sh. *Komintern i kolonial'nyi mir.* Moscow, 1929. A review of resolutions on the colonial question adopted by the Sixth Comintern Congress.

In *Aidit Accuses Madiun Affair.* Djakarta, 1955. A defense of the PKI's role in the 1948 uprising by the party secretary after 1953.

In Aidit, D. N. *The Birth and Growth of the Communist Party of Indonesia.* Djakarta, 1958. Issued on the thirty-fifth anniversary of the PKI.

530

Gen   Akademiia nauk SSSR, *Izvestiia,* Seriia istorii i filosophii, No. 1, 1952; "Khronika v Otdelenii istorii i filosophii ANSSSR v Institute Vostokovedeniia o kharaktere i osobennostiakh narodnoi demokratii v stranakh Vostoka," pp. 80-7. Report of an important meeting of Soviet Orientalists in November 1951; translated in *Current Digest of the Soviet Press,* iv, 20, pp. 3-7, 43.

Gen   Akademiia nauk SSSR, *Vestnik,* No. 1, 1948; "Velikaia oktiabrskaia revoliutsiia i strany Vostoka," pp. 39-46. Incomplete report of an Orientalist meeting in November 1947.

Gen   Akademiia nauk SSSR, Institut Vostokovedeniia, *Kratkie soobshcheniia, vyp.* viii, 1953. Includes articles on revolutionary movements in several Southeast Asian countries.

Gen   Akademiia nauk SSSR, Tikhookeanskii institut, *Uchenye zapiski, tom.* ii, 1949, "Indiiskii sbornik." Includes (pp. 5-56) several controversial papers read at the Orientalist conference on India, June 1947.

Note: For additional publications of the Soviet Academy of Sciences and its branches, see *Periodicals,* below.

Gen   *Allies for Freedom: report of the Second Conference of Communist Workers and Workers' Parties of Countries within the Sphere of British Imperialism.* London: Caxton Hall, 1954. A report by the CPGB on the Second Conference of Communist Parties in the Commonwealth in April 1954.

In   Anderson, B. R. O'G. *Some Aspects of Indonesian Politics under the Japanese Occupation.* Ithaca: Cornell Modern Indonesia Project, 1961.

B   Aung San. "Burma's Challenge." Rangoon, 1947? (mimeograph). Five speeches delivered in 1945-47; the copy consulted by the author belongs to Professor John H. Badgley of Miami University.

Gen   Avarin, V. A. *Politicheskie izmeniia na Tikhom okeane posle vtoroi mirovoi voiny.* Moscow, 1947.

B   Ba Swe, U. *The Burmese Revolution.* Rangoon, 1952. Articles on socialism and Communism by the secretary of the Burmese Socialist Party.

B   Ba Tin (Ghoshal). "On the Present Political Situation in Burma and Our Tasks" (January 1948). Known generally as the Ghoshal Thesis; a mimeograph translation was given to the author by U Thaung Myine.

"Basic Paper on the Malayan Communist Party." *See* Malaya, Federation of.

Gen Beloff, Max. *Soviet Policy in the Far East, 1944-1951.* London: Oxford University Press, 1953.

In Benda, H. J. and Ruth T. McVey (eds.). *The Communist Uprisings of 1926-1927 in Indonesia: key documents.* Ithaca: Cornell Modern Indonesia Project, 1960. A collection of important Dutch documents relating to the insurrection with a lucid introductory essay by the editors.

Gen *Bibliografiia Iugo-vostochnoi Azii.* Moscow, 1960. A listing of over 3,750 Russian articles and monographs on Southeast Asia from the pre-revolutionary era to 1959; indispensable guide to students of Soviet policy in Southeast Asia.

B *Birmanskii soiuz; sbornik statei.* Moscow, 1958. Eleven articles on Burma by Soviet and Burmese scholars.

In Blumberger, J. Th. Petrus. *Le communisme aux Indes Neérlandaises.* Paris, 1929 (translated from Dutch). The author was a former Dutch official in Java.

Gen Boersner, Demetrio. *The Bolsheviks and the National and Colonial Question, 1917-1928.* Geneva: Droz, 1957.

Gen Borkenau, Franz. *The Communist International.* London, 1938; republished in 1939 under the title *World Communism* (New York: Norton).

In Brackman, A. C. *Indonesian Communism: a history.* New York: Praeger, 1963.

Gen Brandt, Conrad. *Stalin's Failure in China, 1924-1927.* Cambridge: Harvard University Press, 1958.

Gen Brimmell, J. H. *Communism in Southeast Asia: a political analysis.* London: Oxford University Press, 1959.

B *Burma and the Insurrections.* Rangoon, 1949. A Burmese government report on the origins of the 1948 risings.

B Cady, John F. *A History of Modern Burma.* Ithaca: Cornell University Press, 1958.

IC Chan Zan Then. *Rasskazy o zhizni i deiatel'nosti presidenta Kho Shi Mina.* Moscow, 1958 (translated from the Vietnamese edition, Hanoi, 1955).

M Chapman, F. Spencer. *The Jungle is Neutral.* London, 1949. Recollections of a British agent in Malaya during World War II.

B   Chzhu Chzhi-khe. *Birma.* Moscow, 1958 (translated from Chinese).

IC   Cole, Allen B. (ed.). *Conflict in Indochina and International Repercussions: a documentary history, 1945-1955.* Ithaca: Cornell University Press, 1956. Includes excerpts from Chinese and Russian sources on the civil war in Indochina.

Gen *Colonial Peoples' Struggle for Liberation: reports to Institute of Economics and Pacific Institute of Academy of Sciences, USSR.* Bombay, 1949. Summaries of reports read at the Orientalist conference on the colonial question, June 1949.

Gen *The Colonies: The Way Forward*; a memorandum issued by the Executive Committee of CPGB (November 1944). London, 1944.
     Communism in the Philippines. See Philippines, Republic of, Congress.
     Communist Banditry in Malaya. See Malaya, Federation of, Department of Public Relations.

Gen *Communist Conspiracy at Madurai: an analysis of the private proceedings of the Third Congress of the CPI with full text of secret documents.* Bombay: Democratic Research Service, 1954. An independent study of CPI policies early in the 1950's.
     The Communist Threat to the Federation of Malaya. See Malaya, Government of, Legislative Council.
     CUFA [Committee on Un-Filipino Activities], *Report on the Illegality of the Communist Party of the Philippines. See* Philippines, Republic of, Congress, House of Representatives.

Gen *Crisis of the Colonial System, National Liberation Struggle of the Peoples of East Asia.* Bombay, 1951. A translation of *Krizis kolonial'noi sistemy*; see below.
     The Danger and Where It Lies. See Malaya, Federation of, Information Services.

IC   Dantzig, A. *Indokitai.* Moscow, 1931. An early full-length study (116 pp.) of Indochina, based largely on French Communist sources.

IC   Das, S. R. Mohan. *Ho Chi Minh: Nationalist or Soviet Agent?* Bombay, 1950.

Gen Degras, Jane (ed.). *The Communist International, 1919-1943: documents,* 3 vols. New York: Oxford University Press, 1956-

Bibliography

60. The first two volumes of this indispensable three-volume collection have been published, covering the period 1919-1929.

IC   *Demokraticheskaia respublika V'etnam, 1945-1960.* Moscow, 1960. A collection of articles by Russian and Vietnamese scholars.

IC   Devillers, Philippe. *Histoire du Viêt-Nam de 1940 à 1952.* Paris: Editions du Seuil, 1952. The fullest treatment by a Western scholar of the period in question.

In   Dingley, S. *The Peasants' Movement in Indonesia.* Berlin, 1927 (translated from French). A *Krestintern* publication.

Gen   Donnison, F. S. V. *British Military Administration in the Far East, 1943-46.* London: Her Majesty's Stationery Office, 1956. An official review of British administration in the China-Burma-India theater during World War II.

Gen   Eudin, X. J., and Robert C. North. *Soviet Russia and the East, 1920-1927: a documentary survey.* Stanford: Stanford University Press, 1957. An important collection of documents, with extensive commentary.

IC   Fall, Bernard. *Le Viêt-Minh: la republique democratique du Vietnam, 1945-1960.* Paris: Librairie Armond Colin, 1960.

The Fight Against Communist Terrorism in Malaya. See Great Britain, Central Office of Information.

IC   France, Gouvernement Général de l'Indochine, Direction des Affaires Politiques et de la Sûreté Générale. *Documents,* 5 vols. Hanoi, 1933-34. Used extensively by I. Milton Sacks (see below); not available to the author.

Gen   Gautherot, Gustave. *Le bolchévisme aux colonies et l'imperialisme rouge.* Paris: Librairie de la revue française, 1930.

M   Great Britain, Central Office of Information, Reference Division. *The Fight Against Communist Terrorism in Malaya.* London, 1953.

In   Guber, A. A. *Indoneziia.* Moscow, 1932. Early full-length study (380 pp.) of Indonesia by a leading Soviet Orientalist.

Gen   ———. *Indoneziia i Indokitai.* Moscow, 1942. Includes chapters on Malaya, Siam, and the Philippines.

In   ———. *Natsional'no-osvoboditel'noe dvizhenie v Indonezii.* Moscow, 1946. Transcript of public lecture, March 27, 1946.

534

In   ————. *Voina v Indonezii*. Moscow, 1947. Transcript of public lecture, August 7, 1947.

IC   Hammer, Ellen J. *The Struggle for Indochina*. Stanford: Stanford University Press, 1954.

In   Hanna, Willard A. "From Jail to Jail: the saga of Tan Malaka," American Universities Field Staff Letter, WAH-1-1959, April 6, 1959. A summary of Tan Malaka's autobiography, written during World War II.

M   Hanrahan, Gene Z. *Communist Struggle in Malaya*. New York: Institute of Pacific Relations, 1954. A detailed study of Communist strategies in Malaya, including several critical documents.

In   Hartono. "The Indonesian Communist Movement, 1945-1948: its development and relations with the Soviet Union." New York: Columbia University, 1959 (Master's thesis).

B, IC   Hinton, Harold C. *China's Relations with Burma and Vietnam: a brief survey*. New York: Institute of Pacific Relations, 1958.

M   "History of the Malayan Communist Party." Singapore (?), 1945. An apparently authentic history of the MCP to World War II, prepared for internal party use; recovered during the Emergency and now in Malayan government files.

PI   Hoeksema, Renze L. "Communism in the Philippines; an historical and analytical study of the CPPI and its relations to Communist movements abroad." Cambridge: Harvard University, 1956 (doctoral thesis). Detailed study indispensable for students of Philippine Communism; exists only in typed manuscript.

Gen   *Iugo-vostochnaia Aziia: ocherki ekonomiki i istorii*. Moscow, 1959. Articles on Southeast Asia by leading Soviet Orientalists.

B   Johnstone, William C. *Burma's Foreign Policy: a study in nationalism*. Cambridge: Harvard University Press, 1963.

In   Kahin, George McT. *Nationalism and Revolution in Indonesia*. Ithaca: Cornell University Press, 1952. Basic study of Indonesian revolution.

Gen   Kautsky, John M. *Moscow and the Communist Party of India: a study in the postwar evolution of international Communist strategy*. New York: John Wiley and Sons, 1956.

Bibliography

B   Kasnacheev, Alexander. *Inside a Soviet Embassy: experiences of a Russian diplomat in Burma.* Philadelphia: Lippincott, 1962. Report of a Soviet diplomat who defected to the West in Rangoon, 1958; see below, *Interviews.*

Gen   Kennedy, Malcolm. *A History of Communism in East Asia.* New York: Praeger, 1957.

Gen   Kheifets, A. N. *Velikii oktiabr' i ugnetennye narody Vostoka.* Moscow, 1959.

        Kolonial'nye problemy. See next item.

Gen   Kommunisticheskaia akademiia SSSR, Institut mirovogo khoziaistva i mirovoi politiki, Kolonial'nyi sektor. *Kolonial'nye problemy, sb.* 1, 2, 3-4. Moscow, 1933-35. The three issues of this Orientalist journal contain a number of important articles on Southeast Asia.

Gen   *Krizis kolonial'noi sistemy: natsional'no-osvoboditel'naia bor'ba narodov vostochnoi Azii.* Moscow, 1949. Nine critical articles on the colonial question by Soviet Orientalists; an important volume.

        Kuusinen, Otto. *See* preceding section of Bibliography.

IC   Lacouture, Jean et Philippe Devillers. *La Fin d'une guerre: Indochine, 1954.* Paris: Editions du Seuil, 1960. Detailed study of Geneva conference of 1954 and its background.

PI   Lava, José. *Milestones in the History of the CPP.* Manila, 1950(?). An official history of the CPPI by its First Secretary at the time; cited as *Milestones.*

Gen   Lenin, V. I. *The National-Liberation Movement in the East.* Moscow, 1962 (translation of *O natsional'no-osvoboditel'nom dvizhenii narodov Vostoka*). Selected articles by Lenin on the colonial question, 1900-1923.

Gen   ———. *Sochineniia,* 4th ed., 1947-50.

Gen   *Lenin i Vostok; sbornik statei,* 2nd ed. Moscow, 1925. A memorial volume by Soviet Orientalists.

PI   Levinson, G. I. *Filippiny.* Moscow, 1953. Early pamphlet on the Philippines.

PI   ———. *Filipinny mezhdu pervoi i vtoroi mirovymi voinami.* Moscow, 1958. The major work of the leading Soviet specialist on the Philippines.

PI   ———. *Filipinny: vchera i segodnia.* Moscow, 1959.

PI ———. "Politika S Sh A i natsional'no-osvoboditel'noe dvizhenie na Filipinnakh v periode 'avtonomii' (1935-1941)." Moscow, 1952. Synopsis of a doctoral thesis, at Leningrad Public
Library.

PI ———. *Rabochee dvizhenie na Filippinakh.* Moscow, 1957.

M Levkovskii, A. I. *Natsional'no-osvoboditel'naia bor'ba narodov
Malaii za svoiu svobodu i nezavisimost'.* Moscow, 1952. Transcript of a public lecture.

Gen Liu Shao-chi. *Internationalism and Nationalism.* Peking, 1948.
First important statement on foreign affairs by a CPC spokesman, November 1948.

M Malaya, Federation of, Department of Public Relations. "Anat-
omy of Communist Propaganda: July 1948–December 1949."
Kuala Lumpur, 1950. Complements "Anatomy of Bandit
Propaganda," December 1948.

M ———. "Communist Banditry in Malaya: the Emergency, June
1948–December 1949." Kuala Lumpur, 1950.

M Malaya, Federation of, Information Services. *The Danger and
Where It Lies.* Kuala Lumpur, n. d. A pamphlet on the early
phase of the Emergency.

M Malaya, Federation of, Legislative Council. *The Communist
Threat to the Federation of Malaya.* Kuala Lumpur, 1959.

M Malaya, Federation of, Special Branch. "Basic Paper on the
Malayan Communist Party," 4 vols. Kuala Lumpur, 1950. Detailed study of Malayan Communist movement to the beginning of the Emergency, based on materials in government files.

Gen McKenzie, Kermit E. *Comintern and World Revolution, 1928-
1943; the shaping of doctrine.* New York: Columbia University
Press, 1964.

Gen McLane, Charles B. *Soviet Policy and the Chinese Communists,
1931-1946.* New York: Columbia University Press, 1958.

Gen McVey, Ruth T. *Bibliography of Soviet Publications on Southeast Asia.* Ithaca: Cornell Southeast Asia Program, 1959.

Gen ———. *The Calcutta Conference and the Southeast Asian Uprisings.* Ithaca: Cornell Modern Indonesia Project, 1958. A
short, but incisive, analysis of the 1948 youth conference at
Calcutta.

In ———. "The Development of the Indonesian Communist
Party and Its Relations with the Soviet Union and the Chinese

Bibliography

People's Republic." Cambridge: Massachusetts Institute of Technology study, 1954 (in mimeograph).

In ———. *The Soviet View of the Indonesian Revolution*. Ithaca: Cornell Modern Indonesia Project, 1957. Focuses on the 1945-49 period.

Manuilsky, D. Z. *See* preceding section of Bibliography.

IC Marshall, R. H., Jr. "The Soviet Union and the Democratic Republic of Vietnam, 1945-1953." New York: Columbia University, 1958 (Master's thesis).

Gen Maslennikov, V. A. (ed.) *Uglublenie krizisa kolonial'noi sistemy imperializma posle vtoroi mirovoi voiny*. Moscow, 1953. Chapters on the colonial world by leading Soviet Orientalists.

M Miller, Harry. *The Communist Menace in Malaya*. New York: Praeger, 1954. A journalist's account of the Emergency.

IC Mkhitarian, S. A. *Bor'ba v'etnamskogo naroda za natsional'-nyuiu nezavisimost', demokratiiu i mir, 1945-1955*. Moscow, 1957.

Gen Motylev, V. *Tikhookeanskii uzel vtoroi imperialisticheskoi voiny*. Moscow, 1940. A standard Soviet study of pre-war diplomacy in the Far East.

Gen Nauchno-issledovatel'skaia assosiatsia po izucheniia natsional'-nykh i kolonial'nykh problem. *Materialy po natsional'nykh i kolonial'nykh problemam*, 1931-1935 (irregular). Includes numerous articles by Soviet Orientalists on Indonesia, Indochina, the Philippines, and Malaya.

Gen Nauchno-issledovatel'skii Institut pri Leningradskom vostochnem institute imeni A. S. Enukidze. *Voprosy kolonial'noi revoliutsii, sbornik statei*, No. 1. Leningrad, 1931. Includes articles on Near East and China and a bibliography of Comintern publications on the colonial question; later issues not located.

In Noor, Gusti Roesli. "Sino-Soviet Attitudes Towards Indonesia, 1950-1955." New York: Columbia University, 1958 (Master's thesis).

Gen North, Robert C. *Moscow and Chinese Communists*. Stanford: Stanford University Press, 1953.

IC Nguyen Ai Quoc [Ho Chi Minh]. *Le procès de la colonization française*. Paris: Librairie du travail, 1925. The first study of the colonial problem by an Asian Marxist.

538

B   Nu, Thakin. *Burma Under the Japanese.* New York: St. Martin's Press, 1954.

M   Onraet, Rene H. de S. *Singapore—A Police Background.* London: Dorothy Crisp and Co., 1947. Memoirs of a former Singapore police officer.

IC   Orgwald. *Tactical and Organizational Questions of the Communist Parties of India and Indochina.* San Francisco(?): Pan Pacific Worker, 1933. A document to guide Indian and Indochinese Communist cadres.

IC   *Les Origines du conflit entre la France et Viêt-Nam.* Paris, 1948. A statement by the Democratic Republic of Vietnam after the outbreak of civil war.

Gen   Overstreet, Gene D., and Marshall Windmiller. *Communism in India.* Berkeley: University of California Press, 1959.

Gen   Page, Stanley W. *Lenin and World Revolution.* New York: New York University Press, 1959.

Gen   Pavlovich-Volonter, M. P. (Vel'tman). *Voprosy kolonial'noi i natsional'noi politiki i III-ii Internatsional.* Moscow, 1920. A pioneer study of Comintern Eastern policy by the leading Orientalist of the post-Revolutionary period.

PI   Philippines, Republic of, Congress, House of Representatives. *Communism in the Philippines.* Manila, 1952.

PI   Philippines, Republic of, Congress, House of Representatives, Special Committee on Un-Filipino Activities [CUFA]. *Report on the Illegality of the Communist Party of the Philippines.* Manila, 1951.

IC   *15 let Demokraticheskoi respubliki V'etnam.* Moscow, 1960. A collection of articles by Russian Orientalists on the occasion of the fifteenth anniversary of the DRV.

PI   "Political Transmissions." Manila(?): 1951 to present. Irregular statements by the CPPI for internal use; most copies have been recovered and are in Philippine government files.

IC   *Pravda o V'etname.* Moscow, 1946. Translation of *Verité sur le Viêtnam,* issued by the DRV Information Service in Paris, 1946.

IC   "President Ho Chi Minh." Hanoi, 1960. Portions of this biography, published in Vietnamese by the Historical Studies Section of the *Lao Dong,* were translated for the author in Saigon in 1960.

539

Bibliography

Gen *Programmnye dokumenty Kommunisticheskikh partii Vostoka.* Moscow, 1934. Important documents relating to Communist parties in the East, including Indochina and the Philippines; edited by Pavel' Mif and others.

Gen Purcell, Victor. *The Chinese in South East Asia.* London: Oxford University Press, 1951.

M Pye, Lucien W. *Guerrilla Communism in Malaya: its social and political meaning.* Princeton: Princeton University Press, 1956.

T Rebrikova, N. V. *Amerikanskaia politika v Tailande.* Moscow, 1959.

T ———. *Ocherki noveishei istorii Tailanda, 1919-1959.* Moscow, 1960.

T ———. "Amerikanskaia ekspansiia v Tailande, 1945-1953." Leningrad, 1954. Synopsis of a doctoral thesis, at Leningrad Public Library.

Report on the Illegality of the Communist Party of the Philippines. See Philippines, Republic of, Congress.

M Rudnev, V. S. *Ocherki noveishei istorii Malaii, 1918-1957.* Moscow, 1959.

IC Sacks, I. Milton, "Marxism in Viet Nam," in Frank N. Trager (ed.), *Marxism in Southeast Asia,* pp. 102-70. Detailed paper on origins of Communism in Indochina.

Gen Safarov, G. *Marks o natsional'no-kolonial'nom voprose.* Moscow, 1934. Discusses also the views of Lenin and Stalin on the Eastern question.

Gen ———. *Problemy Vostoka.* Petrograd, 1922. An early study of the colonial question.

PI Scaff, Alvin. *The Philippine Answer to Communism.* Stanford: Stanford University Press, 1955.

Gen Schwartz, Benjamin I. *Chinese Communism and the Rise of Mao.* Cambridge: Harvard University Press, 1951.

Second Congress of the Communist International. . . . See United States, Department of State.

In Semaun [Semaoen]. *Indoneziia v tsepiakh imperializma.* Moscow, 1927 (translated from Dutch).

In ———. *Indoneziia.* Moscow, 1940. A pamphlet, routine for the era.

Shen Yu-dai. *See* T'ai Sheng-yü.

B   Shnaider, S. S. *Birma*. Moscow, 1951. An early volume on Burma, later criticized and withdrawn.

IC   Sisouk Na Champassak. *Tempête sur le Laos*. Paris: La table ronde, 1961. A Rightist survey of post-war developments in Laos.

In   Siswadji. "The Impact of Comintern Policy on the Indonesian Communist Movement, 1920-1928." New York: Columbia University, 1956 (Master's thesis).

Gen   Skachkov, P. E. *Bibliografiia Kitaia*, 2nd ed. Moscow, 1960. Indispensable for students of Soviet policy in China.

T   *Sovremennyi Tailand*. Moscow, 1958. A collection of studies by Soviet Orientalists, edited by N. V. Rebrikova.

M   "Statement of the Incident of Wright [Loi Tek]." Singapore ? 1948. Translation of an MCP letter to party members on the Loi Tek episode, dated May 28, 1948; in Malayan Government files.

Gen   *Strany Iugo-vostochnoi Azii: istoriia i ekonomika*. Moscow, 1959. Includes articles on Burma, Vietnam, and the Philippines.

Gen   *Strategiia i taktika Kominterna v natsional'no-kolonial'noi revo-liutsii; na primere Kitaia*. Moscow, 1934. Concerns principally China; edited by Pavel' Mif.

Gen   Sultan-Zade, A. (ed.) *Kolonial'nyi Vostok: sotsial'no-ekonomicheskii ocherk*. Moscow, 1924. An early collection of articles on the Near East and China by Soviet Orientalists.

Gen   *Strany Tikogo okeana*. Moscow, 1942. An encyclopedia, including treatment of Southeast Asian countries.

Gen   Tai Sheng-yü. "Peking, Moscow and the Communist Parties of Colonial Asia." Boston: Massachusetts Institute of Technology study, 1954 (in mimeograph).

In   Tan Malaka. *Indoneziia i ee mesto na probuzhdaiushchemsiia Vostoke*. Moscow, 1924 (translated from Dutch). Views on Indonesia by an early leader of the PKI.

PI   Taruc, Luis. *Born of the People*. New York: International Publishers, 1953. An autobiographical account by the leader of the *Hukbalahap*.

Thakin Nu. *See* Nu, Thakin.

541

Bibliography

B   Than Maung, U. "Burma and the Red Star." Rangoon, 1956 ? Manuscript translation of an account of the BCP during the insurrection by a disillusioned former party member.

B   ————. *No Man, Doctor or Lawyer, Is Infallible.* Rangoon, 1955 (in Burmese). Portions of the text were translated for the writer by U Than Maung in 1962; *see* Interview.

IC   Thompson, Virginia M. *French Indochina.* London: Geo. Allen and Unwin, 1937.

Gen   Thompson, Virginia M. and Richard Adloff. *The Left Wing in Southeast Asia.* New York: Sloane, 1950.

      Thuriya Than Maung. *See* Than Maung, U.

B   Tinker, Hugh. *The Union of Burma.* London: Oxford University Press, 1956.

Gen   Trager, Frank N. (ed.). *Marxism in Southeast Asia: a study of four countries.* Stanford: Stanford University Press, 1959.

PI   Troitskii, E. S. "Natsional'no-osvoboditel'naia bor'ba filippinskogo naroda posle vtoroi mirovoi voiny, 1945-1950." Leningrad, 1954. Synopsis of a doctoral thesis, at Leningrad Public Library.

Gen   Trotsky, Leon. *Zapad i Vostok: voprosy mirovoi politiki i mirovoi revoliutsii.* Moscow, 1924. A volume, like *Lenin i Vostok* (1925), affirming the concern of Soviet leaders with the Eastern question; selected writings by Trotsky on revolutionary strategy.

IC   Truong Shin [Truong Chinh]. *Avgustovskaia revoliutsiia vo V'etname.* Moscow, 1954 (translated from Vietnamese). Two articles on post-war developments by a Vietnamese historian.

B   Tsvetaeva, L. "Imperialisticheskaia politika angliiskogo leiboristskogo pravitel'stva v Birme v 1945-1948 gg." Leningrad, 1953. Synopsis of a doctoral thesis, at Leningrad Public Library.

      U Ba Swe. *See* Ba Swe, U.

      U Than Maung. *See* Than Maung, U.

Gen   United States, Department of State. *Second Congress of the Communist International as Reported and Interpreted by the Official Newspapers of Soviet Russia.* Washington: Government Printing Office, 1920. Covers sessions of the Commission on the National and Colonial Question not elsewhere treated.

542

Gen Varga, E. *Mezhdu VI i VII kongressami Kominterna: ekono-mika i politika 1928-1934 gg.* Moscow, 1935. Useful, but un-official, review of Comintern activity between the Sixth and Seventh Congresses.

B Vasil'ev, V. F. "Natsional'no-osvoboditel'noe dvizhenie v Birme posle vtoroi mirovoi voipy." Moscow, 1953.. Synopsis of a doc-toral thesis on Burmese independence, at Leningrad Public Library.

B ————. *Birma.* Moscow, 1954.

B Vasil'eva, V. I. *Birma.* Moscow, 1942. A wartime pamphlet.

IC ————. *Indo-Kitai.* Moscow, 1947. First comprehensive post-war study (273 pp.) of Indochina by the leading Soviet au-thority on the area.

Gen "Natsional'no-osvoboditel'naia bor'ba v stranakh Iugo-vostoch-noi Azii." Moscow, 1949. Stenogram of a public lecture.

Gen *Velikii Oktiabr' i narody Vostoka; sbornik.* Moscow, 1957. A volume published on the occasion of the fortieth anniversary of the Bolshevik Revolution; includes articles on Burma, Indo-nesia, Indochina, and the Philippines.

IC *Vietnam: a new stage in her history.* Bangkok, 1947. An official publication of the DRV; includes an important speech by Ho Chi Minh in October 1946.   .

IC *Le Viêt-Nam en lutte contre le fascisme.* Paris, 1947. A Viet-minh pamphlet; translated into English as *Vietnam's Fight Against Fascism, 1940-1945* (Paris, 1948).

IC Vo Nguyen Giap. *People's War, People's Army.* Hanoi, 1961. A collection of articles and speeches by the Vietminh military leader, including material relating to the war years.

     Voprosy kolonial'noi revoliutsii. See Nauchno-issledovatel'skii institut pri Leningradskom Vostochnem institute.

IC Walter, Gerard. *Histoire du parti communiste français.* Paris, 1949.

     Wang Ming [Ch'en Shao-yü]. *See* preceding section of Bibli-ography.

Gen Whiting, Allen S. *Soviet Policies in China, 1919-1924.* New York: Columbia University Press, 1955.

Gen Wilbur C. Martin and Julie Lien-ying How. *Documents on Communism, Nationalism, and Soviet Advisers in China, 1918-1927.* New York: Columbia University Press, 1956.

543

Bibliography

Gen   World Federation of Trade Unions. *Report of Proceedings of the Second World Trade Union Congress, 29th June-9th July, 1949.* Paris, 1949.

Gen   Zamyslova, Z. A. "Kommunisticheskii internatsional i ego rol' v istorii mezhdunarodnogo rabochego i natsional'no-osvoboditel'nogo dvizheniia." Moscow, 1957. A lecture prepared for party workers, at Leningrad Public Library.

Gen   Zhukov, E. M. "Sharpening of the Crisis of the Colonial System after World War II." Bombay, 1950. An article by the leading Soviet Orientalist after the war, much like his introductory chapter in *Krizis kolonial'noi sistemy* (see above).

PERIODICALS

Aziia i Afrika segodnia. See *Sovremennyi Vostok.*

Bibliografiia Vostoka (published by the Learned Association of Oriental Studies of the Academy of Sciences, 1932-37; irregular). Lists items relating to Indonesia and Indochina.

Bol'shevik (organ of the Central Committee of the CPSU, 1924-52; semimonthly. Renamed *Kommunist* in 1952).

Cahiers du bolchevisme (published by the Communist Party of France; also called *Cahiers du communisme*). Consulted only for 1930's.

Communist (published by the Communist Party of the USA; monthly). Consulted irregularly.

Communist International (English language edition of *Kommunisticheskii internatsional*; called British edition, 1919-35, and American edition, 1935-39).

Communist Review (published by the Communist Party of Great Britain; monthly). Consulted for years 1946-49.

Current Digest of the Soviet Press (published by the Joint Committee on Slavic Studies, New York, 1949 to present; weekly). The *Index* is indispensable.

Eastern and Colonial Bulletin (English language organ of the Profintern, 1927-31; monthly).

Far Eastern Monthly. See *Pan Pacific Worker.*

Bibliography

For a Lasting Peace, for a People's Democracy! (English language organ of the Cominform, 1947-56; semiweekly. Also published in Russian, French, and other languages).

International Press Correspondence, or *Inprecor* (semi-official English language organ of the Comintern, 1922-41; weekly. Also published in German, French, and other languages. Renamed *World News and Views* in July 1939; after 1941, published in London as organ of the Communist Party of Great Britain, 1942-54).

Kolonial'nye problemy. See preceding section.

Kommunist. See *Bol'shevik.*

Kommunisticheskii internatsional (organ of the Executive Committee of the Communist International, 1919-43; weekly, later biweekly).

Krasnyi internatsional profsoiuzov (official organ of the Profintern, 1921-36; monthly). Consulted irregularly.

Materialy po natsional'nykh i kolonial'nykh problemam. See Nauchno-issledovatel'skaia assosiatsiia po izucheniia natsional'nykh i kolonial'nykh problem, in preceding section of Bibliography.

Mezhdunarodnoe rabochee dvizhenie (published by the Profintern, 1925-35; weekly). Consulted irregularly.

Mirovoe khoziaistvo i mirovaia politika (published by the Institute of World Economy and Politics of the Communist Academy, later the Academy of Sciences, 1926-45; monthly. Renamed *Voprosy ekonomiki* in 1945).

New Times (English edition of *Novoe vremiia,* 1945 to present; weekly).

Novoe vremiia (principal Soviet journal on world politics for foreign readers, 1945 to present; weekly. Published also in English, French, and other languages. Successor to *Voina i rabochii klass*).

Novyi Vostok (organ of the Learned Association of Oriental Studies, 1922-30; irregular).

Pan Pacific Worker, also called *Pan Pacific Monthly* and *Far Eastern Monthly* (organ of the Pan Pacific Trade Union Secretariat, 1927-30; irregular. Published in Hankow, Shanghai, and later in San Francisco).

People's China (principal English language publication of the Chinese People's Republic, 1950-57; biweekly. Renamed *Peking Review* in 1957).

Bibliography

Problemy Vostokovedeniia. See *Sovetskoe Vostokvedenie.*

Revoliutsiia i natsional' nosti (publication of the Soviet of Nationality and the Communist Academy, 1930-37; monthly).

Revoliutsionny Vostok (organ of the Research Institute for the Study of National and Colonial Problems, 1927-37; quarterly).

Sovetskoe Vostokovedenie (published by the Oriental Institute of the Academy of Sciences, from 1955; bimonthly. Later renamed *Problemy Vostokovedeniia*). *N.B.* An earlier Orientalist journal of the same name includes no coverage of Southeast Asia.

Soviet Press Translations (published by the Far Eastern and Russian Institute of the University of Washington, 1946-53).

Sovremennyi Vostok (published by the Oriental Institute of the Academy of Sciences, 1957-61; monthly. Renamed *Aziia i Afrika segodnia* in 1961). A more popular journal than *Sovetskoe Vostokovedenie*; both include coverage of Southeast Asia during the period of this study.

Tikhii okean (published by the Pacific Ocean Section of the Institute of World Economy and Politics of the Communist Academy, later the Academy of Sciences, 1927-37; quarterly).

Voina i rabochii klass (published during World War II to fill the gap left by the termination of *Kommunisticheskii internatsional*, 1943-45; renamed *Novoe vremiia* in June 1945).

Voprosy ekonomiki. See *Mirovoe khoziaistvo i mirovaia politika.*

World News and Views. See *International Press Correspondence.*

World Trade Union Movement (organ of the World Federation of Trade Unions). Consulted irregularly.

INTERVIEWS

DR. BA MAW. Burmese Prime Minister, 1937-39, 1942-45. Interviewed in Rangoon, February 25, 1961: relations between factions within the Burmese nationalist movement prior to the Japanese occupation.

BARRÉ, JEAN. Editor, *Réalités cambodgiennes*, Phnom Penh. Interviewed in Phnom Penh, March 4, 1961: relations between China and Cambodia.

BO LET YA. Close associate and aide of Aung San during World War II. Interviewed in Rangoon, January 31, 1962: early Marxist study

546

groups in Rangoon, late 1930's; wartime relations of *Thakins* with Japanese and English.

COLONEL CHAT. Special Operations Officer, Criminal Investigation Division, Bangkok. Interviewed in Bangkok, March 13, 1961: course of Thai Communism since World War II.

DANG DUC KHOI. Formerly a member of the Vietminh; diplomat and liaison officer under the regime of Ngo Dinh Diem. Interviewed in Saigon, February 12, 1962: foreign contacts of Vietminh during World War II; Sino-Soviet rivalry in North Vietnam.

DE CRUZ, GERALD. Former Communist official of the Malayan Democratic Union, 1946-48. Interviewed in Singapore, March 22, 1961, and January 15, 1962: relations of the MCP with foreign parties; Loi Tek episode; activity of Communist front organizations after World War II.

MOHAMMED HATTA. Nationalist leader since 1920's; former Premier and Vice-President of Indonesian Republic. Interviewed in Djakarta, March 27, 1961: early relations between *Perhimpoenan Indonesia* and PKI, 1920's; Communist activity during World War II; Sjarifuddin's role in the Madiun uprising, 1948.

KAZNACHEEV, ALEXANDER. Former Soviet diplomat in Rangoon; defected to West, 1958. Interviewed in Washington, March 23, 1960; Soviet Orientalist studies relating to Southeast Asia; Sino-Soviet competition in Rangoon; activities of Russian Embassy in Burma.

KYAW SEIN. Early Marxist leader in Burma, 1930's. Interviewed in Rangoon, February 25, 1961: activities of pre-war Marxist study groups in Rangoon.

LAVA, JOSÉ. Communist leader in the Philippines after World War II and Secretary of CPPI, 1948-50; arrested October 1950. Interviewed in McKinley Barracks, Manila, April 2, 1961, and January 13, 1962: course of CPPI policies from 1945 to 1950, including intra-party rivalries. *N.B.* José Lava was unco-operative during the 1961 interview, but following correspondence with the author discussed CPPI affairs with some candor in 1962.

MEYER, CHARLES. Aide to Prince Sihanouk. Interviewed in Phnom Penh, March 5, 1961: foreign policies of Cambodia *vis-à-vis* China and the USSR.

Bibliography

NGO DINH NHU. Brother and political adviser of the late President of South Vietnam, Ngo Dinh Diem; assassinated October 1963. Interviewed in Saigon, March 10, 1961: course of Vietnamese Communism; Sino-Soviet rivalry in North Vietnam.

NHOUY ABAHY. Former member of the *Lao Issara* government, 1946; later minister in several cabinets in Vientiane. Interviewed in Vientiane, February 9, 1962: policies and history of the *Lao Issara*, 1945-48.

GENERAL PHOUMI NOSAVAN. Former member of the *Lao Issara*; Rightist leader of several governments in Vientiane. Interviewed in Vientiane, February 9, 1962; origins of the *Lao Issara* and its links with the Vietminh via Prince Souphanouvong; formation and policies of the *Pathet Lao*.

OUN SANANIKONE. Former member of the *Lao Issara*; later active in several governments in Vientiane. Interviewed in Vientiane, February 8, 1962: origins of the *Lao Issara* and role in it of Prince Souphanouvong; Thai-Laotian relations after World War II.

COLONEL PHAM NGOC THAO. Officer in the Vietminh to 1954; Provincial Chief of Kien Hoa during the regime of Ngo Dinh Diem; killed in 1965, several months after abortive coup against Nguyen Khanh. Interviewed in Truc Giang, February 13, 1962: Russian and Chinese advisers and activities in North Vietnam, early 1950's; Vietminh reaction to the Geneva settlement of 1954.

SOEDJATMOKO. Socialist leader and former editor. Interviewed in Djakarta, March 27, 1961: role of the PKI in the resistance movement during World War II; Socialist-PKI relations after the war.

TARUC, LUIS. Former leader of the *Hukbalahap*, 1942-53; surrendered 1954. Interviewed in McKinley Barracks, Manila, April 1, 1961, and January 13, 1962: Socialist-Communist relations in the 1930's; guerrilla strategies during World War II; party rivalries during and after the war; his break with the CPPI, early 1950's.

U THAN MAUNG. Former member of the BCP, 1947-54; subsequently editor, *Mandalay Sun*. Interviewed in Mandalay, January 27-8, 1962: policies of the BCP during the insurrection; intra-party rivalries and relations with Chinese agents. *N.B.* U Than Maung was more restrained during these interviews than in two volumes written shortly after leaving the BCP; *see* listings above.

U THAUNG MYINE. Reuters correspondent, Rangoon, student of Burmese Marxism. Interviewed in Rangoon, February 2, 1962: rivalries in the BCP in 1946-47; party strategies leading to the insurrection in 1948.

THEIN PE MYINT. Early Marxist leader; Secretary of the BCP, 1945-46. Interviewed in Rangoon, January 31, 1962: origins and early course of Burmese Marxism; formation of the BCP; relations of the BCP and AFPFL after the war; intra-party rivalries, 1945-46.

Index

Abdulmadjid, 192, 284, 406
Acheson, Dean, 450
Act of Burma (1936), 330
Aidit, D. N., 416
Algiers Liberation Committee, 262, 267
Alimin, 82n, 86, 91-94, 97-98, 101-02, 131, 283, 417
Allen, James, 224, 228, 230, 300
Alphonso, 99-100. *See also* Tan Malaka
Alsop, Joseph and Stewart, 438
American Federation of Labor (AFL), 120
An (or AN), 102-103
Anglo-Russian Trade Union Council, 65n
Annam, 266, 274-75. *See also* Indochina
Annam Communist Party (previously Vietnam Revolutionary Youth League), 112
Anti-Enemy Backing-Up Society (AE-BUS), in Malaya, 240
Anti-Fascist People's Freedom League (AFPFL), 276, 322-24, 326-28, 331-38, 372, 377n; and Communist Party of Burma, 332-33, 347, 374-75, 379
Anti-Imperialist League, *see* League Against Imperialism . . .
"armed struggle" strategy, 414, 417, 423, 452-55, 465-66. *See also* national and colonial question
Ashleigh, Charles, 27
Atlantic Charter, 267
"Atom" (pseudonym), 194
"August Revolution" (Vietnam), 265-67
Aung Min, 377n
Aung San, 316-17, 320-28, 334-37, 347, 372, 459
Avarin, V. A., 231, 302

Baku Congress, *see* Congress of Toilers of the East . . .
Balgos, Mariano, 177, 419, 426
Baling talks (1955), in Malaya, 462n

Balmori, Joaquim, 126
Ba Maw, Dr., 194n, 318-21, 330
Bandung conference (1955), vii
Bao Dai, 264, 266, 269, 275, 433-35, 447
Ba Swe, U, 321, 377n
Batavia agreements (1949), 413
Ba Thein Tin, 378
Batu Arang (Malaya) coal mine strikes (1937), 237-38
Benteng Republik (Republican Fortress), in Indonesia, 285
Bergsma, P., 81, 90
Blum, Leon, 273
Bognot, Cirilo, 118, 120-21, 129, 171
Bo Let Ya, 316, 317, 319-21, 323-24
Bondarevskii, G. L., 394-96
Borodin, Mikhail, 34-35, 46, 50, 52, 57, 60, 106
Briggs Plan (1951), in Malaya, 393, 397
Browder, Earl, 71, 116, 122, 131, 173, 201, 212
"Browderism," 258, 325-28
Bubnov, A. S., 56n
Buddhism, 195
Bukharin, N. I., 10-11, 53, 56n, 60, 206; at Fifteenth CPSU Congress, 63-65; at Sixth Comintern Congress, 66-70, 98-100
Bulganin, N. A., vii
Bullitt, William, 431, 433
Burma, 451, 465, 471; *to 1935*, 194-97; *1935-1947*, 316-38; *1948-1953*, 371-85, 457-60
Burma Independence Army (BIA), 319, 320. *See also* Burma National Army
Burma National Army (later Patriotic Burmese Forces), 323-24
Burma Road, 243, 318, 330
Burma Workers and Peasants Party (BWPP), 377

Calcutta Youth Conference (1948), *see* Southeast Asian Youth Conference

Index

Cambodia, 275-78, 443-45

Canton uprising (1927), 61, 64-65

Capadocia, Guillermo, 177, 182, 224, 226, 229, 294, 429

Carpio, S., 174-76, 178-79, 181, 186

Castro, Pedro, 296, 419, 421-22

Cawnpore Conspiracy (India), 33

Central Labor Union (Thailand), 341

Chambers, Whittaker, 172

Chan Fu, 112

Chang Fa-kwei, 261-62

Changsha coup (1930), 150

Chen Peng, 310-11, 314n, 316

Chiang Kai-shek, 46, 55, 57, 59, 209, 212, 254

Chiang Kai-shek, Madame, 228

Chicherin, G. V., 34

China, Republic of, 228, 413; as target of Soviet revolutionary strategy, 1925-1927, 33-36, 45-64, 76; neglected at Fifth Comintern Congress, 42, 44-45; discussed by ECCI, 53, 65, 77; soviet movement in, 61-62, 65, 144, 153, 161, 187; and Indochina, 261-62, 268; Stalin's 1925-1927 strategy in China appraised, 481-83. See also Kuomintang

Chinese People's Republic (CPR), 435, 444, 447, 458; and Burma, 384-85, 454; and Indonesia, 415-17; and Philippines, 432; and DRV, 436, 440-42; and Thailand, 449; significance of, in Soviet policy, 468-70. See also overseas Chinese; Communist Party of China

Cochinchina, 108, 220, 275

COF, see Congresso Obrero di Filipinas

colonial policy, see national and colonial question

Commission on the National and Colonial Question, 51; of Second Comintern Congress, 15-16, 21; of Third Comintern Congress, 28, 51; of Fifth Comintern Congress, 88-89

Committee of Good Offices (Indonesia), 290, 402, 411

Commonwealth Conference of Communist Parties (1947), 258-59, 314-15, 337

Communist Information Bureau (Cominform), 289, 351-54, 364. See also Soviet, Comintern and Cominform press

Communist International (Comintern)
Congresses: First, 10-13; Second, 12-24, 47, 83, 103, 479, 482; Third, 27-28; Fourth, 29-33, 84; Fifth, 36-45, 84, 103; Sixth, 66-70, 93n, 94, 98-100, 134-35, 143, 209; Seventh, 152-53, 161, 185, 193, 202, 207-14, 237, 317

1919-1929: and the Eastern question, 17-23, 27-33, 35-45, 49-59, 62-70, 140-41; Stalin's relationship to, 76-78; and PKI, 88-89, 93-94, 98-100; and Vietnamese Communism, 105; operations center in Singapore, 131-36; and Malayan Communism, 133-34. See also Dalburo

1930-1934: and CPIC, 112, 159; and the Eastern question, 143-47; reduced operations in Southeast Asia, 147, 204-06; and CPPI, 169-70, 175, 186-87; and MCP, 202-03; Shanghai apparatus of, 201, 204

1935-1943: and Stalin, 207-08, and Burmese Marxists, 318; appraises Indochinese "united front," 215-16; dissolved, 249

See also Soviet, Comintern and Cominform Press

Communist International, Executive Committee, see Executive Committee of Communist International

Communist Party of Burma (BCP), 320, 347, 372-85; launched, 322-36; and AFPFL, 322-28, 332-33, 336-38; Second Congress of, 325; "Red Flag" Communists, 327-28, 335, 376, 378; "White Flag" Communists, 327-28, 336, 376-77, 457; and insurrection in Burma, 371-85, 457-60

Communist Party of China (CPC, or CCP)
1920-1929: 35-36, 58-65; founding of, 26; allies with Kuomintang, 42, 51-52, 54; and Indochina, 107; and Malaya, 131-33, 135-36

Index

Communist Party of Japan, 62
Communist Party of Malaya (MCP)
  1920's: see South Seas Communist
  Party
    1930-1935: 147, 188, 194f, 197,
    200-03; formed, 136; and strike
    movement, 201-02
    1935-1941: 237-44; and strike
    movement, 237-38; and united front,
    237-39, 242; Fifth Expanded Plenum, 238-39; Sixth Enlarged Plenum, 240-42; Seventh Plenum, 243
    1941-1947: 260, 303-16; creates
    MPAJA, 304; continues moderate
    line after war, 306; directs general
    strike (1946), 308; Eighth Plenum,
    308, 313; Loi Tek episode, 309-13;
    forsakes moderation, 311-12; and
    CCP, 313; and Siam, 344
    1948-1953: 385-401, 461-62, 472;
    Fourth Plenum (1948), 385-87;
    Fifth Plenum, 387; and Emergency,
    388-93, 462; and CPC, 389-91, 399-
    401
Communist Party of Philippines (CPPI
  or CPP)
    1930-1935: 165-88; founding of,
    165; First Congress, 168-69, 172,
    180-81, 187-88; and Comintern,
    169-70; First Plenum, 174, 178,
    181; trial of party leaders, 174-75;
    Second Plenum, 176, 182
    1935-1941: 222-31, 245-46; and
    Sakdalistas, 183-85; resists united
    front policy, 222-23; legality restored, 224; Third Congress, 225-26,
    228; and *Frente Popular,* 227-31
    1941-1947: 292-303; cooperates
    with government against Japanese,
    292-93; post-war leadership struggle,
    295-99; moderate line, 297, 309
    1948-1953: 418-19, 424-31, 461,
    472; conference of May 1948, 418-
    19, 421-23; leads *Huk* rebellion,
    427-29; "Politburo In" raided
    (1950), 428-29
Communist Party of the Soviet Union
  (CPSU), 169, 360; Trotsky-Stalin
  dispute, 36-37, 53, 65, 77; Thir-

teenth Congress, 37; Fifteenth Congress, 63-64. *See also* Communist
International; national and colonial
question; Soviet, Comintern and
Cominform press; Union of Soviet
Socialist Republics
Communist Party of Thailand (CPT),
  Communist activities in 1930's, 197-
  200; legalized after war, 342-45;
  and strike movement (1947-1948),
  446, 448; Second Congress, 448-49
Communist Party of United States
  (CPUSA), and CPPI, 116, 130-31,
  171-86, 228, 299-300; and PPTUS,
  171-72; Eighth Convention, 173; on
  Sakdalistas, 183-84; role in Philippines, 171-86; aids in creating *Frente
  Popular,* 228; Eleventh Convention,
  230; Fifteenth Convention, 431-32
Communist University of Toilers of the
  East (*KUTV*), 26, 43n, 49n, 89
Communist Youth International, 73
Confédération Général du Travail
  (CGT), 158
Conference of Transport Workers of
  the Pacific (1924), 70, 116
Congress of Labor Organizations
  (CLO), in Philippines, 422
Congress of Toilers of the East at Baku
  (1920), 25, 83f
Congress of Toilers of the Far East
  (1922), 25
Congresso Obrero de Filipinas (COF),
  113-130, 165
Congresso Proletario di Filipinas
  (KAP), 128, 165, 168, 175-76
Congress Party (India), 255-56, 319
Constitutional Party of Cochinchina,
  108

Daladier, Edouard, 148
Dalburo (Far Eastern Bureau of Comintern), 50, 107, 119, 136-37, 146-
  47, 162
Dalin, 26
"Dantes," *see* Bognot
D'Argenlieu, Admiral, 273
Darsono, 81, 82n, 101, 284
Darusman Maruto, 408, 411

Dat, 316, 317
Dedijer, Vladimir, 359, 374
de Gaulle, General Charles, 262-63, 265, 267
Dekker, H. V., 81
Democratic Alliance (Philippines), 297
Democratic Party (Philippines), 461
Democratic Republic of Vietnam (DRV), 268-70, 277, 426, 447, 469, 472; formation of (1945), 265-67; war with France, 273-75, 432-45, 462-64; recognized by CPR and USSR, 436; relations with CPR, 440-42
Democratic Union (Malaya), 314
Democratic United Front (Indochina), 217-18
de Ora, Antonio, 166-67
Diakhov, A., 253-64
Dienbienphu, 442, 464
Dimitrov, Georgi, 208, 210, 317
Dohbama Asiayone ("We Burmans" Association), *see Thakins*
Doriot, Jacques, 104-05, 148n
Dridzo, S. A., *see* Lozovsky
Ducroix, Joseph (alias Serge Lefranc), 147, 200
Dulles, John Foster, 439
Dutt, R. Palme, 258

Economic Development Corps (ED-COR), in Philippines, 428f
Effendi, Roestan, 231-32
Eisenhower, Dwight D., 472
Emergency, in Malaya, 385-401, 461-62, 472
Enbay uprising (1930), in Indochina, 147-54, 203f
Engels, Friedrich, 20, 442
Ercoli, 208, 212
Evangelista, Crisanto, 113-15, 117, 131, 171, 182, 226; and *Congresso Obrero*, 113-14, 118, 121-22, 128-30; visits Moscow, 120-21, 125; organizes CPPI, 165-66; arrest and trial of, 167-68, 174-75, 177; released, 224; death of, 294
Executive Committee of Communist

International (ECCI), 27-29, 66, 94-96, 144; Fifth Plenum, 50, 87-90; Sixth Plenum, 51, 91; Seventh Plenum, 53, 55-56, 59; Eighth Plenum, 57-59, 77; Ninth Plenum, 65; Eleventh Plenum, 143, 153, 170; Twelfth Plenum, 143, 176; Thirteenth Plenum, 143, 176, 189-90, 192

Far Eastern Bureau, *see* Dalburo
FDR, *see* People's Democratic Front
Federacion del Trabajo, 113, 126
Feleo Juan, 177, 182
Fontainebleau Conference (1946), 271
Force, 136, 305, 323-24
France, 218-19; and Indochina, 108-11, 148, 158-59, 164, 214-16; and DRV, 268-73, 438-40, 442; and Laos, 276-78, 443-45; and Cambodia, 276-78, 443-45
"Freedom Bloc" (Burma), 318-320
Frente Popular (Philippines), 223-24, 227-31

Gandhi, Mohandas, 195-362
Gapi (Gaboengon Politiek Indonesia, or Federation of Indonesian Political Parties), 234
Geneva Conference, on Indochina (1954), 462, 471, 473
George, Harrison, 114-16, 118, 124-25, 129, 131, 172-73, 183-84
Gerindo (Gerakan Rakjat Indonesia, or Indonesian People's Movement), 234
Ghosh, Ajoy, 453
Ghoshal, H. N., 316-17, 325, 371-74, 376, 378, 381, 385
Graziadei, 18-19
Great Britain, and Burma, 196, 320, 323-24, 331-36, 373-74; and Malaya, 242-43, 303-07, 315, 388-89, 394-97. *See also* Burma Road
Gromyko, A. A., 290, 412
Guber, A. A., 186, 348, 394, 439-40; on Indonesia, 189-91, 285-87, 401-02; on Philippines, 223; on Indochina and DRV, 269-70, 435; on Cambodia and Laos, 443

Index

Hare-Hawes-Cutting bill, 179-183
Harjono, 408
Hatta, Mohammed, 72, 191-92, 233, 278, 282, 286, 401-05, 407, 411, 413-14, 455-56
Ho Chi Minh (alias Nguyen Ai Quoc), 137-38, 149-50, 154-55, 157, 162, 197, 216, 263-64, 271-76, 348, 381, 432-33, 436-37, 469; visits to Moscow, 37, 44, 105; at founding of FCP, 103f; as Comintern agent, 106, 135-36; *Le procès de la colonisation française*, 109; organizes CPIC, 109-12; arrests, 147, 261-62; organizes Vietminh, 220f; elected President of DRV, 266; negotiates with French (1946), 268-71; visits Peking, 441; initiates truce talks with French, 463-64
Ho-Sainteny agreement, 269-73
Holland, and Indonesia (to 1945), 80, 86, 91, 95-96, 139, 191, 232, 278; and Indonesian Republic (after 1945), 284-92, 348, 412-13, 415
Huks (*Hukbong Bayan Laban Sa Hapon*, or People's Anti-Japanese Army or *Hukbalahap*; in 1949 renamed *Hukbong Magpalayang Bayan*, or People's Liberation Army), 293-99, 301-03, 417-31, 466, 472

"Illegal PKI," *see* Communist Party of Indonesia
India, 249-50, 252-55, 256. *See also* Communist Party of India
Indies Social Democratic Association (later Communist Party of Indonesia, or PKI), 80
Indochina, *1920's*, 102-13; *1930-1935*, 147-165; *1935-1941*, 212, 214-22; *1941-1947*, 261-78; *1947-1953*, 432-45, 463, 466. *See also* Democratic Republic of Vietnam
Indonesia, *1920's*, 63, 80-102, 479; *1930-1935*, 188-93; *1935-1941*, 231-36; *1941-1947*, 278-92; *1947-1953*, 401-17, 455-57, 471
Indonesian Nationalist Party (PNI), 102, 190-91, 285, 287, 402, 407

Indonesian People's Congress, 236
International of Women, 73
International Union of Students (IUS), 259, 357, 359
Islamic movement, *see* Pan-Islamic movement
Ivin, A., 199-200

Japan, 62, 86; seizes Manchuria, 205; attacks China, 247; imperialism in Southeast Asia, 183-84, 232, 245-47; defeat of, 266
    wartime relations: with Indochina, 261, 264-68; with Indonesia, 278-80; with Philippines, 292, 294-95; with Malaya, 304-05, 310; with Burma, 319-21, 323; with Thailand, 339-41
Japanese Communist Party, *see* Communist Party of Japan
Japanese Peace Conference (1951), 451, 457, 460
Javan uprising (1926), 56-57, 91-102
Joffe, Adolf, 26-27, 34-36
Jogjakarta Conference of PKI (1924), 86-87
Jorge (alias Frienza), 296, 298, 419
Jusuf, Mohammed, 282, 287

Kamenev, L. B., 37
KAP, *see* Congresso Proletario di Filipinas
Karakhan, Leo, 34-35, 53n
Katayama, Sen, 37, 44
Kemal Atatürk, 195, 362
Kemal Pasha, 29
Khmer Issarak (Free Cambodians), 275-76, 445
Khrushchev, N. S., vii-ix, 460, 483
KNIP (Indonesian National Committee), 285n
Korean War, 437, 439, 463, 466-67, 469
KPMP, *see* Philippine Confederation of Peasants
Krestintern (Peasant International), 25, 73, 89, 120
Krisostomo, Juan, *see* Crisanto Evangelista

556

Index

Index

Profintern (Red International of Trade Unions), 25, 70-71, 138, 259; Third Congress, 72; Fourth Congress, 66, 72, 120, 126; and Indonesia, 96; and Philippines, 113, 126
Proletarian Party (Thailand), 341-42
Pyinmina rally, in Burma, 374-76

Quezon, Manuel, 179-80, 182, 222, 224, 227-30, 292-93
Quirino, Elpidio, 418-20, 422, 431, 461

Radek, Karl, 18, 21-23, 25, 33, 38, 43
Rance, Sir Herbert, 328
Ravensteyn, 29-31
"Red Flag" Communists, see Communist Party of Burma
Red International of Labor Unions (RILU), see Profintern
Renville agreement (1948), 402-04
Romulo, Carlos, 461
Round Table Conference, on Burma, in London (1933), 196; on Indonesia, in The Hague (1949), 415
Roxas, Manuel, 180, 297, 330, 347, 418, 420, 424f
Roy, M. N., 43-44, 52, 60n; at Second Comintern Congress, 14-24; organizes training school in Tashkent, 26-27; at Third Comintern Congress, 28; at Fourth Comintern Congress, 31-33; at Fifth Comintern Congress, 38-40; at Seventh ECCI Plenum, 53, 55, 56n; as Comintern agent in China, 55n
Russia, see USSR
Russian Revolution, 54, 74, 143, 255, 354-55
Ryan, Tim, 173, 175, 177-78

Safrov, G., 161, 190
Saigon Municipal Council election (1933), 155-56
Saigon trials (1934), 155, 158
Sainteny, Jean, 268-69
Sajap Kiri (Leftist Coalition), in Indonesia, 285, 291, 402-03
Sakdal uprising (1935), 183-85, 186, 203, 222

Santos, Pedro Abad, 177, 226-30, 294
Sardjono, 283, 407, 411
Sarekat Islam, 80-85, 88, 102, 191
Sarekat Rakjat (People's Association), 85-86, 89, 95
Saw, U, 320, 335
Saya San uprising, in Burma, 194-96, 203
SEATO (Southeast Asia Treaty Organization), 447, 467. See also "Pacific Pact"
self-determination, see nationalism
Semaoen, 57, 81, 82n, 86, 95-98, 101-02, 141, 235-36; at Fifth Comintern Congress, 44; at Sixth Plenum of ECCI, 91
Serrati, 31, 141; at Second Comintern Congress, 18-23
Setiadjit, 192, 284, 291-92, 406
Shao Li Tse, 56n
Sharkey, Lawrence, 359, 385f, 388, 390, 398
Siam, see Thailand
Sian episode (1936), 247
Sihanouk, Norodom, 275-76, 443-44
Singapore, see Malaya
Sjahrir, Soetan, 279, 283, 286, 290-91, 406, 414
Sjarifuddin, Amir, 278-79, 283-84, 288, 291-92; and PKI, 234, 401-03, 406-08, 411
Sneevliet, Hendrik, see Maring
Socialist Party (Burma), 327, 376-77
Socialist Party (Indonesia), 284-85, 406, 457
Socialist Party (Philippines), 177, 224-27, 229
Souphanouvong, 260n, 276-77
Southeast Asian Youth Conference, Calcutta (1948), 357-61, 367, 369, 374, 376, 388, 390, 404, 418, 433
South Seas (Nanyang) Communist Party (SSCP), 107, 132, 136, 194, 202
South Seas (Nanyang) General Labor Union (GLU), 133-36, 194, 202. See also Malayan General Labor Union
Souvanna Phouma, 277

560

Index

"Teng-fa letter," of CCP to BCP, 326n, 329
Thailand, *to 1935*, 197-200; *1935-1947*, 338-45; *1947-1954*, 445-49, 451
Thakin movement (*Dohbama Asiayone* or "We Burmans" Association), 195, 317-21, 323
Thakin Nu, *see* Nu, U
Thakin Soe, 319-22, 324-27, 332, 335, 347, 376
Thakin Zin, 378
Than Maung, U, 378
Than Tun, 320-22, 324, 326, 359, 374-75, 378, 381-82, 459
Thein Pe Myint, 195n, 316-21, 323, 325-28, 377n, 383
"Thirty Comrades," *see* *Thakin* movement
Thorez, Maurice, 158, 216-17
Trade Union Council (Burma), 377
Tran Van Giau, 154
Trotsky, Leon, 37, 43, 45, 52, 54, 65, 77-78; at Comintern founding, 8-9; at Third Comintern Congress, 28; on China, 58-61
Trotskyists, in Indochina, 156, 159, 217-19, 267-69
Tydings-McDuffie Act, 180, 183, 222

U Ba Swe, *see* Ba Swe, U
Union of Soviet Socialist Republics, resumes relations with China (1933), 205; and United States, 205, 465ff; role in war in Far East (1945), 250-51, 254; supports Indonesia against Dutch in United Nations, 286-91, 412; and Philippines, 303, 462; and Thailand, 341, 345; and Burma, 357-60, 381; and DRV, 381, 436, 439-40; and Indonesia, 404, 414, 457; and Malaya, 462; and CPR, 468ff. *See also* Communist International; national and colonial policy; Soviet, Comintern and Cominform press
united front, 351, 477, 480
1920's: in Soviet Eastern policy, 13-16, 23, 38-39, 64-65; in China, 34-36, 42-43, 45-61
1930's: united front from below, 144; strategy formulated at Seventh

Comintern Congress, 208-14; in China, 211-12, 228, 240, 247-48; in France, 164, 214; in Indochina, 164-65, 214-22; in Philippines, 222-31, 293; in Indonesia, 221-37; in Malaya, 237-45; in Burma, 317; consequences summarized, in Southeast Asia, 245-48. *See also* *Frente Popular*; national and colonial question
United Nations, 265, 345, 349, 467, 469; and Indonesia, 286-87, 290, 403, 412-13; and Burma, 458
United States of America, 113, 252, 255, 437-38; and Philippines, 114, 179-80, 296, 302, 331; and Indonesia, 291, 411; and Indochina, 438-39; and "Pacific Pact," 450-52; and Thailand, 446-48; and Burma, 458-59
United States Armed Forces in Far East (USAFFE), 296

Varenne, Alexander, 108, 110-11, 148, 218
Vasil'eva, V., 348; on Indochina, 152, 164, 218-19, 270-71, 434, 436; on "armed struggle" strategy, 255; on Laos and Cambodia, 277-78, 443-44; on Indonesia, 287, 402, 414; on Burma's *Thakins*, 330; on Malaya, 396
Veltman, M. P. (M. Pavlovich-Volonter), 26, 48-49
Vietminh (*Viet Nam Doe Lap Dong Minh Hoi*, or Vietnam Independence League), 261-75, 346, 433-34, 436-38, 440-45, 472-73, 480; established by Eighth CPIC Plenum, 221, 261; resists French and Japanese during war, 261; and Vietnam Revolutionary League, 262, 268; insurrection by, 263-65; appoints People's National Liberation Committee, 266; establishes DRV, 269-70; aids *Pathet Lao*, 277; reorganized (1951), 444
Vietnam, proclaims independence under Japanese (1945), 264. *See also* Democratic Republic of Vietnam (DRV)
Vietnam Liberation Army, 264-65
Vietnam Nationalist Party, 109, 149